D1474055

God-Fearing and Free

GOD-FEARING AND FREE

A Spritual History of America's Cold War

JASON W. STEVENS

HARVARD UNIVERSITY PRESS

Cambridge, Massachusetts

London, England

2010

Library of Congress Cataloging-in-Publication Data

Stevens, Jason W., 1975–
God-fearing and free : a spiritual history of America's Cold War / Jason W. Stevens.
p. cm.
Includes bibliographical references and index.
ISBN 978-0-674-05555-1 (alk. paper)
1. United States—Church history—20th century.   2. Cold War—Religious
aspects—Christianity.   3. Christianity and politics—United States—
History—20th century.   I. Title.
BR526.S74 2010
277.3'082—dc22   2010024972

Contents

Prologue

T HIS BOOK will help no one to win an election. It will not help to defeat the Christian Right. It will offer no lessons to the secular Left. It
will not, in short, polemicize on either side of the so-called Culture War.

It will help us to understand how these very polemics are themselves
artifacts of discourses forged in the Cold War. The American public, powered by a national religious revival, was purposefully disillusioned regarding the country's mythical innocence and thus fortified for an epochal
struggle with totalitarianism. I have endeavored in this book, by combining cultural, intellectual, and religious history, to capture the ethos of
America during the last period in which its leaders, ministers, and savants
would regularly proclaim that the nation was not free of sin, and in the
first period when the nation, teetering between patriotic adulation and
doubt about the global future, would become a superpower. Throughout
these years, Americans represented both private and public life through a
language of iniquity, guilt, and expiation that intentionally echoed the nation's past religious awakenings.

Key writers and filmmakers played crucial roles both in shaping and in
challenging the theological critique of America's mythic innocence during
the Cold War. This critique was contiguous with, and very much involved
in, midcentury ruminations on the meaning of American force, the responsibility of its citizens, and the future of the globe that Henry Luce had
claimed for "The American Century." These writers and filmmakers ex-

plored whether an orthodox or a modernized form of Christianity was best suited to diagnose frailties internal to the nation as it girded for global responsibilities. Covering a wide selection of narrative and cultural forms—including theology, revivalism, fiction, film noir, liberal conscience movies, Gothic romances, sentimental melodrama, journalism, and confessional biography—I demonstrate how these thinkers succeeded in spotlighting the irony of America's effort to revive faith when the country appeared to have already transferred many religious beliefs and functions to secular contexts, even as institutional religion had become increasingly penetrated by nationalism, mass opinion, the human sciences, and culture. "Culture," in this sense, included especially the arts but was broadly conceived as the sphere of human action, invention, and persuasion.

Prior scholars have written amply on the interplay between Christianity and cultural production in previous eras of American history, but my study is the first comparable project undertaken for 1947–1965, a period in which America underwent its last major religious revival. Increasingly, people interested in our struggles between religious movements and institutions want to know if the current role of faith in American life and American policy is a new development or in continuity with the past. My work argues for continuity, tracing the history of the present to the Cold War era's political and philosophical reaction to Protestant "modernism," the belief that an engaged Christianity must look to cultural expression and political realities for sources of religious revelation, inspiration, and provocation. This was the avant-garde of liberal Christianity. It is in the context of the Cold War that the critical reaction to Protestant modernism, or "counter-modernism," initially forged in the twenties and thirties, led to coalitions forecasting contemporary "culture war" alignments. The terms of a master narrative for American vocation were formed, as modernism was renounced, along with the country's innocence, in the name of forcing the United States to rediscover its own capabilities for evil as well as the evils of its enemies. There was more than one strain of countermodernism, taking forms neo-fundamentalistic evangelical, European-flavored neoorthodox, Jewish prophetic, conservative Catholic, and most prominently the tragic realist, favored by secular ex-radical intellectuals as well as liberals of both Protestant and Jewish persuasions. While I will be situating each, I will be devoting particular attention to the neofundamentalists, exemplified here by Billy Graham, and the tragic realists, epitomized by Reinhold Niebuhr, since the rise of the former must be understood as an effect, partly, of the dystopian recalibration of liberalism under the latter.

The process of cultural repudiation and revaluation I am describing has had ramifications beyond its origins because the Cold War, or, more precisely, the moral and spiritual meanings of the Cold War, have persistently been revived to define American identity, purpose, and power in moments of perceived crisis as well as triumph. By the 1973 cease-fire, the United States had not only lost the Vietnam War but had also severely weakened its economy and lost European sanction for its objectives in Asia and the Middle East. Internally, it had become difficult to justify America's global foreign policy as a moral and even religious obligation, and the long-term interests of the country did not seem to be served by its tax burdens and international blowback. Kissinger and Nixon's realpolitik and nonmoralistic tone were designed to stress the balance of power, rather than anti-Communism, by stabilizing Europe and diplomatically acknowledging China, though neither Washington nor Moscow ever promised or intended detente to mean lasting peace. The Helsinki Treaties (1975), by codifying the European borders of 1945, marked the growth of normalizing trade and cultural links between the superpowers even as new fronts were opened in Afghanistan and Africa. Soviet expansion and human rights violations, combining with post-1967 Israeli-Arab tensions, the assumption of the Ayatollah Khomeini in Iran, a stagnant economy, and the oil crisis, stirred a new militancy in Britain and the United States, where hawks perceived detente as a strategy of weakness and appeasement. In a reprise of John Foster Dulles's pledge to "roll back" Communist advances, Reagan and Thatcher opened a New Cold War, inaugurated in 1982 by Reagan's "evil empire" speech to the National Association of Evangelicals, which shared his opposition to a nuclear freeze.[1] From 1981 to 1989, the Religious Right coalesced with neoconservatives, invoking the early Cold War and yoking that conflict with totalitarianism to the burgeoning culture war, even arguing, as did Irving Kristol in his 1993 editorial for the *National Interest*, "My Cold War," that the war over values, for the nation's soul, was the continuation of the true Cold War: the battle with "the liberal ethos."[2]

In the 1980s the manicheism of Reagan's vision, and his administration's ties with figures such as Irving Kristol, Norman Podhoretz, Tim LaHaye, and Jerry Falwell, summoned nostalgia for the "Christian realism" of Reinhold Niebuhr, as George W. Bush's righteousness, with its own invocations of the Cold War, has since 9/11. My project was motivated by the question of what exactly liberals have been identifying as an object of nostalgia. The countermodernist realism Niebuhr sponsored, as applied in the Cold War, has had a mingled legacy. Its discourses of tragedy and framing of dire choices of "lesser evils," its allegations of the errors of the Red Decade, its foreswearing of utopia, its criticisms of Enlightenment and liberal humanism, its secularization theses relying on encumbering notions of cultural debt and alienation, its pessimistic justifications for relying on consensus and the rule of law, its apologies for American imperialism— these too it has imparted with as much consequence as its touted, yet ultimately soft, critique of Wilsonian idealism and jingoistic nationalism. The long-term effects of realism cannot be fully measured, moreover, by focusing on only the repercussions of diplomacy or policy decisions. Its ideas, alongside others, competed for hegemony within a constellation of beliefs, arts, institutions, communicative practices, and structures of feeling. These afforded a synergy of talent and available discursive formations in which some ideas and modes of expression became stanchions of the Cold War's master narrative, which advised an end to innocence, while other ideas and expressive modes were submerged or driven into temporary exile. I have therefore represented the moral, spiritual, and theological meanings of the Cold War as a dynamic interplay between that period's reflections on the problem of evil and its meditations on the motif of innocence— innocence wished for, innocence lost, innocence imagined, innocence feared, innocence repudiated, innocence forgiven, innocence reconstituted. The imagery of innocence that was associated, in both hopeful and ironic attitudes, with the United States itself—as Eden, as the Garden of the New World—was rife with Judeo-Christian themes for mid-twentieth-century Americans, and the most pronounced of these themes in the Cold War was the biblical problem of sin. Organizing the book around this motif, rather than lines of Right and Left, has allowed me to move the interpretation among texts, and figures, normally isolated from one another and to demonstrate continuities among these texts as well as underappreciated nuances within them.

Much of the language of these texts has become associated with fundamentalism in our time, but during the Cold War, original sin, the Last Judgment, and the problem of moral evil were topical for intellectuals and writers of many persuasions. This is a rhetoric that some liberals today respect for its "toughness" and "complexity." Yet is it worth recovering, even as a counter to fundamentalism's monopolization of Judeo-Christian language in public discourse today? The evangelical Left activist Jim Wallis, in *God's Politics* (2005), tells us that we need a "return to some old-time religion," but the fundamentalist enthusiasm over George W. Bush's use of the word "evil," as if it were a repudiation of the whole culture of postmodernism, surely cautions that this kind of theological language, as liberal icon Reinhold Niebuhr himself suggested in his 1960 preface to *Moral Man and Immoral Society,* may be too liable to misinterpretation and misapplication for progressive democratic voices to communicate their goals and values.[3] The American propensity to conduct cultural life through religious symbols was never more pronounced in the twentieth century than during the Cold War; never since has the meaning of religious terms, such as original sin, been more widely analyzed, more sharply contested, because of their bearings on national character and democratic culture. I propose that to answer the question "Is such theological language flexible enough for appropriation today?" we must consider the range of effects it had on American culture in the Cold War and the tendencies that that period has deposited into America's historical and literary imagination. It has been said that a good conscience is the invention of the devil.[4] The master narrative I am describing—that America must relinquish its illusions of innocence in order to behave responsibly in a world where there are no clean hands—is not an intrinsically pernicious one. It became pernicious, however, in its specific Cold War applications.

Since I am concerned with the legacy of the Cold War period's consciousness upon our own, more religiously polarized environment, I devote much space to exploring the ways that liberals and evangelicals came to view each other in the fifties. The figures who are generally seen as the progressive heroes of this moment—men such as Reinhold Niebuhr—in fact bear much responsibility for the erosion of liberal Christianity, as they opened it to redoubled attacks from fundamentalism. According to received scholarly wisdom, the neoorthodox or realist voices were the countervailing prophetic opinion to American nationalism and fundamentalism, but, in fact, they did not truly represent dissent. My adoption of the term "countermodernist" is designed therefore to invite comparisons between figures such as Niebuhr and Billy Graham, who are usually contrasted with each other. By drawing these generally unsought and overlooked points of comparison, I challenge scholarly distinctions between the "elite/academic/ resistant" and the "popular/normative/dominant." Niebuhr was not a courageously dissenting voice as he has been portrayed, nor was Graham simply a bland and assimilable evangelist fit for the Eisenhower era. Indeed, Graham's rise was facilitated by the brand of reformed liberalism that Niebuhr's generation proffered as an alternative to American innocence.

For better or worse, it seems that we are in a moment when intellectuals cannot simply say, "Kill the gods already." If, as Habermas urges in *Dialectics of Secularization* (2005), intellectuals today have a responsibility to explicate for secular culture the nourishing ideas in religions, recognizing that these are among "the prepolitical supports" of liberal societies, then they must be especially sensitive to the way religions have sought to translate secular culture, whether for apologetic tasks or for the renovation of tradition. This book does not, therefore, foreclose prematurely on modes of discourse, but seeks fruitful points of overlap between concepts of the secular and of the religious. One of the keynotes of the modernist move-ment was the idea that secular culture can be a source of revelation to American religion. The movement had its failings and oversights, and I do not propose that we bypass the countermodernist critique in order to re-turn to what preceded it. Instead, we must consider what was jettisoned and what was preserved in the critique, the rationale for distinguishing the secular and the religious that the countermodernists offered, and how that rationale came to imbricate forces of opinion and institutional structures that now strike us as unhelpful, if not dangerous, given our present climate of cultural warfare. Throughout, the reader will gather that I sympathize more with America's progressive than with its conservative tradition, and that I believe Cold War tragic realism led Americans astray politically and set dubious ethical precedents. Still, there are no heroes in this narrative, nor are there villains. There are voices giving provisional answers to ques-tions generated in the communicative context of the Cold War; some of these answers are still operative today and others are in abeyance—though quite likely to be reactivated if present trends persist.

The book consists of five parts, each dealing with a salient aspect of Cold War discourse: theology, confession, cultural politics, psychology, and prophesy. Their sequence is thematic rather than chronological, and there is chronological overlap between each part, but the time covered in the entire presentation goes no further than the period immediately prior to detente. The New Cold War of the eighties and its long repercussions for the current "war on terror" are beyond the scope of this study, though long-range connections are, I hope, foreshadowed in the book's reflection on the Cold War from 1945 through the Vietnam period. The argument begins by constructing the crucial intellectual and religious precedents for the reclamation of Christianity, tracing it to the critiques of Protestant modernism in the twenties and the conceptualization of totalitarianism as "political religion," or "secular religion," in the thirties and describing how both countermodernism and the political religion diagnosis were refurbished and subtly transformed in the Cold War. The argument then looks ahead to the sixties' widespread rejection, and reversal, of the terms of the earlier decade's religious revival, particularly original sin and related post-Edenic motifs. An America that began the postwar era in a nationwide religious revival turned then to meet the Vietnam era with another type of spiritual awakening, one having its own political implications. With this awakening ensued a new struggle over the symbolic meaning of the Cold War. The young dissidents who made up the counterculture and the New Left wanted to escape the guilt of their liberal fathers, what they saw as the guilt suffus-ing the conduct of the Cold War. I conclude by reflecting on the continuing implications of the Cold War's "end of innocence" master narrative for today's culture wars between liberalism and fundamentalism.

What follows accepts that we have been historically determined by conversations from the directions both of religion and of Enlightenment. I have concerned myself with theology because its contributions to American thought have been unevenly assessed by both sides in a culture war that has occluded more than it has elucidated about the continuing role of faith in this nation. The Calvinist liberal and Pulitzer Prize–winning novelist Marilynne Robinson has said in *The Death of Adam* (2005), "We have entered a period of nostalgia and reaction. We want the past back, though we have no idea what it was."[5] Moved by this remark, I would like, by way of an equally spiritual American author, to make a connection that might strike Robinson as unholy, though it is not, I think, inapt. Brion Gysin, William S. Burroughs's frequent collaborator, once explained his purpose by stating, "I've come to free the words,"[6] referring to the way languages become hardwired to program our reactions to things we believe that we already know. If this book in some small way succeeds in freeing the theological discourses highlighted here from programmed responses on both the Right and the Left, then this project will have done its service.

Introduction:
Going beyond Modernism from
World War I to the Cold War

The Evil I Would Not, I Do: Protestant
Self-Reflection and a Post-Edenic America

Once the My Lai Massacre became public in 1969, *Time* magazine devoted its December cover story to the incident, calling it an "American Tragedy." Folded into the coverage was a feature editorial, "On Evil: The Inescapable Fact," which urged Americans to stop protesting their innocence in the face of such a manifest betrayal of their country's "idealism."[1] The centerpiece of the editorial is a cartoon, titled "The Other Side," showing a hand pointing to its inverted reflection; the mirrored hand, labeled "ATROCITIES," is covered with Guilt, represented as a black slime that drips from the pointed forefinger, which aims back at its accuser. The editorial sets out to explain the contradiction between America's image of itself and the revelation of the events at My Lai.

The editorial gives a curtailed view of American religious history, singling out the Puritans, the pragmatists, and the "young radicals" of the sixties as moral types. Americans, we are told, lost the lesson of the Fall, but retained the Puritans' belief in election, so that over time they have developed an unbounded optimism in human potential: "evil exists in institutions rather than men, and can therefore be legislated away ... dissected and analyzed ... exorcised through education." From describing maladies of the American character, the editorial expands to describe the predicament of mankind.

Man has an enemy within his nature that he denies by imagining evil as if it were a "Wholly Other" to be detested; Hitler, we are told, has served this function for many Americans. The country's failing, it seems, has lain less in positive expressions of evil, such as "the despoliation of the Indian, or the subjection of the black," than in its susceptibility to "Pelagian" philosophies and patriotic myths that have covered over "the persistent dark element in man." Thus the nation has much too eagerly sought to prove its virtue by doing battle with external figures of injustice.[2]

As in Reinhold Niebuhr's *The Irony of American History* (1952), Arthur Schlesinger, Jr.'s *The Vital Center* (1949), R. W. B. Lewis's *The American Adam* (1955), and other classic Cold War statements on the American character, the traits of innocence, optimism, and idealism seem to imply each other, and all three appear to be definitively American weaknesses.[3] Although the *Time* editorial several times mentions "a dark underside to American history," which, when dredged into light, tends to elicit a "'Who, me?'" reaction from citizens, it gives more space to lamenting Pelagian views of sin, which America has supposedly internalized, than it does to scrutinizing the vicissitudes of the nation's counterinsurgency policy in Indochina. The antiwar young radicals, in particular, are singled out for being "typically American" in that they fail to recognize how good and evil are inseparably intertwined. The editorial closes by admonishing and exhorting the nation to practice honest self-reflection:

> According to Christian moral theology, the self-awareness of sin and guilt is a necessary prologue to sanctity. . . . Individuals are not identical with nations, but sometimes they are analogous. And thus it can be argued that only the nation that has faced up to its own failings and acknowledged its capacities for evil and ill-doing has any real claim to greatness.

If Americans can look inward even as they look at their past, then they may be saved from crisis. They cannot be freed of guilt, but they may learn to live without innocence; if they acknowledge their capacity for evil, then they will be less guilty than their enemies. They may even achieve relative virtuousness.

Twenty years earlier, *Time* magazine had named Reinhold Niebuhr America's "leading establishment theologian" and Billy Graham had launched his star-making Los Angeles revival, and only twenty-three years earlier American diplomat George Kennan had written his influential "Long Telegram" in the form, he later said, of "a seventeenth century Protestant sermon."[4] For over two decades, spanning the end of World War II and the onset and escalation of the Cold War, Americans had been urged to lose their innocence. This period was the last time when Americans became versed in the lesson that they were not only favored by God but also under his judgment; it was also the time when the nation, applying the lessons of its re-education in the vicissitudes of sin and grace, became a superpower. During the sixties, the counterculture and sundry activist movements—populist, New Left, and civil rights oriented—had turned to alternative forms of religious self-exploration, often in explicit repudiation of the prior generation's symbols of original sin and the Last Judgment, but the call to end American innocence could still be mobilized, as *Time* illustrated in December 1969, to allege that the most optimistic of nations had occasioned evil because of its people's very idealism.

The Cold War was not the first period in which Americans said that their innocence had ended. In the 1920s, self-critical liberal theologians and writers, based in U.S. metropolitan centers, together believed, with some conceit, that they were the first post-Revolutionary American generation to be skeptical about human progress.[5] The post–World War II generation inherited the theme of an end to national innocence, but, by contrast with their forebears in the twenties, their situation was distinguished by a cultural religious revival, which had as one of its key features a revaluation of original sin, the Christian doctrine that Augustine minted in his early fifth-century masterwork, *The City of God*.[6] In the shadow of concerns about the spread of totalitarian systems, original sin was refurbished and then mobilized in a variety of cultural discourses that aimed to shore up democratic society against threats preying on the nation's internal weaknesses. As the concept of original sin migrated, it generated accounts of evil in which the idea of innocence took on a counterintuitive meaning; instead of signifying clear conscience or guilelessness, innocence became instead a synonym for totalitarian ideologies of the fascist right or the Communist left, with which certain veins of America's heritage—those descending from the millenarian sides of Enlightenment and liberal Christianity—were said to share a dangerous affinity. In the logic of the era's many admonitions tracing chiliastic ideologies to illusions of moral purity, the responsible citizen was one who humbly disclaimed any pretenses to freedom transcending sin. Across the fields of theology, political philosophy, mental hygiene, journalism, aesthetics, literature, and cinema, transactions between the discourses on American innocence had several effects on American society, but the dominant aim was to adjust historical expectations in accord with what I will call "theological countermodernism."

BY CONTRAST WITH its usage in literary and art history, *modernism* here designates an intellectual outgrowth of nineteenth-century liberal Protestantism; it grew into a movement lasting from at least the 1870s to the

1930s and involved a cluster of ideas that called into question traditional distinctions between sacred and secular, the church and the world.[7] This interpenetration of secular and sacred values firmed conservative Christian opposition to liberals, but liberals also disagreed with each other over the extent to which faith could assimilate with secular society before the churches became irrelevant. Certainly the differences between liberals and modernists were subtle to outsiders. In many ways, it was a family dispute.[8] After all, each favored rationalism over supernaturalism, celebrated the humanity of Christ, considered proofs or confessions of personal conversion unnecessary, and supported a broad interdenominationalism united for good works; each believed there were multiple sources of moral authority, that moral perfectionism and postmillennialism were parts of the kerygma validated by the American experience, and that environment conditions the ways that men access truth in history. Following William R. Hutchison's *The Modernist Impulse in American Protestantism*, modernism is most sensitively defined as the name of an impetus within Protestant liberalism that became a self-conscious movement in the early twentieth century; it presumed the acceptance of biblical criticism but added that redemption should be achieved through correlating Christianity with the progressive elements in American society. Modernists did not define themselves as radicals, and some of their ablest defenders actually argued that they were in fact the conservers of Christianity. The University of Chicago's Shailer Matthews stated in *The Faith of Modernism* (1924) that the modernist stood for "permanent Christian convictions" because "Jesus Christ, the Savior, rather than dogma or even the Bible, is the center of the Modernist faith."[9] Rehearsing an apologetic familiar since Friedrich Schleiermacher, Matthews tells his reader that what made Jesus exceptional was his unique consciousness of a dynamically active God (who evinces his creativity in the multitude of natural forms and unique human personalities), not miracles or physical resurrection (115).[10] What makes this consciousness permanent, moreover, is not the identity of its origin, but its vitality and adaptability; the modernist's values, though permanently influenced by the consciousness of Jesus, continuously evolve to help men meet "the actual needs of our modern world" (15, 93). Modernist liberals believed they could discover in secular society's activism, literature, arts, and sciences sources to criticize traditions that conserved doctrines without advancing the spirit of the gospel. They were practicing prophecy in reverse of fundamentalism, reading Christian teachings in terms of progressive revelation rather than interpreting the present with reference to an ancient and predictive text.

This form of apologetic baited fundamentalists, who viewed their differences from modernists as going to the core tenets of Christianity, especially those touching upon the divinity of Christ and the freedom of the human, as Presbyterian John Gresham Machen, of Princeton Theological Seminary, argued in *Christianity and Liberalism* (1923).[11] Machen maintained that Christ was not a mode of human feeling and acting through which man could achieve his own redemption and that only men persuaded of their own god-likeness could make such an assertion in the face of all biblical statements about human iniquity: "At the very root of the modern liberal is the loss of the consciousness of sin" (64). Liberals, according to Machen, circumvent the problem of original sin by their unorthodox interpretation of the doctrine of Incarnation, which treats Jesus as if he were simply the first Christian. In fact, Jesus is utterly distinguished from Christians by his messianic consciousness and the absence in him of a sense of sin (85). To call him the first Christian is to ignore his true condition as the Redeemer of Christians (96). If Jesus is not indisputably the Son of God, then Christianity is without any foundation, its teachings, including its ethics, without singularity.

Modernists, the avant-garde of liberal Protestantism, indeed obviated any basal distinction between man and God that set the church apart from the world. The identification of Christ with culture would redound on the liberal record as a whole once modernism was subjected to powerful censure after the horrors of World War I. Modernists had promised that they were Christianizing secular society by pinpointing its best progressive elements and uncovering the compatibility of these with the gospel—but had they, in fact, been secularizing Christianity and giving the gospel's imprimatur to attitudes that were merely irreverent toward the cautions of the past? Reeling, liberals like Reinhold Niebuhr and his brother, H. Richard Niebuhr (Yale Divinity professor 1931–1962), adapted the critique of neo-orthodoxy, or "dialectical theology," issuing from Germany in the teaching and publications of Protestants Karl Barth, Emil Brunner, Rudolf Bultmann, and Paul Tillich. Their work entered the curriculum of Protestant seminaries in America with such works as *Epistle to the Romans, The Religious Situation,* and *Man in Revolt,* and were received as prophetic disclosures of the crisis in all human thinking about transcendence.[12] Persuaded that there was, to quote Kierkegaard, an "infinite qualitative difference" separating man from God, the dialectical theologians transformed the meaning of idolatry so that it referred less to alien religions than to any system that identified the constructions of time with eternity. The Christian churches themselves were guilty of idolizing their partial, contingent images of God and denying the paradoxical revelation of Christ the Word, which became flesh not so that man could identify and possess God but so God could forgive and save man. Reminiscent of Marx, whose critique of religion (via Feuerbach) developed into a theory of ideology, the dialectical theologians' critique of belief—in this case, of belief as it had been practiced in their own liberal religious contexts—also became their theory of how modern politics came to function as secularized faith. According to Barth and his colleagues, nations, parties, and movements sinned by inventing myths of origins or teleological ends that made it structurally possible for them to identify the spirit of God with a contingent perspective in history's unfolding.

Karl Barth not only attacked the identification of Christ and culture, but he also pronounced liberalism dead. His monumental *Epistle Concerning the Romans* propounded a return to the Bible's witness and to a faith bowing before God's mystery and terrible power. With rare exceptions, such as H. Richard Niebuhr, Barth's radical monotheism did not survive in America in anything close to purity, but his uncompromising work did help to persuade liberal Protestants that their theology was, as many put it, "in crisis."[13] Liberals, said Willard Sperry of his colleagues, had been "sentimental" about mankind.[14] Protestantism, they judged, needed to give up on the perfectibility of culture, an impossible goal based on an innocent, sentimental, ideal of the human. "Instead of a simplified era of final triumph," as Donald Meyer describes it, "Protestantism was entering a period of complexity and defeat—the most complex in its American experience, marked by some of its most serious defeats."[15] In the face of this evidence, Protestant countermodernists (ranging from the neoorthodox to self-critical liberals to fundamentalists) argued that Christianity should testify against the world instead of accommodating it; Christians should recover the God of Judgment who stands over culture rather than pretend to find God in some dialectic of progress. Modernists had devalued, or eschewed altogether, original sin, as they had rejected Calvinism generally, but the countermodernists discovered in the doctrine a profound description of the ambiguity in human reason and the aggression mixed into human creativity. H. Richard Niebuhr, an ex-socialist (resigning the Socialist Party in 1936), stated: "If humanity is what today we believe it to be, what kind of a God is that to whom we can ascend or descend through man?"[16]

THE THEOLOGICAL PROBLEM self-critical liberals confronted is classically defined in H. Richard Niebuhr's *Christ and Culture* (1951), which describes at its outset two polar positions, the "Christ above Culture" and the "Christ of Culture." The first type "emphasizes the opposition between Christ and culture," such that Christ confronts men with "the challenge of an *either-or* decision" between Him and the customs or values of their society. The second treats Christ as the "hero" of human history and cultural achievement, and makes cultural productions themselves expressions of Christ *as* human activity. After modernism, Christ was now *of* culture; as a result, church and civilization were no longer in conflict, tension, or polarity. Both were in bondage to the world and its values. Subsequent accounts of American religious history have adopted the view that liberals conceded Christ's transcendence, made modernity the highest evolutionary expression of Christianity's essence, and naively associated America, the modern, and the Kingdom of God.[17] I do not dispute the fairness of these claims. Whether or not one subscribes to their theological conservatism (which, we will see, did not necessarily correspond to political conservatism), one may appreciate that the critics of modernism initially had legitimate points, for their best spokesmen succeeded at showing how the modernists had overestimated the harmony of secular culture either by covering over the problems of power and inequality or, as in much of the modernist Social Gospel, by assuming that a broad-based, stable moral consensus would overcome these problems.[18] Under the shepherding of such self-rebuking liberals as Reinhold Niebuhr, Willard Sperry, and Harry Emerson Fosdick, the countermodernist critique managed to chasten its own tradition while still affirming that man was a sinner through society and not only in his nature. "Therefore let all modernists lift a new battle cry: We must go beyond modernism," said Fosdick, the pastor of Manhattan's Riverside Church and titular leader of the Northeastern Protestant clergy, "[a]nd in that new enterprise the watchword will be not, Accommodate yourself to the prevailing culture! but, stand out from it and challenge it!"[19] I contend, however, that this initially powerful and necessary critique assumed different functions, with many pernicious effects, in the context of the Cold War, in which the renunciation of the modernist Christ-as-American culture became yoked to a master narrative and its supporting discourses that proclaimed the end to American innocence. This includes especially the liberal version—the tragic realist form—of this national, cultural, and religious evaluation. To understand this historical torsion, one must carefully track how the critique emerged in one generation and how it was subsequently transferred in the next.

There were two analytical consequences of the liberals' countermodernist critique, and each explanation was retooled and redeployed in the Cold War era. As Meyer describes it, first, "the church became a problem for itself."[20] The frustration of the modernist Social Gospel (post-1919), of redeeming mankind and establishing Christ's Kingdom through political instrumentalities, induced "a new stage in Protestant self-consciousness, the ultimate form of which was to be theological. . . . It was a moment when its true destiny, of criticizing rather than extending the culture-religion of Protestant liberalism, was anticipated" (107, 129). The church was seen as itself imbricating secular power and purveying un-Christian ideas about the distribution of wealth, the forms of status, and the tolerance of injustice. Second, this self-dissection and commitment to going beyond the righteousness of mere piety exposed weaknesses in the Social Gospel's own assumption that it "was justified not only by the character of liberal Protestantism but by the character of America" (54). It assumed "the persistence in American society of its basic ethical drive" (113); the national character was more democratic, and therefore more radically committed to equality, than the churches. Over the course of the twenties and thirties, however, the Protestant vanguard that Meyer describes, who eventually called themselves Christian Realists, grew more "tragic" in their estimate of the American character as well as of the churches. America was not exceptional but was itself a nation vying for its self-interest, internally variegated by groups struggling to identify their own interests with the nation. America, too, was tainted by original sin, which manifested itself in groups as both a will to power and as ideological rationalization. The capacity for self-deception, writ large in political ideologies that universalized the interests of the few over the many, was embedded in the very nature of politics, even in democratic systems. For America to pose as God's nation because of its democratic virtue, according to its own national myth of innocence, was to deny its implication in global plutocracy, irrational economics, and imperial conquests.[21]

Whereas America's Adamic myth of the nineteenth century pictured the youthful and beatific nation triumphantly springing free of a hoary, decrepit Europe sagging under History, America's image at mid-twentieth century was becoming a chastened adult's, his visage weathered by the sight of Europe, no longer so far-off, its blight forcing the once callow youth to look inward for his own sin. His innocence would no longer identify the nation with the revelation of Christ, as the second Adam, Adam reborn from History, but with the outgrown illusions of a purity never possessed. Adam was now a tragic hero bearing History as his cross.

Neofundamentalists in the forties and fifties offered their own version of this narrative that was more politically conservative in its underlying logic, and in the process, helped to instantiate the end of innocence as a symbolic interpretation of American experience. The interlegitimation of this master narrative furthered the neofundamentalists' own bid for intellectual and social recognition and power after a period of reconnoitering. In the twenties, liberals like Fosdick, in statements such as his historic sermon "Shall the Fundamentalists Win?" (delivered at First Presbyterian Church, New York City, on May 21, 1922), had confidently staved off fundamentalists' attacks, bringing their movement to national attention and denouncing it at once. During the thirties, moreover, imported neoorthodoxy and "dialectical theology" had supplied self-critical liberals with formidable intellectual ammunition against their foes, since Barth, Bultmann, Brunner, and Tillich upended the fundamentalist argument that the Bible secures knowledge of God. By the words of the Holy Scripture, God had not intelligibly made His will known to man; rather, man, impatient of revelation, had symbolized what it was not his to know in its depth, infinity, or fullness. The liberal self-critique, led in America by the Christian Realists, had also been a self-defense, and such was the success of its rethinking of apologetics (achieved partly through the internalization of neoorthodoxy) that revivalists, premillennialists, ecclesiastical separatists, and opponents of biblical criticism were placed on the defensive by the very culprits whose modernist errors were supposed to be under scrutiny. Neofundamentalists after World War II would be much more effectual at repelling liberal volleys than their predecessors, edging closer to the center of national opinion by interpreting their ideas and values in the light of the pressure points Cold War discourses would expose in American life, its public as well as its private dimensions.

Generated originally in the post–World War I period, Protestant theological countermodernism, and with it the theme of ending innocence about human nature and progress, was recodified and deployed in the Cold War to justify America's emergence as the superpower among Western nations and to instruct American citizens in their new role as defenders of freedom against totalitarian Communism. The new master narrative of the post-Edenic nation, conceived as a guilt-conscious yet responsible Adamic self, sought to explain the contradictions between America's apparent victory in World War II and its sudden entry into, as Auden classically described it, an "Age of Anxiety." The 1951 Samuel Goldwyn film *I Want You* (dir. Mark Robson), which begins on the eve of the Korean War, registers the jarring transition from peacetime recovery to Cold War remobilization. In the movie's opening montage, an aerial camera hovers over an American town and then begins to descend on the streets; a male voice-over (spoken by actor Dana Andrews, known for his role as a World War II veteran in the drama *The Best Years of Our Lives*) tells the audience that the point of view could be either "a bomber pilot" finding his target or else a "low-flying angel." The speaker's equivocation—the angle represents either a heavenly guardian or an agent of destruction—is representative of two perspectives Americans had not wholly reconciled; they were victors blessed for fighting on "the right side" of history in World War II, and yet they were also being told that they were vulnerable to attack from enemies as demonic as those they had just defeated. Cold War countermodernists located the contradiction in a complex trope of moral doubling. "Innocence" came to signify the illusions that America held in common with its enemies, but at the same time it could mark gradations of evil, rooted in original sin, along which America could be favorably located on a continuum of relative virtue and relative evil.

The nation as a whole and Americans individually were invited to practice moral and spiritual self-reflection to stifle the evils bred of innocence. Theologians, Niebuhrian realists as well as neofundamentalistic evangelicals, lamented that totalitarianism and imperialism were signs of a universal guilt, an inescapable complicity, from which America was not free. Seconding Niebuhr, liberal historian and Democratic activist Arthur Schlesinger, Jr. (among Niebuhr's many secular admirers) cautiously praised Americans for having the Christian fortitude to admit that there was potentially "a Hitler, a Stalin" lurking in each of their breasts. Simultaneously, cultural forms, such as modern art and mass culture, and such social institutions as the state, the family, the academy, and, of course, the church and the seminary, were scrutinized for their contribution to maintaining democracy against ideological evils. Christianity had to combat the effects of sin as they were manifested in society; this effort would involve forming alliances, including political commitments, with worldly institutions, leaders, and cultural producers. When the editorial preface to *Partisan Review*'s 1950 symposium "Religion and the Intellectuals" asked the questions "Can culture exist without a positive religion? Is a return to religion necessary in order to counter the new means of social discipline that we all fear: totalitarianism?" it was seriously addressing whether American democracy had, or needed, a religious foundation.[22]

The master narrative describing America's end of innocence, nested in interlocking discourses on modern evil, totalitarianism, and theological countermodernism, shaped interpretation of the effects of secularization on American life; namely, which aspects of American culture could be requisitioned to support Judeo-Christian values and which were antithetical to them. Questions about the purposes of faith, about the nature of evil, about the dissemination of religious energies in American life, were the dynamisms of what David Hollinger, in his reflection on Quentin Skinner's classic, "Meaning and Understanding in the History of Ideas" (1969), has succinctly described as "the communicative context" of discourse:

> Participants in any given discourse are bound to share certain values, beliefs, perceptions and concepts . . . but the most concrete and functional elements shared, surely, are *questions*. Even when one grants that the choice of questions on the part of contributors to a discourse is itself an act of evaluation, and when one grants further that conflicting "answers" to these questions will be structured by the ethical, aesthetic, and cognitive agreements among the participants, it remains true that questions are at the heart of the discourse. . . . Questions are the dynamisms whereby membership in a community of discourse is established, renewed, and sometimes terminated.[23]

Context is not simply a conceptual pasteboard from which ideas and representations are peeled. Instead, it is the process of transactions, or exchanges, between participants within discourses as they compete to provide answers to socially generated questions, and in the communicative context of the Cold War questions were often theologically framed: "Is a return to religion necessary to shore up democracy against totalitarianism? Has America been an innocent among nations? Is sin social or atavistic in origin? Can evil be defeated or only contained? Which is a greater risk to Christianity: liberalism or fundamentalism? Will churches and clergy be compromised if they form alliances with secular culture?" Each of the primary texts that I will discuss in this book functioned as a provisional answer, and we can feasibly describe "conversations" among them even when their producers were not witting peers. These conversations were facilitated by a common language of mobile symbols, most especially original sin, innocence, and prophetic judgment, which proliferated different meanings, different definitions of evil's sources, that were diversely motivated and had conflicting applications. From their contrapuntal dialogue, the terms of the Cold War countermodernist master narrative emerged and were disputed, refined, and challenged.

This dialogue was not peculiar to Protestant theologians: countermodernist themes, reconfigured within the discursive contexts of the Cold War, stimulated discussion across various faith persuasions. I am necessarily foregrounding the Protestant aspects of the revival, for modernism, in the form that was culturally repudiated from the twenties to the Cold War, developed from a Protestant intrafaith struggle between liberals and fundamentalists. This struggle had factionalized American denominations, and it had done so during a period when Protestants recognized that they were indeed, as evangelicals feared since the 1880s, losing cultural and political hegemony under visible pressure from other religious groups laying claim to American identity.[24] One of the purposes of my story is to describe how the master narrative describing America's end of innocence, using terms forged in the countermodernist critique of Protestant liberalism, was jointly constructed by ecumenists, fundamentalists, Catholics, Jews, and humanists.

The role of Jewish theologians, scholars, and intellectuals deserves special mention here because of the impact of their thought in theorizing modernity, in formulating American identity and the bases of its "consensus," and in stating how Hebrew teachings could trammel ideological extremism. For the New York–based intelligentsia who had sought cosmopolitan identities as socialists and Marxists in the thirties, Jewishness was no longer thought a parochial liability to be interred in the ghetto, and one of the narratives this generation of intellectuals would tell of itself after the war was the rediscovery of the possibilities of their heritage.[25] Recent history—the Holocaust, Stalinism, the persecution of Russian and Eastern European Jews, and the founding of the state of Israel (1948)—had opened a reconsideration of what it meant to be Jewish and, moreover, what might distinguish Jewish experience in the United States. Where they were once determined to lose "Morris Bober," the New York intellectuals now asked how they might integrate aspects of the heritage Bober represents into the traditions of American life.[26] These reflections did not lead to the synagogue. Some—notably Leslie Fiedler, Paul Goodman, Norman Mailer, Irving Kristol (of *Commentary,* sponsored by the American Jewish Committee) and Nathan Glazer (also an editor of *Commentary*)—sought to define their reattachment to Jewish religious practices, stories, and rabbinical philosophies, but many of the New York circle sought a strand of Jewishness that was secular, having "no fixed religious or national content," consisting of memory and "blurred complex of habits, beliefs, and feelings."[27] They imagined that the American middle class was undergoing a similar decline of religious orthodoxies, making a more inclusive public sphere. Lionel Trilling, Irving Howe, Sidney Hook, Daniel Bell, Seymour Martin Lipset, Norman Podhoretz, Harold Rosenberg, Robert Warshow, and Richard Hofstadter (whose father was Jewish) believed that America was becoming more secular and, hence, pluralistic.[28] The "civil religion," famously formulated by Will Herberg in *Protestant-Catholic-Jew* (1955), presumes the loss of Protestant hegemony and its displacement by a tri-faith consensus.

Some Protestants themselves came to believe that American life had moved past them, and the knell was not sounded by fundamentalists alone. The sixties became the first decade in which the terms "post-Puritan," "post-Protestant," and "post-Christian" were "popularly applied" in the United States, as the death-of-God theologians—Protestantism's new avant-garde—became short-lived media celebrities.[29] While they wrote insightfully, at times brilliantly, about the Protestant legacy in American life and letters, the New York circle saw the apparent decentering of Protestantism as an inevitable effect of modernization and, positively, as an opportunity for secular surrogates to emerge, for religious energies to be diffused throughout culture, as Dewey had predicted in *A Common Faith* (1934), and for the dissipation of anti-Semitic attitudes. They were all too aware that Jewish Americans had yet to overcome doubts that remained about their loyalty (the majority of the members in the American Communist Party had been Jews), "whiteness," and religious compatibility.[30] In constructing a logic of consensus, they projected, as much as they diagnosed, an image of America. The kinds of prejudice they discerned in fundamentalism and the political far right were "marginal" elements in American life. Judaism, Will Herberg (himself an ex-Communist) would argue, was more centrist in its values, even though a minority faith in terms of affiliation relative to Christians.[31]

The American ecumenical movement, represented by the Federal Council of Churches, had been led by liberals, and after World War II, Jewish leaders joined Christians in crafting interfaith alliances.[32] Efforts at religious cooperation were undertaken, however, in the context of Cold War apologetics for a common Western religious outlook that summoned complex, at times wary, responses from Jewish thinkers. The concept of "Judeo-Christianity," underscoring the continuities between Jewish and Christian monotheism, united both in Western opposition to totalitarianism.[33] It contrasted sharply with the contending view, put forward by the widely read Christian philosopher and Russian exile Nicholas Berdyaev, in such texts as *The Russian Idea* (1946) and "The Religion of Communism" (1932), that Marxism was a secularized form of Jewish messianism, an idea later developed, with debatably anti-Semitic overtones, in the writings of Russian nationalist and Cold Warrior Alexander Solzhenitsyn.[34] In the United States, the concept of Judeo-Christianity saved Judaism from implication in Communism by stressing that it was a transcendent and lawful religion in which the messianic strain, isolated by Berdyaev, was traditionally muted and theologically corralled.

In the 1950s, texts and films designed for mass consumption conveyed the idea that observant Jews, ancient and modern, resisted ideologies alien to the values of the Free World. FBI Director J. Edgar Hoover, in *Masters of Deceit: What the Communist Bosses Are Doing Now to Bring America to Its Knees* (1958), devotes a whole chapter to the thesis, "The Communist Attack on Judaism," with its opening sally: "The people who gave the world the concept of our monotheistic God and the Ten Commandments cannot remain Jews and follow the atheism of Karl Marx and the deceit of the Communist movement."[35] Biblical epics dramatized models of Jewish-Christian ecumenism by taking the global political conflict, which was already being waged in religious terms, and projecting it into an ancient past where enslaving empires could symbolize, even prefigure, Communism facing the West. William Wyler's 1959 Best Picture *Ben-hur,* for instance, stresses Jewish-Christian cooperation and common values rather than Jewish conversion and Christian supersession, in stark contrast with the 1926 silent version of the film, itself based on Lew Wallace's 1880 novel.[36] Symbolically resisting the idolatrizing of the emperor (or any state power), Ben-hur touches the mezuzah as well as the cross.

Ben-hur and Hoover's *Masters of Deceit* are each examples of Cold War nationalism, emphasizing unity at the expense of the particularity of Jewish and Christian dogma. Herberg objected that the centripetal forces of patriotic faith—the notion that "God is champion of America"—could pervert both the civil religion that Americans shared and homogenize the respective faiths they held privately. To Warshow, exchanging "the virtues of the ghetto" for nationalistic conformity, especially when nationalism's terms bespoke the same egocentricity as the political religions of the Left and Right, was not a tantalizing prospect. Intellectuals like Herberg, Trilling, and Boorstin constructed the logic of pluralism, but they also treated Judaism as a sound corrective to messianic, idolatrous, or manichean strains in Christianity and in America's civil religion. In the process of arguing for Judaism's pertinence, they buttressed many of the terms of Niebuhr's Christian Realism: self-restraining irony, respect for the fund of experience, aversion to abstraction, rejection of utopia, honest appraisal of human finitude and atavism.[37] Herberg, former editor of the Marxist paper *Worker's Age,* and Abraham Heschel, of the Jewish Theological Seminary, each admirers of Niebuhr, tempered the Judeo-Christian civil religion with prophetic elements drawn specifically from Hebrew traditions in the Bible. "Pagan" unity around national idols, as opposed to a true pluralism in which all three faiths would be distinct and equal, could not only erode the theological integrity of each religion but also make them a less effectual counsel to the nation. Herberg criticized nationalistic abuses of the trifaith consensus on theological grounds, yoking the work of the Niebuhr brothers on transcendental ethical monotheism, with his own *Judaism for Modern Man.*[38] Reinhold Niebuhr himself frequently cited from the books of Hebrew prophecy, and in such essays as "Jewish and Christian Relations at Mid-Century," he urged that Protestantism must no longer monopolize the reformist impulse in America.[39] In fact, the Hebrew concept of the God of Judgment was a cognate for the Christian doctrine of original sin, and as such could also discipline impulses to national idolatry.[40] Religious pluralism was beneficial not because it promoted multicultural diversity (the terms in which pluralism is often defended today) but because a chorus of voices espousing common values was less likely to be drowned out by extreme ideologies masking a will to power.

AT THE MARGINS of the Cold War revaluation of Judaism, and ramifying the discursive contours of this study, was the fitful lurch of Jewish intellectuals toward neoconservatism, a movement, acquiring its identity in the seventies, that would be helmed by Irving Kristol and that would find its Judaic moralist in Norman Podhoretz. Each man would lose his political "innocence" (for Podhoretz, his first loss; for Kristol, his second); each was a Jewish anti-Communist convert from liberalism after the Democratic Party turned to George McGovern, as if it were following the zeitgeist of the New Left and black radicalism. Once the self-declared heirs of Cold War liberal anti-Communism, once the advocates (in forums like *Public Interest*) of a "realistic" critique of social policy (a "liberalism without a liberal ideology"), neoconservatives since the Reagan era have often adopted a tone that would have startled Cold War peers such as Podhoretz's mentor Lionel Trilling. Contemporary neoconservatives have become the defenders of values-based foreign policy: they are idealists, utopians, and optimists who have faith in American power and the will to rid the world of totalitarianism, especially where its perceived permutations, Russian or Islamic, seem to threaten the sovereignty of Israel.[41] Neoconservatives share this political philosophy, along with a pessimistic estimate of human nature and culture war commitments, with ex-liberal Catholic intellectuals, such as Michael Novak, and with evangelical activists on the New Right, or "Christian Right." Hence, Irving Kristol, recognizing the presence of conservative and fundamentalistic Christians in the Reagan revolution, has extended an open hand to consorts that Cold War liberals would have seen as exhibiting a lethal lack of self-awareness or comprehension of complexity, making them the epitomes of innocence, as men like Trilling, Bell, and especially Reinhold Niebuhr and Herberg defined it.[42] For Niebuhr and Herberg, it was not America's innocence, its New World dispensation, that underpinned its democratic gains, but rather its ad hoc stumbling onto solutions to the problem of power despite its arrogant and child-like innocence that distinguished it among nations. The tragic realist critics of Cold War nationalism are nonetheless part of neoconservatism's genealogy, and neoconservatives themselves have helped to construct this family tree.[43] Herberg's and Niebuhr's "prophetic" irony, meant to remind Americans of their own sinful dispositions to misuse power or their sinful inclination to misinterpret the "responsibility of power" as the possession of righteousness, itself became a rhetoric—and as such, a feature of an intentionally counterhegemonic narrative—that has served national self-acquittal. We hear its repercussions on the New Right and within the neoconservative movement today.

Lest We Be Innocent: The Cold War
and the Uses of Original Sin

For the American intelligentsia, Hannah Arendt's *The Origins of Totalitarianism* (1951) was one of the most widely reviewed nonpsychoanalytic treatments of "radical evil." Arendt, a student of Rudolf Bultmann, discovered in totalitarianism an evil which seemed so profound that, to describe it, she reverted to vocabulary from the Augustinian theology she had written of as a doctoral candidate.[44] Still a foundational work, Arendt's magnum opus is also an example of the postwar intellectual's effort to theorize totalitarianism as a phenomenon of modernity. Theorizations of totalitarianism and secularization were mutually influential, each setting out key questions and tentative answers to the problem of modern evil. Some of these theorizations implicated secularization in the rise of totalitarianism. These did not necessarily have the consent of critics, like Arendt, who had different reasons for indicting political modernity. It was the interpretations of totalitarianism as a political religion bred of the secular age, however, that prevailed in Cold War apologetics for both Christianity and the cause of the Free World.[45]

Arendt argues that totalitarianism consists of both a state apparatus for domination and terror, distinguished from other forms of despotism in its drive to liquidate human freedom and self-regard, and a peculiarly modern mode of thought, ideology, connected to the rise of the mass society. Ideologies explain what "becomes"; they are concerned not with what exists, but with motion and change itself; the final end, the new State, becomes a deductive premise, and the ideology organizes selected facts into an absolute logic that starts from this premise and in turn rapidly deduces everything else from it. Such certainty in logic does not exist in reality, but within the all-encompassing vantage of an ideology, the organic object world of time and change and natality is attenuated by the horizon of the State. Ideology, channeled by the leader, supplies the adhesive where there is no sense of common interest that would otherwise link members into a movement. Its ideas have little empirical basis, but they have powerful psychological appeal since they confer a reason for being on the fragmented mass. There is a kind of metaphysical "idealism" to the mass man's thought processes. Under the sway of ideology, men in the mass lose their capacity for "internal dialogue," the inner conversation in which experience is related to conscience so that the aims and standards of conscience may be rethought in light of living evidence: "Guilt and innocence become senseless notions; 'guilty' is he who stands in the way of the natural or historical process. . . . Terror is lawfulness, if law is the law of the movement of some suprahuman force." The totalitarian mass believes itself the "chosen" of men who "aim at the omnipotence attributed in monotheistic religions to the God who made men."[46]

Having no belief in a Last Judgment at the end of time and thus willing to create images of Hell on earth in pursuit of a lost paradise, the masses in *The Origins of Totalitarianism* are ideal subjects for the totalitarian experiment (Arendt *Origins* 419). Yet Arendt's prognosis was not that men had turned to the State out of a need for God. Although she at times adopted a cosmically tremulous style in her descriptions, Arendt did not see totalitarianism as "a new—and perverted—religion, a substitute for the lost creed of traditional beliefs. . . . There is no substitute for God in the totalitarian ideologies. . . . The metaphysical space for God has remained empty" ("Reply to Eric Voegelin" 81–82). Arendt's analysis of totalitarianism stressed as pre-conditioning elements classlessness, anti-semitism, imperialistic race-thinking, bourgeois political irresponsibility, and the institutional weaknesses of obsolescent liberal nationalist societies, but other intellectuals saw the crisis in contemporary Europe also as "the climax of a secular revolution" (Voegelin 69). For them, totalitarianism was a "political religion," a concept which addressed the now quite obvious fact that modernity has not seen a decline of religiosity, and furthermore, that it has seen the enchantment, or sacralization, of politics as the means to "reassert the primacy of a religious tradition" or to enshrine states and ideological movements with religious symbolism and ceremony.[47] The concept of politics as secular religion, or political religion, was not created in the interwar period (Michael Burleigh traces the first theorization of the idea to Alexis de Tocqueville's *The Old Regime and the Revolution*, 1856), but it rose to intellectual prominence in the contexts of antifascism and anti-Bolshevism among clerical, conservative, liberal, and ex-Communist opponents.[48] It is succinctly formulated in the Swiss Catholic philosopher Denis de Rougement's *The Devil's Share*, widely reviewed upon its first publication in 1944:

A regime is totalitarian when it aims to centralize radically all temporal and all spiritual authority. It then turns into a political religion, or into a policy of religious character. And this is all the more true as the religion it adopts knows no transcendency, and its purely terrestrial aims not only no longer diverge from the normal aims of politics, but become identical with these. . . . There is then no longer any recourse or pardon to hope for: the spiritual community cannot appeal to a tribunal higher than the State, since it is the State which has created it for its sole ends, and there exists nothing beyond.49

The idea of political religion has since had a complex genealogy as both "a metaphor" and "a heuristic device," and Roger Griffin, author of the acclaimed *The Nature of Fascism* (1993), has identified "two of the several contrasting ways that the term religion can be approached in a secular ideological context": (1) the phenomenological, focusing on subjective experience, in which the regime in question "travesties" a traditional religion yet provides "the normative, the motivating, and existentially 'grounding' force" of belonging to a faith community; (2) the Durkheimian, focusing on the functional effects of "an evangelizing political ideology," in which religious elements provide means of social control and legitimation instrumental for a regime. The first view ascended in the thirties and forties among Christian philosophers such as Eric Voegelin, Nicholas Berdiaev, Dietrich Bonhoeffer, Adolf Keller, Jacques Maritain, Pius XI, Paul Tillich, and de Rougement.[50] These thinkers believed in the structural yearning of *homo religiosus* described by the fathers of Western theology, such as Paul and Augustine, who speak of man's soul not resting unless it "reposeth in Thee."[51]

In his classic, *Political Religion* (1938), Eric Voegelin, one of Arendt's critics in the fifties, attributed the religious features of modernity's most fearsome political phenomenon to an alleged de-Christianization of Europe which left "a spiritual yearning, a void waiting to be filled with another content"—"immanentist" ideologies, varying from fascist and liberal nationalisms to communism, each of them the staff of "a spiritual disease" germinating since the Joachite heresies of the Middle Ages.[52] These heresies of a revolutionary Third Age were once contained and refuted in the West, Voegelin, argued, but the forces of political modernity had undermined the authority of the Church to interpret revelation and challenged the power of Christian anthropology to define human nature. In place of these foundations of high civilizations, modern states had substituted a new political science for creating "a millennium in the eschatological sense through the transformation of human nature. The Christian faith in transcendental perfection of man through the grace of God has been converted—and perverted—into the idea of immanent perfection through an act of man." The objections to Voegelin's "Tory-Burkean" theory, Richard Steigmann-Gall has argued, include the record of the continued power and influence of Christianity in Europe, as evinced in Italy's Lateran Accords and the Church's forty interwar concordats; the paucity of evidence showing that Europe experienced "a death of God" or that Nazism's supporters were apostate Christians; and the existing historical evidence that Western nationalism has shown not an opposition between Christianity and nationalistic feeling, but an "affinity" (88–89).

THE LOGIC linking totalitarianism to the corrupting effects of a de-Christianizing secularization was still more torturous as applied to Bolshevism. Nazism and Italian fascism had at least used the vocabulary of Christianity or enlisted the churches' cooperation (as in the enforcement of the Nuremberg Laws), whereas Bolshevik persecution of the Russian Orthodox Church (R.O.C.) and Lenin's militant secular rhetoric—the policy and its tone revived under Khruschev and Brezhnev—demonstrated no displacement of religious belief or feeling that could be inferred from the manifest, or intentional, content of the regime. In the era between Lenin and Khruschev—following his regime's anticlerical terror campaign from 1937 to 1939 and beginning in 1941 after the German invasion—Stalin extended privileges to the R.O.C. in exchange for having the acting patriarch, who was patriotic, recognize the legitimacy of the Soviet Republic.[53] The easing of the state's policy was tactical, intended to co-opt Russian nationalism in wartime, but not, as in Germany's policy of tolerating the Nazified Lutheran Churches, to encourage identification between the official state ideology and Christian faith. The concessions to the R.O.C. were not extended to any other denominations. Dissident author Alexander Solzhenitsyn's 1962 exposé novel *Ivan Denisovich* points to the Machiavellian nature of this alliance, which had nothing to do with promoting Christian belief or values, by making one of the Gulag's prisoners, "Alyosha," a Baptist, one of the groups persecuted by Stalin at the same time that he was making concessions to the R.O.C. It is Alyosha, a religious dissident, named after the Christ-like protagonist of *The Brothers Karamavoz,* who is the keeper of the New Testament, both in his heart and, surreptitiously, in his physical possession. There were sediments of Russian Orthodoxy in the old concepts of Holy Russia and the Third Rome (each dating from the sixteenth century) on which Bolshevism could have drawn, and, in some instances, did. The messianic myth of Holy Rus, of Russia as the suffering servant of humanity, appealed to Solzhenitsyn (and is reflected in Alyosha's characterization), but to Stalin, it was an ingredient of Russia's past that was unwieldy, given his desire to stress the multinational Soviet state above Russian peoplehood. The myth of Russia as the Third Rome, replacing Byzantium, was revived by the R.O.C. after Stalin's leniency, but there is no conclusive evidence that the myth ever decisively influenced policy in Stalin's era or Lenin's.[54] Stalin was not melding the

Crucifixion with the proletariat cause nor was he sponsoring any religious interpretation of Russian history. Had the Soviet regime sought these ends, it could have enlisted priests sympathetic to communist ideals—for instance, members of the schismatic Living Church, which, comparable to "German Christianity," had made religious claims for the ideology of the ruling party.[55] Stalin opportunistically supported the Orthodox institution instead, for motives of military expedience and to consolidate his rule of the USSR.[56] His agreement with the patriarch, "a concordat in all but name," showed how effectively state pressure could marshal what the politburo actually saw as a counterrevolutionary, self-serving medieval institution, an accomplishment allegorically portrayed in Sergei Eisenstein's epic *Ivan the Terrible,* a winner of the Stalin Prize.[57] The State, in short, did not overtly attempt to usurp the functions of the Church, nor ever viewed Communism as a substitute for traditional religion; the Church remained a concern to the Kremlin, even after the decimation of the clerisy, because large segments of the population continued to resist Marxist-Leninist atheism.[58] Soviet Communism did not so much fill a spiritual vacuum left by secularization as define a policy of forced secularization that never wholly succeeded in its revolutionary goal.

Given the paucity of evidence demonstrating that Communism publicly became a substitute for traditional religion in the USSR, the case for diagnosing it as a political religion was largely based on comparative descriptions of religious experience and practices (absorbing the whole man, defining the meaning and cause of life, observing sacred, inerrants texts, having millenarian hopes, myths, public rituals, and cultically worshipping of leaders and martyrs), and was inferred from apparent parallels between Communist ideology and Christian mythology. The very force of the suppression of religion in Russia and its satellites, and the eschatological fervor of "the New Faith," seems to have persuaded commentators such as Niebuhr and John Bennett that Communism was a pseudoreligious system, a heretical reduction of Christianity, having the subjective quality of a faith.[59] Thus the political religion thesis, first mobilized in the thirties to attack fascism and Bolshevism, came to have a direct application in the Cold War, especially when the concept of totalitarianism equated Nazism and Stalinism, as in Arendt's *Origins of Totalitarianism* and Friedrich and Brzezinski's *Totalitarian Dictatorship and Autocracy.*[60] The resulting perspective "implicitly endorsed the claims of the 'Free World' [combining Christian alterity and democratic will] to represent good in the Manichean struggle, against the evils of state Communism."[61]

THE CONCEPT of political religion remains embattled, but relevant here is its reception by intellectuals who evaluated America's claims to lead the

Free World against the political face of modern evil. European commentators who adopted the political religion thesis during the Cold War, in widely read works by Czeslaw Milosz (Lithuanian-born poet, novelist, and essayist), Alexander Solzhenitsyn (anti-Communist Russian dissident author), and Raymond Aron (French journalist and sociologist), disagreed over the relative strength of America to meet the totalitarian threat.[62] All three agreed that Communism waged war on Christianity, that this war was led by alienated intellectuals (including "progressive Christians"), for which they substituted their own religion of immanence, seeking to fill the spiritual vacuum of a modern way of thinking that regarded the transcendent as a subjective "zone of shadow."[63] They were skeptical, moreover, of any Cold War dualism morally and culturally polarizing the West and the East. There were clear differences in the political systems of the Western democracies and those of Russia and the Eastern bloc, but these societies shared prepolitical elements, including traditions like Christianity, which ambiguously supported them. How consequentially preexisting faith traditions could impede political religions was a matter of some dispute. Aron, who was a practical agnostic, believed that America was fit to partner with Britain in leading the Cold War, though not because it had religious fiber. In his *Opium of the Intellectuals,* influenced by American sociologists such as Daniel Bell, Edward Shils, and Seymour Lipset, Aron maintained that America's intellectuals were of a less metaphysical, more pragmatic temperament than France's.[64] Its reform-minded Christians, furthermore, were grounded in the antirevolutionary tradition of the Social Gospel. Most importantly, its society had found technical solutions to the economic problems that might otherwise have placed pressure on a political system that, its intellectuals had discovered, was very sound in its nonideological respect for partisanship. In America, a "substitute religion" like Communism was merely an aberration.[65] Milosz and Solzhenitsyn, in contrast to Aron, saw America as suffering from the same maladies that afflicted secular man in the rest of Western civilization. To the beleaguered Eastern European dissident, Milosz said, hope resides in the West, yet these nations, where the churches receive very little intellectual defense or artistic extension into men's sensibilities, are no more capable of meeting their citizens' "spiritual needs."[66] America could employ its masses, give them better than livable wages, and fill their homes with appliances, but it could not satiate their spiritual hunger ("an inner longing for harmony and happiness," coupled with "a desire for self-immolation," "that lies deeper than ordinary fear or the desire to escape misery or physical destruction") with its materialist ethos (6). Perhaps, Milosz speculated, totalitarian Communism was the pressure Christianity needed if it were to be reborn (42–43). British Anglicans T. S. Eliot and C. S. Lewis were no more confident in the spiritual stores of the Christian nations, for their religion was liberalized, epidermal, its dogma excised.[67] The cultures of the West had themselves impaired the Church's ability to restrain their destructive elements: unrestrained self-interest; an immoral, unregulated economy that, with the recessions and depressions wrought by greed, had opened the door to state capitalism; the primacy of instrumental rationality in the public sphere and the relegation of morality to private life; and the growth of a disinherited mob, "alienated from religion and susceptible to mass suggestion."[68] Mimicking the faith that, if seriously observed, would be antagonistic to them, Western societies had unmoored themselves from tradition and were drifting towards an apparent end in "authoritarian democracy" and the "hell" of "totalitarian worldliness" (Eliot 14, 16, 19).

Stateside, countermodernists, exposed particularly to the literature of Eliot and Lewis, asked how to fortify the West, and, moreover, what, if anything, excepted America from the general spiritual failings of the West. One of the signal intellectual trends following World War II was a genre devoted to critique of the Enlightenment. The better-known examples include Arnold Toynbee's *Study of History* (published in six volumes during the forties, later abridged as *Civilization on Trial*), Adorno and Horkheimer's *Dialectic of Enlightenment* (written in 1942 and published in 1947), Hannah Arendt's *Origins of Totalitarianism* (1950), Richard Weaver's *Ideas Have Consequences* (1948), Peter Viereck's *Conservativism Revisited: The Revolt Against Revolt* (1949), John Hallowell's *Main Currents in Modern Political Thought* (1950), Henri du Lubac's *The Drama of Atheistic Humanism* (1950), Jacques Maritain's *Man and the State* (1951), Eric Voegelin's *The New Science of Politics* (1952), Robert Nisbet's *The Quest for Community* (1953), Chapter 2 of Reinhold Niebuhr's *The Irony of American History* (1952), and Mircea Eliade's best-selling *The Myth of the Eternal Return* (1954).[69] Excepting Arendt's and Adorno and Horkeimer's books, which are resolutely secular evaluations of Enlightenment, these titles assume at least one of three positions central to countermodernism in America. In the first place, religious doctrines and sentiments do not die with secularization; instead, they are displaced into other contexts, so that modern societies are left with an unacknowledged cultural debt to the premodern past. Secondly, nations or empires seem to fall by some inner law when they fail to acknowledge a power higher than themselves. By sundering reason and natural law from Christian revelation, as vouchsafed through biblical symbols or the Church's authority, or by denuding existential man, exposed to the terrors of history, of the resources of faith, Enlightenment allegedly set modern societies on a destructive course. Thirdly, totalitarianism mechanized a will to create a new kind of man, and even a committed secular socialist such as Irving Howe felt as if Nazism and Stalinist Communism urged men toward theological questions: "Inescapably this meant also to reflect upon the nature of mankind, to wonder about the limits of human malleability, whether toward perfection or debasement."[70] Thinkers like Hallowell, Weaver, Voegelin, and Niebuhr offered the assurance that there was something irrefragable in man, a human nature to be worked upon though not limitlessly distorted. Totalitarianism did not succeed in creating, in parody of God, a new man, but was instead the outcropping of—and testament to—man believing, in pride, that he *can* change himself by remaking his world, by trying to change his created nature.

Secular intellectuals in America—those antimetaphysical pragmatists praised by Aron—were attracted to the helminthic and monitory notes of this interpretation, even if they did accept its fundamentalist and reactionary conservative applications. They had become more willing to examine the cultural debts to Christianity of the leading Western nations. Daniel Bell (former trade unionist and labor editor of *Fortune* magazine until 1956), in "The End of Ideology in the West," posited that the intelligentsia, not the religious masses, were the members of society who should be most cautioned in their utopian speculations by the uneven effect of modernization and secularization:

> Other than religion (and war and nationalism), there have been few forms of channelizing emotional energy. Religion symbolized, drained away, dispersed emotional energy from the world onto the litany, the liturgy, the sacraments, the edifices, the arts. Ideology fuses these energies and channels them into politics. . . . Fanaticism, violence, and cruelty are not, of course, unique in human history. But there was a time when such frenzies and mass emotions could be displaced, symbolized, drained away, and dispersed through religious devotion and practice. Now there is only this life . . . [and] politics, because it can institutionalize power, in the way that religion once did, becomes the ready avenue for domination.[71]

Ideology, which Bell associates in the essay with the irrational passions of the East, was still a dangerous quality in American thought, as evinced by the amount of attention intellectuals paid to seeking out and exposing it, and, ironically, by the number of apologies they made to demonstrate that America's mainstream, its national character, was in fact antiideological, despite uneven development (in education, cultural acquisition, technical know-how) across social groups.

Aiming to protect the devices of power from aberrant faiths, countermodernists sought to defuse ideologies by transplanting their corrupted religious contents back to their "proper" frame of reference. By proclaiming the end of innocence, in other words, the countermodernists and their secular counterparts in the social sciences, the humanities, and the arts affirmed the centrality of religion to America's character even as they underscored the likeness of the country's national myths of innocence—of Adamic virtue, idealism, messianism, and perfection—to "pseudoreligious" ideologies, especially Communism. From prewar theological debates, modernists lost prestige for stating that culture supplanted religion; countermodernists were now saying that ideology was supplanting both culture and religion, which need to be distinguished from each other in order to properly nourish each other or (as Reinhold Niebuhr and Paul Tillich asserted) to discipline each other. To equate them, especially through the metaphor of national character, was the Promethean apogee of innocence. These attempts to limn the limits of the secular and the religious, in spite of their admitted and inevitable overlap, were fraught with disagreements over the meaning of secularization, to which "ideology," like "totalitarianism," was so closely affined historically and conceptually. When did the exposure of "ideology" simply point to the effects of secularization in a democratic culture, whereby religious functions—as Dewey and Jefferson had predicted—were to become loosed from historic religions? To what extent was secularization being condemned rather than totalitarianism? To what extent was the secular implicated in the definition of evil?

By uncovering displaced religious meanings in secular contexts, be they political ideology, psychotherapy, familial discipline, or the phenomenology of art, the Cold War–era critic acknowledged the persistence of problems from one era to another as he also asserted their inescapability. In other words, the Enlightenment was simultaneously a moment of ideological rupture with Christianity while, at a deeper level, it remained continuous with the older episteme by its concern with fundamentally religious matters. Christianity might not be able to erase the problems of the modern age, but it could make them more comprehensible than did the arguments of secular thinkers who brushed over man's tragic predicament with an easy conscience. In "A Case of Lost Faith" from *Masters of Deceit*, J. Edgar Hoover recounts the story of a young Midwesterner named Jack who loses faith in God and so turns to Communism to fill his "spiritual vacuum." Hoover extrapolates: "In many instances we know, joining the Communist Party comes from a loss of faith, so to speak, in our Judaic-Christian heritage and earnest, though perverted, seeking for a new faith . . . In America today hundreds of children, growing up in Communist homes, are captives of this alien ideology. These youngsters are taught from the earliest years that God does not exist."[72] Such accounts assume that the human being is structured so that he cannot rest without belief in something that will forgive his guilt, give him hope of continuity despite his finitude, and restore meaning to a reality that appears fragmented to him. If he does not rest in the faith of his fathers, then he will be prey for another which dissembles its will to power.

Since the ethic of power could not be based on reason alone, then the alternatives seemed to be religion or ideology, each of which was mediated by politics, psychology, art, and mass culture. The "radical evil," totalitarianism, was said to combine both alternatives in one volatile fusion. Once the Democratic administration under Truman decided to intervene in Greece and Turkey, Russia was swiftly imputed the traits of Nazi Germany. Even though Russia had just recently been an ally in the war against the Axis, Communism and fascism were now said to possess common totalitarian features and even underlying psychological syndromes. In the annals of American demonology, Communism was an ideological evil.[73] Prior dangers to the American character had been ethnically, racially, or geographically marked, or else pictured by gross imbalances of wealth (as in populist iconography). Communism, however, was a will to power behind an *idea* that invaded the mind and the soul, capitalizing on their weaknesses. The period's dominant types for representing evil, the Demagogue, the Psychopath, and the Mass Man, were all figures defined by a pathological attachment to ideological illusions. This concept of evil was consistent with a general postwar view that moral identity is precarious, assailed by secreted, internal proclivities as well as deceptive invaders. Theologians, statesmen, psychologists, intellectuals, and writers sought grounds, where possible, to cooperate in dispelling American democracy's guilt-free illusions so that the country might "more realistically" act upon honest self-knowledge. The pervasive trope of the moral double, or shadow self, did not undercut the dualism of Cold War thinking, as expressed in the bipolar model of the globe, so much as dualism and moral ambiguity mutually reinforced an atmosphere of surveillance, in which clergy and churches, with the cooperation of other institutions, were encouraged to shore up democratic citizens against any lurking possibility of corruption that might undercut the nation's war with greater evil. The combined watchwords were contrition *and* vigilance.

In the forties and fifties, the national security state and prominent religious spokespersons were both taken by the realization that power was not merely vested in the State but distributed through the fields of culture and psychology. These totalizing Cold War views of omnipresent but rarely visible battles for power, as Alan Nadel and Ann Douglas have suggested, may well have fostered our contemporary hermeneutics of mistrust.[74] This hermeneutic had already penetrated theological countermodernism. Reinhold Niebuhr and Paul Tillich went so far as to say that the Church itself was not independent of ideology, a provocation that ironically affirmed the more neoorthodox Karl Barth's earlier statements that Christ must be the negation of all religions, for these were corruptible man-made systems. The Church and its beliefs, in Niebuhr's and Tillich's readings, were not truly autonomous vis-à-vis structural inequalities, intergroup contentions, or ideological rationalizations; the task of a prophetic theology thus would be not only to judge the world but also the Church, for both were imbricated by power. There are, as today's Foucaultians are wont to remind us, no clean hands.

In 1943, RKO studios released a Val Lewton film, *The Seventh Victim*, which in many ways symbolizes attitudes that would dominate the period after 1947. An ingenue named Mary (Kim Hunter) comes to contemporary Greenwich Village in search of her missing elder sister Jacqueline. Through circuitous routes that bring her into contact with a jaded psychoanalyst, who has ceased to believe in healing, and a melancholy writer, who aborts poems beneath a hellish mural in the "Dante Café," Mary eventually discovers that her sister has been inducted into a Satanic cult. The group, whose leaders speak in European accents, has worldwide reach, but it has gone underground and now secretly uses the instruments of normal American society to further its war against dimmed forces of light. By the end of this exceptionally grim little allegory, Jacqueline, having refused salvation, hangs herself while her younger sister, shocked out of her innocence, is left to seek solace in her sister's earnest ex-spouse, a lawyer. Near the film's end, the writer and the psychoanalyst confront the Satanists with the Lord's Prayer in a rare show of unity. Both of them have been moved by the spectacle of Innocence (Mary), Evil (the cult), and Despair (Jacqueline); armed with this knowledge, both seem to recover a sense of purpose. Yet, lest the audience become overconfident with these examples, the film closes with two grisly sounds: Jacqueline's body stretching a noose hung for her suicide, and a tubercular neighbor coughing as she descends the stairwell to shadow-blackened streets. Though still having tinges of foreignness, evil is pervasive, and it preys on resignation. Art, the law, the science of the mind, and religious faith must rally round lost innocence to preserve what virtue can be retained and make it strong by concerted effort. In Cold War America, the convergence of these forces, it was hoped, would repel the devils, if it could not permanently defeat them. The alliance ended up being more haphazard than achieved, however, and its inevitable chinks and interstices are the subjects of some of the most supple works in the period.

PART ONE

How a Theologian Served the Opinion Elite, and How an Evangelist Startled Them

CHAPTER ONE

Christianity, Reason, and the National Character

Surely, there was never a fairer test of national quality than this. In light of these circumstances, the thoughtful observer of Russian-American relations will find no cause for complaint in the Kremlin's challenge to American society. He will rather experience a certain gratitude to a Providence which, by providing the American people with its implacable challenge, has made their entire security as a nation dependent on their pulling themselves together and accepting the moral and political leadership that history plainly intended them to bear.

—George Kennan, "Sources of Soviet Conduct" (1947)

The so-called free world must cover itself with guilt in order to ward off the perils of communism.

—Reinhold Niebuhr, *The Irony of American History* (1952)

Realists and Crusaders, or the Kennan-Dulles Debate

Totalitarianism was the Other of the "Free World," yet it was also a malignancy that had fed off the failure of the middle classes to persuade the masses that they had once shared common national interests and that they could do so again in the West.[1] As the Truman administration and the intelligentsia each assessed the internal weaknesses in American society, which ranged from military security risks to the apparent psychological condition of citizens, they mobilized narratives to describe how America had managed to weather the Depression in the thirties without succumbing to the forces that had undermined liberal governments in Europe. Some attempts at explanation pointed out how wartime productivity and subsidies for defense contracts had produced the economic recovery the New Deal had been unable entirely to deliver, while others contrasted the sustained dominance of the two-party system in Depression-era America to the European masses' abandonment of their parties for ideological movements. I am concerned with those explanations that stressed the resilience of "the American character," or the heritage of the nation's cumulative experience in the New World.

The moral exceptionalism of these arguments is certainly indebted to the doctrine of the elect and Turner's frontier thesis, but it is modified by admonitions that the postwar world, and America's role in it, have been fundamentally altered. Subscribing to the "legend" of America's pre–World War I isolationism,[2] policy-makers, historians, and political philosophers expostulated that America had been able to preserve its historic innocence by keeping free of entangling alliances and burdensome colonial annexations while enjoying open expansion onto a continent whose vast resources and opportunities for mobility had diffused the class tensions that result from scarcity and social stratification. At mid-twentieth century, however— when industrial overproduction and dangers from abroad threatened crises that could not be averted by political or economic isolation—America, it seemed, would have to exchange its historic innocence for the virtue of "responsibility." Hence, it would have to undergo a process of moral self-examination to meet the challenges of managing advanced capitalism and halting the Communist dissemination of totalitarianism.

At the end of World War II, America was the hegemon of the leading international economic order. U.S. strategy emphasized collective security interests as well as commitment to the Open Door policy, which assumed that foreign markets abroad would be required to sustain an American economy that was no longer domestically sufficient.[3] Under the pressure to expand international free trade, corporate elites rushed to define the world in military terms set by U.S. corporate civilians, including John Foster Dulles, James Forrestal, Robert Lovett, John McCloy, Charles Wilson, and Dean Acheson.[4] Since its inception under Theodore Roosevelt, the logic of Open Door expansion had been accompanied by "a missionary movement" imparting a "theological tone" and a "crusading fervor" to "secular expansion" in the name of civilizing societies so that they would be receptive to Christian conversion.[5] The language of moral and spiritual crusade persisted into World War II and the Cold War, having its classic midcentury formulation in Henry Luce's "American Century" editorial (1940). The crusaders' vision of the Cold War as enabling the spread of a benevolent *Pax Americana* actually summoned up the opposing vision of a group that would come to be known as political realists, including George Kennan, Robert E. Osgood, Kenneth Thompson, Hans J. Morgenthau, and Reinhold Niebuhr, who focused on national interests as a corrective. The realists assailed what they identified as the hegemonic narrative of a blithely innocent and virtuous nation coming abreast of the world and discovering unawares that it had a responsibility to save it from evil. Yet realist cautions that internationalism could not be pursued without political risk or moral ambiguity hardly checked the momentum toward some of the most aggressive foreign policy objectives the country had ever undertaken. The fault lies partly with the softness of the realists' critique of American policy. Thinking back to the debates of 1898, this group asked American leaders to entertain the possibility that the United States could be guilty of imperialism.[6] Yet no sooner did they pose the possibility of imperial ambition than they pardoned America—for even at its most innocent the United States was supposed to be less guilty than its enemies.

"REALISM" had a range of meanings not limited to the pursuit of national interest. Foremost, it referred, as George Orwell aptly described, to a philosophical disposition "to overrate the part played in human affairs by sheer force . . . [and to] argu[e] from this that one cannot apply to politics the same moral code that one practices or tries to practice in private life."[7] Realism was a skeptical attitude characterized by hard-headed, sober, empirical devotion to studying the relations of power, and it had contempt for the false gnosis of ideologies. Realists identified as their antitheses three species of error: idealism, the rational-utopian quest for universally valid standards of justice; perfectionism, the belief that the morality purity and concord of the Kingdom of God can be progressively realized as an earthly estate; and moralism, a conception of morality as a simple exercise of free will which is prone to self-righteousness, and a cognitive style which is rigid, not permitting ambivalence or ambiguity. The country's enlightenment heritage and its revival culture had imbued it with a peculiar optimism and missionary fervor, compounded of assumptions that it was, with one will, the bellwether of democratic equality, the redeemer of history's sins, and the favored of God. Plied with these self-gratifying platitudes, America, the realists feared, could be led to behave in a manner far less innocent than the national ego imagined itself to be, if still far short of totalitarian evil. Congeries of Christian Realists, who included John Bennett (Congregational reverend and Niebuhr's colleague at Union Theological Seminary), Paul Ramsey (Methodist and professor of Christian ethics at Princeton), Kenneth Thompson (political scientist and member of the Council on Religion and International Affairs), and Ernest Lefever (an ex-pacifist minister of the Church of the Brethren, foreign affairs consultant with the National Council of Churches, and understudy of Paul Nitze), contributed to the editorial board of *Christianity and Crisis,* the journal Niebuhr founded in 1941. From the onset of the Cold War until the mid-sixties, these Protestant intellectuals forged a basic liberal anti-Communist consensus at the influential magazine informed by a Biblical sense of man's nature and his prospects. For Reinhold Niebuhr, this basic disposition lent itself to political orientations, from socialism, antipacificism, and defense of civil disobedience in *Moral Man and Immoral Society* (1932) to a later Cold War concern with collective Western security in *The Irony of American History* (1952). In the context of evaluating the proper American response to Communism, Niebuhr's Christian realism was affiliated with a model of collective security based on achieving a "balance of power" in which national interests would be served by forging alliances to protect Western liberal governments and stanch the spread of Russian empire.[8] Christian Realism repudiated isolationism and pacifism, but it also, at least ostensibly, discountenanced national hubris. For support, it turned to Augustine's separation of "the two cities," the City of God and the Earthly City, which acknowledged that in this world, governed by sin rather than love, all peace was essentially a *pax falsa*, based on pressure points, leverage, tension, and credible threat of force.[9] The high church Presbyterian Wilson's effusive crusade for international peace and self-determination had been marked by "hardened utopianism," a confidence in American purpose, to which "modernist religion" had offered mortar instead of resistance (Thompson, *Christian Ethics* 26). The realists were resolved that the clash with communism not become another enterprise for righteousness' sake. In their eyes, America's legitimate motives for its Cold War strategies were security interests and cultural and political solidarity with Western Europe. Its major liabilities moving forward were flaws embedded in its historically formed national character—its idealism-perfectionism-moralism—which turned virtues to vices. Because of its alleged inexperience exerting power internationally and its Christian aversion to force, it could easily veer schizophrenically between bellicosity and ineffective humanitarian rhetoric. Espying the foreseeable world future, realists isolated purity, crusading impulses, and utopian dreaming, rather than any projects for global dominance of the free market or for political supremacy, as probable sources of the nation's downfall if it were not consistently reminded of the misleadingly mythic-ideological nature of its innocence. To coronate America as the world's liberator from Communism, a view most stridently espoused in civilian forums by the ex-Trotskyite James Burnham and, within the White House, boosted by John Foster Dulles, was to allow it a preposterous ambition.[10] Nonetheless, the national-interest realists did not adequately gainsay the crusaders because their leading lights also believed that America's imperial ambitions in the past, what had been its conscious quest for international power, as in the ventures of the 1890s, had only minimal ethical implications for its behavior in the present. It was being forced to seek greater power, defensively "a new and more demoniac expansionism" than the "old imperialisms" (Thompson, *Christian Ethics* 73). In addition, the realists shared with the crusaders basic assumptions about the nature and sources of Communist empire, such as a belief in its deeply, albeit anti-Christian, religious appeal.

The struggle of the realists and the crusaders is epitomized in the breach that developed between two major voices in Cold War–era American foreign policy, George Kennan and John Foster Dulles. Kennan (Republican), diplomat to Russia and member of the State Department's policy planning staff, and Dulles (Republican), adviser to Truman and Eisenhower's secretary of state, were both reared as Presbyterians and viewed their religion instrumentally, as a way of thinking that yielded concrete gains as much as moral uplift. During World War II, Dulles once said that an America armed with Christianity could be a force for global reform because "the Christian approach was a realistic approach."[11] Kennan, imagining religion a bulwark against anarchy, argued that "the great mass of people have always had to have some irrational spiritual solace in the face of their own imperfections and those of humanity in general."[12] Each man was convinced that Christianity could help to nurture international stability in the wake of the revolutions and fascistic movements that had fractured Europe. The tragic side of Christianity was more pronounced in Kennan, however, while its promise of redemption found a secular correlate in Dulles's vision of international peace through capitalist economic integration and Western military alliances.[13] Kennan's grim appreciation of the influence of the "old human ego" in all affairs also cautioned him against one-sided righteousness in dealing with political enemies, a trait which he associated with Woodrow Wilson—Dulles's political hero.[14] When Kennan turned to Calvin's *Institutes* "for guidance" in 1950, it was in the throes of his disagreements with Dulles over Korea, when he feared that the "moralistic" policies of the Truman administration might precipitate, rather than contain, international instability.[15] Kennan's more limited approach to countermanding Russia—by neutralizing Germany, avoiding a rearmament of Europe,[16] offering the Marshall Plan, creating a nonaligned buffer between the Eastern bloc and Western Europe—was shortly displaced by the more aggressive intentions of the Truman Doctrine and the "rollback" envisioned by John Foster Dulles, for whom American democracy was a means of achieving universal economic and spiritual rehabilitation and Communism was a rival heretical faith and an international conspiracy.[17]

Though Kennan by the mid-fifties turned critic of his country's policies, arguing that the evil in the Cold War was not one-sided, he had already, fatefully, defined the Russian character as sinful, anxious, and seduced by its own Communist ideology. Kennan saw a world of sin in which nations, like individuals, would always behave egoistically. Communism was distinct from other types of nationalistic egoism, however, for it was an essentially evil, utterly self-deceiving ideology that led Russia to act against its own best interests in response to internally generated, irrational delusions.[18] This systematic explanation of Russian behavior, as predominantly ideological in motive, reinforced the opinions being formed in the State Department, where Kennan had attracted the attention of George Marshall. In terms he would later regret for the room they left for misinterpretation, Kennan described Russian leaders as ideologues who conserved power by projecting the West as an enemy that was trying to encircle the USSR.[19] Likening the Russian elite's mentality to religious zeal ("a faith no less universal in application than that of Christianity itself") and to psychosis (suggestive of the psychopaths who populate Cold War fiction), Kennan argued that Communism was more than propaganda for galvanizing the masses to sacrifice; the elite themselves had become seduced by their own lies:

> Right and wrong, reality and unreality, are determined in Russia not by any God, not by any innate nature of things, but simply by men themselves. . . . Bolshevism has proven some strange and disturbing things about human nature. It has proved that what is important to people is not what is there but what they conceive to be there. . . . [I]t makes no difference whether "anything" is true, in our conception of the world. For the people who believe it, it becomes true. It attains the validity, and all the powers, of truth. . . . Moreover, it becomes true (and this is one of the most vital apprehensions) not only for those to whom it is addressed, but for those who invent it as well.[20]

Russia would expand because not only because its leaders needed to justify totalitarian government, but also because the Russians—elites and masses alike—could not help interpreting everything through the "prism of the their ideology."[21]

Armed with these assumptions, Kennan's "Long Telegram" (his "seventeenth century Protestant sermon") and his renowned "X" article, "The Sources of Soviet Conduct" (1947), which coined the term "containment," together form a jeremiad, describing a crisis that highlights the naïveté of idealistic assumptions that all countries can be entreated to coexist peacefully with the free West. Kennan's pieces waived several alternatives. Walter Lippmann, himself a realist who believed in the division of the "two cities," gravely disagreed with "Mr. X"'s refusal to consider granting Russia a sphere of influence. Kennan was thus committing America to an indefinitely protracted "cold war," Lippmann proposed in his famous series of

articles discountenancing containment strategy. Kennan's essays also dismissed the "One World" model of the postwar globe identified with
Roosevelt, Henry Stimson, and Henry Wallace, who each believed that a
stable peace with Russian could be achieved through bilateral negotiations, exchange of technology, and free trade.[22] According to Kennan, the
Soviet Union would instead exploit instability and revolution anywhere to
augment its advantage, even at the cost of taking more territory than it
could control politically or militarily. Russia, its satellite governments, and
its provocateurs in other nations, would not abide—and were not even
capable of imagining—a balance of power with the West; under the sway
of Communist thought, thus unable to tolerate freedom, they would try to
devastate the free world.[23] Advisers to Truman, such as Dean Acheson and
John Foster Dulles, concluded that the demonic character of Communism
was such that its threat could not really be limited so long as there were
Communist states or Communist insurgents. Containment, in other words,
was not really an accurate description of the underlying logic of America's
policy.[24] Lippmann and Orwell, who each also assumed that the USSR had
imperial ambitions, doubted the war-ravaged nation's readiness to move
on its goals and prolong the kind of totalitarian mobilization that Orwell
would imagine in *1984*.[25] Their dissenting opinions did not carry the argument within the White House while other civilian cold warriors made a
fervid case for immediate aggressive action. A frequent, and exasperating,
object of Orwell's essays, the "apocalyptic visions" of the American po-
lemicist and realpolitiker James Burnham, in *The Struggle for the World*
(1947) and *The Coming Defeat of Communism* (1950), furthered the case
of Truman's hawks that the only safe world would be one in which Communism had ceased to exist.[26] On such assumptions, a third world war
was imminent and defeat of the United States probable under any policies
of compromise, neutrality, or nonintervention.

To Dulles and Kennan both, Communism was an ideology that justified
a totalitarian state apparatus, enshrining it with a halo of infallibility. It
was a species of political religion. This thesis was flattering to the Free
World, but it also emphasized the difficulty of containing the Communist
threat, since its political ideology subjectively answered to basic and unmet
religious needs of modern man. Just as Fascists manipulated the religious
desires of the masses by transmuting them into the imperial nationalisms
of failed liberal states, so too Communists offered solace to modernity's
disenchanted by proffering a heretical version of Christianity—the promise of a classless, utopian brotherhood—to be won by imperial conquest.
"Actually existing peace on Earth, meanwhile, [is] . . . a sort of simula-

crum of the real thing," because "life on Earth after the Fall [is] inherently tainted by sin, by definition merely temporal."[27] To Kennan, this was inevitably a *pax falsa* that simulated the Kingdom of God, and in *The Irony of American History,* his esteemed colleague Reinhold Niebuhr made the comparable case that Communism was heresy. Communists, using idealistic ends to justify ruthlessly illiberal means, were parodies of Kierkegaard's Knight of Faith, who suspends the ethical for the sake of the teleological. Though nominally atheistic, they had a sacred, apocalyptic sense of history that resulted in a more powerful religious rationalization of politics than did Christianity in a democratic system: "The communists are dangerous not because they are godless but because they have a god [the historical dialectic] who, or which, sanctifies their aspiration and their power as identical with the ultimate purposes of life."[28]

Even in more stable societies, the concepts of nation and class, argued Union Theological Seminary's John Bennett, were ideological "group identities" that "distort all of our ethical judgments."[29] John Foster Dulles, Jacques Maritain, Hannah Arendt, and Dwight MacDonald, otherwise strange political bedfellows, agreed that the regimes of Hitler and Stalin were harbingers of a "new religion of the state," one in which, Maritain and Dulles added, the state had become "a false god."[30] "Since World War I there [had] been increased theological interest in the danger presented by the state, as itself the embodiment of pride and egotism," wrote John Bennett, but "the modern experience of totalitarianism [had] made it more urgent to emphasize the criteria of justice above the law of the state."[31] Arendt's mass men, in *The Origins of Totalitarianism,* casually breach positive law because they recognize no contradiction between relative justice and absolute principles of justice (the sacred order, the rights of man, natural law, or, in Kantian rationalism, the categorical imperative). "By lawful government, we understand a body politic in which positive laws are needed to translate and realize the immutable *ius naturale* or the eternal commandments of God into standards of right and wrong."[32] Since positive law can never attain the absolute standard of justice, since individual cases always attest to the imperfection of human ethical and legal systems, citizens need to believe in something like "the infinite possibility of grace"; moreover, this sense that any social order imperfectly realizes justice was once comprehended in the symbolic meaning of the Last Judgment (462). The higher law lends a "relative permanence" to the laws of government yet still allows for a transcendent source of appeal. To have this outer circle of judgment is crucial since there is always the possibility that a bloc will decree or legislate norms that are manifestly criminal despite the fact that the full might of the state machinery and mass opinion may support them. The attitude of the Last Judgment, however, is alien to the mass man of totalitarian systems.

Prior to the war, commentators—including John Foster Dulles, who collaborated with the Federal Council of Churches from 1940 through 1942 to publicize his "Six Pillars of Peace"—had acknowledged that lasting peace would be impossible to accomplish unless state power could be curbed by international order. One problem was that the doctrine of national sovereignty interfered with principles of universal rights and laws. These laws had only been guaranteed by the positive laws of individual nation-states, and even then only by the consent of nationals within their respective territories. Once the state became the instrument of ideological movements, universalistic standards had no binding force, since spiritual hierarchies (citing race, native origin, or class affiliation) could justify stripping some men of rights while assigning power to others. With states in the Free World bound by the doctrine of national sovereignty not to interfere with the internal policies of burgeoning totalitarian systems, individual victims of totalitarian states had no recourse beyond unheard appeals for mercy or promises of cooperation, while ideologues were free to exploit an essentially lawless environment to prepare for the conquest of foreign territories. After the onset of World War II made the crisis of the nation-state inescapably visible, interest grew in redressing the debacle of the League of Nations and in fostering international cooperation. Models included Dewey's world government of mutual national interests, Wallace's interdependence through reciprocal trade, and Arendt's cosmopolitan "comity of nations." Religious leaders followed suit. Parallel to the establishment of the United Nations, 129 Christian denominations founded the ecumenical World Council of Churches (WCC),[33] designed to facilitate interdenominational consultation based on a global ethic that would be designed to oppose both totalitarianism and imperialism.

THERE WERE RESERVATIONS, however, about the capacity of international organizations to restrain totalitarian states or to prevent their formation. For one, the bipolar world model of Cold War intellectuals presumed that there could be little negotiation with Communist states. Following Kennan's "X" article, Churchill's "Iron Curtain Speech," the Truman Doctrine, and national security document NSC-68, reigning wisdom held that these states were incapable of tolerating freedom and so would enslave or annihilate Western democracies.[34] No amount of legal codes or abstract appeals to universal rights would be able to apply pressure to ideologically enshrined states; if these regimes could eliminate civil laws and silence ethical dissent in their territories, then it mattered little whether similar codes and principles were observed by international alliances. Since the Soviet-based Communist enemy was supposed to be essentially cynical and irrational, contemptuous of bourgeois morality as well as blinded to the prudential benefits of peaceful coexistence, military action by the major Western powers would have to remain an immediate option, leading, if necessary, to "perpetual war for perpetual peace," as John Foster Dulles memorably phrased it.[35] Dulles, who had once stated, after the fashion of his early political hero Woodrow Wilson, that "the moral law" should be inscribed in "international law," came to regret idealists who overemphasized moral suasion at the expense of considering "material force"; without the credible threat of coercion represented by NATO, he believed, the United Nations (an organization that he also helped to plan) would be unable to accomplish international reforms, from which the enemies of "a world of fellowship and love," such as Moscow, would "blatantly" withhold consent. Consistent with the Truman Doctrine, Reinhold Niebuhr thought of the United Nations as essentially a forum where hegemonic Western powers could hear cautions and grievances from countries as yet too weak to defend themselves.[36] The United Nations could act as a counsel to power, warning its custodians against "bogus omniscience," but it could not "change the location of power in the world."[37] *Christianity Today*, the evangelical magazine co-founded by Billy Graham, joined the realists in chiding their disapproval of "the glow of that idealism which characterizes the dream of World Government. . . . Let's be realistic."[38] Liberals in organizations like the NCC or the WCC were "religionists laboring for a monolithic state caricature Galilee"(5). World government would be a veritable Tower of Babel in practice, and, in theory, much like the chimeras of Hitler, Mussolini, and Stalin: "Utilizing the central weaknesses of democracy, dictatorships have gotten miracles out of pelting the mass mind with senseless hopes" (3).

Instead of an international legal system, the nation-state would remain the basic political unit in calculating foreign policy. Realists frankly acknowledged the more ignoble motives of the nation-state, especially when compared to the assumptions of Wilsonian idealism. Power differentials were inherently a source of disequilibrium that nations could only minimize through alliances that checked power by congregating power. Affairs between countries, Hans Morgenthau (another leading realist) pointed out, were Machiavellian in nature, but if nation-states respected each others' "hunger for power" and reasonably anticipated that each would use force to protect these self-interests, then a balance of power—a false peace, of sorts—might result.[39] The basis of this peace would be prudence, a value ethically short of justice, yet the best a "realistic" foreign policy could hope to foster. Alliances, in this logic, would derive from calculations of mutual interest, with foreseeable benefits. A concert of major powers in the West, such as the Euro-American alliance, would be necessary to check totalitarian states and maintain the balance of power, but this alliance was temporary and contingent, not a commitment to binding universal principles. Since the national interest, rather than millennial goals or normative ethics, was to guide America's relations with both its allies and its foes, realists argued further that the country must be willing to compromise its generally anti-colonial sentiments where necessary to accommodate Britain, Western Europe or Israel. As Kenneth Thompson put the matter, Americans would have to accept as "one of the ironies of history" that it would be better, in short term scenarios, to use force to preserve colonial governments or even to resist post-colonial governments rather than alienate necessary friends or permit communism to rush into "power vacuums" that would be left in the wake of old imperialisms.[40]

World government was also unrealistic because it could not hope to alter political behavior within nation-states, and global imbalances of power could be influenced by factors internal to nations as well as relations between them. The actions of nation-states, including even those of the most economically developed countries, were unpredictable, moiled by competing factions within them and by ideologies that were irrational in origin. Despite its organic ties, the nation was internally variegated by vying groups who could unify around foreign affairs issues only when the prestige or honor of the national ego was at stake or when avertable crises had arisen. As the cases of the Spanish American War, the China lobby, and Wilson's interventionist logic had shown, public opinion, since ill-informed and lacking in expertise, was given to swooning with the impulses of the national ego, as fanned by politicians and preachers. Such internal imbalances were inevitable. Yet the realists also believed, as did the more crusading American Cold Warriors, that in the postwar world it was expedient to minimize disequilibrium within nations, for internal tumult and dissension could work to the advantage of Communism and interfere with the prudent calculations of power necessary to defeat it. Nations, Kennan suggested, should work on stabilizing themselves through "domestic regeneration." "We should not lose ourselves in vainglorious schemes for changing human nature all over the planet. Rather we should learn to view ourselves with a sense of proportion and Christian humility before the enormous complexity of the world in which it has been given us to live." If America were to fulfill its responsibility under God, then it would have to relinquish its inherited image as isolated, holy Eden without becoming the missionary, saintly New Israel from another, closely affined strand of its Protestant heritage.[41]

Whether its outlook was realistic or evangelistic, "domestic regeneration" would enhance the prospect of success in the battle against the Free World's enemies by furthering unity at home. The threats to this unity were also in citizens' minds and souls. Although there was still dissension over what to do with social welfare, where to apply pressure for civil rights, and how to conduct domestic countersubversion, there remained a consensus— according to the liberals who disseminated the discourse of consensus— that the postwar establishment, with its expanded cooperation between the federal state, big business, and the Pentagon, had been accepted as the best of all possible worlds, leaving leaders with mainly managerial tasks. Postwar planners noted that America had averted Marxist predictions (no proletariat class had disengaged itself from the nation-state) by restoring productivity and expanding the middle class; so long as the country stayed the course, combining high defense spending and some economic planning with more incentives for wage earners, then it would continue to be an exception to Marx's dialectic of capitalism. If social reform, in essence, were to be a matter of making adjustments within the system that had been bequeathed by the New Deal and wartime reorganization, the less predictable, more tantalizing and elusive objects of reform seemed to be moral and psychological maladies affecting the national character. Americans would have to lose some of their cherished illusions about themselves, especially their belief that innocence would earn them safety as it had in the allegedly isolationist past.

Christians were urged to join the effort to assist the twinned aims of domestic regeneration and antitotalitarianism by reforming America's national character. J. Edgar Hoover trumpeted: "Ministers of America are truly on the front lines of the battle for freedom. On their shoulders, in large measure, depends the future of our nation."[42] It became a staple of apologetics to argue that Christianity was more compatible with democracy than totalitarianism because it comprehended both the virtues and vices of power. John Bennett admitted that contemporary efforts to demonstrate a special affinity between Christianity and democracy were departures from most of the faith's two-thousand-year history: "Christians have generally felt more affinity with constitutional aristocracies than with despotisms *or* democracies."[43] Nonetheless, his own *Christians and the State,* makes the case that recent history has made it possible for "the democratic implications" of Christianity to come to light (154). Christians share three teachings that can prove valuable to democracy: the absolute sovereignty of God, God's love for all persons, and the doctrine of sin (154–155). The first and the third check the power of rulers, thus recommending the political principles of consent and the right of veto. They also caution against the possible tyranny of the majority, thereby recommending the right of minority opposition and the maintenance of a puissant (though constitutionally limited) federal authority. The second tenet, by emphasizing the value of each soul to its Creator, implies the individualism on which equal franchise rests. In effect, the pessimistic side of each tradition, balances its egalitarian optimists, such as Jefferson and perfectionistic Protestants in Niebuhr's similar formulations ("Calvin and the Federalists," 154). Though Bennett expresses these points with unusual care, most of them were not unique to his work or to Niebuhr's; indeed, the "democratic implications" of monotheism, the judgment upon sin, and the priority of the individual soul were part of the public domain of ideas and rhetoric from which religious patriotism drew.[44]

The two theologians who devoted the most service to reforming America's character were Reinhold Niebuhr and Billy Graham, spokesmen, respectively, for the Christian Realists and the New Evangelicals.[45] Niebuhr, from a radical past (now left behind), and Graham, from the far Right, each exerted formative, conservative influences on post–World War II America. Both men shared an aversion to modernism, and, in response, each had turned to a more biblical Christianity in order to correct the theological liberals. For Niebuhr, biblical faith did not mean a return to a common sense meaning of Scripture but to an interpretation of biblical symbols validated by historical experience. "Biblical," in this regard, was not equivalent with "orthodoxy." Indeed, Niebuhr complained that classical Christian doctrine from the early Western Church through Luther had observed a much too dualistic opposition between piety and action, love and justice, pure religion (Christ's selfless ethics) and pure politics (akin to Hobbes's war of all against all), and he assailed Barthian neoorthodoxy for having regressed to this dualism in modern times.[46] For Graham, biblical Christianity meant a return to orthodoxy, conceived as a set of fundamentals deducible from a right reading of God's Word. Orthodoxy, however, did not entail for Graham a dualistic separation of church and world; he too saw this as an error in Christian thought that was not properly historical in basis and into which fundamentalism had wandered after World War I.

Graham thus was an antimodernist conservative external to the world of liberalism, and Reinhold Niebuhr was an antimodernist critic of moral naïveté from within liberalism's ranks. Since each agreed that America had been profoundly shaped, to good and bad effect, by its religious past, the project of reforming the country's character necessarily involved overhauling its Christian beliefs. As traditions were reviewed, revamped, renounced, and reinterpreted, the theological disputes from the post–World War I period shadowed the struggle, as each side fought for some position from which they could combat the effects of sin, as these were manifested in society, without collapsing together the spheres of the sacred and the secular, as in the modernist error, or polarizing them in a dualistic attitude, as evangelical fundamentalists had done. Both opted for the stance that H. Richard Niebuhr called "Christ-Transforming Culture"—bringing Christ to bear on the problems of culture without obviating the tension between Christ and the world—but the Christian Realists and the New Evangelicals offered different versions of Christian reform for America. Apparent agreements on the compatibility of democracy and Christianity, even common emphases on certain doctrines, led to public disputes.

These areas of disagreement are important to remember and to understand, but my major point is that despite their differences in rhetoric, theology, and political goals, the effects of Niebuhr's and Graham's positions were coterminous in ways that have been overlooked. Though there was disagreement and outright antagonism between Niebuhr and Graham—the former committed to liberal pluralism at home and, ostensibly, containment abroad, the latter to anti-New Deal rollback and nationalistic expansion—each was nevertheless broadly supportive of the Cold War consensus regarding the roles of American power and national interest. We should not be surprised to discover confluences between them. Both tried to position themselves as theologically conservative voices with respect to both modernism and fundamentalism. Both tied the rise of totalitarianism to forms of human pride, the denial of sin, and the pretenses of modern philosophies (naturalism, idealism, and bourgeois liberalism). Both sought to be prophets respectful of the Judgment, Atonement, and Christic grace transcending American power, even as they restored to the nation a portion of its exceptional, or elect, status. Most importantly, Niebuhr and Graham each enlisted different portions of the American public for aims that postwar policy-makers acknowledged could have no popular support if presented only as pertaining to national interests. Subtleties abound in Niebuhr, to be sure, but his realism has had enough apologists. Instead of seeing Niebuhr as Graham's foe, we should see both Niebuhr and Graham more clearly as torn halves of the same flag.

Should We Forget Reinhold Niebuhr?
Why Billy Graham Eclipsed Him

Reinhold Niebuhr died in 1971, but ritualistically, liberals and members of the Christian Left continue to revive him as a beacon from the past.[47] Niebuhr's thought enjoyed a small renaissance in the eighties after the publication of Richard Fox's acclaimed biography. During the Clinton years, George Stephanopolous trotted out a Niebuhrian epigram—"it is when we are not sure that we are doubly sure"—to upbraid "the frantic orthodoxy" of Kenneth Starr after the Lewinski scandal, and now in the long wake of 9/11, liberals like Jim Wallis and Arthur Schlesinger, Jr., have tried to refurbish the theologian for the present political contest between liberalism and fundamentalism.[48] During his 2008 presidential bid, Barack Obama identified Niebuhr as his favorite philosopher, which led to the reissue of *The Essential Reinhold Niebuhr* by Yale University Press.[49] But how helpful is it to resurrect Niebuhr at this time and for the purpose, as Schlesinger imagined, of giving sager counsel to power than George W. Bush enjoyed from his faith-based constituency?

A 2000 forum published in the journal *Religion and American Culture* on the ascendancy of "public theologies" since the Cold War abounded with references to Niebuhr, though generally to point out how Niebuhr's influence had waned. By "public theologies" the forum referred to discourses that spoke from within a religious tradition, invoking categories of faith and biblical criteria (as opposed to natural law or social ethics exclusively) to address large issues in the culture, thereby helping "to shape the way problems and policies are addressed in the public domain."[50] Distinguished evangelical historian Mark Noll criticized the failure of the "Niebuhrian type of public theology" to reach beyond the elite secular media and northeastern secular universities in the fifties, so that genuine public theologies had to rise instead from in the South, Midwest, and West, first in the civil rights movement and then via the New Christian Right. These succeeded, Noll proposed, because they were more populist in origin and style than Niebuhr's which never developed "a common theological vocabulary" bridging elite and popular spheres. This argument anticipated the self-criticism the Democratic Party has leveled at its leadership since the 2004 election: liberals need to acknowledge the limits of secularism and to begin talking the language of the people, who are by and large Christian. The forum, in this regard, was an interesting counterpoint to the efforts of liberals like Schlesinger to resurrect Niebuhr as an antidote to right-wing organizations such as the Southern Baptist Convention. Nostalgia for Niebuhr and the liberal consensus of which he was an architect is misplaced, we gather from the forum, since his brand of public theology is passé, ill-suited to addressing today's grassroots religious insurgencies.

Neither Noll nor Schlesinger adequately assess the problems posed by Niebuhr's legacy to American liberalism or to present-day controversies on the proper voice of faith in American civil life. Rather than invoke Niebuhr once again in the ongoing ideological battles between Right and Left, or retire him for the sake of finding a more common vocabulary between the elite and the popular, I contend that it would be more intellectually responsible for us to take a critical approach, analyzing Niebuhr's thought as part of the history of our present crises and as complicit in them. We should understand what brand of religious populism overran the Niebuhrian public theology and recognize that this populism succeeded not because of Niebuhr's elitism or academicism, but because of apologies intrinsic to his Cold War thought, apologies that rendered him a much weaker opponent than Schlesinger imagines and, indeed, that actually made his views available to conservatives who would apply his works, such as *The Irony of American History*, with equal force for the Right. After all, what kind of opposition are we retrieving when *Weekly Standard* contributor David Brooks can favorably invoke Niebuhr in a retrospective on the theologian written to bolster the case for the Iraq War? "If there is going to be a hawkish left in America again," Brooks states, "a left suspicious of power but willing to use it to defend freedom, it will have to be revived by a modern-day Reinhold Niebuhr."[51] To begin to answer the question of why Niebuhr's influence waned and whether his kind of public theology should be revived to speak for liberalism today, I will compare Niebuhr's Cold War career with the rise of the New Evangelicalism, which had the young Billy Graham as its spearhead. Though a colleague, voicing a perception I fear is shared by other liberal intellectuals, once told me that Graham's name is not worthy to occupy the same sentence as Niebuhr's, this yoking of the two men helps to underscore how Niebuhr nested liberalism within conservatism and in the process helped to erode the case for a vigorous resistance to the nascent Christian Right.

By 1957, Billy Graham was the most visible religious leader in America: a spiritual adviser to President Eisenhower (Republican), a State Department–sponsored evangelist to China and India, and a mass media personality reaching millions with a syndicated column, a radio and a TV show, his own movie company, and further revival campaigns on unprecedented scales to record-breaking crowds. When in 1952 Graham first applied to hold a crusade in New York, the city's predominantly liberal clergy refused him for his fundamentalism and his "hillbilly" style. Since that rebuff, Graham had succeeded in positioning himself as a *conservative* leader, neither modernist nor fundamentalist. Acknowledging the modulation in his image, the liberal clergy made major overtures to the evangelist, inviting him in 1954 to speak at Union Theological Seminary, then the bastion of Protestant realism and the academic purlieu of Reinhold Niebuhr. By 1957, then, Graham's celebrity was commanding enough to bring together evangelical conservatives and liberal ministers to organize the Madison Square Garden Revival, the largest ever ecumenical undertaking of its kind.

Clearly, Graham was making inroads in the Protestant mainstream by the mid-fifties, and Reinhold Niebuhr was alarmed by his expanding influence. Both men allowed that the successes of American democracy could be best comprehended through Christian presuppositions, making the faith instructive in the Cold War. They could not, however, agree on the best means of applying Christian teachings to this conflict. In this disagreement, Niebuhr was far more appealing to postwar liberals. A former socialist (though never a member of the Communist Party), Niebuhr's radical past helped to give him credibility with liberal intellectuals like Arthur Schlesinger and Sidney Hook, since the progression from the Left to the Center, in Niebuhr's case, seemed motivated by strong principles and a change of mind about political means.[52] At least, that is how Niebuhr was received and how he wanted to be understood. No such alliance was possible with the New Evangelicals, who seemed to their critics as if they were bringing the lampooned fundamentalism of the 1920s back into the public sphere. The same intellectuals who helped to make Niebuhr America's leading establishment theologian also linked Graham's constituency with McCarthyism and theocracy. The era's major liberal critiques of evangelicalism appeared in the mid-fifties and were followed by pungent film adaptations of *Inherit the Wind* and *Elmer Gantry*. These works warily regarded fundamentalism and evangelical activism, and questioned the deep motivation of Billy Graham and his colleagues to escape from the void of social irrelevance into which their fundamentalist forebears had fallen after the Scopes trial.

Niebuhr was supposed to represent the highbrow and sage alternative to Billy Graham in the fifties, but just how strongly did Niebuhr differ from Graham on both domestic and international politics? I will proceed, first, to discuss the content of Graham's message and the nature of its appeal; second, to address Niebuhr's critique of Graham in his own words; and third, to assert that Niebuhr's charge, that Graham was complacent about injustice, now reads as a vain attempt to differentiate his own political shift to the right.

Since his Los Angeles Crusade, Graham had been sought out by representatives of the National Association of Evangelicals (NAE), an organization founded in 1942 as a competitor to the National Council of Churches (NCC), which was comprised of liberal clergy. Encompassing prominent seminaries (such as Fuller Theological Seminary), the NAE soon established its own publishing mouthpiece, *Christianity Today* (founded in 1956 by Carl F. H. Henry), parroting the title *Christian Century*, the liberal

Protestant organ to which Niebuhr once contributed. From its inception, the NAE and *Christianity Today* had a different charter from the older, separatist fundamentalists of the 1920s.[53] Harold Ockenga, the organizational leader of the NAE, and Carl F. H. Henry, the intellectual leader of the New Evangelicals, both subscribed to the Calvinist doctrine of common grace and shared Calvin's conviction that politics could be Christian tools and that temporal justice could be a godly aim. In *The Uneasy Conscience of Modern Fundamentalism* (1947), which, along with Wilbur Smith's *Therefore I Stand* (1945), opened a "flood" of new apologetic works, Carl F. H. Henry set an agenda for the new generation of evangelicals, asking them to observe fundamentalist doctrines but to go further than had the fundamentalists to carry the gospel's application outside of evangelical enclaves.[54] Christians should not make the liberal mistake of substituting social activism for preaching the gospel, but they could act as advocates, explaining how biblical principles pertained to current social issues.

Graham effectively became spokesman of the organization when he delivered an address at the NAE's annual convention in 1950, just after the Los Angeles Crusade; according to historian William McLoughlin's report of this speech in *Billy Graham: Revivalist in a Secular Age* (1959), Graham told the assembly "that he was proud to be a member of the National Association of Evangelicals and that he believed it to be raised up of God as the medium through which Bible-believing, Christ-honoring Christians might present a united front against the enemies of the evangelical faith and for constructive action."[55] As Graham brought his magnetism to the NAE, the NAE worked to maneuver Graham closer to the citadels of power. And in the 1952 presidential election campaign, he promised to deliver a new constituency: "[T]he Christian people of America will not sit idly by in 1952. [They] are going to vote as a bloc for the man with the strongest moral and spiritual platform, regardless of his views on other matters. I believe we can hold the balance of power."[56]

In retrospect, we can see that the Religious Right did not really materialize until the 1970s with the rise of the Southern Baptist Convention and the Moral Majority. However, Graham succeeded in laying some of the groundwork for a politicized evangelical coalition because, as Bill Moyers commented, he came clothed in traditional symbols. He made core fundamentalist doctrines, such as biblical inerrancy, appealing to a wider constituency of Christians by adorning these doctrines in the timeworn terms of revivalistic American evangelicalism (especially in the fashion of the Second Great Awakening) and its attendant drama of conversion. As in the fashion of revivalists before him, from Charles Finney to Billy Sunday, Graham's message for salvation was always two-pronged, tethering the

destiny of the nation to the morality of its citizens. Though Graham's critics have argued that there was much recidivism among his converts and
that what he truly succeeded in doing was rallying the evangelical subculture rather than winning masses of souls, one still cannot underestimate
the great popular appeal of his message of eternal salvation, a message that
Reinhold Niebuhr neither offered nor was interested in offering.[57]

New Evangelical educator Edward Carnell, anticipating the Madison
Square Garden campaign in *Christianity Today,* pictured Graham as a
Bunyanesque pilgrim primed to slay a giant, the secular metropolis, as
Niebuhr mused from a private box on the sidelines:

> When the man on the street asks about the problem of salvation, he receives
> very little precise guidance from the theology of Reinhold Niebuhr. . . . Rein-
> hold Niebuhr can prove man is a sinner, but man already knows this. Rein-
> hold Niebuhr can develop the dialectical relation between time and eternity,
> but this is beyond the tether of a dime store clerk or a hod carrier. When it
> comes to the acid test, therefore, realism is not very realistic after all. . . .
> Reinhold Niebuhr does not speak about Christ's literal cross and resurrection
> at all. He speaks, at most, of the symbols of the cross and the resurrection.
> But of what value are these symbols to an anxious New York cabby?[58]

Carnell does not accuse Niebuhr of being an elitist, but of lacking insight
into the human appeal of the very orthodoxy his realism would adjust to a
properly biblical view. Niebuhr's failure to fill stadiums is not because he
is highbrow or lacks specious populist sentiment. Rather, he leaves the
New York cabby unphased because his realism cannot promise regeneration. Its reconstructed orthodoxy confers a state of sin upon man while its
modernist legacy still deprives man of an authentic, personal experience of
saving grace. Carnell's is not an ungenerous summary of Niebuhr's theology. Niebuhr was more engrossed in the behavior of nations than in personal piety.[59] The soul's ultimate fate was a matter for God, and men could
not realistically concern themselves with it. The Cross, for Niebuhr, is a
symbol in a grand Christian tragicomedy about man in history's middest
attempting, in all virtue and folly, to justify his actions by projecting himself outside history.[60] History lacks rational unity or moral lawfulness, and
it cannot redeem itself. To imagine redemptive activity working in history,
restraining evil and furthering good, is an assent of faith; although some
faith in meaningfulness of history is presupposed in the very act of imagining it, some faiths more closely approximate a biblical view than others
because they have a more profound sense of irony. How we conceive the
relations between evil consequences and intent, fortuitous consequences
and their causes, yields different patterns of irony. Niebuhr, in other words,
was writing, to borrow Hayden White's term, a kind of "metahistory," in

which he used tropes and genres (irony, tragedy, comedy) to describe how different ways of writing history appeal, implicitly, to our sense of justice.[61] Niebuhr did not argue that his concept of history is empirically true, but that the ironic view is validated by experience, for it apprehends the fragmentary and contradictory sides of human development, and more coherent with Christian sense, for it lies close to the meaning of the myth of the Last Judgment. Irony makes us recognize the validity of "the religious sense of an ultimate judgment upon our individual and collective actions," because it creates an "awareness of our own pretensions of wisdom, virtue, or power which have helped to fashion the ironic situation." In its comic dimension, irony discovers laughter in the disjuncture between human intentions and the outcomes of their actions. In its tragic dimension, irony makes leaders and philosophers aware of "the ambiguity of all human virtues and competencies."[62] From an ironic/biblical vantage, Niebuhr could enframe America's trajectory as a reluctant world power forced to make tragic choices between lesser evils that might, comically, yield fortuitous outcomes.

Niebuhr's work was designed to influence elite decision-making by affecting the opinions of policy-makers. Prior to *Irony*, by the late forties, the chagrined prophet had already become a member of what Ernest May has called "the opinion elite": intellectuals who may be civilians or not and may belong to the power elite or not, but in either case exercise a disproportional influence over policy-makers because they have access to expert information or, as in Niebuhr's case, because they are well-educated, politically active, publicly known, and willing to take strong sides in a division on policy.[63] There were several such divisions that emerged during the forties: on the foreign policy front, whether or not to open reciprocal trade with Russia (the Wallace vs. Truman divide), whether or not to have bilateral negotiations with Russia (the Stimson vs. Kennan split), whether or not to remilitarize Europe (the Kennan vs. Acheson breach), whether or not to contain Communism in Asia (the Kennan vs. Dulles divide); and on the domestic front, whether or not to indefinitely maintain a wartime economy (the Progressive Party vs. the Corporate Liberals debate); whether or not to suspend the civil liberties of Communists and fellow travelers (an issue that opened up an impassioned debate within liberal camps). Niebuhr provided a general orientation, religious as well as political, in which these issues could be evaluated. In the articles he had written leading up to American entry into World War II and then during the dawn of the Cold War, Niebuhr made the case that the use of force to restrain evil is defensible on the grounds of Christian ethics as well as prudence, that defense of the imperialist West is a lesser evil than absolute dictatorship and "slavery," and that Communism is a demonic political religion—its vision of the classless society parodying the Kingdom of God's perfect brotherhood in Christ—that the West must repel even at the cost of heaping guilt upon itself.[64] Realists including Kennan, Morgenthau, and Thompson had argued that the American public in the past had exercised undue influence over policy-making; democracy, it seemed, interfered with complex decisions best left to a well-informed elite.[65] As a self-named realist and celebrity intellectual, Niebuhr cut the figure of an opinion elite who could properly counsel those in power, but as a Christian theologian he also showed an ability to act as a mediator between policy-making and its public interpretation, as he did in such publishing organs as *Time* and *Life*.

Graham, by contrast, wanted to exert pressure on public officials by raising a passion for national repentance, which he tied directly to the spiritual well-being of individuals. His accent on conversion touched roots running deep in evangelicalism and in the idea of American identity, both of which promised transformation of self from an inherited condition into a freedom under God. Evangelical preaching fruitfully blurred spiritual liberty with political emancipation in early America, and, hearkening back to that rhetorical fusion, Graham's message of personal salvation found wide audience in a period of nationalistic fervor.

For Niebuhr, on the contrary, Graham's message of personal salvation hardly made him worthy of a prophet's staff.[66] In his 1956 article, "Literalism, Individualism, and Billy Graham," Niebuhr criticized the evangelist for his simplistic theology, and one year later, he published a follow-up piece after the 1957 Madison Square Garden Crusade. Titled "Frustration in Mid-Century," Niebuhr expressed his concern that the New Evangelicalism equated moral goodness with mere piety and lifted the burden of continuous self-questioning from the Christian: "[Graham's] simple version of the Christian faith as an alternative to the discredited utopian illusions [Christian socialism] is very ironic. It gives even simpler answers to insoluble problems than they. . . . It does this precisely at the moment that secularism, purged of its illusions, is modestly ready to work at tasks for which there are no immediate rewards and to undertake burdens for which there can be no promise of relief."[67] By secularism, Niebuhr was not only referring to belief in the moral autonomy of the rational self but was also emphasizing the sphere of political action too often neglected, he believed, by pious Christians who placed a high premium on personal holiness. Niebuhr admitted that Graham's brand of evangelism was superior to other popular varieties of Protestantism (he had in mind Norman Vincent Peale); at least it "preserved something of the biblical sense of the Divine judgment and mercy before which all human striving and

ambitions are convicted of guilt and reduced to their proper proportions" (21).

Unfortunately, Graham cancelled the meaning of God's Judgment by his
interpretation of grace. At issue here is the doctrine of perfection: the belief
that man, by grace, may attain the perfect love of Christ in this life. In his
tome, *The Nature and Destiny of Man,* so highly influential on postwar
intellectuals, Niebuhr specifies that perfectionism was a Pelagian belief
contrary to biblical Christianity, emphasizing individual piety and utopian
hopes at the cost of complexity and discretion.[68] By promising that "really
good people will be really good," Niebuhr says in 1956, Graham betrayed
the spirit of the Reformation.[69] Since the person, in undergoing a conversion experience, is given an internal power to strive for spiritual perfection,
he has little reason to renovate the institutions of his faith, much less to
criticize their entanglement with the values of unregulated free enterprise
and self-reliant individualism (20). Niebuhr's criticism of Graham's evangelicalism intersects with his representation of Protestant liberalism's
modernistic errors. Postconversion, Graham's Christian believer is in a
sanctified, benevolent condition of willing perfection, much as the modernist liberal Protestant, in Niebuhr's view, believes man in his natural
condition has the endowed ability to will perfection. The two are distinguished from each of other mainly by the temporal sequence of conversion
and sanctification in the latter, and the absence of a belief in the necessity
of prevenient grace in the former. Practically speaking, the evangelical and
the modernist liberal are both perfectionists who exhibit their do-gooding
in different realms, with Graham's evangelical focusing on piety and the
liberal aiming for social utopianism.

Niebuhr's charge of perfectionism is inaccurate, for in Graham's account
of sanctification, the sinful self is not completely eradicated. Graham tempers Wesleyan theology with Reformed.[70] Nonetheless, Niebuhr pinpoints
a significant difference between his conception of human capability and
Graham's. For Graham, grace is a supernatural force added to the human,
assisting man in making a voluntary choice to obey God, whereas for Niebuhr grace is understood "mythically" and refers to the ironic discovery
that men's rational choices sometimes yield just results even when their
motives are biased by illusions that they are more pure than they have right
to claim.[71] These contrasting conceptions of grace, one supernatural and
one metaphoric, follow directly from the two religious leaders' teachings
about the wages of original sin on human nature: on one side, a belief that
the effects of original sin can skew men's reasoning without completely
depriving them of their capacity for ethical thought, and, on the other, a
conviction that the mind ratiocinates in stygian depths unless it begins

from premises that descend from religious authority. Hence, while Niebuhr argued that with the aid of grace working in history, rational man, in his pursuit of justice, can approximate certain values, such as love and mutuality, that rest on religious presuppositions, though the full demand of these values can never be met (in America or anywhere else), Graham and the NAE, beseeching man to call upon God's grace, sought to organize converts in order to win official recognition of the sacred values revealed in the Holy Bible (as specially entrusted to America to defend).

Uniting *The City of God* with Kierkegaard's *Concept of Dread*, Niebuhr argued in *The Nature and Destiny of Man* (1941) that evil was a perversion of the human desire for self-transcendence.[72] To move outside one's ego, Niebuhr observed, is an imperative in Christian, Jewish, Classical, and Enlightenment definitions of the ethical life, yet this demand, he argued, also tempts men to identify their particular self-interests with illusions of universality (a rational error) or perfection (an error of faith). In fact, this is his working definition of ideology: an affiance of self-transcendence and self-deception so close that man cannot recognize the false use of his freedom. The original sin of pride, or "egoism," is, at its root, a denial of the finite character of man's existence with all its anxiety-inducing limitation. Pride results in "self-deception," a formulation not present in Augustine or Kierkegaard, though certainly cognate with the idea, prevalent since Engels, that ideology is false consciousness. Pride, leading to self-deception, and ideology, the systematic rationalization of self-interest, are both aspects of "innocence": a regression from responsible, circumspect judgment to an illusion of moral certitude or righteousness. Niebuhr thus accorded to self-doubt and irony a superior purpose in the exercise of freedom: "Man is most free in the discovery that he is not free."[73] This all-important discovery, nevertheless, is beyond the capacity of most persons. It is hard enough, in Niebuhr's estimate, for an individual to tolerate continuous moral doubt, and it is well-nigh impossible for groups, whose collective wills perilously blend political and religious identities without any corresponding sense of religious guilt.

Since man is willing to give himself only for an absolute value and never for something as provisional as "the common interest," the love of the nation is particularly seductive to his innocence: "The religious instinct for the absolute is no less potent in patriotic religion than in any other. The nation is always endowed with an aura of the sacred" (96). *Moral Man and Immoral Society* had raised the question of why individuals were willing to sacrifice for nationalism, and Niebuhr had concluded there, as in his subsequent work, that nations inspire feelings of altruistic love (91–95). Indeed, he anticipates Benedict Anderson's case that "precisely because

such ties are not chosen, [nationalisms] have about them a halo of disinter-
estedness" that seems ennobling to the political subject.[74] Similarly, the
Marxist revolutionary class has a sacrosanct air because it is supposed to
be the necessity of history's movement toward freedom rather than the
identity of one group's interests versus another's.[75] "The exaltation of class
loyalty as the highest form of altruism," is not, however, ethically pure; it
is simply "a natural concomitant of the destruction of national loyalty," in
which fealty to one absolute is displaced to another (152).

Niebuhr's conception of irony, uniting the problem of human self-deceit
with the analysis of ideology, had its utility for Cold War realism. Czeslaw
Milosz, in *The Captive Mind,* a text widely reviewed in the Western press,
would argue that Communist ideology, in an act of epistemological violence leading to political violence, wrenches history into a logic that Stalin
termed "Diamat" (short for "dialectical materialism"). Since Diamat has
the veneer of science, it cannot be rationally opposed.[76] The intellectuals'
only recourse is dissimulation, but "conversion" to Communism requires
the suppression of irony (20–21). By the forties, Niebuhr had already come
to the conclusion that Communism forced history into a hermetic logic,
and he had parried this dynamic by making the inner meaning of history
ironic. The Last Judgment is a mythical symbol that dramatizes this inner
meaning; it reminds man of the limits of his capacity for rational or romantic self-transcendence, of his predisposition instead to seek spiritual
shelter from history's incongruities. Niebuhr thus, like Milosz, affirmed
that faith can empower men to defy knaves who believe falsely in historical
necessity. However, Milosz had in mind a common class of men, not intellectuals whose refuge was irony (a mode of self-doubling between authentic and official selves he called "Ketman"). *The Captive Mind* envisages
faith as the repository of unlearned, earnest folk spirituality—as it is for
the Eastern bloc's Catholic masses, for whom belief has psychologically
salubrious effects. Niebuhr, on the other hand, was speaking of mankind
as the subject of faith, and of faith conceived as an orientation toward history. Moreover, as Carnell pointed out in *Christianity Today,* Niebuhr's
understanding of the Bible seemed to be directed primarily at the well-
educated since his analysis of it depended upon demythologizing scriptural
symbols. The Last Judgment, for instance, illuminates "a conception of life
and history" rather than an event at the end of time.[77]

For Niebuhr, faith included the tragic recognition of man's complicity
in evil and the comic sufferance of rational pretensions to certainty but
transcended them both through a higher form of irony that affirmed the
moral significance of human freedom from a point of "ultimate perspective"
outside history.[78] This perspective, of divine revelation, of "being judged

from beyond ourselves," is made bearable by the Crucifixion, a symbol showing at once how severely God castigates human rebelliousness and yet how mercifully He reconciles man to Him when he errs from pride. Thus the wise man's doubts about the long-range consequences of his decisions or guilt about his implication in the inordinate self-love of the human heart should only humble him and not discourage him from taking action against the evils of human injustice and destructiveness.

Niebuhr's Everyman thus rejects the posture of "the Yogi" in Arthur Koestler's much discussed essay, pondered by Eastern dissidents as well as Western anti-Communists.[79] One need not choose between Koestler's extremes of the Yogi, the saint devoted to pure contemplation, and the Commissar, the revolutionary devoted to securing justice. The Yogi would be Niebuhr's "Luther," who strives personally to transcend man's power instinct, but at the cost of permitting evil in the world to go unchecked. Niebuhr affirmed instead that one could expose the Commissar's folly without being sapped by the same irony turned against oneself; saved from endlessly negating irony by the perspective of faith, one could challenge the Commissar in action without succumbing, as the russophile does, to the temptation of ideology to purify one's action. Faith properly turns irony against the self as well as against one's opponent in the battle for power, but it allows the subject sufficient grace to secure whatever power is necessary to restrain evil, or, in the logic of political realism, to maintain a balance of power that would protect liberal democracies from Communist encirclement or leverage. Niebuhr had always been antiutopian, even in his radical phase, but once he relinquished socialism, he began to balance the tragic mode of irony with a newfound respect for the comic because it afforded release from "the slavery of pretending to be better than [we] are" so that we need "to have no illusions about the self, and no inclination to appear better than we are."[80] Not incidentally, this new balance in his tone coincided with the onset of his apologies for Western imperialism as a lesser evil than Communist tyranny.

The grave problem with Niebuhr's public theology, as it evolved in the Cold War, is that it stressed the finitude of human thought and its sinful illusions to such a degree that it drastically minimized the creative, ecstatic, incisive powers of reason that could work in tandem with grace. Man could hardly exercise freedom except in terms of the ironic awareness of his ideological pretensions (to innocence, universality, or perfection). Indeed, Niebuhr cast so much doubt on human reasoning that he could no longer provide the kind of sturdy religious apologetic-cum-critique of rational ethics (not, at least, without damage to secularism) and on behalf of a Marxist-limned moral realism that he had once given in early classics like

Moral Man and Immoral Society (1932)—a work that upheld the liberating potential of human rationality and praxis even as it stressed man's liability to sin and error. Already in 1932 he was assaying rationalists and making the pragmatic point that all rational ideals of justice were based on partial understandings of conflicting interests. Troublingly, however, he also denied in *Moral Man and Immoral Society* that reason could ever hope to eradicate traditional sentiments, like nationalism or ethnic loyalties, or transcend egotism. Furthermore, even in these earlier socialist formulations, the political imperialism he passionately opposed then was but the modern expression of a perennial human ailment, since his anthropology identified "the root of imperialism" in all self-consciousness." At whatever phase of human development, rational achievements—abstraction and the ability to adduce universals—became complicit in egoistic dreams of power and conquest. Nevertheless, if Niebuhr saw reason as "the chaplain" of the "will-to-power," then, to his credit, he also noted in 1932 that reason, equally, was responsible for creating the ideal of justice that "operates both in initiating, and in resolving, conflict" and for expanding the public sphere in which "[h]onest social intentions will find more adequate instruments for the attainment of their ends, and dishonest pretensions will be unmasked." Niebuhr's subsequent reduction of his own, more balanced, early arguments helped to pave the efforts of Graham and his ilk to rob Enlightenment reasoning of legitimacy so that they could carve out a greater sphere of action for God's servants to perfect for His glory and America's blessing.[81] Moreover, as Niebuhr assailed the "idealists" and "perfectionists" who equated rationality and progress, equilibrium seemed to become a higher value for him than justice, as the shifting balances of power in the Cold War dictated that Americans condition themselves to accepting "lesser evils" for the sake of social stability or the containment of security threats. Niebuhr's retrenchment on his earlier prewar arguments, his concession to the general evil that limits reason to the choice between evils of greater or lesser magnitude, came to contrast starkly with Graham's galvanic rhetoric summoning Americans to the work of redemption.

Niebuhr criticized evangelists for seeking only to remove immoral influences from private life while ignoring America's structural problems, but Graham certainly did not think himself a quietist about American life. However patriotic he was, Graham also insisted on his autonomy under God to criticize a sinful American culture at a time when centrists were asking for a spiritual affirmation of postwar America—as Graham-supporter Henry Luce was doing in his *Life* editorials. Early in the Cold War, Graham showered invective on American idolatry and vice, and in his sermons, the scourge sent to awaken America from its spiritual complacency is the enemy of the Free World. Graham preached that Old Testament prophecies referred to Communism, in the process drawing parallels between Soviet Russia and the "evil empires" that featured in so many Hollywood biblical epics of the period: "Ezekiel 38 and 39 *may* be well be describing Russia and the mighty power of Communism—the greatest, most well-organized and outspoken foe of Christianity that the church has confronted since the days of pagan Rome!" Graham frequently said that a minister had to avoid being a political partisan, but since Communism was not a political ideology so much as it was a false faith, it fell within the domain of heresy and represented a challenge to Christianity itself. It was imperative to "roll back" Communism, a goal that would require military intervention combined with evangelical missions in Europe and the Third World.[82]

For Graham, the international Cold War and evangelical missions were complementary aims, each in turn tied to the goal of stirring Americans at home to repentance. The threat of international disaster should lead private Americans toward inner reform, the conversion experience through acceptance of Jesus Christ. Graham believed that original sin was a species curse for which each person was individually damnable, but in the terms of his jeremiad, the personal choice for or against Christ had wider ramifications: insofar as its citizens were unsaved, America as a whole baited God's wrath. For the sake of national destiny as well as the salvation of single souls, Graham's message required that he pierce those aspects of American society that dulled men to the message of personal redemption through Christ. The national revival could not consist only in church leadership or ecumenical rallies; it also had to take place in American individuals, since sin of whatever magnitude began not with groups or ideologies but within each heart: "Fascism and Communism [could] find no place in the heart and soul of a person who is filled with the Spirit of God." On such radio and TV programs as "Do We Need the Old Time Religion" (1951), Graham made spiritual pleas to the country's citizens: "If everyone in America were to turn to Christ then 'we would have divine intervention on our side.'" In one of his Sermons of the Month from 1953, he continued the plea: "Only as millions of Americans turn to Jesus Christ at this hour and accept him as Savior can this nation possibly be spared the onslaught of demon-possessed Communism." When he implored "America," Graham was not only addressing leaders and experts. America's fulfillment of God's sacred mission implicated the spiritual condition of each American citizen as much as men of power, such as Eisenhower and Dulles.[83]

At this point, we might return to Niebuhr's question: what were the fruits of all this conversion? After all, Graham and the NAE promised to reclaim secular spheres of action for Christian influence and expression. So how was the convert to cultivate his newfound values within American society? Apart from the international struggle with Communism, what counsel did Graham's preaching offer on matters affecting domestic policy? Though Graham was never as confrontational about social problems as he was about vice, idolatry, or foreign threat, they do receive some airing, as in this passage from *Peace with God*: "What is our attitude toward the race question? . . . What is our attitude toward labor-management problems? What is our attitude toward tolerance? . . . Christians, above all others, should be concerned with social problems and social injustices. Down through the centuries the church has contributed more than any other single agency in lifting social standards to new heights."[84] Graham's statement here, under the heading "Social Obligations of the Christian," rings with topical relevance, and it is certainly out of tone with the fundamentalism of his youth. When one actually examines his teaching on poverty, labor relations, or racial segregation, however, he recommends no means (such as advocacy of specific reforms, organized protest, federal action) apart from the voluntary Christian compassion that Niebuhr had challenged in the thirties. Labor and management should apply "the Golden Rule" to each other, the poor should receive help from social workers or local charities, and racial integration should be encouraged by the teaching of brotherhood. On race relations, the social issue he was most frequently asked to address, Graham preferred the role of mediator to prophet. A registered Democrat from North Carolina, Graham acted as a conscience of white Southern moderates, and he recieved censure from civil rights activists as well as racist demagogues, both of whom he considered extremists. He waffled in his criticism of segregationists until *Brown versus the Board of Education,* and not until 1957 did he openly endorse anti-Jim Crow legislation. Losing respect among black leaders for his tepid gradualism in the sixties, Graham at no point condoned any form of resistance, even nonviolent, in the protests for civil rights or for black liberation.[85] In fairness to Graham, he did shift slightly to the left when he threw his support behind President Johnson's War on Poverty. But in the fifties, he was deeply suspicious of New Deal social policies as well as labor unions and direct action politics. Prior to his revisiting the teachings of the Social Gospel in the sixties (which enduringly altered, and liberalized, his views on the causes of poverty), Graham was swayed by positions inherited from the much earlier (pre–World War I) fundamentalist bouts with modernists over the meaning and method of salvation; modernists had been accused, accurately, by their opponents of substituting social service for individual conversion and identifying social perfection with regeneration from sin (conceived by modernists as a shared, corporate guilt). After modulating his position on welfare legislation during Johnson's Democratic presidency, Graham would still maintain, as the Christian Right does today (even at its moderate fringe, for example, with a figure such as Rick Warren), that spiritual salvation resides in the individual's relationship with God, although social service may follow as a fruit of one's conversion.

To return to Graham's statement that he was offering a "spiritual platform" for Christian voters in the fifties, it now appears as if the platform he then had in mind, one which has had a virulent afterlife even though Graham has himself moderated, bore much resemblance to what is now called the New Right. In an essay titled "New Conservatism in America" (1956), sociologist Irving Horowitz presciently diagnosed the emerging ideology: a revolt against social welfare liberalism and secularism, and an adoption of the expansionist foreign policy objectives of liberals.[86] In contrast to "old style" conservatives, the new breed is not nostalgic for a precapitalist past. It also rejects utopianism, but it does not seek security from the fallen world by isolating the nation-state. Rather, it is committed to hegemony and expansion. Since these processes are motivated by business interests, the new conservative "no longer makes paramount the critique of the bourgeoisie" (161). Instead, like the editors of the *National Review,* the new conservative aims to make business leaders aware of "ultimate goals" so that capitalism, whose private property relations are often expressions of sin, can be instead an instrument of "heavenly sanction" for spreading the moral values and social norms of the hegemonic power (148, 156). It gives imperialism "theological imprimatur" (161). Within the hegemon, national "harmony," rather than national unity (which can be artificially imposed) is the goal of society (153). In this regard, new conservatives appropriate the liberal discourse of consensus, though with an important additive; consensus must be achieved not through pluralities or by rational agreements on shared interests but by education in "patriotism, love of God, and national heroes" (153). The teaching of proper attitudes instills, supposedly, a moral orientation that checks man's febrile rationality.

AT THE TIME Horowitz composed his essay, Billy Graham's brand of neofundamentalism deviated significantly from the elitist conservative tradition being refurbished by William F. Buckley and the *National Review.*[87] His comparable aspiration to broker a broadly illiberal religious consensus, with sufficient voting power to get its opinion a serious hearing and, more importantly to him, change Americans' perceptions of their culture's spiritual direction, led him to adopt a style of public religion that carried the conservative agenda to a mass base more effectively than his intellectual counterparts outside the New Evangelicals. The conservative intellectual movement, which began to percolate post-1945, faced many obstacles, not least of which was the threat of sectarianism. The movement was a baggy assemblage of libertarians, interventionist anti-Communists, and antisecular traditionalists.[88] Buckley's strategy to rally the polyglot, contentious house (what he called "fusionism") was initially the raison d'etre for his famous magazine.[89] Secondly, many conservative leading lights were Catholics or Catholic converts in an atmosphere where the baiting of the Vatican as an un-American and even totalitarian entity was still tolerated in such serious publications as the *Nation* and the *Christian Century* (Nash 87–93, 219–220, 238–243, 271–274). Thirdly, under a political establishment where the reigning consensus was liberalism, conservatives strove to demonstrate that America's political traditions (as grounded in the Constitution, *The Federalist Papers*, natural law, and Christian revelation) were in fact antimajoritarian and antiequalitarian. These conclusions placed their exponents in the rhetorically difficult position of arguing for the Americanism of a governmental philosophy that was, in fact, less democratic than liberalism held. Compounding the difficulty, many of the new conservatives were also cultural elitists and Europhiles who believed that a good society was properly stratified to afford leisure and cultivation to a learned, tasteful (meaning, "classical" rather than mondaine) class that would lead—or as the *National Review*'s James Burnham had it, *deceive*—the have-nots and keep their power and influence properly minuscule, thus ensuring political stability and choking off the many-headed Public (51–84, 287–339, 390–391). For conservatives, Buckley's bon vivant anti-Communism modeled a way of living (harpsichord lessons optional) as well as a political stance. Their patrician hauteur seemed perpetually on the verge of discomfiture, however, since many of the *National Review*'s orbit were persuaded, glumly, that America was already a mass society in pandemonium. As the traditionalist, anti-Communist icon Whittaker Chambers had discerned in the fifties, these problems would gravely complicate any effort the new conservatism made to expand its social base beyond isolated cognoscenti. Indeed, Chambers (despite his own ingrained despondency about the future of the West) taught Buckley that in order to make itself a viable political agent, the new conservative movement would have to reach out via mass media to a broader constituency with a populist message—making cause with the people—later adopted by the Barry Goldwater campaign in 1964 and subsequently Ronald Reagan.[90] In the fifties, when Buckley's intellectual circle was as yet unexcited by the GOP, Graham was already modeling such a style of conservatism and shepherding it toward the Republican Party.

Graham's populism, in the universalist spirit of American evangelical-ism, concluded that the equality of souls in God's eyes led necessarily to the idea that each man, regardless of origin, enjoyed the wherewithal to be a strong individualist and an active agent of Christ in the world. In this respect, his message dovetailed with the interventionist anti-Communism of Chambers as well as the libertarian elements of the conservative move-ment. Buckley's *God and Man at Yale* (1951), defying liberal Catholics' anticapitalist, pro–social welfare interpretation of papal teachings, adroitly yoked the Church's long-standing antistatism to a defense of the free mar-ket and an attack on Keynesian principles, but the book speaks in the tone and setting of academic, Ivy League privilege, legacy, and donors' largesse. Graham was actually closer to our contemporary neoconservatives, who have shown themselves as adept at co-opting populist language, symbols, and myths in religion as in politics. In other respects, especially his attacks on secular culture, his blessings to deregulated capitalism, his appeals to traditionalism, and his tendency to see the world as a territory to be har-vested for democracy and Christianity, Graham's theology and his ethics were also well-suited to the emerging positions subsequently adopted by the New Right as well as by the neoconservative confreres who defected from the Left. Since morality was an eternal set of truths passed down through the faithful, moreover, a key voting criterion had to be whether or not the candidate was sufficiently Christ-influenced—or, as it turned out in the case of Eisenhower, the candidate who was sufficiently friendly and susceptible to Graham's religious counsel. What Buckley hoped to procure through "fusionism," Graham thus accomplished by melding the new con-servatism's themes (libertarian, anti-Communist interventionist, and tradi-tionalist) while extending their audience to the White House. Moreover, he invited a broadening of their interreligious base when the conservative movement was still parochially Thomist. In the ecumenical spirit of a re-vivalist, Graham demonstrated openness to Catholics as brethren in Christ beginning in the early sixties, and also, in an interface that the conservative intellectual movement would not make until such figures as Norman Pod-horetz and Irving Kristol migrated right in the seventies, tendered his bless-ing to Jews in the state of Israel.[91]

At this point, we can compare Graham's message to Niebuhr's in or-der to point up the pretensions of Niebuhr's critique. On the question of foreign policy, Niebuhr's *rhetoric* departs from Graham's. Niebuhr never deviated from saying that if America is truly under God's Judgment, then

its foreign policy objectives cannot be identified with God's will, which is
what Graham came perilously close to suggesting. Throughout the Cold
War, Niebuhr cautioned that the identification of God and country could
lead to national self-righteousness and the overextension of American military commitments in an ill-fated effort to save the world for democracy.
His distinction between God and country was intended to dissuade America from overextending its power and to cultivate a mood of fear and
trembling before the vicissitudes of history. Thus, Niebuhr's counsel was
supposed to be the wiser alternative to Graham's apocalypticism, since his
rhetoric appeared to discourage military commitments in the Third World.
In fact, Niebuhr, no more than Graham, provided an ethical position
clearly condemning America's expansion of its global anti-Communist objectives. In *The Structure of Nations and Empires* (1959), a summation of
his thoughts on politics since the onset of the Cold War, Niebuhr judged
Western imperialism "morally ambiguous" rather than "morally evil" like
Communist "universal empire"; since the effects of "strong nations" upon
"weaker ones" are "creative as well as baneful," America, as the hegemonic nation of the Western democratic alliance, should not be dissuaded
from using necessary power (economic and military) by the hue and cry of
liberals whose anti-colonial principles were too pure to guide the nation's
actions in world affairs: "The U. S. must frankly acknowledge the imperial
dimensions of its power and accept the responsibilities which are the con-
comitants of power."[92] Since Niebuhr also assumed that Marxist revolutions anywhere were threats to the national interest, he believed that
America was obliged to prevent nonaligned countries from being turned
Communist.[93] Since the "realist" Niebuhr as much as the "crusader" Graham agreed that Communism would be a form of enslavement much more
severe to colonial subjects than what they had endured under Western
paternalism, wars of counterinsurgency were justifiable in both of their
philosophies. Niebuhr would always add the caveat that ironic hindsight
might later reveal errors in America's tactical judgment, but wherever national interests or Western freedom appeared to be at stake, the country
had to assume pragmatic justification, albeit tainted, if its actions were
measured against the standard of Christic purity. This moral paradox,
conjoining guilt and virtue, was no surprise given the "pattern of ironic
failure" recurring in history, in which the value of rational interest is always irresolvably at tension with perfect love, and the human shortcoming
of Christ's example is masked as some innocence-preserving ideal: "That
we should be less innocent as a nation than our fathers hoped; that we
should be covered with guilt by assumption of the very responsibilities that
express virtue . . . all this fits very well into the pattern of ironic failure. In

all of them human limitations catch up with human pretensions."[94] Between action and its long historical ramification, the degree of America's guilt would remain uncertain, a mystery that only time would solve.

Niebuhr failed to convert *Irony*'s negative appraisal of American idealism (a target he still shared with Kennan) into a critique of the United States' bipolar world model and its attendant reliance on military force to maintain an equipoise of power, primarily because he could not divorce his thought from his hardened, post-1945 image of Communism as an ideological nemesis having the persuasive force of an absolutist faith. By the early fifties, Niebuhr had joined Kennan as a frequent visitor to the Foreign Policy Planning Staff and Dulles as a planner for the World Council of Churches (238–239).[95] These collegial contacts probably did not alter any of the three men's opinions, which were already well formed. Niebuhr's own deductions, however, led him to pivot from Kennan towards Dulles on matters of U.S. strategy. Despite his rhetorical differences with Dulles, Niebuhr—who once called the Secretary as "stupid" as his President—nonetheless came round to several of Dulles's strategies for combating Communism, including the use of nuclear deterrence, support for the French colonial war in Indochina, the counterrevolutionary classification of East Asian nationalisms as totalitarian-controlled, and tolerance of right-wing dictatorships over rebel insurgencies: "The argument between the mass of American 'liberals' and 'conservatives' was reduced to one over means. . . . The 'realists,' as many of those who agreed with Niebuhr liked to call themselves, criticized Dulles for not keeping means and ends in balance. This criticism was beside the point, for both sides agreed that, first, the underdeveloped world was becoming the focal point of the Cold War, and second, the neutrals, unless closely tied to the United States, could become 'virtual allies' of Communism."[96] Both the United States and the Soviet Union were expanding world powers that claimed to be antiimperialist, and each failed to see how its actions were dialectical responses to the other's. The point here is not to excuse Soviet imperialism but to point out how Christian advisers excused America's own brand of imperialism by greatly exaggerating the threat of Russia to America's direct security interests, while at the same time swathing U.S. actions in the language of millennialism and tragedy. The two attitudes toward American behavior were not exclusive.

On the issue of imperial intervention, Niebuhr's Zionism is also a significant portion of his legacy, though one often glossed over by his defenders. The close affinity between Zionism and certain strains of evangelical fundamentalism is well-known, and so we are unsurprised to learn that Graham's film company, World Wide Pictures, circulated *His Land: A*

Musical Journey Into the Soul of a Nation (1969), a movie depicting the evangelist's conviction that the restoration of Israel had fulfilled Old Testament prophecies.[97] But it is more troubling to recognize that Niebuhr, supposedly the voice of temperance, staked "realist" positions as extreme in their bias as Graham's dispensational millenarian view. A former coleader of the Christian Council of Palestine, Niebuhr had been the chief Protestant proponent of Zionism in the forties, and, though he would remain uncomfortable with the messianic claims of certain Zionists, he would consistently refuse to criticize Israel's actions, even when fellow *Christianity and Crisis* editor John Bennett took more circumspect positions, citing concern for Arab refugees. Arguing the necessity for what he would elsewhere call "imperialistic realism," Niebuhr willingly acknowledged that the establishment of a separate, sovereign Jewish state in Palestine would entail injustice to Arabs but asserted that "the collective will" of Jews to survive as "a nationality" outweighed the abrogation of Arab rights.[98] His case for Zionism (and his rejection of a binational state) in the forties drew upon the crisis in Europe for its urgency, but he was equally adamant in his support of Israel when it expanded its territory in the 1948 Israeli-Arab war, when it occupied Gaza after the Suez War, and when it captured lands nearly three times its original size during the Six-Day War (Niebuhr opposed the proposal of a UN sanction against Israel in 1967). His often overlooked, but startling analogy in *The Irony of American History* likening the rise of Communism in the twentieth century to the rise of Islam and "its challenge to Christian civilization in the high Middle Ages," further likening the Sultan of Turkey to Stalin—the first a theocrat, the second the head of a false state religion—suggests perhaps that aside from the obligations of "imperialistic realism," Niebuhr's championing of Israel's rights at the expense of Arabs' also rested on an unstated but deeply biased religious prejudice shared in common with Graham.[99]

Furthermore, Niebuhr's record on domestic policy in the fifties is less aggressive than his critique of Graham implies. True, Niebuhr was concerned about racial oppression and opposed to dismantling Roosevelt's social programs, but the edge of his rhetoric in the fifties was no longer directed against class and racial injustice.[100] His chief target was America's mythical image of itself as God's innocent bearer of democracy. When it came to criticizing systemic problems in American life, Niebuhr assumed a much tamer voice than he did as a myth-buster. He rarely went further than to join other liberals in saying that "imperfections" in American democracy would, he hoped, be improved on by pragmatic compromises in the near future; he quite often said, however, that these imperfections were less frustrating if one recognized how much worse conditions could be given the ineradicable nature of original sin, which taints all rational endeavor: "the purity of idealism . . . must always be suspect. Man simply does not enjoy pure reason in human affairs; and if such reason as he has is given complete power to attain its ends, the taint will become the more noxious."[101] For all his continual remarks about the need for men to resist evil in secular life as well as in the soul, Niebuhr basically accepted that the postwar compact, with its permanent war economy underwritten by large defense expenditures, was really the closest approximation of the good society Americans could expect so long as the Communist threat existed.

In retrospect, it seems that Niebuhr was less a critic of the establishment than he was a public relations man for it. When he eventually unscrewed his Cold War armor in his writings on the Vietnam War, Niebuhr did achieve a level of self-criticism, as he saw the folly of anti-Communist interventionist policies he had shielded a decade earlier.[102] But the ironic insight came late. He had been one of the premier deradicalizing intellectuals of his generation, and by criticizing Graham in the fifties, he was flanking himself from his critics on the Left, such as A. J. Muste, who had pointed out how much he had compromised his earlier principles: "Considered as political phenomenon, it is not an accident that Reinhold Niebuhr, the radical, and John Foster Dulles, the Wall Street attorney and one of the chief architects of the bipartisan foreign policy of the United States, should now be virtually a team."[103] In our own time, when liberal Democrats like Schlesinger are invoking Niebuhr's example to parry the rhetoric of the Religious Right, it is doubly important that we remember this chapter from Niebuhr's and Graham's careers. Graham and the New Evangelicals were soon able to eclipse Niebuhr's brand of Christian liberalism because the latter's gloomy apologetics could offer no robust alternative to the traditional appeal of Graham's clabber of populism, conversion, and national covenant. Graham promised a dynamic engagement with contemporary crises through the immediate choice for a new, regenerate life in God, whereas Niebuhr, in effect, said that any action for substantial changes in the American system and its foreign conduct were circumscribed by the wages of sin. The ex-radical liberal, in other words, had adopted the language of eternal caution, whereas the conservative had taken up the banner of active mission. Between them, the two men effected a reversal of image from which liberalism in American faith and politics is still suffering today.

CHAPTER TWO

Origins of an Ailing Polemic

There is in Graham's preaching, as in that of all pietistic revivalists, an authoritarianism which stems from the belief that the best
possible political system is after all a theocracy.

—William McLoughlin, *Billy Graham: Revivalist in a Secular Age* (1959)

Looking Backward from the "Culture War": McLoughlin's *Billy Graham*

After attending Billy Graham's revival crusades in the fifties, historian William McLoughlin published two studies of the evangelist, the final chapter
of *Modern Revivalism* (1959), titled "The Engineering of Mass Consent,"
and a book-length critical biography, *Billy Graham: Revivalist in a Secular
Age* (1959).[1] In both studies, McLoughlin portrays Graham as a charismatic leader and his revivals as mass rallies that disturbingly blend political content with apocalyptic prophecy and liturgical symbols. The
evangelist wants to reunite church and state: "There is in Graham's preaching, as in all pietistic revivalists, an authoritarianism which stems from a
belief that the best possible political system is after all a theocracy."[2]
McLoughlin believes Graham's revivals and sermons together make for a
Christian mimesis of totalitarianism: "Graham's willingness to emulate the
disciplinary measures and ideological indoctrination methods of the totalitarian systems . . . [quoting Graham] 'They have an ideology. They
have a control.' . . . Graham is not, of course, advocating a dictatorship in
America. He is urging young people to dedicate themselves to Christ. Yet
this authoritarian presentation of Christianity as an ideological alternative
to communism is scarcely the appeal to individual freedom which, on other
occasions, he portrays as the central theme of Christian teaching" (89–90).

Turning from this sketch of Graham's ideology to the revivalist's followers, McLoughlin speculates on the underlying sources of Graham's appeal
to the audience. How does Graham win their consent by means other than
rational persuasion? According to McLoughlin, Graham taps a psychological complex that is latent in his flocks: namely, the status-anxiety of
groups who are bewildered by modernity. Disoriented by the sudden social
proximity of competitive out-groups and the threats to their traditional

norms, they now must dominate what they fear will absorb them: "The scapegoats [of fundamentalists like Billy Sunday] in the 1920s were foreigners, labor agitators, and Roman Catholics. In the 1950's the scapegoats were any and all non-conformists."[3] Through the unifying example of such leaders as Graham, who take the "authoritarian and patriarchal tone of the Bible" literally, these siege-mentality Protestants are now "only a short step away" from "anti-intellectualism to the self-righteousness of bigotry."[4]

McLoughlin's studies of Graham, in short, condense most of the elements of the liberal analysis of evangelicalism that intellectuals developed in the Cold War, especially through the work of Richard Hofstadter, Daniel Bell, and Talcott Parsons in *The New American Right* and *The Radical Right,* in addition to several "liberal conscience" films about fundamentalism. According to McLoughlin, Graham and the evangelical masses regress from modernity; they are irrational, herd-like, resentful, paranoid, hostile to a democratic open society, hotly anticipating crises in the social order as signs of God's impending return, conflating the old revivalistic task of converting souls with the political task of winning recruits to a radical mass movement, and totally obeisant to their leaders, who act as the Messiah's regents preparing for a Kingdom of God that will resemble a fascist or totalitarian regime. Much attention has been devoted to Protestant anti-Catholicism and open accusations by secular publications, like the *Nation,* that the Church was an authoritarian structure unsuited to democracy, allegations fomented by certain Catholic leaders' support for McCarthy.[5] What has not been given due examination, apart from the last chapter of Leon Ribuffo's 1983 study, *The Old Christian Right,* is the liberal profile of evangelicalism and how this influenced diagnoses of McCarthyism and the radical anti-Communist right.[6] It is important to revisit these analyses, and their dominant motifs, because they are pioneer efforts to interpret the sources of the Christian Right at a moment in American history when Protestant leaders, such as Billy Graham, were moving to mainstream fundamentalism.

The differences between the fundamentalists of the 1920s and those of the 1950s are crucial to understanding the context in which Cold War liberals forged their critique. The earlier fundamentalists were a separatist movement consisting of conservatives, biblical literalists, premillennialists, and revivalists that had coalesced after World War I, united by opposition to theological modernism and the Social Gospel. They were known as ecclesiastical separatists who wanted to purge their denominations of liberal Protestants and their modernist theology, but they also emphasized their apartness from secular American culture.[7] The Old Christian Right from the 1930s, consisting of right-wing populist demagogues such as Gerald K. Smith and Gerald Winrod, was fundamentalist in its background but not representative of fundamentalism's social ethos. While the campaign of Catholic Al Smith for the presidential nomination, the temperance movement, and Darwinism in public education involved fundamentalists in public—and unflatteringly publicized—issues during the twenties, the fundamentalists were not political activists. In fact, after their pyrrhic victory in the Scopes trial, which climaxed with the passing of their most eloquent spokesman, William Jennings Bryan, fundamentalists developed what Randall Balmer has called a "bunker mentality": a subculture formed by their own denominations, colleges, seminaries, and publishing houses.[8] By 1925, fundamentalists were calling themselves the authentic voice of Christianity in America, but their voice, they felt, was not the consensus of the country. Bryan was dead, his grave publicly danced on by H. L. Mencken in a typically excoriating obituary, "In Memoriam: W. J. B," designed to inter the movement he had defended.

After World War II, the complexion of the Christian Right was changed by the movement of neofundamentalistic Protestants, or New Evangelicals, who believed that their counterparts in the twenties had inadvertently damaged the authority of American evangelicalism. One of their chief goals was to overturn the impression that they were modernization's losers. To accommodate a broader appeal to conservatives, the National Association of Evangelicals (NAE) reached out to Jews and Catholics, and to unify evangelicals and to reopen theological debates, they made adjustments to their eschatology and to their theory of biblical inerrancy in hopes of recapturing denominational leadership from liberals.[9] These changes alienated old school fundamentalists, such as Carl MacIntire, the first president of the American Council of Christian Churches (ACCC), who claimed that Graham and the NAE were not really fundamentalist. They responded by defining themselves as "conservatives."

While theologically somewhat more liberal than hard-line fundamentalists, hence justifying the appellation "conservative," the New Evangelical leadership was politically activist on the Right: anti–United Nations, anti-Communist, and anti–New Deal. Moreover, the New Evangelicals rose to prominence during a decade when liberals felt as if the legacy of the Roosevelt administration was under siege and when Christian anti-Communist groups more extreme than the New Evangelicals, such as the John Birch Society, were helping to mobilize a right-wing counterreaction to the liberalism of the postwar consensus. The fifties had inherited a passel of images defining fundamentalism that were now complicated by the resurfacing of revivals, premillennial prophecy, and biblical inerrancy, all combined with opposition to the liberalism of the defunct Popular Front. From the twenties and the thirties, in the contexts of debunking Puritanism and raising the Brown Scare, there were the satires of H. L. Mencken and Sinclair Lewis (*Elmer Gantry* [1927], *It Can't Happen Here* [1935]).[10] The iconography of their writings would endure through major film productions that capped the Eisenhower years. Stanley Kramer's filmization of Lawrence and Lee's play *Inherit the Wind* (1960) and Richard Brooks's adaptation of *Elmer Gantry* (1960) were liberal conscience films that used the twenties, especially the period immediate to the Scopes trial, as a screen for projecting speculations about the filmmakers' own political environment. Like the creators of these films, liberal intellectuals seemed to be revisiting this venerable iconography to contrast the recent past with its extensions in the present, searching for continuity, as if readying for a rematch with old enemies, all the while recognizing, sometimes dimly, that contemporary evangelicals were not in fact the same foes as before. At the very least, as Richard Hofstadter admitted, they were more respectable and better organized:

> Fundamentalist-evangelical America was, in fact, so long divided or quiescent as a political force that many intellectuals have forgotten that it still exists. . . . [T]his is not to say that the old cultural issues of the 1920's are important manifest issues under the present conditions, but rather that ascetic Protestantism remains a significant undercurrent in contemporary America, and that its followers have found newfangled ways of affirming some of their convictions. . . . The participants in this revolt against modernity are no longer rubes and hicks, and they gained something both in sophistication and in cohesiveness.[11]

Clearly, "the participants in this revolt" could not be dismissed or simply ridiculed, as H. L. Mencken had done when he lampooned what he zestily called "Bible-wallopers." How much was the resurfaced evangelicalism alike and how much was it different from the sort of mentality that Clarence Darrow had challenged in Dayton, Tennessee, a generation earlier? The question prompted urgent review of the interrelationships of attitudes, motives, and beliefs among right-wing Christian activists, including Catholic supporters of McCarthy but most especially evangelical Protestants.

The analysis that antievangelical critics provided in such texts as *The New American Right* or *The Radical Right* can no longer be accepted. These works were seriously skewed in their original context by key assumptions of Cold War liberalism, and even though the academic Left has since repudiated much of the liberal consensus model of American politics, it has continued to use some of the idioms forged by that generation of intellectuals, especially pertaining to the Christian Right. The flaws of the antievangelical critique have not prevented the fifties' analysis from enjoying a long legacy. The themes and motifs were subsequently recycled in the early eighties, amidst concerns about the mobilization of the New Christian Right in the Reagan Revolution, and they have continued to color the multiple monographs that have been published to explain the phenomenon of conservative evangelical activism within the Republican Party, most recently in Chris Hedges's book, *American Fascists: The Christian Right and the War on America*.[12] In the polemical battles of today's so-called Culture War, the association of the Christian Right with fascism, totalitarianism, or extreme, irrational regression from modern life has devolved into a rhetorical weapon of center Democrats and left-wing forums like the *Nation* just as bluntly driven as the terms "secular humanism" and "liberal-fascist" are wielded by culture warriors on the Right. By examining the polemic we have inherited, at the point of its Cold War formulation, we can understand how urgently we need to develop more precise analytical criteria to talk about the religious ferment on the Right. We will consider how Cold War liberals set out models of the role religion should play in American life, how neofundamentalists deviated from these models, and how liberals responded by theorizing the deviation.

The Holdouts from "Civil Religion"

One of the most ambitious and financially successful religious films of the fifties was MGM's *The Next Voice You Hear* (1950), produced by liberal anti-Communist Dore Schary. The film uses an unusual narrative device to present an image of faith consistent with the consensus-based pluralism espoused by the liberal center. A suburban American family begins receiving exhortative messages from God through its living room radio. The family is lower middle class, struggling, and discouraged. Fearing downward mobility, the father is becoming hostile to his superiors at work, while his bad attitude has begun to harm his son's performance at school. When God begins emitting New Testament scripture over the radio, the family at first suspects a Communist plot but gradually realizes that families across America and of many faiths are also receiving God's broadcast. Listening now in hope, they learn to trust as a unit in the American political system, which depends on a spirit of cooperation between labor and management, institutions and individuals. This deity, who honors American productivity, technology, and middle class aspirations by speaking through the radio, like FDR, is clearly not a God of judgment and wrath. The one character who believes in such a God is the family spinster, Aunt

Martha, who toils in church but without receiving any assurance of peace in herself or her family. God, she thinks, is broadcasting to remind her of the curse upon her sins and to warn of an impending apocalypse. Even her pregnant sister's false labor is a sign of doom, sending her into hysterics. Her brother and sister-in-law respond initially with frustration, but then follow with compassion, recognizing that intolerance and the failure to empathize would be a sin as serious as the aunt's hopelessness and anxiety. Fundamentalism, in the person of the aunt, is thus rebuked, yet invited to assimilate with the rest of the family. The aunt is more to be pitied for her irrational fears than resisted for her severe beliefs. The radio God in *The Next Voice You Hear* is implicitly an ecumenist who speaks to all faiths and does not expect conformity of men but urges them to do the good that they will, as they understand it.[13]

Schary's film could well be a dramatization of the thesis in Will Herberg's *Protestant-Catholic-Jew*, published five years later. Herberg famously argues that in America, European immigrants have tended to accentuate their ethnic differences not through language or dress or customs, but through their religious identity. Although European observers, habituated to established churches, might have expected this situation to result in anomie, instead American society developed a pluralism sustained by a common lay religion. The three "major" faiths have developed an informal, ecumenical belief in the American way of life that they observe in addition to their internal traditions. This "civil religion" reflects an underlying consensus among Christians and Jews that (1) the liberal, democratic, and middle-class values of the American people are honored by God, and (2) that the basic agreement on these values outweighs the historic hostilities and theological disputes that have wedged apart religions in Europe. Americans agree that though groups worship God in their own way, Deity is not the exclusive property of any one of them. Having no priests, rabbis, or pastors, this lay religion sacralizes civic life without challenging the separation of Church and State.

Herberg's position was entirely compatible with that of Daniel Boorstin's *The Genius of American Politics* (especially Chapter 5, "The Mingling of Political and Religious Thought") and the opinions of the participants in the *Partisan Review*'s 1950 Symposium, "Religion and the Intellectuals," who imagined a tolerant secular state and a public sphere in which each religion is permitted its voice while being politically weak and (preferably) nonpartisan. "So long as religion is freed from authoritarian institutional forms, and conceived in personal terms," Sidney Hook states, "so long as what functions as a vital illusion or poetic myth is not represented as a public truth to whose existence the once-born are blind . . . it seems to me to fall in an area of choice where rational criticism may be suspended."[14] The Church and the synagogue occupy a separate sphere of choice than that of the state, and within that sphere alone religion could be safely entertained: "[T]he only way to make the Church an ally of freedom is to keep it permanently weak among a multitude of freely competing religious faiths."[15] The secular state could discourage any faith from becoming so sufficiently hegemonic that it could spell a rival to the state.

WHAT THE PLURALIST MODEL of civil religion did not accommodate was precisely an alignment of biblical values and eschatology with the Cold War's partisan right wing. This alignment was the upshot of several confluent developments, and the first of these was the yoking of fundamentalism and nationalism. In *Protestant-Catholic-Jew*, Herberg devotes no serious attention to fundamentalism and mentions Billy Graham only in passing and with mildness.[16] He is much more concerned with American secularism and its tendency to substitute a general lay ethos, mere belonging or sociability or "religiousness," for the specific content of the country's religions. This lay ethos sanctifies the "national self-will" (263). More biblical Judeo-Christians, by remembering their orthodoxies, might be more personally exacting and less likely to equate God with the nation than mainline Protestants (the most accommodationist demographic in his findings). Herberg's hoped-for sources of theological renewal, however, were figures like the Niebuhrs and Paul Tillich (121). His prognosis did not take into account the looming fact that a large contingent of neofundamentalists, who also specified their version of orthodoxy, were choosing not to be separatist. The redefinition and mainstreaming of neofundamentalism was evolving in a syncretic fashion, without sectarian purity or backwardness. Neofundamentalistic evangelicals, like those affiliated with the NAE, were vying to identify themselves more closely with national values and interests in order to gain prestige and political contacts that would boost their faith's stature as a cynosure of American society's mores. They were not disrupting the calmly rolling waters of a civil religion, but profiting by fractures that belied the image of plurality. The touted lay faith did not rest on as broad a Judeo-Christian consensus as Herberg and Boorstin were wont to say. President Eisenhower and Joseph McCarthy equally observed a vague, patriotic ecumenism, but pluralism, as a cultural ideology celebrating diversity, was not yet in ascendence. The national religious revival of the postwar years had actually drawn attention to the historic theological tensions between faiths and within Protestantism itself. All beliefs were equally protected under the law, but not all were equally aligned with the nation, its history, its heritage, its norms, and its myths.

In this environment, the New Evangelicals identified themselves with the national character by learning to combine cultural politics with a brand of anti-Communism that, unlike the politics of the Old Christian Right, could be integrated into the Republican Party because it indicted liberalism without embracing fascist imagery or themes. Billy Graham was instrumental in this process, as he did more than any other figure to change the image of evangelicalism after the bruising controversies of the twenties and thirties. Though Graham seemed extreme to some observers at the time, he was actually a conservative activist rather than a radical demagogue. In McLoughlin's profile of him, Billy Graham identifies his conscience with God's, and wherever a difference exists between his conscience and positive law, he asserts a contradiction that must be negated either by God's hand or, more frighteningly, by human pressure on behalf of God. The fact is that Billy Graham never expressed impatience with bureaucratic rules and procedures until the late sixties, when he appealed to the idealism of the Pentecostal "Jesus Movement" (or young evangelical counter-counterculture),[17] nor did he ever challenge the distribution of socioeconomic power, except to appeal for individualism against conformity and materialism, in the fashion typical of fifties middle-class, Babbitt-like rebelliousness. Instead of attacking "the power elite," Graham reserved his vitriol for the intellectual "elites" of liberal universities, who were Christianity's cultured despisers. New Evangelicals in the fifties were not a revolutionary right-wing movement, nor was Billy Graham attempting to establish a theocracy. He did not, in other words, advocate that the state enforce religious laws or that state funds should be used to establish a national church. Even when he suggested that a candidate's moral values should be a criterion for elective office, he did not go so far as to specify denomination or creed. He believed that the pedagogical function of the church was not the same as the disciplinary function of the state; these were complementary, but not unified, offices.

Billy Graham and the NAE also tried diligently to leave the embarrassing skeletons of fundamentalism in the tenuous past. They avoided overt prejudice, being sensitive to the trenchancy of anti-Semitism and white racism that adhered to evangelicals because of the ties that had existed between numbers of fundamentalists and the nativist movement, the KKK, and Gerald Winrod's The Defenders of the Christian Faith.[18] Contemporary evangelicals were more willing than the former fundamentalists to criticize segregation and disenfranchisement,[19] and Graham also reached out to conservative Catholics for cooperation in the battle with secular society, and sent "decision cards" for Christ to Jewish synagogues, moves that offended the more hard-line fundamentalist constituency.[20] Though by no means Freedom Riders or subscribers to *Commentary*, white evangelicals after World War II did show more ethnic, religious, and racial tolerance, just as they showed more ecumenism, than had earlier, more militant and controversial, figures on the Christian Right.

Today, when we turn to cable news stations, surf the Internet, or go to our local Wal-Mart and see and hear the likes of Pat Robertson's *The New World Order*, the fiction series *Left Behind*, or the legal advocacy group Alliance Defense Fund, or when we discover that wealthy televangelist Kenneth Copeland and thirty-six other ministries were campaign donors to Mike Huckabee, well, Billy Graham probably looks like he was a moderate. Nonetheless, we can see in the New Evangelicals a tendency toward the sacralizing of political ideologies, as if these are extensions of clerical theology, and this tendency has justifiably caused alarm in light of the some of the trends now vocal on the Christian Right. In particular, New Evangelicals tested Sidney Hook's version of the boundary between church and state by trying to win special recognition for their "voting bloc" from representatives of the federal government and by devising occasions to advise congressional and executive opinion on matters of faith. In his autobiography, *Just As I Am*, Billy Graham downplays his partisanship in the 1952 election and omits the many topical remarks on Cold War policies that featured in his sermons. McLoughlin's biography, written in the fifties, and William Martin's later, more comprehensive biography (1991) each correct this view with numerous quotations and interviews showing that Graham regularly violated his own dictum, frequently repeated, that men of his vocation should not take sides with political parties, for God's concern was with men's salvation. The evangelist himself initiated contact with Eisenhower in 1951, when he sent the general a letter proposing that he make a presidential bid. Persuaded by his public relations man, Sid Richardson, to cultivate a contact with Graham, Eisenhower met with his admirer in person, and thereafter Graham acted as though he were the candidate's spiritual adviser, calling him a type of "Daniel" or "Moses."[21] This symbolic union of religious conscience and state, in the year that the Republican party retook the presidency and the Congress, was sealed during the inauguration, when Eisenhower became the first president ever to lead the nation in a prayer and then retired to the White House, where Graham baptized him in the Oval Office (161).

There was "no necessary correlation" between conservative theology and right-wing militancy; indeed, the premillennial dispensationalist eschatology of most fundamentalists and revivalists like Billy Sunday had tended to discourage activism.[22] On the other hand, liberal evangelicalism, including the Social Gospel, had been postmillennialist; it aimed to realize the

Kingdom of God here and now. Graham's premillennialism succeeded in marrying the two themes, preparation for Christ's return and immanent reform, by subtly modulating eschatological symbols. Graham eschewed the deterministic dispensationalist scheme (the seven epochs of history leading to the End) and stressed instead human agency and stewardship (a Calvinist theme associated with the doctrine of "common grace"). He did so, moreover, without diminishing the prime importance of converting the soul. Instead, he mined an old analogy rhyming individual conversion and national (re)birth, freedom from sinful nature and freedom to serve democracy. In the post-Revolutionary era, American evangelicals had endowed man with more agency to choose God's grace, and they thereby accommodated republican ideas of virtue and freedom. Graham reactivated this core idea of what Mark Noll has called "American theology," while dissociating it from Enlightenment and uniting it with anti-Communism.[23] America was battling an enemy whose existence signified national sin, God's Judgment, and the need for Christ's return (traditional premillennialist themes) as well as conversionist hopes for culture (postmillennial themes).

WHEREAS PROPONENTS of the civil religion theory like Boorstin and Herberg preferred to point out the democratic implications of certain Christian or Jewish tenets, the Cold War Christian Right asserted that America's democratic character had its foundations in biblical revelation rather than in a complex meshwork of Enlightenment and religious influences, and, hence, that it could not survive without recognizing the centrality of faith to its purpose.[24] Thus, interpreting anti-Communism as a test of national vocation and as an occasion for spiritual rebirth, Billy Graham and the editors of *Christianity Today* vowed to regain the cultural hegemony they believed they had lost in the previous generation when other Christian groups, such as the leadership of The Federal Council of Churches and the National Council of Churches, had wrongly persuaded Americans that liberalism, theological modernism, and the Social Gospel were the vanguard of twentieth-century Christianity. The deception, they contended, even if not willful, had been detrimental to American values, for it had shifted the culture from the grounds of its legitimacy, and at a critical historical juncture. The NAE was not above the Red-baiting of the liberal clergy that McCarthy's staff director, Joseph Matthews, a former Methodist evangelist, practiced when he reported that the mainline Protestant churches were full of Communists.[25] All the while, they avoided the xenophobia and religious bigotry of the Old Christian Right. Instead, the New Evangelicals borrowed from the cultural and political mainstream, opposing socialistic collectivization with national unity based on moral identity. Here again, the New Evangelicals were very agile at outpacing the pluralists' rhetoric of harmony through inclusiveness. The union they preached was not a *volkish* unity, in which the nation is a mystical body based on racial descent, but a community of finality and action in which members collaborate for the common end of purification, restoration, and the resistance of tyranny. This community was identified by its principles, as witnessed in the American past and in the Bible, rather than specified to a confessional identity: the Church, the visible saints, the body of Christ, or the Kingdom of God. The New Evangelicals, in other words, did not preclude the possibility of some rapprochement with conservatives of other persuasions, so long as they were Judeo-Christian. Instead, they positioned themselves as the presumptive leaders of a scripturally based, antimodernist movement with a potentially broad fundament, in which dogmatic rigidity was less important than a common sacred text combined with a common definition of values and national purpose. Thus, by owning the scriptural authority that liberal theologians had allegedly jeopardized, New Evangelicals maneuvered to place neofundamentalism inside the American character as the chief defender of the source of its fortifying virtue and its telos. Accordingly, the shapers of public opinion, education, and policy who had claimed the "vital center" since Hoover were deviant, alienated from the country's vocation.

In retrospect we can see how the New Evangelicals, despite their relative moderation in some areas, were helping to lay the ideological, theological, and methodological groundwork for more radical movements and groups on the Christian Right. With Billy Graham as their national and their world figurehead, New Evangelicals built a nationally recognized organization, made political contacts, erected respectable institutions in Washington,[26] created voluntary associations along with high-profile radio, television, movie, and newspaper outlets, and brought together the techniques of revivalism with those of social consciousness-raising, which not only gave the merger of neofundamentalism and activism a measure of clout but a model of organizational strategem that proved instrumental to building the New Christian Right in the seventies and eighties. The John Birch Society, which married themes of McCarthyism and evangelical fundamentalism, also gained much attention from commentators in the fifties and sixties, but the Birchers never achieved legitimacy within the Republican Party since they attacked the Eisenhower administration itself as part of a conspiratorial Establishment.[27] Their successes were at local levels (chapters and associations), not at a national one. The Birchers, moreover, aggressively named names of individuals and institutions that were, allegedly, parts of Communist plots, whereas New Evangelicals relied mostly on common motifs vaguely linking liberalism with Communistic ideas, such as atheism, humanism, materialism, and collectivism. The New Evangelicals were far more important than the Old Christian Right or their contemporaries on the far Christian right in sheperding neofundamentalistic evangelicalism toward the Republican Party and in helping to effect an overall rightward shift in American politics. Conservative Christian activism had not only moved closer to the center but had also brought on its coattails, without always condoning, more dissident religious agendas.

By helping to transform American political attitudes to such an extent that social liberalism is now considered far Left by many, the success of the "Billy Graham evangelicals" has made more acceptable ideas that were once considered extremist or fringe elements. These ideas have included a resurgence of postmillennial prophecy combined, somewhat incoherently, with conspiracy theories about a global totalitarian government, called the New World Order, that will parody the one thousand years of peace and righteousness predicted in the Book of Revelation.[28] Moreover, there has been a change of strategy from the Cold War era. The New Evangelicals exerted moral influence on government primarily through advocacy and the enhanced visibility and prestige of its affiliations, whereas the New Christian Right has moved to shape public policy through efforts to place like-minded believers in positions of power where they can use the state as an instrument for morally regenerating the nation and preparing the world for the coming Kingdom of God.[29]

ANOTHER FEATURE of the radicalization of neofundamentalism that has taken place since the initial activism of the New Evangelicals is the rhetoric of "cultural warfare." The term "culture war" was introduced by sociologist James Davison Hunter in his 1991 book, *Culture Wars: The Struggle to Define America,* in which Hunter proposes that polarizations in American society over values and worldviews, and the politicization of these disagreements, seriously call into question whether there is an American civil religion.[30] Hunter was describing what he believed was the deplorable state of our public sphere, created by vociferous members of both the religious Right and the secular Left, but the exponents of cultural warfare soon came to wield the concept, and the dualistic imagery of battling for America's soul, in order to fight for a new consensus in which liberalism and secular humanism would be excluded as an enemy ideology. The architects of the new consensus have built on Graham's melding of anti-Communist nationalism, biblical infallibility, conversionist tropes, and eschatology, but they have departed from the apologetic purpose that attended the Cold War cultural politics of the earlier activists. Spokesmen like Harold Ockenga had urged New Evangelical scholars at Fuller Theological Seminary to acquaint themselves with modern knowledge in order to challenge more effectively liberal Protestants on theological and exegetical questions raised by the natural sciences, secular psychology, or historical criticism of the Bible; this was a strategy that Ockenga called "infiltration," as opposed to older fundamentalist "separation."[31] In the seventies, however, lecturer and writer Francis Shaeffer, author of *The Christian Manifesto* (1981), encouraged evangelical scholars to become "fluent" in "secular humanist" thought so that they could undermine its "presuppositions" and "deceptions."[32] Secular humanism, a coinage of Shaeffer and a watchword for the New Christian Right since the eighties, refers to any and all of the intellectual presuppositions that undergird liberalism in theology, social philosophy, or cultural mores. Its prime conduits, putatively, are education and informational media, which together comprise a competing world view not only contrary to the biblical one but also compatible with totalitarianism. The opponents of secular humanism do not seek to show gaps or errors in secular thought in order to correct or delimit them. Instead, they strive to dismantle secular thought, conceived as an interlocking hermetic system, by demonstrating that it is a false faith, promoted by high-placed atheistic savants, with an implicit political program inimical to Judeo-Christianity, democracy, and nationhood. This critique of secular logicality and hegemony amounts to "right-wing Gramscianism,"[33] and it has contributed immensely to the sacralization of partisanship we can now observe in America, often justified through the rhetoric of cultural warfare.

When we attempt to locate Cold War New Evangelicalism within the ideological spectrum of the Christian Right today, it seems more moderate than it was at the point of its emergence. Billy Graham himself now represents the middle of the Christian Right rather than the far Christian Right (or New Christian Right) that has come into ascendancy within the core of the Republican Party along with neoconservatives and traditionalist conservatives. This is an effect partly of the shift in American political attitudes in the past fifty years and also of Graham's own move towards moderation of his rhetoric, his social message, and of the degree of his involvement in politics. Graham is rightly praised for having signed the Lausanne Covenant (1974), an evangelical document recognizing international human rights, and for having given his blessing to the NAE's endorsement of the 2004 Evangelical Call to Civic Responsibility, which earmarked such issues as poverty and AIDS.[34] This does not, however, erase his accountability from the historical ledger. Assessing Graham's role, and that of the New Evangelical movement he did so much to launch, has been hampered by commentaries, including recent books by Jim Wallis, Charles Marsh, and Chris Hedges, which have driven too sharp, and historically too ill-informed, a distinction between Graham and the New Right, preferring to use the moderate Graham of today to condemn his Protestant contemporaries on the far Right without recognizing his legacy to them.[35] It is as if the Billy Graham of the Cold War has been forgotten. Graham's own mea culpas have not clarified matters. His admissions that "he had a weakness for politics"; that "he was so caught up in anti-Communism it distracted him from the gospel"; that "after Nixon he became aware of the damage [politics] could do to the ministry," seem to have encouraged contemporaries to confuse forgiveness with amnesia.[36] Contemporary valorizations of Graham as America's spiritual dean and the confidant to its presidents excuse, as they must, the critical legacy of his brand of neofundamentalism. In this respect, Williams McLoughlin's early studies of Billy Graham from 1959 and 1960 remain prescient and valuable, even if Graham was not quite the theocrat or demagogue that McLoughlin portrayed him to be. The studies capture Graham in the period of his mobility from callow evangelist to American icon, though they are unfortunately skewed by many of the same analytical assumptions as the better-known books, *The New American Right* and *The Radical Right*.

Initial Efforts at Diagnosis: *The New American Right* (1955) and *The Radical Right* (1962)

The *New American Right* and *The Radical Right* are the most influential liberal statements on evangelicalism written during the Cold War. The immediate catalysts of these volumes, published respectively in 1955 and 1962 and each edited by Daniel Bell, were McCarthyism, the John Birch Society, and the Goldwater insurgency (which was mistakenly seen as evangelical in style). *The New American Right* introduces a classic set of essays by historians and sociologists including Richard Hofstadter, Talcott Parsons, David Riesman, and Seymour Lipset, which were subsequently expanded in *The Radical Right* to accommodate additional reflections, including more antievangelical commentary. Liberals had inherited two clusters of images from earlier depictions of fundamentalists: hicks and fascists. The latter predominates in these studies, though with significant modifications. As Leon Ribuffo has shown, the terrorism of the KKK and the visibility of the Old Christian Right during the Brown Scare "widely disseminated" "the convention associating fundamentalism with bigotry and reaction, created during the 20s."[37] The essays in *The New American Right* and *The Radical Right* argue that the Old Christian Right was not just an aberration in American politics; instead, the Old Christian Right expressed recyclable attitudes in American life that could be mobilized through mass politics in periods of crisis, or perceived crisis. Reviewing the ambitious theory of these texts, one feels sympathy for the effort as well as vexation with it, not only because the essays fail adequately to grasp the problem before them but also because they ceded so much of American political idiom to the Right. This second failing has more to do with their Cold War model of democracy than with the complexity of the phenomenon they analyze.

To liberals like Bell, Hofstadter, and Parsons, McCarthyism represented the possibility that a radical demagogue might use the liberties of a pluralistic democracy to undermine it. It could siphon from perennial American attitudes, including parts of the country's religious heritage, to undo the qualities of American politics—rationality, bargaining, and competitive parties—that gave plural interests, including ethnic and religious minorities, some means to prevent prejudiced groups from amassing absolute power. The locus classicus of the liberal interpretation of McCarthy is Richard Hofstadter's "The Pseudo-Conservative Revolt" (1954), later republished as the keynote essay in *The New American Right*. Hofstadter introduces the diagnostic term "pseudo-conservative," taken from Theodor Adorno's *The Authoritarian Personality* (1950), which was based on a study by social scientists at the University of California at Berkeley. Hofstadter quotes from Adorno in his text: "'The pseudo-conservative is a man who, in the name of upholding traditional American values and institutions and defending them against more or less fictitious dangers, consciously or unconsciously aims at their abolition.'"[38] The pseudo-conservative scorns the status quo, but he labors under the illusion that he is actually committed to defending the status quo's basic values. As Adorno describes it, the pseudo-conservative cannot bring himself to attack traditional institutions because he is psychologically obeisant to symbols of authority. In order to express and rationalize his destructive aggression, he projects his unsocialized impulses upon other groups, who become his scapegoats. Particularly under a liberal democracy, where citizens are raised to hold strong beliefs in individualism, pseudo-conservative authoritarianism may go unrecognized, but in a social crisis, as in a breakdown of legal or economic order, the pseudo-conservative might try to assert order by totalitarian means. From Adorno, Hofstadter extrapolates the theory that the modern American right wing is comprised of pseudo-conservatives who have grown angry with the transformations in American society since the thirties. As such, the pseudo-conservative functions as a kind of a shadow fascist lurking within American attitudes; he has an authoritarian personality syndrome, activated by resentment and anxiety, and harbors reactionary ideas already at large in American society, though these are not linked into a coherent, radicalizing ideology until a leader unites them for him.[39] The pseudo-conservative is a sociological variation on the Niebuhrian profile of the self-deceiving moralist, who is lacking in redemptive self-irony, though Hofstadter's version restricts the field of subjects. The unintentional hypocrite of *Irony* describes Everyman, but the pseudo-conservative has an authoritarian syndrome that sets him apart from the normal populace.

Leo Lowenthal and Norbert Guterman's *Prophets of Deceit* (1949), which Hofstadter also cites in "The Pseudo-Conservative Revolt," suggests that right-wing Christian "agitators" could very well serve as this unifying force. Demagogues like Gerald Smith and Gerald Winrod create an "artificial fusion with Italian and German notions" and "certain forms of religious revivalism . . . which exploit such rigid stereotypes as the distinction between the damned and the saved."[40] By combining predictions of America's collapse with affirmations of American values, they lead the public away from rational insights into their social dissatisfaction to "pseudo-protests" that never rise above furious, resentful outbursts at enemy figures.[41] Though Hofstadter does not go so far as to call the modern Right engineers of "hoaxes" on the masses, he does extract from *Prophets of Deceit* the overarching point that the agitator's main concern is "'a sphere of frustration . . . and moral uncertainties.'" Like the pseudo-conservative in *The Authoritarian Personality,* the agitator offers "'attitudes, not bread.'"[42]

Following "The Pseudo-Conservative Revolt," Hofstadter would identify evangelicals as key elements of the new right wing in his essays "The Paranoid Style in American Politics" (1964) and "Pseudo-Conservatism Revisited" (1965), and in his book *Anti-Intellectualism in American Life* (1964), his most extensive critique of evangelicalism. The first 150 pages of *Anti-Intellectualism,* are devoted to a history of Puritanism's devolution and its displacement by fundamentalists, with their extremist "one-hundred percent mentality . . . fusing absolute religion and absolute patriotism."[43] Hofstadter's critiques of evangelicalism in 1964 and 1965 built upon the collective work of *The New American Right* and *The Radical Right,* which found more to fear from evangelical Protestants than from Catholics, even though, according to these studies' own statistics,[44] Catholics numbered higher among McCarthy's supporters than Protestants, and some Catholic spokesmen, such as Cardinal Spellman, had attacked Protestants for being less patriotically anti-Communist than they.[45] In general, Bell, Lipset, Riesman, and Hofstadter treat American Catholics more delicately than they do evangelicals, as they blame much of Catholic overzealous anti-Communism to status-anxieties inflicted on them historically by intolerant Protestants.[46] Though Daniel Bell is aware of McCarthy's own Catholicism, for instance, he does not attempt to tie the senator's message to his faith. On the contrary, he argues that Catholicism is a religion "focused on heaven" that is tolerant of "human foibles," while "schizoid" evangelical Protestantism has hardened into a moralistic, intolerant religion.[47] McCarthy, in other words, has more in common with evangelicals than his Catholic supporters. In *The New American Right* and *The Radical Right,* the pseudo-conservative revolt, visible in McCarthyism, the Birch Society (where Protestant fundamentalists did in fact number high), and the Goldwater insurgency, is in a sense the irrational apogee of the evangelical spirit.

My purpose here is not to replay the baiting of Protestants and Catholics over the issue of which was the most anti-Communist, but to show where the writers of these studies allotted responsibility for the pseudo-conservatives' religious beliefs and to point out that their criteria had less to do with statistical evidence, certainly in the case of McCarthyism, than with their evaluation of a belief system's underlying character or what they believed to be its psychological and social underpinnings and the ideological extensions of its theology. The most fatefully formulated charge, to my mind, links evangelical "moralism" and populism: what evangelicalism enforces in the populist tradition is bigotry, nostalgia, and conspiracy. In part, the writers of *The New American Right* and *The Radical Right* are reacting against the Progressive historians, such as Charles Beard, who had favored more direct forms of democracy, and emphasizing instead an old Federalist caution—that popular impulses are not democratic—which had been given new credence by fascism. However, they are clearly choosing to emphasize the right-wing applications of populist idioms, at the cost, their critics have argued, of discrediting populism altogether.

In his major monograph of the fifties, *The Age of Reform: From Bryan to FDR* (1955), Hofstadter's concern is with the "extremism" of Left populists, agrarian reformers, and labor movements rather than right-wing pseudo-conservatism, but his underlying analysis is similar. According to Hofstadter, the populists were "unrealistic," "innocent," and self-defeating buffoons who were determined to return America to a simpler, less bureaucratic form of capitalism.[48] Unlike McCarthyism, populism originated in the 1880s and 1890s, periods of economic crisis, so it had more licit causes.

Nevertheless, its intellectual style and social objectives, Hofstadter argues, were virtually the same as the modern Right's. Then, as in the 1950s, differences in the distribution of wealth and office were being turned into ideological melodramas by men unable to rationally accept that their interests lay with modern bureaucracy and the cooperation of government and big business, for, whatever the flaws of this arrangement, its tide could not be reversed. As Hofstadter sees it, the big difference in the melodrama is the change of villains: instead of the virtuous poor versus the corrupt rich, there is the virtuous anti-Communist versus the liberal intellectual elite. The commentators of *The New American Right* and *The Radical Right* join Hofstadter in urging liberals to sagely gravitate away from the class ideologies that characterized the country's earlier Democrats, especially in the figure of William Jennings Bryan, who—conveniently for Hofstadter and Bell—combined both populist, agrarian reform, and fundamentalist legacies.[49] In his character sketch of Bryan in *The American Political Tradition,* "The Democrat as Revivalist" (the most brutal essay in the entire volume), Hofstadter uses his subject to represent "the shabbiness of the evangelical mind." Bryan's "socially liberal brand fundamentalism" was a minority position among the movement's leadership in the twenties, and fundamentalists were not major constituents of populism or progressivism, but the fact that Bryan's political ideals and religious convictions were "strange bedfellows" makes little difference to Hoftstadter's case, since, in keeping with the methodology of *The New American Right* and *The Radical Right,* he is concerned with the thought-residues and emotional traces of ideological themes as these are reclaimed in American life, often in the service of opposing causes. As portrayed in *The Age of Reform,* Bryan epitomizes the way reform-mindedness in America, untempered by liberal realism and given to evangelical moralism, actually becomes as shabby as the Right in its apocalyptic fervor.[50]

According to Hoftstadter, fundamentalists have a conspiracy theory of history, populated by invisible principalities.[51] If McCarthy, the Birchers, and Goldwater looked for signs of evil Communists everywhere and Bryan's populists looked for signs of class conspiracy in all niches, the fundamentalist predates both with a scheme of history that sacrifices truth for maximum logical coherence and projects a moral intentionality behind all events. In "The Paranoid Style in American Politics," transparently referencing Barry Goldwater, Hofstadter compares a populist ideologue with a fundamentalist preacher: "Like religious millenarians, he expresses the anxiety of those who are living through the last days and he is sometimes disposed to set a date for the apocalypse. . . . Properly expressed, such warnings serve somewhat the same function as a description of the horrible consequences of sin in a revival sermon: they portray that which impends but which may still be avoided. They are a secular and demonic version of adventism. . . . [W]hat is at stake is always a conflict between absolute good and absolute evil."[52] What is being rejected in this anticipated conflagration, moreover, is a return to the past, the Golden Age that is also the Kingdom of God. As in populism, the iconography of fundamentalism is nostalgic for a premodern past, for village idiocy, homogeneity, and conformity. Imagine Gopher Prairie in Sinclair Lewis's *Main Street,* and you will have pictured Hofstadter's ideal type of the populist and fundamentalist version of paradise.

The argument that populism and evangelical fundamentalism are copacetic, while very suggestive, and in light of contemporary American politics seemingly inescapable, actually did a disservice to liberalism in the terms that *The New American Right* and *The Radical Right* formulated the case. Bell, Hofstadter, and company were recognizing, in their own time, the Right's skillful co-opting of populism. Yet in our eagerness to join them in tracing continuities, especially when the connections seem prophetic of our present, we must also be aware of how the continuities have been drawn and why. David Plotke has stated that the commentators of *The New American Right* and *The Radical Right* were simply pointing out that populism is an enduring discourse that becomes "available later to other forces that may not be identical in purpose" to the original movement.[53] If this statement were true then I would have no argument, but I believe Plotke is giving the writers more than the due benefit of doubt. One of the chief purposes of both volumes, as Michael P. Rogin has argued in his book *The Radical Specter* (1967) (the first major rebuttal of Bell and Hoftstadter), was to represent pseudo-conservativism as an authoritarian syndrome that unites apparent ideological opposites, mirroring the Right into Left.[54] This was a Cold War strategy to shore up the liberals' claim to be the voice of centrist America. By casting pseudo-conservativism as radicalism in disguise, as shadow fascism, while also linking it to the populist iconography of the Left, particularly the Popular Front, the authors of *The New American Right* and *The Radical Right* could disparage class politics as well as right-wing activism.[55] Each group was essentially authoritarian, catering to mass politics and mischaracterizing what were merely administrative problems of capitalism.[56] From Hofstadter's extremely unsympathetic portrait of Bryan (since revised by Lawrence Levine) to Riesman's and Glazer's dispossessed prophets, the comparisons to evangelical fundamentalism underscored the mediocrity of the populist imagination.[57] In the assessment of *The New American Right* and *The Radical Right,* populism's opposition to entrenched economic and social elites had evolved into the self-righteous, disgruntled, delusional gibes of the irrational at the progressive. Overstating the peripheral association of fundamentalism with populism helped to recast the latter as reactionary: suspicious, antimodern, moralistic—in sum, pseudo-conservative.

In a country as historically antisocialist as the United States, populism has been an alternative idiom of protest capable of expressing popular dissatisfaction with unjust distributions of wealth and resources in American society, as populist themes and motifs served the radical working class and multi-ethnic politics of the Popular Front. With texts like *The New American Right* and *The Radical Right,* Cold War liberals effectively ceded the discourse of populism to the Right. Furthermore, they misunderstood the skillful revision of its themes by leaders like Billy Graham, who successfully blended populism with nationalism through conversionist, revivalistic tropes of awakening and rebirth. Graham's message avoided overt bigotry of the kind that Hofstadter and Bell exaggerate in their accounts of populism, and, above all, his message was not nostalgic. It venerably blended American vocation with millennial hopes. Instead of looking backward to Main Street—Sinclair Lewis's Gopher Prairie—it envisioned a triumphal pax Americana under God.[58]

The Christian Right has furthered expansionist nationalism and crusadership not by reviving America's mythical innocence, as Reinhold Niebuhr had feared in the fifties, but by making national sin a symbol anticipating the renewal of national vocation and by identifying that vocation with an eschatology mixing premillennial and postmillennial themes. Eschewing the customary polemic and refining our terms, loosening them from the encrustation of Cold War liberalism, helps us to see a continuity between fundamentalism in the past and in the present that does not have as its mediating term "fascism," but instead a syncretic dogmatism.[59] Though seemingly a contradiction in terms, this concept speaks to the blend of elements that has made for the successful presentation of a neofundamentalistic evangelical agenda. It is compounded of impurities though it claims to be about fundamentals. The renascence of neofundamentalistic evangelicalism in America is a response to the secularizing process in which many of the phenomena of modernity—mass media, mass politics—have been utilized to defend and purvey an interpretation of modernity that will rival liberalism, socialism, and fascism, an interpretation that sacralizes Americanism as an extension of its theology, yet claims not to be authorized by nationalism, but by values and cultural meanings derived from an inerrant sacred text. The Cold War was the testing ground in which this politicized religion was forged, and its endurance, through cycles of legitimation and radicalization, reminds us of what liberalism was not equipped to anticipate, and what it has ever since struggled to understand.[60]

PART TWO

Narratives of Blindness and Insight in an Era of Confession

CHAPTER THREE

Guilt of the Thirties,
Penitence of the Fifties

Ours, a "twice-born" generation, finds its wisdom in pessimism, evil, tragedy, and despair. So we are both old and young "before our time."

        —Daniel Bell, *The End of Ideology* (1960)

[The Devil]: My revolutionary thought was to destroy man by seducing him through good.

        —Whittaker Chambers, "The Devil," *Life* (1948)

There but for the Grace of God:
Whittaker Chambers's *Witness*

The tragic imagination, core to realism's moral philosophy, provided an interpretive framework for liberals that was compelling at several levels, not least in its reclamation of pragmatism.[1] Cold War liberal intellectuals owned the pragmatic tradition as the most vital philosophy in American life, implicit even in the reasoning of the founding fathers; however, it had certain embarrassing features. Its Emersonian impulses needed to be curbed to make it more congenial to the realist vision. The tragic was the remedy of choice.[2] Pragmatism, already prized for its progressive, yet temporizing and meliorist, approach to conflict, was denuded of William James's flair for the heroic and of John Dewey's optimistic prognosis for a fully democratic public sphere continuously improved by the method of intelligence. The pragmatic theory of value and its concept of a pluralistic universe were married to a tragic view of history and a consequently ironic attitude toward human idealism: "for those who take on responsibility, who forgo the sin of pride, of assuming they know how life should be ordered or how the blueprint of the new society should read, one's role can be only to reject all absolutes and accept pragmatic compromise."[3] Pragmatism, was still regarded as a method for maximizing man's power to transform life short of the use of force; however, as Sidney Hook argued in "Pragmatism and the Tragic Sense of Life," the threshold of human contentment, not to speak of happiness, had to be realistically adjusted for current circumstances, in which the threat of force often made the lesser evil rather than the ideal good the only worthy choice.[4] That which strove to envision, much less enact, an immanent historical possibility that was not "evil" in some qualified sense fell outside the limits of rational discourse as "ideology." Tragic pragmatism's utility in bracketing dissent as ideology and ideology, in turn, as an illegitimate dissent, made it functionally akin to Reinhold Niebuhr's objection to "perfectionism" in the theological tradition and to Bell's and Hofstadter's repudiation of "fundamentalism" and "populism." As such, it stressed compromise within a consensus model of politics and provided an apologetic framework for America's neo-imperial foreign policy. The tragic was also appealing in the context of domestic anti-Communism because "pragmatic" ex-radicals of the thirties recanted and moved for rapprochement with social welfare liberalism by blaming their former errors on human pride, especially as comprehended through the Christian symbol of the Fall.

Certainly many intellectuals who became anti-Communists after the thirties genuinely felt a sense of complicity with Stalinism. Their staunch opposition to totalitarianism, of the Left as much as the Right, resulted from having once actively supported or sympathized with the actions of the USSR in the belief that it was the revolutionary vanguard for the masses and against injustice; it stood, in the words of the Comintern: "for the overthrow of the international bourgeoisie and for the creation of an international Soviet republic as a transition stage to the complete abolition of the State."[5] The USSR was supposed to represent the anti-imperial alternative to National Socialism, which was an inauthentic, fascist hijacking of socialist ideas; instead, it had committed comparable state crimes, including the scapegoating of Jews, if short of Germany's genocidal campaigns.

The intellectual generation that came of age in the thirties, feeling implicated in "radical evil," redefined themselves through changes in party affiliation, shifts in political strategy, and ideological (at times religious) conversions. Many of them, especially those who clustered around the *Partisan Review* after its founders Philip Rahv and William Phillips officially broke with the Communist Party in 1937, had experienced their first loss of innocence long before the onset of the Cold War. Trotskyism was their recovery: an alternative anticapitalist, anti-imperialist position to official Communism that repudiated Stalin while maintaining that the original Leninist impulse of 1917 was legitimate. Rebuking the Popular Front's compromise with Stalinism, radicals like Sidney Hook, who had divorced himself from the Communist Party earlier than had the *Partisan Review,* still maintained that socialism was the route to economic and political justice.[6] Support for antifascist intervention in World War II, along with a growing awareness of Stalin's expansionist intentions after the war, forced a Niebuhrian reconsideration of "lesser evils" as well as a revaluation of the virtues of the American system. After this turnabout, for some a second loss of innocence, even anticapitalism became an error of the thirties.

Some who departed from the *ancien* Left, such as Max Eastman, James Burnham, and J. B. Matthews, became ardent right-wing anti-Communists; Burnham and Eastman signed on to the *National Review,* while Matthews ricocheted onto the House Un-American Activities Committee (HUAC) as its chief investigator. For liberals, their decision to become anti-Communist was not simply a hegira to the New Deal Democratic center. Socialist goals were not being condemned wholesale, though socialist political movements might be rejected on pragmatic grounds. The British Labor Party and the German Socialists each relinquished the goal of the nationalization of industry, and both Britain and Germany were acceptable models of mixed economies that did not seek absolute centralization through the state. It remained important to hold a firm line against laissez-faire. Niebuhr, who had never been a Communist of any stripe, was firm in his rejection of revolutionary Marxism, but he remained an opponent of libertarian conservatives who identified any state intervention as totalitarian. Chagrined at the inviolable value that Americans accorded to private property yet convinced that the combining of political and economic power would create a dangerous new administrative class, Niebuhr was only slightly to the right of members of the Old Left, such as Daniel Bell and Sidney Hook, who remained social democrats in principle, favoring ad hoc state-corporate planning and high state spending. A wider gap existed between their persuasions and the radicalism of Labor Party activist Irving Howe, for whom "an unqualified and principled opposition to Stalinism" was "an effort to salvage the honor of the socialist idea."[7] Yet even Howe would reject Marxism for social democracy in the pages of *Dissent* by the early fifties.

Amidst disputes over what the proper form anti-Communism should take, whether the anti-Communist position was consistent with socialist ideals, whether socialism was compatible with liberal anti-Communism, they asked: What had caused the Old Left to overlook or minimize the evils of Stalinism in the first place? Why had they mistakenly believed in the continuity of revolutionary and reform-minded methods of achieving social justice? Why had they lost faith in liberal democracy? One major strain of interpretation said that they had overladen social justice with metaphysical meanings and thus had become impatient with partisanship, compromise, and gradualistic reforms, since these could never release modern man from his alienation, or what the consummate dialectician

Georg Lukács, in a famous phrase, called modern man's "transcendental homelessness."[8] In 1931, ex-Communist Benjamin Ginzburg, reporting in the *New Republic,* decried the new "messianism" among intellectuals who had turned away from cultural criticism to political reform.[9] In the wake of Stalin's purges and the German-Soviet Non-Aggression pact, many on the former Left turned this same epithet against themselves, as did their critics. They were able to draw on earlier debates among socialist intellectuals who themselves had posited that Marxism, most especially its theory of social change in history, was tinctured by secularized religious concepts. Edmund Wilson, influenced by Max Eastman's *Marx, Lenin and the Science of Revolution* (1926), concluded in 1940: "The dialectic then is a religious myth." Eastman's critics had argued that he was conflating the method of historical materialism with the vulgar Marxism of Soviet Communist theory, but Wilson nonetheless accepted Eastman's case that Marxism's "dialectic" was really a faith in "a semi-divine principle of history." Widely read European critics of Marxism made comparable claims in the fifties. In *The Captive Mind* and *The Opium of the Intellectuals,* Czeslaw Milosz and Raymond Aron, respectively, argued that political religions had taken hold among the unchurched intellectuals, not the masses. Communism was the faith of the professorates, the literati, the progressive theologians, the philosopher kings; the folk, the proles, having more humble aspirations, were relatively unscathed.[10] It was the intellectuals and the pro-labor clergy, alienated from bourgeois society and misunderstanding the conservative impulses of the masses with whom they identified, who were the priests and acolytes of political religions. The class politics of the Left were, in Arthur Koestler's words, *The God That Failed* (1950), but its prophets were never the industrial workers for whom God had revealed Himself in the desert.[11] It was the elite, their heads spangled by angelic figments, who saw gnosis in Marxism's counterfeit gleam. For all their touted realism about the capitalist order, they were unconsciously the worst of Hegelian idealists.

SOCIALISM may or may not have been a workable thesis in America, but what the Old Left, with few exceptions, did not dispute was the evil of Marxist ideologies that had assumed the penumbra of a spiritual quest after salvation, perfection, or harmony.[12] They were understood, moreover, as surrogate faiths for the thinking class that had rejected parochialism and ritual, on the one hand, and bourgeois Christianity—sentimental good will and paternalistic charity—on the other. It was well known that many figures on the old Left had come from inherited religious backgrounds that they were either trying to lose or to renovate: Norman

Thomas, Socialist Party candidate for president, was an "ex-Presbyterian, ex-seminarian"; Earl Browder, executive secretary of the Communist Party of the United States of America (CPUSA), came from a family of Methodist ministers and gave speeches at Union Theological Seminary; A. J. Muste, after aligning himself with American Trotskyists, returned to the Fellowship of Reconciliation and its pro-labor, pro–civil rights Christian pacifism; Granville Hicks, the Communist literary critic, was an ex-Unitarian minister; James Burnham, member of the Workers Party, was formerly a Neo-Thomist Catholic whose encounter with Trotskyism was "suggestive of a conversion experience"; Max Eastman, editor of the *Masses,* was the son of two Congregational ministers in the Calvinist line; Henry Ward, United Front activist, was a professor at Union Theological Seminary and a Methodist cleric; J. B. Matthews, contributor to various radical labor journals, had formerly been a Methodist evangelist to Malaysia; F. O. Matthiessen, Christian Socialist, who despite avowed intellectual ties to Perry Miller and Reinhold Niebuhr, and having undertaken a herculean reclamation of the tragic imagination in American literature, was still perceived as an apologist for Stalinism; and Niebuhr himself, who ran as a Socialist Party candidate for Congress, was a professional theologian and ex-pastor.[13] Beleaguered liberals likened their former Marxist commitments to alienated religious passions and ideals. Alfred Kazin testified: "I thought of socialism as orthodox Christians might think of the Second Coming—a wholly supernatural event which one might await with perfect faith."[14] Former *New International* contributor and ex-Trotskyist Irving Kristol said that he had anticipated "a secular redemption" (56). Daniel Bell, who took up reading Kierkegaard and Niebuhr after the war, remembered feeling as if socialism had replaced his lost Judaism: "When I was thirteen years old and being at that time an orthodox Jew, I had a *bar mitzvah* . . . I had joined the Young People's Socialist League and I felt that I had found the truth. You see, I had lost my belief in God. So I went to the rabbi who had prepared me for the *bar mitzvah* and I said to him, 'you know, I'm not to going to put on *tvillum*. I've found the truth; I don't believe in God'" (48).[15] Marxism, meanwhile, having demythologized religion as false consciousness, as ideology, actually resumed all the "old millenarian, chiliastic goals of the Anabaptists" (280–281, 394).

Some components of this narrative were not specific to America: the intellectuals' burden of guilt for the Red Decade, their impossible secular fusion of political and spiritual aspirations, their deconversions and reconversions.[16] These were standard themes of the era's self-reflection. However, American intellectuals peculiarly expressed their guilt in post-Edenic themes pronounced in America's Protestant past and, as they were wont to comment, in classic American literature.[17] Murray Kempton, a former member of the Socialist Party and a liberal journalist for the *New York Post* and *Newsday,* wrote confessionally of his generation that they had replaced one deity with another without finding a cognate in the new faith for Augustinian doctrine: "For Communists offer one precious, fatal boon: they take away the sense of sin. It may or may not be debatable whether a man can live without God; but if it were possible, we should pass a law forbidding a man to live without a sense of sin."[18] Disillusionment, or "the loss of innocence," said Daniel Bell, "is America's distinctive experience of the thirties."[19] The American Left confessed that it had taken a tragic stumble comparable, it seemed, to the Christian story of Adam. The error was mitigated by the nature of the seductive fruit, which promised political utopia. Liberals adopted as an apologia the Nieburian analysis (seconded by Niebuhr's colleagues Paul Tillich and John Bennett) that Communism, however evil in its methods and deluded as to the possibility of its goals, was distinct from Nazism insofar as it was a perfectionist heresy rather than a cynical creed that denied human equality. Since Communism was not a callous choice against good, but the fruit of innocence, in which sin was the perversion of good, its evil had an ambiguous continuity with virtue. Thus, reformed liberals could cover themselves in guilt while also extenuating their moral lapse, for they could show that they had condoned iniquitous acts and leagued themselves with a fallacious regime (as fellow travelers or as Communist Party members) because they had actually intended justice. Since they had known the taint of the enemy, having yielded their own liberal values and standards of civil conduct to defend the ends of revolution, only to then have their ideals betrayed, they were now inoculated against further pollutants by tragic experience. Their rhetorical strategy was to turn this sense of failure to their moral advantage. They now knew the sting of tragedy, so ran the main line of defense, and so were wiser enemies of totalitarians. By outwardly signifying penitence, the ex-radicals not only assuaged their private sense of moral error. They also tried to absorb the issue of anti-Communism.

The liberal anti-Communist position was formally represented by the Americans for Democratic Action (A.D.A.), founded 1948. Exponents of this position, such as A.D.A. co-founders Reinhold Niebuhr and Arthur Schlesinger, Jr., argued for a pragmatic, interest-based, rather than an ideological, analysis of America's imbalances of power that excluded Communism while allowing that liberalism would be able to achieve some social democratic goals by nonrevolutionary means, as the prudent reforms of the Roosevelt administration had already demonstrated.[20] In *The Irony of American History* and *The Vital Center,* for example, the historic tensions between democracy and industrial capitalism had been resolved through serendipity in the form of the New Deal, its wisdom of the mixed economy, which allowed for some redistribution of income, over the illusions of a classless order, which was a "utopian" notion. As opposed to the totalitarian, who believes that successful seizure of power will prove that revolution was justified from the first bomb detonated, Schlesinger and Niebuhr's American citizen accepts that each of the nation's various "pressure groups" (versus the Old Left's politicoeconomic "classes") has a right to compete for its interests, and he does so out of a tacit recognition of his fallibility as free being, an attitude that is analogous to Christian humility.[21] Since Communism was not a pressure group, but an idolatrous "political religion" (254), American labor (under the C.I.O.) and liberalism were aggressively to purge their ranks of any fellow travelers, most especially Social Gospel Christian and Progressive Party candidate for president Henry Wallace, unjustly branded a dupe of the Communist Party.[22]

But they had not paid enough penance yet. No sooner had Henry Wallace been purged than the legitimacy of liberalism was put into question by two highly publicized cases of conspiracy on the former Left: the trial of Alger Hiss and the conviction of Julius and Ethel Rosenberg for treason.[23] There was serious division over how to respond to the Hiss case, in particular, because of Hiss's profile in the Roosevelt administration, at Yalta, and in the United Nations. Those who believed the case was a right-wing maneuver to discredit the legitimacy of liberalism came to Hiss's defense, while others chose to make the Hiss case an occasion for exculpating the new liberalism from the errors of the thirties. Several reformed liberals, notably Leslie Fiedler (in succession, a member of the Young Communist League, the Socialist Workers Party, and, until 1941, the Workers Party) wrote mea culpas treating Hiss and the Rosenbergs as doubles of their anterior selves, which they could now look upon with edifying irony.[24] Finding universal drama in Augustinian motifs, notably of *The Confessions*, Fiedler likened his intellectual odyssey to that of Simone Weil, the Jewish-born convert from Communism to a mystical, idiosyncratic Christianity. Weil, he said, had experienced the inner existential meaning of Christian myth, as present crises have exposed its core to the secular mind:

> She speaks of the problems of belief in the vocabulary of the unbeliever, of the doctrines of the Church in the words of the unchurched. The *askesis*, the 'dark night of the soul,' through which she passed to certitude, is the modern intellectual's familiar pattern of attraction toward and disillusionment with Marxism, the discipline of contemporary politics. The day-to-day struggles of trade unionism, unemployment, the Civil War in Spain, the role of the Soviet

Union, anarchism, and pacifism—these are the determinants of her ideas, the unforeseen roads that led her to sanctity. . . . The fate of the world, she knew, is decided out of time; and it is in myth that mankind has recorded its sense of its true history, the eternal 'immobile drama' of necessity and evil, salvation and grace.[25]

Weil never formally converted to Catholicism, and, as one of "the Unchurched," she is a spiritual comrade as much as an exemplum to Fiedler, who, having no sacred community, has also had to quest vagrantly after enlightenment having lost the false religion of radical politics. Fiedler does not believe he has attained the purity of Weil's suffering, but in her self-effacing reach after perfection residing in the empathetic tradition of *imitatio christi* rather than a Gideon-like moral striving to fell evil, he sees a version of sainthood continuous with his own profane absolution, his moral reconciliation to the gap between is and ought: "I have never dealt with a personality so painfully and inexhaustibly contemporaneous as Simone Weil; though ten years dead, she remains living in a way that Alger Hiss, for all the resurrection of his name in the press and on the radio, is not. Beside her, the Rosenbergs, McCarthy seem ghosts, less real than what one has written about them" (31). Weil irradiates an aura of authenticity because, unlike the other benighted souls Fiedler lists, she has been touched by the grace that comes of having her ego wounded by history and then gratefully enduring self-alienation and mortification. In her penitence, she has seen her implication in the guilt of mankind, whereas a fool like Hiss, who denies any complicity with evil (whether or not he has actually spied), cannot even recognize his individual wrongdoing. Thus Fiedler rewinds Hiss in Lazarus's shroud, returning him to the funereal ground of ossified causes from which the media, irreverently, have dragged him to reticulate old radical errors, while he resurrects Weil in Hiss's stead.

For Diana Trilling, grace had protected liberals from stumbling into the most egregious error of radicalism, treason, though this blessing still may not have saved them from obloquy. In "Memorandum on the Hiss Case" (1950), Trilling argues that post-Hiss, even to identify oneself as a liberal is to call down suspicion of a guilty past. Even before the accusation is leveled, her hypothetical liberal, she fears, may feel complicity, for if he did not actually commit espionage, as did Hiss, then he likely sympathized with the pro-Communist position. Similar to the adulterer Jesus admonishes in Matthew 5:28, Trilling's liberal had sinned in his heart if not in act. The proper reaction, she advises, is not self-laceration, which would demoralize liberalism and discredit its real gains, but grateful humility. Speculating that she speaks for many in her generation, Trilling considers Hiss and says, "There but for the grace of God go I."[26] This sense of a "common . . . complicity" that is both individual and collective—covering a generation of an intellectual class—pervaded the writings of the New York intellectuals and attracted the ire of former Progressive Party member and Wallace supporter Norman Mailer, henceforth to become a persistent irritant to, and occasionally stirring witness against, the liberal establishment.[27] In *Barbary Shore* (1951), a mournful allegory about politics after the Old Left's demoralization, which has the Hiss case as one of its subtexts, Mailer parodies the moral masochism of the ex-radical in the character of Lannie Madison, an ex-Trotskyist, neurotically fixated on the bleeding Christ, who welcomes an intrusive FBI agent into her bed with the invitation: "I love you even if you torment me."[28]

Many ex-radicals did indeed speak of Hiss with a shock of rueful self-recognition, but since he maintained his innocence, he could symbolize only the fall and not the redemption of the penitent liberal.[29] Hence, Hiss's accuser, Whittaker Chambers, gained more sympathy from liberal anti-Communists who seconded his charge that the liberal Left coalition in the thirties had been inveigled into condoning and in some cases cooperating with evil. By 1948, ex-Communist Whittaker Chambers would be a celebrity in the case of treason and espionage, but prior to his testimony, he was known mainly as an editorial writer on religion and politics for *Time* and *Life* magazines, where he had contributed, among other pieces, a review of the first volume of Reinhold Niebuhr's *The Nature and Destiny of Man, Human Nature,* in which he praised Niebuhr for "put[ting] sin back in the spotlight."[30] When he accepted Henry Luce's assignment to write an additional essay on Niebuhr's theology in 1948, only six months prior his testimony, he composed a piece, "Faith for a Lenten Age," which appeared in the March 8 edition of *Time,* with an unmistakable autobiographical subtext. After being a Stalinist and a spy, Chambers had broken with the Communist Party in 1938, ending a thirteen-year affiliation, and had since become a Quaker who espoused a kind of Christian neoorthodoxy. As he later acknowledged, the 1948 Niebuhr piece, chocked with citations of Barth, Dostoevsky, and Kierkegaard lamenting that man is inescapably guilty and self-deceiving, was a dry run for the exposition of his newfound faith in the extraordinary *Witness* (1952).[31] Assuming the stance of Everyman, Chambers would manage to make his singularly bizarre declension from Communism, replete with microfilm-stuffed pumpkins, into a spiritual odyssey for America's instruction. Like Chambers himself, the book was taken as an emblem of its generation, leading the acerbic New York art critic (and former anti-Stalinist Marxist) Harold Rosenberg, in his "Couch Liberalism and the Guilty Past" (1955), to deem the fifties "the Confession Era" and the age of "radical penance" versus "radical politics."[32]

Using Christian typology, Chambers had crafted in *Witness* a fresh—and, as it turned out, voguish—narrative suitable for the purposes of the informant's personal and public apotheosis. If Hiss and the Rosenbergs were converted into emblems for collective guilt, Chambers, by his own narrative devices, became an emblem of private redemption. Chambers invented a new "model of guilt" that would become a prevalent trope of the first half of the fifties: the symbol of the informant as *Micro-Christus* rather than Judas. In the preface to *Witness*, "The Letter to My Children," Chambers reinterprets the Crucifixion in light of his own life's revelations. "In this book I am giving you my hands," he says. "I am leading you, not through cool pine woods, but up and up a narrow defile."[33] The end of the defile (a ponderous pun) is Golgotha, and that "is the meaning of the journey" (22). With this image, the informer becomes the thief (the Communist) who is saved by turning to Christ. At the same time, the informer is himself Christ, for like the Savior in his own time, he has been misunderstood as a criminal by his naive countrymen, who cannot distinguish the true American from the subverter.

Some of the most prominent of Chambers's defenders extended the Christian *figura* in *Witness* to their own accounts of the informer and alleged traitor. For Kempton, Chambers was the Christian son who had fled his origins for an alternative faith, only to be persecuted by the conscience of his old one. Hiss, by contrast, was the man from "shabby genteel" background who had been educated above sin to a Jay Gatsby–like "Platonic conception of himself." Stalwart atheist Sidney Hook's support of Chambers was the most astonishing given his earlier criticism of the intellectual vogue for neoorthodoxy and other conservative theologies (including, at the time, Reinhold Niebuhr's), but he saw in Chambers an exemplar of the new resolve of prodemocratic anti-Communism rather than the "The New Failure of Nerve" he denounced in 1943.[34] Defenders of Hiss, as chronicled in *Witness*, did not choose to overlook Chambers's religiosity, as Hook did, but instead accused him of being a charlatan who hid behind his God. Taking advantage of what he saw as a tragicomic situation, as the center fought within itself over whether to partner with the Right, Norman Mailer ridiculed Christian anti-Communism, including in *Barbary Shore* an undercover FBI agent named "Hollingsworth" who carries a Bible and a tacky "phosphorescent" cross signifying that he is anti-Bolshevik, to show that the state was cynically appropriating priestly robes in the name of battling an apostate faith.

Rahv and Schlesinger, who offered two of the most thoughtful retorts to Chambers, did not accuse him of being disingenuous. They saw Chambers as terribly sincere, ideologically the inverse of Hiss, but morally his double, for he had sloughed off one system of illusions for another just as hermetic. Rahv, who had been defending literature from the sort of "religio-aesthetic attitudes" that Chambers expounded in *Time,* warned that this Christian "conservatism" could legitimate state authoritarianism.[35] Schlesinger, who took umbrage with Chambers's quotations from Niebuhr, said that he was self-righteously arrogating to himself antinomian claims of revelation: "Mr. Chambers himself hears voices [from God]; so did Joan of Arc; but so did Hitler."[36] Columbia University Professor of English Lionel Trilling, one of America's leading public intellectuals and, with Reinhold Niebuhr, one of "the representative men" of "the generation of the thirties," was equally disturbed by Chambers's religious intemperance, and equally concerned to protect the legitimacy of liberalism, in his only novel, one of the most remarkable and representative documents of the liberal conscience in the postwar years.[37]

Self-Deception and Wisdom in Lionel Trilling's *The Middle of the Journey*

Four years earlier than the publication of *Witness,* before Chambers had converted himself into a typological figure, Lionel Trilling left an indelible image of Chambers as "Gifford Maxim," a key character in his semiauto-biographical novel about the prewar Left.[38] Trilling based part of *The Middle of the Journey* (1947) on Chambers's conversion from Communism to conservative Christianity, and the novel speculates on the shock-waves such a personal change of conviction might have sent through a Left-liberal coterie gathered in New England during the thirties. Trilling, for his part, showed obvious disappointment with Chambers, first in the portrait of Gifford Maxim and then in a 1976 retrospective on the writing of the novel.[39] Whittaker Chambers was not a fundamentalist, and he never endorsed a state church or a theocracy—structures that would have been anathemas to the version of Quaker faith he ended up adopting.[40] Chambers nonetheless linked New Deal and Popular Front liberalism to the Christian "heresy" of Communism, and on the basis of these parallels, advanced in such pieces as Chambers's *Life* magazine fable "The Devil" (1948), Trilling saw in the soon-to-be notorious convert a figure of modern regression. One year before the Hiss case broke, *The Middle of the Journey* expressed Trilling's reservations that Chambers's example—which would shortly be applauded by many high-profile ex-radicals—might portend an intellectual "pendulum swing" from utopian visions to theological pessimism: "The time was getting ripe for a competing system. And it would be brought by the swing of the pendulum, not by the notion of growth."[41]

In his novel's pages, Trilling dramatizes his own marginal involvement in thirties' politics, first as an anti-Stalinist Marxist and later as a member of the Trotsky Defense Committee, as well as his reasons for leading the deradicalization of intellectuals after the war.[42] *The Middle of the Journey* is, as often noted, a contemporary novel of ideas, but it is also an exploration of the inner life of intellectuals in the thirties. Not satisfied that his colleagues had probed themselves deeply enough to appreciate what had happened inside their souls when they became fellow travelers, Trilling describes Communism as a malady of modern man, his longing for transcendence and his irresponsible flight from social actuality. In this display of self-examination, however, Trilling did not see the depravity that Chambers had discovered in his own radical past.

In an early reading of *The Middle of the Journey,* Nathan Scott, Jr., stated that Trilling was intensely "resolved" to "uphold the secular legacy of the Enlightenment."[43] A review of Trilling's writings shows that he was actually searching for a humanism that would incorporate some of the insights of Western religion while remaining agnostic on questions regarding the existence or nature of God. From his Ph.D. dissertation on Matthew Arnold, his commentaries in "Reality in America" on Dreiser's religious conversion, in "The Fate of Pleasure" on Augustine's ascetic morality, and in "Little Dorrit" on Dickens's anti-Calvinism, to his meditations on theodicy in Wordsworth and Keats, Trilling often took the part of interpreting Christianity for the middle class.[44] In the debates over faith's role in the modern age, he intervened by training attention on the nineteenth century, which he, like Arnold, saw as a period when reason and culture began to supplement the functions of a religion whose orthodoxy was fast losing its intellectual and social authority, as "the Sea of Faith" retreated from "earth's shore" with "a melancholy, long, withdrawing roar."[45] Throughout his work, from the early books on Arnold (1939) and E. M. Forster (1944) to the essay collections of the fifties that highlighted Henry James and the Romantics, Trilling searched for a consensus of feeling and thought while resisting any academic case for an official religion, of the sort being aired in the United States by New School sociology professor Ernest van den Haag (who had a set-to with Sidney Hook in the *Partisan Review*), or for the elite defense of religion as a means of maintaining social stability as proffered by University of Chicago political science philosopher Leo Strauss.[46] Trilling joined Meyer Schapiro, and most of the other contributors to the *Partisan Review*'s "Religion and the Intellectuals" symposium, who opposed any argument that intellectuals should justify religion because it is a "useful fiction in maintaining morality and the social order, particularly for the ignorant and the poor," a position recommending the teaching of "a 'double truth' one for the elite and another for the simple," which was no improvement on the Marxist analysis of faith.[47] In *Matthew Arnold*, Trilling resists the Englishman wherever his criticism tends to verify culture by its consistency with High Anglicanism, and, like the plurality of the *Partisan Review* symposium, he accepted no justifications for state church establishment. These were, he believed, generally predicated on a pessimism about democracy, one that was founded on a deeper pessimism about human potential often expressed religiously through the doctrine of sin, "the specious position in which all injustice is laid at the door of the original Old Adam in each of us, not to be done away with until we shall all, at the same moment, become the New Adam."[48] Arnold's writings, on the other hand, commanded Trilling's admiration because they are not preoccupied with the problem of the sinful will (a focus of Puritanism), but moved by the condition of human suffering.[49] The contrast between a Christianity concerned with how we endure pain and mortality versus one riveted upon the control of our evil nature is a theme that returns in Trilling's later work and culminates in his eloquent essay, "The Poet as Hero: Keats in His Letters." Trilling elaborates upon this theme in *The Middle of the Journey* through the protagonist John Laskell's reflection on the meaning of his own recent brush with death and through his verbal blows with Maxim, who gloats that his newfound religion reprises "the *old* knowledge" of human fate.[50]

It is clear that the liberal Protestant church, weakened by its modernist compromises, cannot be a help to Laskell in his quest after a secular theodicy. *The Middle of the Journey* describes a parish where the Arnoldian priority on ethics and fraternity above dogma and fear has been debauched by an excess of good will and ignorance unleavened by any respect for the complexity of the moral choices facing modern men. In the New England town where John Laskell retires after convalescing from his near-fatal illness, the local Congregationalist minister has gone so far left of Calvinism that he flirts with Communist ideology. Mr. Gurney, the pastor, says that though he is not an extremist, he is "sympathetic to what he called The Great Experiment that was going on over One-Sixth of the Earth's Surface. . . . Mr. Gurney went on to say in some ways religion could be said to be an effort for social justice. He said that it was significant that Jesus Christ had been a carpenter and his apostles of a similarly proletarian origin" (287).[51] In the exchange that follows, Maxim easily eviscerates

Gurney, slighting the minister's intellect and suggesting the weakness of his convictions:

> "In short, sir, you do believe in society and social justice and sociology but you do not believe in God." . . .
>
> "It depends on what you mean by God, Mr. Maxim. If you mean a being who may be understood as some divine purpose in the world, or some principle that is at bottom good—"
>
> "Suppose we say that God is the Being to whom things are rendered that are not rendered to Caesar."[52]

Maxim's challenge to Gurney is very much like Chambers's ideological reversal in *Witness;* whereas Communists, in eliminating God, refuse to obey Caesar and deify a state that the revolution will bring in its stead, the Christian man, whose god transcends all political authority, obeys Caesar and looks to eternity for his freedom from the ramifications of sin. Though Maxim's statement is unremarkable in the context of Cold War discourse, the reaction it elicits from Gurney in Trilling's narrative is very telling. Whereas Maxim, consistent with his punning name, is unshakably firm, the minister, who stalls for a moment before fumbling with some cod theology, seems self-conscious about offending his college-bred guests: "Everything about Mr. Gurney was clear—that he was not learned, that he was not intelligent, that he was decent. Equally clear was his desire to be approved of . . . it must have been very confusing for him, for it had long been part of his view of the world that intelligent people were sure to be atheistic or agnostic and, if they spoke about God at all, were likely to attack even so complicated and modified a belief as Mr. Gurney himself held" (288). Mr. Gurney, whose name (by contrast with Maxim's) suggests a movable stretcher for reclining, has become so comfortably ensconced in his role as a middlebrow metaphysician and ethicist, even on matters as dire as world revolution, that he has forgotten the passionate center of belief and overlooked the potential for danger in mingling simplistic morality with political theory.

Gurney is a composite of the traits identifying him with the weaknesses of liberal Christianity. To dabble in politics armed only with moral sympathy, Niebuhr had argued, was irresponsible because the clergy were intellectually ill-equipped to parse the ends from the methods in radical theories that might highlight the worthy aim of justice but advocate either ineffectual means (a charge leveled at the Social Gospel) or destructive ones (the charge leveled at Communism). Secondly, Gurney's simpering modernism has underestimated the subrational, emotional component of man, a topic of great concern to Trilling in his writings from *Matthew Arnold* forward.

Modern man, as represented in *The Opposing Self*, *Beyond Culture*, and *Sincerity and Authenticity*, is so mindful of his selfhood that he cannot endure doubt and suffering, for these emotions attest to his impermanence as a temporal being and to the vulnerability of his inner life to circumstance. Hence the modern self romanticizes the activity of negation, for in emptying of all value the mutable world he has been given, he shows himself transcendent to it.[53] In *The Middle of the Journey*, the religious passion for the ideal, versus the actual, has passed into radical ideology, which expresses a typically modern attitude in blaming society for man's perennial anxieties over his transitoriness.

Liberal Protestants like Gurney, whose church notably has "a short steeple," may not remember the force of the human desire for transcendence, but Maxim, a Communist at one moment, an equally devout Christian in the next, embodies it at two extremes.[54] When Laskell, an agnostic, curiously leafs through Gurney's ecumenical manual, *The Pastor's Helpful Funeral Guide*, he takes the book as a symbol of how modern Protestant churches, in setting aside the theological battles of the past, have grown sapless, homogenized, and muzzy: "All three faiths [Episcopal, Presbyterian, Methodist] lived very comfortably in the small black book and Laskell thought how many passions had died, how much belief had attenuated, to make this possible. The book contained all the scriptural texts that were relevant to the occasion, and prayers, and poems, and lines of poem that could be quoted to advantage" (333). By contrast, Laskell is impressed—and dismayed—by the ferocity of Maxim's response to Gurney, which recalls his initial ruminations on Maxim's personality early in the novel: "Gifford Maxim was the man of the far future, the bloody, moral, apocalyptic future that was sure to come" (65).

Though Maxim appears "the blackest of reactionaries" to Laskell, he is, in spite of having "lost" his "nerve," a person who transfixes radicals by his example because he uncannily thinks and sounds like them, even as a Christian convert (183, 340).[55] When Kermit Simpson, editor of a progressive magazine called the *New Era* (Simpson's character is probably based on Dostoevsky scholar and *Partisan Review* founder Philip Rahv), leaves a bedridden Laskell some fiction reading, *The Possessed* (later translated as *The Devils*), the allusion to contemporary revolutionary socialists is unmistakable (51). Dostoevsky's character Shatov, Rahv had noted in a well-remembered essay on the novel, says to Stavrogin, "It is difficult to change gods," acknowledging the paradox of his own conversion from nihilism to Eastern Orthodoxy and romantic nation worship.[56] As in Dostoevsky's novel, world-abjuring and demonic idealism in *The Middle of the Journey* is pandemic among political radicals as well as religious sectarians. Maxim's brand of religiosity shocks and offends his friends, the pro-Stalinists Arthur and Nancy Croom, but their own idealism matches his in its "clandestine negation of the political life," of "contingency, conflicts of interests and clashes of will and the compromises they lead to."[57] Trilling encapsulates his critique of the Crooms in a seemingly innocuous scene between Laskell and Susan Caldwell, the child of the Crooms' handyman, Duck. For the Sunday church bazaar, the little girl is preparing a recitation of the preamble to Blake's *Milton*. In an England blackened by industry, the poet is emboldened by his mental image of Jerusalem, the holy city where "the Lamb" walks:

> And did that Countenance Divine
> Shine forth upon our clouded hills?
> And was Jerusalem builded here
> Among these dark Satanic Mills. . . .
>
> I will not cease from Mental Fight
> Nor shall my sword sleep in my hand
> Till we have built Jerusalem
> In England's green and pleasant land.

With its imagery of a Satanic industrial order, the sword of God's justice, and a New Jerusalem on earth, the stanzas, in the novel's context, clearly imply the utopian faith of radicals who may be tempted by Stalinists to convert "the Mental Fight" into a literal war on capitalism. To underline the allusion, Susan's practice is interrupted by some pregnant remarks from Laskell, who believes the child's elocution suggests a misinterpretation of the poem. On the phrase, "I will not cease," Susan stresses "not" and stamps her foot in a show of defiance, eliciting this response from Laskell:

"I don't think you ought to do that."
"Why not?" she said in reasonable surprise.
"Because it's as if you were a child being stubborn. . . ."
"But I am a child, really."
It was certainly a point. Laskell thought about it. "Yes," he said. "But you haven't said any other part of the poem as if you were a child, and then suddenly, just at the end, when the poem gets so determined, you change the character of the speaker." (190)

Intellectuals like the Crooms are impatient with political life and wish to hasten the Marxist dialectic of progress, as if the New Jerusalem could be realized on earth. Trilling underlines the immaturity of this view—its stubborn refusal to see its own will as anything less than absolute truth and goodness—by extending the metaphor of childishness from little Susan to the Crooms, especially Nancy, the more adamant in her support for Stalin. Upon reuniting with his friends, Laskell reads Nancy's face with some misgiving: "her clear eyes . . . showed a child's wonder but could also show a child's strong, demanding anger" (12). In the presence of his old friends, he is startled by the "differentiation between the Crooms and himself . . . What had happened to Laskell, all at once, was that he realized that you couldn't live the life of promises without yourself remaining a child. The promise of the future might have its uses as a way of seducing the child to maturity, but maturity itself meant that the future and the present were brought together, that you lived your life *now* instead of preparing and committing yourself to some better day to come" (163). Nancy can imagine no scenario in which present and future can meet because the world she anticipates will dissolve rather than meliorate the actual conditions under which men now labor. Laskell ponders Nancy's trust that she stands on the noble side of history: "What she did hope for she was passionately sure would come, for she knew that most people had her own clarity of spirit. It was a very large faith, a very large involvement with life. But now Laskell saw her as he had never seen her before—in an aura of self-deception. It was that which made her so very girlish today. . . . For the desire to refuse knowledge of the evil and harshness of the world can often shine in a face like a glow of youth" (121). In her desire to leap beyond the present in preparation for the advent of a Marxist utopia, Nancy is not only childlike. Similar to the "Children of Light" Reinhold Niebuhr describes in a famous essay, she is also willing a return to a kind of second childhood, in which she might have the moral purity of innocence, of being able to name with certainty the party of virtue and motion from the parties of self-interest and stasis.[58] Anything less than total commitment to the future makes one a bourgeois intellectual, "shilly-shally[ing]," non-committal, and guilty.[59] Laskell summarizes the atmosphere on the Left in the thirties, in the process his thought shading Communists into Nazis:

> Laskell thought how much of life was being conducted as a transaction between guilt and innocence. Even among people who were devoted only to ideas of progress and social equality and not at all to action, there had grown an unusual desire to discover who was innocent and who was guilty, who could be trusted and who needed to be watched . . . the events in Germany would seem to show that even among those terrible people there was a preoccupation with guilt and innocence—so many words to explain the wrongs done to them, for the wronged and the weak are the innocent; so much cruelty to separate themselves from the guilty, for those who are punished are

guilty and those who punish are innocent; so much adoration of strength, for the strong who were once weak are never guilty (169–170).

The illusion of innocence, earned through identifying with the weak against the wrongdoer, relieves the Left from the obligation to ask whether its ends are realistic and its means proportional. The Crooms bristle when Laskell finally tells them that only a child has absolute freedom from the responsibility to distinguish the good from the bad in any social system, even if that system includes inequality (354).

Maxim's own critique of the Left ends up drawing unexpected parallels between his otherworldly dualism and the Crooms' secular eschatology. In an essay on *Billy Budd,* written for Kermit Simpson's the *New Era,* Maxim uses Melville's novella as an occasion to present his dialectical theology, in which the Spirit of Christ (Billy) is sacrificed to the Law of God (Vere) for the sake of preserving man from total absorption in Evil (Claggart). The allegory, called "Spirit and Law," anticipates *Witness's* explanation of Communism as a Christian heresy. Painting a propertyless world in which each man serves his neighbor, the Communist tempts the Christlike part of man—the Lamb from Susan's impatient recitation—only to deliver this spirit over to anomie. The cunning of Communism consists in its teaching men that they must flout the Law in order to give Spirit its complete expression at once in the temporal realm. This deep meaning of the story is lost on the modern bourgeois liberal and radical mind, which assumes that Billy should be exonerated for striking Claggart and may even be tempted to see Billy as a beleaguered member of the proletariat: "For such people, Billy Budd will be nothing more than an oppressed worker. . . . And Captain Vere will seem at best a conscience-ridden bourgeois, sympathetic to a man of the lower orders but committed to carrying out the behests of the established regime" (181). This reading, Maxim continues, fails to grasp that without submission to the Law, Spirit would go over to its opposite, becoming evil in its effort to destroy Evil. Law is Necessity because Spirit, being free, cannot sustain Christlikeness; indeed, Spirit's striving to make Christ actual in human institutions is precisely what could lead Spirit to revolt and violence. Hence, man has a tragic recognition to make: "As long as Evil exists in the world, Law must exist, and it—not Spirit—must have the rule" (182).

Responding to Maxim's article, the Crooms ignore the theology as rubbish, but, to Laskell's surprise, they do not agree that the piece is utterly bumptious. Arthur extracts a "core of realism" from Maxim's extreme dystopian vision: "The great danger to the progressive movement these days, as I see it, is that liberals are going to confuse their dreams and ideals

with the possible realities . . . they begin shouting for immediate political democracy, forgetting the realities of the historical situation" (185).
Though Arthur is still the benighted fellow traveler, apologizing for Stalinism by blaming historical exigency rather than the totalitarian nature of
the regime, his willingness at least to confront the utopian illusions of his
intellectual coterie and to respect the Niebuhrian "paradoxes of power"
suggests that he may be eventually redeemed from his political misjudg-
ment: "Laskell thought of his friend as the kind of man who was going to
dominate the near future—not the far future when the apocalyptic days
would come, but the time now at hand before things got very bad" (272,
64). Arthur has the makings of a liberal who will later come to his senses
(the events of the novel predate the Hitler-Stalin Non-Aggression pact) and
join other ex-radicals in renouncing the "guilty past." Nancy, on the other
hand, seems irretrievably innocent. Misinterpreting Maxim's article in
terms of Communist Party propaganda, she concludes that it is a justification of Stalin's purges:

> If you think about it, you see that it is really quite applicable to the Moscow
> trials. Even if those men were subjectively innocent . . . they may have had to
> be executed for the sake of what he [Maxim] calls Law in the world of Neces-
> sity. . . . Certainly before they [Stalin's political enemies] died they had a
> proper appreciation of Law. They realized that the dictatorship of the prole-
> tariat represented Law. Of course, God wasn't mentioned, but it was the same
> thing in effect and they said that their punishment was necessary. (184–185).

Nancy's gloss on "Spirit and Law" completely overlooks how the condemned men's final statements may have been coerced or how the trials
themselves may have been staged. Her dogmatic attitude recalls Laskell's
chilling observation that he could hear "Armageddon in her voice," the
same voice that steels her more careful husband with a spirit of "absolute
intransigence" (204, 272). Nancy has also considered joining the Communist Party (a measure Arthur has never taken) and even has had a conversation with the preconversion Maxim about helping him with espionage
(174–175). Despite the differences in ideology, the Crooms and Maxim are
each caught up in dialectics of redemption whose ideals of Good are conceived as the motors of history rather than the products of it.

Both views are deterministic, denying what Trilling, following his teacher
John Erskine, would call "the moral obligation to be intelligent."[60] Regardless of the subjective intentions behind it, the good or evil of an act is
entirely beyond the reasoning of the doer to judge. Its value is either objec-
tively ascertained by the Marxist teleologist, who scientifically analyzes its
effect on political economy in a given stage of capital, or else it is resigned

to the mysteries of Providence, which only the Divine can reveal in His own time. In neither case is there room for independent reflection; man is an absolutely sinful union of freedom and pride who must await the Father's eternal dispensation, or he is a product of social forces who, at most, can urge the chosen agent of revolution to complete history's inevitable movement. Though only Maxim's position is explicitly theological, each has its own "God-terms," to borrow from Richard Rorty, that guarantee the meanings of the stories they wish to impose on society.[61] Since the Crooms do not subscribe to Maxim's doctrine of "common guilt," they cannot see in Maxim an alienated version of themselves. The ex-radical, however, makes the grotesque connection for them when he proposes an alliance: "We must go hand in hand. Let it be our open secret. You will preach the law for the masses. I will preach the law for the leaders. For the masses, rights and freedom from blame. For the leaders, duties and nothing but blame, from within and without. We will hate each other and together we will make the new world."[62] At first cryptic, these remarks make more sense in the light of Maxim's essay, "Spirit and Law." Laskell, by contrast with the Crooms, is appalled by the piece because its defense of law and discipline seems to give the state virtually unlimited authority in the temporal sphere by making it the embodiment of tragic Necessity (355). The Crooms, it seems, can groom the masses for revolt so that Maxim's party of theological pessimists can lead a near-fascist counterreaction in which the state is strengthened by the fear of anarchy. Nancy's endorsement of party dictatorship and her expressed disgust with "civil liberties" and "Jeffersonian democracies" suggest that she, too, would identify Necessity with the martial state if she believed there were no other means to postrevolutionary order (216). The religious vision of earthly tragedy and the secular imagination of utopia once again seem to meet despite their mutual antagonism in theory (340, 341).

The intellectual protagonist of the novel, the one who understands the "moral obligation to be intelligent" is John Laskell. Having recently come close to death, he has had all of his illusions tinctured by the sense of his mortality, and so he can estimate the pretensions of both the Crooms and Maxim. For Laskell, neither of their systems allows any latitude for the doubt that will enable self-reflection. Maxim's "Spirit and Law" performs a necessary critique of the Crooms' idealization of Stalin, but it too closely resembles their own dialectic of redemption in its failure to confront the ambiguity of freedom. Equally rejecting Maxim's belief in the common guilt and the Crooms' hope for postbourgeois innocence, Laskell is the novel's free thinker (he belongs to no parties or committees) who wants liberal reform, but balances speculation about social change with meditation on perennial problems, such as mortality and existential suffering, which each self must face. Implicitly in the novel's logic, Laskell would defuse the idealism and masked egoism of both the Crooms and Maxim by making the self, its will, and its anxieties objects of intellectual contemplation. Laskell believes that his will is mysterious, since it is compounded of both personal and conditioned elements (301). Its full disclosure (to himself or to another) is not possible. Yet he does not give up trying to affirm the resilience of the self to all the modern forces which would deny its depth or growth.

In his essay "The Poet As Hero," which expands themes from *The Middle of the Journey*, Trilling's reading of Keats throws into relief Laskell's virtues. The essay is his deepest meditation on the theology of suffering, culled from Job and the Gospels and blended with the wisdom writings of the *Pirke Abboth*, a text he acknowledges in "Wordsworth and the Rabbis" as a boyhood find and a continuing source of inspiration. In "The Poet as Hero," evil is not an opponent or a structure to be surmounted. Trilling proposes that Keats instead gives to men a theodicy in which the self grows in empathy and strength through the endurance of suffering. Evil originates not in "the vale of tears," but in a flight from finitude into "the egotistical sublime," the nonempathic self that lords mind over world, the abstract over the actual. Revisiting the manifesto for a reformed liberalism that he had offered in the preface to *The Liberal Imagination*, in "The Poet as Hero," Trilling holds up Keats's "negative capability" as a model for thought, open to ambiguity and complexity, which is lacking in the modern egoism of both the Right and the Left: "Negative capability, the faculty of not having to make up one's mind about everything, depends upon the sense of one's personal identity and is the sign of personal identity. Only the self that is certain of its existence, of its identity, can do without the armor of systematic certainties."[63] Keats develops Trilling's diagnosis of ideology, but negative capability, or the capacity to reside in uncertainties, is also a principle of Trilling's secular humanism. Keats writes with "an animus against Christian doctrine," but what he is giving, Trilling says, is "a sketch of *salvation*" (40; Trilling's italics). Eschewing doctrine, Keats makes the fall from grace into ambiguity and pain a *felix culpa* through which man gains an identity and a soul (41). His poet implicitly neutralizes the egoistic longing for transcendence, for the desire absolutely to negate the actual, by making salvation into an open process of "'provings and alterations and perfectionings'" (41).[64] As the self collides with circumstances that resist it, the redemptive response is to "bless" what is given, even if this be terrible, for without opposition to its will, the self would remain hopelessly incomplete and lacking the "spiritual and moral health" for community.[65]

When it describes the nature of egotism, Trilling's reading of Keats shows a debt to Reinhold Niebuhr (a friend whose work is cited in "The Art of the Novel").[66] Yet he adds nuance to *The Nature and Destiny of Man* that Chambers did not begin to imagine in his own *Time* and *Life* pieces on the theologian. Particularly, Trilling shows in the figure of Maxim Gifford that the preoccupation with sin can be as egoistic as the preoccupation with liberation, for it ultimately leads to the renunciation of what is given, what exists; it, too, speaks to a human desire for a grand rupture with the ambiguous, diurnal world of relative and limited freedom. For Maxim, the avowal of his sin makes his life an exemplum for the epoch (what Chambers was to call "the terrible division of our age" between Christianity and atheism, freedom and slavery), but, through Laskell's impressions, Trilling cautions the former Left against adopting Maxim's confessional pose, unless it is willing utterly to condemn the liberal imagination.[67] Rebuking oneself for the sins of the past, an action that might publicly authenticate a Gifford Maxim because of the extremity of his deconversion/new conversion, could make a reformed liberal, unprepared to disclaim humanistic values as sources of iniquity, seem still tainted, still anxious, still defensive. The novel imagines an attitude of humility (what Trilling will later link to the ethic of "sincerity") that can persist with an ethic of ambiguity, or "negative capability," without the former being construed as penitence for sinful blemish. In *The Middle of the Journey*, Trilling foresees the possibility of liberalism becoming trapped in a confessional mode, where the exposure of the radical past continually pressures men of liberal conscience to ask forgiveness for their failures to achieve self-understanding or to fully disclose themselves to others. In Keats's hero, as in John Laskell, Trilling discovers an alternative to Chambers's rhetoric of confession, with its excessive emphasis on the problem of sin, and thereby aims to protect liberalism from being permanently caught, and demoralized, in the admission of self-deception.

Trilling did not expect that this form of secular theodicy would replace belief. In romanticism, as in Arnold, he appears to have been looking for some grounds of reconciliation with religious thought, and his tone in discussions regarding the secular versus the religious (see, in particular, "Wordsworth and the Rabbis") betrays the attitude of one who is doubtfully making a case for dialogue instead of participating in one. *The Middle of the Journey* leaves the reader uncertain whether any entente cordiale of reformed liberalism and Christianity will succeed against the influence of the utopian Left and a counterreactionary religious revival. For the foreseeable future, Maxim says, people like himself and the Crooms will dominate the world, while "humanistic critical intelligence" like Laskell's must submit to a moratorium: "'Maybe we will resurrect John Laskell. But resurrection implies—' And he shrugged."[68] Despite the tentative note of *Middle of the Journey*'s conclusion, Trilling's ongoing efforts to eke out a space for reformed humanistic liberalism and an enlightened religion show that he was less resigned than Maxim would have Laskell be. Trilling's resolve, however, was purchased by heightening the emphasis on moral and aesthetic means of "criticizing life" while treating moral life and art as contemplative realms where freedom could be preserved regardless of the distribution of social power, a move present not only in his own work but also common to ideology of the emerging Cold War liberal establishment.[69] In 1952, the *Partisan Review* published a symposium, "Our Country and Our Culture," asking if intellectuals had "actually changed their attitude toward America and its institutions" to accord with "the reaffirmation and rediscovery of America" that seemed to be "under way" (118). The majority of the contributors, including Lionel Trilling, promised that there would be no continuation of Depression-era opposition. Having given up even on the Popular Front strategy of forming a third-party coalition (combining trade unions, small farmers, minorities, and the organized poor) to apply pressure on the Democratic party from its Left, liberal intellectuals redefined opposition as creative consumption, search-and-destroy raids on ideology, and nonconformity.[70] The freedom of thought they defended would protect democratic society from varieties of false consciousness, while the hope of preserving democratic gains would rest with the middle class, which would exercise a stabilizing, civilizing influence on American culture. This middle-class-led consensus was to be the bedrock of Trilling's humanism.

As a spokesperson for this view, Diana Trilling criticized Mailer's *Barbary Shore,* upon its publication in 1952, for placing the "alternative to a fascist triumph" so remotely from "political actuality" that Mailer had to look "for salvation elsewhere than in politics."[71] Certainly the mass, as illustrated in the novel by the greedy and inconstant Guinevere, a Jehovah's Witness, promises to be no Marxist agent, and the principle of hope can be sustained only at a macrocosmic level, in the battle between Light and Darkness, Life and Death, while America's Guineveres (vulgar masses) and Lannie Madisons (self-flagellating ex-radicals) remain in thrall to the fascistic Hollingsworths.[72] Mailer's rejection of the tragic and his embrace of the eschatological, however, was only the inverse of the penitential liberal narrative, and needling to the extent that it called attention to liberalism's own rapprochement with the permanent war economy, motivated not only by attacks from the Right but also by a profound loss of faith in the mass as an agent of change. *The Middle of the Journey* in this regard is symptomatic of the postwar intellectual's alienation from the working class and the poor for which he can no longer speak. In a novel about the prewar Left, labor has no representation apart from the unsavory handyman Duck Caldwell, who is really a middle-class dropout (and therefore delinquent in Trilling's eyes) rather than a worker. The character's chief function in the novel, as a chronically lewd and disheveled figure, is to undercut the Crooms' illusions of a virtuous proletariat. In the characterization of Duck, Trilling may be pointing out the facileness of kitsch pity that sentimentalizes its object, a point that he made five years earlier in his fascinating review of James Agee's *Let Us Now Praise Famous Men;* this critique from 1942, however, balanced Trilling's irony toward Agee's sentimentality with his compassion for Agee and Walker Evans's subjects.[73] *The Middle of the Journey* concentrates solely on the self-deceptive egoism of the intelligentsia and its seemingly irrational aversion to appearing bourgeois. The Left, one gathers from Trilling's novel, was less guilty of being Communist than it was guilty of being guilty about being bourgeois. His study of *Matthew Arnold* shares Arnold's fear of working-class anarchy (*Culture and Anarchy* was occasioned by the Second Reform Bill of 1867), but it also respects Arnold's genuine sympathy for labor and his wish to save society from a "mercilessly individualistic and isolated Economic Man."[74] John Laskell's quiet brooding on mortality, which extends into the secular theodicy of "The Poet As Hero," gives us instead the crisis of a man discovering the fragility, and even the folly, of ideals which propelled the middle class to dissent on behalf of a disgruntled and uninspired proletariat. Parrying the Left and the Right by comparing their illusions with each other, Trilling in the process palliates the problem of class injustice and displaces human suffering under the category of the existential or, in "The Poet as Hero," under the tragic. Thus his recovered middle-class thinker, epitomized in the eminently amiable Laskell, can find salvation by learning to be content with the kind of self-affirmation and critical nonconformism that passes for engagement in "Our Country and Our Culture."

In the context of the ex-radical mea culpa, Trilling's is a cautionary intervention, a tocsin to intellectuals of his generation about the risk of a "pendulum swing" from opposition to confession and a nuanced, though reposeful, effort to stake the "vital center" for the university-educated middle class. Drawing upon the influences of realism and newly atoned pragmatism, *The Middle of the Journey* arrives at an equally tragic humanism, estimable for its prescience in recognizing Chambers's fundamental hostility to liberalism, but regrettable for crafting a style of resistance to the Right that was neither honest about the "guilty" past nor robust enough to silence the far Right's own indiscriminate imputations of collective guilt. Liberalism, dodging flak from the Hiss case and countersubversive measures like HUAC, flanked itself by confessing to self-deception, but this apologetic stance was not adequate to repulse the case of the far Right. The far Right did not charge liberalism with error, misplaced idealism, or human egoism, but with willful and concerted deceit. Liberalism and subversion were virtually conterminous. As Fiedler and other masters of the confessional rhetoric maneuvered to meet these characterizations, McCarthy became to liberals, variously, a vigilante and a psychopath, even taking on the contours of a melodramatic villain. These are the collection of images that one of the era's great films, *The Night of the Hunter,* was to ridicule, but not escape.

CHAPTER FOUR

McCarthyism through Sentimental Melodrama and Film Noir

Did he destroy men and truth with no trace of guilt or remorse? Did he create tumult to no purpose? Was he deranged? A psychopathic personality? . . . He lied with poise and spontaneity, but he was obsessed with the problem of truth and falsehood.

—Richard Rovere, *Senator Joseph McCarthy* (1957)

"Now, children, I know you haven't forgotten 'Judge not lest ye be judged' or 'Beware of false prophets, for though they come in sheep's clothing, they are ravening wolves.'"

—Miz Cooper in *The Night of the Hunter* (1955)

The Dark Woods at Pipe Creek Farm

Clasping each other's hands, a little boy and his baby sister hasten along a lonesome river bank.[1] Rimmed by twilight and mist, the penumbral woods behind the tiny figures lower the sky. Every few paces, the brother looks about fearfully and tugs on his sister, who yawns and hugs her dolly. Where they once enjoyed childhood innocence, they are now orphans and exiles. The children's evil stepfather has convinced all other adults that his wards are liars, and, enjoying the mask of his false virtue, he hunts the unoffending little ones in the night. Betrayed and helpless, the boy and his sister have fled home to find a skiff that will carry them downriver, as the stepfather, thrashing through the woods that in their ominous darkness seem identified with him, bellows for them to stop or else endure his wrath. Cast upon nature's mercy and God's, the children's suffering is their only plea for justice since everyone in the world they knew has been fooled by deceit.

This sentimental outtake from Charles Laughton's *Night of the Hunter* (1955) is striking for a movie often classified as a film noir. The knife-wielding evangelist in Laughton's now-acclaimed film, based on Davis Grubb's best-selling 1953 novel, stalks two waifs through a Depression-era countryside for money stolen by their father. Filled with such noir motifs as the psychopathic liar, *Hunter* is a thriller set apart by its pervading religious context, shared only by Edmund Goulding's *Nightmare Alley* (1947) in the Cold War period. Yet for all its crime and thriller elements, *Hunter* also contains material from sentimental melodrama. Childhood and nature are enclosed, pastoral spaces of innocence from which brother (John Harper) and sister (Pearl) are forcefully ejected by villainy (the evangelist, their stepfather). The adult world is subsumed by underlying moral forces, but evil spreads deceiving signs everywhere, so that virtue, in the shapes of babes and women, may be wronged and then treacherously accused. The villain seduces and manipulates the community (Cresap's Landing), while the virtuous (John and Pearl) are tormented. The victims of evil leave their home (a rural hamlet) to escape calumny, and in the course of their journey eventually find a new haven (Miz Cooper's farm) where their innocence may be recognized. These are no small parts of *Night of the Hunter.* Nonetheless, the contribution of sentimental melodrama to the film's unique texture has gone unnoted, despite even obvious cues such as the presence of Lilian Gish, playing the film's heroine, and the filmmakers' well-known, publicized interest in David Wark (D. W.) Griffith.[2]

THE UNFASHIONABLENESS of sentimental melodrama, in *Hunter*'s own era as well as our present, may have encouraged the oversight. In the postwar period, the form and its ethos were already dismissed by critics, who included some of *Hunter*'s reviewers as well as some of Cold War America's leading intellectuals. Indeed, the terms "sentimental" or "melodrama" were bandied pejoratively by Reinhold Niebuhr, Leslie Fiedler, Richard Hofstadter, Arthur Schlesinger, Jr., and Lionel Trilling. Comparing fellow travelers to the egotistical social reformer Hollingsworth in *Blithedale Romance,* Schlesinger rues that the prewar Left was so "innocent" and "sentimental"—like Hawthorne's villain, unable to understand that well-intending men often do the worst.[3] The very title of Niebuhr's *The Children of Light and the Children of Darkness* (1945) mocked the Marxists and bourgeois liberals who painted the world as a dualistic struggle between selfish rulers and virtuous victims of power. Because these "sentimentalists" failed to understand that virtue is always tainted by the egotism they decried in their enemies, they represented to Niebuhr the most excessive aspects of the nineteenth-century liberal Protestant heritage that he had repudiated. Childhood, in Niebuhr's *Human Nature,* is but an inexact symbol for perfection, which should properly be associated with the tragedy of the Cross; in fact, Augustine better comprehends the meaning of perfection than Jesus because *The Confessions* associates children with human corruptibility rather than the harmony of the Kingdom, as in unfortunate quotations from the Gospels.[4] Having clung to its image of itself as the Kingdom, America, in assuming ambiguous world responsibility, was like a gawky adolescent called to a father's duties out of the cradle of egoistic, illusory "child-like innocence."[5] Leslie Fiedler called Ethel and Julius Rosenberg "melodramatic" and Alger Hiss's defenders "sentimentalists" because they persisted in seeing the Old Left as idealists and called American anti-Communists "monstrous, insenate" oppressors.[6] Through his own studies of American anti-intellectualism, Richard Hofstadter espied in populist mythology, chiliastic religion, and the radical right a common "melodramatic" imagination that is impatient with ambiguity and adverse to pragmatic reason.[7] Like Niebuhr's children of light, these anti-intellectuals divide the world into an absolute moral contest for justice where good must triumph over evil. In *The Middle of the Journey,* Lionel Trilling develops the novel's maturity theme by counterposing John Laskell's "negative capability" with the wonder and innocence of the Crooms, especially Nancy, who live by promises of a better day, as a child does, rather than committing to life in the present.[8] The boy hero of *Huckleberry Finn,* in Trilling's 1948 essay introducing the novel, earns our pathos as well as our affection because we know he must grow up, learn to lie not "innocently," as a child does to another, but to lie as adults do, "to themselves," out of "the depravity in man's heart."[9] In each of these examples, sentimentality or melodrama is solidly opposed to realism, the perspective of the innocent and reckless to that of the wise and skeptical.

Despite the low intellectual estimate of sentimentality, the milieu of anti-Communism certainly produced scenarios inviting melodramatic interpretation. Coalescing around Wisconsin Senator Joseph McCarthy (Republican) between 1949 and 1954, exhortations to engage in anti-Communist countersubversion, as well as rumors of cloaked subversives being aired from pulpits, stumps, Rotary Clubs, and even academic halls, created a crisis in which virtuous figures could appear threatened by obloquy. We can better appreciate the persistence of sentimentalism in the heyday of Niebuhrian realism and countersubversion by returning to one of the period's key texts, Whittaker Chambers's *Witness* (1952), an ex-Communist confessional published at the heart of the McCarthy years, which strikingly incorporates elements of sentimental melodrama and noir thrillers.

Chambers's spiritual autobiography is, on the one hand, and by its author's own description, a "crime drama" or "a spy case" in which true-life events eerily parallel situations from film noir such as *Kiss of Death* or *House on 92nd Street:* "foreign agents, household traitors, stolen documents, microfilm, furtive meetings, secret hideaways, phony names, an in-

former, investigations, trials, official justice."[10] *Witness* takes familiar
trappings of noir thrillers—including Chambers as "psychopath"—and
transforms these into signs of the spiritual alienation Niebuhrian realists
appreciated, that permanent doubt wherein the lonely man, knowing the
weakness of his own heart, must mistrust the will of other men: "What is
irreparable is the faith between man and man which is the arterial pulse of
the community; for henceforth the conspirator is indistinguishable from
the man beside you" (34). From this world of suspicion, Chambers permits
himself no permanent escape. His conversion from Communism does not
restore his trust in his world or his world's trust in him. Though he accepts
God's grace and pays penance by testifying before the House Un-American
Activities Committee (HUAC) in 1948–1950, he remains a pilgrim in a
fallen place where his allies doubt his veracity, his liberal "psychotic" enemies call him a liar, and Alger Hiss's defense team actually names *him* a
"psychopath."[11] *Witness* redeems Chambers's sinful errors of the past,
transforming the ex-spy into a *Micro-Christus*, but even in the state of
grace, he continues to suffer, enduring the accusations of the deceitful (Hiss
and his defenders) and the misunderstanding of the foolish (benighted liberals). It is from the perspective of abused virtue, as much as confessional
guilt, that *Witness* interprets Chambers's history. Although Chambers
never excuses his pre-Christian duplicity, indeed requires that the public
acknowledge his past sins, his converted protagonist-informer laments
that men mistrust his sincerity in the Hiss case. From being the fallen
example in a tragedy in which appearances deceive all men about their
wills, he becomes a victim in a melodrama in which individual dissemblers
deliberately misrepresent and persecute him for his good intentions.

Chambers insists throughout that his is a tragic, realistic story, and his
one mention of "bad melodrama" is disparaging (50). His sentimentality
is not self-conscious. When *Witness* becomes fully sentimental, Chambers
is expressing, with resort to very familiar icons, a wish for his vindication
in a language that moves him despite—or perhaps because of—its bygone
flavor. Chambers underscores his plight by retreating at intervals to the
Arcadian, childlike idyll of Pipe Creek Farm, where the dissemblers have
not penetrated. Through memory, as Chambers-the-narrator, and through
physical escape, as Chambers-the-informer, he finds solace and hope on
the farm he and his wife have made for their children far from "the false
standards and vitiating influences of the cities" and of the urban elite (88).
Here the night imagery that covers Washington and New York is dissi-
pated by "golden" light over the pastoral "kingdom," which is protected
from the "far beyond world" by "the far blue Maryland hills" and by
"walls thrown up by work and love" (18). Here "guiltless and defenseless"

children, cradled by nature and maternal care, inspire their weary father with their natural "reverence and awe" of God's creation and their natural revulsion at its desecration (21, 18). More than just a way of life that Chambers has chosen after his break from Communism, Pipe Creek Farm is a topos of innocence. Chambers's yeomanry is part of his "witness against the world" where men misconstrue and slander him.

Pipe Creek Farm is, however, finally overshadowed by the pensiveness of the narrative voice, which already knows, as the farm's children do not, the fragility of innocence in the world of deception. Chambers's narrator shockingly interrupts his nostalgic reveries to remember his small daughter, perhaps restless at night, coming upon her father as he loads a pistol to guard against assassins, and to wince at the grimness of the babes frolicking over the pumpkin patch where their father has buried stolen microfilm (19). These moments disturb Chambers's memories of "the golden days," but they save the integrity of *Witness* as a testimonial (17). Chambers's wish to recuperate innocence after his fall can find expression, and then only fleetingly, in a utopia so antique it would be pastiche if the narrator did not permit the contradiction between the noir-like majority of his story and the sentimental, melodramatic portions to emerge. On the one hand, Pipe Creek Farm interrupts the mood of suspicion and complicity the narrative elsewhere illustrates; its little boy and girl are symbols of the sincerity few men can recognize in Chambers's testimony before HUAC. They are guiltless, as is he, of evil intentions that actually belong to his wily accusers. On the other hand, the farm's children enjoy a prelapsarian condition from which Chambers, like Everyman, is eventually barred by his sinful pride. They are defenseless, as was their father, to prevent their fall once they leave Pipe Creek and the near-Edenic state it represents. The crepuscular woods at the farm's border not only mark the edge of the family's territory but also the passage between childhood grace and adult tragedy. In these woods, "where it was darker, lonelier, and in the stillness . . . the voices louder," the children approach the dreadful truth of adulthood: that all men become guilty and then confuse the penitent with the proud deceivers (21). The existence of innocence, in *Witness*, protests the deception that comes of man's sin and clouds men's judgment, but, by its very weakness, the same innocence serves to remind the narrator that he cannot truly escape suspicion.

Though *Witness* builds to the events of 1950, when Alger Hiss was convicted for two counts of perjury, it was published in 1952 amidst escalated anti-Communist countersubversion on the domestic front. Despite his own sentimentally conceived sense of persecution by the Left, Chambers earnestly believed subversives had so deeply penetrated the liberal establishment that government probes could not assume the innocence of anyone.[12] Once Hiss was sentenced for perjury, liberals felt they were on the defensive, being forced to deny guilt by past association with Red politics or by mere sympathy with Marxist or socialist ideas.[13] For liberals who now felt they were being unfairly suspected, Senator McCarthy became the lightning rod for criticism. Against the calls for liberal "subversives" to acknowledge their guilt, there was a countervailing liberal attack on McCarthy's power that could itself invite sentimental as well as noir representation.

Inaugurating his war against domestic Communism with the infamous Wheeling, West Virginia speech for the Republican Women's Club (February 9, 1950) announcing the beginning of the "final, all-out battle between Communistic atheism and Christianity," McCarthy called for Americans to awaken to the evil in their midst only to become, to his liberal opponents, himself covered by guilt. Appointed to investigate and judge others' veracity, McCarthy was accused of being a liar and a blackmailer, and, by the time he was defrocked, the senator had become symbolic of the excesses of state anti-Communism. To some degree, he was also its scapegoat, for McCarthyism was presaged by the Smith Act, the policies of the Truman administration, and the efforts of J. Edgar Hoover.[14] Nonetheless, McCarthy was the most aggressive, the most reckless, and perhaps the most dubiously motivated advocate for institutional purges and the investigative methods of professional anti-Communism—in the form of HUAC, the FBI, the Loyalty Review Board, and the Senate Internal Security Subcommittee, which were eventually matched by McCarthy's own chairmanship on the Senate Committee on Government Operations. Until his censure in 1954, McCarthy stoked anti-Communism by satisfying the political need to put names to the Right's demonology, and he defended his secrecy about his methods and his sources by appealing to a higher goal than government should dare to delimit, the godly nation cleansed of un-Americans.[15]

In his 1952 presidential bid, Democratic activist Adlai Stevenson, who had no Communist past, found himself hotly under attack from McCarthy, and he publicly retaliated that the professional hunters after dupes and fellow travelers were "rudely, carelessly" invading "the field of conscience, of thought, the field that belongs to God and not to senators."[16] God's prerogative had become an elite technic, and, in theory, anyone could be guilty unless he had already confessed.[17] Since the demons professional anti-Communists sought were ideological, the "subverter" had no visible markings disclosing his conscience.[18] Hoover expends an entire chapter of *The Masters of Deceit* decoding apparently straightforward

Communist language to reveal its true malignant purposes, and the overall tenor of the book is that no one—except perhaps the "insiders" of professional anti-Communism—is immune to becoming a Communist dupe because the enemy can only be decoded by professionals.[19]

In a political culture where the loyalty of citizens could be thrown into question by mere allegation, where suspected traitors could acquit themselves only by confessing a guilty past, where the pursuit of subversives had a theological imprimatur, McCarthyism involved the delegation of gross power to a judge of no demonstrable authority who had suddenly been appointed to detect liars and unearth dual identities by elite methods and secret avenues having no oversight. Throughout McCarthy's career, there were reservations about his techniques and the basis of his allegations, and by the time the senator slipped from power, in humiliation, between 1953 and 1954, the question of how he had gained influence, how he had created the mystification on which his authority depended, was paramount to his critics and onetime supporters.[20] For sociologist Edward Shils, as for the analysts in *The Radical Right,* McCarthy had blessed himself with a theological mandate, drawing to anti-Communism backward and desperate Americans seeking in "political enthusiasm" the expression of "half-mad angers" and "grudges" that other radicals had found in "in religious revivals."[21] They were "moral desperadoes" who cultivated "symbolic secrecy," the nonfunctional (from a national security estimate) publicizing of information simply to maximize passions for loyalty, as "part of the war of fantasy which the pure and good conduct incessantly with corruption and evil until the Last Day": "Their image of the world as the realm of evil, against which they must defend themselves and which they must ultimately conquer, forces them to think of their enemy's knowledge as secret knowledge" (16, 235, 234).

McCarthy exasperated even some of his congressional supporters for his admixture of evasiveness and contempt for due process, on the one hand, and of animadversion and lie detection, on the other, but he was especially offensive to liberals who believed they were being falsely pursued for past errors of judgment rather than continuing sins. The authority in charge of ferreting out subversives thus himself became the evil dissembler, and the trope of the suffering innocent could therefore transfer from the ex-radical conservative (Chambers) to the liberal victim of McCarthyism's attacks. To lump reformed liberals together with the likes of traitors, Leslie Fiedler objected, was certainly unjust and preposterous: "Surely the chief evil of McCarthyism consists in branding honest men as Communists out of malice and stupidity."[22] In "McCarthyism and the Intellectuals," Fiedler depicts Joseph McCarthy, a cloddish parody of "the Grand Inquisitor," imagining himself the hero in the paranoid political right's anti-Communist "melodrama." The senator finds plots and villains, yet, Fiedler adds ironically, he never espies the human evil in himself. At the same time, liberals who called anti-Communists a greater threat to American liberties than Stalinists and fellow travelers were exhibiting Alger Hiss's gross "sentimentality,"[23] which denied that the Left ever did anything immoral; in fact, the Left's "whole dream of absolute innocence," when in fact, "there is no innocent 'we' and a guilty 'they,'" showed it to be as sentimental as the vitriolic McCarthy. In "Hiss, Chambers, and the Age of Innocence," Fiedler, speaking for his generation, reminds readers that, like Chambers, many American intellectuals in the thirties had erred because they were dazed by virtuous intentions which Communists had exploited. Unlike Alger Hiss and the Rosenbergs, the wise among them had since left their "garden of illusion" and accepted responsibility for their error (24). As in *The Middle of the Journey,* the passage from innocence to responsibility is described through a rhetoric of "growing up," with overtones of the *felix culpa.*[24] Alger Hiss and his defenders do a great disservice to reformed liberals by insisting on their moral high ground instead of "speak[ing] aloud a common recognition of complicity" and accepting "the great privilege of confession."[25] As Morris Dickstein comments on these passages, the public repentance of the guilty liberal becomes analogous to an adolescent "rite of passage" from "childish things" to adult values.[26] The terms here anticipate Fiedler's major work, *Love and Death in the American Novel* (1959), in which he unfavorably contrasts sentimental melodrama to America's "Calvinistic" Gothic novels to demonstrate that American culture has failed to mature because it has not accepted the loss of heroic innocence that any serious expression of the problem of evil would oblige. In effect, the earlier piece on the "Age of Innocence" accuses unrepentant liberals of having the childish imaginations of a sentimental melodramatist.[27]

If the liberals' plight invited a sentimental reading in which they are harassed by evil accusers, the sinuous bases of McCarthy's authority, its mystification through secrecy and lies, lent itself to interpretation by the noir themes of duplicity, coercion, and pathology that Chambers had turned against his Left enemies, the Communists as well as the liberal "elite." The two modes highlighted in *Witness,* sentimental and noir, could both be adapted to attack McCarthyism's culture of suspicion rather than the liberal subversives vilified in Chambers's narrative. My case in point will be *The Night of the Hunter,* the eponymous novel and the film having been created over the two year span (1953–1954) when McCarthyism was on the defensive, after having accumulated great influence and then having flagrantly abused it.

Thus far we have been alluding to certain melodramatic tropes and discussing sentimentality as an attitude or world view. These tropes can also be specified to a theatrical and narrative tradition, "sentimental melodrama," which the filmmakers would have understood at least from D. W. Griffith, Charles Dickens (from whom Laughton read aloud on set), and Laughton himself, whose background included Victorian drama. Designed to mediate between the visible order of bourgeois social manners and a sacred, still basically Christian order whose symbols and rituals no longer controlled the public sphere, melodrama strove to express an underlying contest between good and evil, now concentrated in human actors rather than angels and demons, by making the surfaces of nature and society signify polar moral values.[28] Evil has no life apart from the innocent perception that it perverts; it exists by mimicking the good and thereby scrambling the signs the community trusts for its moral legibility. This trust is virtually a natural contact, signified by the rural or semirural environ the villain invades. In the United States, melodrama was the province of the sentimental literary tradition and of the Victorian theater, where, in both media, it was used to promote and honor the middle-class, Christian cult of domesticity above the old masculine Calvinist ethos, which placed spiritual truth wholly beyond the realm of appearances. The sentimental melodrama, which we here designate, to set it apart from other, derivative "melos" (romantic or Gothic melodrama, for example), makes the family its emblem of natural community, the cradle of moral feeling, and also the point of narrative departure and its closure.[29] Victim and redeemer in these scenarios tend to be female; typically, where an innocent child or daughter falls prey to deception, it is a compassionate mother (or a maternal surrogate) who guides, forgives, and recuperates the faith of the innocent while the villain is exposed and, often, expelled by the virtuous.

The sentimental melodrama continued to be popular through the turn of the century, as productions like the original stage version of *Way Down East* still sold out shows and received tribute from ministers who promoted them in sermons.[30] D. W. Griffith became the silent screen's most famous American filmmaker by crafting sentimental sagas out of the popular melodramatic theater where he had honed his talent as writer. Such movies as *Birth of a Nation* (1915), *Broken Blossoms* (1919), *Way Down East* (1920), and *Orphans of the Storm* (1922) exemplify sentimental melodrama in their idealistic moralizing ("nearly all good pictures are good," Griffith said, "in that they frequently show the triumph of good over evil"), feminized Christianity, and rural populism.[31] By the 1940s and 1950s, however, the traditional sentimental melodrama had become passé, superannuated by the contemporary, Freudian family melodrama, where the central cause of suffering was not evil's mimickry of goodness and its willful persecution of virtue, but the maladjustment of characters to their gender roles, age levels, or social status.[32] Vestigial traces of sentimental Christianity, especially Sheldon's *In His Steps* (1897), still shape Douglas Sirk's *Magnificent Obsession* (1954), but the problem of evil deception, for which sentimental melodrama had provided a kind of popular theodicy, had become the possession of other discourses, neoorthodox and realist, more compelled by perpetual ambiguity than by moral legibility.

In contrast to sentimental melodrama, which was now an antique form with nineteenth-century origins, the emerging film noir was a recent creation of World War II–era Hollywood. Not a distinct genre so much as a deviant mode in the Hollywood cinema between 1940 and the early sixties, "film noir" names a constellation of visual styles, themes, motifs, and narrative devices that filmmakers applied to established genres, altering the mood and look of these forms and the ways they told their stories. Reflecting the substantial auteur influence of directors (Orson Welles, Fritz Lang, Billy Wilder, Robert Siodmak, Anthony Mann, and Alfred Hitchcock), cinematographers (Nicholas Musucara, John Alton, Gregg Toland), producers (Jerry Wald, Mark Hellinger, Louis de Rouchement), and "hardboiled" writers, film noir brought to American cinema an exceptionally grim attitude toward the modern secular world as well as "a solipsistic and modernist preoccupation with the laws of aesthetic mediation."[33] Noir is characterized by the rejection of such classical Hollywood traits as the clear duality of goodness and villainy, the moral authority granted the family, the basically benevolent representation of "common men," the use of linear plotting to express and justify the protagonist's desire, and the reification of social harmony through the happy ending. These it replaces with narrative patterns and visual schemes that, at their most expressionist, create environments mystified by irrational authority or haunted by the insane, where guilt is omnipresent and men collude out of fear or cunning. Visually, noir techniques create the impression of the viewer's being trapped inside a deviant subjectivity and make the antinaturalism of the mise-en-scène connote a character's insanity, his unconscious, or his angst. By contrast with the Depression-era gangster cycle, crime bleeds outside the underworld ghetto to render the surface of mundane reality unstable, as if to veil crouching aggression, and at the close of the films, when secrets have been divulged to authorities, justice is muted by the sense of pervasive evil.

These preoccupations with authority, secrecy, duplicity, and deviance show film noir's origins in the early forties, amidst wartime speculations on the enemy, the nature of his mind, and his moral resemblance to citizens on the home front. In its most significant contribution to the imagination of evil in popular culture of the forties and fifties, film noir adapted these wartime speculations on the "enemy" to help imagine the duality of peace-time America, ranging from large-scale conspiracy and countersubversion (domestic fascism, Communism, government intelligence, crime syndi-cates) to the subterranean life of private citizens (conformity, bigotry, sex-ual pathology, scandal, murder). Mirror or shadow figures, such as the psychopath, allowed filmmakers to explore the capacity of evil to blend with normality, as in such films as *Pitfall* (1948) or *Shadow of a Doubt* (1943). The psychopath is the night-side of the self, the side that, in the psychoanalytic logic of noir, the superego punishes into concealment. He is also a chronic, compulsive liar whose duplicity spreads suspicion across "phonies" and good citizens alike. By the end of Hitchcock's *Strangers on a Train* (1951), the aptly named Everyman, Guy, is so shaken by his ordeal with Robert Walker's psychopath that he does not even trust the minister who shares a dining car with him. Despite the fact that film noir exhibits a predominately demythologized, desacralized, and irreligious universe—in which God is silent, inscrutable or, more often, forgotten—its themes of uncertain justice, floating blame, double selves, and mutual suspicion could easily elicit the theological symbolism Chambers transfers to noir motifs in *Witness*.[34]

   If sentimental melodrama hopes that goodness can be separated from evil and that deception can be cleared, film noir has a sensibility closer to the tough-minded postwar realism that called for an end to innocence. Like many realists, noir filmmakers were compelled by the wartime/post-war meditation on the ubiquity of guilt even if they did not accept Cham-bers or Niebuhr's biblical presuppositions. For the intellectual Left who have written much of the criticism and scholarship on film noir, the mov-ies' powerful depictions of evil have been very important because these are both secular—uncoupled from any system of the sacred—and centered in American society. The category "film noir" has assumed for Left movie critics and scholars a function somewhat analogous to the role Niebuhr's theology played for the realists. As Niebuhr turned a theory of human sin against America's historic moral exceptionalism, noir criticism exploits film images of irrepressible depravity, chaos, and subterfuge to demystify what it alleges are deceptive idealistic images of American life.[35] Where Niebuhr challenged America to let go of its pretenses of innocence and acknowledge its potential for evil, noir critics often employ the films to show America's underside, finally depriving the nation's life of even the ironic virtue Niebuhr allowed it. Noir, in sum, seems closer to our contem-porary critical sensibilities, with their preference for subversion and moral ambiguity, than to sentimental melodrama, which bears the trappings of

Victorian domestic culture and populist mythology. When one adds that noir, in addition to its modernist sensibility, is also frequently credited with being the aesthetic pinnacle of pre-1970s American cinema, it is not surprising that some of *Night of the Hunter*'s admirers have been willing to claim it for the company of such classics as *Double Indemnity* while minimizing *Hunter*'s sentimental elements.

Night of the Hunter is an unprecedented hybrid of noir and sentimental melodrama, and its original, often ironic mixture of the two dissonant modes necessitates that the critic take a dialectical course, contrasting how each diverges from a common concern with the sinister intentions behind dissembling appearances. Each mode assists the film to indict misplaced faith in "false prophets" and their culture of distrust. Depending on the persuasion of the onlooker, McCarthy was either a Christian patriot or a casuistic—perhaps even "psychopathic"—demagogue.[36] Those he accused seemed either guilty prevaricators or misconstrued victims. It is a crisis of trust in crusaders and an air of darting suspicion that *Night of the Hunter* conjures through the image of a fundamentalist revival community. It is a wish that conscience be relieved of the anxiety of defending its innocence that the film expresses through scandalizing the revival community and juxtaposing that community with the heroine Rachel Cooper's world. Pitched between a noir nightmare of demonizing, pathological authority and a melodramatic vindication of wronged virtue, *Hunter* transfers the children John and Pearl from an environ where the deceit of the human heart makes all men complicit with evil prophets to another where evil prophets alone deceive and willfully do so.

Night of the Hunter evinces a wish to forgive "the guilty past," as Harold Rosenberg derisively termed it, and repudiate those like McCarthy who capitalized on that past to persecute others. In demystifying self-righteous leaders and acquitting the virtuous of evil intentions, however, the film nearly tears itself into two incongruous worlds. By using film noir to invert the fundamentalists' perceptions of themselves, the filmmakers show that the revival community, despite its obsession with naming sin, is actually far more evil than it estimates. By thrust of the noir mode, however, the film also succeeds in tinging every space around Cresap's Landing with the sense of ubiquitous guilt and mistrust that Cold War realists had assumed was man's inevitable state. These images of a fallen world sharply contradict the passages foregrounding Rachel Cooper's world, where evil is an invader and secreted guilt has no place. In the Griffithian sections, *Hunter* risks betraying the film's earlier, more pungent portions, and we will ask how adequately Miz Cooper, especially in the finale, shapes an alternative to the Preacher's demonology. *Night of the Hunter* incorporates a vintage genre whose world view opposes a McCarthyite culture of suspicion, but the film cannot fully ward off the era's doubts about the moral legibility of postwar society.

The Master of Deceit

Ever since working with him in *Crossfire* (1947), Robert Mitchum believed he had learned from Robert Ryan (his co-star, who played a fascist GI) how to play an evil character, but apart from *Track of the Cat* (1954), Mitchum had had no opportunities to show a villainous side, for RKO had kept him locked in a string of "two-fisted tough guy" parts. When he was finally granted the chance to portray, as Laughton put, "'a diabolical *shit* of a man,'" Mitchum did not give a Ryan-styled performance.[37] Under Laughton's direction, his Preacher is frightening, but he is also broadly theatrical, even funny, using an extroverted pantomime style that complements Stanley Cortez and art director Hilyard Brown's expressionistic mise-en-scène, which projects the Preacher's fantasies into the outer world. The performance, as directed, played, and shot, astonishes because it combines qualities of the criminal psychopath and the melodramatic villain. Robin Wood and Leo Braudy have both commented on the "stunt casting" of Mitchum, closely associated with crime thrillers, opposite Lillian Gish, iconic of Griffith's oeuvre. Wood has actually ventured that the casting constitutes an alienation effect, since the viewer is aware of Mitchum's displacement in the Arcadian world of rural virtue.[38] I prefer to emphasize the irony internal to Mitchum's character, which borrows from two discursive frames for representing evil and dissimulation, and the ways Mitchum's performance exploits this irony for effects that are, by turns, terrifying and blackly comic. In the process of realizing Preacher Harry Powell, the filmmakers and Mitchum have created a liar who is fanatically sincere in his fundamentalist belief that he is above human law because God has called him to mete out divine justice.

Other than Edmund Goulding's 1946 adaptation of William Lindsay Gresham's novel *Nightmare Alley*, Roy Del Ruth's *Red Light* (1949), Alfred Hitchcock's *I, Confess* (1953), and Gerd Oswald's 1956 adaptation of Ira Levin's *A Kiss Before Dying*, *The Night of the Hunter* is the only film noir that presents the psychopath in an explicitly religious context.[39] The evangelist in *Night of the Hunter* is distinguished from these examples in that he uses faith—beliefs that he himself shares, no less—to deceive an entire community. Harry Powell masks his own secrets—what authority ordained him, how God communicates with him, what means he uses to support his ministry—by appealing to the people's trust that a holy man who denounces the Devil must be accepted on faith. When Ben Harper asks the Preacher what religion he professes, Powell flourishes his switchblade, which he calls Jehovah's Sword, and answers cryptically, "The religion worked out betwixt the Almighty and myself." *Hunter*'s self-ordained evangelist, sincerely believing he is God's executor, stealthily murders, blackmails, and plunders so that he can erect a tabernacle where he will tell the world of *other* men's evil. The Preacher is also dedicated to the idea of purity (personal, sexual, communal), and he sees no contradiction between this ideal and the illegal, immoral means he uses to achieve it.

As one who talks familiarly with God, the Preacher betrays no irony. Rather, Powell seems convinced that he is indeed a prophet granted the power to tell others about the truth beneath appearances. The Preacher's one sermon, incessantly repeated, is "the story of Right Hand and Left Hand, the tale of Good and Evil," illustrated by the fingers of his own two hands, the right tatooed with L-O-V-E and the left with H-A-T-E. The story of mankind, he expounds, is the relentless war of these two hands, whose fingers he constantly threads, but Love, he promises, will win the struggle, a point he illustrates by crashing down his left hand on whatever kitchen counter or fence post is available. The Preacher never explains how one distinguishes good from evil, for the point of the sermon is simply to replay a dualism in which the truth, once God has revealed it, is as evident as telling one's right hand from one's left. In a world where "salvation is a last minute business," however, only holy judges like the Preacher have the revelation permitting them to discern men's hearts. In the logic of the anti-Communist crusade, there existed an underlying moral duality comparable to the tale of Right Hand/Left Hand, but conspirators and liars had allegedly confused the truth, so that citizens, especially liberals, could be either subversive or American, heretic or faithful. The demonized sides of these binary pairs could blend perniciously with their legitimate, moral counterparts. Thus the authority to distinguish Good from Evil had to reside in "a position outside the system; in other words, it had to be theological."[40] Powell's channel to God is a wish-fulfilling fantasy in which transcendent authority guarantees the interpreter's judgment. Betraying a mistrust of McCarthy-like claims that the countersubversive possesses exclusive insight into citizens' hearts, *Night of the Hunter* undermines Powell's intimacy with divine will by showing that his God is the figment of his psychopathic imagination.

Preacher Harry Powell not only claims to receive the Word directly from its source, but also consults with God, who "speaks" to him many times about what actions must be taken. For the first time since the early silent

epics, the Lord had spoken in Hollywood films twice during the fifties—
The Next Voice You Hear (1950) and *Red Planet Mars* (1952)—and He
would speak again in *The Ten Commandments* (1956). In these cases, the
conceit of having God speak is naturalized by making the voice audible to
other characters in the diegesis and also to the viewer, but *Night of the
Hunter* provides no evidence that God speaks apart from Harry Powell's
own testimony. In *Hunter*'s opening montage, Powell, bumping over the
dirt roads of Depression-scourged West Virginia in a stolen Model T Ford,
raises his eyes skyward and addresses an invisible listener: "Well, now, what's
it to be, Lord? Just say the word, Lord—I'm on my way!" There is no response on the soundtrack, but Powell tips the brim of his hat in respect and
smiles that he is understood. The Preacher will speak to God and listen for
His response many times in the film, but only he hears the answer, which
is always a directive to "go forth and preach the Word" or to annihilate
those who stand in the way of that mission: "The Lord's a talkin' to me!
He's sayin' 'I cannot abide a liar!'" As the Preacher listens for God's Word
in these scenes, Mitchum affects a trancelike mad gaze common to psychopathic characters in this period, as if he is enthralled by his hallucination.

In addition to the disjunction between the Preacher's words and God's
silence, the film's visual devices also undercut Powell's sense of his divine
election by identifying him with the underworld and the unconscious. The
opening shot sequence of the film descends from the heavens to a cellar
where the Preacher has deposited a corpse. As Rachel Cooper, superim-
posed over a starry sky, quotes the Sermon on the Mount, the camera dissolves to an aerial, God-like vantage (filmed from a helicopter), and then
makes an arc through space (dissolving to a crane shot) towards an open,
pitch-black cellar from which protrudes a freshly killed woman's ankles.
While the Gospel comes to us from the sky, the Preacher's work goes on
underground in the shadows. Continuing the sequence, the camera cuts
again to an aerial view that descends to discover the Preacher in his car.
The vantage shifts dramatically across the next set of shots, moving from
the Godlike point of view to an extremely voyeuristic vantage. The camera
cuts to a baroque long shot of a burlesque dancer, framed by a keyhole
shaped aperture and filmed with Tri-X stock, which adds an exaggerated
phosphorescence to the stage lights. The next two shots in the burlesque
hall scene establish the Preacher's vantage, as the camera tracks to a medium close-up of the glowering minister, seated in the audience, and then
cuts to another phosphorescent keyhole shot of the dancer. The repeated
shot of the dancer is distinguished by its perverse mise-en-scène, which
creates the illusion that the Preacher is looking at the dancer from the opposite side of a door. By contrasting the perspective from the exterior aerial

shot to the view from within Preacher's deviant subjectivity, the sequence rhymes with the spatial descent from sky to cellar depicted in the previous pair of images; both pairings, each juxtaposing high to low, light to shadow, the heavens to hidden recesses, associate Harry Powell with the obscene rather than the holy.

In the process of demystifying Preacher's fundamentalist claims to speak for God, *Hunter* follows the logic of noir in suggesting that the unjust, deceitful authority figure suffers from madness—an implication that risks remystifying Preacher's power, just as Shils mystifies McCarthyism's by calling it "madness," "lunacy" and "paranoia."[41] *Night of the Hunter* enriches its vision of Preacher's leverage over his victims by modulating his psychopathic features with those of the melodramatic villain. Each type is a master of deceit, but the psychopath works his schemes in the big city (where Harry Powell eventually meets his fate) rather than the small country town. The villains of sentimental melodrama, by contrast, often penetrate enclosed rural settings, where domestic values of harmony, sympathy, and trust prevail, where faith in goodness seems as natural as the love between maternal characters and their children. Among the feature-length Griffith films at the Museum of Modern Art (MOMA), where Laughton, Agee, and Cortez each viewed the director's work, is *White Rose* (1923), about a Southern minister (Joseph Beaugarde) who seduces and impregnates an ingenue (Bessie Williams). The minister, in the tradition of other Griffith predators like *Way Down East*'s Lennox Sanderson, disturbs the natural trust not only of the victim but also of the rural hamlet. Preacher Harry Powell may not be a sexual seducer, but he wins the faith of Cresap's Landing by first charming its Christian women and then acquiring a family where he can prey upon the children John and Pearl. As much as Preacher refers to noir's criminal madmen, he also belongs to melodrama's line of seducer-hypocrites, and Mitchum's performance incorporates their theatrical affectations. The allusions to sentimental melodrama, through Mitchum's portrayal, Harry Powell's villainy with women and children, and the iconography of the country town, show the ironic discrepancy between the genre's image of a harmonious community and the gullible, devil-fearing people of Cresap's Landing. In *Hunter,* the community betrays the very images of sentimental idyll, to which the film alludes, and in effect becomes Powell's accomplice. The Preacher's power depends as much on the people's knavery as it does his self-mystifying dissimulation.

Harry Powell's prey, Willa Harper, is less the virtuous victim of melodrama than she is a timid woman who accepts Preacher's lies because she is ridden by guilt and scandal following her husband's bank robbery. "Help me to get clean," she prays on her wedding night, "so I can be the way Harry wants me to be." Fearing that the bloody money may "still be amongst us, tainting us," she throws herself wholly into the evangelist's ministry, even submitting when he bullies her into making a false confession before a hysterically assenting congregation:

> *Willa:* You have all sinned!
> *Congregation:* Yes! Yes! [men and women both featured on the pews]
> *Willa:* But which of you can say as I can say—I drove a good man to *murder* because I kept a-houndin' him for clothes and perfumes and face-paint. And he slew two human beings and he come to me and he said: 'Take this money and buy your per-fumes and paint!' But brethren, that's where the Lord stepped in! *That's where the* LORD *stepped in!*
> *Preacher:* Yes!
> *Congregation:* Yes! Yes!
> *Willa:* And the Lord told that man—
> *Congregation:* Yes! Yes!
> *Willa:* The Lord said, Take that money and throw it in the River!
> *Congregation:* Yes! Yes! Hallelujah!
> *Preacher:* IN THE RIIV-ER!
> *Congregation:* IN THE RIVER![42]

Helping to underscore the discrepancy between the sentimental social idyll and the fundamentalists' world, the lighting of this revival meeting sharply contrasts to the appearance of the sunlit church picnic of a few scenes earlier. Where mothers and children had frolicked outdoors in spacious long shots, the men and women now shouting in the revival are slashed by shadows thrown by torchlights, leaving the front row mostly black from the neck down and the back rows completely in silhouette, while the hellfire torchlights dominate the foreground and constrict point of view, making the meeting seem claustrophobic. The crammed and indistinct bodies seem joined together by threat of damnation, and Willa, airing her coerced confession, has become their paragon.

Mitchum's performance also accentuates the fundamentalists' gullibility, a feat the actor accomplishes by playing Harry Powell like a silent movie villain traveling through a sound film. Mitchum accentuates his character's menace with his body: crouching, glowering wide-eyed, curling his lip in a snarl, gritting his teeth, shaking his fists, shifting his eyes, pointing his finger above his head, chasing the children with arms outstretched and hooked fingers. Similarly, when he pretends to be a saint, Mitchum exaggerates Preacher's acting by adopting much too typical gestures: wiping his dry eyes with his palms (in imitation of sobbing), turning up his hands (to show good will), looking heavenward (for hope), hanging his head (for humility), tilting his head on his shoulder (to show sympathy). Mitchum's affectations are throwbacks to the melodramatic style common in early silent cinema. Pantomime as well as gestures and expressions with obvious signification belong to melodrama, and they serve its purpose of stamping appearances with legible moral meanings. The genre derives suspense and irony from evil's appearance *qua* evil, replete with physical clues, and evil's astonishing ability nonetheless to mimic the signs of goodness. The villain must be recognizable as such, so that when he deceives other characters, audiences may observe the effects of his hypocrisy on the innocent.[43] These conceits were less quaint when directors like Griffith began making pictures. Before the invention of the close-up and the advent of sound made possible more naturalistic acting styles and slower character development, visual signs displayed by the film actor's body and clothing facilitated storytelling by indicating his character type to the audience.[44] Melodrama, conveniently, covered early cinema's technical limitations with a mode of communication that was entirely consistent with the genre's conventions. In a late sound film like *Hunter,* however, the histrionic, heavily typed techniques are inessential and grotesque; the excessive overstatement does not compensate for the actor's inaudibility or his distance from the audience, but, instead, creates an extreme incongruity between the audience's perception of Preacher's clearly marked evil and the fundamentalists' mistaken perception of his righteousness. The effect is often satiric, depriving Preacher's dupes of the sympathy normally afforded the victims of the seducer-hypocrite. When Preacher tells the Spoons the tall tale of a lascivious Willa absconding in the night, Mitchum sheds crocodile tears, rolls his eyes to heaven imploring the Lord, then lays his head on his Bible, prompting Icey to wonder aloud what could have driven the newlywed to run away. Mitchum spreads his hands wide and answers, with eyes bleeding sincerity, *"Satan."* "Ooh, mmhmm," says Icey, nodding gravely and crossing her arms. Filled with pity for the weeping man of God ("I tried to save her; Lord knows I tried to save her"), Icey overlooks Preacher's immediate reversion to a villain's pose—lowered face, arched brow, narrowed eye, frowning lip—as he mutters: "She won't be back—I promise you that." Icey, like the rest of the faithful, does not appear to be sadly fooled, but utterly foolish. For their willingness to follow the dissembling crusader, the fundamentalists are not innocent of evil—indeed they are obsessed with sin—but deluded by their religious ideology.

In its portrait of Cresap's Landing, *Hunter* deftly borrows from noir to show the psychopathic character of Preacher and the instability of his followers, while its ironic allusions to sentimental melodrama protest the noir-like community's fall from the social idyll where hypocrisy, suspicion, and fear are unnatural. In this postlapsarian environment, where adults are morally unreliable, it is the children, John and Pearl Harper, who are the victims, and neither child will enjoy safety or sincerity from adults until they reach Miz Cooper. Like the innocents approaching the dark woods in *Witness*, the brother and sister are ushered into an adult predicament where good and evil are suddenly confused, and the two children are tempted to "sin" by swearing secret oaths and deceiving confessors. Though neither John nor Pearl intends evil, they are nonetheless drawn into the plots of lawbreakers and dissemblers. For these errors, their right to defend themselves, even to exist, is jeopardized, as they are accused of being willfully deceitful and hunted by the false prophet. Through John and Pearl's ordeal, *Hunter* makes a plea for misunderstood and persecuted virtue, whose sentimental shape underscores its fragility in a noir world of evil judges.

The Perils of Virtue

Our first glimpse of John and Pearl is what the screenplay specifies as "a sentimental picture."[45] A crane shot descends to show the brother and sister playing on a sward dotted by white daisies and bordered by apple trees, suggesting the Garden of Eden. It is a classic topos of melodrama, which "typically opens with a presentation of virtue and innocence, or perhaps more accurately, virtue *as* innocence. We see this virtue, momentarily, in a state of taking pleasure in itself."[46] The children's fete is interrupted by the sound of a Model T, which crashes into a fence post and spills out their father, Ben Harper, bleeding from a gunshot wound he has sustained in his bank robbery. Ben stashes ten-thousand-dollars into Pearl's doll, and then asks each child to swear an oath never to tell where the "cursed, bloody gold" is hid, bidding John particularly to hold one hand aloft and to place the other over his heart. From the moment the children take the oath to protect their father's secret, the imagery of the Garden is deferred. Until the film's final scene, they are never shown at play, except when Pearl "does a sin" by making paper dolls out of some of the stolen money. The doll (Miss Jenny) with which Pearl plays in "the sentimental picture" becomes an object of struggle and fear, the children's sleep is disquieted by horror, and their very imaginations, as reflected in their fairy tales, are troubled by loss and hazard.

Like the imagery of the violated garden, the swearing of oaths to family is a melodramatic convention designed to demonstrate the trust of the innocent in their elders, but by the time of *Hunter*'s production, oath-taking had also become a familiar and troublesome symbol in America, connecting the radical politics of the thirties and the countersubversion of the Cold War. The Truman administration had required government employees to take oaths of loyalty to the United States, initiating a policy that several private businesses and universities followed as well, and confessed ex-Communist party members could also be asked to take loyalty oaths along with making public renunciations and naming the identities of other suspects. The oath in these scenarios, theoretically, exonerated the subject from suspicion, though swearing, as Alan Nadel has pointed out, signified true fealty only to the extent that everyone involved, the citizen and witnesses, seriously accepted the act as a kind of religious ceremony (83). An oath is "a conditional curse" in which the swearer calls God to witness his promise by placing his own fate in balance.[47] Apart from any juridical penalties for perjury, the act of swearing carries perlocutionary force because it is sacramental, identifying the sincerity of one's statements with the status of one's soul. But what if subjects, with equal sincerity, swear by different gods? What if different gods each promise goodness and justice? How, except with mature hindsight, to tell the good from the evil promise, the good from the evil motive? Zealous Communists, as *Witness* showed, had required the taking of oaths to the Party in the name of a false god, a utopian moral order that concealed a wicked, secular-totalitarian character. Now, anti-Communist organizations such as the Loyalty Review Board demanded oaths to certify the patriot and the Christian, the kind of God-fearing American that Joseph McCarthy claimed to be.

Ben's entry into the "sentimental picture" casts the children into a state of divided loyalty, where the confession of their secret will betray their oath to their criminal father and the refusal of confession will disobey those representing law-abiding adult authority. That this authority seems untrustworthy only further befogs the morality of the oath John and Pearl have sworn to Ben, whose pitiable fate in the state court at Moundsville sets a pattern for denying images of paternal authority their foundation in Law. Compounded by the film's unflattering treatment of Preacher's "divine" jurisdiction, Ben's trial deepens the moral ambiguity threatening to overwhelm John and Pearl's virtue. The children's suspended fete is interposed between two scenes juxtaposing the fates of Preacher and Ben Harper in court. In these scenes, noir imagery later extended to the church congregation is applied to the state courts, whose judges, like the church's "Sword of Jehovah," seem intolerant and double-edged.

Like Harry Powell, Ben Harper has taken the law into his hands and committed a mortal crime, but he is nonetheless a sympathetic, if very flawed, character—"a good man in an evil season."[48] Driven to violence by want, Ben is the figure in *Hunter* who suffers directly from the Depression, and he recalls iconic Left-populist images from the thirties.[49] A hard-bitten "common man," like those celebrated in Agee's classic, *Let Us Now Praise Famous Men* (1941), Ben has a seasoned doubt of pretension and promises, which he displays in his conversation with Preacher; he immediately detects Powell's fakery and sarcastically refuses to confess his secret. Ben, in short, recalls a type with which many Left liberals in the thirties identified and in the name of which some turned to radical, even revolutionary, politics.[50] Ben's desperate robbery could have elected him a hero in Left-populist fiction two decades earlier (a type of Jesse James rather than Duck Caldwell), but by 1955, his violence taints him and makes him a double of the Preacher, as implied by the rhyming shots of their separate sentencings. Each man is positioned exactly as the other and before the same judge in the same chamber.

Although John Harper's father and future stepfather are both marked as fallen men, the film nonetheless generates pity for Ben while making the courtroom judge who condemns him appear a dubious character. When Ben Harper is sentenced to hang, the judge closes by saying, "May God have mercy on your soul," but the legitimacy of this judge, like that of God's other "judge," Harry Powell, is undercut by the film's mise-en-scène.[51] The interior of the courtroom, where both Harry Powell and Ben Harper are sentenced, is lit expressionistically. Heavy contrast bisects the judge's head down the middle, so that one half is obscured by deep shadow, which brushes an American flag situated at the judge's left. The illuminated half of his face is adjacent to a portrait of Abraham Lincoln, the only completely visible countenance in either of the two shots in which Ben and Preacher receive sentencing. The judge is a split figure, divided between two oppositely lighted national symbols, the bright portrait of Lincoln and the bedimmed American flag, which is itself doubled in the shot by the shadow it casts to the camera's left.

By suggesting that none of the adults outside Miz Cooper's farm—even delegated authorities—are without shadow, the film enhances sympathy for the trials John and Pearl suffer after swearing their oath of secrecy. When policemen arrest Harry Powell, wounded by gunshot, John—in shock—mistakes the evangelist for Ben and begins flailing him with the money-filled doll: "Take it back, Dad! Take it back! I don't want it, Dad, it's too much!" The scene becomes a tableau of suffering virtue, as the boy bows over the handcuffed Preacher's body while onlooking policemen freeze at attention. As John pleads to be released from the oath, the spectacle becomes symbolic of his moral confusion in a world of scrambled signs where no one can be certain of impunity. John and Pearl's story at every point reinforces the fact that they have become accomplices to Ben's desperate crime as a result of innocent error and not from willful sin, though they are unforgiven by God's judge, Harry Powell, who vilifies them to their mother, to Icey, and to onlooking migrant laborers at an orchard. The possible destruction of the children is dire because they embody virtuous innocence—faith, good will, sincerity—and it is the right of these qualities to exist that is at stake. If they cannot survive, then the hope of a morally legible society, where good and evil can be properly recognized, will be lost; or, noir will swallow sentimental melodrama. Pearl's name alludes to Christ's parable, of the pearl of great Price (*Matthew* 13:45–46), and the quality that gives her precious value, her innocence, is also what endangers her in the adult world that has fallen short of virtue, a world where false prophets have authority.

The Nightmare Passed? A Sentimental Utopia

Hunter stresses the contrasting religious attitudes of Preacher and the film's heroine, the children's protector, Miz Cooper, by setting the characters in two worlds marked by clashing iconography. In the second world, childlike innocence is recuperated under Rachel Cooper's sheltering Christianity in a wish fulfillment expressed, formally and thematically, by allusions to D. W. Griffith. In a scenario familiar from Griffith's *Way Down East* (1920), a film featured in *Hunter*'s promotional materials and directly quoted within the movie, Rachel's sincere, long-suffering Christlike heroine collides with a punitive, wrathful religion easily deceived by villainy.[52] When *Hunter*'s two orphaned children, John and Pearl, show up on Miz Cooper's property, she asks them, "Where are you from? Who's your folks?" the very lines the kindly grandmother in the Griffith film asks Gish's orphan (Anna) when she appears on the farmhouse doorstep. In *East*'s scenario, the waif Anna has been wandering friendless after being seduced and abandoned by a lying city rake (Lennox Sanderson). The villain turns the staunchly Old Testament village squire against the helpless Anna, before the squire's gentler, New Testament–quoting mother and her grandson adopt the orphan into their family through marriage. In *Hunter*, Gish's Miz Cooper is herself the spirit of the Word and the redeemer of virtuous victims, while the narrative's transferral of innocence from a childlike heroine to actual children enhances its sentimental plea for the victims' justice.

Once John and Pearl escape Cresap's Landing in Ben's skiff, the long river passage prepares for the entrance of Miz Cooper and makes the transition from a nightmarish world to an idyllic one. After the film's prologue, in which Miz Cooper is briefly shown teaching Christ's words, she is absent until the skiff, drifting oarless, providentially comes to rest on a sandbar below her farm.[53] On their graced journey to the farm, the orphans' grief for Willa and their longing for a new home is evoked by Pearl's fairy song about the "pretty fly" and the voice of an unseen country woman singing a lullaby for her baby. During the lullaby, the mise-en-scène becomes misty and abstract, showing the outline of a farmhouse and a barn that seems a dreamlike prefiguration of Miz Cooper's place.[54] The association of home and safety with the children's good dreams—versus the nightmarish noir world—continues when John awakens from slumbering in the skiff to discover Miz Cooper, aglow in the morning light, standing before him and telling both children to go to her house where they can be bathed. As in the first shot of the children, when they are at play, Pearl sits among daisies in a meadow, where Miz Cooper (to Pearl's right) calls to John; the screenplay specifies that the three shot, showing the old woman and the two children, should look like a "nursery frieze." The melody of the country woman's lullaby resounds as John takes in the new lady. The good dream, it seems, has continued into waking life.

The first shots of the new home, a haven for abandoned children (Mary, Clary, and Ruby), recall the orphan Anna Moore's arrival at the farm in *Way Down East,* but the iconography belongs as well to Chambers's Pipe Creek Farm and a host of other sentimental topoi. Though the neon-lit city of New Economy is only a ferry ride away from her home, Miz Cooper seems to live untouched in a valley. Children delightedly fill baskets in a garden, a mother goose and her gaggle troop past the white picket fence, and the ring made by the mountains and the river hem the place. High-key lighting, balanced compositions, and frontal framing set apart the look of the farm from the style of the city scenes as well as Preacher's. The vintage imagery, completely free of expressionism, underscores the notion that Miz Cooper is a bygone figure belonging to an ideal past, much as her association with dreams and childhood generates nostalgia. An "Eternal Mother" like the figure Gish represents in *Intolerance,* "old, yet ageless" Rachel Cooper, her first name alluding to the Old Testament woman who prayed for the miracle of children, has sheltered orphans for nearly twenty-five years.[55] To purify her character of motives besides maternal love, Rachel's character has been simplified from Grubb's original.[56] In the film, Miz Cooper is quite simply "our heroine at last."[57]

Miz Cooper gives back to the children Christianity unspoiled by fundamentalism, even reclaiming Preacher's leitmotif, "Leaning on the Everlasting Arms," by singing to herself, "Leaning on Jesus." Just as the good grandmother in *Way Down East* teaches the judgmental Squire that he must learn humility since he too can be deceived, so Rachel Cooper emphasizes sympathy and forgiveness along with the wisdom of knowing people "by their fruits" rather than their words. Miz Cooper's beliefs have a special burden in *Hunter,* because they counter Preacher's psychopathic faith, its hypocritical and bigoted religiosity and its overlap with vigilante justice. Her handling of guilt-troubled John shows how her personal faith lies beyond the confessions common to reformed liberals as well as the self-righteousness of the anti-Communist Right. Contrary to Niebuhrian realism as well as the Preacher's fundamentalism, Miz Cooper never mentions the word "sin," and after she wins John's trust, she asks him to bring each of them an apple—a highly symbolic object by this point in the film. Apples appear throughout *Hunter,* evoking nature and temptation, innocence and sin; in the Harper home's cellar, earlier, when John deceives Preacher about the money's hiding place, Powell throws him across a bushel of apples and shouts that God Himself calls the boy an evil liar.[58] In his face-to-face with Miz Cooper, however, John bites into the apple, enjoying its sweetness, and, on Christmas Day (the Redeemer's birth), he will hand another apple to Rachel, who tells him "it is the best gift a body can have." The symbolic exchanges of the apples between Rachel and John coincide with John's growing confidence in Rachel's good will and his guilt-releasing divulgence of Ben's secret. Through Rachel's gentle ministry, which recognizes John's true virtue, the boy undergoes forgiveness in terms provided by sentimental melodrama; he lets go of unfair guilt and returns to childlike faith.

Especially in *Hunter*'s penultimate passages, forgiveness facilitates the restoration of childlike traits in the sentimental tradition, as the recovery of John's innocence helps to set off a quality key to Rachel's world: sincerity. In *Sincerity and Authenticity* (1974), Trilling's threnody for an ethos antiquated by the Cold War realism he helped to perpetuate, the belief in sincerity, we are told, is crucial to melodrama, where the nature of villainy is to refuse truthfully representing oneself to another. The modern temper's distance from melodrama and its "hypocrite-villains," Trilling says, coincides with its devaluation of sincerity; we have become accustomed to suspecting the insincerity of public speech and to doubting our ability to tell truth from misrepresentation, reality from ideology.[59] In its preoccupation with unstable appearances, the McCarthy era already knew the condition Trilling described. Alluding to "canine philosophers" in *The City of God,* Richard Rovere remarks that McCarthy was both a true cynic and a true mountebank because he not only had disbelieved "in the possibility of sincerity" but also had "corrupted his spirit" with fraud so heinous that he paid the price by being obsessed with lie detection.[60] In their opposition to McCarthy, however, liberals did not try to rehabilitate sincerity from his cynical dissimulation so much as they fell back to defending themselves as less "innocent," in Niebuhr's ironic sense, than McCarthy. Seemingly, the only credibly sincere statement in the anti-Communist climate was one disclaiming innocence by taking the "great privilege of confession" or admitting to the common complicity.[61]

According to wisdom and tough-mindedness, the intelligentsia's guilt, while particular in content, sprang from a predisposition to self-deception endemic to all men. According to the Cold War liberal narrative, the recovering intellectuals of the thirties at least had the "maturity" to acknowledge their fallibility. Seared by experience, enlightened and ironic, they had fortuitously suffered the Fall. Their perspective was not in every case as acherontic as noir, but they appreciated the shock of having intended good and having seen "evil" result; after the errors of thirties radicalism, virtue now entailed the responsibility of renouncing sinless utopias. By confessing to the pride and finitude of common mankind, down to the most well-intending Communist Party sympathizer, ex-radical liberals both extenuated their sentimental errors ("we were guilty of being innocent") and routed the realist philosophy of Neibuhr's *Irony of American History* against McCarthyism's quest for evil outside itself. Edward Shils, though having no radical past, fell into the cadences of the liberal apologetic when he likened the "perfectionists of security and loyalty" to "the perfectionists of justice and freedom" to prove them equally wanting in "matter-of-factness, the acceptance of the intractability of the world and the obstinacy of the Old Adam in us."[62] If citizens could adjust to the truth that doubt and ambiguity were ineradicable, then society might discern that its evil could be restrained but not expelled, and the honest individual would be advised to maintain a vigil over his own will by intending limited good rather than the justice of a "crusader." As he criticized "hateful," "frantic" anti-Communists for failing to consider that they could be themselves capable of error or sin, Niebuhr describes a state of suspicion consistent with the noir depictions of Cresap's Landing, Moundsville, and New Economy in *Hunter*.[63]

Yet these spaces cast no shadow on the Miz Cooper passages. "The children look at her with complete trust," the screenplay specifies.[64] Rachel addresses everyone with the same directness and probity she displays when speaking to herself of the Lord, and secrecy and hypocrisy yield themselves before her. Ruby willingly confesses to Miz Cooper the secret of her journeys into New Economy, and once John pours out the secret of Ben's bloody money, Miz Cooper takes him into her arms. When Harry Powell arrives at her doorstep, she "senses in a flash" that he is lying and reads the truth in John's eyes when the boy says, "He ain't my Dad"; "No, and he ain't no preacher, neither," adds Miz Cooper, unimpressed by Powell's attempt to tell her "the story of Right Hand and Left Hand."[65] Rachel is the first adult who has trusted John's sincerity when he calls the Preacher a liar. The most emphatic testimony to the mutual sincerity Rachel cultivates, however, is John's recovery of his voice. Terrorized by what he has endured, the boy is mute for the first few scenes with the old woman, and he communicates only by nodding. Once Miz Cooper wins his interest with the story of Moses, he speaks for the first time, just before biting into the apple, so that he regains his desire to communicate at the moment he begins to recover his innocent faith. Having had every adult disbelieve him and having himself resorted to lies out of fear and concealment, John can speak again because he has left an atmosphere of suspicion for one of trust.

After the children's discovery of false appearances, the signs of sincerity are poignant and fitting, but they are also very fragile. Based on *Hunter*'s representation, characters can be true to themselves as well as each other only in the absence of the adult world the film has elsewhere manifested from the church to the courts. Like the innocent children who express it, sincerity seems to be nurtured only within the ideal space of Miz Cooper's farm. By associating the farm and Rachel with dreams, nostalgia, and childhood, *Hunter* bolsters the sense that innocence and the traits that sustain it, forgiveness and sincerity, have no place in the world other people have created. In its effort to protest the adult world's falsity and injustice, the film nearly wishes them away, as is evident in the very language of the country woman's lullaby, which suggests that Preacher's threat is as unreal as a passing nightmare.

Leo Braudy has deemed the ending, which erases all stylistic traces of noir, a "return to an Eden of aesthetic innocence" and likened the effect to parody. Braudy's reading is tempting to the postmodernist, but it actually misses the problem presented by the film's entire last third.[66] Laughton was very fond of Miz Cooper, and the success of the film's final half hour depends on our acceptance of the ideals she and the whole topos of the farm embody.[67] The passages fail, however, because they overstate the utopian element within sentimental melodrama. Narratives like Griffith's *Way Down East*, *White Rose*, *Adventures of Dollie*, *Intolerance*, and *Orphans of the Storm* hold out the possibility that virtue may once again be made secure from the villainy that has temporarily gained power over the innocent and scrambled the signs of good and evil. Virtue may safely come to exist in an idyllic domestic community, as in *Way Down East*, or it may require more sweeping transformations; in the apocalyptic ending of *Intolerance,* a host of archangels descend to end the weeping of the Eternal Mother who, while rocking the cradle of Time, has seen unjust men produce a history of calamity. Laughton, taking his cue from Grubb's novel, opted for an ending after *East's* example, where virtue finds contentment in an ideal present rather than hope in an eschatological vision (as in *Intolerance*), but he failed to understand that *East's* ending succeeds because its drama transpires in a context less complex than *Hunter's*. The Evil that Lennox Sanderson represents is concentrated in his villainy, and once it invades the idyllic community, he needs only to be expelled for harmony to return. In some of his mannerisms and schemes, Harry Powell belongs to the Lennox Sanderson tradition, but he is also a psychopath from the noir universe, and, consistent with noir attitudes, the adult world he touches is ambiguous and tainted before he enters. It is this ironic contrast with sentimental melodrama that the passages in Cresap's Landing highlight in *Hunter's* earlier portions. Because the problems raised in its fallen adult world cannot be expunged by Preacher's elimination, the film instead creates an alternative social space—Miz Cooper's—from which evil can be more simply repelled.

The limits of the Miz Cooper passages, their inability to finally suppress the noir environment surrounding Rachel's special realm, emerge in the climatic exposure of Preacher's evil that precedes the Christmas finale. In a proper melodramatic structure, these recognition scenes would be purgative, expelling evil and securing justice for the innocent. Given the sway of Tartarean influences the film has almost everywhere represented, however, the return of earlier figures from Cresap's Landing and Moundsville instead makes the happy ending that follows seem more wistful than satisfying. When Preacher enters the farm, the noir imagery of the film's earlier sections comes with him: low-key lit night scenes, arching shadows, acicular shapes on walls, silhouetted figures against luminous backdrops. Quite contrary to his earlier appearances, however, Preacher is easily deposed by his would-be victim, and the imagery associated with him shortly diffused by morning sunlight. The confrontation with Rachel—a long, suspenseful sequence in the novel—is played for comedy, with Preacher "scuttling out of the house in good Mack Sennett manner, hooting and hollering as he grabs the seat of his pants."[68]

The lightness of these scenes may imply that Preacher has been deprived of force by Rachel's incorruptibility, but the following sequence, which shows the Preacher's trial and its horrid aftermath, abruptly reverses tone, as the sober themes of uncertain justice and overpowering hypocrisy reenter the film. The shock of the evangelist's reappearance recalls the guilty doubleness of fathers and authorities in the world John has fled. The camera dissolves from Rachel's farm to the state court in Moundsville, where Ben was sentenced to hang, and John, terrified in the witness stand, has resumed his muteness. It is here in Moundsville that the Spoons lead a lynch mob to administer the Lord's punishment to the false prophet. Where Rachel seemed to have defeated Preacher, she is no force to quell the self-righteous vigilantes who become as mad as he is. The crowd of vigilante Christians, with the Spoons at the fore, shows one community's failure to restore its harmony or its moral legibility after Preacher is expelled. In fact, the Spoons, representing Cresap's Landing, help to foment violence in another space, the city of New Economy. These scenes thus throw a special onus on Miz Cooper to represent the power of good, but her portrayal in the sequence instead shows how much she is supplanted in this other world. After having been the source of authority and the principal speaker ever since her entrance in the film, she is speechless in Moundsville, where Icey Spoon's voice ("He's Satan hiding behind the Cross!") predominates. Rachel's response is to gather the children around her skirts and march them to the train where they can be whisked back to the farm for Christmas Day. Occurring on the eve of the holiday commemorating the Savior's birth, Preacher's death sentence and the mob's vengeance seem yet another challenge to Rachel's Christic teaching of "judge not," but the dictum is hardly compelling by this point in the film. Who is responsible when judges themselves seem dubious, intolerant, or blind? How to make moral choices when perfect justice seems out of reach? Can one afford to be sincere when the trust between a community's leaders and its citizens is violated by reciprocal accusations of guilt and deceit?

Unless one is willing to accept Miz Cooper as a solution, the issues raised by the film, problems very close to the intellectual and political culture of the McCarthy period, appear to be left behind as the representatives of goodness and innocence withdraw from evil rather than counteract it. Film noir, with its tendency to frustrate narrative closure by scattering guilt across the cast of characters, does not provide more viable solutions to the issues *Hunter* raises than melodrama does, but neither does noir try falsely to transcend the problems. *Hunter* is most effective when it centers on Preacher's power over those he fools, zealotry's warping effect on perception, or judges who identify God's justice with their own. In these passages, the relationship between sentimental melodrama and film noir is dialectical, for they bolster each other's vision of a postlapsarian state where appearances mislead and evil holds sway, even as the allusions to melodramatic innocence, chiefly symbolized by the children, protest this state and animate some hope that virtue will be vindicated. So long as the

film does not attempt to materialize this hope, the narrative benefits philosophically from the struggle between the noirish tendency to disseminate
responsibility for evil and the melodramatic tendency to concentrate blame
on singular hypocrite-villains. As soon as the film offers its idyllic vision,
the narrative suffers the same stasis that Pipe Creek Farm introduces into
Witness, though Chambers, at least, acknowledged that the innocents
would eventually have to wander "the dark woods" alone. After John and
Pearl have experienced their "nightmare," the idyll of Miz Cooper's farm
overly strains sentimental motifs in order to eclipse the children's bad
memories. Rather than the melodramatic purgation of evil and the restoration of virtue's safety that seems intended, we have instead retreat and
withdrawal.

SOME TEXTS are telling for their flaws as well as their achievements. *The
Night of the Hunter* is an important artifact of the fifties because the problems that eventually overtake the narrative stem from the filmmakers' very
success at envisioning a complex fictional correlate to the McCarthy era's
excesses. So inventive and salient are the first two-thirds of the film that the
Miz Cooper passages often look as if they deflect what has gone before.
The utopian ambitions of *Hunter*'s last half hour, in particular, move fatefully beyond the film's liberal-friendly premises—disgust with vigilantism,
sympathy for the wrongfully persecuted, support for personal belief above
fundamentalist ideology—as the narrative tries to achieve precisely what
realists had said was not only impossible to realize but also naive to dream:
a reversal of the Fall, a return to innocence. Though its form in Rachel
Cooper fails to persuade, *Hunter*'s utopian wish is nonetheless poignant
when considered against some of the spectacles of the early fifties and their
damaging repercussions on American political life for years to come. With
McCarthyism fanning the flame, HUAC had summoned individuals, including hundreds in the movie industry, to a bar where they exonerated
themselves from suspicion by confessing to guilt and accusing others.[69]
McCarthy had accused liberals of being saboteurs and subverters only to
level the same charges against previous allies in his own party, and his critics, Democrat as well as (in fewer numbers) Republican, responded by
accusing him, in turn, of being a guilty liar. In the Cold War world the filmmakers had witnessed, trust and sincerity may have appeared so enfeebled
that perhaps only dreaming children and eternal matrons seemed their fitting symbols. This observation does not excuse the ending's serious flaws,
but it does remind us that *Hunter*'s anomalous mixture of sentimentality
with noir is more richly appreciated in the context of the controversy

stirred by the right wing's abuses of countersubversion and the liberal intelligentsia's defensive posturing. Preacher's segments of *Night of the Hunter* may be more compelling to us today for their noir sensibility, but the wistfulness of the Miz Cooper passages reminds us that sincerity is a principle of hope and its loss a condition of a politics fatefully predicated on mistrust.

PART THREE

Cold War Cultural Politics and the Varieties of Religious Experience

CHAPTER FIVE

The Mass Culture Critique's Implications for American Religion

America is a nation where at the same time cultural freedom is promised and mass culture produced.

—Editorial Statement, "Our Country and Our Culture,"
Partisan Review (1952)

For the first time, too, there has grown up an elaborate mass pseudo-culture, plus a frightening antagonism to genuine culture, which organized religion can no longer challenge, only imitate, in order to survive as an institution.

—Alfred Kazin, "Religion and the Intellectuals," *Partisan Review,* (1950)

Authentic and Pseudo Spirituality, Elite and Mass Taste

Thomas Merton's spiritual autobiography, *The Seven Storey Mountain* (1948), was one of the decade's best-selling works of religiously themed nonfiction. The story of his conversion to a Trappist monk, after a youthful marriage with Communism in the thirties (he worked with the Young Communist League and the National Socialist League), Merton's narrative repeats an Augustinian pattern, from false faith to the true faith, that *Witness* fully wrought in 1952. His text is distinguished by the role he accords to art in effecting his authentic conversion.[1]

AN ASPIRING literary critic who pursued a graduate degree in English at Columbia University, Merton remembers, during his days taking Shakespeare with Mark Van Doren and writing his thesis on William Blake, how he viewed his upbringing, divided between his middle-class Protestant grandparents in New York and his artist father in Europe. "Pop," as Merton knew his grandfather, made money persuading his employer, Grosset and Dunlap, to print "the books of popular movies illustrated with stills from the film [titles included de Mille's *The Ten Commandments* (1923)] to be sold in connection with the publicity given to the picture itself" (21). This was not only a source of income to Pop, but also a way for him to indulge his love of the movies, which "were really the family religion"

(22). The grandson's theological education under Pop's auspices amounted to little more than watching him stuff envelopes with donations for the Salvation Army and the Zion Church (25). His grandparents' California trips to mingle with movie people, on the other hand, were "in the nature of a pilgrimage," and their "two gods" were stars Douglas Fairbanks and Mary Pickford, to whom they paid "a somewhat corrupt form of hyperdulia" (22). The son of painters who instilled in him a love of the fine arts, Merton, even as a boy, sensed the folly of his grandparents' movie-love. He and his brother, he recalls, innocently preferred comedian W. C. Fields's pratfalls to the "heavy" and "sentimental" melodramas, and the voice of Merton's adult, postconversion narrator turns sarcastic when describing the "immortal masterpiece" they once saw Gloria Swanson filming on Long Island (21). Thus, with nervous affection, Merton derides this aspect of his childhood, which comments upon the tastes of the American middle class and the limp devotions of worldly Protestantism.

It was in reaction to these attitudes and in seeking ultimate values, which Columbia's "pragmatists," New Dealers, and "liberals" could not supply him either, that the young man Merton found Communism, and in the process, ended up repudiating temporarily some of the instruments of his eventual salvation (141). One of his painful memories is the afternoon he spent "going into the Columbia Bookstore and selling them a copy of T. S. Eliot's essays and a lot of other things which [he] was getting rid of in a conscious reaction against artiness—as if all that were too bourgeois" (138). Yet the very suppression of his aesthetic nature for the sake of what seemed at the time like a spiritual goal, served, with the adroitness of Providence, to deepen his hunger for God. While attending meetings about world justice, accosting people on corners, and handing out pamphlets, his sensibility sought solace in the memories of his travels in France and Italy with his father, amidst the frescoes, museums, Byzantine mosaics—the infinite love, wisdom, and power of God "implicit in every line of the pictures"—and memories closer of reading Blake, Hopkins, Baudelaire, Joyce, and Eliot. Without his knowing anything substantial about Christian doctrine at the time, these works of art spoke to him, or rather, another did: "it was He who was teaching me Who He was, more directly than I was capable of realizing" (110). Merton's eventual withdrawal from Communism, as he describes his odyssey, is a miracle of grace that makes aesthetic taste its accessory. The path from the picket line to Our Lady of Gethsemani Monastery led through the museums at the Baths of Diocletian and the halls of Columbia, where Merton was exposed to works opening levels of being that most of the English Department's instructors (who sullied literature with psychoanalysis, economics, and sociology) could not have conceived, and unable to conceptualize, could not feel (180). Literature was not scripture, museums were not vestibules, and sacred painting was not incarnate image, but in the stillness of contemplation these afforded Merton an intensified perception of beauty and, in the beautiful, a heightened sense of man's connatural affinity with God's Being.[2] Nothing in Communism, mass culture, or any other form of materialism could replicate these experiences.

Merton would distinguish himself in the sixties as a courageous advocate of peace and civil rights, but, in 1948, the cultural politics underpinning his spiritual journey were not simply uncontroversial, but almost too traditional to be reassuring. Reading *The Seven Storey Mountain*, one imagines that art, religion, and entertainment commodities are in their owns spheres, as fatefully as God is in Heaven; thus Merton as narrator can look back on embarrassing features of his upbringing with humor (and slight condescension) rather than foreboding. His mood of confidence was not shared by some of his contemporaries. In Cold War projections of the mass society, consumers feature as weak democratic subjects, and mass entertainment as a substitute for an archaic and cultlike religion. Mass cultural forms, regardless of whether they had religious subjects (such as the biblical epics), allegedly induced a state of reversion to primitive mass identity, prior to individuation and the negative power of self-consciousness.[3] The chance that democratic leveling could actually produce a mass society of Eliotic incubus seemed to have grown because the boundaries between religion and entertainment, art and entertainment, aesthetic experiences and faith, were not so self-evident as Merton regarded them.[4]

The editorial preface to *Partisan Review*'s symposium "Our Country and Our Culture" (1952) asked, "Do you believe that a democratic society necessarily leads to a leveling of culture, to a mass culture which will overrun intellectual and aesthetic values traditional to Western civilization?" Reinhold Niebuhr answered in the affirmative, deploring "the synthetic and sentimentalized art of Hollywood" and "the lower depths to which television has reduced this art." These epitomized the "cultural and spiritual crudities of a civilization preoccupied with technics." Theological critics of Protestant modernism, from Eliot's New Critical acolytes, "the neo-Christians," to religious socialists like Paul Tillich, extended the stakes of such discussions into the domain of religious experience, questioning whether Christian institutions in America were more or less autonomous from mass culture and mass opinion than the provinces of elite taste.[5] There was also a general alarum that Americans were relying on inferior sources, such as Hollywood films, more than the churches for religious inspiration, succor, or even instruction on the meaning of the Bible or the leading of a holy life. In a review written for the *Christian Century,* T. S. Driver, Union Theological Seminary's instructor in religion and drama, tried to dissuade ministers from promoting de Mille's latest bread and circuses, *The Ten Commandments* (1956), for it stressed epic spectacle over the inner meaning of history, which is personal faith: "This three-hour-and-ninety-minute-god must be rejected quite as absolutely as the god of the Golden Calf was rejected by Moses." In the secular press, sociologist Frederick Elkin said that Dore Sharey's religious film, *The Next Voice You Hear* (1950), was appealing to the same childish dependency on an "all-loving sympathetic God" as did Billy Graham, who similarly drew "tens of thousands." William Whyte's "organization man" glossed the ads for Twentieth Century Fox's *A Man Called Peter* (1955) from Catherine Marshall's best-selling biography; Marshall's husband, the first chaplain of the U.S. Senate, is billed in the ads as a real swell: "He was everybody's kind of guy. . . . He was God's kind of guy." For Whyte, this ad line was characteristic of God in mass culture: He "likes regular people"; He is "gregarious and he can be found in the smiling happy people of the society about you. As the advertisement puts it, religion can be fun." So much for Barth's Wholly Other. The fans of *A Man Called Peter* worship society as a deux ex machina and their "higher-ups" as godlike. They are the parishioners who go to "The Church of Suburbia" (the title of Chapter 29 in Whyte's *The Organization Man* [1956]) where the Sunday School of Tom Sawyer has become an expensive community center for newly affluent white collar families.[6] The churches and mass culture seemed to be exchanging values and styles. In the pages of *Commentary,* William Phillips wondered if ministers and popular media were making a success of faith by making a faith of success.

This was not, of course, the first time that cultural commentators had told a tale of declension about American religion. Concerns over the domination of religion by commerce were older than America and had been mounting since the Civil War and industrialization. By the 1870s, it had become "axiomatic" to many observers that "religion had been reduced to a 'kind of sacred amusement,' 'an aesthetic entertainment.'"[7] Historian Laurence Moore has demonstrated that middle-class Protestant religious leaders responded by pursuing a project analogous to genteel reformers' efforts to uplift consumers' tastes for better culture. Religion mixed with entertainment could educate the populace to choose instructional commodities that were better for them, and thus create a demand for more edifying goods that reflected the Protestant consensus (172–237). Aesthetic taste and moral values were inseparable in this model.[8] According to Moore, this project, in the perception of mainline Protestant leaders, had been completed by the fifties: "Protestant leaders were more relaxed with the institutions of commercial culture after World War II than they had been at any time since they had first tried to set rules for the market" (236). Conditions were not so much relaxed as they were a choreographed calm. As Frank Ninkovich and Frances Stonor Saunders have shown, this was a period in which America (specifically the State Department, UNESCO, the CIA, and the Division of Cultural Relations) was interested in exporting a self-image through "cultural diplomacy" that was based on a "practical combination of national interest, anti-Communism, and bureaucratic activism."[9] Moore's abbreviated account of the Cold War period gives the impression that the fluid exchange of religious and commercial markets was relatively undisturbed, as Americans learned about, and learned to export, the benefits of democracy, capitalism, and biblical ecumenism. In the years after World War II, "[r]eligiously inspired commodities" did indeed "saturate the American cultural landscape" in paperbacks, magazines, entertainment, and gifts, and much of this spending was ratified by appeals to antitotalitarian religious nationalism, even if the effects were sometimes to inspire intense devotion exceeding the Cold War rationale.[10]

Predictions and diagnoses of the mass society, however, acted as a counterbalance to the facile optimism Moore finds in the era's synthesis of mammon and manna. Theorists of the mass society challenged "the cultural nationalism" of "the American Way of Life"; moreover, they regarded with grave suspicion the "fast media"—"technologically oriented, populist in its partiality for undifferentiated mass audiences"; in short, the stuff of commercial mass culture—that state-sponsored cultural diplomacy favored for its apparent ability to "achiev[e] immediate results in the form of altered opinion or attitudes."[11] Speculations on the mass society, in other words, perceived a gap between the image of American culture compatible with national interests in the battle of Cold War ideologies and the quality of culture actually produced, as well as its effects on American attitudes and psyches. Mass culture catered to America's innocence, its moral nostalgia, lack of reality-testing, dreams of heroism, and simplistic view of evil; more insidiously still, it corroded the inner fiber of American citizens, making them more susceptible to ideological self-deceptions. Where would a spirit of resistance to the makings of mass society be located? Within the churches, traditionally viewed as buttresses of the American values, or outside of them? The critique of culture implied, and led to, a reflection upon the churches' complicity in packaging and selling culture-religion, producing mass men, coarsening citizens' sensibilities. It mobilized the logic of theological countermodernism to refuse the protototalitarian mass man whose stained glass was the window of a box office, whose church was an arcade and a revue.

Just as critics, such as Paul Tillich or Eliot and the New Conservatives, conceived high culture in some antithetical relationship to "middlebrow" or "kitsch," which imitated the intelligentsia's culture and blurred the distinction between commodity and art, so too, they warned, the spirit of Christianity now had to be preserved from its brummagem versions, which borrowed the kerygmatic symbols but deprived them of depth, such that the Gospel, or, as Tillich preferred, "the Protestant principle," had to burst against mass tastes and needs. Any honest reckoning with the lonely crises of conscience and faith was enfeebled by the market influence of consumer veto.[12] By the end of the decade, in *The Death of God* (1961), the neoorthodox Gabriel Vahanian had declared that America had entered a "post-Christian era," and in *The New Shape of American Religion* (1959), associate editor of the *Christian Century* Martin Marty stated that the country had entered a "post-Protestant time." Ours is certainly not a post-Christian or a post-Protestant culture, but Vahanian and Marty were responding to a then widely held perception that, as H. Richard Niebuhr had long feared, the "Christ of culture" had been swept along by the nationalistic revival of the fifties, its character deliquescent, having little more than entertainment value, its doctrines purposefully vague, and its theology incoherent.[13] By the end of the decade, the Christian novelists John Updike (a neoorthodox Presbyterian of Barthian persuasion) and Walker Percy (a Southern Catholic) were writing, respectively, about protagonists in *Rabbit Run* (1959) and *The Moviegoer* (1962) who must venture outside the modern church before they can feel the motions of grace. The ambling laymen Harry "Rabbit" Angstrom and Binx Bolling may not be confessing believers by the end of either novel, but they nearly realize the necessity of faith by the very depth of their alienation.

For Paul Tillich, this kind of estrangement from both church and society could be a more truthful evocation of spirituality than bishops or priests leading congregants to peace. In his "Communicating the Christian Message" (1952), it seems that people are now being deprived of their opportunity to make a genuine choice to accept or reject the Gospel, since the ministers, believing they must make converts, are turning into Norman Peale-type public relations men, who make the Gospel more appealing by deleting elements that are not compatible with the middle class way of life or the American success narrative: "Ours is a society which tries with all its means, unconsciously and sometimes even consciously, to standardize everything by means of public communication which every moment fills the air we breathe. So here participation is very easy! In fact it is so easy that in order to communicate the Gospel we need non-participation. Ministers need withdrawal and retirement from these influences beating upon them every minute. This, perhaps, is the most difficult task. Ministers belong to those who participate, and have only weak weapons to resist this participation." Under these pressures, ministers have misconstrued the purpose of evangelism: "The question cannot be: How do we communicate the Gospel so that others will accept it? For this there is no method."[14] Tillich calls for the professional ministry to have a moratorium before it succeeds in compromising the Gospel, and for religious leaders meanwhile to listen to critical voices outside the denominations. By a "historical providence," at this very time the arts (most especially the modernist painting, drama, and literature Tillich favored) have shouldered the mission that the organized church, in its overeagerness to participate and evangelize, is in danger of miscarrying. Though many philistine Christians might dismiss them as agnostic or atheistic, the contemporary arts, in their evocations of human consciousness straining against demonic objectifying structures, are actually ahead of the organized churches in prophetically diagnosing the predicament of man in an industrial, conformist society.[15] Art was subsuming the role in which Rabbit's pastor and Tillich's overeager reverends had failed, as it collided with the layman's dulled sensibility, his glutinized thought and chafened heart, while also, crucially, helping to preserve a space for the existential questioning that faith answers, a space that had already been contracted by liberal theology or biblical literalism and was now being puttied with mass tastes.

Achieving, or prizing, art that spoke to the alienated ego of faith (credo), while warily regarding the community of believers in Christ (credimus), marked off one's sensibility from the mass society, but the exaggeration of otherness in religion, as in aesthetic experience, also risked reducing the inwardness of both to moments of negation within a radically isolated subjectivity. A pilgrim might have wondered *where* the Mystical Body of Christ was to be joined, since communion—or, in more modish terms, "intersubjectivity"—seems tainted with overtones of the conformity. Nonetheless, in the zeal to resist the commodity's infiltration into the form and content of both culture and religion, critics definitely sought in art an accent on paradox and ambiguity, dissonant composition and broken form, properties inducing a sense of apophasis, kenosis, horror, guilt-consciousness, estrangement, or "a Barthian exaggeration of God's transcendence," as British expatriate W. H. Auden put it.[16] Outside the crucible of negation and angst, symbols like sin, grace, and the cross too easily lended themselves, in the nominally Christian culture, to false consciousness. Christian artists writing in a secular society, Cleanth Brooks observed, must presume that all audiences, whether or not they profess faith, are uncomprehending "gentiles," no more receptive to revelation than were the original heathen reached by the early church, because the language of belief has been darkened and distorted, its spiritual context lost: "Not only do the Christian symbols that most people would expect the poet to use fail to convey his meaning; they may actively distort his meaning."[17]

The elite repudiation of mass culture as well as kitsch religion, in often exchangeable terms, betrayed doubts about the churches' autonomy but, more fatefully for subsequent reflections on the sources of neofundamentalism's populist appeal, it did nothing to discourage misconceptions that there were psychological correspondences, authoritarian in disposition, between popular religious revival and regressive mass entertainments, as exemplified in historian William McLoughlin's work on Billy Graham, his colleague Richard Hofstadter's writings on religious fundamentalism and the radical Right, and Stanley Kramer's famous liberal conscience film *Inherit the Wind*. Their explanations of popular and commercial religiosity, by comparing psychological regression in both consumers and communicants, actually obscured the most significant features of evangelicalism's occasional appropriation of the styles and techniques of mass culture.[18] They misunderstood the desire of evangelical leaders such as Billy Graham, representing many constituents outside the middle class or newly moving into it, for cultural capital, these leaders' own suspicions of mass culture, and their willingness to adapt both elite art and entertainment commodities for the same kerygmatic purpose.

The Specter of the Mass in Hillsboro, Tennessee

During an emergency in Stanley Kramer's *Inherit the Wind* (1960), the film's liberal protagonist, defense attorney Henry Drummond (Spencer Tracy), affronts prosecution, judge, and jury by confessing that "Right," being "a grid of morality," "has no meaning whatsoever," but "Truth has meaning, as a direction." Drummond's opposition in the trial is Matthew Harrison Brady, a United States senator and an evangelical fundamentalist whose grandiloquence appeals to the faith of the "common people" and their right to protect future generations from ideas challenging values bequeathed to them by biblical tradition. Though Brady believes he speaks for God and the virtuous rural folk, Drummond reproves Brady as a "self-appointed prophet" whose constituents are "fanatics" and "bigots." Speaking to his client, Bertram Cates, a schoolteacher jailed in Hillsboro, Tennessee, for teaching evolution rather than the biblical creation myth, Drummond characterizes Brady's supporters: "You killed one of their fairy-tale myths, and they'll bring down the wrath of God, Brady, and the state legislature to shut you up." Drummond defends the conscience of a single man possessed of intellectual doubts, and Brady champions what the film portrays as a mob. Drummond's scruples are independent of his client's, but Brady's are identified with the crowd.

The film, of course, adapts Lawrence and Lee's play of the same title, and, like the play, it revisits the Scopes trial of 1925.[19] Bert Cates is John Scopes, Matthew Harrison Brady is William Jennings Bryan, and Henry Drummond is Clarence Darrow. At the end of a decade in Hollywood that had abounded in biblical epics and stories of religious miracles, *Inherit the Wind* was the first polemical American film on religion and politics and one of the few movies that actually dealt with religion *in* America. Only the second American film since 1931 to unflatteringly portray American religious leaders, *Inherit the Wind* simply could not have been made under the old integrated studio system.[20] Even though he produced it independently, Kramer had a difficult time finding a distributor for such a commercially risky venture. On the strength of the source play's Broadway run and his previous successes with uncommercial properties, such as *The Defiant Ones* (1958) and *On the Beach* (1959), Kramer eventually sold the project to United Artists, one of the smaller distribution companies.

Like his other work (including *Judgment at Nuremberg* and *Guess Who's Coming to Dinner?*), Kramer's *Inherit the Wind* is a "liberal conscience" or "liberal consensus" film, a type of postwar message movie, usually independently produced, that addresses such problems as bigotry and social inequality.[21] *Inherit the Wind* was designed in part as a civics lesson in First Amendment liberties and as a defense of democratic pluralism.[22] During the filming, "the conflict within the story caused conflict for [Kramer] the producer," as "fundamentalist" groups petitioned United Artists to abandon the project on the grounds that it was an anti-God movie (174). According to Kramer, these groups did not believe that he would be "scrupulously fair to both sides" in the story. They did not abate, and he "reconciled [himself] to being hounded throughout the filming of the picture" (174). The occasional shrillness of the film may be due partly to this outside interference, for it is not the objective presentation of both sides that Kramer indicates. It is stacked against the fundamentalists, whom it portrays as an authoritarian mass unified by a star personality.[23]

Several scenes establish that the townspeople of Hillsboro, where the drama takes place, are authoritarians whose wrathful God seems invented, as Bert Cates speculates, to protect them against their own hatred for nonconformists. The town holds two demonstrations protesting Cates's nonbelief, the first a prayer vigil that turns into pure invective:

Reverend Jeremiah Brown: Do we believe?
Mass (in unison): YES!
Reverend: Do we believe the Word?
Mass (unison): YES!
Reverend: Do we believe the truth of the Word?
Mass (unison): YES!
Reverend: Do we curse the man who has sinned against the Word?
Mass (unison): YES!
Reverend: Lord, strike down this sinner. . . . Let him know the terror of Thy
    sword! Let his soul for all eternity writhe in anguish! We ask the same curse
    of all who ask mercy for this sinner!
Mass (unison): YES! YES!

Throughout this scene, Kramer inhibits the viewer's identification with any townsperson in the gathering. He cuts between long shots of the mass and medium close-ups of individual faces, but from either distance the people look grotesque, with oblique angles and harsh, masking shadows. He etches the crowd in chiaroscuro, rimming the heads at the crowd's forefront with light but making the bodies meld together in darkness; heads at the rear of the crowd are backlit, appearing in silhouette only and seeming to flow out of the inky center. All of the people in the crowd appear linked in space, implying their conformity to one another's mass belief. The close-ups do not individuate them but accent their collective monstrosity. Kramer cuts in to a close-up of a different townsperson each time the crowd assents to the reverend. The close-ups are low angled and canted at about thirty degrees, adding to the distortion of the spectator's view of faces already obscured by the baroque lighting. None of these shots is held longer than the duration of the crowd's intoning "YES!", as though the chant predominates over each speaker. The spectator cannot attend to the peculiarities of the face so much as to the mimed movements of the mouths, one after another. The dehumanizing style here is the director's comment on the crowd's message. The Hillsboro fundamentalists treat dissent as sin, and rather than forgiving that sin, they would prefer to eradicate the sinner and preserve their unity. When Bert Cates's fiancée, Rachel Brown, breaks free of the mass and pleads for his soul, the Reverend damns her, his own daughter, even though she "be flesh of [his] flesh."

Kramer trumps this "prayer meeting" with his culminating mob scene, a mass demonstration in the Hillsboro streets where citizens form what resembles a pogrom. The demonstration is foreshadowed by Henry Drummond's speech to the trial judge that Hillsboro is marching backwards to the terrors of the sixteenth century, when "bigots burnt men of the Enlightenment." A few moments later, Kramer fades from the courtroom to an image of Bertram Cates burning in effigy before a mob. Marching in time with torches and the effigy, the mob chants a parody of "The Battle Hymn of the Republic": "We'll hang Bert Cates from a sour apple-tree / We'll hang Bert Cates from a sour apple-tree / *Our* God is marching on / Glory, glory, hallelujah / *Our* God is marching on." Kramer cuts to Henry Drummond's motel room, as newspaperman E. K. Hornbeck (based on H. L. Mencken and portrayed by Gene Kelly) pops in derisively donning a Klansman's hood.[24] With this scene, Kramer manages to parallel the fundamentalists to the Inquisitors, fascists, and the KKK, the analogies united by each group's loathing for nonconformity, which they treat as heresy, treason, or impurity.

Bert Cates's defender is an agnostic lawyer who has made a career of challenging public opinion on a variety of issues. That Henry is an agnostic does not make the film anti-God. Drummond's character does not make an argument for disbelief but for independent judgment. He is portrayed by Spencer Tracy, a star with a well-established thirty-year-long screen persona (from *Boys Town* to *Bad Day at Black Rock* to *The Old Man and the Sea*) of stern, courageous, resolved but not reckless or pugnacious men who act on personal principle. The character type of Henry Drummond, however, has its own legacy. Within the genre of liberal conscience cinema, Drummond's closest ancestor is Henry Fonda's juror from *Twelve Angry Men* (1957), who is not a loner content with his own private code but a rationalist desiring to convert others to his opinions. Tracy is excellent casting for Drummond, as the actor manages to balance in his performance the impression of robust will wedded to social scruple. Inside the world of *Inherit the Wind*, Drummond emerges as a dogged optimist, working from the margins not by choice but because mass opinion endangers the form of government in which he believes. Democracy, a realistic form of government in Drummond's estimate, has become so jeopardized in the film that for him to continues believing in it is heroically idealistic. He still holds that democracy can be a consensus of free thinkers: "Conform, conform, conform!" moans Drummond: "What do you [Brady] want to do? Run all the members of the jury through a meat grinder and have them come out the same!" Just as Drummond prizes difference, he also values moderation and ambiguity, earmarks of his role as liberal spokesman and precisely those subtleties that Hillsboro lacks. Responding to Rachel Brown's worries that Bert Cates may be doing "something bad" to the town, he replies: "It's not as simple as all that: black or white, good or bad." Drummond does not refer here to Cates's trial alone; he is stating a general presupposition about all conflicts of interest. He is not moralistic. Over dinner with Brady's wife, an old friend, he jokes: "You know, looking back, I don't think Matt would've made a good president. But I would've made him king, so that you could be queen." She plays along: "Then what would that make you, Henry?" He gives a sure nod: "Your Majesty's loyal opposition." Drummond agrees to respectfully disagree so long as the right of disagreement is reciprocal, and since he accepts that another man's free thought may check his own, he expects compromise rather than purity from the law: [to Hornbeck] "I've been a lawyer long enough to know that there are no total victories."

The populace of Hillsboro, however, is not so democratically minded as Drummond. They may chant national anthems like "The Battle Hymn," but their American society would be ruled by the ideology of the folk. Thus the inner demon that Drummond must overcome is pessimism about democracy, an attitude posed in the film by E. K. Hornbeck. A caricature of H. L. Mencken, Hornbeck is the intellectual displaced in America, the elite critic and acid wit whose distaste for the mass verges on misanthropy: [Referring to the torch-bearing mob in the streets] "Well, those are the boobs that make our laws. It's a democratic process. . . . Oh, why don't you to wake up, Henry. Darwin was wrong; man didn't evolve. He's still an ape. His creed's still a totem pole." Drummond finally upbraids Hornbeck for lacking empathy for the less educated, but given the film's grotesque portrayal of the fundamentalists, Drummond's reprimand is more appropriately an indictment of Kramer's editorial camera.

Unlike Hornbeck, Drummond refuses to identify mass opinion in Hillsboro with the nature of a democratic society, but despite the attorney's oft-reiterated conviction that one Bert Cates is a greater testament to democracy than all of Hillsboro, Kramer's visual rhetoric nonetheless makes the fundamentalists overshadow the conscientious schoolteacher. They are more ominous still when assembling with their idol Matthew Harrison Brady in scenes that invite comparison between Hillsboro's faithful and the consumers in mass society theories. Kramer's representation of the Matthew Brady cult becomes an assay into the problem of stardom in mass religion, or the pseudoreligion of mass experience. For the part of Matthew Harrison Brady, Kramer cast Fredric March, an actor much more multifaceted than Tracy and lacking an established star persona. Texturing the Brady character's effusive vainglory with dreamy sentiment, his piety with hysteria, March's performance enhances Kramer's conversion of the populist Bryan into a pitiable demagogue. Kramer chose March for the role because he had worked with him on the Broadway stage production of *Death of a Salesman,* and the Brady of Kramer's film does possess some Willy Lomanesque pathos; Brady lives to dream of former success, tries to proselytize others with his delusions, needs to believe in his popularity and charm, goes to die not knowing who he is. Willy Loman's panache finally exists only in his own imagination, however, while Brady's can be affirmed by his fans and apostles. As embodied by Tracy's invisible acting style, Drummond's convictions seem intrinsic to him, whereas March's grand-standing bombast and Kramer's camera suggest that Brady's confidence requires the crowd's assent. During his speeches, Tracy usually keeps his head down, while March always turns to the audience, which punctuates his words with applause or nods. Tracy's close-ups isolate his visage in space. Even when the actor moves about the courtroom, Kramer's camera tracks him in tight close-up, as when Drummond makes his contempt-of-court speech to the judge. By contrast, March is physically stationary, pre-ferring to exert his voice, but he never seems to be speaking alone. He is framed by medium close-ups, so that we are aware of people flanking Brady or of the crowd backing him. While Tracy is usually filmed in me-dium or close shots, March is several times filmed in extreme long shots, to show him at the center of a crowd, as during the rally welcoming him to Hillsboro. He is never given close-ups isolating him in moments of ru-mination, as Tracy is granted when Drummond pauses to consider how to parry his opponent or to introduce a point. When Kramer grants March facial close-ups, these are moments in which Brady is mortified and pan-icked: as he hears his wife cry out that he cease his abusive examination of witness Rachel Brown, as he tries to regain the floor after Drummond dis-misses him from the witness chair, as he shouts out his pyrrhic victory speech while the radio broadcasters and newspapermen ignore him. These are moments when Brady is overplaying his zeal and losing approval from the audience.

While the film throughout depicts Brady as a charmer of the crowd, its finale suggests that he actually siphons life from it. The medical cause for his death in the courtroom finale is "a busted belly," but the metaphorical cause is his loss of the crowd's attention. In a dither, Brady whimpers to his wife that the crowd laughed at him (in fact, only the newsmen and crowd's teenagers—not the hard-core supporters—are shown laughing): "Mother, they laughed at me! I can't stand it when they laugh at me!" Brady's wife cradles his head and rocks him, murmuring, "O, baby, baby." Brady's de-pendency on the crowd is a near infantile fixation, as the mass, in some sense, substitutes for Mommy. After Cates's sentencing, Brady takes the center floor to deliver a speech for the nation, but in the commotion, he is ignored. Brady begins orating for any who will listen, as the camera tracks forward to an extreme close-up isolating him spatially. At this point, Bra-dy's eyes, desperate, roll back in his head, and his face falls, mortally, out of the frame. The demagogue cannot live without the crowd.

Drummond's tribute, in the final scene, is *Inherit the Wind's* one concession to Brady's past, and it transparently alludes to William Jennings Bryan's early political career. Elsewhere in the film, there are scattered
references to Brady's former bids for the presidency, as the candidate who
"fought for the common man," but this phrase, even when it comes from
Drummond's mouth, oscillates in connotation, for the film cannot finally
separate Hornbeck's cynicism from Drummond's sympathy. Its antipa-
thetic portrayal of the Hillsboro fanatics implicates popular democracy. If
the film asks us to pity Brady more than the crowd, it is because the delusional demagogue is less to be feared than the popular mass mentality that
requires him and helps to create him.

The crowd's star worship mistakes the famous for the messianic, the
mythical for the true, the common for the prophetic. The senator rides into
town under a banner that reads "BRADY WILL SAVE US." During his
welcoming rally, a legion of church ladies marches down mainstreet singing the classic evangelical hymn, "The Old Time Religion"; after Brady's
speech, they once again troll the hymn, but with a change in the refrain,
from "If it's good enough for Jesus then it's good enough for me" to "If it's
good enough for *Brady* then it's good enough for me." When Drummond
steps off the bus, Hornbeck makes explicit the crowd's identification of the
celebrated fundamentalist with the savior whose Gospel he preaches:
"Their Messiah arrived yesterday." Asked to swear an oath on the Bible,
prospective jury member Jesse Dunlop, farmer and a member of the town
council, goes one oath further: "I believe in the Holy Word of God. And I
believe in Matthew Harrison Brady." A chorus of amens and hosannas
follows. In so many of the film's images of the Hillsboro people, each citizen seems to mimic the other. Brady's voice too is essentially theirs, though
he seems set apart by his power to draw the crowd's energies towards himself. That energy does not ultimately reside in him, but in the mass experience he induces by lending his fame and oratorical power to dramatize the
people's dualistic myths in God and the Devil.

Fundamentalism as Authoritarian Mass Culture?

Brady's star power is predicated upon a kind of idealism, though of a different quality than Drummond's. If the defense attorney's idealism is actually faith in a realistic democracy of compromise solutions, Brady's
resembles what Theodor Adorno, in his "Freudianism and the Theory of
Fascist Propaganda" (1951), described as the matrix of fascist mass demonstrations, in which people take pleasure in surrendering their individual-

ity to a mob. According to Adorno, an individual enjoys sacrificing his self-control, as in primitive cults, when his ego can no longer hold together his impulses. As the fascist agitator solicits the audience's abstract identification by acting out its conflicting emotions, the mass cultural product, by conglomerating unassimilated parts of the mass personality, brings about the same effects of submission and arousal in the anonymous consumer. The modern individual regresses to this archaic state because mass culture has broken down his ego, so that he must choose the will of the leader, who is imbued with the aura of the mass. This is the crucial dialectical turn in the essay: mass culture, a product of late industrial society, has helped reproduce the conditions of archaic religion by homogenizing the ego. Alluding to McCarthy as well as Hitler, Adorno asserts that fascists need only reify what mass culture has already accomplished. American intellectuals in the Cold War would have recognized that Adorno was reworking the theses of his earlier mass culture critique, "The Fetish Character of Listening and Popular Music" (1938), where he had argued that mass culture was characterized by superficiality, formula, and a cult of personality, all of which indicated a weakness in the democratic subject.[25]

After the recent, and long overdue, American publication of Adorno's World War II–era study of the Depression-era Southern radio demagogue, Reverend "Martin Luther" Thomas of the Christian American Crusade, we can see that in the 1951 piece Adorno was also drawing on his analysis of revivalism as a species of propaganda and mass culture.[26] Identifying Thomas as (debatably) a "fascist" and (accurately) a "fundamentalist" like Gerald Winrod, Adorno discounts the content of the reverend's "obsolete," "illiberal," anti-"modernist" theology as sheer ideology that deviates from the "Christian ideals" it invokes.[27] As in Hitler's ceremonial addresses (to which Adorno continuously refers the reader), the state of consciousness Thomas induces is irrational and perversely un-Christian—"pagan" and "primitive": "the collective religious wantonness of the Holy Rollers may be consummated by the pogrom" (7). Where Thomas stresses the pragmatic benefits of orthodoxy for his faith "movement," Adorno studies the rhetorical function of his "religious medium," or his "racket" (75–103). The reverend sells his propaganda in a religious package by tailoring Protestant idiom, especially of the fundamentalist and revivalistic strains, to the medium of mass communications and "advertising." Inspired by his chief models—Billy Sunday, Gerald Winrod, Father Coughlin, and, above all, Hitler—Thomas has intuited how psychological effects, conventionally induced by religious stimuli ("aura," "charisma," the "magical halo") but now enshrined in products and glamorized personalities, can be transferred from the marketplace to ideological politics, from the fetishistic commodity to the fascist leader. These will culminate in the totalitarian system of complete domination. Adorno's conclusions anticipate Lowenthal and Guterman's thesis, in the more widely known *Prophets of Deceit* (1949), that Christian Right "agitators," who are nascent fascists, borrow the emotionally excitative techniques of mass culture to fan anger at a sense of social malaise. This is an unrest induced by the industrial, administrative, instrumentalizing conditions that are coming to dominate all aspects of capitalist society, including cultural production and reception.[28]

Adorno's piece on "Fascist Propaganda" confirmed what he had surmised in the earlier World War II–era studies: Joseph McCarthy's success shows that the democratic subject is not autonomous of mob influence, and America's own culture industry, as much as its psychologically regressive revivalism and extreme anti-Communist politics, is to blame for the right-wing subversion of its liberal government. Of all the work produced by the Institute of Social Research,[29] Adorno's critique of mass culture, along with Lowenthal's and Herbert Marcuse's, had the greatest impact in America, for "it came at a time when Americans themselves had begun to fear the realization of those dire prophecies that foreign visitors since Tocqueville had made about the effects of mass democracy."[30] The absence of a precapitalist, aristocratic tradition of cultural patronage was long seen as an advantage in America, but in the nineteenth century this view was impugned by what Lawrence Levine has called "the sacralization of culture," which produced a hierarchical model of cultural distinctions excluding commercial art from reverence. Prior to the thirties, commercial art had been attacked by old elites, who argued that it undermined moral values and leveled barriers (manners, lifestyles) between classes, and by genteel reformers, who thought it interfered with efforts to improve the mentality of laborers; both of these views saw culture as a bulwark against the marketplace and the mass public. High art, a category itself constituted in the nineteenth century, was ringed around with "sacred language and religious analogies" by cultural leaders. A notion of popular art had been very important to American populists, such as Whitman in *Democratic Vistas,* and remained so for cultural progressives, such as Gilbert Seldes who asserted in *The Seven Lively Arts* (1924) that culture was not the property of hereditary superiors or an isolated fetish.[31] With vested interest but vast influence, Hollywood, too, argued that popular art intermingled classes and celebrated mutual prosperity. As capitalism became the principal mode of disseminating culture in the twentieth century, the rise of mass culture, of what Dwight MacDonald, in 1944, defined as commodities impersonally produced to reach the widest possible markets (like Hollywood films), met with rising opposition from intellectuals on the Left, who associated it with social oppression, as well as the Right, who associated it with anarchy. In the age of mass culture, the ideas of "popular" (of the people) and "commercial" were increasingly opposed to each other by observers, memorably in the works of Nathanael West, F. Scott Fitzgerald, and the hard-boiled school of James Cain and Horace McCoy. In the thirties and forties, mass culture, defined in opposition to popular indigenous art (as celebrated in the Federal Writers' Project and the Popular Front), was attacked by antifascists and anti-Stalinists for its subversion of democracy. According to the critiques of the Frankfurt School and its American equivalent (Bernard Rosenberg and David Manning White), the democratic subject had been weakened by brutalizing factory labor and by the concentration of power in corporate monopolies and state bureaucracies; now mass culture promised to complete social domination by transmitting ideology through private consumption, where the aesthetic needs unfulfilled by alienated labor were displaced to the commodity.

Although the Frankfurt School's critiques of mass culture had always treated the consumer as rather mindless, they had also possessed a utopian dimension in common with the thinking of John Dewey. Art, Dewey wrote, would be generally accessible only in a "better-ordered society" where the "compartmentalization" of art from ordinary life had ended, when individuals had been freed from drudgery to enjoy aesthetic satisfaction in work and educated to perform the intellectual labor of experiment and solution.[32] Adorno differed from Dewey in assuming that until the methods of capitalist production were transformed to eliminate the alienation of labor and the commodity fetish, the autonomy of art would depend on an aesthetic elite, who must insist that mass culture was an instrument for administrative affect-control and the purveyance of false consciousness.[33] Lacking the utopian component of either Dewey or the Frankfurt School, the American cultural theories of the fifties turned from the issue of class inequality to the more nebulous concept of conformity.

THE POSTWAR cultural pluralists who displaced Marxist analyses listened to conservative voices, most especially T. S. Eliot's, in hopes of rehabilitating the quality of liberal thought and feeling so that its intelligentsia could more effectually counter the potentially leveling impact upon culture of democracy in a capitalist system. Their conservative counterparts conceived of culture as a whole way of life, sown and suffused by a breathing Christian world view, harmonizing functional classes.[34] As Eliot specifies in "Religion and Literature" (1935), conservatives were not defending a "highbrow" as against a "lowbrow" art, but an integrated cultural sensibility.[35] Eliot, Kirk, Kenner, and the former Agrarians resisted the bourgeois model of art as strongly as the Marxist Left; both views mutually repudiated idealist aesthetics and the aesthetics of genius, which, since the late eighteenth and the nineteenth centuries, had defined art in terms that made it reminiscent of a sacred object, inasmuch both were supposed to be separated from everyday life, born from a nonrational source, and received in an attitude of disinterested contemplation.[36] In contrast to their Marxist opponents, however, they located the dissociation of art and life in the roots of modern revolution, in the Reformation, the spirit of 1789, the unrest of 1848. The isolation of art, its confinement to museums for the literati, to the classrooms of the academe, or to the private collections of the nouveau riche, was the result of the dissolution of organic society and its replacement by the image of society as a machine of human intention without final form, a clanking Frankenstein monstrosity animated in the Jacobin, empiricist imagination of the eighteenth century and released, hulking, patched, and bolted, into the industrial age. Lionel Trilling had recommended Eliot's religious cultural philosophy to Marxist radicals as a corrective to their mechanistic view of society; nonetheless, he remained sufficiently influenced by John Dewey that he did not, even in doubt, proclaim the project of democratic culture a folly. In one of his more grim pieces, Trilling describes "unlettered" pontificators, with mundified sensibilities, who approximate Eliot's pessimistic estimate of democratic capitalist man, but he does not indulge in dystopian mass society images of deindividualization, atomization, and fragmentation.[37] Like Daniel Bell, Trilling resists the mass society thesis as an undemocratic and foreign imposition.[38] One could adopt Eliot's high concept of sensibility as educated emotion, or the fine extension of feeling into disciplined thought, without believing that sensibility required the base of a unified hieratic precapitalist culture.[39] Perhaps what Eliot defined as the conditions of "dissociation"—secularism, broken traditions, absence of orthodoxy, emphasis on personality—could be construed instead as aspects of an open society. Trilling's fellow pluralists, Leslie Fiedler, David Riesman, and Robert Warshow, positively appraised the diversity of patterns of education and consumption under industrial capitalism. They did not absolutely relativize cultural distinctions any more than Trilling or Bell, but they focalized America's capacity to accommodate various "taste-markets" and sensibilities, for this was evidence that it had not yet become the mass society of so many dire predictions from the Marxist Left and the conservative Right.[40] Since they denied that America was in fact a mass society (at least yet), pluralists treated the figures of "the mass men"—minimally conscious, ugly little machines of desire, preconditioned for totalitarian activation who consumed gobbets of mass culture—as a dystopian invention of conservatives and prewar

Marxists more appropriate to the European imagination. Just as there were many denominations in American society, so there could be many kinds of cultural knowledge and appetite, though some were clearly more deserving of institutional nurture and preservation than others.

The danger of mass culture nonetheless remained that it could expand its taste market, depressing the growth of other levels and becoming a substitute for what unifying orthodoxy and tradition had been in earlier stages of cultural development. In contrast to the Marxist Left of the thirties, moreover, liberals indemnified the audience as a major source of cultural recidivism. Whereas Marxists had analyzed the taste for mass culture as indicative of the "dehumanizing" effects of industrialization on workers' sensibilities, liberal pluralists interpreted taste as almost exclusively an effect of the structure of the commodity itself: inferior formal qualities, marked by the profit motive and standardized industrial production, which falsified reality.[41] Mass culture was too crude to bear the anxiety for meaning and certainty in modern life, as high art did, yet it was this very "experience of an alienation from reality" that gave it dreadful appeal.[42] Its kitsch lifted the consumer's fardel of misery without making him strain even a bit at the psychic cantilever. Almost irresistibly, mass culture insinuated itself into his worldview and became the epoxy of his inner life. Riesman was one of the few intellectuals in the period, along with Leslie Fiedler and Robert Warshow, who wrote with some degree of sympathy about movies, comics, or genre fiction, and he argues for the potential liberating aspects of mass culture, especially the star personality in Hollywood movies. Anticipating American Cultural Studies, he makes the creative possibilities within consumption a refrain of his *Individualism Reconsidered*.[43] This modest, and politically neutered, dissent notwithstanding, one source of consensus among liberal pluralists, conservatives, and socialists in the Cold War era remained a shared belief that mass culture must be contained, a belief summarized by Philip Rahv: "the proliferation of kitsch in this country under the leveling stimulus of the profit-motive is a liability of our society which is not be wished away by pious appeals to democracy and the rights of the 'common man.' But if under present conditions we cannot stop the ruthless expansion of mass culture, the least we can do is to keep apart and refuse its favors."[44] Under present conditions, egalitarian attitudes were designated as naively sentimental, subject to "Hornbeckian" superciliousness.

Seen in the context of the mass society theories that proliferated in the fifties, Kramer's troubled representation of the fundamentalists, as it vacillates between specifying their psychology to fanatics (as does Drummond) or generalizing it to the common man (as does Hornbeck), seems finally to protest itself. Although the film conveys esteem for Drummond's idealism, it betrays more fear of the star Brady and his fans. While fundamentalism, as a creed, seems restricted in the film to the rural Bible Belt, the underlying authoritarian mode of thought is not so clearly isolated. Rather than focus on Hillsboro's sectarianism, *Inherit the Wind* stresses via the Brady character—senator, onetime presidential candidate, renowned orator—the national ramifications of the town's aggressive conformity. Drummond's own arguments—in the courtroom or in private sessions with Bert Cates or Hornbeck—repeatedly underscore that what happens in Hillsboro has wider repercussions for American life. The Brady cultists are a mass phenomenon on a local level, but could their example also imply a national mass mentality? It is not necessary to insist on Kramer's final answer, since my intent has not been to establish an identity between situations in the film and theoretical positions, but instead to use *Inherit the Wind* as a way of staging how its Cold War liberal image of evangelicals resembles a democratic populace leveled by mass culture. The indiscriminate democratic consumer, precariously poised between utter dissolution and conformity to mass culture icons, is explicitly linked in Adorno to archaic religious experience. Kramer's film similarly associates the mass phenomenon in Hillsboro with an archaic breed of religion, and his antievangelical film—in its characterizations and its editorial camera style—has equivalents to the images of mass culture in Adorno's essays and Lowenthal's *The Prophets of Deceit*.

While not enveloping Kramer's liberal center, fundamentalism in the film is a breeding ground for cultural pathogens to which more of American democracy would be susceptible, if not for the secular faith of men like Drummond. The analogy between fundamentalist evangelicals and mass entertainment, moreover, is present in sources other than Kramer's film, explicitly in Richard Hofstadter's *Anti-Intellectualism in American Life* (Chapters 4 and 5), which emphatically equates evangelicalism with mass culture. Hofstadter believes the loss of Calvinism led less to a revaluation of Protestantism than to a devaluation of theology generally, as evangelicals threw more emphasis on the personality of ministers than on the creeds of learned exegetes: "[T]he work of a minister tended to be judged by his success in a single area—the saving of souls in measurable numbers. The local minister was judged either by his charismatic powers or by his ability to prepare his congregation for the preaching of some itinerant ministerial charmer who would really awaken its members. The 'star' system prevailed in religion before it reached the theater."[45] The lay "itinerant charmers" proved even more damaging than the local ministers, for in their efforts to carry religion to the western settlements, "the elite upon which culture depended was . . . debased by a rude social order" (80). The evangelical effort to procure souls outside of established ecclesiastical orders evolved into a religion of "vulgar populism" that has peaked in modern fundamentalism (127–128). The post–World War I fundamentalists suffered the first shock at the penetration of modern ideas into the schools, the arts, and the press. Their combative reaction to advanced secularization was "the first consequence for religion of the development of a mass culture, and of its being thrown into contact with high culture" (118). The lowbrow religion of these fundamentalists has returned in the contemporary far Right, whose near-fascism was seeded by generations of anti-intellectual cultural production. Hofstadter's initial observations, that with the passing of Calvinism seminaries also suffered the loss of much logical rigor and erudition, thus give way to less substantial claims that American mass culture, opposed to Enlightenment and progressive politics, practically developed with evangelical fundamentalism. Mass culture did exert pressure on the style of Protestant ministers, especially urban revivalists, but it was not an extension of backwoods religious populism. Rather, it was a production of the industrial society that churches confronted in the second half of the nineteenth century.[46]

Like Adorno's study of Martin Luther Thomas, Hofstadter's analysis is skewed by the Brown Scare imagery of the thirties. His interpretation seems overdetermined particularly by Sinclair Lewis's *Elmer Gantry* (1927), in which the resourceful heel-turned-evangelist Elmer (based largely on Billy Sunday) and his partner, Sharon Falconer (based on the flamboyant revivalist and radio star Aimee McPherson), satisfy the low church's illiterate tastes with the mass-market appeal of formats inspired by Hollywood, vaudeville, radio, and pulp. Believing in the same God of success as WASP moguls and imagining that he has been ordained to keep the lower classes appeased with "high-class preaching," meaning—with an irony he misses—the clabber of kitsch, entertainment, and the Bible gelled by his showmanship, Elmer steadily graduates from a half-believing hypocrite to a monomaniacal demagogue who brings hundreds of people to kneel before him in the street. The mass psychology of fascism is already incipient in the lowbrow style of worship.[47] After World War II, Lewis's Brown Scare visions received a renewed intellectual lease from the analysis of totalitarian state-culture. In the imaginations of traditional cultural conservatives such as T. S. Eliot as well as pluralists and left-wing cultural conservatives such as Dwight MacDonald, the protofascist banal culture that Elmer Gantry brings from the countryside to his fictional capital of Zenith became a "spreading ooze" that seemed to carry to extreme consequence the egalitarian and populist tendencies of liberal democracy, as "cultural leveling"

produced conformity—or worse, protototalitarian collectivity.[48] Fundamentalism was a metonym for this spreading ooze, yet, as the next chapter
partly examines, New Evangelicals also objected to "conformity," as did
liberal sociologists like David Riesman. They too disclaimed the influence of
mass culture and sought positions of resistance to it.[49]

In the process of imagining the mass society and bugbears to pluralism,
Cold War intellectuals tended to vilify mass culture for razing critical
thought and isolating elite culture rather than, as in Lewis, for habituating
the lower classes to their oppression.[50] The evangelical response, though
drawing on sequestered populist themes, was no serious alternative to that
of either the Eliotic conservatives or the liberal pluralists. It lacked the
former's powerful insights into the grinding, disintegrative effects of industrial capitalism upon labor, traditional communities, and the poor, while it
shared the latter's willingness to monitor the health of democratic society
by attending to what the middle class was consuming. It is important
to correct the distorted images of evangelicals in Kramer's, Lewis's, or
Hofstadter's depictions, but it is equally crucial to note that Billy Graham
and *Christianity Today* did little to dispel the impression that Americans
were evenly enjoying the era of "affluence" and "abundance." In their focus on the effects of Amercians' disposal of their leisure time and surplus
spending, the neofundamentalists and their liberal critics each elided the
Cold War corporate economy's unequal social distribution of wealth, welfare, and productive power, a problem that the era's theories of consumption also occluded. The long-term upshot, facilitated in part by the vagaries
of liberal pluralist cultural politics, has been the ascendance of an evangelical referendum on commercialism, or "materialism," that implicates
corporate power but guiltlessly celebrates free-market ideology as both a
populist and a godly instrument. Kramer's *Inherit the Wind* crystallizes the
idiom of liberal cultural politics, while Richard Brooks's film adaptation of
Elmer Gantry, explored in the next chapter, discloses its limiting assumptions and offers a more perspicacious, and indeed more jeremiadic, view of
the problem posed by popular evangelicalism and its quite conscious imitation of the market.

CHAPTER SIX

Jeremiads on the American Arcade and Its Consumption Ethic

> Like it or not, we are in competition with the entertainment industry.
>
> —One minister to another, *Elmer Gantry* (1960)

Adapting the Protestant Ethic to an Expanded Spiritual and Leisure Market

In the forties, Richard Brooks, a novelist and a screenwriter, contacted Sinclair Lewis about his desire to film *Elmer Gantry,* and the author gave his blessing.[1] After trying for nearly fifteen years to bring the project to fruition, Richard Brooks, now a director with several films to his credit, and the film's lead, Burt Lancaster, convinced United Artists in 1959 to back a film adaptation of *Elmer Gantry* that would retain some of the muckraking purpose of Lewis's novel.[2] Brooks embeds his adaptation in social contexts highlighted by Lewis's original, though these are newly configured within Cold War discourses on evangelicalism and on mass entertainment. While alluding to the showmanlike career of Billy Graham, the film levies its own judgment on American innocence, associated, strikingly, with the avowal of sin rather than its denial. Like Kramer's *Inherit the Wind,* the movie faced preemptive censorship from conservative Protestants, including a Baptist executive at Paramount who pushed Columbia to buy its way out of the contract, only to have Brooks and Lancaster refuse the offers.[3] The project's survival resulted in a film that offers the decade's most trenchant view of revivalism and the paradoxes of American churches' struggle to participate in secular culture by attracting a mass audience.

The chief of these paradoxes would be evangelicalism's fusion of the ethic of consumption with the legend of the political neutrality of the market as well as the conservative theology the New Evangelicals had promised to defend, even against doubters among old fundamentalists. Graham's style of revivalism anticipated this fusion even as David Riesman and William Whyte were proclaiming the timely, but by no means tranquil, end of the Protestant ethic amidst the society of high "productivity," "abundance," and "affluence." The Protestant ethic, at one time necessary to nineteenth-century capitalism, had devolved into a mere "success ethic," and was now being superseded by the consumer ethic of "the other-directed."[4] Though the development of this new personality type contained the danger of conformity, it was rehabilitable,[5] and a welcome alternative to the outmoded "success ethic" of which Lewis's George Babbitt, according to Riesman, was already a caricature in the twenties.[6] The Babbitts of America lived on, however, in the complex psychology of the middle class, for whom the old success ethic, with its traces of puritanical guilt and self-abnegation, interfered with the invitations of the ascendant consumer ethos (37, 208, 219–220). According to Riesman, the major domestic problem for the American in the mixed economy was overcoming his guilt and anxiety over how to spend his leisure time, a spiritual trial that thankfully affected youth less than it did older members of the middle class. Substituting for Veblen's theory of "conspicuous consumption," which indicts the irrational disposal of wealth from industrial productivity in private consumption to aggrandize an elite, Riesman effusively touted the democratic possibilities of "creative consumption," for which the suburbs, in contrast to the old robber barons, were to be the vanguard (273–285). Consumption was the new frontier where Adam could escape his guilt; as in the classic Western, "the pioneers" range over the "self-service market" where "the shopper's caprice and imagination can roam without interference" (211, 213).

Riesman believed the Protestant ethic was now the bane of American life, and Fredric Jameson (from further left of the political spectrum) has quipped: "There is no such thing as a booming, functioning market whose customer personnel is staffed by Calvinists and hard-working traditionalists knowing the value of the dollar."[7] However, there have been plenty of evangelicals who have successfully bridged consumerism and the Protestant ethic for which Riesman so hopefully delivered a requiem; they have succeeded, moreover, by accepting a Cold War market ideology, central in later neoconservative thought, to which liberalisms like Riesman's, and indeed liberalism since the Great Society experiment, have failed to offer a forceful retort. Indeed, the "New Democrats" of the nineties advanced this ideology themselves. Legendarily, the market performs the functions of the state without the risk of concentrating power in the government, which should be avoided because of "the evils of freedom and human nature itself" (273). The state raises the specter of totalitarianism and the market that of unruly self-interests, but evangelicals have preferred the assumptive populism of the market even while recognizing the market's own potentials for evil. The Neofundamentalists, particularly, are afraid of the concentration of economic power in organizations that could supersede the nation-state; the

New World Order of conspiracy theories à la *Left Behind* is clearly a phantasm of global finance capital and multinational corporations as well as One-World government.[8] Nonetheless, neofundamentalists accept the Cold War Right's structure of presenting the problem such that third alternatives are excluded as "Communism"; between the "lesser evil" of the potential imbalances of market control and the oppression of the absolute state, they choose the market and attempt to make it an instrument of God. They do not see the market as a mechanism only for checking the human will to power. Instead, Christian principles of stewardship and charity can restrain the urge to greed and self-interested self-reliance, while also directing spending and investment into religious niche markets with hoped-for crossover appeal where the products may serve to evangelize "outsiders" even as they act as devotional art to "insiders." One can spend on, or invest in, "good" goods. If commodities can be used both to proselytize and to celebrate prosperity, then one can separate the meaning of the marketplace as an instrument for evangelizing from the pursuit of economic self-interest, which, historically, Christians have placed under the sign of sin.

Moreover, the crossover appeal of Christian commodities, now recognized by major industries and retailers, has led to a new form of identity niche marketing, exemplified by *The Passion of the Christ* and Sony's distribution of the DVD release of *Left Behind III,* which makes the system seem egalitarian to believers. As the neoorthodox and the Althusserian Marxist each argue, no institution, no matter what authority it cites, enjoys full autonomy from its culture's reigning concepts or its socioeconomic base. The problem faced by modern revivalists, and augmented by developments in evangelical subculture since Graham's heyday, has been the risk that Protestants who engage modernity by competing with its attractions, undertaking operations involving outside investors, talent recruiters, pollsters, public relations staff, advertising men, and finance managers, as well as the imagery, techniques, and glamor of the entertainment industry, will lose whatever semiautonomy their institutions have had by virtue of their traditions, teachings, and confessions; or, in a more neoorthodox parlance, they risk losing the prophetic vision to judge culture rather than take an immanent view of it.

Identifying ethical responsibility for the depredations of the market becomes more difficult in a society of apparent affluence. Images of consumer choice and pleasure bombard audiences even as abundance and equality remain separated in fact.[9] Sympathetic with the adaptational pressures on churches, yet critical of their effect on the quality of American conscience, Richard Brooks's *Elmer Gantry* is distinguished by its focus on the diminution of guilt-consciousness in religion that is run like showbiz in a spiritual marketplace. It suggests that "sin is in" because Americans like to confess, even publicize, their guiltiness so that they can feel absolved for worshiping material success at human cost. Brooks's *Elmer Gantry* imagines how showbiz makes sin digestible, providing the necessary dose of guilt without alienating the audience or making it think critically about the capitalistic sources of its guilt. The film does not imply that the revivalists are aberrations of a potential mass society but sees them instead as epitomes of American enterprise, which makes success rather than integrity the measure of both culture and religion. *Gantry*'s emphasis on hypocrisy versus integrity, an ethical value untinged by association with any demonizable Marxist critique of capitalism, makes it a centrist liberal film. *Gantry* does not stand fully outside the cultural politics of Cold War liberalism, yet it does achieve sufficient distance to function as a criticism of the latter's assumptions. Addressing the fusion of popular evangelicalism and popular mass entertainment, *Gantry*'s representations disclose much more of this union's sources and implications than *Inherit the Wind*. *Elmer Gantry* stimulates us to view its protagonist's story with a prophetic eye cast toward possibilities beyond the conditions depicted, whereas Kramer's film implies a cozy agreement between filmmaker, liberal hero, and audience in which each is superior to the objects ridiculed.

Two Types of Jeremiads: Revivalism as Epitomizing American Commerce and Revivalism Bidding to Transcend It

Brooks had originally intended, like Lewis, to follow Elmer Gantry into academic as well as showbiz circles, but he wisely decided not to begin the film in Bible college and seminary. These passages of the novel had weighed the intellectual worth of theology, but the film, Lancaster convinced Brooks, should concentrate on Elmer's mature career as a religious con artist and showman. The screenplay telescopes the narrative to the midsection of Lewis's book, in which Elmer joins forces with Sharon Falconer, and interpolates relevant material from other chapters, such as Gantry's "frame-up" with a prostitute. Lewis's narrative is structured as a series of encounters in which Elmer ingratiates himself to different communities, manipulates them, and then narrowly escapes by the cooperation of amoral fortune and his own wits. Drawing on the novel's theatrical allusions, Brooks's film is structured instead around Elmer's and Sharon's performances. The movie opens with Elmer's impromptu Christmas Eve sermon in a saloon and closes with his improvised song service for Falconer's mourners. In between, the film is divided by six other shows, with the off-stage action (private seductions, revival planning, and business deals) counterpointing Elmer's and Sharon's star roles. In place of Lewis's satire, the film is appropriately gaudy and direct. Lewis's sustained irony, speaking critically through Elmer's self-acquitting point of view, is only possible in a literary medium, which permits for free indirect speech and hidden polemic. Making the most of film's limitations, Brooks lets Lancaster's acting style for Elmer—broad and nonnaturalistic, closer to pantomime and live theater than film—enhance the themes of showbiz and seduction. Lancaster plays the scenes outside the revival services (love interludes, business meetings, press conferences, police raids, train rides) in the same register as those inside, and the continuity emphasizes the way most of the characters around Elmer mirror him, always performing or making a pitch—wooing an audience, a lover, a church committee, a newspaper, or a business donor. The atmosphere inside the revival services and their rehearsals pervades the rest of the characters' lives.

A nearly broke traveling appliance salesman when the film opens, Lancaster's Elmer is a charlatan who gets into revivalism because he frankly wants to be a success, and is visibly astonished by his effect on audiences. He discovers the enchantment of being at the center of attention (Lancaster once said that Elmer is "basically a ham") as well as his star power, managing to convert 450 people out of 1200 in his first revival sermon. Elmer knows that the spirit moving inside him is not divine. After one of his glib "God is Love" messages, he turns to Pulitzer Prize–winning investigative reporter Jim Lefferts and cracks, "Think that was divinely inspired, Jim-boy!"[10] Yet he has discovered that he can succeed as an entertainer who excites people about the Gospel. Elmer does not really answer Jim's question, "Do you believe in *God?*" but he does answer affirmatively for religion: "Prayer's the cheapest first-rate medicine I know." Elmer's medicine, it turns out, packs a dose of quinine as well as honey. Sharon opens her meeting by promising that she is no scare preacher, but when Elmer gets his first chance to address the audience, he takes a drastically different tack: "I'm gonna give you all the hell in the Bible! I'm bringin' back the Old Time Religion!" Jim Lefferts comments: "I've seen many a good Bible-walloper in my day, but you not only put the fear of God into 'em, you scare the Hell out of 'em!" Elmer's "Old Time Religion" nets him the biggest mass conversion of Sharon's revival, including one man who runs screaming into the aisle begging for salvation and another so mortified that he is reduced to barking like a dog. Sharon's manager, Bill Morgan, believes Elmer's style of preaching is in bad taste, but Sharon and Elmer synthesize their presentations in a manner Morgan well summarizes: "One minute you're preaching a perfume-scented heaven, the next minute Gantry terrifies them with a stinking hell. . . . Like two cops working over a guy; Gantry scares him with the electric chair, then he confesses and you save him."

The fear Elmer strikes into the crowd is not so much the fear of God as the fear of material failure coupled with guilt over greed and hustling. Elmer introduces the topics of sin and damnation after a long, fabricated testimonial about his own salvation from corrupt salesmanship. God, he says, teaches him "the good, hard, dollars and cents value of Christ in Commerce. . . ." After a hard week of dishonest business and poor sales, his broken businessman prays for redemption over a Gideon Bible and in reward reaps bigger profits than ever before: "Thank ya' Lawd. I didn't make that sale—You did." Elmer's apocryphal salesman finds success through salvation and in the process expunges the guilt over his materialism. Responding to this self-exculpatory message, the sinners in the crowd flock to the altar, occasionally in paroxysms. After Elmer helps to refurbish Sharon's revival machine with his message of sin, salvation, and success, it joins forces with big business in the figure of George Babbitt, a character cleverly folded in from an earlier Lewis novel. As in *Babbitt* (1922), the eponymous character in Brooks's film is a social-climbing, flag-waving real estate man, on the Zenith city council as well as its committee of Protestant churches. Acting as the Falconer troupe's go-between in Zenith, Babbitt explicitly ties the Old Time Religion's idea of salvation to free enterprise and bad conscience. Elmer's sermons in the small towns make a success of guilt, and in the city Babbitt gives Elmer new ways of showing people how to be penitent without contradicting free enterprise. Outside the Zenith revival tent, picketers wave signs reading, "God does not support labor unions," and Elmer and Babbitt both rail at socialists and "anarchists," while Babbitt buys Elmer radio time to drub the muckraking "yellow press" and its "atheistic" sympathizers at the universities: "Darwinism, Harvardism, Yalism, and Princetonism." Investigative journalism, a threat to Babbitt's business practices, is damned by association with the intellectuals. After the fashion of Billy Sunday, Elmer rallies the people to defend Prohibition and the sanctity of the streets, so long as they stay out of precincts where Babbitt, visible at all of Elmer's public events, owns property, including speakeasies and brothels. Babbitt, like Elmer, believes that religion is good for business and good for American society, and so long as he publicly supports it, his mendacity is balanced in the moral account.

DESPITE his likeness to Babbitt, Brooks's Elmer always remains more sympathetic than the businessman or Elmer as he appears in Lewis's novel, even though all three are hypocrites. Lancaster's input helped to reshape

Gantry, whom he, like Brooks, believed was too dehumanized in the book: "Sinclair Lewis wrote Elmer Gantry as a caricature; he made him so one-sided and so bad that it was hard to identify with him. . . . With Dick Brooks I felt that an audience had to recognize something human in him."[11] That "something human" is a capacity for self-recognition, which Lewis's character sorely lacks. As in the novel, Brooks and Lancaster's Elmer can connect with his audience because he shares their lust for financial and social mobility. What separates him from the other Christians on the make, as reporter Jim Lefferts well understands in the film, is Elmer's honest recognition of his egoistic drive. When Jim slugs a heckler for Elmer, he pays his begrudging respect to the evangelist's hard-boiled self-analysis, which—albeit saddled to hypocrisy—is preferable to the escapism of other Americans who believe that quick and painless penitence atones for exploitation, that ruthlessly gotten success is the reward for accepting salvation. In Jim's estimate, Elmer at least knows he is playing a bunko game, whereas Lewis's Elmer remains half convinced that Providence is on his side. Such blinding justifications are necessary to Lewis's Elmer, for the evangelist has imbibed so much phoniness so adeptly that he cannot help but remain an accomplice of evil. By contrast, Elmer in the film is finally capable not only of seeing the false values of his religious culture, but also of renouncing his role as its performer. After Sharon burns in her tabernacle, the chastened Elmer greets her mourners by quoting from Paul: "When I was a child, I spake as a child, I understood as a child, I thought as a child; but when I became a man, I put away childish things" (1 Corinthians 13:11). In the context of the epistle, Paul is telling the believer to humbly await the day when God will reveal His mysteries more fully to man; in the context of the film's conclusion, Elmer quotes the apostle to admonish Christians against the idolatry of their own beliefs, which identify righteousness with all-too-human forms of religiosity. The evangelist himself has undergone a kind of conversion that has matured him. He can no longer playact the role of the Lord's agent, the Professional Good Man. The film's final image brings to mind a scenario that Frank Shallard fantasizes in Chapter 28 of the novel: "I *am* going to get out of the church! Think of it! A *preacher,* getting religion, getting saved, getting honest, getting out. Then I'd know the joys of sanctification."[12] The last shot shows Elmer, after declining to stay and continue the revival, donning his hat and leaving the site of the tabernacle. Whether his decision to "put away childish things" entails the renunciation of Christianity altogether is openended. As Elmer exits the frame, he walks beneath a cross, charred but still aloft.

Elmer is at the very least abandoning revivalism, as the *sine qua non* of commercially corrupted religion; he is renouncing, as well, the example set by the career of the world's best-known evangelist. Brooks researched the lives of Billy Sunday and Aimee McPherson, but he also kept a separate file labeled "Billy Graham." Brooks would later deny that Graham had been a model for any of the film's characters, but he had in fact amassed "newspaper and magazine articles on which he pencil-marked the salient characteristics" of Graham's pulpit techniques.[13] After a long interim—the professional city revival had been defunct for twenty years—Graham's success dredged up memories of past excesses and Sinclair Lewis's monument to them. As with his predecessors, Graham's personality was magnetizing, extended by mass media outlets (TV chiefly) unavailable in the twenties. On the heels of the L. A. revival, the Luce magazines *Time* and *Life* sounded that Graham was the successor to Billy Sunday and Aimee McPherson. Gossip columnist Louella Parsons conducted an interview with him, and director Cecil B. DeMille *(The Ten Commandments)* offered him a screen test for his next biblical epic.[14] However, European newspapers, in terms Lewis would have appreciated, scoffed that Graham was "a Hollywood version of John the Baptist" and "a salesman in God's company" (186). These were accusations that would dog Graham through the fifties, in America as well as Europe. In *Billy Graham: Revivalist in a Secular Age* (1959), McLoughlin makes much of the fact that Graham was a Fuller Brush salesman before entering seminary, and he believes that Graham has the high pressure techniques of a colporteur.

Certainly there was no denying the many mercantile aspects of his revival enterprise, compounded by his use of the William F. Bennett Advertising Agency, celebrity galleries, and big business donors, and nowhere more obvious than in the way he advertised: "Sixth Great Sin-Smashing Week," "Dazzling Array of Gospel Talent," "Hear America's Sensational Young Evangelist," "God's Ball of Fire." Neofundamentalistic evangelicals have been great beneficiaries of one of keynotes of both secularization and corporate capitalism: the phenomenon of consumerism in which in religion itself is a commodity in "a spiritual marketplace."[15] Instead of commodification leading to the demise of official religion, as some twentieth-century theorists, such as Walter Benjamin, once predicted, we have seen official religions increasingly produce commodities to carry their message.[16] Billy Graham Ministries pioneered in the areas of television and filmmaking, yet, throughout his enterprises, Graham insisted that the evangelicals were appropriating secular culture on their own terms: "Clearly the Lord was setting our course for the immediate future. In the one year between Los Angeles and Atlanta, we had developed an organization, a radio broadcast, a film ministry, a financial policy, and a compatible Team."[17] Graham, like other revivalists, believed that the conversion crisis was powerfully emotional, but the guilt, release, and joy the convert underwent were effects of the Spirit's persuasion rather than passions stimulated by his devices. The ministry roused emotions that made the sinner malleable— Graham, like other professional revivalists, was direct on this point—but eventually the sinner was taken by the Spirit of God. Of course, those like McLaughlin who contended that Graham was a showman or a showman-demagogue were least inclined to accept his explanations that his success had nothing to do finally with artifice, sensational forms of persuasion, or the selling of consumable emotions.[18]

Clearly more persuaded by Graham's critics, Brooks's film extends Lewis's critique of showbiz and commercial values in American evangelicalism by staging an incisive debate not contained in the novel. It is featured in perhaps the film's most remarkable scene, which moves fifties boardroom drama fare into the unexpected setting of a church committee meeting.[19] It ensues when the Falconer revival campaign is invited to Zenith by George F. Babbitt, who requests that Zenith's committee of Protestant churches vote to bring the revival to the city. When a minister educated at the Harvard Divinity School, Reverend Philip, protests that the revival is a mockery of Christianity (words from the film's prologue), he is rebutted by another parson desperate to increase attendance at his church: "But, Phil, my churches are half-empty. Like it or not, we are in competition with the entertainment industry." When Philip demurs to liken religion to entertainment, Babbitt persists: "But, Phil, you oughtta. It's up to us to make a success out of Christianity. Christianity is a going concern. It is an international enterprise." The tacit assumptions of the revivalists are laid bare; the profit motive is now the Apostle's creed. Adding that churchmen must make a thriving enterprise of Christianity not only for the sake of Zenith, but for the sake of America, Babbitt makes an appropriate enough plea, since red, white, and blue are the dominant color motifs of the revival.

As a metaphor of American mores, the film's many confidence games (a metaphor steeped in Melville, Twain, Hammett, Fitzgerald, and W. C. Fields as well as Lewis) illustrate the paradox of success for churches that evangelize in a society where religion, like most other forms of culture, is on the market. To what extent they can negotiate that market and remain both doctrinally sound, evangelistic, and critical of society is the film's enduring question. Urban revivalism, McLoughlin and Brooks charge, was one wrong answer. Yet to comprehend the long-term implications of Graham's success for subsequent evangelical forays into mass culture, one must grasp how the evangelist himself combated charges of commercialism. Graham did want to be seen as a cultural authority and a prophet of culture's weaknesses, and not simply one of its marketable products. His authority, he believed, was moral rather than intellectual, but he was not unwilling to assume the role of public intellectual where it complemented the premises of his faith. By acting this part, Graham could also distance his image from mass entertainment, which continued to shadow his ministry.

Early in his public career, Graham's attacks on American culture were largely pietistic, like those he had directed at Hollywood in his Los Angeles Crusade. Movies, music stars, and pulp writing inspired rebellious youth, juvenile delinquency, crime, illicit sex, profanity, and disrespect for the home. Here Graham was following a line of criticism in common with the Catholic Legion of Decency and those Protestant reformers who wanted to protect citizens from the sinful influences of the movies and other urban distractions. He also denounced consumerism and commercial values for their spiritual impoverishment: "The American way of life' we like to call this fully electrified, chrome-plated economy of ours—but has it made us happy? Has it brought us the joy and the satisfaction and the reason for living we were seeking? No."[20] As he became ensconced in the Protestant establishment, Graham would also adopt the mass society thesis in his judgments about secular culture. No longer scrapping for prestige, now an adviser to presidents and in polls recognized as one of the world's most admired men, Graham had the clout to mimic the part of a cultural critic while leaning on the moral authority of a religious leader. In *World Aflame* (1965), Graham diagnoses the "symptoms of Madison Avenue's and Holly-wood's power of suggestion":

> The movies and television with equal ease lead and change the nation's thoughts on politics, morals, and social questions of great importance. In the darkness of a living room or theater, where people sit relaxed to give undivided attention to the flashing pictures, psychological conditions are perfect for insinuating ideas into the mind. In test after test among high school and university students, it has been proven that a movie or a television program can brainwash. . . . The movies, television, radio, the sensual novel, the cheap magazine all have combined to make it almost impossible for the masses to do any real individual thinking. . . . Are we becoming a robot civilization, manipulated by mass media, pressurized by conformity and pushed by political maneuvers? . . . Are we collectivizing the mentality of America?[21]

The phrases here are well-worn and were certainly passé in 1965 when the pop and camp movements were accelerating. Graham's belated cultural critique is nonetheless interesting because he uses it for ends obverse to those of Adorno, Trilling, Brooks, Tillich, or Dwight MacDonald. Graham is not interested in protecting elite culture, but its presentation of an alien and degenerating modern world seems to him yet another call to repentance. In Chapter 20 of *World Aflame*, "Signs of the End," he warns of the

Anti-Christ, a "World Dictator," who will dominate the people and use modern technology to control their minds (190–195). Mass culture is preparing the people mentally for the impending conspiracy, and the only protection from "brainwashing" is a commitment to Christ the Almighty, who is above culture. Paul Tillich tried to save "the name of God" from its "unembarrassed use" in the national revival by finding religious depth in high secular culture; Graham tried to save American citizens for Christianity by goading them from the gloss, conformity, and depthlessness of secular culture to the churches.[22] Graham's commitments were to Christian and especially evangelical institutions, and his criticism was designed to affirm their autonomy from the culture industry, even as he borrowed some of its means of attracting audiences.

Moreover, Graham, too, used modern literature as a source for forms of prophecy, though in this capacity he construed them as cultural warning signs of the Apocalypse. He found much support for the premillennial motifs of his message in high culture, especially modernist art and philosophy, to which he alludes frequently in *World Aflame*. In "Signs of the End," he points to several writers who have described the true "mental state of the world": "[Jesus] said the generation before His return would be under severe pressure from every point of view and there would be no apparent way out. This sounds very much like something written by Sartre, Camus, Huxley, Hemingway, or some other modern writer. In fact, Jean-Paul Sartre wrote a book called *No Exit*."[23] Huxley's drug-abusing characters in *Brave New World* show how modern men, unable to cope with "life's rough edges," numb themselves with artificial, escapist pleasures (119). The famous lines from the conclusion of T. S. Eliot's "The Hollow Men," "This is the way the world ends, / Not with a bang but a whimper," chant of "man's ultimate failure" and the terrible judgments upon his pride (168). However much these writers share his dystopian view of the present, Graham does not intend them as examples of a latent Church, for their prophetic tone seems accidental to their decadence. The existentialists, he laments, have either destroyed absolute values or resigned themselves to this destruction; Albert Camus has seen man's reason for existence disappear (40, 54). Because they have no faith in an afterlife, the writings of "William Faulkner, James Joyce, Ernest Hemingway, Eugene O'Neill, and many others are filled with pessimism, darkness, and tragedy" (110).

As in articles writers contributed to *Christianity Today*, Graham's allusions give the (rather transparent) illusion that he too is inside the elite's cultural circuits and capable of distilling the truth in high modern art for those less educated.[24] In the works of Eliot and others, he respects the denial of cultural affirmation and the intimations of apocalypse, but this truth is partial, needing the supplement of faith. In effect, Graham is demystifying high culture for his readers. They do not need to feel at a disadvantage to the intellectuals, for they already know what is worth knowing in modern literature. As for the aesthetic experiences of ambiguity and alienation, Graham has no use for them. His cultural criticism does exactly what Trilling had chastised in *The Liberal Imagination*: it bases its judgments of value solely on the moral correctness of ideas. To dismiss this side of *World Aflame* as kitsch criticism, however, is to argue with Graham on grounds he would not have honored. Kitsch was a value category for making formal distinctions between genuine and pseudo culture, regardless of its sacred or secular origin, while Graham held all culture subject to the kerygma of the Holy Bible, and it was the Bible's message, its values, not its poetry, that made it sacred. Tillich, theorizing the "God above God," conferred sacred meaning on art that confronted men with their existential condition. For Graham, though some cultural products might express disaffection with the modern world, these artifacts could not be taken as revelation. They are not ways to faith but symptoms of the world's faithlessness. Graham, in sum, does not cross the bridge between aesthetics and religion.[25] While Tillich, Brooks, and Merton believed art could broach spiritual states, Graham placed no value on aesthetic experience in his writings because he did not categorize faith as a mode of imagination, contemplation, or expression. Faith must be expressed, but it is not expressive; it is an experience of grace mediated by the Holy Spirit.

Liberal defenders of art and intellect against the lords of kitsch would have undoubtedly found the terms of Graham's resistance to the secular mass mind quaint, at the mildest, yet they offered no compelling alternative to his interpretation of the culture of commodities. Riesman, together with liberal pluralists like Trilling and Fiedler, sought to cantilever Americans' cultural demands and judgments, without implicating, aside from shadowy allusions to "the profit motive," the corporativist control of ownership, supply, and distribution or that system's creation of artificial needs to maximize profit and colonize leisure. Improved taste, where possible, could offset, perhaps even alter, the habitual intake of bad mass culture and thus have a salubrious effect on democratic society as a whole. This diagnosis resulted in merely a descriptive analysis of mass culture's effects on consumers, generally supported by paltry ethnographic evidence. Corporate capital's role in building a "power elite," as classically analyzed by C. Wright Mills, was minimized by liberals like Bell, who dismissed Mills as "conspiratorial" and Riesman, who countered with a theory of pluralistic "marginal" groups saved from ideological politics by creative consumption or "the opportunities of the audience to individuate responses to canned, mass-distributed products."[26]

Even Brooks's film, which decries the pro market, antilabor bias of revivalism, differentiates the levels of cultural capital it represents in mass-psychological rather than class-economic terms. Brooks's evident fascination with the worship services is mixed with suspicion of the crowd's irrationality, and in the final scene, as the Waters on the Jordan Tabernacle smolders, fire pours on everyone gathered in a setting that looks like Hell, with the false Christians burning and wailing. Brooks roasts the congregants, for they are the demand side of the Falconer troupe's business equation, and they are a mob of irretrievable ignoramuses.[27] Presumably they do not read Tolstoy as Jim Lefferts admits he does in his leisure moments. As an intellectual who is also a minister, Reverend Philip suggests a bridge between faith and high culture, but his credentials on both sides are elite ("HAAAARVard!" mocks Babbit, with a shrug). As for Jim, it is impossible on the basis of the film's evidence to ascertain how he became a savant, whether by college education or autodidactic regimen—this very ambiguity is significant. The liberal voice in these postwar social problem films is typically an intellectual (compare Drummond in *Inherit the Wind,* for instance) who is more enlightened than most folk simply because he has had the curiosity, the will, the fortitude, and the courage to ask questions. Complex thought does not help to individuate him; he thinks complexly because he is individuated. These presentations of the intellectual as individualist obscure the relation of taste to cultural capital, which is highly correlated to socioeconomic class and status.[28] There is a comparable disconnect between taste and privilege in the representation of the mass audience, whose pleasures derive from some interface of desire and ideology that is conditioned by nothing, it seems, besides bad culture itself. Much as Graham offered a spiritual nave for Christians to vertically transcend American materialism, the Cold War liberal critique of American life made high culture into a realm of speculative freedom, existential drama, and moral nurture by uncoupling it from the limiting conditions of property, income, pedigree, family, and peerage. In the "mixed economy," with its open society and plural taste markets, class was *deus-absconditus.* Evangelical populism, feeding on antielitism and bad conscience yet articulating no class consciousness, benefitted (and continues to do so) from the same analytical ellipsis.

Though it also trucks in ill-founded mass-psychological representations of taste, Brooks's film ultimately avoids the smugness of the scenario in Kramer's *Inherit the Wind,* where the stouthearted hero is pitted against the susceptible mass. Unlike so many other liberal films of the decade, *Elmer Gantry* has no moral center like Henry Drummond in *Inherit Wind* or Rick Dadier (Glenn Ford) from Brooks's own *The Blackboard Jungle* (1955). Instead of transcending his society, Jim Lefferts is bemused by it, and he does not seek to redeem it but to embarrass it. However chagrined he is by American greed and boobery, he empathizes with its pipe dreams, even its religious ones, and for all his astringency on the printed page, he is also charmed by Elmer and Sharon's con game. Jim admires the way Gantry "strings words together: America—home—mother—heaven—hell." The newspaper man sees American society as a sort of bunko-game with every man on the make, and Elmer is Horatio Alger par excellence. When Jim publishes his devastating exposé of the Falconer business, he continues to smile at Elmer like some wayward progeny and exchange ripostes with him during Prohibition marches. "Nothing personal," he says to Elmer, as he offers him a friendly swig of whiskey. In Brooks's film the society is so thoroughly corrupted by the quest for success that even the ostensible liberal spokesman is not unscathed by it. He drinks with the devil he damns.

It is tempting to say that the film expresses the bad conscience of liberal pluralism. Yet it seems more likely that the film is straining to find a preserve in high culture from a pervasive confusion of orders of value—market and salvational—that it has the perspicacity to link to evangelicalism's efforts, then finessed, now stertorous, to accommodate its conservative theology to market ideology and the ethos of consumption. The film, to its credit, revives from Lewis's novel its criticism of the complicity of both market values and commercial culture in creating false consciousness. Thus, innocence, as self-deception and pretense, is the *avowal* of sin that minimizes the guilt of the market and of the plutocratic control of product and investment. It is perhaps because Brooks and Lancaster make this crucial connection that the film also registers doubts about the pluralist position that so long as mass culture could be confined and high culture sealed, the diversity of taste-markets would demonstrate the democratic fruits of national abundance. Of the many films that have since addressed evangelical popular religion, from *Angel Baby* (1961), *Wise Blood* (1979), *Oh God!* (1977), *Leap of Faith* (1992), to Robert Duvall's wonderful *The Apostle* (1997), Brooks's *Elmer Gantry* is still singular for representing its title character as an icon not of the pernicious side of mass religion, but of the American quest for innocence from the guilt which its scrambling self-makers cannot avow without indicting the social effects of their success.

Before leaving *Elmer Gantry* (1960), I must comment on the film's ending, which hauls a literal miracle and damnation by flame into its universe. The night Sharon dedicates her Waters on the Jordan Tabernacle, she sees a shooting star and takes it as a sign of God's blessing. After delivering a short sermon on faith, "without which we are morally sick," she performs a faith healing on a man struck deaf years ago during a thunderstorm. Laying her hands on his head and asking for God's mercy, she does indeed open the man's ears. There is no evidence that the healing has been staged, and even Jim and Elmer seem awestruck. Suddenly, a bucket of paint and spattered rags explodes (someone has carelessly tossed a cigarette in the just recently finished building), setting afire the awning and banners. Soon there is a conflagration, and the crowd of Christians in panic begin stampeding each other. "Please wait! You are in the house of God!" cries Sharon, "You must have faith! If you only have faith, all will be okay!" In reply, one of the Christians swats the Bible from Sharon's hand and then belts her in the face. Elmer and Jim are carried by the stampede out of the tabernacle and into the river, while Sharon burns to death inside. Following the miracle, the blaze seems less accidental than divinely fated. What is one to make of this sequence? God grants Sharon's prayer, affirming the people's idea that she is a saint, and then incinerates them. What could have possibly induced Brooks to make the supernatural God manifest and then make His intentions mysterious? The heavy symbolism of the fire makes clear the moral judgment on the crowd, but what kind of deity is punishing them? Sharon keeps shouting that they lack faith, but faith in what kind of Christian God, if He makes an entertainer into a saint only to destroy her minutes later or grants the crowd a miracle and then brings down the rafters before anyone can make it to the altar for repentance? One gathers the impression that Brooks has created an American Arcade so defiled that at the climax he has brought in a literal deus ex machina to give it just desserts, and while I do not want to push hard for any particular theological orientation, this force resembles the enigmatic, terrible, and crushing God of Judgment in the Calvinist imagination. By resorting to Reformed images of hellfire and wrath, the liberal Brooks seems to show that he is more rankled by "moral sickness" than are the prostituted churches. The spectacular and divine explosion at the end of *Elmer Gantry* (1960) may be a shrill demonstration that however much cheap salvation may take the onus off guilt, sin—unshrifted—remains.

PART FOUR

Versions of Inwardness in Cold War Psychology and the Neo-Gothic

CHAPTER SEVEN

Controversies over Therapeutic Religion

Americans have forgotten the Biblical rule, "Chasten thy sons while there is hope, and let not thy soul spare for his crying." . . . We have turned to the psychiatrist and we have all sorts of books on the home . . . on how to rear children . . . [but] there are more unhappy homes today than ever before in our history. . . . You know what the devil's philosophy is today? Do as you please. Kick up your heels. Modern psychology is going along with the present program and psychologists are saying, "Don't spank your children, you'll warp their personalities."

—Billy Graham, quoted in McLoughlin, *Billy Graham: Revivalist* (1959)

Christine Penmark, the heroine-victim of William March's Gothic thriller *The Bad Seed* (1954), rises on a summer morning to the sounds of an awakening neighborhood: "an automobile starting in the distance, the twittering of sparrows in the live oaks that lined the quiet street, the sound of a child's voice raised suddenly and then hushed."[1] As she moves about the house, she is pleased by how orderly it is, nothing amiss in any of the rooms or cluttering the "wide elaborate hall with its elegant, old-fashioned parquetry floors." Her home is tasteful, but not exceptional for the shoreside community of Pelican Bay, where comely facades line up neatly on each lane. Neighbors debate over whether to receive guests in their "paneled dining-rooms" or "the little alcoves off [their] living rooms" trimmed with ferns and violets (41). Parents send their children to the Benedict Grammar School, which has reasonable enough rates for lower-income middle-class families like the Daigles as well as the more affluent households like the Penmarks. During the school year, the Fern sisters instruct the children in "the niceties, even some of the elegancies of fastidious living" and the "practical matters," while they pass their summers holding community picnics on their school grounds (20). Over these frolics and neighborly parties, the people in Mrs. Penmark's orbit talk casually about "the age of anxiety," make mincing jokes about the hydrogen bomb, and venerate the "inspired" Dr. Wertham (30, 27, 44).[2] The neighborhood in Pelican Bay seems as impeccable and placid as Christine Penmark's fair, bovine reflection in the bathroom mirror, where mornings she practices "putting on her first, tentative trial smile of the day" (5). Never one to attend Sunday School or even read the Bible (which she finds violent and primitive), Christine has chosen to preserve a positive image of God by shearing Him of any "of the bloodier precepts": "She had never been religious in the accepted sense of the word, but she'd always believed in the power that had once shaped the universe, and guided it now. She chose to think of that power as benign" (107).

In these opening images, which establish Christine Penmark's milieu, March presents a caricature of the secure postwar home, the place where many Americans thought they "might be able to ward off their nightmares . . . control their destinies and perhaps even shape the future."[3] The narrator's tone is never satiric, but as it accumulates details about the neighborhood's perfection, the description becomes grotesque, a picture of ideality so achieved it is alien. The dreamy air of Pelican Bay, where the small talk treats war, nuclear annihilation, and delinquency as matters of finesse, recalls many other vapid, predisaster communities in fifties' pop fiction, from Linda Rosa in *The War of the Worlds* to Santa Mira in *Invasion of the Body Snatchers*. Pelican Bay, however, is not set in the Southwest, where desert winds and mountain shadows are ominous with massing alien invaders or natural forces about to go amok. A well-bred community that has opened its sanctuary to up-and-coming families, Pelican Bay is insistently "the locale of the good life, the evidence of democratic abundance" (162).

Within the Penmark home, all is staid as Christine, having perfected her smile, greets her daughter Rhoda, so prim and organized that she is already dressed, her hair combed and plaited, her face "fixed in a solemn expression of innocence."[4] "I never deserved such a capable child," Christine marvels, "When I was eight years old, I doubt if I could if I do anything" (5). Dr. Spock might have disagreed with Christine's modesty, for the Penmark home is appropriately child-centered, all adult effort geared toward making little Rhoda a success. Now that Mr. Penmark has departed for South America to do work for his steamship company, Christine will have even more time to shower on her prodigy, and if Rhoda should want for another playmate, the next-door divorcée and lay psychoanalyst Mrs. Breedlove, who finances the local psychiatric clinic, will snap to entertain the little girl, who is fascinatingly devoid of childhood neuroses. On this June morning, as Christine prepares to take Rhoda to the Ferns' picnic, she cannot foresee that weeks from now the picnic will seem the hour when "the bad seed" became manifest. For now, only the narrator's proleptic vantage can appreciate the vanity of the adults as they fawn over Rhoda, whose braids are tied "in two thin hangman's nooses," the macabre description foreshadowing executions the desperate mother and the cool child will carry out. Within a few weeks, precocious little Rhoda will have slain two people, the second and third victims of her budding career, and driven her mother to attempted murder and suicide.

The child's evil comes from an original stain, a curse, and not from any lack of love or positive reinforcement, which abound in her environment (85). The bad seed she carries is an "inborn, predestined thing" (151). The theologically evocative language points less to a positive corruption than to an absence. Lethally innocent, the child is dangerous because she is mentally prelapsarian, guilt-free. March's novel offers several theories (including congenital insanity) for Rhoda's remorselessness, but, as *The Bad Seed* depicts the beliefs of adult characters, it continually circles the idea that Rhoda's symptoms are actually common to the human race. The novel builds a case that Rhoda Penmark is no mutant, but the natural man given full rein in an overindulgent, consumerist, therapeutic environment. Mixing equal parts *Totem and Taboo* and John Calvin, the story's pop-Freudian mythology, with bloody origins pursuing the civilized present, complements its theological pessimism, which might be likened to the cry of the typical Gothic protagonist: "God, why hast thou made me thus?"

Called a "baby gorgon" in one memorable review, Rhoda Penmark, the outrageous fictional scion of Alabama-born William March, who set out to become the South's next great novelist and ended up being remembered for his ace thriller about family dementia and sin, was a cause célèbre as well as a commercial triumph. Possibly the most lauded potboiler of its era, the source of both Maxwell Anderson's long-running, Tony-winning play and an MGM film (1956), March's novel, like its permutations in theater and film, is a broadside at most of the premises of what would shortly be defined as "the therapeutic" and was already being called America's new secular faith.[5] One can imagine the novel's favorable reviewers, who included the old cultural rebels Malcom Cowley and Ernest Hemingway, topplers of the Victorian matriarch in their generation, gleefully releasing Rhoda from her barbed-wire playpen to stomp on the domesticators of Freud.[6] Today, "the therapeutic," a term we have inherited from such critics as the Catholic conservative Philip Reiff, describes the fateful transference of the values of mental health to those of religion.[7] Even in the fifties, as scrutinized in highbrow, professional, and expressly religious forums, the postwar cooperation of Christians with the therapeutic movement was described as the undoing of orthodox belief. Actually, it contained some of the most complex intellectual achievements of Protestant modernism. "The therapeutic," as we have come to call it, should be more appropriately restricted to naming the simplistic ideological and pop-psychological extrapolations of this serious body of thought. "The therapeutic" is justly caricatured by Billy Graham and *The Bad Seed*. The intellectuals whose ideas the ideology of the therapeutic trammels, however, were avowedly realistic—rejecting sentimentality and cultural innocence— yet, in contrast to other realisms, nontragic in their outlook. Exchanging diverse secular and religious viewpoints on human nature, they imagined the remedial possibilities of nurture (medicinal, familial, institutional) in a democratic society.

One of the salient attitudes of the Cold War was the liberal confidence that psychological expertise could have a large hand in nurturing and adjusting Americans to their image of democratic fitness, imagined in tandem with personal well-being and social equilibrium.[8] During the forties, and under the auspices of the National Mental Health Act (1946), government-funded research into "syke" warfare, crowd management, and treatment for "war neuroses" had raised psychology to unprecedented levels of accreditation and respect.[9] Psychologists, especially such clinicians as Harry Stack Sullivan, did not simply argue for reforms of asylums, but yoked social reform to the prognosis of the American public's mental health. Mental illness, its definition expanded to a variety of "neurotic" behaviors and feelings besides acute psychopathologies, was now a dysfunction that pointed to the lag between culture and science. These sources of imbalance could, however, be cured and even prevented by early and sustained treatment. Dissolving "conventional distinctions between positive mental health and social welfare," individual "adjustment" and "public policy," the national mental health movement had the imprimatur of the liberal intelligentsia, who imagined that the authoritarian exercise of coercive state power could be averted by methods of "psychological management on a social level—releasing uncomfortable tensions here, adjusting sources of strain there—and transforming the exercise of power into something resembling psychiatric treatment" (25).[10] Psychotherapy, in forms ranging from consumer-friendly manuals to outpatient private care, particularly benefitted from close cooperation with mental health professionals, and ascendent among its schools was psychoanalysis, its influence extending beyond medicine to become a cultural logic. During World War II, the influx of refugee analysts from Germany had made America the world's "center of psychoanalysis,"[11] and by the mid-fifties, Lionel Trilling had placed Freudian thought at the center of "the American educated middle class, expressed in that class's theories of education, child-rearing, morality, and social action."[12]

Though it did not endorse the idea that the new "secular religion" could substitute for faith, liberal Protestantism nonetheless played a substantial role in the heavily theorized and popular shift towards therapeutic psychology among the middle class.[13] The most ballyhooed of the psychological schools, psychoanalysis also had the most anti-Christian lineage because of Freud's candid atheism and his assertions that Western culture's religious moralism was murderous in origin and neurotic in tendency.[14] Nonetheless, through the modernist torsion within American Protestantism and the writings of theorists, including members of the New York Psychology Group (NYPG), liberal Protestants sought a rapprochement with psychoanalysis as they honed new techniques for pastoral training, or "the healing of souls," a process broadened to include parishioners' problems with family, sexuality, and self-esteem.[15] Freud, rather than Kierkegaard or Pascal, both dear to the neoorthodox, seemed to offer a deeper perception of the psychology of faith, though his is the view of a pathologist. By internalizing, rather than assailing, Freud's critique of religion as illusion, liberal Protestants were actually reasserting the relevance of Christianity to the mental-health-conscious domestic sphere. Moreover, they were assisted by secular intellectuals who saw psychotherapy as the companion to religion or an alternative to traditional, "puritanic" or "authoritarian," religion.

Psychology could investigate the formation of conscience, its relationship to irrational authority, and its evasion by psychic defenses. Best-selling author and Baltimore-based clinician Robert Lindner, for instance, diagnosed one of his cases, named "Mac," as a subject plagued with oedipal self-hatred first inflicted by his evangelical fundamentalist upbringing and then acted out through his affiliation with the authoritarian Communist party.[16] Lindner, like other advocates and practitioners of psychotherapy, believed that his cure could achieve the best effects of religion minus its primitive, punitive, and ultimately unhealthy overreliance on guilt to produce social discipline. For the sake of mental health and antitotalitarian social planning, therapists sought to snip hypertrophied guilt consciousness at its neurotic root, in the psychosocial dynamics of the family. By contrast with America's Puritan legacy, which founded social discipline on a profoundly internal sense of man's positive corruption, psychoanalysts, especially the revisionist neo-Freudians, humanists, and "ego-psychologists," hoped to make conscience more pliable to reason by tempering and even dissolving the superego, the product of what Freud called "the family romance."[17] These researches into the bases of morality stimulated significant theological redaction among liberal Protestants, emptying original sin of any residue of natural depravity, or dispensing with it altogether, and taking the moral onus off forms of guilt that were neurotic in kind, those seeming to stem from damaging oedipal dynamics and sexual training. This theological revisionism drew fire from such critics as Reinhold Niebuhr, who believed the cultural impact of the therapeutic movement and its humanistic offshoots diminished man's consciousness of evil.[18]

Niebuhr's opinion of the Protestant adaptation of psychotherapy is substantially Donald Meyer's in his well-known *The Positive Thinkers*.[19] Superior to Meyer's book (including the updated 1988 edition), Allison Stokes's *Ministry After Freud* properly distinguishes between "religious pop psychology," a limp form of apologetic, and the serious effort by pastors and theologians to integrate the latest research and clinical methods of the science of the mind with the permanent features of Christianity in the modern world, which Stokes designates the Religion and Health Movement. Having precedents especially in Harry Emerson Fosdick's advocacy of mental hygiene, beginning in the twenties and culminating in his book, *On Being a Real Person* (1943), this movement, Stokes argues, must be seen as a product of "the modernist impulse" in American Protestant liberalism, especially in its aspects of cultural adaptation, immanence, and progressivism.[20] Stokes touches upon the wartime conditions under which the religion and health movement advanced, especially the intelligentsia's cosmopolitan receptivity to ideas migrating from Europe-under-siege, but the postwar and Cold War discursive contexts are equally crucial. I am concerned here to show how Protestants positively incorporated Freudian diagnoses of neurotic guilt into their theology during a period when liberalism, especially its modernist tendencies, was in disrepute for having preached man's Christlikeness to an "innocent" American nation. When America was being urged to shed its innocence and accept its unrighteousness, how could Protestants already under indictment for their excessive renunciation of the country's Calvinist past settle the psychoanalytic prescription for a remission of religious guilt with their "responsibility" to correct liberalism's errors?

Our point is not Meyer's, that Protestants merely substituted mind cure for the social Christianity of Reinhold Niebuhr and Rauschenbusch, nor is it a vulgarly Foucaultian one, that Protestants were simply assisting the therapeutic regime to imprison man's body in an imago of his soul. Rather, the alliance of liberal Protestants and mental health made for a potential counterhegemonic discourse to the period's "end of innocence" master narrative. The Left Freudians, in fact, would imagine a new eschatology and new utopianism that refused tragedy without calling for a return to moral innocence. The full emergence of this counterhegemonic discourse was deferred by the gender politics of the Cold War, as highlighted in the clinical recognition of momism and the pathologizing of feminine domestic maladjustment, and the gender deterrent will be the subject of my discussion of author Shirley Jackson.

Treating Guilt: "Orthodox" Freudians, Neo-Freudians, and Humanists

Psychoanalysis incorporated "the conscience," a category of rational psychology, with its premises of free will and conscious choice, into a dynamic model in which much of the stimulus for moral action is below awareness. The superego contains both the conscience, the taboos that an individual learns from its society, and the ego ideal, the goals and identifications that the ego experiences as esteem. Aggressive drives, which the superego siphons from the id, enforce obedience of the conscience and punish any shortfalls of the ego ideal by making the person feel pain, smallness, and grief. These are affects attached to adult teachings, combined with parental imprints, or "introjects," which the child retains from the psychic trauma of the family romance. Since Freud conceived the family structure as a basically nuclear one, in which available love objects are few, the hapless child in the oedipal scenario becomes a rival to his parents for their affections, particularly to his father for his mother's attention, and wishes to destroy the parent that he also loves. Its will torn by incompatible impulses towards the father, the child's organism, in self-preservation, inhibits the aggressive impulses the child cannot express and submits the will to the ends of parental authority, developing the instinctual renunciations on which civilization unhappily relies. The child thus identifies with the figure that threatens him, and his destructive fantasies are repressed along with his guilt, which henceforth resides in him as the superego. This traumatic experience creates internalized discipline for the child, who is now prepared to be instructed in other forms of renunciation.

The social compact that the child enters through successive repressions is not a rational agreement to do good for the whole, nor is it a prudential contract among rival self-interests.[21] It may take these guises, but it is actually a mass projection of the superego and the social symbols that attach to guilt.[22] These projections do not ensure an ethical society, however, for the superego's exacting punishment of the ego forces the organism to find neurotic remissions of guilt, which leave the subject more, not less, vulnerable to submersion in irrational authority. Modern politics only convinced Freud that most men were psychically too weak to be rational, for the collective superego, in the form of mass identities, was gathering puissance as individuals sought remissions from punitive guilt by resurrecting the primal father in autocratic leaders.

Since the superego could assail the ego to such a degree that it could not responsibly develop its own value judgments, liberals sought to dissipate its force and thus make the ego more resilient and its reasoning more supple. In 1954, the Group for the Advancement of Psychiatry met in Topeka, Kansas, to discuss the harm McCarthyism could wreak on democratic culture by impairing the nation's psychic health. In his summary of the proceedings, Lionel Trilling suggested that the democratic values of an open society coincided with therapeutic principles:

> This tendency of suspiciousness and repressiveness is no doubt latent in all cultures; in American culture it has periodically made itself manifest in dramatic ways; its most recent manifestations we came to call McCarthyism. . . . The consensus at the conference was that the tendency of repressiveness must inevitably have a bad effect upon our national psychic health. It was not merely said that individuals would be made the prey of intense anxiety. The harm was said to be of a far deeper kind and likely to be perpetuated in the culture. For the ego is the aspect of the mind that deals with the object-world, and one of its most important functions is the pleasurable entertainment of the idea of adventure. But if part of the object-world is closed off by interdiction, and if the impulse to adventure is checked by a restrictive culture, the free functioning of the ego is impaired. No less subject to injury is the superego—it was said at the conference that 'a mature super-ego can optimally develop only in a free and democratic society.'[23]

Opposed to the frontier spirit of democracy is the immature superego of McCarthyism, perpetuating insecurity, suspicion, isolation, and intolerance. Liberals, such as David Riesman, argued for the progressive application of psychotherapy to culture by positing two conceptions of conscience: first, a humanistic one that is normal; and, second, a pathological one that is essentially the superego in classical Freudian theory.[24] The second is the mentality of an authoritarian like McCarthy rather than an atavism of human development as Freud had believed. With a national mental health initiative, such culturally regressive influences would be replaced by more rationally balanced and tolerant peer groups open to the object-world.

Despite Trilling's efforts to recuperate Freud as a humanist, as in *The Liberal Imagination, The Opposing Self,* and *Beyond Culture,* there was little support for his hopes in the Viennese philosopher's own writings. In theory, Freud allowed that people undergoing analysis could master their guilt, but he actually believed that very few were able to successfully complete analysis because self-knowledge would be too disturbing for them to look honestly into their unconscious. Moreover, Karen Horney explained of Freud, man was netted in opposing instinctual drives that "had the stamp of finality": "Man has therefore at bottom only the choice of suffering and destroying himself or of making others suffer and destroying them."[25] Uncomfortably for advocates of psychoanalysis, such as Trilling and Riesman, Freud's anthropology did not meld with democratic thought, and, indeed, his speculations about man's political future tended resignedly to a kind of Hobbesian autocracy gelled by charisma, national ideology, and scapegoats rather than rational assent.[26] By contrast, the revisionists—neo-Freudians, or "ego psychologists," and "humanists," such as Carl Rogers and Rollo May—aspired to strengthen the individual's self-understanding and make him more independently creative with respect to his own aims. Whereas Freud argued that anger, fear, and guilt arise from within the matrix of the child's instinctual ambivalence and the repressions of these conflicts, the revisionists argued that individuals have greater intrapsychic freedom, with more power centered in the conscious, thinking portions of the ego. This freedom, moreover, could be expanded and given supporting conditions by altering cultural practices and mores. Neuroses were caused by both self-repressions and interpersonal conflicts, and in either of these formations symptoms could be relieved and outgrown, allowing a more constructive course, by changing both the patient's perception of his "real self" and the culture's ideas about man's reality. D. E. Roberts, chairman of the Commission on Religion and Health (1953), citing the work of Horney, Fromm, and Sullivan, succinctly puts the differences in prognosis for mental health and social environment:

> Earlier psychoanalytic thought sounded a definitely fatalistic note insofar as it attributed to man an instinctual equipment which had to be combated by society and the individual's own conscience in order to maintain any kind of stable civilization. The difference between the older and the newer view can be expressed quite simply. In the one case civilized man is fated by his very nature to be torn inwardly by serious conflicts. In the other case such conflicts are related to modifiable circumstances; granted the establishment of favorable conditions, there is nothing in man which prevents him from reaching emotional stability and a satisfying use of his capacities.[27]

Criticizing Freud for his biological determinism, the "new view" largely disposed his theory of the instincts and of infantile sexuality (for which Norman O. Brown roundly criticized the neo-Freudians in *Life Against Death*) and reconceptualized complexes and stages as attitudes and symbols transmitted from culture via the family. "Home reflects the culture" (28).

AN IMMEDIATE cultural factor necessitating change was thus family discipline, through which the germ of guilt was implanted. In *Childhood and*

Society (1950), Erik Erikson ruminates on the infantile "core of human tragedy": "For the super-ego of the child can be primitive, cruel, and uncompromising, as may be observed in instances where children overcontrol and overconstrict themselves to the point of self-obliteration. . . . The suspiciousness and evasiveness which is thus mixed in with the all-or-nothing quality of the super-ego, this organ of moral tradition, makes moral (in the sense of moralistic) man a great potential danger to his own ego—and to that of his fellow man."[28] The child must learn "the horizon of the permissible" without sacrificing his initiative, lest he grow up to become one "intolerantly turned against others in the form of persistent moralistic surveillance" (257). In his "psycho-history" of Protestantism, *Young Man Luther* (1958), Erikson argues that Luther's theology is an interpretation of a typical neurotic conflict, acutely felt in Luther's time, which the Reformation successfully integrated into Christianity. According to Erikson's stage theory, the human being passes from a preoedipal phase, in which he faces the crisis of trust versus mistrust, to the oedipal phase, in which he must cope with the crisis of initiative versus guilt. In the first phase, the mother's role is all-important, for she reassures the child of the essential goodness of his instincts and the stability of his cosmos, while in the second, the father assists the child in taking responsibility for his person in spite of his irrational guilt and fear of punishment. Psychologically speaking, the Reformation addresses an imbalance in the oedipal phase that resulted in Luther's fixation on guilt, which was so strong that it nearly paralyzed his initiative and obliterated his trust in himself and all known values; theologically speaking, this fixation was taken up into an almost exclusive stress on man's evil rivalry with "the divine Father-Son" (263). The primal motive of all religion is to reaffirm the basic trust—and the victory over mistrust—that the mother gives the child in its infancy (263). Without this confidence in his safety from evil, the child will have difficulty bearing down oedipal guilt and accepting himself again after having felt a bad creature. He will develop a "negative conscience" in which the super-ego is completely antithetical to the ego identity, much as God's judgment is always contrary to man's self-appraisal in Lutheran dogma. Where a "sincere" conscience makes for a holistic ego that can tolerantly blend opposites in the psyche, the negative conscience rigidly separates man's psyche into "good" and "bad," and it identifies the self solely with the *impure* psyche. According to Erikson, Luther's doctrine of undeserved grace through absolute faith is designed to restore basic trust, but his doctrine of depravity works contrarily to preserve the negative conscience—a curse, it turns out, from an overmastering pater familia. As Roger Johnson has pointed out, the demonic principle in Erikson's account (though not in

Luther's theology) is the punitive father, represented in *Young Man Luther* by the theologian's sire Hans, a "moralistic" and inhibiting "authoritarian."[29] From his father's behavior toward him, Luther internalized a hateful image of himself and expiated for it by turning his father's aggression inward against his ego.

Erikson, however, does not insist that the dictatorial superego is the child's destiny; it is a possibility that can be averted by teaching the child the proper ethos of reward for tangible goals achieved.[30] Doctor Spock, in *Baby and Child Care,* a manual for parents, similarly addresses the problem of initiative versus guilt: "You don't want a small child to develop a **heavy** sense of guilt. The job of a parent is to keep the child from getting into trouble rather than act as a severe judge after it's happened" (Spock's boldface).[31] When children are naughty, they are not trying to offend, and so they must not be made to mistake their bad behavior as proof that they are intrinsically bad beings. Such feelings are damaging because they do not facilitate learning how to rationally differentiate between right and wrong and instead alienate the child from itself.

WHAT INTERCEDED between rational value judgment and superego compunction, impairing the one and aggravating the other, was "moralism," the set of attitudes symptomatic of the authoritarian personality syndrome in *The New American Right* and *The Radical Right:* the idea that man just needs to try hard, using will power to make the ethical parts of himself dominant over his lower nature; goodness consists in resistance to and triumph over flesh. Moralism leads to the formation of bad conscience, as the person internalizes dictates he cannot possibly fulfill without extreme repression, and adopts authoritarian rigidity to check and control the impulses he cannot express without incurring pain. Inevitably, neurosis results from bad conscience, as thoughts and wishes pass into the unconscious where they cannot be felt as the self's property or rationally examined as sources of constructive or obstructive patterns. To Karen Horney, for example, the resulting neurosis causes "self-hating" guilt to cleave from appropriate guilt feelings and interfere with their elimination, since the former is unassuagable, being inspired by no specific misconduct. Appropriate guilt involves remorse and a decision to make amends for the specific wrong behavior. Self-hating guilt is a sense of having failed the "perfectionistic" demands of a too powerful super-ego.[32] As shown by "the frequency of neuroses" in our civilization, with its "Christian injunction ('Be ye perfect . . .')," men are not predisposed to do evil, but suffer from a superabundant sense of contempt, Horney says in "A Morality of Evolution," the Introduction to *Neurosis and Human Growth*. Intending to

curb the instincts, the older ascetic moral traditions have been overweening. In trying to make men godlike, they have in fact enjoined them to "the
devil's pact": "an individual in psychic distress [from his superego] arro-
gates to himself infinite powers, losing his soul and suffering the torments
of hell in his self-hate."[33] Before a child ever wanders from its family, the
organism, in its flight from guilt, has already installed a primitive persecu-
tor more awful than any god or demon: "we do not need an inner strait-
jacket with which to shackle our spontaneity, nor the whip of inner dictates
to drive us to perfection. There is no doubt that such disciplinary measures
can succeed in suppressing undesirable factors, but there is also no doubt
that they are injurious to our growth" (13–16).

Fromm connects this intrafamilial dynamic to structures of religious and
political authority in *Man for Himself* (1947), a text written after his participation in the NYPG: "The most effective method for weakening the
child's will is to arouse his sense of guilt."[34] Children who cannot accept
their own individuality or take pride in their own power and strength are
prone later to internalize values because of "charismatic" authority rather
than rational judgment: "The prescriptions of authoritarian conscience are
not determined by one's own value judgment but exclusively by the fact
that its commands and taboos are pronounced by authorities. . . . A believer in Hitler, for instance, felt he was acting according to his conscience
when he committed acts that were humanly revolting." The ego ideal of
such children contributes to the projection of authority: "For such conscience is always colored by man's need to admire, to have some ideal, to
strive for some kind of perfection, and the image of perfection is projected
upon the external authorities" (150). Fromm, who favored Aquinas to
Protestant theologians for Thomism's recognition of natural law, argued in
The Escape from Freedom (a key theoretical text of the NYPG) and *Man
for Himself* that the Reformation bred authoritarian personalities, filled
with "self-hatred" and "self-contempt," by instilling the anxious bourgeoisie with superhuman, unattainable ego ideals and unbearable doubt
about their salvation: "According to [Luther and Calvin] the greatest obstacle to man's salvation is his pride; and he can overcome it only by guilt
feelings, repentance, unqualified submission to God, and faith in God's
mercy. . . . The idea of man's worthlessness and nothingness found a new,
and in this time entirely secularized, expression in the authoritarian systems in which the state or 'society' became supreme rulers, while the individual, recognizing his own insignificance, is supposed to find his fulfillment
in obedience and submission" (214). From Luther and Calvin to Hitler is
a linear development.[35] The cosmic terrors of faiths like Calvinism, like
those of recent authoritarian ideologies, had only succeeded in reinforcing

the organism's fear of itself. Fromm's conclusions dovetail with Erikson's in *Young Man Luther*. The evil that Hans bequeathed to his son is similar to the psychic damage in which "totalitarian" ideology, a late perversion of Reformation theology, Erikson suggests, plants roots.[36] Since Luther remained fixated on guilt, he could only rationalize action in the pursuit of total, moralistic reform, and it is this tendency towards "totalism" that Hitler carried to a global crisis.[37]

Freud's oversight, according to the neo-Freudians, was to identify the superego of this "totalistic" type with man's essential psychic structure, which can, at best, be tempered only a bit. Fromm, however, states in *Man for Himself* that "the authoritarian conscience is what Freud has described as the Super-ego."[38] Horney, citing Fromm, adds in *Neurosis and Human Growth*: "Freud can aim merely at reducing the severity of the super-ego, while I aim at the individual's being able to dispense with his inner dictates ['the tyranny of shoulds'] altogether and to assume the direction of his life in accordance with his true wishes and beliefs. This latter possibility does not exist in Freud's thinking."[39] Thus, therapy can achieve what Freud never imagined, the psychic equivalent of political reorientation: "The effect is to be compared with the moment when a youngster who has grown up under dictatorship learns a democratic way of living" (350). Where primitive, irrational, unconscious guilt does not block or deflect energy, the ego can afford to be more resilient in the face of change, and thus make ethical judgments on the basis of "mutual concern," "productivity," and clear "reality-testing" rather than moralistic (or ideological) reactions (364–365). The "humanistic conscience," as Fromm preferred, is buoyed by an overall character orientation in which morality is not eradicated but in which archaic elements do not predominate.

Behind all of these precautions lies a key assumption: knowledge of good and bad is not damaging, nor is remorse and desire to make restitution, but guilt that results in repression will stunt maturation. The key to the child's moral development is not punishment and mortification but encouragement of the child's potential for the cooperative virtues of trust and love, which are assumed to be more basic to its born nature than aggression and deceit. Until wounding experiences cause him to react with defensive mechanisms (projection, denial, rationalization, ego inflation), there is nothing in the child's nature for which he needs to atone. Each natality introduces a new Adam. The theological implications of therapy were not lost on psychologists, the churches, or secular commentators, all of whom were quick to recognize the new movement's contrast to the classical psychoanalysis of Sigmund Freud. It is revealing in this regard to look at a special supplement of the *Atlantic Monthly*, titled "Psychology in

American Life" (1960), a collection of articles that includes authors such as sociologists John R. Seeley and Philip Rieff, who here offer excerpts or early versions of their seminal works, Seeley's *The Americanization of the Unconscious* (1967) and Rieff's *Freud: The Mind of the Moralist* (1959) and *Triumph of the Therapeutic: Uses of Faith After Freud* (1966).[40] "Psychology in American Life" presents two images of psychotherapy, one the heir to conservative Protestantism, the other a makeover for liberal humanism and democracy.

The editor, Charles Rolo, prefaces the collection with a fusillade against the excesses of the Freudian revolution: "the awful movies depicting quasi-miraculous psychoanalytic cures; the slick novels and dramas in which bad Daddy and possessive Mummy are the source of all evil; the cocktail party sages who have translated gossip into solemn psychoanalytic jargon." These "vulgarizations" and "corruptions" of psychoanalysis mirror the *decline* of religion.[41] Seeley, in his article "The Americanization of the Unconscious," agrees with Rolo that the Freudianism of postwar America is not that of Vienna, but rather than trace a declension, he pursues an analogy between America's religious pluralism and the country's relaxed absorption of schismatic psychoanalytic schools. Freud's ideas, like the major Western religions, have undergone a revision in the United States, and, in turn, psychoanalysis has transformed many Americans' perceptions of themselves in ways as epochal as religious revivals. The American "sects," represented by Horney, Fromm, Sullivan, and others, grant the ego much more agency and accentuate the role of culture in ego formation rather than the clash of the instincts with consciousness. This "rival episcopate" is nearly a "new systematics," but enough of Freud's original ideas persists in the innovations that Seeley imagines a "distant ecumenical reunion." In the meantime, America fosters both "the orthodox church" and the revisionist, sustaining "inter-sect antipathy," but, "characteristically" discouraging any "wars of religion."

O. Hobart Mowrer, former head of the American Psychological Association, also distances Sigmund Freud from American "ego-psychology," especially its popularizations, but contrary to Seeley, he does not envisage an "ecumenical" reunion. In Mowrer's "Psychiatry and Religion," Freud is the antithesis of the new school, for he shares the moral determinism of John Calvin. While the revisionists seek to make men doubly responsible for their actions, their choices for good as well as evil, Freud substitutes "neurosis" for "sin" and makes men doubly irresponsible for their neurotic behavior. Calvin's "medieval sophistry" had at least permitted men to be accountable for their wrongful actions; Freud's "momentous further step" was to erase both sides of the moral ledger (89). The contemporary turn in "ego-psychology" towards semi-Pelagian rather than Freudian or "Calvinistic" notions of character and will power may avert the "tragic consequences" of Protestantism, which has left "us without a clear and effective means of dealing with personal guilt"(89).[42] Mowrer's contention, that psychotherapy has interceded in a liberal culture that has been without functional remissions for guilt since Calvinism disabled religion by making moral life unbearable, seconds the opinion of Erich Fromm.

Philosopher of ethics at Chicago's Center for Advanced Behavioral Study Philip Rieff, in "The American Transference: From Calvin to Freud," shares Mowrer's opinion that the mainstream psychoanalytic crusade has become "a self-help movement . . . a doctrine suitable to a post-religious age." As such, the movement does not break with Freud or Calvin, however, but continues the limited adjustments Freud had made to a culture raised on conservative Protestantism. Whereas Mowrer asserts that Freudianism and American Protestantism are both doddering moral systems, Rieff believes Freud and Calvin remain powerful influences, though paradoxically related to each other, as Freud fortifies the Calvinist ethos and at the same time denies its guilt-releasing concept of salvation. Freud and Calvin warn man that he has a hidden self, for all purposes unknowable, which impels all of his actions. Calvin counsels men to monitor their behavior, for, however inconclusively, "only the outer actions [can] give even a hint of the inner condition, whether that be of grace or damnation." In the secular age, Freud referred to "sin" as "neurosis" and made all signs point away from the cosmos and downward into the "dark" and "sinister" unconscious.[43] Like Calvin, Freud believed that each man's inner mystery captivated him because it contained the answer to his plaguing guilt, but he offered the secular man a chance, slim yet real, that Calvin never could; under psychotherapy, a faithless man might find self-knowledge and thereby console his anxiety.

Herein, however, lies the problem with psychoanalysis in Rieff's estimate; when men have ceased to believe in grace, then guilt-consciousness may appear as if it is a sign of emotional weakness, ill health, rather than a sign of hidden, but unforgiven, misconduct. In its ultimate effect upon the interpretation of culture, Freud's alternative to religion does not make men better, only more at ease with their general ethical failure in modern society. Undergoing analysis, they receive no path to redemption, but learn endurance to "function more adequately in a situation essentially competitive from cradle to grave" (107). With some ambivalence, more evident in *Freud: The Mind of the Moralist* (1959), Rieff accepts the Freudian adjustments to conservative Protestantism because these realistically estimate "the universality of human weakness," from which Americans are not exempt (107). The liberal self-help and child-conditioning therapies, however, attempt to go beyond Freud to create new "doctrines of salvation," promising complete rational control of anxiety and release from guilt. Compared to his charges in *The Triumph of the Therapeutic*, Rieff is generous to liberal psychologists in "The American Transference." In the later book, by contrast, "the rise of psychological man" has signaled a new naïveté among intellectuals, who have made freedom from guilt a moral end in itself.[44]

Rieff's remarks about the new wave of psychotherapists, like other claims that they were replacing superego values (such as self-restraint) with id values, are not quite accurate since, as observed earlier, the neo-Freudians, ego-psychologists, and humanistic analysts made a crucial distinction between genuine guilt and its neurotic variety, a difference that I will shortly discuss at more length. Yet Rieff, and the other pundits in the *Atlantic Monthly* issue, did grasp the underlying spirit of the therapeutic movements when they spoke of its secular religious aspirations. Some of the leading psychotherapists turned to their vocations quite deliberately to repudiate elements of historic Christianity, especially the Augustinian doctrine of original sin. As Paul Vitz has noted, Carl Rogers's *On Becoming a Real Person* (1961) seems intentionally titled to echo *On Being a Real Person* (1943), written by a man he esteemed.[45] Before getting his degree in psychology, Rogers attended Union Theological Seminary, where he had hoped to break from his conservative Protestant upbringing. He ended up breaking with Christianity altogether and turning to John Dewey for inspiration. Nonetheless, deeply moved by certain theologians, he frequently cites Kierkegaard in his essays, and he carried on dialogues with Paul Tillich and Martin Buber. Rollo May, author of *The Springs of Creative Living: A Study of Human Nature and God* (1943) and editor of *Existence: A New Dimension in Psychiatry and Psychology* (1958), was also an aspiring theologian at Union Theological Seminary and a Congregational minister before he became a psychotherapist, lastingly influenced by Paul Tillich.[46] Trained as a rabbi, Erich Fromm also hoped to lead men away from a Christianity morbidly obsessed with evil, and especially away from Luther and Calvin, towards a "sane society" in which repression would not be necessary. Towards this task, Fromm intricately translated religious systems into formulae for secular utopias founded on a passionately felt humanism and on psychosocial theory, as in *The Development of the Dogma of Christ* (1963) and *You Shall Be as Gods* (1966).[47] Horney looked at the clinical process from the perspective of "moral and spiritual values," citing Kierkegaard, William James, and Albert Schweitzer to describe how man reaches toward the infinite and how man can affirm his potentialities when he fails his idealized image.[48] When comparing liberal Protestants with these secular psychotherapists, especially those who were members of the NYPG at Union Theological Seminary (Rogers, Fromm, May), it is difficult to assess the direction of influence between theory and theology. What is clear is that secular psychotherapists of the new wave were not deeply critical of religion per se, as Freud had been, but of moralistic, perfectionist, or deterministic beliefs, and furthermore, that the cure of these neurosis-inducing and neurotically encaging beliefs entailed the sharp criticism of Freud's own assumptions about mankind.[49] Fromm, consistent with Rieff's later comparison between Freud and Calvin, finds in classical, or "orthodox," psychoanalysis a pessimism about human nature that uncomfortably resembles the view of predestination, for Freud believes "that morality is essentially a reaction formation against the evil inherent in man. . . . This theory is the secularized version of the concept of 'original sin.'"[50] Rogers too, who disaffiliated his "client-centered" therapy from psychoanalysis, stated that Freud is philosophically more similar to Calvin than to Augustine, for his theory has "a basically Calvinistic view of the evilness of the natural man."[51] The liberal project to disseminate therapeutic ideas and practices for the promotion of democratic stability had facilitated the visible emergence of revisionists to Freud, and these revisionists' ideas, along with Freud's own, mingled with a modernist turn in Protestantism—owing less to Christian political realism than to pastoral concerns—that was interested in the cure of souls instead of declaiming liberalism's "innocence."

The God of Judgment Goes to the Consulting Couch: Tillich and the Implications of Psychoanalysis for Counseling and Preaching

John Seeley's and Charles Rolo's opinions notwithstanding, the patterns of psychoanalysis reception show that it never was a replacement for official religion in America. In the fifties, no Catholic or Jewish leaders espoused psychoanalysis with the fervor it enjoyed from liberal Protestantism, and certainly none made special claims for the congruence of Jewish or Catholic religion and Freud's theories. The reception of Freudian thought, so firmly associated with the demystifying spirit of modernity, clearly marked the different patterns of intellectual assimilation among Catholics, Jews, and liberal Protestants.

Although the majority of practicing psychoanalysts were Jewish, there was no comparable effort in Judaism to commend Freud or neo-Freudians to renovating traditional religion. One exception was New England radio rabbi Joshua Loth Liebman, who broadcast coast-to-coast on NBC, ABC, and CBS (1939–1946) and published the best-selling *Peace of Mind* (1946), in which he rejoices that "prophetic religion" now has a secular ally.[52] Having "two strategies, one goal," Jewish ethics and psychoanalysis (he cites Fromm, Horney, Menninger, and Freud) are united in leading man to self-understanding rather than the self-condemnation instilled by "punitive religion," in which the conscience is like "an angry father" "keeping us in the posture of boys" who fear "woodshed ministrations" (37). The psychic and spiritual maturation of its citizens can help America to throw off "the helpless, poverty-stricken, powerless motifs in European culture" and become a revelation for all religion: "Let us not seek to defend democracy on earth and yet demand moral tyranny from Heaven . . . it will be from the democratic experience of our century that mankind will first learn its true destiny as independent and necessary partners of God" (172). Despite Liebman's popularity, and the agility of his rhetoric, which anticipates Herberg's integration of prophetic Judaism into the civil faith of postwar democratic consensus, *Peace of Mind* inspired few immediate imitators outside the Protestant-dominated "positive thinking" genre. Gregory Zilboorg's posthumous *Psychoanalysis and Religion* (1962), for instance, compiles essays written after his conversions (from Jewish Orthodox to Quaker and then Catholic) and makes arguments against atheism aimed broadly at a Christian audience, the group in which the book had its impact. Fromm's *The Development of the Dogma of Christ* and *You Shall Be as Gods* display a regard for rabbinical wisdom writing, Jewish mysticism, prophecy, and Hebrew exegesis already evident in *Man For Himself* (1947), but Fromm does not attempt to argue specifically for the Jewishness of psychoanalytic thought, as a few contributors did in *Commentary* and *Judaism*.[53] The Menninger Foundation's seminars and its summer program, Institute for Mental Health (1954–1973), hosted at the monastic St. John's College, were attended by Jewish and Christian clergy, fostering interfaith dialogue about the Religion and Health movement.[54] However, these meetings did not issue in any Jewish literature comparable to the Protestant outpouring of material on the new science's applications to priestly offices or its implication for theology.

By the end of the fifties, the Religion and Health movement had not penetrated very deeply in the Catholic Church either. Proportionate to its membership, Catholics accounted for far fewer American psychiatrists in 1959 than did Protestants or Jews.[55] Despite some early progress by such figures as Thomas Verner Moore, Catholicism was slow in absorbing psychodynamic theory because of the papal oaths against modernism

(1907), which seriously hampered Catholic intellectual life, restricting it to a neo-Thomism that had no space for the unconscious.[56] Pius XII opened channels during the fifties in a series of speeches to the clinical community, though he continued to voice the Church's long-standing (drawn in the twenties) reservations toward psychoanalysis for seeming to undermine natural law and focus attention on sexual wishes that could easily become lascivious.[57] The pope, however, did not condemn psychoanalysis,[58] and Pius's overall tone of congeniality to clinical psychology, combined with the influence of European Catholic scholarship, promoted more receptivity to the studies of psychotherapists, most especially Carl Rogers and certain neo-Freudians, such as Erikson and Horney.

Yet vociferous reservations persisted in high-profile outlets. Whatever overtures Pius XII may have made in the scientific community, and whatever progress was marked by Jesuit universities, or programs like the A.C.P.A. (American Catholic Psychological Association), or the positive clerical reception of Presbyterian John T. McNeill's classic *A History of the Cure of Souls* (1951), these were publicly overshadowed by the radio-TV star Bishop Fulton Sheen, who routinely blasted Freud's "materialism" in the same breath that he disparaged Marx's.[59] Not hostile to psychology per se, Sheen expressed esteem for Carl Jung (the collective unconscious suggested to him the universal, mystical substratum of the human soul) and even outlined a possible route of cooperation between "psychiatrists" and "moralists," but his consideration could not extend to psychoanalysis, which submerged man in a libidinal underground instead of ascending "the interior Sinai of conscience," where the law is given. In his sermons, Sheen tended to dismiss Freud (whom he never differentiated from neo-Freudians) with sarcasm, suggesting psychoanalysis was merely a trend of the "bored," too enervated by modern moral lassitude to even yawn at guilt: "Some probably believe the reason why Cain turned out so badly was because Eve had no books on child psychology"; "If [Lady Macbeth] lived today, she would say all she had to do was to be psychoanalyzed to get rid of that 'false feeling of guilt.'"[60]

Despite his facetious tone, Sheen's repeated on-air and in-print attacks on Freud betray a worry, pronounced in his extremes but shared by Catholic psychologists, that the consulting couch would eventually usurp the office of confession.[61] In fact, some of the earliest opposition to psychotherapy rose from the belief that "Catholics were coming to view psychoanalysis as a substitute for the confessional," a concern that Pius XII echoes in his address, "Psychotherapy and Religion": "[N]o purely psychological treatment will cure a genuine sense of guilt. . . . The means of eliminating the fault does not belong to the purely psychological order. As every Christian knows, it consists in contrition and sacramental absolution by the priest."[62] The Church's concern, to protect moral theology from being medicalized and priestly intercession from being white-coated, would eventually be resolved into a model of respectful complementarity, though this was slow in coming. When Catholic psychologist Harry McNeill had a set-to with Sheen in *Commonweal* (Summer 1947), excerpted in *Time*, he suggested, prophetically, that "it was high time that Catholics and Freudians got together and swapped their trade secrets" instead of the Church "facilely" claiming "that Catholics have confession, therefore do not need psychoanalysis."[63] Nonetheless, it was not until the sixties, as Carl Rogers's humanism became its own movement and as Europeans discovered Erikson's stage theory of character, that therapeutic concepts—even psychoanalytic strains like Erikson's—began to assist changes in the confessional.[64]

Why was there no clamor earlier from Catholic parishioners eager to take advantage of the touted mental health movement? Foucault would have us consider, as many before him recognized, that the confessional served an analogous function to therapeutic consultation;[65] and although a number of the religious were clearly afraid that this office would become secularized and then outmoded, Catholics nonetheless seem to have been slower to absorb psychotherapy because they already had a time-honored means of disclosing their guilt to a human authority who could act as an intercessor.[66] According to Protestant theology, by contrast, confession is supposed to be a private dialogue with God, who alone can forgive the sinner and transform his motives. In the Protestant churches, the closest approximation to the confessional was pastoral counseling, which received a tremendous boost during the fifties, and seminaries chose forms varying from psychoanalysis to family counseling to Pealesque positive thinking.[67] Liberals formed the vanguard, theorizing not only pastoral care, but using insights of the *cura anima* to build apologetics for the gospel and cooperate alliances with secular psychology. David Roberts takes an explicitly anti-Barthian and antifundamentalistic stand in *Psychotherapy and the Christian View of Man* (1950): "If the Church is really interested in curing sin, instead of merely calling attention to its ineradicability, it will not despise the effective help which 'worldly' agencies can offer, even though the agencies in question do not use the word 'sin.'"[68]

Planning to foster more conversation among ministers and professional therapists, a committee of the Federal Council of Churches, later a branch of the National Council of Churches, solicited opinions from the National Medical Association for Mental Health, which resulted in a pathbreaking book, *The Church and Mental Health* (1953). The coda by Union Theological Seminary's David Roberts, then Chairman of the Commission on Religion and Health, acknowledges the contributions of Harry Stack Sullivan, Erich Fromm, and Karen Horney for raising awareness of the "social, ethical, and religious authoritarianism which tend to keep man enslaved and estranged from himself" (284). So great was the demand for psychological theory in liberal seminaries that in 1956 the exiting president of the American Psychiatric Association, R. Finley Gayle, Jr., gave his farewell address on the "Conflict and Cooperation between Psychiatry and Religion." Ever since the thirties, some seminaries had been sending students to hospitals and mental institutions to learn from the mentally sick, but during the fifties, more seminaries began building these field trips into course work.[69] In 1953, the Menninger Foundation began giving clergymen a "clinical orientation" through the Edward F. Gallahue Seminars on Religion and Psychiatry and chaplaincy services at hospitals associated with the Menninger School of Psychiatry.[70] In such high-ranking seminaries as Union Theological Seminary, the number of courses in pastoral psychology increased, as students tried to bring old "priestly" offices of the clergy up-to-date with the mental health sciences. The bastion of Christian Realism, Union Theological Seminary, set a precedent for other divinity schools when it established a full-time psychology faculty chair in 1956, the same year that the Cathedral of St. John the Divine held an interdenominational observance of Freud's centenary. At the highest level of organized liberal Protestantism, the National Council of Churches gave its official approval to therapeutic rationale by supervising symposia, conferences, publications, clinics, and fifty nationwide seminars (in 1958)—all measures bringing together clergy and psychiatrists.[71]

Unphased by conservative evangelicals and neoorthodox thinkers, both of whom saw man and God as irremediably in conflict outside the transcendent relation to Christ, liberal Protestant pastors, theologians, and seminary students adapted psychoanalysis to redact the Christian doctrine of man and reconceptualize the meanings of sin and grace, incorporating the therapeutic emphasis on achieving reconciliation within oneself.[72] What Freud called religion—obsession compulsion, wish fulfillment, guilt-laden symbols—actually provided the critique of pseudoreligion, beliefs and practices that instill an authoritarian conscience impressed by "an authoritarian father figure" rather than "the loving father figure of Christianity."[73] Freud, inadvertently, gives Christians criteria to reform their faith. They must remove from it the elements of neurosis, such as projecting God as "an omnipotent *Fuehrer* who takes all responsibility, leadership, and control" (217). The relationship between psychology and faith was not merely critical, however; it did not leave Christians with only the scraped hull of their faith. The revisionists—neo-Freudians, ego-psychologists, humanists—offered a more optimistic prospect for therapy and provocative statements on Freud's short-sighted perceptions about man and ethical life, which proved compatible with the progressive, immanentist impulses within liberal Protestantism. By internalizing both Freud's critique of faith and the revisionist's critique of Freud, the Religion and Health Movement articulated a hoped-for renewal of Christianity. The positive definition of religion, as opposed to pseudofaith, was concerned less with teaching morals than with transforming the whole personality, removing obstructive inner defenses and releasing constructive energies, to provide the individual a new orientation, a new spring of motives for making moral judgments. As in the nineteenth-century liberal theologian Horace Bushnell's restatement of salvation in his classic, *Views of Christian Nurture* (1847), this transformation was to be a persuasive process of growth, rather than a crisis conversion. Indeed, one of the appeals of therapeutic models was their congeniality to the liberal preference for "once-born" versus "twice-born" Christianity.[74]

THIS WAS NOT a purely pragmatic decision on the part of liberals, nor was it intended to reveal the hidden religious coherence of modern thought. It was an effort at mutual cooperation between the Church and mental health professionals that solicited theological reflection and enlisted a theological defense. Among the most influential voices for the movement, Paul Tillich, in *The Courage To Be* and "The Theological Significance of Existentialism and Psychoanalysis" (1955), argued for its continuity with the Christian existentialism he had traced in modern art.[75] Ministers and psychotherapists, Tillich proposed, should pool their resources: "Neither the medical nor the priestly function is bound to its vocational representatives: the minister may be a healer and the psychotherapist a priest. . . . The goal of both of them is helping men to reach self-affirmation, to attain the courage to be."[76] Cooperation toward a common goal, however, should not be construed as a complete merger of method. While clergymen and psychotherapists assist each other, "their functions should not be confused and the representatives should not try to replace each other," for the first deals with "ontological guilt" and the second with "neurotic guilt." The neurotic form should be avoided, and the ontological one overcome: "For man to be freely and creatively a self, he must not be inhibited by guilt (77)."[77]

To become mature persons, we must give up our "dreaming innocence" and leave a state of mere "potentiality" for "actuality," yet this actualization of our freedom necessarily differentiates us from our essence (the good of Creation) and its source, the divine ground of creativity, and therefore involves us in ambiguities of meaning and conflicts of value.[78] Since it is an aspect of the divine creativity and the source of estrangement, freedom fills the individual, in his finitude and temporality, with dread and guilt for being divided from his ultimate ground, which is Being itself, or "the God above God" (the divine conceived erroneously as a person). This ontological guilt is inevitable and incurable, and the resulting anxiety can only be endured through the Lutheran paradox of justification by faith, in which the sinner does and does not possess the righteousness he anticipates. Justification is the reconciliation to one's self in its freedom to contradict itself; thus Tillich can insist that "all-acceptance of the self is what the Reformers really meant by grace."[79] Yet this foundation of the Reformation, what Tillich elsewhere calls "the Protestant principle," has too often been suborned. Many "moralistic" versions of Christianity misappropriate the meaning of "the profoundly true but badly named doctrine," original sin; properly, it refers to the turning of finitude to evil under the condition of existence.[80] The finite self's flight, through egocentricity, illusions, and lies, from the *Urangst,* "the ontological basis of anxiety," turns into horror and despair in the state of sin.[81] The *Urangst* is directed toward nothingness, symbolically "the demonic." Instead of the Devil and his hordes, the demonic is conceived structurally as nonbeing resisting being. Moralistic religions hold individuals personally responsible for the demonic, thereby instilling an extreme horror of being condemned. These religions instigate a pathological avoidance of the demonic instead of acknowledging that as existent beings we will necessarily contradict (or "negate") our selves. If a person suffers guilt from his anxiety or doubt over this condition, it is because he fails to accept that nonbeing is part of the dynamic of existence. Since no moral regimen can heal estrangement from the divine (Being itself, or "the God above God"), the individual must subdue his anxiety of the demonic again and again by choosing to exist rather than destruct. When he quails before the choice and ceases to affirm himself, it is because he experiences the demonic as if it were an immoral temptation, leading to the neurotic delusion that he is guilty of a sinful will instead of a failure of courage. For security he looks to forces outside himself to define his values, but these do not truly abolish his anxiety since he is now accountable to externally determined standards that his very spirit—his freedom—negates.

The task of the psychologist, Tillich counsels, is to pierce these superficies and remove the onus from the subject's self-division, so that the minister can lead him to understand the grace of his paradoxical situation. With the psychologist to cure his neurosis and the minister to correlate his existential problems to kerygmatic answers, the individual will be capable of accepting his "ultimate concern": whatever value affirms his being despite the anxiety and guilt of his estrangement. The ultimate concern is analogous to the supervenient grace that orients one's will toward the divine. Though not all propsychoanalytic liberals adopted Tillich's ontology, they did appropriate the basic argument that estrangement was not blameworthy and that neurotic guilt, or self-damnation, could not be countenanced as a sign of virtue. Moral guilt, properly speaking, should refer only to specific misconduct, though these "sins" are often, far more than the religious have previously realized, the results of neurotic guilt that has formed in response to both developmental conflicts (leading to illness) and from anxiety of the demonic (or, angst stemming from the state of sin). Here Protestants of the religion and health movement follow Brunner, Tillich, Bultmann, and Niebuhr in demythologizing the Genesis account so that Adam's sin stands for a universal, but not inherited, condition: the contradiction in man's freedom between inclination and "ought."[82] Sin is not transmitted to man as a legal burden of guilt. Sin is alienation from God, experienced as contradiction-in-freedom, which man does not will and needs help to overcome. The psychologist and the minister can each be instruments of grace, by releasing man from a moralistic superego on the one hand, and from divine estrangement on the other, though Tillich, like his colleague Dr. Seward Hiltner, believed these allied functions should be carried out by separate offices.[83] Many Protestants, however, sought to combine both.[84]

An insightful application of Tillich's two types of guilt is Louis Gross's *God and Freud* (1959), an apologia for the Protestant-psychotherapeutic alliance as well as a treasure trove of interviews and stories with clergymen and theology students who have turned against "moralistic religion." The older liberals had swaddled theology in ethics, according to Gross; now the therapeutic liberals are bracketing ethics and making the parishioner's wellness their sacred responsibility. Before men can become ethical beings, he asserts, they first have to overcome estrangement from themselves. Written as a kind of "manual for pastors," Gross guides his reader through "the theology of psychology" and makes a sympathetic case for dismissing the "God of Wrath" and installing full time the "God of Love."[85] "The progressive element in U.S. Protestantism" has learned from psychoanalysis that all ethics presupposing the Fall and natural depravity are un-Christian: *"The sin is wicked, never the sinner. God accepts you for what you are. . . . The psychiatric method dramatizes the religious idea of acceptance"* (9, 14; Gross's italics). As Seward Hiltner, Reuel Howe (Virginia Theological Seminary), and Dallas Pratt outline in *The Church and Mental Health*, the minister prepares the parishioner for analysis and receives him afterwards by offering him, as a therapist does his patient, a demonstration of unconditional acceptance that is analogous to Christ's teaching of loving sacrifice and the example of the Cross.[86] If Christians truly honor the meaning of the Crucifixion, then they will not heap scorn where God has already forgiven, for this stifles the life-altering effects— love, humility, gratitude, compassion—that spring from man's realization that he is already accepted in his imperfection. The Atonement makes man free to do the good that he creatively seeks and wills to completion without the resentment bred of guilty compunction to obey "the tyranny of shoulds." It is the difference between genuine faith and self-deceiving pseudo faith.

According to Gross, ministers who have been disheartened by their parishioners' unhappiness can now recoup the Gospel, for psychotherapy has taught them that its message is not ineffectual. It has only been misperceived. Where they had suspected some of the old doctrines of insufficient subtlety, they now have medical confirmation of their reservations, for such concepts as the oedipal complex show the adverse, long-lasting effects of insufficiently loving families and peers; in many cases, the ministers report, they are asked to address parental, conjugal, and youth issues, such as sexual promiscuity, infidelity, neglectful spouses, juvenile delinquency, chronically misbehaving children, excessive discipline, and sibling hostility. In response, the ministers have *de*secularized domestic and sexual problems by withdrawing them from ethics and reclaiming them for religion, which is properly therapeutic instead of morally prescriptive.[87] If these problems are "sins," they are also, more importantly, evidence of neurotic guilt stemming from the individual's anxiety about his self-worth, and until ministers and psychologists help him to understand his personal potential for good, to accept his particular endowment of prevenient grace, he is not free from defensive mechanisms or destructive patterns (27). To reach the realization of what Atonement means for him, the individual must first be released from those inner conflicts that impede the acceptance of himself, as he is in his freedom, and the rationalizations that deceive him as to the true bases of his conduct, which are often unconscious.

SEVERAL MINISTERS Gross interviews concur that the "old-fashioned" Protestant axiom of "free will but not free" did more harm than good because it unfairly insisted that men were condemnable for being sinful creatures, the old Adam. David Roberts, in *Psychotherapy and the Christian View of Man*, says that the new findings require Christians to revise the meaning of "bondage to original sin," if the doctrine is to be retained: "every child is influenced by both heredity and society before he has an opportunity to exercise moral discrimination. . . . The moral capacities of the individual are so powerfully determined by his constitution and formed character structure that often the only way to alter the effects of early conditioning involves the retracing of the past."[88] The precept of "free will but not free" rightly expressed the notion that men are often bound by forces that escape rational control and bend their motives to destructiveness, but it misidentified the source of the deviance by faulting men's spiritual inheritance rather than analyzing how repression constrains the will at a preconscious level.[89] "'Moral accountability,'" a clergyman adds, "'should normally be expected from those who have the capacity to control their moral behavior, but one can hardly be held responsible for unconscious behavior which one is powerless to control.'"[90] As in the reassessment of Atonement, the redefinition of accountability entailed a modification of ministerial practice, and the thrust of the liberal therapeutic position was clearly self-restorative. Wrongdoing, as the Protestant Freudian Karl Menninger pointed out in his classic, *Man Against Himself* (1938), may be a method of self-crucifixion or invitation of punishment motivated by guilt-feeling that is seemingly without means of remission. If the parishioner is suffering from neurotic guilt, then he must be shown his neurotic patterns, for only then he can be persuaded from being one of Kant's oafs, who attribute Job's pain to his sins, and instead focus on working through the conflicts that cause him to behave in harmful ways and so develop a sense of ethical responsibility as opposed to mere guilt-feeling.[91]

If the notion of an essentially sinful spirit is only disciplinary and not curative, it follows that those who preach a God of Judgment are inhumane. One of the most remarkable portions of *God and Freud* describes young ministers who are seeing therapists to protect themselves from becoming "authoritarian" preachers.[92] In terms mirroring Hofstadter's and Bell's profiles of fundamentalism, liberal ministers describe the baleful old-school preachers who accosted their congregations with "moralistic, puritanical codes." The descriptions delve below concrete examples of "hatred" in the pulpit to a general pathology: "hatred is symptomatic of the preacher's unconscious guilt, hostility, or anxiety" (144). These sermonizing preachers have ruined the lives of many with "sin," but only recently has the enlightened ministry begun admitting that men in their own midst are wretchedly neurotic: "Religious bodies have come to realize in the last two decades that numbers of ministers have tended to use their offices as outlets for their own emotional difficulties" (144). For these unfit and tormented ministers, religion is, in fact, an illusion, as Freud charged, and it prevents the attributes of the image of God, *the imago dei*, from being taken into the self as creative potential. In hope of saving their parishioners' health as well as their own, says Gross, some upcoming pastors are being analyzed so they can honestly, without inhibition, spread the gospel of acceptance. Gross cites Reverend Burkhardt of Columbus, Ohio, who notes: "the theory of original sin is a lazy excuse for not doing what love ought to do from the moment a baby is conceived" (86). Psychoanalysis had permitted liberal Protestants to undermine Calvinist theology by turning it into a projection of the hellfire preacher's abnormal unconscious. The God of Judgment was now the superego writ large, a holdover from a less hygienic period before men had learned honestly to look inward.[93]

The Left Freudians: Imagining Eschatology and Utopia without Innocence

After regarding Freudian psychology with initial suspicion in the twenties and thirties, many Protestants internalized Freud's critique of religion and his theory of the family romance but also made significant modifications to Freud's ideas. Inasmuch as they adapted modern psychology, especially psychoanalysis, liberal Protestants participated in the diffusion of psychoanalysis through a national mental health movement sparked by wartime speculation on the benefits of applying psychological treatment to the civilian stateside population. Although funding for national security interests aided the dispersion of neo-Freudianism and ego-psychology, liberal Protestants were also readied to receive "the secular religion" by their own theological modernism, which was an intellectual legacy existing prior to the Cold War rationale. While many of the military and psychiatric lobbyists for a mental health program had been motivated by plans to medically engineer democratic morale and social stability, liberal Protestants absorbed the discourse of preventative psychotherapy because it promised to renovate "outworn" methods of spiritual healing.[94] Pre–World War I modernism did not prescribe psychoanalysis, but its logic of reforming Christianity through the adaptation of secular culture certainly anticipated such positions as Paul Tillich's and Louis Gross's, which argued for the complementarity of medical and pastoral goals. The ministers in *God and Freud* therefore insist they are not justifying their roles by capitalizing on a vogue; rather, discouraged with the results of more traditional religion, they have begun experimenting with the psychological method, and they are exhilarated about the positive feedback parishioners have given the new approach.

Much of the criticism the therapeutic movement received in the fifties came from social conservatives (Philip Rieff, Billy Graham), liberals hectoring conformity (William Whyte, Reinhold Niebuhr), or from the artistic and political unrepression of gadflies (such as Norman Mailer). Norman O. Brown attacked from the cultural Left, and as a Left Freudian.[95] Though he is overlooked in the literature on religion and health, Brown is an important and unique voice in the debate of this period because his *Life Against Death* (1958) offers a critique of both neo-Freudianism and theological liberalism by drawing on neoorthodoxy as well as Freud. An intellectually rambunctious classics professor with a self-confessed Protestant background, Brown approached his subject—psychoanalysis as an advanced phase in the historical return of the repressed—with no particular religious affiliation, but a commitment to the prophetic meaning of Freud that inspires him to seek religious avatars.

THE PREFACE to *Life Against Death* opens with an allusion to Reinhold Niebuhr's Gifford Lectures (1938–1940) and proceeds to call for a new eschatology:

> In 1953, I turned to a deep study of Freud, feeling the need to reappraise the nature and destiny of man. Inheriting from the Protestant tradition a conscience which insisted that intellectual work should be directed toward the relief of man's estate, I, like so many of my generation, lived through the superannuation of the political categories which informed liberal thought and action in the 1930's. Those of us who are temperamentally incapable of embracing the politics of sin, cynicism, and despair have been compelled to reexamine the classic assumptions about the nature of politics and about the political character of human nature. (xvi)

In turning for eschatological meaning to Freud, whom so many had deemed a pessimist, Brown does not apologize for his hero's refusal to attribute evil to culture but offers it instead as tough-minded honesty: "In traditional ethical terms, identifying love with good and hate with evil, Freud's fundamental perspective is that the evil in man is not to be explained away as a superficial excrescence on a basically good human nature, but is rooted in a deep conflict in human nature itself" (98). Neo-Freudianism, by contrast, is too sentimental, explaining away aggression and the death drive with the fatuous Enlightenment rationalism of liberal theology (98, 210, 227). As opposed to the unpleasant truth of *Civilization and Its Discontents,* in which man is at war with himself as in Augustine's *City of God,* neo-Freudians serve up "lullabies of sweetness and light," "the liberal optimist position . . . that man is inherently good and peaceful" (98). Brown rehearses the rhetoric of the neoorthodox critique of liberalism—for its sentimental optimism, watery humanism, Pelagian moralizing—but applies it to psychoanalysts who try to purge Freud of those traits that link him, in other critiques, to the radical moral determinism of the Reformation. In fact, Brown finds the greatest historian of repression prior to Freud in Luther, the very figure that Fromm positioned as a crucial link in *Escape From Freedom*'s genealogy of fascism (203). Brown does not dismiss religion in any form as neurotic, but sees it as a phase of the return of the repressed to consciousness. Before psychoanalysis became self-conscious of this process, the Reformation represented the greatest breakthrough of repressed content into historical symbolization, for in Luther's theology, it discovers a "new relation to the Devil" (210). As described in Brown's chapter "The Protestant Era," Luther's Devil is "persistently anal in character," and thus He is the Lord of "filthy lucre": capital, which (theologically speaking) is a weapon of heresy and (psychoanalytically) a symbol system of anal-sadism and the death drive. Brown breaks from Fromm by turning Weber's *The Protestant Ethic* (a key source of *Escape from Freedom*) on its head; instead of accumulated capital being the sign of godly stewardship, it is extreme alienation from God. Indeed, Luther is more radical than Marx, in his diagnosis and in his eschatology. Property is the sign of bondage through original sin, making men themselves property of the Devil. So pervasive is His filth—usury, interest, commerce—that Luther declares, with a theological novelty truly epochal in Christianity, that "the world, in all its outward manifestations, is ruled by the Devil" (217). In his scatalogical images of Satan and of the earth as Satan's fecal dominion, Luther arrives at the conclusion of prophetic psychoanalysis, that "culture is a diseased reification of body metaphors [in this case, anal-sadistic] born of repression at the deepest instinctual level."[96] Luther thus imparts a lesson to the Left, which logic-chops with its historical dialectics; the emergent capitalist culture of Luther's time (and so much more pervasive now) is so foul that there is no power of redemption within it. The world must be remade by the Kingdom of God. The secular version of this hope would be utopia.

In his world renunciation, Luther is the most extreme and the most revelatory of religious prophets; his Protestantism, unlike Calvin's, is properly apocalyptic.[97] But where is there an equivalent today to Luther's radicalism? "Current psychoanalysis has no utopia; current neo-orthodox Protestantism has no eschatology."[98] Neoorthodoxy qualifies "the superficial view, with its implicit philosophy of progress" that "identifies Protestantism with the modern age" (227). However, Karl Barth and his kind leave us stagnant, because they "give the devil his due" (unlike the liberals) while lopping off the positive feature of Luther's theology: the imminent expectation of the Kingdom which his world-renouncing diabolism necessitated (217). Neoorthodox Protestantism vindicates the power of the demonic, but puts the Kingdom at such an infinite distance from man that it "consigns this earth to the eternal dominion of Satan," leading to "acceptance," not the "realism" it claims for itself (218). Ultimately, Brown himself turns from millennial or utopian hope to a mysticism presupposing his own revision to Freud, a recasting of the much-maligned theory of the drives; Freud's dualism of Eros and Thanatos becomes a dialectic when man accepts death as a part of life and thereby releases the libido from its dammed-up reservoirs in fetishes and sublimations, such as capital.[99] In place of Christ, Brown gives us the Dionysian "resurrection of the body": "the abolition of repression. . . . a union with others and with the world around us based not on anxiety and aggression but on narcissism and erotic exuberance" (308). Further, since time itself is a projection of the body repressed by the death drive, Paradise is regained with the abolition of temporal consciousness.

The psychoanalytic meaning of history is perversely the end of historical thinking. Brown aims to succeed the chiliastic Reformation by evacuating time altogether, but, under such a prognosis, the subject in his theory cannot attain to what Herbert Marcuse, with secular intent, called "transcendence": the Logos capacity within human reason to see possibilities, ideas and values, realizable in an alternate historical situation.[100] Transcendence in Marcuse's dialectic is a politically achieved as well as a speculative utopia, but Brown is as skeptical of political utopias as the neoorthodoxy he criticizes. Moreover, his naturalistic mysticism, which reduces culture to the pathology of unhealthy instinctual man, would deny liberals the basis for their own, admittedly milder critique of culture, specifically of elements of conservative Protestantism that they had detheologized. The image of atomized man, each a will unto himself, before God the Judge could no longer be treated as revelation, though it was part of Christianity's repository of tradition. Instead, liberals, in keeping with some of the insights of the Social Gospel, argued that man, from birth to death, was a social being as well as a spiritual one, and the sins that he committed, even those rooted in unconscious conflict, were remediable by changes in attitudes and practices, just as they had been perpetuated by them in the past, as neglect, ignorance, and abuse: "we can understand how collective evils get transmitted from one generation to the next."[101] The interdependence of the psychological and the cultural was the condition of possibility for restoring man's capacity to have moral life without resentment and to make ethical choices without bad conscience.

Brown's indulgence notwithstanding, his point remains that the therapeutic movement lacked an eschatology, and, with the arguable exception of Tillich, this was true of therapeutic liberal Protestantism as well. In "The Political Meaning of Utopia" (1951), Tillich calls for a transcendence of utopia, since it sets man the impossible hope of eliminating all the negativities of his existence and regrafting his essence. Tillich's alternative, the New Being, is the divine intrusion of something apocalyptic and unintelligible from history, and, like utopia, it has political implications, since love, power, and justice are united in the New Being that breaks into man and against him. However, Tillich had grown tepid on active politics, and his lecture sounds none of the righteous anger at institutional power or the sense of imminent, decisive renewal that had characterized his Berlin "*kairos* circle" in the thirties.[102] As in his other late writings, his emphasis falls almost exclusively on the courage internally to withstand irruptions of nonbeing (meaninglessness, isolation, mortality, thinghood). Neither the therapeutic movement nor therapeutic liberal Protestantism followed the implications of its culturalist assumptions through to revolutionary prognoses because neither perceived social relations in America on a model of political domination, and this centrist attitude had its pros as well as its cons. Neither fell victim, for instance, to the hyperbole of Norman Mailer's diatribe, "The White Negro," in which revolution must begin inside the passional self, the inner authentic "psychopath," because American society is virtually totalitarian.[103] Such apocalyptic rhetoric, which was by no means confined to Mailer's glamorization of psychopaths as "saints" (though fanned by it), audaciously transvaluated the choices of greater or lesser evil, Armageddon or realism, anarchy or balance, criminal madness or sanity, through which the postwar establishment had validated itself as the best of all possible options. But, like too much of the countercultural politics on the Left, the effect of statements like "The White Negro" was mainly performative, subverting dominant systems of meaning rather than moving actual power relations, and not succeeding in the latter because its chiliastic rhetoric promised to annul the democratic work of dissent in the name of infusing it. The revisionists to Freud and liberal Protestants thankfully avoided this extreme, but their progressivism did lack a politically utopian dimension, one that would have connected the ideal of "a therapeutic community," as Seeley put it, with the ideal of a more equitable social system. Instead, the utopian spirit survived in the connotations summoned by "mental health," the images of "undivided man" in "his childhood, his era of innocence, his paradise among his peers," finding his home in "an undivided society."[104]

Horney, in her early classic, *The Neurotic Personality of Our Time* (1939), disposes of Freud's biological theory of anxiety by pointing out that relations in modern life are competitive and thus generate "hostile tension" and "constant fear," an observation that implied a psycho-social critique of capitalism,[105] but it was in the work of Herbert Marcuse and Erich Fromm, each of whom had once been attached to the Frankfurt School, with its pioneering attempts to bridge Marx, Weber, and Freud, that the two utopian ideas, the healthy community and the just one, are uniquely conjoined, particularly in *Eros and Civilization*'s demands for the repeal of surplus repression, the liberation from repressive desublimation, and the affirmation of The Great Refusal.[106] The last concept, like Marcuse's "transcendence," is quite deliberately a secular response to an otherworldly eschatology: a refusal to accept death as an escape from the suffering of this world, or to be resigned to the existent in exchange for eternal peace and reward. It is a refusal in favor of transcendence, the reimagining of the present from the standpoint of its immanent potential, or the theoretical projection of a society in which labor is no longer alienated and full productivity enjoyed, made possible by the conditions of affluence under rational planning. Never an important thinker for the Religion and Health Movement, Marcuse's critical Marxism more than his militant secularism would have been an obstacle to his inclusion in a project that was somewhat narrowly, if legitimately, focused on renovating the teaching and priestly functions of ministry. Even Erich Fromm, more sympathetic to Christianity than Marcuse, was attractive to the movement for the humanism of *Man for Himself* (which includes a chapter entitled "Faith") rather than *Marx's Concept of Man* (1960). Liberal Protestants, moreover, followed the mainline of clinical theory in focusing on the family as the institution where psychology would effect significant transformations in the baby-boom generation. As a result of these biases in method and interpretation, a shortcoming of the Religion and Health Movement remained its hesitation to connect the project of internal cure with a more thoroughgoing protest of the structures of power and not only cultural attitudes, as Left Freudians argued to greater receptivity in the sixties.

W HERE liberal Protestants have previously been attacked for abandoning Niebuhr's realism and caving into post-war America's consumer ethos (identified by Donald Meyer with the new therapeutic sensibility), the case from the Left could be made that they were too realist in their interpretation of figures like Horney and Fromm. One of the liberals' major contributions to rethinking moral theology from a therapeutic vantage, the insight that ego identities should not be identified with the perfectionist drives and ideals of the superego, could be construed as consistent with Niebuhr's own realism, which recommended that Americans shed their innocent expectations of purity. In fact, David Roberts, one of the leading figures of the Religion and Health Movement and often one of its most perspicuous voices, cites *Human Nature* frequently and explains New Testament eschatology in quite Niebuhrian terms. Christ's sacrifice relieves men from the impossible task of fulfilling His eschatological ethics—a dispensation that perhaps even Christ Himself did not fully comprehend: "To hold such standards as universals as well as absolutes is to make the guilt-ridden feel even more guilty. If such standards are accepted in an imperfect world a vicious cycle is set up, a cycle of failure followed by guilt, followed by new failure . . . the standards of Jesus seem indisputably stated in absolute terms. Can they be preached wholesale in a society of ambiguities and compromises without working against, rather than for, mental health?"[107] The question begins from the most problematic assertion of Niebuhr's Christology: Christ's perfectionist ethics and command to love perfectly are secondary to his message of salvation, and so the latter, "Christ for us," can be made to check the former, "Christ in us," from being perverted in the state of sin. Niebuhr's irony, like Freud's and Rieff's, is to suggest that man's ability to imagine ideals makes his guilt-consciousness possible, while his need to elude guilt-consciousness makes ideals necessary.[108] *Imitatio Christi*, in this case, would lead to neurotic guilt or, worse, deflect religious yearnings for the absolute into "totalitarian" and conformist identities.[109] However, Niebuhr's objectionable Christology was not the word of the movement as a whole, and even Roberts seems to qualify his interpretation of the *eschata* when he states that he believes in "divine immancence": God moves through his Creation now, fulfilling human love in divine love and freeing man from his "anxieties and old strategies of defensiveness."[110]

Psychologists were making an intervention into the fields of philosophical ethics and religion by way of therapeutic medicine, and the resulting debates made some question whether the new rationale would only effect the end of prophetic Christianity or succeed in renewing parishioners' confidence that faith was still relevant to their responsibilities and needs in all parts of their lives. Certainly the eagerness of so many churchmen to shed the concept of original sin for self-actualization strongly contrasts with the gloom of the realists who, in their heyday of the late forties and early fifties, had proclaimed with *Time* magazine that "man's story was not a success story."[111] Skeptics of the revisionists to Freud employed logic similar to the countermodernists' arguments with the radical Enlightenment, as when D. E. Walker compared his colleague Carl Rogers unfavorably to Rousseau, and Rogers's predecessor Freud to the wiser Augustine.[112] In view of modernity's revelation of human evil, it seemed ill-advised to set expectations for a new image of man too high. Rieff and Niebuhr worried that the psychologist might not only heal the person's neurotic errors, but also make him carelessly blithe regarding the crises in liberal culture or in the Cold War at large. Though their view was not always understood, the revisionists to Freud did in fact believe there was a moral and social im-

perative behind psychotherapy, for it could save patients from disproportionate, excessive guilt that made them more likely to destructively "act
out" on society or to become psychically dependent on absolute (even "authoritarian") moral systems immune to intergroup compromise.

APART FROM the postwar puff given to therapy because of the theorizing
of democracy and mental health fitness, a powerful source of the therapeutic movement's appeal was also its promise of complete honesty and
self-understanding. The patient and the parishioner could overcome the
distortions of an immature conscience and see the truth of the personality,
in all its rationalizations, its underlying needs, its wishes, and its resources
for growth and actualization. This was not the honesty of "irony," or the
honesty admitting man's rational and moral limits. It was the honesty of
preparing to respond freely to God's grace, acting through natural abilities
that had been damaged, dammed, and undiscovered. In this respect, despite superficial resemblances between psychological and Nieburhian critiques of perfectionist morality, the Religion and Health Movement departed
from Niebuhrian realism's doctrine of man and from the rhetoric of the
postwar critique of liberal "innocence." The movement did not promise
a return to innocence, a recovery of childlike harmony between self and
Other, virtue and will, but it did promise to dispel the self-deception that
was synonymous with "innocence" in the critique of modern and liberal
pieties. Self-deception, in the therapeutic accounts, is an aberration of
pseudofaith, which fosters or reinforces egocentricity, insecurity, and the
need, therefore, of moralistic illusions. Faith, properly grasped in one's total
being, is a release from dishonesty. It outgrows the anxious evasion of the
limits of self-consciousness, replacing pride with the desire for fellowship
unencumbered by guilty self-absorption or irrational idealism. An uneasy
conscience is not the only good conscience; on the contrary, in the healthy
psyche, the good conscience is not guilt-haunted because in it self-love
does not selfishly deny love to man. The true self-love the healthy psyche
enjoys is impossible without feeling love for man. As expressed in the
movement as a whole, these positions never graduated to being truly counterhegemonic since they did not theorize the relationship between cultural
attitudes and structures of power with the intensity that they theorized the
relationship between culture and neurosis; hence they did not arrive at a
necessary alliance of political instrumentalities and therapeutic modalities.
Yet in an age where moral realists "honestly" appraised self-deception as
congenital to man's fallen nature and offered the recognition of this tragic
condition in apology for "ambiguous" conduct and "lesser evils," the utopian impulse of the religion and health movement must stand out more

strongly than its lacking eschatology or its fears, then and subsequently aired, of the "hypertrophy of the therapeutic attitude" that "sickness accounts for badness."[113] Envisioning a therapeutic community based on mutual regard and loving acceptance, using the rational to heal the emotional and the analytical to release the creative, the movement did transcend the end of innocence narrative that saturated other areas of intellectual production, albeit this was transcendence of a speculative and politically incomplete nature. Certainly there were pop-religious derivatives—the magazine articles with their headlines asking "Sin or Symptom?"—as well as some abuses in the application of mental hygiene to ministerial goals, as Karl Menninger, a proponent turned friendly critic, had pointed out years later in *Whatever Became of Sin?* These half-assimilations of therapeutic ideas do not invalidate the achievement or undo the potential that lay in the alliance of religion and health.[114] The danger to human well-being lay not in psychology's diminution of sin-consciousness, but in the relation of psychology to compulsory gender formations, which, perhaps more than any other cultural pressure, hampered and deferred the potentially liberating applications of therapeutic methods.

CHAPTER EIGHT

Locating the Enigma of Shirley Jackson

> We are afraid of being someone else and doing the things someone
> else wants us to do and of being taken and used by someone else,
> some other guilt-ridden conscience that lives on and on in our minds,
> something we build ourselves and never recognize, but this is fear,
> not a named sin. Then it is fear itself, fear of self that I am writing
> about . . . fear and guilt and their destruction of identity. . . .
>
> —Shirley Jackson, unsent letter to Howard Nemerov (1960)

The Attraction of the Satanic

Though she was raised by a Christian Scientist, Shirley Jackson's fiction
bears no trace of Mary Baker Eddy's theology. Her recurring theme, she
once stated, is "'the insistence on the uncontrolled, unobserved wickedness of human behavior.'"[1] Evil is no mental illusion for Jackson, and her
narrators share knowing attitudes about the multifarious guises that evil
may take, especially in a modern world where the Devil, as Baudelaire
observed before Jackson, has succeeded in convincing most men that he
does not exist. With her caustic slant on the pretenses humans assume in
love and morality, which one critic has compared to Swiftian misanthropy,[2]
as well as her frequently mordant and rococo subject matter, Shirley Jackson was sometimes taken for a celebrant of medieval diabolism rather than
the anatomist of human deception that she was in fact. Particularly after
the scandalizing publication of "The Lottery" (1948) for the *New Yorker*,
some rumored that Jackson herself was quite literally devilish, but these
indignant reactions and their parody by middlebrow literary critics, such
as Harvey Breit, missed the author's ironic relation to traditional symbols
of evil.[3] Although Jackson's reading habits betray a long fascination with
the figure of the Devil,[4] she was not persuaded that modern people could
respond to such a literal-minded personification. She preferred instead to
encourage readers to play the game of imagining the cracks the Devil might
see in their world were he looking for signs of recidivism that could be
turned to hell's profit.

   In the only story where Jackson directly portrays the prince of darkness,
the results are notably burlesque because the youthful human characters,
both members of the up-and-coming baby-boom generation, are too much

the wiseacres to be either hoodwinked or frightened when the Devil comes with the standard contract for their souls. In "The Smoking Room," the Devil materializes in a girls' college dorm where the strict housemother's injunctions against cigarettes seem more awe-inspiring to the students than horns and hooves.[5] The two girls, for whom the underworld of eternal torment is nothing but a slang word (they casually say "what the hell" and "raise hell" in the Devil's presence), easily outwit their guest. The Devil is missing his forked tail (an allusion to folk stories in which clever humans cut the tail off), and, with a little sly double-talk, one of the girls manages to bamboozle him into losing something else; he obliviously signs over *his* soul to her terms. In the end, the girls have reduced their haggler to looking like Old Scratch rather than Mephistopheles, though the Devil snorts enough brimstone to make him seem nearly infernal—until the housemother orders him from the dorm because he constitutes a fire hazard. The story intrigues because its playful tone mocks the humans as well as the more obviously foolish Devil. The image of Satan, adversary of God and man, is clearly a butt of satire, but the girls' trick is not a victory of human wisdom as much as it is a sign that humans have become better at the Devil's confidence game than he.

Though her works were reviewed in the mainstream press, Shirley Jackson was overlooked by academic literary intellectuals who were then placing the Gothic at the center of the (newly invented) American canon as both a national countertradition and the main artery of the classics.[6] Critics like Harry Levin and Leslie Fiedler praised the American Gothic as the masculine alternative to moribund liberalism, with its deadening mixture of Enlightenment and "sentimental" Christianity.[7] Only in the Gothic had American fiction produced tragic figures of Faustian dimension, who learn that "our dream of innocence" and the "self-deceptions of positive thinking" never truly abolished evil, only "drove the devils inward" to "a hidden world of nightmare."[8] Critical studies like *The Power of Blackness* and *Love and Death in the American Novel* were written more or less in sympathy with Cold War liberalism, but while they berated the quondam sunlit optimism that had traded the "darker wisdom" of the Puritan legacy for the cooing of "Mr. Smooth-It-Away," Shirley Jackson, taking the modern American family as her laboratory, was saying "'No in thunder!'" more gravely perhaps than liberals would have cared to hear.[9] Jackson does not stop at digging a grave for the old Emersonian optimism and the pieties of Little Eva. She turned her theme of humanity's "uncontrolled, unobserved wickedness" on the period's compulsory gender formations with perspicuity embarrassing to the oversights of both the therapeutic movement and tough-minded, masculinized realism.

Combining concern for the victims of social power with a dystopian attitude keen to pretenses about the moral progress of modernity, Jackson was a postwar thinker recovering from the crisis of liberal philosophy that had led certain intellectuals to Niebuhrian realism.[10] Although Jackson had bona fide liberal credentials, which her fictional worlds delimit, to discuss her only as a voice within the liberal self-critique would not reveal her uniqueness. Jackson was one of the few postwar American women writers—others include Flannery O'Connor, Patricia Highsmith, and Sylvia Plath—who made the problem of evil central to her work. Theology had historically been male-authored, and the discourses on evil in Cold War America were conducted by males, save for the influence of Europeans Hannah Arendt and Simone de Beauvoir. Setting herself apart, Jackson wrote about iniquity and placed that sin within women's lives. She extended the postwar dissections of deceit and self-deception, guilt and its evasion, barbarity and regression, into the experience of "domestic containment."[11] Jackson's overt liberal sentiments, such as her disgust with insipid xenophobia and intolerance, were rarely explicit outside of her first novel, *The Road through the Wall* (1948), as she chose instead to describe how individual women in their families served functions analogous to the surrogate victims in larger social networks.[12] This was not the stuff of the liberal reflections on evil that made press during the Cold War, when there was "no legitimating cultural vocabulary for troubled housewives."[13] Hence Jackson early on courted the impression that she identified with witches, the Devil's vessels, for the witch was a female outsider whose imagination, like magic, challenged the reality principle that others accepted on convention.[14]

Blood of Atonement: Domestic Rituals, Sacred Patterns, and Psychic Disturbances

Jackson does not set the violence in her stories apart from the mundane. Instead, her stories show barbarism's continuity with arid social behavior, as if the author had discovered "the banality of evil" years before Hannah Arendt formulated it. The unidentified community of Jackson's celebrated, career-launching story "The Lottery" indefatigably follow a bloody custom with a lost ceremonial origin that none of the villagers can identify.[15] The story's imagery, its victim's name (Tess *Hutchinson*), and the characters' asides imply several different sources: pagan fertility rites, the Crucifixion, the Puritans' expulsion of antinomians, the ancient Hebraic practice of stoning lawbreakers.[16] By netting so many religious traditions, the sto-

ry's symbolism implies that all rites are united in the sacrifice of the surrogate victim. The allusions to the Crucifixion in the ritual of lots, moreover,
challenge Christianity's central conceit that the Lamb's offering was the
consummate sacrifice, putting an end to all previous covenants requiring
sacrificial offerings of blood and introducing a new covenant based on
love.[17] Jackson once explained that she was writing about the possibilities
of "order" and "adjustment" in "an inhuman world," but where ego nat-
urally vies with ego, order itself becomes an inhuman necessity.[18] Order
does not maintain the instrumentalities of justice, nor does it protect the
powerless; it is but regulatory violence imposed upon indiscriminating destruction.

Tess Hutchinson in "The Lottery" differs from other female victims in
Jackson's fiction since she publicly refuses, at the last, to comply with the
sacrificial order, but subsequent Jackson heroines have much more difficulty identifying what imperils them since they are not affronted with an
open communal rite, but immured in the ostensibly private relations of the
home. To conform within one of Jackson's groups is to give up oneself to
the will of another, and in the home, the person who surrenders most, under pressure of rejection and censure, is typically female. Her female characters, moreover, are often daunted, even stymied, by ambivalence about
domestic life as much as fear of tangible reprisal from family members
or society at large. "Madwomen" or "witches" like Natalie Waite, Clara
Spencer, or Eleanor Vance cannot resolve whether their repressed desires
consist only of dissociated libidinal wishes incarcerated by the family order, or else a damnable evil within them denied by the home's rituals and
by idyllic domestic fantasy. Through the prisms of their fantasies, we discern how their theological anxiety enforces their self-fear, for each woman
wonders whether her unconscious consorts with evil or merely harbors the
narcissism and aggression that are less appropriate for the feminine role to
express. Unable to know, they hesitate to flee. Since the home is repressive,
it may, paradoxically, seem both a safeguard against evil and a prison for
the self. Through her own sensibility, Jackson was grappling with a problem that feminists a decade later would pose as the question, "how have
women learned to comply with their self-sacrifice?"

To approach this issue in Jackson's writing, it is not enough to work
with sociological categories, as in Elaine May's important work on gender
in the Cold War, or with psychoanalytic ones, as in so much of the criticism devoted to Jackson specifically. These approaches, while valuable in
some applications, usually minimize the strong presence of evil that Jackson discovers in the family and in Christian society at large; feminine self-
sacrifice, for Jackson, was one more example—one literally "close to

home"—of the invidious tendency of human communities to sacrifice life in exchange for maintaining order that is neither disinterested nor equitable. In the short story cycle of *The Lottery, or the Adventures of James Harris* (1949) or in such novels as *Hangsaman* (1951), *The Bird's Nest* (1954), or *The Haunting of Hill House* (1959), the characters have not truly advanced beyond the order of sacred violence, in which a sacrificial victim guarantees the stability of the society.[19] The sacrifice may be a literal immolation (as in "The Lottery") or it may be a renunciation of self, which the victim registers as a malevolent possession—"being someone else and doing the things someone else wants us to do and being taken and used by someone else."[20]

In a haunting letter to Howard Nemerov that is key to understanding the psychology of her heroines, Jackson defines guilt nonmoralistically as "self-fear," which leads to dispossession by conscience and the destruction of identity. By "identity," Jackson perhaps intends some continuity between the meaning one has for others and the meaning one has for oneself. It is precisely, however, this coincidence of inner sameness and outward demands that guilt dislocates, even "destroys," in victims who are selected to give their happiness, or their very lives, for the sake of maintaining social congruence. Having learned only too well the "fear of self," her female characters face situations that dare them, against guilt, to commit "the unnamed sin" of being themselves. They can find no release from their guilt by seeking absolution, for Christianity is hypocritical, nor by soliciting the aid of mental health professionals, for psychotherapy is merely an arm of the sacrificial order.

Near the end of her life, when Jackson was approaching a nervous breakdown, Stanley Hyman and friends encouraged her to see a psychotherapist.[21] Eventually she consented to outpatient care, but only after considerable resistance. Whereas her husband was a doctrinaire Freudian and an exponent of psychoanalytic literary criticism, Jackson was skeptical: "The obvious choice was psychotherapy, but Shirley feared and distrusted the idea. 'I always felt it was a little bit like Christian Science'" (251). The comparison to the religion of her mother, Geraldine Jackson, which Shirley had long rejected, might seem cryptic unless one remembers Mary Baker Eddy's belief that the mind, being sovereign over all that existed by it and for it, could be self-curative if only it would put aside the illusions of sin and fear that stood in the way of its power. Although postwar psychotherapy was rational rather than mystical, it also aimed to heal the mind by making the psyche's contents less fearful and more self-integrated. Jackson's "mad" heroines, by contrast, suffer psychological fragmentation in which parts of the psyche are alienated by guilt, only to return in horrifying forms. Yet, in Jackson's imagination, this condition is preferable to integration. In a culture where diagnoses of momism could trace evil to women's influence even as mental hospitals were shown sequestering women for mental diseases in literature and film, Jackson asked whether the new "secular religion" was more cruelly efficient than the Christian morality of the Dark Ages since the therapeutic gaze could effectuate conformity without preaching fear of the Devil.[22]

The postwar pact with psychology inspired a host of fiction and films introducing, in some cases exploiting, the new theories of the mind, and one of the wave's major motifs was the madwoman whose presence not only showed a genuine fascination with the bewildering inner world of the ill but also stressed the imperative for medical intervention in women's lives.[23] Shirley Jackson successfully entered this market for mental case study literature with her self-nominated "psychological horror novels," *Hangsaman* (1951) and *The Bird's Nest* (1954). These books, her second and third, extend the themes of order, self-fear, and feminine fantasy, and they look forward to the characterization of Eleanor Vance in *The Haunting of Hill House* (1959). The two novels each treat a different syndrome— *Hangsaman* dealing with schizophrenia and *The Bird's Nest* with multiple personality disorder. For both, Jackson did independent research with the help of a psychiatry faculty member at Bennington College, and this knowledge clearly informs each book.[24] *Hangsaman*'s central character, a seventeen-year-old woman named Natalie Waite who is embarking on a college career, exhibits many traits resembling the diagnostic profiles that sociologist Carol Warren has reconstructed in *Madwives: Schizophrenic Women in the 1950s*. Natalie too has experiences that mimic "delusions and hallucinations," "paranoia and fear of conspiracy," "irrational talk," "wandering," and "suicidal threats," but such parallels underscore Jackson's self-conscious appropriation of phenomenal descriptions of illness rather than point to the clinical key to the character.[25] The novel is narrated solely from Natalie's point of view minus any intervening medical interpretation, and her strange perception of situations creates patterns that indict banal and manipulative social networks rather than point to a disease transpiring in herself. Contrary to so many other examples of mental case study fiction, Jackson's psychological horror novels trust the patient rather than the doctor.

Natalie Waite, a female fantasist who wishes to transfer her experience into writing is a rare case in Jackson. This ambition is choked, however, by the girl's fear of revealing what she thinks and sees, a predicament that Jackson specifies as feminine by contrasting Natalie's attitudes towards writing to her father's. Aware of his daughter's aspirations, Natalie's father, an accomplished author, regards her as his protege and offers commentary on his daughter's notebooks. Consistent with his own views of his craft, Mr. Waite has taught Natalie to think of imagination as a private activity that has no bearing in a society where one must learn, he instructs Natalie, the business of "strengthening your artistic integrity and fortifying you[rself] against the world."[26] Mr. Waite, who compares himself jestingly to "the Old Testament God," treats his art as a way of protecting the purity of an inner world that he takes for granted and needs no reciprocal voice to confirm (424–426). In many ways an early version of Hugh Crain, the sinister artist-patriarch of *Haunting of Hill House,* Mr. Waite, godlike in his aloofness, uses his mind to obviate the activities around him and to display his contempt for conventions, particularly those of his wife, whose maternal solicitude he finds positively trite. In contrast to Mr. Waite, Natalie cannot simply resolve to keep her interiority whole, for she suffers from a fundamental insecurity, foreign to her father's experience, that she lacks a free self with a continuous identity. Although she feels alone, it is not in the confidence of self-possession but in the terrible anxiety that if she asserts herself among people, she will either cease to exist or else commit some wrong for which she will be punished, damned, or locked away. Natalie hesitates to write her fantasies because they are not partitioned from her environment as her father pretends of his own; instead, they mediate her extreme dispossession by her social relationships.

An example of a guilt-ridden consciousness that confuses suffering with punishment,[27] Natalie believes, as Wyatt Bonikowski points out, that she is marked by some anterior "original crime."[28] Unable to identify what interdict she has violated, for it is actually her whole person that is implicated, Natalie imagines that her estrangement and depression are symptoms of retribution returned for an unknown evil. Rather than let herself suffer dumbly, as in a cry, Natalie prefers to have the meaningfulness of guilt, even if she cannot avow her transgression. As we join her at the beginning of the novel, amidst the family's preparations for one of her father's literary parties, she is having the first of her many fantasies, one in which a detective interrogates her for a murder she does not remember committing. The interrogation takes place in a library amidst books on demonology, the first of several clues that Natalie's creativity makes her a kind of modern witch subject to persecution.[29] The criminal fantasy recurs in one of the novel's most telling passages, when Natalie imagines that she has been interred in a mental hospital for some offense: "Or even suppose, imagine, could it be true? that she was confined, locked away, pounding wildly against the bars on the window, attacking the keepers, biting at the doctors, screaming down corridors" (468). Inhaling ether, with a policeman as well as a nurse in attendance, Natalie imagines fading in and out of a delirium in which reality is the hospital chamber, and dream the life she has known for seventeen years. A vision in which asylum and prison converge, Natalie's reverie about "mad women" does not represent a self-diagnosis so much as it reveals the girl's terror of the external world where her behavior as a young woman is evaluated. That world, she thinks, is made of appearances concealing darker, controlling forces that people overlook because they have been subdued and anesthetized, either literally, as madwomen are treated by doctors, or else figuratively, like the normal people who expect her to grow up. Natalie's fear of psychiatric help extends even to private consultation. Suffering from depression during her first year at college, she contemplates going to a campus therapist, only to reject the idea because she suspects her mind would be taken from her: "I wonder what I would say to a psychoanalyst. . . . I think if I could tell someone everything, every single thing, inside my head, then I would be gone, and not existing anymore, and I would sink away into that lovely nothing space where you don't have to worry anymore" (411). Psychotherapy would reduce her to a nonentity, a prospect that has some appeal to Natalie because it would release her from the dread of others, though it would also make her mind the property of an investigator, who would have the power to use it without giving up any of his own thoughts in return (412). These fantasies of confession suggest Natalie's desperation for intimacy as well as her flight from it. She imagines being drawn, by force if necessary, into revealing herself so that she might be saved from loneliness and have her "crime" and her "madness" divulged. At the same time, any revelation will be processed by people whom, she imagines, will annihilate all the personal anomalies that make her secrets worth preserving in the first place.

Carceral and medical authorities have become Natalie's models for human communication because she has found no reciprocity in private relationships, which have instead resulted in her objectification. It is important to recognize that Natalie begins having fantasies of being investigated or destroyed prior to the sexual molestation that takes place during one of her father's literary parties, when an older male guest takes the drunk girl into the garden. Judy Oppenheimer has suggested that the sexual abuse, and the family's subsequent denial that it took place, precipitates the girl's schizophrenic reactions, but this shocking incident serves rather to demonstrate an emergent pattern of coercion that characterizes Natalie's life. Just as the rapacious party guest feigns an interest in Natalie's unusual mind so that he may extort her body, so too her acquaintances, at home and at college, pretend to involve her in their lives only to exact demands that would nullify her difference from others.

The opening vignettes of *Hangsaman* quickly establish Natalie's milieu: an unhappy middle-class family in which the self-absorbed father is the center of attention, the mother alcoholic, the son nearly invisible, and the daughter (Natalie) afraid of adult life. When Mr. Waite is out of earshot, Natalie's mother has surreptitious conferences with her daughter, whose fate, she fears, may become like her own—deceived by someone she now regards as an enemy: "All he wants is no one to think that they can be the same as he is, or equal to him, or something. And you watch out—the minute you start getting too big, he'll be after you too. . . . First they tell you lies and they make you believe them . . . Then you find out you've been tricked, just like everyone else, just like *everyone,* and instead of being different and powerful and giving the orders, you've been tricked just like everyone else" (348). Mrs. Waite's speech, the only long passage of dialogue given her in the novel, moves from an indictment of her marriage to a general statement in which the manipulation between husband and wife, as well as father and daughter, characterizes the trickery practiced on *everyone,* the pronoun repeated and italicized in the text of the speech. Under the rubrics of psychopathology in Jackson's day, such a statement would have likely been labeled paranoid, especially coming from a housewife, but in *Hangsaman* it describes the situations Natalie experiences, from her English teacher's adulterous relationships with his students, to the family of Arthur and Sue Langdon, whose antagonistic marriage mirrors her mother and father's relationship; to the rounds of college initiations designed to enforce conformity and ostracize deviates; to the homogenous township where everyone seems to have become an "automaton" serving "the harmony of discipline that control[s] a huge, functioning order" (515). Granted, these are Natalie's visions, and no external narrative voice affirms them, but the visions are corroborated by the view of social groups shown elsewhere in Jackson's work, *The Road through the Wall* and the short stories collected in *The Lottery* as well as the later fiction, such as *The Sundial* and *We Have Always Lived in a Castle.* Natalie's fantasies are haunted by one of the recurrent themes of Jackson's fiction, a theme underlined by the novel's very title, which alludes to a sacrificial figure, the Hanging Man, from the tarot deck.[30] Through her firsthand experience of exploitation and deceit at home, Natalie has been granted traumatic insight into the workings of an aggressive principle in human relationships by which some forfeit their lives so that others may assert their ego.

The Hanging Man is pointed out in a shop window by Natalie's college friend and spiritual double, Tony, whom she suspects a witch. Possibly an efrit of Natalie's own imagination, Tony shares most of Natalie's impressions and invites Natalie to reject forever the adult life, the alien world of others' wishes, that has been plotted for her (522). As a "witch," Tony is a figure of imaginative empowerment in Jackson's oeuvre, but the character's audacious, self-pleasuring nature appears dangerously amoral to Natalie, who knows no compromise between complete egoism and utter self-abnegation. The novel closes on an uncertain note. As Natalie leaves the woods where she has renounced Tony and made her vanish with an incantation ("one is all alone and evermore shall be"), she has a final fantasy, poignant in its irony, that the first car approaching is her mother coming to take her home, even though nothing in the novel suggests that Natalie can be anywhere both at home and in herself. Unable to accept the dare to join her magical double, and yet unprepared to return to society, her final wish to rejoin her mother may veil a longing for regression to childhood, in which fantasy is tolerated as natural rather than mad, and the individual, as yet, has committed no crime that requires payment.

ELIZABETH, THE FRAGMENTED heroine of Jackson's psychological horror novel about multiple personality syndrome, *The Bird's Nest* (1954) has her own childlike regression interrupted by psychiatric care only then to face the oppression of her recovery. Jackson's novel encompasses the perspectives of the subject Elizabeth's four personalities as well as those of her guardian (Aunt Morgen) and her psychotherapist (Dr. Wright). Whereas in *Hangsaman* a godlike father tries to make his introverted daughter "grow up," in *The Bird's Nest* the paternalistic psychotherapist attempts to reduce a girl's dissociated personalities into one malleable soul. *The Bird's Nest* gainsays therapeutic closure, however, instead disclosing how the doctor supplants the patient's defenses so that she and her surrogate parents can coalesce into an obligatory family unit. The supernatural splashes in the pompous doctor's rhetoric call attention to the similar functions of ancient religion and modern medicine, while Jackson associates Elizabeth's "healing" with sacred violence only her "sick" imagination was able to resist.

When the reader joins twenty-three-year-old Elizabeth Richmond and her three other personalities—Bess, Betsy, Beth—they have been living together alternately in one body for over four years, ever since the death of Elizabeth's alcoholic mother precipitated her disintegration.[31] The orphaned child has been in the foster care of her unmarried and jobless Aunt Morgen, who, unable to handle her charge's increasingly erratic and abusive behavior, has finally dispatched her to Dr. Wright, a prim, aging psychotherapist. After a couple of hypnotic trances, Dr. Wright becomes acquainted with two of Elizabeth's personalities, Beth, whom he adores, and Betsy, whom he regards as evil incarnate. Beth moves him to "fa-therly" devotion: "I thought of myself frequently, as fatherly," he remarks in his log, "and often found myself addressing her as a fond parent speaks to precious child."[32] When Beth mutates before his eyes into Betsy, who is mischievous and taunting, Dr. Wright recoils as if he has "raised demons": "As I watched her in horror, the smile upon her soft lips coarsened, and became sensual and gross. . . . and she laughed evilly and roughly, throw-ing her head back and shouting, and I, seeing a devil's mask. . . . thought only, it cannot be Beth; this is not she. . . . What I saw that afternoon was the dreadful grinning face of a fiend" (192). Jackson appears to be alluding here to a passage from Freud's "Dora" (1905): "No one who, like me, has conjured up the most evil of those half-tamed demons that inhabit the hu-man breast and seeks to wrestle with them, can expect to come through the struggle unscathed."[33] A treatment that famously went awry because of the male therapist's ham-fisted approach to his female patient, Dora's case is an apt comparison for Dr. Wright's handling of the antagonist Betsy. In fact the liveliest and most inventive of all Elizabeth's personalities, Betsy is the woman arrested in childhood, at the point her father died and her mother disappeared for a series of affairs. What the doctor mistakes as "sensual" and "evil" is actually Betsy's understandable disrespect for adults and those, like her sister persona Beth, who want to obey them. After Dr. Wright determines to cast out "the possessing demon," he suc-ceeds only in shutting down the treatment, and, exasperated, he tries to jettison Elizabeth's case. Betsy's rebellion is the first crisis that results from the doctor's design to select and mold those parts of Elizabeth's fourfold personality that he deems fit for a young lady.

Once the psychotherapist deserts, Elizabeth's warring personalities at-tack each other with escalating violence, promising to kill off their host's body in their efforts to possess her mind, until Dr. Wright, who shows no remorse over having abandoned his patient, returns to the case with undi-minished pomp. Unexpectedly, the doctor and Aunt Morgen find them-selves bizarrely attracted to each other, and a sort of family triangle forms around Elizabeth, who has not had two supervising adults in her life since the passing of Mr. Richmond. Together, Dr. Wright and Aunt Morgen force the second major crisis of Elizabeth's treatment, as they make her confront her unconscious guilt over her mother's death and her seduction by one of her mother's lovers. Once Dr. Wright and Aunt Morgen pressure Eliza-beth's unconscious traumas to the surface, her four personalities melt away, leaving a neophyte who has memories of her past lives but no emo-tional cathexis to any of them. The new being, who, according to Dr. Wright, warrants another name altogether, seems well on the road to full recovery, but as the doctor and the aunt converse about her future, the fresh "Elizabeth" seems very vulnerable. "You have just eaten your four sisters," the doctor tells "Elizabeth," whose recovery, he muses, illustrates some cannibalistic principle of existence.[34] He entertains the theory at a party later the same afternoon: "Each life, I think, asks the devouring of other lives for its own continuance; the radical aspect of ritual sacrifice, the performance of a group, its great step ahead, was in organization; *sharing* the victim was so eminently practical" (378). Diverted by conversation, Dr. Wright rambles from "the custom of human sacrifice" to the practice of magic: "'The human creature at odds with its environment must change either its protective coloration, or the shape of the world in which it lives. Equipped with no magic device beyond a not overly sharp intelligence . . . the human creature finds it tempting to endeavor to control its surroundings through manipulated symbols of sorcery, arbitrarily chosen, and frequently ineffectual'" (379). Such is Jackson's subtlety that she buries her key motifs in the doctor's party conversation, which is frequently sidetracked by snippets of other characters' dialogue. Despite the apparent sangfroid, however, the doctor's gabbing contains irony that escapes him, for Elizabeth's story has been, at one level, about the clash between "sorcery" and "sacrifice."

Both demon possession and ritual sacrifice are the reverse of psychoanalytic transference; rather than projecting memories of past figures onto another, as the patient theoretically does to the analyst, the victim undergoes an "extreme alienation in which the self absorbs the desires of another," whether the other is a demon who invades the soul or a group that makes the scapegoat its surrogate.[35] The processes recall Natalie's perception of psychotherapy, in which the patient does not project onto the analyst so much as she lets herself be absorbed by him until she has become hollow. In *The Bird's Nest*, as well, psychotherapy functions like the superstitions it purports to have superseded, despite Dr. Wright's enlightened opinion that these ancient practices are "generally deplored today."[36] Elizabeth's self-splitting—and Betsy's imaginative diversions—have been a magical protection against bewildering guilt as well as adult authority, represented by Dr. Wright and Aunt Morgen, who each want to place claims on her being. In Elizabeth's sickness, there was chaos, regression, and even mortal danger, but her cure is only a relative betterment, for it leaves her subject to the propriety of Dr. Wright and the emotional blackmail of her Aunt Morgen. Having sacrificed, or devoured, her sisters, "Elizabeth" is now subject to sacrifice herself for her newly formed family. Dr. Wright and Aunt Morgen, who have begun to joke about being parents and an old married couple, have plans for their ward; whereas before Elizabeth was "possessed by demons," she is now an "empty vessel" for them to permeate. Dr. Wright observes, "*Our* responsibility is, clearly, to people this vacant landscape—fill this empty vessel, I think I said before—and, with our own deep emotional reserves, enable the child to rebuild. We have a sobering duty. She will owe to us her opinions, her discriminations, her reflections" (374). Dr. Wright's charter for the trio's future, to be played out upon the identity of "Elizabeth," follows a passage that intimately describes the recovering girl's own revelations, perceptions, and new acquisitions. In the novel's final scene, as "Elizabeth" names the stars and the flowers on her path, Dr. Wright and Aunt Morgen, talking—literally—over the girl's head, discuss betwixt themselves what *they* should rename their ward. The novel's closing line, Elizabeth's "I know who I am," rings hollow (380). She has passed from one shattered family structure to a freshly formed parental set who, in the name of health and duty, will use guilt to mold her.

Jackson's implicit defense of madness, and its association with witchery, in many respects anticipated the next decade's influential "anti-psychiatrists" Thomas Szasz and Phyllis Chesler, who both struck parallels between the psychological labeling of social undesirables and the religious persecution of witches, stigmatized first by the Catholic Church and later by Protestant reformers.[37] Citing the biblical injunction, "Thou shalt not suffer a witch to live" (Exodus 22:18) as well as two of Jackson's favorite texts, the Book of Leviticus and Frazier's *The Golden Bough*, Szasz argues that witches were imprisoned, interrogated, tortured, and killed for the sake of preserving the prevailing, theological, ideology of social control, which was made visible by sacred ritual. The modern world is only more subtle, not more ethical, than the medieval Church; the "scapegoat" for society's violation of its official norms is now the mad person, whose counterexample is emphasized by stigmatizing medical labels that imply the threats of force and expulsion, actuated if necessary through hospitalized internment and compulsory treatment.[38] Between "the Age of Faith" and "the Age of Therapy," the "human predator" has thus redefined "sin" as "mental illness": "The differences between these two perspectives, one theological, the other therapeutic, are ideological and semantic, rather than operational or social. . . . Ancient religions are thus restored in new psychiatric ceremonies of inclusion and exclusion" (268, 265). Incorporating Szasz's parallels between religious inquisition and modern mental hygiene, feminist Phyllis Chesler stressed the feminine gender of the witch and noted that in the twentieth century, an overwhelmingly disproportionate number of women, as opposed to men, had been classified as mental patients.[39] Drawing upon a striking case history, Chesler notes that the first person to make "the analogy of Institutional Psychiatry and the Inquisition" was nineteenth-century author Elizabeth Packard, interned in an asylum by her minister husband because she disagreed with his Calvinism (9–11). In the contemporary world, Chesler asserts, the pieties women are coerced to observe, on threat of being labeled abnormal and sick, are domestic rather than religious; expecting a sacrificial servant, the patriarchal family follows Reverend Packard in giving love on the strictly observed condition of obedience.

In light of Szasz's and Chesler's theories of scapegoating and the power-inscribing effects of discourses on illness and gender, Jackson seems remarkably prescient, though even in this regard her work remains politically elusive. While the revolt in the sixties against the therapeutic was libertarian and feminist, Jackson writes from no theoretical position about patriarchy, preferring instead to develop witchcraft and madness as multilayered metaphors for the feminine imagination's entanglement with extreme repression. From her readings of witchcraft theory, Jackson would have known that the Church had classified magic as "the counter sacred" and the sacred as "counter magic," the inverse categories assuming that necromancy was an evil perversion of holy ritual.[40] Inasmuch as an abnormal feminine imagination envisions an alternative to the prevailing order, it is "counter sacred," heretical and blasphemous, like witchcraft, and some of Jackson's imaginative heroines, who are racked by guilty fear, actually conceive of themselves as dallying with the Devil and risking damnation.

In "The Tooth," a story ostensibly about a trip to the dentist, the heroine, Clara Spencer, a suburban wife and mother, dreams of escaping from her domestic cycle. Woozy from anesthetic, Clara awakens to tell the nurse that the blood that filled her mouth during the operation has defiled her: "God has given me blood to drink."[41] In any Christian or Judaic context, the consumption of actual blood would be blasphemous, since only God is permitted to shed blood or receive it in sacrifice, but in Satanic rites, with which Jackson would have been familiar from her voluminous witchcraft library, the ingestion of blood is a countersacrament, wedding the soul to Satan rather than Christ.[42] Forgetting plans to return home, Clara wanders off to a netherworld with the dark stranger from her anesthetized dream, a man who may be a projection of her own imagination—or else the Devil incognito as "James Harris," the demon lover from an old ballad, who leads women into hell.[43] The figure of Faust, as discovered in the Cold War liberal's American Gothic, was a masculine hero learning to grow up, with pangs to his Adamic ego, by playing the Devil's game. Jackson's Faustian protagonists are typically female, and they do not attain the grandeur of the Fall, but intuit psychosocial connections between scape-goating, the mechanism of guilt, and domestic ideologies of feminine self-sacrifice. If imagination could lead to madness, Jackson resisted the thought of cure, for she did not relinquish the idea that fantasy, however perilous to the feminine dreamer, contains insight lost to the normal, "counter magical" order. It might be the Devil's truth, but it might be also be a refusal of domination and death in life.

An Anatomy of Deceit More Radical Than Niebuhr's

Since she saw through the devilish con games of "good" people, Jackson herself was willing publicly to court the pose of flirting with Satan, but some of her heroines hesitate, fatefully, to transgress home's boundaries and wish to sustain the illusion of domestic safety even after they have per-forated it. Showing a woman's schizoid descent through a trio of loveless families—one biological, another improvised, and one spectral—Jackson's penultimate novel, *The Haunting of Hill House* (1959), turns the material of psychoanalytic case study into a supernatural mystery (one of her few forays into the marvelous) that functions as her most profound meditation on the lies that regulate power in the home.[44] Clara Spencer dares to es-cape; Natalie wavers between submission and witchery; "Elizabeth" is forcibly reintegrated into a family; Eleanor's end, however, is the cruelest example of sacrifice in Jackson's oeuvre since Tess Hutchinson's stoning in "The Lottery."

Hill House's designer, Hugh Crain, and its guest, Eleanor Vance, are paired by the novel's key metaphors of madness and dreaming. The novel opens and closes on a symmetrically repeated, anthropomorphic descrip-tion of Hill House, alone, dreaming, and insane, its personality foreshad-owing Eleanor's fate and implying Hugh Crain's sensibility. The mirroring descriptions of the house punctuate the theme that reason is illusion, and readers encountering these lines the second time, after Eleanor's sojourn in the house is over, will appreciate the narrator's irony: "Within, walls con-tinued upright, bricks met neatly, floors were firm, and doors were sensibly shut."[45] In fact, this description is deceptive, as is the apparent orderliness of the house, for Hugh Crain, contemning "other people and their sensible, squared-away houses," made a house "to suit his own mind" (105). In a scrapbook Crain had prepared for his daughters, he included a Goya etch-ing that appears to be "The Sleep of Reason Produces Monsters," in which a writer, asleep at his desk, dreams of winged ghouls that fly about his head

(168). Crain designed Hill House to emancipate his imagination—take what hideous shape it might—rather than to prepare a domicile for his wife and children. His rebellion against the reality principle is exalted by his sublime revolt against the laws of reason and God, whereas Eleanor's rebellion is aborted by guilt. His insanity is privileged by romantic conceit, while Eleanor's invites suspicion of sickness. The Byronic Crain comes from the mold of Gothic hero-villains, but the narrator's interest in Eleanor's counterbalancing example underscores how Crain's form of rebellion is unavailable, in Jackson's universe, to the feminine gender unless the female risks destruction by the family ideal she is supposed to serve. A nonconformist masculine artist, Crain defied convention and suffered tragedy, but the violence fell upon him indirectly, wasting his wives and pursuing his children. Eleanor, by contrast, is devastated by her dreams, which she can neither don heroically nor even accept as part of herself.

As in past works, Jackson suggests the social coercion beneath pretenses of closeness and righteousness by likening life in the home to taboos and laws that are justified by the order of the sacred rather than mutuality or any measure of love. The iconoclastic Hugh Crain, who was intrigued by religion and obviously irreverent toward Christianity, inscribed a scrapbook to his first daughter, decorated with scenes of torture from Foxe's *Book of Martyrs* as well as lurid visions of the spirit world by Goya and William Blake, which is designed to emphasize the violent polarity of orthodoxy and heresy. All four characters who leaf through the scrapbook are shocked by its contents, which are patently satiric, even blasphemous. Hacked apart from many volumes on religion and glossed with his own mock teachings, Crain's scrapbook reveals a flair for extreme duality, of redemption and damnation, of purity and sin. Although the scrapbook has many notes of false humility ("my feeble effort," "humbleness of spirit"), its author shows his hubris when he puns on "father" (paternity, godhead) at the end of the illustrated sermon on the Seven Deadly Sins, addressed to his eldest daughter Sophia Anne. Godlike, Crain enjoins his daughter to "a sacred pact" whereby Sophia Anne must preserve her "meek" and "virtuous" father's laws lest her soul be lost. Crain has signed the pact in his own blood, parodying Christ's bloodshed for man's redemption (171).

With his blasphemous pact, sealed in his own unhallowed fluid, Crain shifts the analog for the parent-child bond from merciful God and erring sinner to an older sacrificial covenant, as in "The Lottery," based on the taking of life rather than the proffering of love (171). By mocking the New Testament covenant, which supposedly ended ritual sacrifice for Christians, Crain's scrapbook flamboyantly points up the principle of sacred violence that runs through the domestic order in Jackson's earlier fiction.

It is appropriate to the theme of the sacred that one of the recurring metaphors for Hill House's evil is "leprosy," a disease quarantined in the Bible
by taboos that could not be broken without entailing strict atonement.
Crain's creation, Dr. Montague speculates, is "unclean or forbidden," like
the "houses described in Leviticus as 'leprous,' *tsaraas*" (70). When the
visitors in Hill House happen upon a sculpture of St. Francis among the
lepers, Theodora, a psychic, quips that the figures represent Crain's family,
and the House returns Theodora's flippancy by staining her room in a
scene that evokes images from the Leviticus passages. In Leviticus 14:33–
54, to which Dr. Montague alludes, God instructs the Israelites in Canaan
that a leprous house can be identified by the greenish and reddish streaks
upon its walls; Theodora's walls are papered green, and the stains are red.
Repulsed, she panics, fearing that she cannot be cleansed, and Eleanor responds by offering to wash her clothes, further alluding to Leviticus 14,
which specifies that all who sleep or eat in the leprous house must wash
their belongings (157). Although this method of cleansing (washing clothes)
significantly resembles the domestic labor to which Eleanor has become
accustomed, the portion of Leviticus that bodes more ominously for her is
the specification that leprous dwellings must be purged by an offering of
blood.[46]

Since all but one its victims have been women, Hill House seems to be
sated by specifically female blood, and, indeed, one of the females in the
new "family" (including Dr. and Mrs. Montague, Luke Sanderson, and
Theodora) gives up her life to the home, completing the immolation predicted by the Levitical allusions earlier in the text and by Hugh Crain's
blasphemous pact.[47] It is Eleanor who is doomed to act the sacrifice. Standing in the foyer, she hears a "sick voice" inside her whispering *"Get away
from here, get away,"* and later she will describe the impression that the
house wants to "consume" someone (35, 139). These misgivings notwithstanding, Hill House has power over Eleanor because it weaves her repressed psychology into its own dreams. Having adapted to the pattern of
self-sacrifice as if it is her lot, and a virtuous one at that, Eleanor is the
weakest and most susceptible of the visitors, and Hill House understands
her psychology too well to let her go.

ELEANOR IS the most theologically sensitive of Jackson's heroines, and
like her literary sister Esther Summerson in Plath's *The Bell Jar* (1966), her
fears of hell are validated by her suffering in this life. When she is introduced to the reader, Eleanor is apprehensive of any deviation from habit
that might reveal the unreconciled, refractory parts of herself and lead to
her mortification. Her mother's death has freed Eleanor from responsibil-

ity to home for the first time in eleven years of caretaking, and when she departs for Hill House, she almost musters a rebellious attitude, though it is short-lived. Hill House offers Eleanor the first adventure of her life, but from the moment she decides to take her sister's car without permission, contemplating the first "crime" of her life, she is anxious that in escaping from her birth home she may be risking evil. Given to "[seeking] out omens everywhere," Eleanor's imagination causes her to misperceive a fairground sign reading "DAREDEVIL" for a message, "DARE EVIL," which makes a pun of the original spelling. Eleanor is in fact being given an opportunity to dare the unknown, and she conceives her chance as a spiritual test that could implicate her in some deviltry seeming to spring from her secret resentment of the family regimen. She is unshielded, moreover, by most of the "magical" defenses that sustained Jackson's previous "madwomen." In place of those subversive visions of horror and regression, which Eleanor experiences only intermittently (227–234) or expresses as poltergeist activity resembling hysterical symptoms (73, 141), her mind is permeated more diffusely with the moralistic fantasies of her upbringing and the banal reveries of her stunted girlhood, typical fantasies mocked in Jackson stories like "The Demon Lover": a fairy princess returning to her palace, a lady awaiting her lover, a house decorated for a girl's own. Eerie for revealing her arrested adolescence, Eleanor's conscious dreamworld remains a young girl's enchanted rehearsal for feminine comportment, replete with the accessory of a handsome domicile.

As in prior works, Jackson uses the Gothic device of the double to reflect on the possibility of a feminine imagination that has transcended convention and its psychic compunctions, though in this case, the double survives the heroine, whose alienation from her counterpart results in slaughter. Having a name that echoes the masculine Theodore, Theodora ("Theo" for short) is the only visitor in the house who combines in herself Hugh Crain's daring, his amorality, and his imagination. In her relationship with Eleanor, as in Natalie's and Tony's pairing from *Hangsaman,* the two personalities complement each other, one enjoying freedom and the other bearing the sense of fault: "Theodora was not at all like Eleanor. Duty and conscience were, for Theodora, attributes which properly belonged to Girl Scouts" (8).[48] Theo, in fact, has a positively irreverent attitude towards theology (her short name is itself a pun on the Greek root for "God"), and her gaiety makes her capable of taking the imaginative dare that Eleanor cannot assay for fear of wickedness. With whimsy that strikes Eleanor as bravado, Theo taunts Hill House, and, later, when Luke parodies a medieval morality play, she accepts the part of the Devil vying for Nell's soul.[49] Having shades of the demon lover who tempts Clara Spencer, Theo confronts Nell with all that the weaker girl suppresses in herself so that she can earn the companionship of family, which Theo has foregone for most of her adult life, having severed all ties with her relatives. When Theo adds that God can be trusted no more than the Devil (123), she echoes Jackson's pictures of unreliable fathers, such as Mr. Waite and Hugh Crain, who claimed to be God in sardonic admission of their egoistic disregard for their daughters' happiness. Rather than hide from the narcissism that these fathers enjoy, Theodora nurtures her self-love, decorating her apartment mantle with a signed photograph of herself (8). She is also an artist figure (a sketch artist, living with a sculptor) who initiates games of make-believe and alternate identity. Her fantasies do not vault as high as Crain's, but, at a lower pitch, they are mischievous retellings of fairy tales, in which her princess masquerades as an ordinary mortal in the clothes of a maid, in order to escape her lord father's plot of forced marriage.[50]

Since Theo is one of Jackson's few female artists and drawn in sharp relief to Eleanor's repression, some readers have erroneously interpreted her, rather than Eleanor, as the novel's heroine. Along with the Montagues, Luke Sanderson, and Eleanor, however, Theodora also participates in the group's manipulative surrogate parent-child-sibling relations, and her behavior toward her "sister" Eleanor is occasionally jealous or cruel, as when she taunts Nell about blaming herself for her mother's death.[51] Like the other members of the household, living and dead, she appears to share in the house's bad will, and why should Theo be exempt from that original selfishness which Jackson, in her grimness, always detects beneath human behavior? Moreover, Theo's amorality, which the narrative underscores several times, also warrants comparison to the ambiguous figure of fellow fantasist Hugh Crain. An authorial double of sorts, Crain's example recalls Jackson's own dallying with a "Satanic" reputation to accentuate her occasionally scandalizing creative activity. By shading Theo's imagination into Crain's while contrasting both Theo and Crain's egoism to Eleanor's guilt, Jackson shows up a moral risk that her staid females, such as Eleanor's conservative mother and sister, never plumb and that Eleanor, at least, cannot resolve. Between Eleanor's overweening conscience and Theo's insouciance, there is no purity to be had, for implicit in freedom from convention is the danger that one's egotism, unbridled by lies of intimacy and togetherness, will assume the proportion of Hill House's evil: callous, contemptuous, baleful, manipulative, rapacious.

Yet the medical, religious, and familial orders established to regulate such unruly, devouring emotions seem more unjust than any damage their chaos might cause. "It's not fair," Tess Hutchinson cries as the first ceremonial rock caves her head. Whatever raging and unrequited feelings may roil in Eleanor's unconscious, they are finally less dangerous than the fantasies of domestic security that provide her no preservation against the narcissism and aggression in her families or Hill House's amoral sacred principle, which scapegoats the weak and the mad. When the alternative is Eleanor's unbearable renunciation, Theo's ignoble self-love, for all its hints of human blemish, is more tolerable. Jackson is too pessimistic a subversive, and too skeptical a liberal, to be less than frank about the dark choice facing an Eleanor or a Theodora; for a female character to escape, or at least survive, the evils that finesse women's repressive guilt, perhaps she must embrace the evil of egoism. Twelve-year-old murderess Merricat Blackwood, the heroine of Jackson's last completed novel, *We Have Always Lived in the Castle* (1962), carries this logic to a startling conclusion, deciding to poison her family (like her hero, Richard III) rather than be insulted by kindred who tell her what to do and then withhold the attention she feels she deserves. Merricat is the apotheosis of feminine "witchery," and her rebellion, extremely ruthless though it may be, simply owns the risk of damnation that faced Jackson's earlier heroines. Better to take the dare and join the Devil, it seems, than to pledge constancy and pray for love.

Eleanor, however, is the heroine of *The Haunting of Hill House* rather than Theo, and the novel is ultimately about her tragedy rather than her double's moxie. In contrast to the fantasists Hugh Crain and Theodora, Eleanor is too afraid to dare the devil because she equates evil with risk itself rather than the influences in the house, which has dreamt itself into a symbol of the dishonestly loving family she can no longer resist. Her flight from evil into domestic fantasy ultimately leaves her without defenses against her abiding guilt. When the caretaker of Hill House, Mr. Dudley, nearly turns away Eleanor from the driveway gate, she thinks to herself, "Hill House, you're as hard to enter as Heaven" (34). By the end of her sojourn, Eleanor has imagined that she is one of the elect: "The house wants me to stay. . . . Hill House means for me to stay" (245). To be chosen is a dubious honor, however, for the elect are sacrificed—not saved. Eleanor's self-abnegation is total, literal, and suicidal, her fate all the more horrifying because she accepts it as the debt for belonging to a home: "No, it is over for me. It is too much, she thought, I will relinquish my possession of this self of mine, abdicate, give over willingly what I never wanted at all; whatever [Hill House] wants of me it can have" (204). Eleanor's wish to belong and her desire for oblivion are no more powerfully illustrated than in the novel's climax, when the Montagues, along with the rest of the makeshift family, oust her from the house because she fails to behave sanely. Still protesting the group's decision and citing Hill House's wish that she stay, Eleanor fatally steers her car into a tree, and, up to the last moment before impact, she cannot understand why her hands are turning the wheel toward death: "This is me; I am really really really doing it by myself . . . *Why* am I doing this? Why am I doing this? Why won't they stop me?" (245–246). After deteriorating through successive families (biological, improvised, and spectral), Eleanor no longer clearly distinguishes home from annihilation, and in seeming to choose both at once, she plays into the ruse that Hill House has been practicing on women for seventy years. Having sacrificed her life, she is still without the companionship she craved, for whatever walks in Hill House, the narrator reminds us, "walks alone" (246).

Jackson rescues feminine fantasy from the discrediting labels of pathology, but she stops short of equating madness with personal triumph, contrary to Judy Oppenheimer's suggestion in *Private Demons*.[52] Whereas R. D. Laing and some of the confessional psychiatric literature of the sixties (for example, Doris Lessing's *The Golden Notebook*) make the madwoman a mystic revolting against patriarchal mental hygiene, Jackson sees the human costs as well as the originality of her heroine's flights from normality.[53] Natalie's and Elizabeth's fantasies and self-fragmentation are not voluntary choices but traumatic defenses—involving depression, suicidal impulses, and self-inflicted violence—and there are no clear avenues to transcendence or even survival. For them, as for Eleanor, the only way to manage the feminine psyche's centrifugal forces—the claims of home, the promises of love, the desire for self-expression, and the power of a punitive conscience—is through complete withdrawal or utter self-renunciation. There is no suggestion in Jackson's writings that her heroine's breakdowns are to be celebrated as signs of independence or afflatus. It is a dubious, if not an "unhealthy," distinction to be able to see that the family too is permeated by a universal and evil sacrificial principle.

In *Hill House*, the *unheimlich* is not just the return of the repressed; it is "a view of reality in which man is taken to be an unwelcome guest in the world. . . . 'one who is thrust out of doors.'"[54] Most of Jackson's heroines are as unwelcome guests in the world, and some of them make the mistake of believing they can leave their estrangement outdoors if only they can enter a home. Her more daring women escape into madness or identify with wickedness, and Jackson herself, of course, had the imaginative outlet of writing. Even when its unconscious subverts the banal fantasy life of an Eleanor Vance, however, feminine imagination is still a fragile defense against the forces of order, and Jackson deviates from fellow liberals by counting mental hygiene among the methods of coercion. If others called the therapeutic a "secular religion," capable, perhaps, of succeeding Christianity or complementing it, Jackson saw instead a more rationalistic version of the same sacred principle that Christianity had never truly transcended. She does not single out liberal Protestantism, which had actually incorporated therapeutic goals into its teaching, but pinpoints the core dogmas of Christian orthodoxy. In teaching that Christ's atonement has put an end to sacrificial violence and made possible a community based on love, churches, it seems, have also deceived men as to the irrepressible nature of egoistic aggression. Fatefully, Christianity has in common with postwar mental health programs the pretext of altruism and the purpose of releasing persons from guilty suffering—each of which has immured the faith in false perceptions of its power to heal the heart. Indeed, as she depicts sacrifice as an inversion of Eucharistic symbolism, selfless love as a dupe for devouring "O-gape," and a universe in which God, if He exists, is a tormentor like the Christian's Satan, Jackson has motifs in common with Plath, the contemporary writer with whom she bears closest comparison, though Jackon's anti-Christianity is more decisive.[55]

JACKSON was a postwar liberal whose sense of human self-deceit was more radical than the Niebuhrian realists'. Her art is in fact a counterhegemonic, but profoundly dystopian, challenge to Cold War liberalism's dominant narrative of evil, as self-deceptive innocence. *Hill House* begins with the phrase, "no live organism can continue for long to exist under conditions of absolute reality . . . even larks and katydids are supposed by some to dream."[56] Beneath life's banality there is its evil radix: an instinctual drive in each organism to feed on other life for its survival (larks eat katydids, katydids eat plants); in humans, an egotism that says one devours or one is consumed. Against this "absolute reality," no one can continue "sane," and so no wonder we must dream, though only some dreams are reified. Our self-deception lies in our incapacity to live without dreaming and in society's selective pathologizing of those very dreams that most profoundly register the contradictions between absolute reality's red-toothed terror and the fantasies by which people recognize normality. When her heroines manage to turn away from compulsory roles and homogenous dreams, they do not gain a sinless innocence, an ideal that would have drawn opprobrium from Jackson as well as any Niebuhrian, but nor do they, as in the postwar liberal theodicy, achieve an ironic comprehension of the virtue that may reside ambiguously in comparative sin. The anxiety in Jackson's universe does not lie in moral choices between relative degrees of evil but in the fundamental amoral choice between risk that invites reprisal and conformity that rewards with effacement. In Jackson, a good conscience is not the invention of the Devil; the Devil is the invention of a bad conscience, which is the only conscience that lives on and on in us. For the guilt-riddled, the Devil may be an ally in which Faustian creativity and freedom are realized along with the capacities of one's own aggressive, unsated desire. Jackson's anatomy of human deception repeatedly begs an analysis of sexual oppression, from a feminist perspective falling outside the masculinized anti-sentimental interpretive framework of Cold War liberalism, that her dark anthropology deprives of any hopeful appeal. For all the depth of her sympathy for the weak and the exploited and the near prophetic lament that sounds in her naming of "wickedness," she protests inhumanity by peeling back illusions that only reveal inhumanity more nakedly. To speak of an "inhuman world" is to imply a measure of humaneness that is undiscoverable, even as a possibility, in the fiction.[57] Yet Jackson's flirtation with moral nihilism springs from the same fount as her subversive energy, and we would hardly trade the former at the loss of the latter. By turning an unrepentantly Satanic perspective on the fifties' domestic idyll, she uniquely, and disturbingly, challenges us to see injustices that liberalism, for all its claims to "realism" and "honesty," was not yet educated to perceive and also the extremity of denial that the investiture of power in regimes of health and productions of identity can drive an artist in her refusal to affirm power's lies.

PART FIVE

The Styles of Prophecy

CHAPTER NINE

Voices of Reform, Radicalism, and Conservative Dissent

For where there is inspiration and prophecy, there are false prophets and true prophets; thieves aiming to dominate men and servants aiming to set them free; inspiration from dark instincts and inspiration from genuine love.

—Jacques Maritain, *Man and the State* (1953)

Servants and Thieves

While radical rhetoric in the Enlightenment tradition has cited natural law to appeal for the inherent rights of the disenfranchised, prophecy reproaches injustice by invoking sacred law or else some special intuition of a higher good. Each tradition adduces an authority exceeding positive law, but prophecy is a specific message from a divine authority directed to an audience, whereas natural law is a general axiom that has as its authority the "state of Nature," a description of man's original condition before sin or political oppression enslaved him. Though natural law refers to God-given functions and ends in the political theories of Aquinas and Richard Hooker, within the modern secular state the notion of natural law is deployed, after the fashion of John Locke and Thomas Paine, primarily as a rights discourse relatively free of any religious mandate.[1] Prophecy, in the Hebrew Bible and the Christian exegesis, may be applied to the defense of justice against tyranny, as the abolitionists combined God's higher law with natural law to assail slavery, but it is primarily a language of general moral indictment that uses specific grievances, which may include social injustice, to exemplify the iniquity of a people who must be exhorted to transform themselves.[2] Where natural law represents humanity in its abstract being (what man, freed from tyranny, possesses in his original condition), prophecy in the Hebrew Bible is a language of angry witness to a particular people. The prophet is not the alienated visionary that Bertrand Russell, for instance, imagines in *Authority and the Individual* (1949), but is himself a member of a people who, by their failure to respect a transcendent demand, are calling down a crisis on themselves.[3] The prophet's language is emotive, direct, and confrontational; it requires a response from the accused, who must either deny the message's import or else alter their situation. Assuming the prior establishment of a bond—a covenant—between speaker, addressee, and an obligation, the prophetic emphasis on both individual-to-group encounter and unconditional imperatives at once personalizes values and makes them the content of communal choices for life and death.

Although our cultural memory readily associates prophets with the sixties because of the images of the civil rights movement, Black Power, and the various charismatic sects that Robert Ellwood has lovingly cataloged in *The Sixties Spiritual Awakening*, not only was the dissenting prophet topical in the forties and fifties, but, as the diversity of examples suggest, there was also dispute over the efficacy and risks of prophecy in the public sphere. The tragic realist discourses calling for the end of American innocence had interred class politics while trying to safely corral the issue of racial inequality within the logic of pluralism. Daniel Boorstin and Sidney Hook joined Reinhold Niebuhr in yoking Dewey's well-taken criticisms of eighteenth-century natural rights doctrines to an almost Burkean respect for the cumulative wisdom of tradition, the organic bonds of the past, and the narrow interpretation of constitutional precedent.[4] The language of "oppression" and "deliverance" connoted the radical Left of the thirties and the radical Right of the fifties, and liberals preferred to speak of those "left-out but starting to move in" rather than speak for the "disinherited."[5] Their tone and assumptions were fundamentally at odds with radical prophecy, which speaks for oppressed groups and identifies divine and secular justice such that eschatology expresses utopian aspirations. The pedigree reaches back to the Social Gospel, itself an outgrowth of Abolitionism, and forward through Progressive-era Reformed Judaism's concern for the rights of labor to Muste's Fellowship for Reconciliation and Niebuhr's (pre–World War II) Christian Realism to the black liberation theology, exemplified by James Baldwin and James Cone, which emerged from the civil rights and Black Power movements.[6] Prophets, in this line of descent, are not alienated from the mass, as Russell's prophet is from "the herd," but from the centers of social power. These "prophetic souls," to borrow a phrase from the Social Gospel's Walter Rauschenbusch, speak to the dominant group on behalf of the disinherited.

Rather than use the Hebrew books of prophecy only to identify Jesus as the Christian Messiah and Israel as the body of Christ, prophets for the oppressed more closely aligned Jesus with the Old Testament precedents in their contexts of slavery and bondage, hoping to awaken a spirit of dissent that Christendom had traded for institutional power. Their critics, which included fundamentalists, the neoorthodox, and Niebuhrian realists, responded on theological grounds. They deferred to the Augustinian exegesis of the Old Testament prophets, in which the New Covenant transforms the meaning of the Hebrew covenants, so that the messianic promise ceased to refer to a specific, politically oppressed people. From this standpoint, the historical traumata of the Hebrews—their exile, captivity, and military domination—were actually allegories of a spiritual disinheritance, bondage to original sin, exacted because of the wrong exercise of man's will. Thus, for its tendency to place Providence on the side of the oppressed, radical prophecy stood accused of minimizing the sinful condition of all men, and for its proclivity to make political protest a redemptive expression of Christlike love, it was chided for too closely identifying the New Covenant's Gospel with this-worldly social activity.[7]

Each of the figures I will be discussing in Part V positions himself relative to the orthodox Christian exegesis of the Old Testament prophets, as either a revisionist of this tradition or as its modern bearer. Though the arguments over the proper exegesis of the prophets are predated by the antislavery debates that led up to the Civil War,[8] the terms had been restated, with great sophistication, by Reinhold Niebuhr's response to the Social Gospel preacher Walter Rauschenbusch. Influenced by Thoreau, Marx, and liberal evangelicalism, the major point of Rauschenbusch's message (through his first book, *The Righteousness of the Kingdom,* in 1893; and his last and most famous book, *Theology of the Social Gospel,* in 1917, one year before his death) was to shift the emphasis in Christianity from the sanctification of the personal soul to the transformation of the social order. He conceived the Social Gospel's "prophetic spirit" as a rediscovery of Christ's true revelation: "an experience of religion through a solidaristic social feeling" of both sin and salvation.[9] People inspired by God would take measures to redeem their neighbors from the "super-personal sins"—monopoly and finance capital and exploitative wage systems—that had produced the modern-day "Job living in a tenement."[10]

Rauschenbusch pitted the example of Jesus's ministry in the Gospels against the theological traditions that had descended from the Roman Church. The Jesus that Rauschenbush "salvages" from tradition is not "the mystic impartation of divine life and immortality," but "a personality able to win hearts, dominate situations, able to bind men in loyalty and make them think like himself, and to set revolutionary social forces in motion."[11] To describe Jesus's personality, Rauschenbusch culls from the Written Prophets of Israel's Fall, Captivity, and Exile as much as from the synoptic Gospels. These Old Testament sages "were the revolutionists of

their age. They were the dreamers of Utopias . . . in them all is the prophetic hope: a mighty uprising of Jehovah, a casting down of the powerful
and the wicked, and then peace and prosperity for the poor and the righteous" (70, 73). The prophets emerge not only as precedents for Jesus's
ministry but also as authentic expressions of the same Spirit of God that
animated Jesus and that Jesus, as the revelation of history, has made a
concrete, human example for all "inspired men": "The prophets of the
Old Testament were not lonely torches set aflame by the spirit of god. . . .
Genuine prophecy springs wherever fervent religious experience combines
with a democratic spirit, strong social feeling, and free utterance."[12]

In effect, Rauschenbusch, much like black liberationist James Cone decades later, was accusing Christian theology of harboring the Docetite heresy: the Hellenic idea that in Christ's person God-the-Logos had taken the
appearance of an individual man without ever becoming a particular human being. In consequence, Jesus, who walked ancient Palestine under the
Roman rule, was accidental to the Incarnation, and had no bearing on the
revelation of the Word made Flesh.[13] Rauschenbusch was impatient with
the ancient Church's response to the Docetic heresy (the Chalcedonian
Definition of A.D. 451) because he felt as if it still placed too much emphasis on the mystery of Christ's incarnation and too little on Jesus's historical
ministry: "The speculative problem of christological dogma was how the
divine and human natures united in the one person of Christ; the problem
of the social gospel is how the divine life of Christ can get control of human society." By giving more thought to metaphysical christology than to
Jesus's historical and spiritual heritage from the prophets, the Church has
protected its internal hierarchy and its common interests with the dominant powers (the Roman empire, feudal lords, owners of capital) that have
permitted the Church an institutional role in their social order.[14] And
where the Reformation has tried to purify faith by separating the Church
from worldly affairs, it has no less contravened the example of the prophetic Word made Flesh: "If the Reformation laid the stress of its preaching on dead works and living faith, it may be that our age must spurn the
dead faith and demand live works."[15]

Niebuhr's quarrel with Rauschenbusch begins with the ways the Social
Gospel teacher related two further, crucial theological points: (1) the "corporate" nature of sin, and (2) the Kingdom of God on earth. By the time
he wrote his major theological treatise, *Theology of the Social Gospel,*
Rauschenbusch had dissolved the doctrine of original sin for another explanation of why sin persists in the human species. Accurately noting that
neither the prophets nor Jesus, for all their consciousness of men's sins,
allude to the Fall described in Genesis (apart from one allusion in the

fourth chapter of John, which belongs to a separate tradition from the synoptics), Rauschenbusch concludes that original sin is derived basically from the Apostle Paul, who was the first to put Adam's fall to "full and serious" theological use.[16] Turning from Paul to the prophets, Rauschenbusch argues that they show no interest in sin's primal origins. Instead, they conceive of sin as the corporate transmission of evil behavior through successive generations. Man's collectively ill-made environments help to perpetuate sin as much as individual human weakness does.[17] Just as men, together, create the crises in their societies through their commission and toleration of sin, so they also affect their salvation by the actions they take to alleviate these conditions: "The life of the individual cannot be perfected except by seeking the perfection of society" (115). Christians, in particular, must cease to rely on charity to ameliorate the oppressed lower classes and begin to advocate measures that would instead eliminate the need for charity.[18]

Niebuhr was deeply influenced by Rauschenbusch's conception of corporate sin, but he criticized Rauschenbusch's perfectionism, which had led the Social Gospeler to revise messianic eschatology. The Kingdom of God, for Rauschenbusch, is not the apocalyptic hope of the early Christian sects nor is it Aquinas's sovereign Church. It is holiness spreading over the whole of society through reform.[19] "We need a restoration of the millennial hope," Rauschenbusch's proclaimed. Niebuhr responded that the Social Gospel suffered from liberal theology's great mistake of severing Jesus's attitudes about human nature from Paul's; the resulting liberal doctrine of the Incarnation, as the perfection of the *imago dei* in man, laid the premise for an equally unbiblical view of political possibility in history. The love ethic of the Kingdom of God, Niebuhr said, was "involved in every moment of history" as mercy and as judgment, but, in the struggle for justice, it was a leavening norm to steer men's actions rather than the description of any politically realizable community. In Niebuhr's *Human Nature,* Raushenbusch's teleological reduction of eschatology is leagued with Dewey's and Schleiermacher's "anemic" theory of "cultural lag" because all three of them, Niebuhr claims, attribute sin chiefly to the transmission of bad patterns through social institutions.[20] The self-alienation of man could not be traced solely to particular man-made evils or to natural scarcities since sin perpetually enters history through the human spirit. The bourgeois class may have a bad conscience, as Marx charges, but insofar as Marx ignores sin, he grants mankind as a whole a much too "easy conscience" (*Human Nature* 93, 97).

In *Moral Man and Immoral Society* and Niebuhr's work of the thirties, the moral God of the prophets makes Himself known to the oppressed in human history.[21] Niebuhr had criticized Social Gospel–style liberalism largely for its failure to use adequate political instrumentalities, including class struggle, to achieve socialist ends. After the German-Soviet Non-Aggression pact in 1939, Niebuhr broke with the Socialist Party, and, while remaining committed to socialist goals, his prophetic stance began to shift considerably partly in response to international developments but also as a result of his deepening study of Augustine and Reformation theology, reflected in the articles collected in *Christianity and Power Politics*. While he was refurbishing the doctrine of original sin in his Gifford lectures (delivered at the University of Edinburgh 1938–1940), he showed that his disenchantment with the image of man in socialist theory had reached a point that he had begun to doubt whether its utopianism, which socialism held in common with the ferocious political religion in Russia, was a greater liability to the world than Western nationalism and imperialism.[22] Niebuhr had never equated proletarian revolution with Providence or exalted class loyalty as ethically pure, but he had defended, albeit hesitantly, the "eschatalogical emphasis" of the proletarian radical.[23] In his Gifford lectures, Niebuhr maintained that the biblical prophets were anti-aristocratic and suspicious of the powerful, because the sin of pride was more pronounced in them, even as he faulted the Social Gospel and Christian socialism for having in common with revolutionary Marxism the "self-righteousness of the weak," as if the sin from which the oppressed suffer is "a peculiar vice" of his oppressor.[24] By 1941, when he had decided to support American intervention in Europe, Niebuhr had fully formed his opinion that socialists, alongside the pacifistic Protestant clergy who opposed war as morally indefensible, were minimizing the heritage of sin in the oppressed (the world proletariat) while overemphasizing it in Western colonialist, liberal capitalist countries.[25] As the critic of the Left's "innocence," Niebuhr was settling into the role he would play in the Cold War, the prophet who uses history's paradoxes to pierce idealist or utopian pretensions of virtue, rather than continuing to be *Moral Man*'s voice of the disinherited. As Niebuhr grew to emphasize the inexorable judgment in history while attenuating the promise of redemption, the stern moral fervor of his earlier voice would be tempered by a cool skepticism that searched out human folly, the voice that would preside over *The Irony of American History*.

Like Sidney Hook and so many other ex-radicals, Niebuhr ceased to believe in the mass as a historical agent, for it seemed that charismatic leaders with millennial ideologies had upended the Marxist dialectic. Had he been inclined, Niebuhr could have turned for support to a number of sociologists and historians who were persuaded of the liabilities of radical prophecy. In studies by Shils, Lasswell, and Cohn, in Arthur Schlesinger's essays on native fascism, in *The End of Ideology*'s historical genealogy of "chiliasm" from religion into politics, in Lowenthal and Guterman's *Prophets of Deceit*, or in Eric Hoffer's best seller, *The True Believer* (1951), charismatic leaders may discern legitimate grievances, but they use these to feed a cynicism towards public institutions; the governing authority appears so lethargic and decadent that only an acceleration toward crisis will accomplish any result.[26] Max Weber, whose work was introduced in the United States in the thirties by the sociologists Talcott Parsons, H. E. Barnes, A. Salomon, and Edward Shils, provided one of the most influential models of charismatic leadership, which emphasized the prophet's nonrational powers of persuasion and his likeness to the political demagogue.[27] Discounting theophany, Weber naturalizes theories of "grace," "revelation," or "divine election" with his concept of charisma, adopting the terminology of early, Pauline Christianity.[28] Where Paul's charismata distinguish each member for the edification of the whole, Weber's charisma separates an individual from the mass so that it can be united through obedience to the newfound prophet: "Charismatic domination means a rejection of all ties to any external order. . . . Hence, its attitude is revolutionary and transvalues everything."[29] Weberian charisma functions like Pauline charismata only in its "opposition to institutional permanence," conceived by Paul as the Greek cultus or the Jewish law and by Weber as any traditional, legal, or rational routine (21). The mass responds to the prophet's presence and his message out of a "fundamental re-orientation of their emotions" that he inspires by his opposition to the average and the habitual (53). Gone is the agonistic relationship between prophet and audience in the Bible; Weber's is a leader at the center of a crowd rather than a Jeremiah lamenting his people's obstinance. Thus, the Weberian demagogue, who would make the masses impatient with the slow, self-correcting justice of consensus, reared itself in the Cold War imaginary as a spirit of anomie to be then countered by the Niebuhrian prophet of irony.

Belonging as it does to "revolutionary," "millenarian," or "Messianic" promises, radical prophecy, in this light, emerges as fundamentally antagonistic to the constitutional democracies of the West. Jacques Maritain, a leading Catholic theologian and a *Partisan Review* contributor, acknowledged in *Man and the State* that totalitarian states had made the image of prophecy "sinister" to the West, and in his chapter "The Prophetic Shock-Minorities," he protects true prophets from false—Messiahs "trying to force the people to free"—by recommending that leaders focus on "ideas rather than electoral success," and that they operate within "small dynamic groups," rather than large mass movements, which can "act as ferment either inside or outside the political parties." In other words, he makes his "prophetic shock-minorities" equivalent to the democratic "pressure groups," which were supposedly ideology-free alternatives to the class and racial politics of the prewar era.[30]

Flannery O'Connor, the American author most closely identified with prophets in the fifties, made no such distinctions as Maritain to accommodate liberal democracy. Her prophets are Christ-haunted nomads, carrying Jesus festering in their heads like a bee's stinger. Singularly uncharismatic, they are fixed on the vertical relation to the absolute that they deny; thrust, impaled, upon the God whose name they blaspheme. They are subject to God's irony without being ironically conscious, rejecters of worldly materialism who could never become Social Gospel progressives because they reject modernity as well. O'Connor is as eccentric as her prophets, and her art and thought suggest affiliations in the Cold War intellectual climate but align cleanly with none of them. When O'Connor dissents from American triumphalism and its market values, she bears comparison with two fellow Southern conservatives, historian C. Van Woodward and man-of-letters Robert Penn Warren, who also disclaimed American "innocence" from the "ironic" and "tragic" vantage afforded by their regional identities.[31] Yet, unlike O'Connor, who writes as a prophetic seer and in sympathy with her avatars in the Bible and in the contemporary South, Warren and Woodward suspiciously regarded prophets and their inspired rhetoric, associating them with demagogy, "higher law" abolitionists, New England philosophes, fascists, and black nationalism.[32] O'Connor's aesthetic, fusing New Critical principles with Thomas's *Der Veritate*, is closely affined with the sensibility of her friend and literary booster Allen Tate, who also shared O'Connor's horror at the impersonal relations of capital; O'Connor is distinguished from Tate and other conservative Catholic intellectuals of the period by her penchant for seeking out—or inventing—Protestant prophets in a contemporary American landscape.[33] This predilection drew her, in a heterodox act of imaginative empathy, to Southern fundamentalists. It is tempting to see O'Connor's "strange alliance" as anticipating subsequent culture war coalitions between neofundamentalistic evangelicals and conservative Catholics, but her repudiations are more consummate than expostulations over cultural values, and her Augustinian distinction between the transcendental order and the orders of men ultimately places her fundamentalists closer to John the Baptist than Billy Graham.[34] In an era marked by suspicion of prophecy and revaluation of the biblical prophets, her dissent is one of the most idiosyncratic, illiberal, and deeply felt.

Eating the Word: O'Connor's Poor (1952–1963)

> The writer who emphasizes spiritual values is very likely to take
> the darkest view of all that he sees in this country today. For him,
> the fact that we are the most powerful and wealthiest nation on
> earth doesn't mean a thing in any positive sense. The sharper the
> light of faith, the more glaring are apt to be distortions the writer
> sees in the life around him.
>
> —Flannery O'Connor, "The Fiction Writer and His Country" (1952)

No American author of the fifties was more closely identified with the
biblical prophets than Flannery O'Connor.[35] A devout Catholic who preferred to write of sectarian fundamentalists rather than priests or saints,
she startled readers by creating fierce, vital protagonists from the rural
evangelists, faith healers, farm hands, and drifters that others would have
cast as rubes or bigots.[36] While the first generation of O'Connor readers
frequently misunderstood her work to be a lampoon of rural evangelicals,
the publication of the essays collected in *Mystery and Manners* as well as
the interviews she granted before her early death established, in fact, that
she identified with her "backwoods prophets." Five decades of criticism
later, sufficient attention has been given to the integral relationship between
prophecy and social class in O'Connor's work. The author's identification
with the poor and laboring classes is as pronounced as her fascination with
prophecy, so much that one disgruntled reader sent her a message in protest: "'Tell that girl to quit writing about poor folks. I see poor folks every
day and I get might tired of them.'"[37]

As Robert Coles remarks in a classic study, "She knew which 'social
scene' was hers: not the upper class South; not really, with a few exceptions, its professional and business cadres; but overwhelmingly, its 'poor
white' rural and small town folk, or its ordinary working-class men and
women."[38] Noting that O'Connor's prophets always come from this social
stratum, Coles describes how the religion of the rural poor is no mere opi-
ate that makes their predicament endurable. Taking the sermon of an actual itinerant Georgia evangelist as his example, Coles tries to evoke the
spirit of protest in this religion:

> And those who are on top, who think they have certain rights, obligations,
> privileges by virtue of books read, capital accumulated, lineage of one sort or
> another inherited, had best know how radically, violently egalitarian this mes-
> sage [the Gospel], this story [Christ's], this mandate [redemption], this per-
> sonal remonstrance of our Savior was meant to be.... These humble
> southerners, these dirt-poor men and women, scorned nationally, and some-
> times scorned regionally, too, have had every reason to search the skies and

ask why. Why their fate—not only their material fate, but their fate at the hands of their judges? . . . Theirs is a country, spiritual radicalism that denounces the rich. A radicalism addressed to the poor. A radicalism that stresses an egalitarian hope. (71, 102–103)

Certainly fundamentalistic evangelicalism can be strongly egalitarian, as grasped by such O'Connor stories as "Revelation," but I have a difficult time translating the consciousness Dr. Coles ascribes to most of the characters in O'Connor's world.[39] Nowhere in her fiction is there any righteous anger directed at the rich for their social privilege. O'Connor's poor characters do not see themselves as unfairly scorned by the rest of society because they are economically destitute or lack family name or education, nor does society seem to scorn them for their disadvantages. When her educated liberal characters condescend to the underprivileged, they do not slight them for their poverty or their awkward manners so much as for their spiritual beliefs, associated with illiteracy. To O'Connor, however, this slight was a serious enough offense, for religious sensibility was the quality she most prized about the lower classes and their prophets. Like her farmers, laborers, and drifters, the ragged prophets in O'Connor's stories are troubled by the meaning of Christ's sacrifice because their imaginations are still permeated by biblical myths: "Where you find Catholics reading the Bible, you find that it is usually the pursuit of the educated, but in the South the Bible is known by the ignorant as well, and it is always that *mythos* that the poor hold in common that is most valuable to the fiction writer. When the poor hold sacred history in common, they have ties to the universal and the holy, which allows the meaning of their every action to be heightened and seen under the aspect of eternity."[40] That this sacred history is remembered by the South's indigent rather than its better-off citizens is a grim comment upon affluent, secularized culture. O'Connor's poor are not disaffected from society because they feel injustice or class prejudice, but separated from it because they still have an attachment, part superstitious and part devout, to the Bible that her large landowning or propertied characters neglect because they have begun to absorb modern values.

O'Connor's uncompromising fictional prophets dramatize her own image as a religious dissenter in an America where modernity has chucked the crucial issues of sin and spiritual salvation, which are kept by the forgotten lower classes in her universe. In the sectarian, frequently ramshackle, but always "Christ-haunted," religion of the Southern rural lower classes, O'Connor found bastions for a spiritual consciousness that could help brace people against modern values (32, 44). The very violence with which

O'Connor enforces the separation of the poor, as sources of prophetic dissent, from the modernized world, with its promises of social amelioration, makes her a fascinating antithesis to the Social Gospel line of radical prophecy.[41]

Efforts to define what kind of dissent O'Connor voiced in the Cold War have been only partly successful because they have not adequately taken account of the prophecy theme and its interrelationship with social class. In the nineties, two books taking a cultural historicist approach, Thomas Hill Schaub's *American Fiction in the Cold War* (1991) and Jon Lance Bacon's *Flannery O'Connor and Cold War Culture* (1993), opened new contexts for O'Connor studies by placing her among post–World War II America's dissenting intellectuals. Schaub and Bacon correctly point out that O'Connor resisted the model of religious consensus outlined by Will Herberg in *Protestant-Catholic-Jew,* and they also accurately describe her disgust with "sentimental" culture, consumerism, and conformity. When comparing O'Connor to other intellectuals of the period, however, Schaub and Bacon both erroneously align her with Leftists, such as Norman Mailer or C. Wright Mills, and reformed liberals, such as Reinhold Niebuhr or David Riesman.[42] The basic problem with Schaub's study is that he compares O'Connor to other Cold War intellectuals based on the similarity of the objects they criticize rather than on the motives for their criticism. Schaub, for instance, argues that O'Connor was "a Christian Realist" criticizing liberals, as "guilty" liberals like Niebuhr were criticizing the assumptions of the former Left. This parallel fails to be very instructive. Christian Realism originally developed from a Protestant quest to balance the demands of love and justice through politically efficacious, yet morally proportional, instrumentalities, and while it attacked the "sentimentality" of the Social Gospel, it retained certain liberal commitments to supporting social welfare. Niebuhr believed that he was saving liberalism from its "utopian" excesses while still providing a biblical basis for Christians to be politically engaged. Never herself a theological liberal, O'Connor was uninvolved with the Left legacy of Protestantism, never countenanced the Church becoming an advocate for labor or any social cause, and did not believe, as Niebuhr did, that Christianity was a this-worldly faith. When Jon Bacon, in his study, likens O'Connor to David Riesman, William Whyte, and C. Wright Mills, he partly avoids Schaub's error because he considers how much O'Connor's resistance to "national homogeneity" reflected her commitment to local religious subculture.[43] However, he places a high valuation on "individualism," which was less important to O'Connor than it was to Riesman, Whyte, or Mills, who were each writing about the psychological and moral tensions of the newly affluent middle class—

decidedly not the group that concerned O'Connor. In contrast to the intellectuals that Schaub and Bacon select, O'Connor portrays dissent from modern culture in prophetic terms that frequently take evangelism as a contemporary correlative to prophecy. Since they discuss her attitude of dissent in terms borrowed from humanists or else from theologically less conservative thinkers, Bacon and Schaub do not appreciate how her antagonism to much of postwar American culture actually reflects a much broader opposition to secular modernity, the ways it diminishes the mystery of grace and mistakes ethical goodness for salvation.

To demonstrate that O'Connor's was a voice of dissent, Schaub and Bacon both showcase her indignant reply to Henry Luce's 1955 *Life* editorial, "Wanted: An American Novel."[44] According to Schaub and Bacon, O'Connor's response is comparable to Norman Mailer's retort to *Partisan Review* ("Our Country and Our Culture," 1952), when he charged that the intellectual in the United States was becoming domesticated by pressures to affirm American life. A closer look at O'Connor's reply to Luce, "The Fiction Writer and His Country," shows instead that she was less interested in defending the autonomy of the intellectual—an identity she was uncomfortable owning—than she was in testifying to her Christian values and the ways these were being subverted by mainstream modern culture.[45]

Luce's editorial complains that contemporary American writers are failing to faithfully represent their period. If in the twenties and the Great Depression such talents as F. Scott Fitzgerald and John Steinbeck wrote novels of social criticism that appropriately showed the fraud and hardship of those eras, then in the present, American writers should follow the same realist aesthetic in accurately describing the prosperity, power, and near-classless equality that define America in the fifties. Weary of the dourness in American letters, Luce calls for a writer who "speaks for America today," who recognizes that "the time for social criticism is past." This last statement would have piqued a writer like Mailer, a Progressive Party campaigner in 1948 whose recent work included a novel about socialism *(Barbary Shore)* and another about the Hollywood blacklist *(The Deer Park)*, but O'Connor was more offended by a phrase that lauded "the redeeming quality of spiritual purpose" in America. "The Fiction Writer and His Country" begins by acknowledging that critics of many persuasions have been incensed by Luce's "loud" remarks, but then O'Connor immediately stakes her position as religious:

> This [the *Life* editorial] was irritating enough to provoke answers from many critics, but I do not know that any of those who answered considered the question specifically from the standpoint of the novelist with Christian concerns, who, presumably, would have an interest at least equal to the editors of

Life in 'the redeeming quality of spiritual purpose.' . . . The writer whose position is Christian, and probably also the writer who is not, will begin to wonder at this point if there could not be some ugly correlation between our unparalleled prosperity and the stridency of these demands for a literature that shows us the joy of life. He may at least be permitted to ask if these screams for joy would be quite so piercing if joy really were more abundant in our prosperous society. . . . My own feeling is that writers who see by the light of their Christian faith will have, in these times, the sharpest eyes for the grotesque, for the perverse, and for the unacceptable. In some cases, these writers may be unconsciously infected with the Manichean spirit of the times and suffer the much-discussed disjunction between sensibility and belief, but I think that more often the reason for this attention to the perverse is the difference between their beliefs and the beliefs of their audience.[46]

O'Connor adds that the editors of *Life* are requesting a "soggy, formless, sentimental literature" that no self-respecting writer, certainly no Christian writer, can honor (30). O'Connor's objections to "sentimental" literature do not imply, however, that she commends those socially critical novels, *Gatsby* or *The Grapes of Wrath,* which Luce consigns to the past. Nowhere in the response does she make a case for the continued relevance of Steinbeck and Fitzgerald or suggest that Luce's prosperous, powerful society be judged because it overlooks the other Americans, the Joads or the George and Myrtle Wilsons, who have not enjoyed any economic windfall.[47] Her dissent is based on different grounds. The true Christian writer is strongly shielded from the lure to affirm Luce's vision because her faith sets her apart from the beliefs of so many readers of *Life,* who suffer from the "Manichean spirit of the times."

THE TERM "Manichean" often coincides in O'Connor's essays with "sentimental," and the words describe two interrelated modern heresies that the Luce editorial abets. Reaching back to Augustine's teachings on the Manichees, O'Connor uses the term "Manichean" in an ontological rather than a moral sense. Her Manicheans do not divide the world between good and evil, but separate spirit from matter. In effect, they deny the capacity of God to intervene in nature, as He did through Christ (who fused Word and Flesh), and thus they cancel the miracle of the Incarnation that made Christ's sacrifice an atonement for perverted nature. The modern world, according to O'Connor, commits a version of the Manichean heresy by denying man's need for grace and describing his actions in purely naturalistic terms (68, 147–148). With Man reduced to the scale of his own perception, ethics generally becomes man's highest standard of self-judgment, and, in liberal Christian thought, even Jesus Christ is reduced to human components that make the Savior capable only of behaving ethically, like "a golden-hearted" person (192). This diminution of cosmic perspective, by excising God's life from His creations, has the consequence of "sentimentalizing" ethical judgment rather than strengthening it, as many modern men mistakenly believe.[48] To O'Connor's thinking, when men measure their moral aspiration against humanity's accomplishments, they begin to apologize for their "imperfection" and cease to endure the humility God demands: "sentimentality is an excess, a distortion of sentiment usually in the direction of an overemphasis on innocence, and that innocence, whenever it is overemphasized in the ordinary human condition, tends by some natural law to become its opposite. We lost our innocence in the Fall, and our return to it is through the Redemption which was brought about by Christ's death and our slow participation in it. Sentimentality is a skipping of this process in its concrete reality and an early arrival at a mock state of innocence" (148).[49]

Though her rhetoric may echo Niebuhr's, O'Connor's prophetic style positions her closer to Billy Graham's than to any of the dissenting intellectuals that Schaub and Hill cite for comparison. Graham never so strongly aligned his vision with the poor as O'Connor does, but he did treat evangelism as a correlative for prophecy and chastised modern idolatry as it was reflected in the spiritual, intellectual, and consumer trends of the day. O'Connor's fundamentalists, however, are not neos like Graham. Since he took the American nation as his audience, Graham reached out to its center. Even though he reserved the right to criticize the nation, he modulated his prophetic tone by allowing America a special grace. Though the country is not exempt from God's judgment, as he emphasized, its democratic values and its freedom of worship have spared it the catastrophes that the Law has levied upon other nations. The country's history thus remains exceptional even when its policies or its cultural trends warrant prophetic attack. O'Connor struck at modern values and liberal theology, as Graham did, but quite unlike him, she did not blunt her prophetic ire when speaking about America the leader of the Free World. In contrast to Graham's efforts to mediate between his Christianity and a broad national audience, O'Connor was free to criticize without moderation because she felt no need to appeal to the country's center. She imagined herself a voice at the margins of modern culture, like the poor in her universe. In contrast to Billy Graham and the New Evangelicals, she did not believe there was a cultural hegemony for her to regain, and unlike nationalistic Catholics, such as Fulton Sheen, who received Graham as a fellow agent for conservative interfaith ecumenism, she saw no reason for the Church to assimilate American ideals.[50] Hers is a world of Augustinian kingdoms in which there is no concept of the nation-state, but instead an eschatological dualism separating the universal Church, as the revelation of Christ's regenerate body, from all worldly governments. Whatever aspects of America smacked of modern heresies, O'Connor belittled them without qualification because she valued the prophet for his dogmatic truth rather than his facility at persuading groups that American society was peculiarly indebted to Christianity. In *Wise Blood,* for instance, Hazel Motes's inability to make charismatic contact with anyone actually seems a sign that he is committed to truth rather than success, and according to a letter O'Connor wrote before the publication of *The Violent Bear It Away,* the protagonist Tarwater, she speculates, will not succeed in converting anyone in the city where his uncle Rayber lives.[51] O'Connor embraced such characters, as she did their real-life fundamentalist sources. Their "fanaticism," their "one-notion minds," and their "madness" testified to the persistence, in however distorted or fragmentary a form, of "the blind, prophetical, unsentimental" faith.[52]

The most excessive sentimentalists in O'Connor's fiction are the liberal rationalistic crusaders, such as Rayber in *The Violent Bear It Away* or Sheppard in "The Lame Shall Enter First," but sentimentality, or the state of "mock innocence," is also indulged by the modern attitude that matches human progress with the expansion of material goods and services and the elimination of want. In the Luce editorial, for instance, there is a sense of paradise regained after the travails of two world wars and economic depression. For O'Connor, however, Luce's prosperous, plentiful, triumphal America has merely multiplied the means for people to indulge the illusion that the increase of this-worldly happiness is man's spiritual end. Against the Manichean cleavage of nature from grace and the sentimental assurance that men's social progress expunges sin, O'Connor developed her own "prophetic vision," or "deeper realism."[53]

Her statement that prophets "recall men to forgotten truths" shows how much she appreciated Bruce Vawter's 1961 study, *The Conscience of Israel:* "Twentieth century Biblical criticism has returned the prophets to their genuine mission, which was *not to innovate,* but to recall the people to truths they were already well aware of but chose to ignore" (italics added).[54] The prophets whom Social Gospel advocates such as Walter Rauschenbusch called radical progressives for their denunciations of the rich and powerful could also be construed as radically conservative reformers who reproached men for their idolatry, their indifference and skepticism toward the covenants, and their flouting of the Mosaic laws. O'Connor clearly leans to the latter interpretation. She is inspired by the prophets' warnings to people who have fallen away from the values of the past, for she confronts "an age" "whose prevailing attitudes" "run counter" to hers, even though much of the culture still calls itself Christian.[55] Like Rauschenbusch, she contrasts the biblical prophets with a lethargic contemporary Christianity, but her own prophetic function is not to repeal the Church's teachings for a more authentic rendition of the Gospel so much as it is to restore an excessively modernized, nominally "Christian" culture to the world-changing dogma of the historic universal Church. Thus she speaks of the Church as the safeguard and transmitter of prophecy rather than its suppresser: "it [the prophetic vision] is also a matter of the Church's gift, which . . . is safeguarded and deals with greater matters. It is one of the functions of the Church to transmit the prophetic vision that is good for all time" (179–180). Her dogma follows the Pauline-Augustinian exegesis of the New Covenant (Jeremiah 31:31) and the messianic promises, so that "the fundamental doctrines of sin and redemption and judgment" refer not to Israel's historic destiny, but to original sin and the dispensation provided by Christ's incarnation and sacrifice.[56] O'Connor's difference from a Social Gospel advocate like Walter Rauschenbusch can be measured by the example she took from John the Baptist, a prophet mostly ignored by Rauschenbusch but befitting O'Connor's orthodox Christology. In such works as *The Violent Bear It Away,* O'Connor sees the contemporary prophet as an outsider to a culture that has become as lost as was John's in the days before Christ's ministry began.

Perhaps because her prophets renounce modernity, O'Connor has been interpreted as a reactionary whose conservatism reflects her genteel, ethnocentric background, but I believe her imagination is more complicated than such an ungenerous description allows.[57] O'Connor's politics were not so far right of center. She ignored McCarthy and other professional anti-Communists (in a period when many conservative Catholics, like Cardinal Spellman, supported them), voted for Adlai Stevenson rather than Eisenhower and for Kennedy over Nixon, expressed approval for Lyndon Baines Johnson, and allowed that Martin Luther King, Jr. was "doing what he has to do."[58] Politically she was more liberal than Billy Graham in the fifties even though the fundamentalists in her fiction are more extreme premillenialists than he. Her caricatured liberals, such as Rayber and Sheppard, are not appealing, but it is important to recognize that what O'Connor holds up to ridicule in each of them is less their good intentions than their presumption that goodness is innately human. Although nothing in her writing suggests that raising the poor's quality of life was a priority for her, nothing asserts or even implies that such an effort would be an unworthy human endeavor if it were possible to preserve the biblical mythos that the poor, more than any other class, had managed to retain by force of their low circumstances. For O'Connor, the defining feature of modernity was not its prosperity nor its technological capacity for alleviating want and suffering, but the substitution of confidence in these advances for the hard demands of her faith.

Progressive reformers in O'Connor's fiction founder on their self-love. Rayber first appears in her fiction in a very early short story, "The Barber," in which he is one of the few liberals in a small Southern town where he is campaigning for a democratic integrationist ticket against a racist demagogue. In the story, Rayber fails to win the reader's trust because his political ideals seem to be based less on compassion for blacks than on his desire to feel superior to the uneducated men at the local barbershop where there is support for the segregationist ticket.[59] In "The Barber," Rayber is a pathetic figure whose vanity defeats his own cause, but by the time he reappears in *The Violent Bear It Away,* he is a dogged prophet of the false liberal faith. His transformation from a comically improvident crusader into Tarwater's adversary shows how O'Connor had come to connect the sin of pride to the idolatry of sentimental humanism.

The issue of social amelioration had to be partitioned from the prophetic message of salvation, for when the aims were confused, men became "innocent" and lost the sense of the paucity in their depths. O'Connor reads the prophetic books selectively, as she chooses not to exploit their several references to the unrighteousness that neglects the poor's *physical* needs and finds in physical poverty a symbol for "the state of all men," for original sin, a poverty "so essential that it needn't have anything at all to do with money."[60] In "The Teaching of Literature," O'Connor explains that the material lack of her poor characters was not itself worthy of art; however, inasmuch as poverty reminded man of his finitude, his creaturely dependence, it was the wellspring of the novelist's imagination: "I am very much afraid that to the fiction writer the fact we shall always have the poor with us is a source of satisfaction, for it means, essentially that he will always be able to find someone like himself. His concern with poverty is with a poverty fundamental to man. . . . When anyone writes about the poor in order merely to reveal their material lack, then he is doing what the sociologist does, not what the artist does" (131–132). On the one hand, O'Connor obviates class differences in her fiction by strictly separating art and sociology, while, on the other, she restores the significance of class privilege by making it delimit the possibility for a more immediate experience of man's finitude before God. As such examples from her fiction as Sarah Ruth in "Parker's Back," the Misfit in "A Good Man Is Hard to Find," Francis Tarwater in *The Violent Bear It Away,* and Rufus Johnson in "The Lame Shall Enter First" show, O'Connor's poor in their mean environments, "with less padding between them and the raw forces of life," can more likely feel the "hunger" of the prophet for the Word, while the well off are better insulated from feeling the spiritual lack they have in common with man. In his raw and desperate state, O'Connor's prophet directly experiences the hollowness of concupiscence, despairs of quenching his lawless desire. This modern world of mammon, of illusory plenitude, is a vomitorium; in the Word's body and blood there is satiety. Like John (or for that matter, Ezekiel or Jeremiah), O'Connor's prophet discovers that it is not his purpose to satiate his hunger, but to *spread* it.[61]

O'CONNOR'S rigorous demarcation of the cause of social justice from the message of the Christian kerygma was challenged by the theology and the language of the civil rights movement, which she received with suspicion. Like fellow Southern moderate William Faulkner, O'Connor believed that integration would occur through a voluntary, gradual transformation of conventions between blacks and whites who would locally develop new systems of manners without the need for federal intervention.[62] Alongside her concerns for the consequences of the movement on Southern identity, however, O'Connor objected to its sanctification of the pursuit of the good society on dogmatic grounds, as when she objected to activists calling King a saint, even though she supported integration. Unlike King or James Baldwin, whom she did not respect, O'Connor did not believe that the movement warranted prophetic speech, for this should be restricted to its proper, kerygmatic, function.[63] Moral attitudes in the South could be altered informally by pressures and counterpressures felt, and addressed, at local levels, but the human heart, in its terrible opposition to God and thus to its essence, could be transformed only through Christ's abrogation of original sin. While the benighted souls in her universe move slothfully (if at all) towards the Christian revelation, her poor blacks, like her poor whites, remain in the spiritually advantageous position of being shielded from modern heresies and the atmospheres that cultivate them. Her only story in which a major black character is urban, economically independent, and Northern also portrays him as an atheist. In "Judgement Day," the black actor, who lives in a high-rise apartment next to a white woman, is insulted when her father, an old man recently migrated from the South, calls him "Preacher"; the black man (unnamed in the story) screams in exasperation: "I'm not no preacher! I'm not even no Christian. I don't believe in that crap. There ain't no Jesus and there ain't no God!"[64] By contrast, the poor rural blacks who appear at the beginning and the end of Tarwater's story in *The Violent Bear It Away* serve as agents of the prophet's destiny. Buford Munson and his wife, who are black, meet Francis Tarwater as he is leaving Powderhead (his great uncle Mason Tarwater's home in the woods) for the city, and they encounter him once more when he returns. In the first case, Buford's wife has had a vision of Mason's death, and her husband urges Francis Tarwater to bury his great-uncle in the ground as the Lord intends, for souls will rise from their graves in the Rapture. Young Tarwater rebels by neglecting to the bury the body and instead burning the house, thinking the body will also be incinerated. When Tarwater returns, he learns from Buford Munson that his uncle was never charred; the black farmer, doing his Christian duty, retrieved the body before the fire and interred it in the ground with a cross set above it. Tarwater takes Buford's revelation as evidence of some miraculous design, and it is the last, critical link in a series of shocking events that break the boy's resistance to God so that he accepts his calling. In the conclusion, as the newly ordained Tarwater marches toward the city and Buford crosses the fields into the woods, the novel's prophet carries a message to the spiritually impoverished that the black man, as one of the redeemed, already understands, but this message cannot encompass the social disinheritance—the actual poverty—that Buford endures as a Christian servant.

By the standards of the Social Gospel, O'Connor's prophetic vision seems to leave the Christian mantra "love thy neighbor" unfulfilled. Like other pietistic Christians, however, O'Connor takes the teaching quite seriously but reserves it for the province of charity.[65] Charity and prophecy were interrelated in her thinking even if they were separated in function. She understood charity in a double sense, referring to acts for the benefit of others (especially for the poor or the weak), and to *caritas*, the Christlike spirit of love for fellow men from which all charitable acts are said to flow. In a little discussed piece, the introduction to *A Memoir for Mary Ann*, O'Connor meditates on charity, taking as her chief example an event from Nathaniel Hawthorne's life that inspired his daughter, Rose Hawthorne Lathrop, to later found the Dominican order, the Servants of Relief for Incurable Cancer.[66] Hawthorne was haunted enough by the incident that he wrote about it in his journal as well as in his book, *Our Old Home*, and O'Connor weaves together the two accounts to illustrate how her favorite American author had been compelled to show charity under the most loathsome circumstances.

Hawthorne was touring a Liverpool workhouse worthy of a Dickens novel when an orphan hideously disfigured by scurvy took "the strangest fancy" to him. Of the two accounts that O'Connor excerpts, the version from Hawthorne's journal is the more vivid: "It was a wretched, pale, half-torpid little thing . . . I never saw, till a few moments afterward, a child that I should feel less inclined to fondle. But this little sickly, humor-eaten fright prowled around me, taking hold of my skirts, following at my heels, and at last held up its hands, smiled in my face, and insisted on my taking it up! . . . It was as if God had promised the child this favor on my behalf, and that I must needs fulfill the contract. I held my undesirable burden for a while, and after setting the child down, it still followed me. . . . I should have never forgiven myself if I had repelled its advances."[67] The narrator in *Our Old Home* adds to the end of the story, "[I] am seriously of the opinion that he did a heroic act and effected more than he dreamed toward his final salvation when he took up the loathsome child and caressed it as tenderly as if he had been its father" (217–218).

O'Connor's gloss on these passages defines the difference between true charity, which begins with "fear" and "searching," and modern "tenderness," which smooths its objects with "cliches" of "simplicity" and "innocence" (226, 227). Though Hawthorne did not feel tenderly for the child, even admitted how repulsed he was by its deformity, he yet managed to behave "Christ-like" because he feared having "ice in his blood" (217, 227). He was not motivated by pity, but by an honest admission of his repulsion that unlocked some need for self-transcendence, an emotion he associated with man's hope for salvation. Modern men, by contrast, blame God for children's suffering, as "Ivan Karamazov" does, and imagine that their pity makes them more feeling than those who affirm grace in the face of horror. In fact, they can feel pity for other humans only because they cover over the "grotesque" features of man's moral nature and idealize them, discovering "innocence" and "simplicity" where, at best, there is only "good under construction" (226). Although he was not a Christian believer, in O'Connor's estimate Hawthorne nonetheless understood that good can only begin when man recognizes how much he lacks the capacity to love what offends his ideals. The hope of redemption, which Hawthorne understood intuitively even if he did not think doctrinally, is the only true source of charity, and this hope cannot be fulfilled unless men first accept their deficiency of love's full demand. While modern men are so "busy cutting down human imperfection" that "they make headway also on the raw material of good," Hawthorne manages to see with a vision akin to "the blind, prophetical, unsentimental eye of acceptance, which is to say, of faith" (227). Prophecy does not exhort men to do good; it shocks them into awareness of their sinful inadequacy, so that they may receive the saving, reconciling, transforming grace that will help them to be charitable even when their ideals are shorn. If Rauschenbusch's formula was justice always in tandem with charity, O'Connor's was charity only after redemption.

CHAPTER TEN

James Baldwin and the Wages of Innocence

> It is not my impression that people wish to become worse; they really wish to become better but very often do not know how. Most people assume the position, in a way, of the Jews in Egypt, who really wished to get to the Promised Land but were afraid of the rigors of the journey; and, of course, before you embark on a journey the terrors of whatever may overtake you on that journey live in the imagination and paralyze you. It was through Moses, according to legend, that they discovered, by undertaking this journey, how much they could endure.
>
> —James Baldwin, *Nobody Knows My Name* (1961)

Identity, Self-Knowledge, and the Limits of Irony

During an address on minority rights at Kalamazoo College in 1960, James Baldwin ventured to explain why Americans associate their national identity with a specific image of whiteness. The "national self-image" is a "cross between a Celt and a Teuton," who worships a "Puritan god," imagines he inherits the wisdom of "New England aristocrats," and hopes to enjoy a high material status. These myths shape the "social forms" and "manners" as well as the "interior life, the life of the mind," and it is this second sphere, the inner life, that proves elusive. Baldwin continues, turning to a story that has a long lineage in black preaching, spirituals, and literature. In this tradition, the Hebrews' deliverance from Egypt and their travel to Canaan describes the experience of bondage (through slavery, Jim Crow laws, systemic poverty, and political disenfranchisement) and the hope of liberation.[1] In Baldwin's allusion to Exodus, however, he shifts the figural parallel from black historical experience to white Southerners; as the speech expands in scope, the whole of American society stands in relation to Baldwin as the Jews did to Moses, as Baldwin coaxes the people to discover, with him, what prevents them from undertaking a journey to discover who they are and who they might become. The transfer of the biblical analogy from blacks' bondage by whites to whites' captivity as a result of their own self-images reveals a crucial aspect of Baldwin's prophetic message in the civil rights movement. For black freedom to be complete, white Americans must acknowledge the deep psychic and cultural interrelationship they have with blacks. Baldwin's insight here, as in his other explorations of American identity, is that whites do not really know who they are because they are afraid of understanding why they oppress others. There is a truth about themselves in black misery that whites have excluded from their consciousness through their distorted representations of American history and American life. "Whiteness," in Baldwin's work, is an investment in a version of American identity that prevents those who choose its myths from examining history from the perspective of the dispossessed and disinherited, whose experience denies that democracy has truly existed, nor its humanistic and Christian values truly honored, in the United States.[2]

Assailing the "myths," or "lies," of whiteness, Baldwin turned the Cold War era's end of innocence narrative against Americans whose Christian culture, he charged, had not saved them from damning illusions of moral purity. There are similarities to Christian Realism in Baldwin's thought: sin as denial (or "innocence") of sin, the critique of American character as innocent in the ironic sense of blindness or pretense, liberal universalism as false transcendence of self, the tragic sense of life as the burden of facing reality, the rejection of fundamentalism and sentimentality. Yet Baldwin's concerns with racial identity and national identity, the way these identity formations are inscribed by power, and the means for resisting these inscriptions and their supporting social structures, propel him beyond the limits of Niebuhrian irony.

Baldwin's intervention in the hegemonic end of innocence narrative of America's Cold War years makes an instructive parallel to Niebuhr's, for Baldwin reminds his reader that a philosophy of American history cannot abstractly ascribe innocence, even in an ironic sense, to the national character if it is to truly account for the kinds of self-deceit that whites have practiced toward other groups governed by the state. Such historians as Taylor Branch have shown that Niebuhr was a significant intellectual influence on the civil rights movement, for King credited Niebuhr's Christian Realism (especially as argued in *Moral Man and Immoral Society*) with helping him to synthesize thoughts from Gandhi, Thoreau, and Walter Rauschenbusch.[3] King indeed was inspired by Niebuhr's ethical weighing of different political instrumentalities, which rejected saintly martyrdom (the "Lutheran" position that politics, being concerned with power, is worldly and sinful) for a praxis that admitted the possible moral uses of force and favored civil disobedience as a nonviolent form of political coercion that does not contravene love. These debts aside, however, Baldwin's exploration of American innocence suggests why Niebuhrian irony, in its

Cold War cast, would have been very problematic for the civil rights movement and Black Power.

In *The Irony of American History,* Niebuhr portrays America as if it were guilty chiefly of lacking irony about its national ideals; because Americans, through their myths and intellectual traditions, have been made to believe the aim of democracy is perfect equality between free men, they have usually overlooked the evidence that their political gains were achieved by realistic assessments of how to share power distributed disproportionately among competitive groups. Thus, Niebuhr says, Americans have discredited their actual pragmatic achievements by glorying in a false image of America as the promised land. The basic problem with Niebuhr's view of the American past is that it is a critique of the majority view from within the majority, not from a true plurality. In articles published throughout the fifties, Niebuhr reprobated racial bigotry as a sin and stood up for black voting rights, though he disapproved of civil rights activists whose demands for immediate legal desegregation, he felt, gave no heed to existing power relations and communal mores. While it was important to advocate for anti-Jim Crow laws codifying equal rights in schools and public accommodations (which were not, Niebuhr argued, as basic as the franchise), local and national leaders should also, and perhaps primarily, work to carefully evolve a new moral consensus respecting interracial community. Methods would include, but not be limited to, boycotts and non-violent protests. Unfortunately, Niebuhr's polemic in *The Irony of American History* tended to obscure the very realities that elsewhere he chided civil rights activists for overlooking, while substituting its own mythical construction of American history. When he speaks of the national character in the famed 1952 book, he seems to project, by omission of race, a common vision of the past, and when he attacks the innocence of that vision, he does so by measuring it against "realities of power" without noting how much racial minorities have been shut out of these realities. A group who has had only surrogate representation in politics by privileged whites cannot be said to have shared power with anyone.[4] When Niebuhr tells Americans to check their ideals of perfect justice in *Irony,* he does not also state that blacks have been prevented (by barriers legal, political, and economic) from applying the pressure of their interests to the making of consensus.

One of Baldwin's tasks is to remind Americans that those who have been excluded from participating as whites in society do not share the same myths about the past and, in fact, have much more serious judgments about that past than a merely ironic attitude toward democratic idealism. Niebuhr proposes that America, in its self-deceived innocence, has tended to flee from the tragic, but crucial, recognition that having the responsibility of temporal power does not exempt a group from sin, but further involves it in mankind's finitude and imperfection. Baldwin suggests that white self-deceit, while it may indicate weakness common to men, has also been necessitated by the choices against blacks that the dominant racial group has made in order to enjoy the safety of power. Self-deceit and power are intricately related for Baldwin, for they are both means to the condition that he typically calls "safety"—an escape from the fear of self-knowledge. Power furnishes the material support for whites to preserve their national myths of innocence, while these myths, in turn, ratify the injustice that has enabled whites to invest themselves with privilege. If Niebuhr concludes that in all groups self-transcendence and egotism are inextricably bound, Baldwin concludes that whites must lie to themselves to avoid the truth of their specific historical record. Niebuhr in *Irony* chides Americans for fantasies of do-gooding that obscure the nature of the good they have actually accomplished, whereas Baldwin asks white Americans to lose their fantasies so that they might confront the repugnance of their actual deeds. As we engage with Baldwin, *The Irony of American History* should stand revealed as itself a terribly innocent document.

Baldwin's Modernism and the Pentecostal Sources of His Imagination

Partly as an effect of his meditations on Christianity, Baldwin has been criticized for drawing the issue of race out of political theory and into the discourse of moral seeking and exhortation. In his landmark *The Crisis of the Negro Intellectual* (1967), Harold Cruse, for example, deplores how Baldwin jokes about his amateur grasp of "'that sociology and economics jazz,'" as if he can rely on merely moral suasion to alter the situation of blacks.[5] Cruse argues that the main power blacks have had historically is moral argument, and this has proven a weak source of social change. By his reckoning, any black spokesmen needs now to recognize that a hard analysis of political economy must replace pleas for changes of heart. Like Cruse, many readers have been drawn to the power of Baldwin's witness though not compelled by his spiritual appeals. In response, they have stressed solely the political side of Baldwin's thought, leading them to sever the connection between Baldwin's exploration of whiteness and his prophetic, revisionist encounter with Christian tradition.[6] It is rare for Baldwin to attack white civilization without also inveighing against Christendom, and we cannot fully appreciate his critical intervention unless we are willing to see how whiteness represents to him a deviation from spiritual values Christian civilization itself has betrayed.

Baldwin did not make his choices about what to retain from religious tradition based on clearly stated presuppositions; instead, he asked himself how acting on religious ideas would affect the moral contexts in which men seek goods and formulate means. According to George Shulman, in *American Prophecy: Race and Redemption in American Political Culture* (2008), Baldwin thus "secularizes" and "de-theologizes" prophecy: "non-theistic because he does not announce god's words or point of view as a messenger, but prophetic because, on the basis of avowed experience, social position and artistic vision, he announces what is disavowed and unsayable, and testifies to what he sees and stands against it. I call him non-theistic but prophetic because he announces the vicissitudes of human finitude not by way of God's righteousness in a providentially ordered universe, but by the exemplary meaning or 'truth' of his experience as a human being."[7] Largely these are agreeable premises, but as they are developed in *American Prophecy,* the conclusions become objectionable; Shulman's account of prophecy's "secularization" does not permit Baldwin to be, at once, damning of Christendom yet still, as he was in so many respects, a Christian thinker.[8] Baldwin's biblical words are not merely rhetorical devices, but categories of his thought, though significantly revised, as all prophecy is for the pressures of historical crisis. It is intrinsic to prophecy, especially as it has been revived by Protestants, to be critical of an established church or of a dessicated, outmoded Christianity. Baldwin assails *false* Christians, reveals *the Church's mimicry of evil,* renounces a *theology of terror* that denies a Johannine one of Love, declaims *perverse* proclamations founded upon *the Christ* rather than upon the example of Jesus.[9] As for the claim of "de-theologization," if Baldwin's writings are compared, as they should be, to the Protestant modernist movement and the Social Gospel, then it is quite clear that a prophetic voice can be non-theistic, and yet Christian in its basic ethical orientation and anthropology. For a modernist like Shailer Matthews, God was not the antecedent and man the predicate.[10] Theology was an expression of human culture's striving after spiritual fulfillment and not a revelation of something transcendental above it. As defenders and enemies both were wont to point out, Protestant modernists kept the ethical values of Christ while making over Christianity as a gradational humanism in which man redeems himself by degrees through historical evolution. Since Baldwin believed that the modern world could make no substantive progress until it emancipated the colonized and the racially disenfranchised, he did not share the cultural immanentism of the modernists (any more than did Walter Rauschenbusch), but inasmuch as he put Christian creeds to pragmatic tests and, implicitly, interpreted religious dogmas as culturally dependent expressions instead of revelations from a sovereign being, he reflected the modernists' conviction that our estrangement from divinity was essentially separation from alienated potentials in man. Any specific image of God was a symbol for human ends, which would be judged by their effects on modern culture and society. As Baldwin would later pronounce in *The Fire Next Time*, if Christendom's God cannot help men to love, "then it is time we got rid of Him."[11] Indeed, this is to "secularize" in the original, Christian sense of the term (from *saecularis*, "generation" or "age"): to remove from ecclesiastical control or influence, to move into the world outside the Church's institutions and properties. It is not, however, to de-Christianize or to become antireligious or atheological.

Baldwin's case is further complicated, and requires a more subtle application of the term "secularization," by his continual engagement with Pentecostalism. Modernists, including those in the Social Gospel camps, had left mostly untouched the problem of racial inequality, taking positions that were, at best, moderately progressive compromises with segregation.[12] Baldwin's contemporary and senior, Martin Luther King, Jr., was trained in these schools of thought (Rauschenbusch was especially influential) as well as in the schools of their critics (such as Niebuhr and Tillich), though in the sixties he would adopt more radical positions than those of modernism, Niebuhr's Cold War realism, or Tillich's mediating theology. Using the Social Gospel initially to give a theoretical praxis to the message of deliverance in black preaching, King would gravitate in the last two years of his career toward socialist, anti-imperialist politics and a radicalized image of Christ compatible with the liberation theologians Albert Cleague and James Cone, who wanted to justify biblically the self-help nationalism of Malcom X.[13] Although King impacted Baldwin's thinking, he represented a fusion of black prophetic, evangelical preaching with academic liberal theology, which distinguishes his intellectual development from Baldwin's.[14] Independent of any contact with liberal Protestant theologians such as Reinhold Niebuhr or Paul Tillich, Baldwin's prophetic voice would evolve instead through a complex process of modernistic reimagining of his Pentecostal heritage, as powerfully presented in *Go Tell It on the Mountain* and subsequently in *The Fire Next Time* and the plays *The Amen Corner* and *Blues for Mr. Charlie*.

Pentecostalism, now the world's fastest-growing, and most racially diverse, Christian denomination, began as a charismatic movement concerned primarily with the experience of the "baptism in the Holy Spirit," accompanied by "gifts of the Holy Spirit," especially speaking in tongues, prophecy, and healing.[15] The Azusa Street revival in Los Angeles, the first institutional practice of Pentecostalism, would endure for three years (1905–1908), drawing curious Christians from around the world. While the movement eventually split into two major denominations—one black, the Church of God in Christ, and one white, the Assemblies of God—Pentecostalism was originally multiracial in worship, and many worshipers saw the revival's racial integration as a sign of God's presence. One participant famously proclaimed that the color line had been "washed away in the blood," and William Seymour, the black leader of the revival, prophesied that the baptism in the Spirit of God was an eschatological sign of Christ's imminent return to found a biracial Kingdom of God. As Harvey Cox has discussed in *The Fire from Heaven*, Pentecostalism has since been pulled not only between racial groupings, but also between fundamentalist and experiential strains.[16] The fundamentalist strain emphasizes strict conformity to the Word of God, legislated by commonsense understanding of Scripture and observance of the rules of behavior deducible therefrom, the experiential strain the witness of the Spirit over the Letter, as illumined by the indwelling of grace and evinced by fruits of mystical, transformative Love. Baldwin had to discover the prophetic voice in black Pentecostalism by repudiating its fundamentalist strain and reimagining its experiential one through a complex reimagining that bears fruitful comparison to modernist theological revisionism. Each stage of his thinking involved a return to and a revaluation of the Pentecostal influences he knew while growing up in Harlem.

The best source for understanding Baldwin's intrafaith conflict is his first, semi-autobiographical novel, *Go Tell It on the Mountain* (1953). Following three generations in a black family, from Reconstruction to Northern migration, the five-part novel is framed by the story of a third-generation adolescent boy, John, who undergoes a climactic conversion experience in a Pentecostal church—a church very similar to the one where young Baldwin used to preach when he was a teenaged minister, as described in *The Fire Next Time*.[17] The first section of *Go Tell it on the Mountain*, "The Seventh Day," introduces John Grimes as a youth whose future seems special to the members of his father's church: "it was said that he had a Great Future. He might become a Great Leader of His People."[18] Yet John "is not much interested in his people and still less interested in leading them anywhere," for he has internalized the loathing and self-hatred of his fundamentalist stepfather, the Reverend Gabriel Grimes, who vocalizes his hatred for whites, but inwardly shares his oppressor's subhuman, bedeviled view of blacks. Gabriel is a tragic figure, a former slave-woman's son whose hypocrisy, wrath, and pride testify to his inchoate sense of helplessness and outrage in a post-Reconstruction America. The Northern migrant church, by failing to transform its theology from the Southern church's premillenial dispensationalism, has done little more for parishioners than help them to cope with the ghetto. Through the tragic portrait of Gabriel and the carefully laid irony of John's religious conversion, *Go Tell It on the Mountain* contrasts false or incomplete models of Christianity with Baldwin's emerging consciousness of prophetic alternatives.

While the periodical press and postwar civil rights films hissed at Southern bigots, the poverty of blacks in Northern cities, unimproved and in some ways worsened by the social democratic policies of the New Deal, received much less political attention.[19] Harry Truman's Fair Employment Practices legislation was derailed by the Korean War, and the NAACP's legal fights to end racial discrimination could not create occupations for undereducated blacks, who were losing jobs due to the expansion of the white-collar class and the corporate divestment in unskilled factory labor. Although Baldwin's novel is set in Harlem during the 1930s, it presents a picture of economic segregation that had been little changed by the fifties, as Baldwin would witness in such essays as "Notes from a Native Son," in which he describes the aftermath of a Detroit race riot in 1943, or "Fifth Avenue Uptown," in which he charges Northern liberals with being innocent about the troubles just a few blocks above Saks. John's anger towards whites over their unequal privilege, as well as the despair over his future from which this anger springs, are presented sympathetically by the novel's narrator, but the church has taught John to mistrust his indignation about the squalor of the ghetto, as if such feelings are sinful marks of the "natural man." When the youth bitterly quotes a passage from Revelation 22:11, "He who is filthy, let him be filthy still," he chokes on his irony: "the phrase turned against him like a two-edged sword, for was it not he, in his false pride and his evil imagination, who was filthy?"[20] John's enervating moral hesitancy is only bolstered by Gabriel's brazen hatred for the boy, whom, in disowning, he has treated like a damnable bastard.[21] His stepfather's hatred compounds the sense of social inferiority John bears for being black, and his church's theology makes his painful self-doubt seem the inevitable lot of one who is not covered by Christ's blood.

Angered by the world outside but also afraid of himself, John is brought to an emotional crisis during a Saturday night service, as parishioners "plead the blood" for his soul. The description of John's crisis is narrated in free indirect discourse, and from the youth's subjective view, he appears to be undergoing a conversion. Initially John's consciousness is divided by two voices, one that he identifies as the Holy Ghost, and another "malicious, ironic voice," unidentified, which reminds him of his misgivings about the church and goads him to "rise—and, at once, leave this temple and go out into the world" (196). The ironic voice seems vicious to John because it draws him away from the light and down into darkness, but as the two voices compete, it is not clear that the light redeems rather than simply dazzles. Throughout the novel, Baldwin plies biblical references with double meanings, so that the underlying feelings of loss and deprivation in his characters can be detected along with traditional Christian virtues of long-suffering and patience. The church's inability to give an honest voice to the inner conflict in John tempts the youth to scorn his religion before he emotionally succumbs to the Saturday service, and the closing passages, with their glimpses of poverty unchanged, do not promise that he will escape his stepfather's fate, preaching the Word publicly while secretly hating his life of "hunger and toil" (28). Interpretations of John's conversion thus divide into an ironic camp, which explains the event in purely psychological terms and completely rejects the black church and Christianity, and an affirmative camp, which asserts that the experience is an authentic act of grace.[22]

Although I support the ironic interpretation, I believe its double consciousness of Christian doctrines, as they have been applied by white Christendom and black evangelicalism, anticipates later phases of Baldwin's prophetic voice. The novel's irony is internalized by Baldwin the prophet in order to renovate Christianity and disentangle certain of its values and symbols from the theology of terror. After his conversion, John does not turn first to his stepfather, the false prophet, but to the younger prophet, Elisha, his compassionate boyhood friend and potentially his beloved, who combines a faith in Christian brotherhood and also the capacity to love John as an individual. The allusiveness of John's name, moreover, implies that he may have a special relationship to Christianity, for all three Johns in the Bible appear in the New Testament; moreover, each of the three—John the Baptist, John the Apostle, and John of Patmos—bear the message of Christ at various stages in His revelation: preparing for His coming, witnessing to His ministry, and prophesying His return.[23] As Baldwin came to sift parts of Christian faith from the historic church, he located the possibility of salvation in Christ's teachings of universal love, a theme strongly pronounced in the Gospel of John, which contains the amaranthine passage in 3:16, "For God so loved the world that He gave His only begotten son." Yet Baldwin also recognized that the Christic ideal of loving brotherhood was more easily a hope of the oppressed than it was an incentive for the oppressor to alter his way of life. As he forged his prophetic voice, he urged that social justice be implemented before the oppressed's blighted hopes of mutual love could lead to a day of Judgment.

To assume this prophetic voice—the persona of *The Fire Next Time,* modified in *No Name in the Street* and in Reverend Meridian from *Blues for Mr. Charlie*—Baldwin parsed the doctrines of the evangelical church portrayed in *Go Tell It on the Mountain* and revised its motifs of deliverance. Baldwin firmly rejected the teaching of original sin, which plays no part in his subsequent messages, but his rationale for purging this piece of evangelical doctrine goes further than the modernists' because it portrays the idea of inherited depravity as especially dehumanizing for blacks, who were debased under an ideology equating them with the moral blackness of the natural man. In *Go Tell It on the Mountain,* for example, the idea of inherent sinfulness fills John with self-doubt and hesitation. While such ambivalence may be itself a sign of wisdom in Niebuhr's theology, it inhibits John from taking his negative emotions seriously, except as involuntary manifestations of "malicious irony" or "false pride." Baldwin still found much to mine from the church's idea that "innocence" itself could be a form of evil. Where the faithful in *Go Tell It on the Mountain* associate "first innocence" with original sin, Baldwin jettisoned the Augustine doctrine while refurbishing the trope of innocence. From the evangelical interpretation of "first innocence," his writings retain the notion that the sinner does not recognize his guilt, but Baldwin further charges that the sinner is guilty of lying from the need to protect his power and safety. As he reconfigured the motif of innocence, Baldwin also took "deliverance" out of the Pentecostal contexts of premillennialism and personal salvation, and instead projected the oppressed's victory over suffering in the imminent, global future. Throughout *Go Tell It on the Mountain,* Baldwin shows how Gabriel's congregations cling to the Gospel stories of Christ's ministry as well as the Old Testament stories of people released from captivity in the Hebrew histories and the prophetic books. Yet, where Gabriel's church uses the New Testament to pacify the idea of deliverance, by transforming it into a wholly inner condition (salvation from the curse of sin), Baldwin instead located the common thread of both Testaments in the oppressed's struggle for liberation. Using the trope of righteous wrath, his writings confer moral dignity on the anger that John's faith tells him to overcome with forbearance.

Protest or Revolution: Is there a National Identity that Love Can Make?

When Baldwin speaks of deliverance to come, his mood matches the prophets of the Babylonian and Assyrian captivity, but when he addresses white innocence, his voice is similar to the preexilic cries of the prophets, as they warn Israel and Judah of the coming crisis in the hope that belated reforms might still spare them disaster. Both attitudes mingle in Baldwin's best-known nonfiction work, *The Fire Next Time* (1963), the first full-dress example of his prophetic style. From the apocalyptic promise of the book's title to the image of its first section, "My Dungeon Shook," alluding to God's rescue of the shackled Apostles in Acts 12, *The Fire Next Time* is a warning as well as an expostulation.[24] The book's two parts were originally published in 1962, after the year of the Freedom Riders and two years into Kennedy's presidency, as the Democratic administration, cautious after the Party's retaking the White House, was still wavering about whether to support a civil rights bill.[25] Meanwhile Black Muslim activism in the urban North and revolutions for independence in the Third World had emboldened black nationalists to seriously entertain separating from white society in the United States, perhaps by means of force. *The Fire Next Time* weighs the gradualist-integration and the nationalist positions and finds both solutions wanting.

Baldwin could not accept the prophet's role of articulating national history as a trajectory from sacred origins that confer a covenanted identity. Nor could he, in adapting prophecy to his purpose, easily accept that national identity could be collectively invented within history. George Shulman has suggested that Baldwin's prophetic attitude toward the past could be instructively compared to Perry Miller's argument in *Nature's Nation* that American identity has never been something inherited, as the Puritans preached of New England in their jeremiads.[26] Miller and Baldwin, instead, both conceive of national identity as something continuously in the process of being achieved now with an eye to the future as well as the past. Insofar as Baldwin sees national identity as uncovenanted and created by each generation's reckoning with the cultural consciousness of the previous one, this is an acceptable parallel, but if one examines Miller's formulations of how a national identity is achieved, the comparison raises difficulties. In Perry Miller's well-known essay "Nature and the National Ego," the ego in question evolves through an experience (in this case, the change from wilderness to city) that brews inside of Americans until some gifted individuals give it a collective expression, thus making historical transition into an object of self-reflection. Miller describes these collective meditations by personifying America in the singular, so that, notwithstanding his careful delineation of each text he introduces, we are given the impression of a conversation beginning and ending on an underlying consensus. Whether Miller intends it as a category or as a metaphor, the phrase "national ego" deters the reader from conceiving the American past as driven by contradictions between groups; the very application of the phrase already suggests that disagreements were transcended by a higher unity. Baldwin recognized that the appeal of a concept such as "national ego" ("American identity" or "national character") is its implicit promise of consensus, though he could never invoke it in order to make consensus seem a forgone conclusion.

Racially separated within America yet joining himself to its destiny, Baldwin endured—and portrayed—the contradiction of being a supplicant and a pariah among, a testifying witness against as well as a conscience for, his "countrymen."[27] He expresses this division, within himself and within America, by employing the prophetic trope of antithesis.[28] Calling for reform as he announces judgment, promising salvation as he assures men of God's wrath, blaming the Hebrews for their fate even as he chastises the nations who conquer them, the prophet is a bearer of contraries. He responds to divine action in history, as God makes and unmakes Israel's suffering, by both denying and affirming the nation's inheritance, eventually reconciling this tension by renewing the Abramic and Mosaic covenants through the Davidic. In certain personifications of divine speech (Isaiah 52:7), we hear the tension between denial and affirmation of the nation's inheritance expressed as God's pathos rather than the prophet's, but in other passages, the contradiction clearly lies within the prophet's heart.[29] Jeremiah is the richest source for examples, for at some moments he rues his mission and resents his unlistening, unregenerate audience, while at others he mourns the "irrecoverable judgment" that strikes the nation.[30] Inasmuch as the prophet's message concerns the Hebrews, it necessarily grasps him as a member of the community, whether or not the people heed him. Ezekiel actually makes his body symbolize the Hebrews' crises, and Hosea names his children after the phases of the nation's judgment and future salvation.[31]

In adopting the trope of antithesis from the Bible, however, Baldwin necessarily alters its temporality, such that redemption is not oriented towards the recovery of the past but the making of a future. The Hebrew prophets address the nation as covenanted members of that national identity, even when they are persecuted by their group, and they remind the people of God's will as it has been revealed in a history that is also the prophet's inheritance. The Hebrew prophet finally interprets the vicissitudes of history by the promise of the covenant, unbroken by God, and hence, he sees redemption as a return to, or renewal of, the sacred laws and practices of the past. God transcends the nation, but at the same time, God's values are immanent to the nation's past, and all change to tradition is essentially extension or fulfilment rather than rupture. Baldwin does not believe the nation is a covenanted identity, on the model of the Old Testament prophets, but an imagined one that a group holds about itself; it is a form of moral and cultural self-definition that can legitimate or protest the actual institutional and economic structures that organize society. In America, Baldwin speaks of the nation in two senses, one pejorative and the other visionary. Where the nation in the pejorative sense refers to ethnocentric ideology, encouraging amnesia and blindness, the nation in the second, visionary sense is a truly inclusive identity, and Baldwin confers on this idea of an American nation certain "spiritual" values culled from his modernization of black Pentecostal tradition.

King had been the great prophetic avatar of this tradition in Baldwin's time, but in *The Fire Next Time,* Baldwin's temporalization of prophetic antithesis gives him a different understanding of redemption than King. The Reverend preached that black civil rights were a crucial step toward realizing black human rights, which were based on Christian spiritual values that lay at the core of American identity. King was essentially calling white Americans back to the moral sources of the national character and asking them to extend their own values to blacks. John F. Kennedy was clearly borrowing from King's rhetoric in his 1963 televised speech on civil rights: "We are confronted primarily with a moral issue. . . . It is as old as the Scriptures and is as clear as the American Constitution. The heart of the question is whether all Americans are to be afforded equal rights and equal opportunities, whether we are going to treat our fellow Americans as we want to be treated."[32] King's prophetic rhetoric at this stage, in other words, was compatible with liberal pluralist arguments for racial inclusiveness. Baldwin, by contrast, asserts that black exclusion from full legal and human membership in the United States has disqualified American identity from being a source of moral values. How, Baldwin begs, can one penetrate the collective innocence of a Cold War superpower that elects itself, in God's name, to defend the rights of man globally even as it denies freedom to indigenous black Americans? Writing against the country's Adamic myth, Baldwin continues that America has so far thrown its chance to be exceptional, the redeemer of nations, because it has imitated Europe's theology of terror and its "shame" of color, as exemplified by the counterrevolutionary policies the United States had been pursuing as part of its Cold War strategy.[33]

It was precisely these sentiments—that America was essentially unethical—that irked Robert Penn Warren, who felt that America's faults, albeit considerable, did not disqualify its countrymen from using their professed humanistic, Christian, and democratic ideals as standards for judging the society and justifying the renegotiation of power relations.[34] Allowing for his critique of certain Christian dogmas, Baldwin does not reject these ideals in their entirety, especially if they are understood as goals and not achievements, hopes rather than the country's heritage. His persona in *The Fire Next Time* is dually identified as black as well as American, but, contrary to liberal pluralist models of American identity, Baldwin does not reduce blacks to an "interest group" within American society. Instead, as a black subject, he presents himself as a member of an oppressed population speaking to a society whose national identity he does not yet share, since to ground his appeal for national change on the identity that currently exists would be tantamount to sharing white lies about America's pure intentions. As Lawrie Balfour states, Baldwin believes that American democracy is not "an idea to be returned to," for until blacks stand inside the promise of full citizenship and human rights, American democracy "will not have been genuinely tried."[35]

In order to prophesy a future where whites and blacks can honor one another's mutual humanity, Baldwin urges Americans to look not toward King's mythical image of their original ethical selves, but toward an as yet undiscovered America, one that will not exist until black freedom is a reality: "The price of the liberation of the white people [from their immoral myths] is the liberation of the blacks—the total liberation, in the cities, in the towns, before the law, and in the mind. . . . In short, we, the black and the white, deeply need each other here if we are really to become a nation."[36] Since most Americans still do not know the truth of their past, the America that Baldwin envisions does not yet exist (88–89). Hence, he aligns his vision with a nation that would transcend its presently deformed image, predicated on lies, by uniting the mutual ends of liberation and self-examination.

Self-knowledge emerges in "Down at the Cross" as itself the beginning of freedom, a concept that is quite distinct from the legal goal of equality. It is a reckoning with fear that calls itself innocent, but that expels and denies experience: "The person who distrusts himself has no touchstone for reality—for this touchstone can be only oneself. Such a person interposes between himself and reality nothing less than a labyrinth of attitudes." To decide what society Americans, black and white, should together share, they must be willing to search themselves: "Whatever white people do not know about Negroes reveals, precisely and inexorably, what they do not know about themselves" (43, 44). The prophet must initiate the process of coming into self-knowledge, and this process begins not with the American people's confessions, but with Baldwin's personally. It is by confessing, rather than by casting a charismatic net, that the prophet establishes his sincerity, and thereby his right to be heard as a truth-teller to power. Baldwin voices his intent to be honest and guarantees that intent by his inescapable, though unsought, submergence in the reality of pain. From the long description of growing up in Harlem and the account of his ambivalent meeting with Elijah Muhammad, both in "Down at the Cross," to the ploy of presenting "My Dungeon Shook" as if it were a personal letter to his nephew, also named James, Baldwin creates the impression that his prophetic ire and anguish stem from his *sincerity.* He seems moved to speak, in other words, by his direct involvement with "Harlem's empty lots," the "urine-stained hallways," the "children parceled out here and there," the "knife and pistol and fight" (20, 104). In such powerful pieces as "Notes of a Native Son" and "Fifth Avenue Uptown," Baldwin had perfected the technique of using personal reminiscence and firsthand accounts to describe in "local," "individualized" contexts the effects of social and political policies, the suffering and loss unseen by the white world.[37] One of his rhetorical feats in *The Fire Next Time,* as in the earlier testimonial pieces, is to persuade the reader (for instance, the white interlocutor in "My Dungeon Shook") that her ignorance of the situations he describes is itself a justification for his passionate need to speak, for, by contrast with her, he cannot afford (economically or emotionally) detachment from these scenes. Writing as if spurred to retort to those who call him a "bitter" black man, Baldwin's memories of family survival encourage empathy until the sudden change in tone and in time perspective, which shifts focus to "James"'s brother's affliction, and through his suffering, to that of Baldwin the speaker, who retaliates in anger that seems to flow inexorably from years of having indelibly observed a family member decay. Where charisma bestows a special power on the speaker who commands his audience's obedience, the Baldwin persona's sincerity persuades the reader that his message is a continuation of his personal witness, and this message warrants her attention because the evil presently affecting black Americans like himself has for too long been undisclosed.

MAKING the confessional the prelude to the prophetic, Baldwin strikes a balance between accusation and self-scrutiny. Although whites, having more self-distrust, resist honesty more forcefully and with greater panic, the failure of biracial freedom in America is still an example of a "human truth"—that men "of whatever color" are reluctant to bear freedom.[38] In "Everybody's Protest Novel" and "Many Thousands Gone" Baldwin had begun to develop his own idea of the tragic sense of life. It is not the condition of having to choose between lesser evils, but a human refusal to bear the stigmata of mortality, the flesh, and all its associated frailty because these are signs of creaturely vulnerability to suffering and loss.[39] The suffering that comes of this vulnerability cannot be removed from human life, and Baldwin, in essays beginning with "Everybody's Protest Novel" and going forward, had also traced even remediable social evils, political and economic inequality, to a common root in the human desire to deny tragedy. The dread is a mortal, and not strictly a socially structured, condition, as is the innocence that covers over it. Innocence emerges as a particular form of an existential longing for purity, which is doomed to result in hypocrisy because it cannot cope with the wounding nature of life. Through splitting and projection, it purifies the self while punishing another for all the woes borne of existence. Indeed, love in *The Fire Next Time* is opposed to a form of Christian theology, imbricating slavery and imperialism, which may have helped to engender the mentality of racism. It is a theology that denies the tragic character of life, tragedy that can be accepted and overcome only by love, and instead makes Western men fixate on evil as a cosmological principle, entailing the grueling prospect of damnation. Filled with spiritual dread,[40] whites project onto blackness all the weaknesses they abstract from themselves in a psychic split that renders Christian compassion towards the racially subjected essentially hypocritical, since it does not flow from charity but instead from mortification and self-fear. Evil is not a primal taint but the refusal to acknowledge that the Other is the disavowed self. Beneath the liberal conscience of *Uncle Tom's Cabin*, for instance, Baldwin sees a "theological terror, the terror of damnation": "the spirit that breathes in this book, hot, self-righteous, fearful, is not different from that spirit of medieval times which sought to exorcize evil by burning witches; and is not different from that terror which activates a lynch mob."[41] The lynching, like the burning of religious heretics, is a ritual of purification, parodying the Crucifixion, in which the blood spilled denies a common finitude and frailty, and falsely purchases safety from the diurnal world of flesh and time. "Down at the Cross" is the culmination of Baldwin's meditation that purity always comes with the price of another's freedom, for a group, or a person singly, can only rest in the lie of innocence if another is made to bear the stigma for suffering.

Innocence thus covers over a darkness common to all in which each is tempted to turn human suffering into rancor rather than overcome tragedy by love. Baldwin rejected original sin because of the doctrine's applications in proslavery apologies, but he did speak of "the individual horror, carried everywhere in the heart. Which of us has overcome his past? And the past of the Negro is blood dripping through the eaves. . . . But this past is not special to the Negro. This horror is also the past, and the everlasting potential, or temptation, of the human race. If we do not know this, it seems to me, we know nothing about ourselves, nothing about each other."[42]

Although he highlights here the experience of black double consciousness (exemplified by Richard Wright in "Alas, Poor Richard"), Baldwin also underlines that some horrifying desire for "fantastical violence," which would "wash away" tormenting memories, flows from the cumulative outrage and dread that each man, black and white, carries in his past. So long as humans evade knowledge of tragedy, no one, it appears, can long avoid being made a surrogate in which someone else reposes his rancor.[43] As any number of confessional passages show, Baldwin did not exempt himself from this horror. In a telling reflection in "Notes of a Native Son," he describes his reaction upon hurling a water pitcher, with intent to kill, at a white waitress in a segregated diner: "I had been ready to commit murder. I saw nothing very clearly but I did see this: that my life, my *real* life, was in danger, and not from anything other people might do but from the hatred I carried in my own heart."[44] The scenario, which begins with a victim confronting bigotry, startlingly turns to self-accusation. The passage in no way apologizes for the behavior of the whites in the diner, but it does demonstrate that for Baldwin rightful wrath and hatred are alarmingly intimate with each other, and hatred implicates even the victim of racism in the ubiquity of human failing. Indeed, Baldwin's sensitivity to the ever-present desire to overcome suffering with evil, by hoarding power or by avenging one's hurt, made him imbue the capacity of love with a quality akin to grace, since the horror in each human heart seemed to militate so strongly against it.

The exhortative emphasis on love in these passages seems designed to abreact what Baldwin perceives as the self-interestedness of most political strategy, which typically takes as its premise (and note the Cold War phraseology) "the realities of power."[45] Although he admits that the disenfranchised must utilize political means since they cannot trust the "sloppy and fatuous nature of American good will," Baldwin describes typical political logic as a cynical calculation of interest without moral judgment: "[Hard problems] have been dealt with, when they have been dealt with at all, out of necessity—and in political terms, anyway, necessity means concessions made in order to stay on top" (87). The *Brown vs. Board of Education* decision, for instance, appears to the speaker in *Fire* as a concession made by a superpower to gain diplomatic leverage. Without the Cold War pressure to woo Third World nations from Communism, he charges, American liberals would have still been saying "wait" on ending segregation in schools (55, 58, 87). Baldwin simply (and somewhat simplistically) strips liberal "realism" of its tragic sobriety; there is no ambiguity in power politics—only moral rhetoric accompanying the conservation of privilege by those who dominate out of fear. Blacks, he argues, have learned to regard politics cynically because whites have so often masked self-interest as high principle. The danger is that blacks will also learn to regard the discourse of universal human rights (as these principles had been ratified by the United Nations in 1948) with equal cynicism. Thus he makes abundantly obvious, especially in his assessment of Elijah Muhammad (a double to Baldwin's own prophet persona), that blacks must not retaliate by internalizing their oppressors' will to domination. People in any future society, he insists, must achieve more than simply a reversal of the present distribution of power (87). Human rights will not be secured, it seems, unless political strategy is supplemented by some awakening that transforms the attitudes of individuals towards each other. Changes affected by protest or rebellion without a corresponding spiritual rejuvenation will leave the process of liberation incomplete, for a new society cannot be free unless its members individually accept one another as a moral end—and do so because, not in spite, of the tragedy and weakness they see in one another: "I speak of change not on the surface but in the depths—change in the sense of renewal" (92).

The Fire Next Time devotes lengthy passages to describing why Baldwin renounced the Pentecostalism of his upbringing, but its argument no less borrows from the evangelical emphasis on being "born again," in which the individual, having confronted his heart, undergoes a complete reorientation of motive. Baldwin nowhere states that conversion can accomplish justice, which, *Fire* admits, will likely require some measure of political coercion, nor does he have in mind the kind of instantaneous conversion that dazed John Grimes into almost forgetting how much he resented his family's poverty. For the prophet persona in *Fire*, one cannot be "born again" outside of a community in which members understand that injustice is a sign of their fear—not their incapacity—of baring themselves. It is the fear that plagues *Fire's* white liberals, who desperately want to ask forgiveness from blacks before fully confessing the sins they have done against them, and so, against themselves. In effect, Baldwin here reads his Pentecostal heritage through a modernizing lens. In place of a vertical, divine-to-human downpouring of grace, the individual can be truly converted only through relationships of mutual self-examination and self-revelation. Where political action can affect legal definitions of justice and the social distribution of power, the spiritual bonds Baldwin has in mind would alter the motives of change, replacing Niebuhrian prudence or subaltern *resentissement* with the responsibility to love individuals unmediated by the illusions of innocence.

Baldwin's position is difficult because love at one and the same time must dispel illusions and also create the motive that will survive their loss. Blacks, moreover, have to assume more responsibility for the work of love.

In "Down at the Cross," the second part of *Fire*, the white man might be released from his innocent self-image—from the "tyranny of his mirror"— by the Christic ideal of saving love that accepts men in all their paradox of grace and horror: "Love takes off the masks that we fear we cannot live without and know we cannot live within. I use the word love here not merely in a personal sense but as a state of being, or a state of grace" (95). Whites might be awakened to the possibility of mutual, biracial freedom if they are able to truly perceive how blacks have nurtured love despite all the suffering and dread from which white men have tried to insulate themselves by "staying on top" of "the Negro" (8–10, 98–100). The idea that blacks are more capable of the love that whites need if they are ever to be released from their false identities seems derivative of King's teaching that blacks, through love, should set a moral example for whites—a position that many even in 1962–1963 regarded as impractical folly.

BALDWIN'S BELIEF in common guilt and the reciprocality of love did not, however, minimize his sense that the oppressor bears a special accountability for having manifested his self-deceit in such systematic, inveterate, and lethal forms. The speaker in *The Fire Next Time* does not downplay the resilience of innocence in its capacity for self-deception, and he balances his message of love with impeachments of systemic evils that innocence excuses, much as the black Christ, in Baldwin's later writings of the sixties, never promises love without also extolling his wrath toward liars. By holding, furthermore, that personal innocence can only be sustained by collective lies, Baldwin redeems political action. If white hypocrisy and Cold War calculus might reduce politics to the semblance of a "necessary evil," Baldwin claims politics for the responsible exercise of Christic love.

Because Baldwin continually resorted to the generalization of "white innocence" as he assailed the United States and Western civilization, he offended Robert Penn Warren, as he had other critics, who argued that his disregard for making moral discriminations within groups, other than blacks, deprived his later work from the sixties forward of subtlety.[46] As Patricia Schnapp has noted, Baldwin's hyperbolic rhetoric owes to the tradition of the Old Testament prophet, "for it is the nature of the prophet to rail, to direct his attention only to the failures, and to avoid palliating remarks."[47] However, Baldwin has also modified the terms of biblical invective in ways that his critics, in their quickness to attack him for generalization, have not always appreciated. The prophets levy judgments of collective guilt, which hold the whole of Israel, each and every member, accountable for the cumulative sins committed by the populace. Since all are morally guilty of contributing, in deed or in spirit, to Israel's unrighteousness, all are subject to the same punishment. God's reprisal strikes all, and no one can protest, because, as members of Israel, all are sinners. It is a similar kind of logic, however, that Baldwin rejects in both Black Muslim theology as well as white racist Christianity. Replying to Elijah Muhammad's prophecy that whites, because they were without virtue, would be collectively destroyed for the evil that the race has perpetrated, Baldwin says: "There is nothing new in this merciless formulation except the explicitness of its symbols and the candor of its hatred. Its emotional tone is as familiar to me as my skin; it is but another way of saying that *sinners shall be bound in Hell a thousand years.*"[48] Baldwin does not proclaim that whites are collectively guilty for all of the sins that certain whites have committed; instead, he charges that whites are collectively guilty of innocence, of hiding within and promulgating the myths of whiteness that support inequality. By showing whites that their identities as Americans or Europeans are based upon lies, he may persuade them that they can choose to negate the structures those lies conserve. So long as whites guard their innocence, through the insulation of social separation, political power, and ideology, they are guilty of condoning black suffering, whether or not they actively violate individual blacks or own businesses exploiting black communities.

It is worth recalling here the distinction Hannah Arendt draws between "collective guilt" and "political responsibility" in her conclusion to *Eichmann in Jerusalem.* The first concept she rejects as a deviation within the Christian Church, which by spreading guilt everywhere holds no one in particular accountable.[49] When judging group behavior, one cannot hold each individual member culpable for acts certain members commit; however, one can assert that "every generation, by virtue of being born into a historical continuum, is burdened by the sins of the fathers as it is blessed with the deeds of the ancestors" (298). This burden is "political responsibility," and although Arendt reckons that this kind of accountability is too impersonal to be morally binding, the concept is actually very much compatible with the heart of what Walter Rauschenbusch called *The Theology of the Social Gospel,* when speaking of "corporate sins" being transmitted between generations. The very notion of corporate sin bridges the distinction between what the Puritans called "sins of omission" and "sins of commission." Corporate sins, belonging to the structural relations of society, are perpetuated not only by individual agents in positions of control but also by the choice of people to leave intact structures that could be justly altered. Simply put, certain interests could not use the status quo to exploit men if others did not omit their political responsibility to prevent particular groups from being deprived of their human (Rauschenbusch would also say God-given) rights. Whether or not one is the author of a social injustice or actively intending wrong to a group, one inherits a responsibility to alter the corporate relations, and if one omits to act, one fails the obligation of love and becomes guilty of evil's continuum. Like Rauschenbusch's belief in corporate sin and the guilt of omission, Baldwin's notion that evil comes of "collective innocence" makes the acceptance of political responsibility a moral choice rooted in a spiritual orientation where love is the paramount motive.

Returning, in the last pages of *Fire,* to his theory that whites secretly want release through love, Baldwin does not relinquish hopes for a nonviolent solution and, in fact, he provides no justification for force. Instead he insists that whites must respect the sources of black anger—the sense that there is "nothing to lose"—while he warns of the violence that will come if whites do not assume their moral and political responsibility: "At the center of this dreadful storm, this vast confusion, stand the black people of this nation, who must now share the fate of a nation that has never accepted them, to which they were brought in chains. Well, if this so, one has no choice but to do all in one's power to change that fate, and at no matter what risk—eviction, imprisonment, torture, death."[50] This penultimate judgement of America's crisis led him to the final paragraph's exhortation, what Harold Bloom calls "the prophetic core" of the book and what Robert Penn Warren mistakenly called a wish for cosmic vengeance:[51]

> When I was very young, and was dealing with my buddies in those wine- and urine-stained hallways, something in me wondered, *What will happen to all that beauty?* . . . When I sat at Elijah's table and watched the baby, the women, and the men, and we talked about God's—or Allah's—vengeance, I wondered, when that vengeance was achieved, *What will happen to all that beauty then?* I could also see that the intransigence and ignorance of the white world might make that vengeance inevitable—a vengeance that does not really depend on, and cannot really be executed by, any person or organization, and that cannot be prevented by any police force or army: historical vengeance, a cosmic vengeance, based on the law that we recognize when we say, "Whatever goes up must come down." And here we are, at the top of the gaudiest, most valuable, and most improbable water wheel the world has ever seen. Everything now, we must assume, is in our hands; we have no right to assume otherwise. If we—and I now mean the relatively conscious whites and the relatively conscious blacks, who must, like lovers, insist on, or create, the consciousness of others—do not falter in our duty now, we may be able, handful that we are, to end the racial nightmare, and achieve our country, and change the history of the world. If we do not now dare everything, the fulfillment of that proph-

ecy, re-created from the Bible in a song by a slave, is upon us: *God gave Noah the rainbow sign, No more water, the fire next time!*[52]

Harold Bloom has praised the "rhetorical movement" of the passage, "from the waterwheel to the ambivalent divine promise of no second flood, the promise of the covenant with its dialectical countersong of the conflagration ensuing from our violation of covenant," an alternation of contraries (water/fire, love/vengeance, beauty/destruction, ignorance/duty) comparable, one might add, to the tropes of antithesis in the Old Testament prophetic books.[53] However, Bloom does not recognize how Baldwin's allusion to the Noahic covenant points to difficulties troubling the whole passage. Baldwin, of course, alludes to God's promise to Noah's family in Genesis 9:9–17 that He will never again use rain to deluge the earth. The Noahic covenant, however, is quite a different promise from those with Abraham, Moses, and David, which the prophets invoke during the Babylonian-Assyrian sieges of Israel. More than guaranteeing that there would never again be Flood, these later covenants sealed the unity of the Hebrews as a nation under one God whose laws they were bound to obey. It is in the absence of a similar "covenant," one unifying blacks and whites as a nation involved in the realization of common values, that Baldwin must prophesy from a position outside the American identity, as he voices the wrath of a people once called the sons of Noah's offspring Ham by white masters and, like Ham's progeny, still disinherited.[54] One of the underlying, and troubling, ironies of the allusions to Genesis 9 is that Ham's children, later in the same chapter (9:25–27), are cursed into slavery by the same God who gives Noah the rainbow sign. It is a crossed divinity, a deity who destroys and curses as well as promises no Flood, that the ending of *Fire* evokes, and, by contrast with the God of Isaiah or Jeremiah, He observes no national covenant that tempers vengeance with love for the people He has unified as one body.

The difficulties of the passage, which are deepened by the complex allusion to Genesis 9, stem from the ambivalence about rage and the political use of force that trouble the last third of *Fire*, which culminates in Baldwin's rescinding of the Noahic code, whereby God disqualifies Himself from ever again destroying the earth. Baldwin's characterization of vengeance earlier in the passage—as if it were cosmic or historical law intending that everything going up must also come down—actually seems more compatible with Greek ideas of nemesis than with Jeremiah's or Christ's teachings of a loving God's Judgment.[55] There may be a justice in this vengeance, but it is not the vision of freedom that Baldwin has discovered in his spiritual values or imagined in America's future. If love and mutual responsibility cannot produce liberation, he worries, then will a solution by violence afterwards be able to spiritually right itself or will it be merely a *lex talionis?* When Baldwin asks, "What will happen to all that beauty" he is not referring to "the beauty of the beasts and the fowl" from Genesis 9 (as Bloom speculates), but to the beauty in blacks engendered by years of having withstood suffering.[56] He asks whether that beauty, perhaps out of necessity, will be marred by a desperate confrontation with whites. A liberation movement predicated on hatred of the oppressor rather than hope of a biracial solution, he worries, may debase itself, embodying the horrific irony of a God who saves Noah's family from wickedness only to do the inhumanity of cursing Ham's progeny. And if "the fire next time" has the magnitude of the Flood, then it will not create or unify, but only destroy. At the same time, Baldwin cannot attach moral obloquy to the oppressed who may, with or without Elijah's logic, retaliate for despair that whites will ever make redress for their collective innocence. *Fire* closes with a prophet trying to balance his commitment to social liberation with his commitment to a New Testament vision of America, unified through Christic love, one that the facts of white society and the lies of white civilization may finally extinguish.

Baldwin here grapples with a Niebuhrian theme: an individual may be capable of sincerity, but can a group ever be? In Baldwin's terms, can a people see a reality, admit a history, confess a truth, that indicts it for a catastrophic failure to love and a willful choice to be innocent? The escalation of violence in America and abroad compelled Baldwin to consider whether there were limits to the work that love could effect. Could the theology of Love coexist with a liberation message in which wrath must sound louder in warning? If love failed to effect the escape route from violence, would force be necessary to remove the illusions of innocence from the oppressor's eyes? In *The Fire Next Time,* Third World revolutions (at the time Baldwin was writing, most recently in Algeria) give urgency to the book's other major theme—the coming liberation. If King's domestic strategy of nonviolence does not awaken white men to assume political responsibility in a spirit of love, then perhaps the wrath released in Cold War "hot wars" may reveal to them how they are seen by blacks and other nonwhites around the world.

Baldwin had been sensitized to Third World revolutionary politics during his self-imposed exiles in the fifties, when he had contacts with Algerians in France and attended the Conference of Negro-African Writers and Artists (1956). His cross-identification with nonwhites battling for independence in other countries becomes a pronounced theme in *No Name in the Street* and "White Racism or World Community." These works are complicated, however, by his denials of a pan-African diasporic identity. As he revealed in his response to the Negritude movement, Baldwin believed that opposition to colonialism was an insufficient basis for an identity and a culture. Opposition to a common source of oppression was a foundation for a political organization or movement. Identity, however, was more profound than the political; it was not an instrumentality, but a value to be achieved for itself, in the coalescence of love and freedom. The African American quest for identity was exceptional, because there was no mother country, or mother culture, to return to as an origin, before the colonizer. As Kevin Birmingham has discussed: "Baldwin boldly asserted [at the First International Congress of Black Writers and Artists, 1956] that African Americans have had their roots viably (if not justly) transplanted in a unique slave experience. Cultural roots are as important as ever, but the relevant soil for African Americans is in the United States."[57] Baldwin's exceptionalist claims for black experience in America placed greater pressure on the work of love. If the quest for identity was still rooted in America rather than being international and diasporic in scope, caught up in a common history with white America rather than consciously forming in opposition to an oppressor, then violence as a political means for black power was even less defensible on American soil. It would undo the very conditions that *The Fire Next Time* lays for the possibility of a genuine, meaning biracial, American identity.

In 1963, Baldwin held still to his exceptionalist position that black Americans were culturally in a very different situation from the revolutionaries in colonized nations: "They [American blacks] are not in the position of the Africans, who are attempting to reclaim their land and break the colonial yoke and recover from the colonial experience."[58] Although outraged by savage attacks on nonviolent protesters and black citizens (the brutality was epitomized by the bombing of Birmingham's Sixteenth Street Baptist Church in 1963), Baldwin still participated in peaceful projects, such as voter registration drives, that were overseen by the SNCC and CORE, both groups that, at this point, still supported civil disobedience. The question for him was what kind of pressure, short of threatening rebellion, blacks could use to impel swifter legislative response and more legal protection from the federal and state governments. On this matter Baldwin had no clear theoretical position, but despite his doubts about King's methods, he had not entirely given up King's and his own vision of a redeemed, mutually free America united by love. The preface to *Blues for Mr. Charlie* (1965), in addition to condemning the plague of white racism, also speaks of rescuing "our children," and the possessive plural refers to future generations white and black. Throughout the preface, Baldwin refers to Americans as "we," as though invoking a time when the national identity would be racially inclusive. In light of Baldwin's prefatory remarks, when Reverend Meridian takes up his murdered son's weapon, his speech seems less a clarion call to militant violence than another instance of the author warning that continued social lethargy could carry America beyond its crisis to regrettable bloodshed.[59]

THE DIAMETRICAL VIEWS that Baldwin affords of John Brown between 1956 and 1972 expose the development of a major fissure in his politics and in his prophetic message. In a 1956 review of J. C. Furnas's *Goodbye to Uncle Tom*, the author of *Go Tell It on the Mountain* concurs with Furnas's villainous version of the abolitionist folk hero: "Perhaps the worst thing that can be said about social indignation is that it so frequently leads to the death of personal humility. Once that has happened, one has ceased to live in the world of men which one is striving so mightily to make over. One has entered into a dialogue with that terrifying deity, sometimes called History, previously, and perhaps again, to be referred to as God, to which no sacrifice in human suffering is too great."[60] Baldwin's picture of John Brown in this review anticipates his portrait of Black Muslim leader Elijah Mohammed in Part II of *The Fire Next Time*. Both exhibit the innocence of a theological dualism that denies any responsibility for evil, and seeks only its purification. Baldwin, in the civil rights era, could not imagine, with Franz Fanon, a dialectic of revolution in which violence was intrinsic and necessary. He could foresee an untenable situation in which the Manicheism of innocent whites—their Bigger Nigger stereotypes arrayed against their Uncle Toms—would summon up an equally strident, fierce Manicheism on the part of blacks, but he could not imagine, as Fanon does in that handbook of Third World revolution *The Wretched of the Earth* (1961, translated 1963), the resulting violence forcing the oppressor to recognize the subjecthood and claims for freedom of the oppressed. He could see only "an emotional tone that is as familiar to me as my skin; it is but another way of saying that *sinners shall be bound in Hell a thousand years.*"[61] However, sixteen years after writing his review of *Goodbye to Uncle Tom*, in a 1972 interview, Baldwin calls John Brown a "true American prophet" for trying to free "a whole country from a disastrous way of life."[62] Baldwin's John Brown, in 1972, is a "great American prophet" who had been released from self-deception, and so was capable of doing "an act of love. Love" (255, 264). Concerning Brown's means to his goal, his sacrificial storming of the Harper's Ferry armory, Baldwin excuses "the prophet" from familiar charges of extremism and accepts that the "bloodshed" was an "act of conscience" breaking upon the guilty land (255,

256). It may have been necessary, even, to make real the immorality of slavery (256). Within a few pages, however, he adds that Brown's act of love, however pure in its motive, "failed" to "change institutions" or instigate "progress" (264, 265). Certainly, Baldwin makes clear that the failure inhered in the inertia of the American character, but whether Brown's choice of political violence contributed, in 1859, to undoing what forgiving and liberating love, as it is described in *The Fire Next Time*, aims to achieve short of war, Baldwin does not clarify; much less does he commit to whether Brown's marriage of love and force is a suitable precedent for contemporary America. Thus he leaves inconclusive, in the 1972 interview, whether political violence can be part of love's redeeming work. Baldwin, in such texts as *No Name in the Street*, dallies with justifying violent resistance, and this tentative flirtation introduces an instability in his conception of the Judgment, and its relation to love, that his comments on John Brown only underscore. In *The Fire Next Time*, revolutionary violence is the Judgment to be avoided, its ominous stirring an urgent warning to radically reform. Revolutionary violence in America would exile blacks and whites both from the goals of identity and freedom, and indefinitely defer redemption. After *The Fire Next Time*, Baldwin's writings pose a question: is violence instead a judgment chiefly upon liars and *their* civilization; a regrettable exigency by which freedom and identity are imperfectly purchased from entrenched power and its lies? Subsequently in Baldwin's prophetic prose, revolutionary violence does change in its complexion, yet without ever earning his full commitment. The method of violence and the goal of biracial, national redemption still seem opposed. The question for Baldwin was whether he would retain the same goal or adopt another that would cancel his exceptionalist belief in the racial situation of America. As the strategy of nonviolence failed to deliver more than civil rights legislation, and no solutions to the problems of black poverty, deficient housing, white monopoly of businesses, the paucity of black representatives in government, the harassment of black leaders—issues which struck more directly at the interests of white elites and also the dreams of working-class and petty-bourgeois whites who aspired to higher status— Baldwin was theoretically stymied: how to realize liberation without staying or contravening love's work, yet how to resist forms of political domination that deny love's invitation to mutual self-knowledge and mutual freedom?

Baldwin's political identification with the Black Panthers in the late sixties did not resolve the contradiction but exacerbated it, and in his effort to bridge the spiritual and political, the realm of love and the realm of freedom that would harmonize in the Kingdom of God, he identifies with

Jesus.[63] Inspired by Malcom X, Stokely Carmichael and the leaders of the Black Panther Party for Self-Defense (Eldridge Cleaver, Huey Newton, Bobby Seale) had enlarged the context of the American black nationalist struggle for liberation to an international, anti-imperial battle for human rights and self-determination.[64] Baldwin, in adopting the Black Panthers as the prophetic agents of *No Name in the Street*, did not reject finally Christianity, as Stokely Carmichael did, but continued revising it in order to justify the ends of black freedom, though the ends of national redemption and black power, American exceptionalism and international revolution, remained poles of tension. At the end of *Blues for Mr. Charlie*, after leaguing himself with the younger militants, who are impatient with "the white God," Reverend Meridian carries his Bible out of the sanctuary and into the streets, where scripture will be interpreted in light of the obstacles and necessities ahead; as Baldwin himself had said in *The Fire Next Time*, if God cannot help us to love, "then it is time we got rid of Him."[65] In his last major prophetic statements of the sixties, "White Racism or World Community" and *No Name in the Street*, Baldwin replaces "God" as his imagination settles on the figure of Jesus. Indeed, it is Jesus, rather than any of the Black Panthers, who is the hero of *No Name in the Street*. Love itself replaces, becomes, God in *Fire*, but the Jesus of these later reflections, after King's assassination, is a character who endures the conflict of love and wrath that Baldwin felt in himself, as he was torn over the question of political violence. Tracking the figure of Christ, from the mystical presence of love in *The Fire Next Time* to its reembodiment as the incarnate Jesus, permits us to see the continuity of questions that Baldwin never ceased to frame with reference to the theology of Pentecost. Through his Jesus, Baldwin tries to unite the themes of black power with redemption, renewal, self-revelation, compassion, and biracial harmony.

Baldwin's Jesus: Witness to Love's Betrayal

Baldwin's early essays denounced Stowe's Uncle Tom as a Christlike redeemer of the white man's civilization, but in *Go Tell It on the Mountain*, he began to evolve his own version of the Messiah, making a Christ figure from a black atheist driven to suicide by racism. In Elizabeth's analeptic narrative (section IV of the novel), she remembers how her lover Richard, John's biological father, was jailed for a crime he did not commit because his black skin made him suspect. Richard is accused in a police lineup between two black youths apprehended for stealing from a white man—an allusion to the two thieves crucified on either side of Jesus—and then beaten by cops until welts raise on his flesh, a further allusion to Christ's wounds after being scourged by Roman soldiers. Unable to defend himself against charges that he is a criminal, Richard bitterly tells Elizabeth: "Maybe you ought to pray to that Jesus of yours and get Him to come down and tell these white men something."[66] Earlier in the section, when Elizabeth tries to share her faith with Richard, he replies by saying, "You tell that puking bastard to kiss my black ass!" (172). By the time he is released on lack of evidence, Richard has been demoralized, and after a night of weeping, he slashes his wrists. In contrast to Uncle Tom's suffering (in Baldwin's reading of Stowe's novel), Richard's anguish testifies to the hypocrisy of Christian civilization. Its white Jesus, as described in "Everybody's Protest Novel" and "Many Thousands Gone," is meant to cleanse men of all the spiritual "darkness" that whites have associated with black culture and have symbolized by the black subject's skin color. The Christlike black man cursing the white Jesus, however, is paradigmatic of Baldwin's complex response to Christianity—on the one hand, condemning its dogmatic and racist abuses, while, on the other hand, recuperating some of its values and motifs to dignify black resistance to oppression and sustain hope that, through love, a nation not yet created would come of a freedom not yet ventured.

In Shulman's "secular" reading of the meaning of love, Baldwin empties the concept of Christic associations by analogizing the redeeming power of love to the actions of the sexual lover, and, by analogy, the artist: "he analogizes lover and artist to secularize prophecy: as the lover reveals the beloved to himself, so the artist reveals the collective subject its disavowed otherness as well as its capacity for love."[67] According to Shulman, Baldwin's subject encounters its Other by becoming immersed in the dionysian aspects of experience, where identity may be dissolved, the self regenerated, and identity remade without its being premised on violent expulsions (136–151). By offering Nietzsche's Dionysus as the Crucified of the Christian imaginary, however, Shulman overlooks the risk of the dionysian: its sacrificial violence too closely resembles the logic of Manicheism that he has already rejected in the figure of Elijah Muhammed. True, the lover's/artist's openness to the imperfection of the Other may be a model for redemption, but the model for the lover/artist, and the likeness is clear in the saintlike Eric of *Another Country* (1962), is also the redeeming, revelatory Love of the New Testament, which is "apprehended in and through experiences of release from conditions of fatedness as well as reconciling forgiveness."[68] Baldwin's subversion of Christian dogma lies not in his adoption of a dionysian self-shattering, which permits a necessary return of the repressed, but in his decision that Christic love no longer could be symbolized by the Christ of tradition. Instead, Christic love is given form as Jesus the disreputable Hebrew.

Baldwin's revisionist Jesus has a long pedigree in his work, but it is in *The Fire Next Time* that Baldwin first explicitly differentiates the historical Jesus from the Jesus of Christendom, as Albert Cleague and James Cone, respectively, were to do shortly in *The Black Messiah* (1968), *Black Theology and Black Power* (1969), and *God of the Oppressed* (1975). In place of the Pauline exegetical tradition, Cleague and Cone describe a "black Jesus," Jesus the deliverer, who came with the moral fervor of Hebrew prophets before him to protest Roman social injustice and the hypocrisy of the Jewish priesthood. Arguing that the history of the suffering of the world's most systematically oppressed minority has made the revelation of biblical prophecy uniquely discernible to blacks, Cleague and Cone retake Jesus from church dogma and academic theology, which have proclaimed and studied "Christ" but obscured the meaning of the savior's Resurrection: God's identification with the poor and the persecuted in their quest for freedom.[69] The early Christian converts, who were attacked by the Roman cultus and state, courageously faced violence and heresy charges because they believed Jesus had come to free them from Rome and from irrelevant, politically conservative ceremonialism. If the Crucifixion at first seemed to dash their hopes, it is because they did not understand that the Resurrection was itself a "political event": "When God raised Jesus from the dead, God affirmed that Jesus's historical identity with the freedom of the poor was in fact divinity taking on humanity for the purpose of liberating humans from sin and death. . . . The politics of resurrection is found in its gift of freedom to the poor and the helpless" (115). By promising liberation to all men (not exclusively the Hebrews), Jesus widened the relevance of God's justice, so that the poor and downtrodden of any generation may embody His Spirit.

For Baldwin, the Jesus of Christian faith and the historical Jesus of social protest have also been split by the idolatry of the Western Church. Like Cleague and Cone, moreover, Baldwin relies little on scholarly evidence to substantiate his historical Jesus because the figure is chiefly meant to invert a Christian tradition that has been aligned with ruling interests. Truths about the Savior that are hidden from whiteness, because it is too comfortable with privilege, now stand revealed to blacks, since they have been forced into a historical role parallel to Jesus's, and so the black messenger carries these truths to the benighted, who, if they do not pay heed, will either self-destruct or be destroyed. Baldwin pauses during his anti-Church invective in *Fire* to observe that long before white Christians invented "the Negro" in order to make a racial property out of "their virtue and their power," their own professed Savior had been executed because another imperial-minded people were seeking to preserve their virtue and privilege: "White Christians have also forgotten several elementary historical details. They have forgotten that [Christianity] . . . came out of a rocky piece of ground in what is now known as the Middle East before color was invented, and that in order for the Christian church to be established, Christ had to be put to death, by Rome, and that the real architect of the Christian church was not the disreputable, sun-baked Hebrew who gave it his name but the mercilessly fanatical and self-righteous St. Paul."[70] The Apostle Paul is a well-chosen target, for his epistles are the earliest theology in the Bible postdating Jesus's death, and he essentially invented the concept of the "church." Baldwin understands that Paul is the forefather of Christendom, and by attacking Paul as if he were a belated interpreter whose teaching warped Jesus's example, Baldwin implies that the religious tradition is illegitimate, for it has not truthfully examined its own Savior's character. In his address "White Racism or World Community" (1968), delivered to the National Council of Churches (NCC), Baldwin warns ecclesiastical bodies that they must either recover Jesus Christ or else suffer "doom."[71] His preface to the speech, to which he returns at its close, comes from Jesus's analogy of the sheep being separated from the goats in Matthew 24:40: "Insofar as ye have done it unto the least of these, you have done it unto me" (749, 756). In this apocalyptic vision, Jesus describes how he will reward those who attend to the needy and the sick, the stranger and the prisoner, and cast into fire those who have attended only to their own flocks and wares. Baldwin subversively implies that the churches themselves will be burned, for inasmuch as they have helped to plunder and insult black humanity, they have also betrayed their Savior.[72]

Two ideas about the "real" Jesus emerge. His ministry began long before white men invented the myth of "color," and, being a "sun-baked Hebrew," he was himself dark-skinned, contrary to the white-complected Savior of Christian art. Secondly, he was a "disreputable" man, indeed a criminal and a heretic to many, whose death was a concession to prejudice and power. These observations about the pre-Pauline Jesus, his darkness, his disrepute, and the vested interests for his murder, make the Savior available to Baldwin as a parallel to the careers of black leaders in the sixties. In *The Fire Next Time*, "My Dungeon Shook" had alluded to a prophet praying for release from metaphorical chains, but within four more years, Baldwin had witnessed actual incarceration and worse fates for many fellow black social activists. In the course of the decade, Medgar Evers, Martin Luther King, Malcom X, Bobby Hutton, Fred Hampton, and Mark Clark would be killed, Frederick Lawson shot, Stokely Carmichael and Huey Newton jailed, and Bobby Seale publicly chained and gagged in a Chicago courtroom. By the late sixties, according to James Campbell, Baldwin had begun to fear for his own life and rightly suspected that he was under FBI surveillance.[73] In the atmosphere following King's assassination especially, it seemed to Baldwin as if a sacrificial burden had been laid upon black leaders to offer themselves for an example to the poor and the nonwhite around "the world—which does not accept the American version of reality as gospel."[74] By the time he began drafting *No Name in the Street,* black revolutionaries seemed to be bearing the common spirit of the Hebrew prophets and the "disreputable" Jesus, a spirit Christendom obscured with its theology of terror and now more than ever would do its utmost to destroy politically. Like early Christians, hounded by the empire into hiding and meeting secretly, blacks seemed to be faced with a similar trial as the primitive converts: "In spite of our grim situation, and even facing the possibility that the Panthers may be smashed and driven underground, they—that is, the black people here—yet have more going for them more than did those outnumbered Christians, running through the catacombs: and digging the grave, as Malcom put it, of the mighty Roman empire" (463). In contrast to the corrupted Church Baldwin elsewhere attacks in *No Name in the Street,* these early, pre-Byzantine Christians were closer temporally, and, he implies, closer spiritually, to the Savior for which they chanced imprisonment and death.[75]

By aligning his spiritual values now with Jesus and using the spiritually revolutionary Hebrew to undercut the Church that proclaimed "Christ," Baldwin seeks to divest the West of its moral authority and challenges whites to consider whether their societies indeed conform more to imperial Rome or to the community of Jesus and the early converts. By lashing the Church with a refurbished image of its own Savior, Baldwin absorbs that Savior's moral authority into his own persona, but he does not then proclaim, with anything like Cone's confidence, the liberating power of the Resurrection. In *The Fire Next Time,* love is the precondition for mutual freedom, love is the power that dispels the lies of innocence. For the liberation theologians, it is freedom, won by forcefully (if necessarily) ripping away the veils of innocence, that makes the precondition for love to thrive. Indeed, Cone and Cleague were avowed black nationalists, inspired by Malcom X's message of "self-help" and "self-defense," who justified the use of political force against a racist Western imperialism. *No Name in the Street* perceives the justice of Malcom's charges, and even the justness of the arguments for more aggressive resistance, but Baldwin never unqualifiably endorses black nationalist revolution in America. Nor, however, does he condemn it. Baldwin's Jesus is a figure of the East condemning a colonizing Church of the West on behalf of all dark races, and he is the embodiment of Love, familiar from earlier works, speaking for a Kingdom of God in the image of a renewal of America. The goal of the Kingdom, Baldwin painfully realizes, may be thwarted so that the international struggle for racial justice can be furthered. Thus, Baldwin's message must continue to alternate between hope and wrath, dogged efforts at awakening whites and exasperation before the undying lies of whiteness, not only those of the West but also the specific American innocence that falsely believes its virtue consists in its identity as the exemplar of democratic civilization. The close of *No Name in the Street,* his last major prophetic statement of the sixties, sounds again the contrapuntal notes that ended *The Fire Next Time:*

> To be an Afro-American, or an American black, is to be in the situation, intolerably exaggerated, of all those who have ever found themselves part of a civilization which they could in no wise honorably defend—which they were compelled, indeed, endlessly to attack and condemn—and who yet spoke out of the most passionate love, hoping to make the kingdom new, to make it honorable and worthy of life. There is a level on which the mockery of the people, even their hatred, is moving because it is so blind: it is terrible to watch people cling to their captivity and insist on their own destruction. I think black people have always felt this about America, and Americans, and have always seen, spinning above the thoughtless American head, the shape of the wrath to come.[76]

If black readiness for deliverance were much longer ignored, then whatever political leverage the Panthers or their nationalist counterparts might purchase would likely underline rather than transform the division between blacks and whites in America. In the near future at least, Jesus's righteous anger rather than his vision of brotherhood might necessarily predominate. Under the pressure of the decay of the civil rights movement, campaigns of domestic political persecution, increasing antagonisms between black radicals and white liberals, racial polarization in the rhetoric of Black Power, and counterrevolutionary violence in the Third World, Baldwin's voice strains to sustain the tension between the promises of Judgment *and* Redemption. The prophetic trope of antithesis nearly dissolves into a nondialectical choice of either-or. Baldwin fights to avoid picturing historical crisis in terms of the familiar Cold War trope of the "lesser evil," in which reality dictates that the demands of justice defer those of healing and perfecting love, but his Jesus can only dramatize the contradiction of Love being in the world of power; Jesus cannot resolve it.

Through his invented Jesus, Baldwin was grappling with the problem Niebuhr had raised in his objections to the Social Gospel: must love be powerless in history? If power and love resist each other, since power is the assertion of self-interest and love the capacity for self-transcendence, then love, in its most pure form of Christic perfection, is powerless in history. By recourse to the tragicomic, Niebuhr developed a philosophy of history in which perfect love is perpetually thwarted by the reality of power even as human love, imperfectly, works alongside prudent rationality to restrain the injustice of man's will to power.[77] Perfect love in human history, the dream of the Kingdom of God, is a noble illusion, but one that can inspire men to just action so long as they are ironic enough to realize their political choices are never for love versus power, but for one form of power versus another, in which love may find some small expansion. Baldwin does not resort to the tragicomic; instead, his Jesus is planted within history as a criminal, whose fate does not point to the irony of grace (that love in its purity must be destroyed within history in order to redeem it; that love in its purity can only stand outside history as a judgment upon the impurity of all of history's actors) but instead testifies for the outrage of love, its anger over innocence (as when, echoing Jesus' rebuke to Satan in John 8:44, Baldwin cries "ye are liars, and the truth is not in you!") and its despair over the prospect of force begetting force (*No Name in the Street* in *Collected Essays*, 424, 468). There are no degrees of sanctification, no spectra of love in quest of an impossible perfection in this life. For Baldwin, there is only love.

Christic love is frustrated by innocence, but this frustration does not find symbolic expression in original sin. Innocence is the belief in lies perpetuated, at a partially unconscious level, by specific groups to exculpate them from responsibility for specific, generationally transmitted forms of injustice. There is a common, human root from which all evil, individual and collective, seems to stem, and this is the denial of tragedy, but this denial comes of fear and not pride. Love can overcome fear, but can it pierce the systematic lying of generations? Can it disturb the illusions of safety when these are supported by the structures of power, media, and knowledge? The human heart, in Baldwin, can come to know itself in the Other, but only if the Other can be released from his captive self-perception. In *The Fire Next Time,* love beckons with the integrationists; in *No Name in the Street,* Jesus shouts with radicals; but in each voice, the priority of power costs love's betrayal.

Epilogue:
Putting an End to
Ending Our Innocence

Norman Mailer once said that he could be "the Jeremiah of our time," and at the close of *Armies of the Night* (1968), his Pulitzer-winning tour de force, he finally takes the role.[1] The self-described "religious revolutionary" gives a prayerful coda, "The Metaphor Delivered":

> Brood on that country who expresses our will. She is America. . . . [C]an she, poor giant, tormented lovely girl, deliver a babe of a new world brave and tender, artful and wild? Rush to the locks. God writhes in his bonds. Deliver us from our curse. For we must end on our road to that mystery where courage, death, and the dream of love give promise of sleep. (304)

The book's subject is the 1967 March on the Pentagon, organized by Jerry Rubin in the last year before the prospects of building a viable New Left coalition broke down in sectarian rivalries. The March was host to religious speeches, presences, and symbols—Yale Chaplain William Sloane Coffin, Jr., invoking the "rights of a man of conscience," the gathering at the Church of the New Reformation, clergymen condoning the immolation of draft cards, Protestant-haunted Catholic-convert Robert Lowell reading poetry, and, notoriously, Abbie Hoffman trying to exorcise the Pentagon—all of which Mailer keenly observes, adding his opinion that "the protesters might be touched with the Lord's grace" (18, 33, 59, 60, 88, 120). In Book II, Mailer's heroes are the nonviolently resisting "saints" who are arrested for not leaving the Pentagon after the March's permit has expired, and for a communal symbol to express these 160 demonstrators' sacrifice, Mailer mines the country's Christian legacy. The ending of Book II rhymes with the end of Book I; after Mailer closes the first book with his impromptu sermon on the bleeding Christ that Americans have killed, he visits Christ a second time, at the end of Book II, in order to plead, in the Savior's name, for remission of the country's sins. In spirit, his narrator joins the jailed Quaker activists who prayerfully beseech America to earn forgiveness, to come back from its sinful lapse in order to renew its founding ideals: "America—the land where a new kind of man was born from the idea that God was present in every man not only as compassion but as power, and so the country belonged to the people; for the will of the people—if the locks of their life could be given the art to turn—was then the will of God. Great and dangerous idea! If the locks did not turn, then the will of the people was the will of the Devil!" (287–288). Strikingly, for a pundit who expended so much breath on the theme of ushering in a new religious consciousness, Mailer here weds his destiny to his country through the very symbol that the postwar "end of innocence" theology had refurbished: America as God's fallen nation.

Mailer's conclusion to *Armies of the Night* was not a statement of Christian faith. His career since World War II juxtaposed the early Cold War religious revival with moods that would soon befit the New Left and with a style of post-Christian eclectic spirituality anticipating the counterculture.[2] Mailer became a writer in an alienating period of political oppression, when the radical values he defiantly held were supposed to be humbled by tragedy. Whereas the spiritual Left in the sixties often felt as if they were marrying partisan causes with religious experiences, Mailer turned to theology and spirituality to supplement or to right deficiencies in the early Cold War political climate. In his effort to try to start his own religious underground (what he called "Hip"), Mailer succeeded instead at introducing some innovations into key Cold War tropes of evil, apocalypse, and moral crisis, which made these available for a more unorthodox interpretation while never entirely unmooring them from their prior frames of reference.

No doctrine of original sin anchors Mailer's theology, but guilt, in his universe, is as inescapable as redemption is uncertain. In his desperate novel, *American Dream* (1965), published just two years prior to *Armies,* one has the impression that two cosmic superpowers are vying for the hero Rojack's person like America and the Communist menace for some piece of nonaligned territory. The Cold War of good and evil, "God" and "the Devil," is being waged within Rojack's psyche. In Rojack's (and Mailer's) sense that sometimes one must league with the Devil in order to serve God, moreover, there are echoes of Kennan's, Chambers's, and Niebuhr's "tragic" insight that defenders of democracy might have to borrow some methods of the enemy in order to defeat him. Mailer's paradox, of course, is that the enemy is Cold War America as much as Russia, while God and the Devil are aligned with neither. An evil principle, which is imperial, "totalitarian," joins both superpowers. Published in the wake of the Bay of Pigs fiasco and the downing of the U-2 spy plane, the novel's frequent allusions to invisible government and secret agencies point to what John Bennett called "the moral underworld" where America could resort to the unrestrained and "lying" methods of its totalitarian enemies while relieving the public and its elected officials of responsibility and preserving a façade of virtue. With "plausible deniability," the game of lesser evils could be played without even the twinge of tragic guilt.

To exempt himself from American totalitarianism, the Mailer hero—be it Rojack, the persona "Norman Mailer"—incongruously joins the Armageddon rhetoric and "spiritual anxiety" of the late forties to the mystical militancy and millennialism of the sixties' awakening. In a theological punning upon "grace under pressure," he feels *kairos* and purity in the moment that free action, uncoerced by the needs of utility, labor, law, or authority, intersects with the deep Self, but before he can be filled with Being and thus morally cleansed, he must first tarry in a noirlike cosmos of murk and doubles. God is an opposing principle to the Devil, which provides Mailer's cosmos with its dualistic tension, yet He is also personified as the grandest version of the Mailer hero who suffers from the sin of self-estrangement. He strives to be authentic by uniting self-expression and courageous action, and He recruits men to actualize His spirit, acting as His saints and His warriors. The Christ symbol which closes *Armies* is a case in point. America is cursed not because God above is angry, but because He is enchained by men's failures to act intrepidly on democracy's behalf, and Christ's forgiveness is not mercy accepted, but grace earned by wrestling with the Devil.

Purity never extends itself in time for Mailer. It remains a momentary reprieve, already receding before it is fully apprehended, that fortifies the self for another moral test. It is an intimation of a state of innocence that is poignant so long as that Edenic self is recognized to be an image of impossible desire. Mailer believed the nausea of guilt pushed him on his moral uppers; innocence would be the opposite of moral action since it could only be maintained dishonorably through stasis or projected through self-deceit. Yet it is in their longing for purity extended in time, as a new eschaton purchased through radical commitments, that Mailer empathizes with the young activists at the Pentagon, and for their spiritual convictions, less than their agendas to demobilize unjust power structures, that he memorializes them. In asides, he skeptically regards his younger cohorts since their political theories, warmed over from Mao, Castro, and Che, strike him as simplistic in their own way as the old Marxist Left's iron logic of historical necessity. They fail, moreover, to be the vanguard of his theology of dread, since they acknowledge the Devil only as a totalitarian principle in American society and not as an element coursing in themselves. Mailer is nonetheless moved by the gathered young. He senses in them a strikingly different air from the realism of what Daniel Bell had called his "twice-born generation." Indeed, they wanted to escape the guilt of their fathers, the guilt of the Cold War itself.

They did not see themselves implicated in a torn and bleeding Christ broken out in stigmata. Jesus, in his many musical and hippie renditions, was a populist hero in the sixties, but the doctrine of man's inevitable corruption was distinctly absent from the new expressions of myth and symbol.[3] Niebuhrian ambiguity had apparently been lost on the children of the generation it was meant to purge of idealistic and apocalyptic longings. Death-of-God theologians William Hamilton and Thomas Altizer were taking the pulse of the counterculture and the New Left, and their essays, such as "The New Optimism—From Prufrock to Ringo" (1966), are enlivened by references to the civil rights movement, freedom songs, James Baldwin, the Beatles, and John Cage.[4] All are harbingers of change that usher out the "Eisenhower period," "fashionable neo-orthodoxy," "Old Niebuhrians," "existentialism," "tragedy," "Oedipus," and, in Altizer's reasoning, even polarized Self/Other identities (44, 158, 166–169, 171–191). Radical historian Theodore Roszak, editor of *The Dissenting Academy* (1968), proposed, approvingly: "it may be that the most strategic bastion of traditional values the counter culture is attacking is precisely the bourgeois Christian pride in a well-developed guilty conscience."[5] In contrast to Niebuhr's and Graham's pleas that Americans acknowledge their common sinfulness, the mood of the various countercultural spiritualities was a return to innocence, evinced in the mythology of childhood freedom and perception.[6] In his memoir, *Making It* (1967), Norman Podhoretz reflected on the prevalence in postwar American literature of the imagery of growing up and growing old: "[in] the imagery of American writing from 1946 and 1956 on subjects as diverse as psychoanalysis, theology, politics, and literature . . . the idea of youth came to be universally associated . . . with the idea of neurosis . . . and the idea of maturity with mental and spiritual health."[7] Youth and maturity were transvalued in the sixties,[8] but Adam was not reinstated as a national symbol. In a sense, the counterculture believed that much of America had indeed lost its innocence, for childhood could be recovered only outside of the corrupted society, in the precultural phases of human development (for example, the philosophies of Norman O. Brown and R. D. Laing) or among romantic Others, such as the Indian, and in romanticized spaces, such as the pastoral, the road, the ethnic ghetto, or inner space.[9] As in the Popular Front's cultural nationalism, the true America was innocent, but this innocence now was to be found exclusively among the folk at the country's social margins.[10]

The somber covenant-making God that was to have presided over the Judeo-Christian consensus represented but one variety of belief, less credible because its cautionary view of man's finitude had not, it seemed, prevented civilization from reaping war and suffering and apathy. By contrast, Hoffmann's half-mocking, half-serious tone at the Pentagon (he names "the Tyrone Power Pound Cake Society in the Sky" as one of the deities arrayed against evil) revels in the possibilities of human imagination—in all the gods it has invented and has yet to invent.[11] The Port Huron Statement (1962), the declaration of Students for a Democratic Society, calls for a revival of "idealistic thinking" to replace the "defeatism that is labeled realistic": "The decline of utopia and hope is one of the defining features of social life today. . . . To be idealistic is to be considered apocalyptic, deluded. To have no serious aspirations, on the contrary, is to be 'tough-minded.'"[12] Typical of the style of sixties' utopianism, the Port Huron statement offers an ethical rather than an instrumental version of politics; if there is not always a clear, programmatic sense of how changes in the social order should be enacted, there is a very strong conviction of where change should begin. The vision must precede the program, and the vision will come from those groups alienated by the elite power structure (186–194). The arguments outline an undemocratic society that could be reborn through local initiatives, much as the counterculture was representing an America whose grey battle-scarred God should be splintered into so many lights hidden within men.[13]

These arguments were inspired by C. Wright Mills and Herbert Marcuse, but not limited to their influence. The sixties gave broader voice to the tiny Christian Left of the fifties. The Christian Faith and Life Community (CFLC) at Austin, Texas, incubated several activists in civil rights, SNCC, and the student Left during its ten years (1952–1962). These included Casey Hayden, an executive of SDS and member present at the Port Huron conference with her husband Tom, who called the CFLC "a liberated zone."[14] Evangelical in charter but breaking away from the fundamentalism of Bill Bright's Campus Crusade for Christ, the CFLC "reflect[ed] a modernist conviction that religion had to change with the changing times," though its definition of change would draw freely from the example of the primitive church as well as the more contemporary, therapeutic lan-

guage of liberal Protestantism (63). To resist the conditions of totalitarianism (individual isolation, social conformity), it sought to create "intentional
communities," having as its internal goals self-acceptance, authenticity,
transparency, and the restoration of basic trust (68). These would be
achieved through a common acknowledgment of sinfulness, recognized
not in priestly office or private meditation, forgiven not through penance or
mortification but through mutual disclosure (70). The CFLC held Baldwin's
hope in the possibility of rebirth in relationships of joint self-examination
and self-revelation, and as in Baldwin, the quest for confessional honesty
with one's fellows raised ethical implications, namely a commission to
mitigate those conditions that alienate men from each other: poverty, star-
vation, sickness, oppression, and imprisonment.[15] It forewent Baldwin's
speculations, in his moments of despair, that the human heart may be unable to confess a truth that condemns it.

Via the writings of Dietrich Bonhoeffer, A. J. Muste, and, selectively,
Paul Tillich, young affiliates of the Christian Left were discovering what
H. Richard Niebuhr, addressing his brother's theology, had said many
years earlier immediately following World War II.[16] Richard, a theological
conservative as cognizant of original sin as any thinker of his generation,
worried that Reinhold was seeing the contemporary experience of God as
disillusionment rather than hope.[17] God expresses himself in his elder
brother's theology as a negative principle, as a No to human pretension.
Grace is not present in our ideals, as Christ is in us, but in their ironic re-
versals, as reminders of Christ crucified because of us; not in our utopian
intentions, as stirred by the Resurrection and Pentecost, but in the unforeseen consequences of human freedom, as the Father's Judgment. We have
the impression that God enters time chiefly through refusal, chastisement,
and limit. It is Christ's perfection against which we are continually found
wanting by the Father, yet that perfection is denied us in time as glimmer-
ings of a *pax falsa*. The wages of sin, Richard reminded, should never be
accentuated to the point that they silence the Gospel's witness to the positive power of grace, of Christ released into history, of discipleship in the
world. In listening only for God's No, he said, we muffle His Yes. The leaders of the Christian Left affirmed the redeeming effects of love, hope, and
the valuing of community over the constraining effects of sin manifested in
machtpolitik, and as a result, they refused to accept the Cold War argument for choosing, tragically, the "the lesser evil." Muste, who nurtured
many of the leaders of the SNCC, SDS, and CORE and energized the anti-
war movement until his death in 1967, said not to behave like the Devil in
the name of restraining him. Cold War realism was "using Satan to cast
out Satan" :

The neo-orthodox writings . . . sometimes impress one as based on a single text: 'The good that I would I do not; the evil that I would not, that I practice . . . Wretched that I am, who shall deliver me?' . . . It is true, as they insist, that even where grace abounds, sin still also persists. (They seem to me sometimes to come very close to saying that where grace abounds, sin abounds much more!) But this is not the Christian last word; it is the statement of the paradox in its negative, non-creative form. The Christian, scriptural, creative statement of the paradox is ever: 'Where sin abounds, grace much more abounds.[18]

Muste summarized the youthful radical's view of the Cold War establishment's dystopianism: when politics is defined as a domain in which men do evil of tragic necessity, then it becomes easy for them to apologize for ever greater measures of evil.

THE POST–WORLD WAR II renascence of interest in original sin had been a feature of the general religious revival in America, and the Augustinian concept was in several ways a casualty of developments within that religious revival as well as the pressures exerted by the sixties. Countermodernists described a bipolar world of mirroring superpowers in which the United States was compelled to make tragic decisions that implicated it in guilt (Niebuhr) or else engaged in liberation struggles that could save it from the sins its national character shared with the Russian double (Graham). The theological emphasis on guilt also imbued American civil politics with an aura of dread and crisis, relieved by faith in rational consensus. Contritely practiced within civil law, social action possibly served God; carried above civil law, social action made for a sinful escape from guilt. The "pragmatic" self-doubt this line of reasoning encouraged seemed to be threatened, however, by the hidden radicals within the nation—whether they were Communists, psychopaths, or fundamentalists—who might so confound men that civil law would look like injustice, legitimate authority like oppression, and evil behavior like means to good. In the religious terms of both international and civil affairs, the discourses of original sin actually thrived on the instability of the bipolar model (America/Russia; democracy/totalitarianism; free citizen/mass man) constructed in the postwar years. Over the course of the postwar years and into the sixties, the bipolar model was challenged abroad by anticolonial revolutions, nonaligned Third World nations, and the growth of Communism independent of Russian tutelage, as it was also contradicted in the United States by protest groups (most visibly, black activists) and later by a young radical intelligentsia, who together exposed that the globe could not be determined by the balance of two powers and their respective allies. The young, with the New Left at the vanguard, were discovering that the dualistic rhetoric of anti-Communism distracted from the fact that the Cold War, nominally between America and Russia, was in fact a series of "hot wars" being fought with various nationalist insurgencies. In a world where multiple centers of political agency and quests for self-determination seemed to be moving history rather than a shadowy battle between agents of good and minions of evil, countermodernist rhetoric became less compelling as a description of Cold War realities. As the United States was forced to deal with pluralism as a fact, the old paradigm of rivalry between binary ideologies was shaken, and with it, the myths of doppelgangers and tragic misprisions that had shaped Americans' "spiritual anxiety." The Niebuhrian version of the vital center could not hold indefinitely, and, in light of the international Cold War's evolution as well as domestic policy fractures, it deservedly fell. The Armageddon fears raised by Kennedy's nuclear brinksmanship and the Cuban Missile Crisis instigated the creation of SDS rather than talk about the necessity of lesser evils.[19]

The New Left, thus, was not incited to action by America's counterrevolutionary policy in Vietnam, though this was a key catalyst. It came into being out of a fundamental disagreement with the morality of liberal anti-Communism and as a reinterpretation of the Cold War's symbolic meaning for America. The New Left saw the Old Left as guilty, not only because it had been tainted by association with Stalinism, but because it had endorsed philosophical positions that warded off innocence, in the double sense of shunting it away and demonizing it, and had plunked for policies designed to gird democracy against the vicissitudes of sin and error. This was a generational dispute that was waged in moral terms borrowing the imagery of youth and age, light and shade, Eden and post-Eden. The Old Left had lived with the burden of complicity (or the perception of complicity) with totalitarianism; the New Left said the ex-radicals and social democrats had become the accomplices of the postwar liberal establishment.[20] Survivors of the Old Left reacted to Tom Hayden and SDS much as they had to their brethren in the Popular Front a generation earlier, or to the defenders of Alger Hiss during the drama of confession in the fifties; the young activists were innocents, but suffering this malady in a significantly different situation than had the Old Left. The generation that came of political age in the thirties had known totalitarianism at the center of its intellectual world and its historical experience, whereas the young radicals had seen only the pernicious effects of liberal anti-Communism, and so judged their forebears unflinchingly and, it seemed to their intellectual elders, with foolhardiness.[21] Irving Howe, still a socialist and by no means a subscriber to Christian Realism or its secular liberal variant, fell into the cadence of

by then familiar Cold War rhetoric when he said that the New Left, lacking experience, had no knowledge of the tragic: "The emerging new sensibility rests on a vision of innocence, an innocence through a refusal of our
and perhaps any culture. . . . There is no need to taste the apple. . . . it exists only in your sickened imagination" (318). The new radicals are antinomians inasmuch as they are perfectionists; they follow an internal
authority whose voice, echoing their own preciously esteemed ideals, seems
pure because it is narcissistic.[22]

Moreover, Howe argues, in another Cold War turn, that the New Left is
investing politics with misplaced spiritual passions. He credits Paul Goodman's analysis, in "The New Reformation," that the New Left is "satisfying formless religious hungers."[23] "The purpose is not politics," Goodman
had argued, "but to have a movement and form a community. . . . Religiously, the young have been inventive, much more than the God-is-dead
theologians. . . . In the end it is religion that constitutes the strength of this
generation" (90, 93, 95). Paul Goodman's essay was a sympathetic endeavor, in the grain of all of his work, to explain the radix of youthful
alienation (the consciousness of which he calls "Lutheran") in the postwar
system of efficient consumption and bombs-on-demand, an effort begun
with his novel *The Empire City* (1947) and continuing in his short story,
"Adam," written just prior to *Growing Up Absurd*. The new dissidents,
like Goodman-Everyman in the aforenamed story, long to return to "paradise" from exile; Adam would turn his "trust-drunken face" toward the
young and, just as he has told Goodman, assure them that paradise is
within their own souls, while adding that they must not be content only to
look inward, but must also deliver America, their "only world."[24] Their
rescue tactics so far have been "bad politics," "without coherent proposals
for a better society," Goodman explains, but he nonetheless defends their
utopian images, in rapport with his own anarchist tradition, that spring
from the Western "religious crisis."[25] Howe, on the other hand, had altogether different motives in citing "The New Reformation." Borrowing the
trope of the Fall, which Goodman explicitly rejected in "Adam," Howe
was prodding the New Left to grow up and leave the phantasms of the
Garden. As giddy utopians, they were "trying to satisfy religious needs
through radical politics," and this displacement "represented a confusion
of realms damaging to both."[26] Religion, investing affective faith in sacred
values, should not actively trespass upon politics, a domain properly concerned with clashing interests, inequities, and uneven distribution of power.
This was a Cold War belief, shared by realists and pluralists alike, for
which Niebuhr had provided theological support by reading the books of
prophecy forward from the Fall and backward from the Crucifixion. The

"innocent" identification of this-worldly and otherworldly aims showed a
lack of biblical insights: the Bible's ironic view of history and its lesson of
transcendence. There is a qualitative difference, not in degree but in kind,
between any earthly kingdom and the *pax vera*. Howe did not accept the
political conclusions of Niebuhr's Augustinianism (indeed, he formed the
Democratic Socialist Organizing Committee in the 1970s), but, in essence,
he was invalidating the New Left by turning upon them the Niebuhrian
critique of Communism, much as the "twice born" generation attacked
the Old Left not for being atheistic, but for being a secular political religion.[27]

It might have startled Howe to learn that Billy Graham read the movement the same way. In *The Jesus Generation*, Graham diagnoses the baby-
boom generation as "alienated, uncommitted," having "a deep vacuum
within them" and needing community, identity, and ultimate purpose.[28] In
contrast to Howe, he attributes their crisis to secular life, in yet another
rendition of the conservative, fundamentalist, and neoconservative assertion that modern modes of meaning-making are indebted to religious presuppositions and therefore illegitimate. The natural consequence one of his
title chapters indicates: "The Devil Is Alive and Kicking." Yet, as in Graham's preaching from the fifties, he is offering the "fiery-eyed, long-haired
radicals" his own kind of utopianism, concentrated in the Christian
kerygma (28). Join "the youth revolution" and "the Jesus revolution," he
says, by "preaching the Gospel in the contemporary language of modern
youth" (16). This modest adaptation will divert them from rebelliousness
that, he eminently surmises, will do little more good than the Children's
Crusade of the thirteenth century (148–150).

Both Howe and Graham characterized the young political and cultural
radicals' utopianism as unformed religion, and each did so for the purpose
of delegitimizing the radicals' utopian aspirations as the worst excesses of
their movements. Each rhetorically deploys one of the two major adaptations of the political religion thesis in the Cold War: Graham, linking modernity to totalitarianism, as modern thought and culture, indebted to
religious traditions that it disavows, fragments society into atomic individuals who need substitutes for belief and ritual; Howe, stating that politics
have become unrealistically laden with meaning-making and millenarian
hopes, when religion should be properly restricted to the private sphere
where its irrationality can be tolerated. The second assumption should be
challenged as much as the first.[29] Regardless of whether one accepts Goodman's case that a Western religious crisis propelled sixties' activism, Christianity and other world religions were indeed important cultural sources
for the New Left and the counterculture's themes of love, community, and

quest for contact with the ultimate. Religious inspiration, symbolism, and affective relation to values were not why the Left went wrong. The counterculture was egalitarian and voluntaristic to the point that it scorned organization as the shell of slithy institutionalism. It succeeded in briefly reproducing communal milieus, in subverting mass media, and, if we are to believe the testimonies, even in restoring a sense of inner harmony to many communicants, but its overreliance on schism, charisma, "organic" associations, and sheer good will made alliances, planning, and mobilization very difficult to achieve, as the New Left discovered when it attempted, with mixed results, to combine countercultural styles with effective political praxis.[30] The New Left, too, often squandered its energies in performative gestures, but also broke its back in sectarianism, ignorance of historical precedents, insensitivity to the working class, naive identification with Third World revolutionaries, apologies for "transitional" dictatorships, and, embarrassingly, the Weathermen's nihilism. As a result of these missteps, it damaged its credibility and achieved limited lasting influence outside the academy. There were many missed opportunities in this decade, as those who were part of its ferment, such as Todd Gitlin, have acknowledged, but the failing was not utopian vision. It was inexperience meeting the complexity, as in all nonreformist movements for social change, of identifying instruments—beyond existing institutions, parties, or single-issue pressure groups—to realize an ethical vision. These are situations that call for more utopian thinking, not less. To assail utopianism by likening it to inchoate spirituality or displaced religious modes of affect and thought ("ideology"), especially in conjunction with imagery of the Fall, is meretricious rhetoric, whether practiced by the political Right or the political Left. It was already artifactual of the Cold War when Graham and Howe repeated it; today, it is the invidious parlance of our Culture War.

Additionally, if the counterculture's response, to return to a more innocent self, or to a more innocent, because unofficial, part of America, now seems quaint, I do not here wish to support any refurbishing of the Cold War's master narrative. We do not need any more urging to ward off our national innocence, accept our responsibility, and face hard, tragic facts, especially when this same logic has been mobilized in recent times to support American imperialism in the Middle East. As a revision of national prophecy, the close of *Armies* is far less searching for us now than James Baldwin's work. Mailer's symbol of the nation as Christ bleeding, combining soteriology and secular history, still makes America peculiarly responsible to God, still makes God the American people's reason for bearing freedom. Our deliverance is His vision, our bondage His alienation. In calling America back to its mythical past, these old strains do not dare to ask, as Baldwin's art does, whether God's vision was ever ours to lose in the first place. Baldwin's prophetic voice was prescient then and a witness today. In light of recent events, we may take his Jesus's provocation—*ye are liars, and the truth is not in you!*—to tell us not simply to shed our innocence, but to put an end to ending our innocence. We must stop what has become a national ritual that functions as self-acquittal through self-accusation.

Baldwin's melding of modernist Social Gospel and evangelical themes, moreover, points to the possibility of mediation between equally erroneous forms of countermodernism, represented here, respectively, by Niebuhr and Graham. Cold War debates did not resolve the theological and political differences separating conservative evangelicalism from liberal Christianity, but in the exchanges between Niebuhr and Graham, there was at least conversation, and, for a brief time in the sixties, there was unity around the goal of civil rights for disenfranchised Americans. Even as New Evangelicals revitalized conservative Protestantism in the Cold War, the crises in the period also made them listen to voices that hearkened back to the evangelical legacy of social reform, including abolition and populism. These movements, which were often evangelical in style as well as leadership, did not accept that the Kingdom of God was fulfilled in an America where oligarchy or social inequality were left untouched. They rejected the notion that God's glory could only overflow when economically and racially disadvantaged groups were passive objects of established power. Would evangelicals recover more fully the memory of their own past, then perhaps they would be more willing to consider that a country fractured by widening gaps between rich and poor, continued institutional racism, infringements on civil liberties, and even efforts to deprive some groups of civil rights, has no place in singularly owning the moral authority to wage unilateral "wars of liberation." If evangelicalism, as the University of Chicago's Robert Fogel has asserted, is in the midst of another "Great Awakening," then perhaps those on the Left should also reconsider some of the critical potentials within it rather than foreclose on the movement because it is presently encrusted with far-right policies.[31] An evangelicalism teaching that all nations stand under God's Judgment, for none are without injustice, none certain of Providence's favor, would be a strong asset in building the multiconfessional collaboration that will be necessary to forge "the global ethic" that we desperately require.[32] To reject a dialogue out of hand is merely to accept the terms of the Culture War and again forget the legacy of the postwar meditation on modernism.

Notes

Acknolwedgments

Index

Notes

Prologue

1. I have taken the appellation "New Cold War" from Martin Walker, *The Cold War: A History* (New York: Holt, 1995), 252–277.
2. Irving Kristol, "My Cold War," *The National Interest* 31 (Spring 1993), 141–144.
3. Jim Wallis, *God's Politics: Why the Right Gets It Wrong and the Left Doesn't Get It* (New York: Harper, 2005), 37.
4. Albert Schweitzer, *The Philosophy of Civilization* (1923), ch. 26 [trans. C. T. Campion (Buffalo: Prometheus, 1987), 307–329].
5. Marilynne Robinson, *The Death of Adam: Essays on Modern Thought* (New York: Picador, 2005), 206.
6. Brion Gysin, *Mektoub: Recordings 1960–1981* (Perdition Plastics, 1996), Track 1: "I've Come to Free the Words."

Introduction

1. *Time*, (December 5, 1969), 26–27.
2. Pelagius (b. AD 354) was a Christian opponent of Augustine. He said that grace supports the will, whereas Augustine said that grace transforms the will. See Hans Küng, *Great Christian Thinkers* (New York: Continuum, 2002), 82–87.
3. See, especially, R. W. B. Lewis, "The Contemporary Situation: Adam as Hero in the Age of Containment," the epilogue to *The American Adam: Innocence, Tragedy, and Tradition in the Nineteenth Century* (New Haven: Yale University Press, 1955), 195–198.
4. George Kennan, *Memoirs, 1925–1950* (New York: Pantheon, 1967), 293.
5. Ann Douglas and Henry May have each described this generation's mixture of adulation and pessimism, especially as reflected in modernist art and letters; see Douglas, *Terrible Honesty* (New York: Farrar, Strauss, and Giroux, 1995); and May, *The End of American Innocence* (New York: Oxford University

Press, 1959). T. Jackson Lears traces the attitudes of modernist artists to various modes of fin de siècle antimodernism that opposed secularizing liberalism and to the rise of the consumption-driven economy and the bureaucratic megastate. Among the more profound modes of anti-modernism, in his estimate, was the recovery of Christianity's sense of the tragic, of the need for self-transcendence, and of the longing for the infinite. He notes, however, that this recovery was largely unheeded, or else (in the cases of Henry Adams and T. S. Eliot) voiced through the symbolism of Catholicism or the Middle Ages in conscious rejection of optimistic, acculturated, and therapeutic Protestantism. See Lears, *No Place of Grace: Antimodernism and the Transformation of American Culture, 1880–1920* (Chicago: University of Chicago Press, 1994), 309–313, also, 32–47, 142–215, 262–297.

6. For statistics on growth in church attendance, construction, and denominational growth, see Robert S. Ellwood, *The Fifties Spiritual Marketplace* (New Brunswick, N.J.: Rutgers University Press, 1957), 5, 23. For discussions of the postwar revival of interest in religion, including books and films, see Mark Silk, *Spiritual Politics: Religion and America since World War II* (New York: Simon and Schuster, 1988); Martin Marty, *Modern American Religion, vol. 3: Under God Indivisible, 1941–1960* (Chicago: University of Chicago Press, 1996), 115–476; Paul Carter, *Another Part of the Fifties* (New York: Columbia University Press, 1983), 132–133; William Lee Miller, *Piety along the Potomac: Notes on Politics and Morals in the Fifties* (Boston: Houghton Mifflin, 1964), 30–32, 41–48. Of particular interest is Andrew Finstuen's *Original Sin and Everyday Protestants: The Theology of Reinhold Niebuhr, Paul Tillich, and Billy Graham in an Age of Anxiety* (Durham: University of North Carolina Press, 2009). Finstuen shows that rank-and-file Protestants, or "lay theologians," also evaluated postwar experience through the categories of original sin and grace, and that this broad interest in Christian orthodoxy, which was a major facet of religiosity in the postwar revival, supported the spread of Niebuhr, Tillich, and Graham's influence on American culture. Together, these men interpreted ordinary Protestants' anxieties in classic terms already in use. Finstuen finds the three thinkers' public theologies more salutory than do I (particularly in the cases of Niebuhr and Graham), and while the Cold War provides historical bookends to his study, the decade's ideological and political conflicts are negligible factors in his analysis. His book does, however, affirm that the religious revival was a cultural dialogue in which intellectuals and the public, evangelists and professional theologians, shared common symbols and questions.

7. Modernism has a complex genealogy in American religious history. Originally describing a turn-of-the-century Catholic version of higher criticism closely associated with an "Americanizing" movement in the church and shortly struck down by papal oaths (1899, 1907, 1910), the term was subsequently appropriated by evangelical fundamentalists who used it derogatively to characterize liberal Protestantism and the "higher criticism" of the Bible; it was then transvalued by liberal Protestants, who, parrying fundamentalist attacks, used it to name a progressive, this-worldly, and positively Americanized experience of

Christianity. The papal oaths were Leo XIII, *Testem Benevolentiae,* January 1899; Pius X, *Pascendi Dominici Gregis,* 1907; Pius X, "The Oath Against Modernism," September 1, 1910. Fundamentalists, from the twenties forward, have observed no serious difference between "liberal" and "modernist."

8. Acknowledging the dispute, Kenneth Cauthen distinguishes between "evangelical liberalism" and "modernistic liberalism," but William R. Hutchison persuasively argues that the differences between these types were not fundamental and uses the general classification "modernist"; Cauthen, *The Impact of American Religious Liberalism* (New York: Harper and Row, 1962); Hutchison, *The Modernist Impulse in American Protestantism* (New York: Oxford University Press, 1976), 7n and 7–9. Martin Marty refers to liberals collectively as modernists: "[they] were agents of the modern, progressives who actually wanted to advance the processes of change from within the Protestant core-culture"; Marty, *Modern American Religion, vol. 1, The Irony of It All, 1893–1919* (Chicago: University of Chicago Press, 1991), 13. Marty justifies the common label in part because it follows the practice of newspapers in the twenties, which used "Modernist" to stand for "anti-Fundamentalist"; *Modern American Religion vol. 2, The Noise of Conflict, 1919–1941* (Chicago: University of Chicago Press, 1991), 155.

9. Shailer Matthews, *The Faith of Modernism* (New York: Macmillan, 1924), 15, 93, 144.

10. See Friedrich Schleiermacher, *The Christian Faith,* 2nd ed. (1830–1831); and *Life of Jesus* (1864). On Schleiermacher's apologetics, see Wayne Proudfoot, *Religious Experience* (Berkeley: University of California Press, 1985), 9–40; Hans Küng, *Great Christian Thinkers,* (New York: Continuum, 1994) 155–184; Albert Schweitzer, *The Quest of the Historical Jesus* (Baltimore: Johns Hopkins University Press, 1998), 62–68; Hans Frei, "Barth and Schleiermacher: Divergence and Convergence," in *Theology and Narrative: Selected Essays,* ed. George Hunsinger and William C. Platcher (New York: Oxford University Press, 1993), 177–199.

11. John Gresham Machen, *Christianity and Liberalism* (New York: Macmillan Co., 1923). On the continuities joining Pelagius and modern liberals, see Langdon Gilkey, *On Niebuhr* (Chicago: University of Chicago Press, 2001), 125–126, 128, 132.

12. Karl Barth (b. Basel) first published *Epistle to the Romans* in German in 1919. The first English translation, published by Oxford University Press, was issued in 1933. The English translation of Brunner's *Man in Revolt,* originally published in German in 1937, was published by Lutterworth Press in 1939. Brunner (b. Zurich) lectured at various American seminaries in the thirties and took a two-year visiting position at Princeton in 1937–1938. German-born Paul Tillich, who moved to the United States in 1933, was the first nonnative intellectual to be exiled from Austria by the Nazis, and the leading theologian of the wartime European migration to America. His achievements as a systematic theologian earned him posts at Union Theological Seminary (where he was invited by Reinhold Niebuhr), Princeton, and Yale. Tillich's ideas received important exposure in the United States after H. Richard Niebuhr translated *The*

Religious Situation (originally published in German in 1926; Niebuhr's translation was published by Henry Holt in 1932). German-born Rudolf Bultmann, also associated with this group of theologians, though more liberal on the doctrine of sin than Brunner and Barth, achieved wider influence in the English-speaking world after World War II, when a greater selection of his works was translated; from the thirties, see *Jesus and the Word* (New York: Charles Scribner's Sons, 1934), (originally published in German in 1926). Like Bultmann, Tillich was uncomfortable with being called neoorthodox, since his method of correlating the New Testament with contemporary culture and politics often placed him at odds with the more purely kerygmatic theology of Barth and Brunner. In his essay "Protestantism," originally published in the *The Protestant Era* (1948), he called himself a "mediating," or "neo-dialectical" theologian; *The Essential Tillich*, ed. F. Forrester Church (Chicago: University of Chicago Press, 1987), 85. On Tillich's differences with Barth, see his autobiographical piece, "What Am I?" in *The Essential Tillich*, 256; and Wilhelm and Marion Pauck, *Paul Tillich: His Life and Thought* (San Francisco: Harper and Row, 1989), 95–96, 192, 194, 238.

13. For Barth's discussion of "Krisis" and "the Guilt of the Church," see *Epistle Concerning the Romans*, 6th ed. (New York: Oxford University Press, 1968), 362–391, 502–526. An important conduit for Barth's ideas in the United States, Reinhold's brother H. Richard Niebuhr would become known for his work on "radical monotheism," the loss of which is the thesis of his classic, *The Kingdom of God in America* (1937). For H. Richard Niebuhr's statements on Barth, see "Theology in a Time of Disillusionment" (1931); and "The Kingdom of God and Eschatology in the Social Gospel and in Barthianism" (written for presentation to the Theological Discussion Group convened at Union Theological Seminary, beginning in 1931); H. Richard Niebuhr, *Theology, History, and Culture*, ed. William Stacy Johnson (New Haven: Yale University Press, 2007), 102–116, 117–122.

14. Willard Sperry, *The Disciplines of Liberty: the Faith and Conduct of the Christian Freeman* (New Haven: Yale University Press, 1921), 4–5.

15. Donald Meyer, *The Protestant Search for Political Realism, 1919–1941* (Westport, Conn.: Greenwood Press, 1960), 10.

16. H. Richard Niebuhr, "Theology in a Time of Disillusionment," 105.

17. Stephen R. Prothero adopts Niebuhr's typology in *American Jesus: How the Son of God Became a National Icon* (New York: Farrar, Straus, and Giroux, 2003) 3–19, 291–303; Donald Meyer makes a book-length case for the "realism" that succeeded liberal optimism in *Protestant Search*; Ann Douglas describes liberalism's "loss of nerve" in *The Feminization of American Culture*, Noonday ed. (New York: Farrar, Straus, and Giroux, 1998), esp. 12–44, 327–344; Martin Marty argues that liberalism became a culture-religion of good intentions, lacking irony or fire, and favors "the age of realism" in *Modern American Religion*, vol. 2, *The Noise of Conflict, 1919–1941*, 303–340.

18. May, *End of American Innocence*, 12–14.

19. Harry Emerson Fosdick, "The Church Must Go Beyond Modernism" (1935) in *The Riverside Sermons* (New York: Harper, 1958), 362. By Reinhold Niebuhr,

see especially *Leaves from the Notebook of a Tamed Cynic* (1929; repr. New York: Meridian Books, 1957); and *Moral Man and Immoral Society* (New York: Charles Scribner's Sons, 1932). By H. Richard Niebuhr, see "Toward the Independence of the Church," in H. Richard Niebuhr, Wilhelm Pauck, and Francis P. Miller, *The Church Against the World* (Chicago: Willett, Clark and Company, 1935); *The Kingdom of God in America* (New York: Harper, 1937); and his translation of Paul Tillich's *The Religious Situation* (New York: Henry Holt, 1932). By Harry Emerson Fosdick, see also *Christianity and Progress* (New York: Fleming, 1922). By Willard Sperry, see *The Disciplines of Liberty* (New Haven: Yale University Press, 1921). See also Hutchison, *Modernist Impulse*, 225–256; and Meyer, *Protestant Search*, 10, 54, 107, 129–130.

20. Meyer, *Protestant Search*, 107.

21. Christian Realism was forged in the thirties and then became solidly identified with its best exponents, Reinhold Niebuhr and John C. Bennett. Its ideas, antipacificist, antifascist, and, initially, anticapitalist, formed the editorial consensus of *Christianity and Crisis*, the magazine Niebuhr founded in 1941 to rebut *The Christian Century*'s pacificism; see Mark Hulsether's history of the publication's founding, *Building a Protestant Left: Christianity and Crisis Magazine* (Knoxville: University of Tennessee Press, 1999), 1–48. By John Bennett, see *Christian Realism* (New York: Charles Scribner's Sons, 1941). See also Robin Lovin's philosophical explication of Niebuhr's corpus, *Reinhold Niebuhr and Christian Realism* (Cambridge: Cambridge University Press, 1995). Lovin discusses the several facets of realism in Niebuhr's thought (moral, religious, political), though his analysis is synchronic and thus ignores how Christian Realism's applications and relative emphases (on the weight of sin and the power of grace) develop over the course of Niebuhr's career.

22. Arthur Schlesinger, Jr., *The Vital Center* (New York: DeCapo, 1949), 250. The symposium, published in four installments through the spring of 1950, was a weighty exchange, featuring twenty-five contributors that included John Dewey, Hannah Arendt, W. H. Auden, Dwight MacDonald, Clement Greenberg, Sidney Hook, Irving Howe, Meyer Schapiro, Alfred Kazin, Philip Rahv, James T. Farrell, James Agee, and Paul Tillich; *Partisan Review* 17, nos. 2–5 (1950). It was preceded by a series in *Commentary*, "The Crisis of the Individual" (1945–1947), prefaced with such questions as "Where did our Western civilization go wrong? . . . Is the contemporary crisis due . . . to a distortion of basic ideals which would require a renascence of religious belief or some other inner revaluation of values?" Contributors included John Dewey, Reinhold Niebuhr, Sidney Hook, and Hannah Arendt. Quotation from *Commentary* "The Crisis of the Individual" in Michael Leja, *Reframing Abstract Expressionism* (New Haven: Yale University Press, 1993) 244. *Commentary* v. 1 (December 1945), 1–8; (January 1946), 1–8; (February 1946), 27–35; (March 1946), 1–8; (April 1946), 7–11; (May 1946), 9–16; (June 1946), 51–57. *Commentary* v. 2 (September 1946), 201–207; (October 1946), 339–345; (November 1946), 436–447; (December 1946), 537–546. *Commentary* v. 3 (March 1947), 210–221; (April 1947), 378–385; (August 1947), 137–147; (November 1947), 416–422.

23. David Hollinger, "Historians and the Discourse of Intellectuals," in *New Directions in American Intellectual History,* ed. John Higham and Paul K. Conkin (Baltimore: Johns Hopkins University Press, 1979), 43; Quentin Skinner, "Meaning and Understanding in the History of Ideas," *History and Theory,* 8, no. 1 (1969): 3–53.

24. In the late nineteenth century, Catholicism and Judaism did see the emergence within their ranks of some progressive theologians who sought to integrate belief with the findings of science and the opportunities of democracy. As James Davison Hunter and Martin Marty have argued, however, there was also a countervailing trend in each faith against modernism that would eventually lead, post-sixties, to ecumenical organizations among conservatives and fundamentalists across Protestantism, Judaism, and Catholicism. See Marty, *Modern American Religion,* vol. 2, *The Noise of Conflict* 193–250; Hunter, *Culture Wars: The Struggle to Define America* (New York: Basic Books, 1991), 67–106.

25. Jonathan Sarna's *American Judaism: A History* (New Haven: Yale University Press, 2005) surveys postwar reaffirmations of Judaism and provides a valuable context for situating the stances of Jewish intellectuals when secularism was increasingly unacceptable in their wider community; see especially 272–356. Also helpful, and more broadly canvassed, is Howard M. Sachar, *A History of the Jews in America* (Knopf: New York, 1992), 672–712, 748–787. The following biographies, memoirs, and social histories give ample insights into the Jewish intelligenstia's grappling with its ethnic and religious heritage: Mark Royden Winchell, *Too Good to Be True: The Life and Work of Leslie Fiedler* (Columbia: University of Missouri Press, 2002), 6, 50, 119–123, 196–97, 233–234, 319–320, 322–323; Thomas L. Jeffers, ed., *The Norman Podhoretz Reader* (New York: Free Press, 2004), 114–130; Norman Podhoretz, *Ex-Friends: Falling Out with Allen Ginsberg, Lionel and Diana Trilling, Lillian Hellman, Hannah Arendt, and Norman Mailer* (San Francisco: Encounter Books, 2000), 139–177; Robert Warshow, *The Immediate Experience,* enl. ed. (Cambridge, Mass.: Harvard University Press, 2001), 25–52, 79–96, 213–220, 265–272; Irving Howe, *A Margin of Hope* (San Diego: Harcourt Brace Javonovich, 1982), 247–282; Nathan Glazer, *American Judaism* (Chicago: University of Chicago Press, 1957), 79–129; Alfred Kazin's autobiographical trilogy, *A Walker in the City* (New York: Harcourt, Brace, 1951), *Starting Out in the Thirties* (Boston: Little Brown, 1965), and *New York Jew* (New York: Knopf, 1978); Donald Kaufmann, ed., *Norman Mailer: The Countdown, The First Twenty Years* (Carbondale: Southern Illinois University Press, 1969), 99–110; and Norman Mailer, *The Time of Our Time* (New York: Random House, 1998), 1228–1236. On Trilling's postwar statements about Jewish identity, see his contribution to "The Jewish Writer and the English Literary Tradition," *Commentary* 8, October 1949, 368–369. Trilling's reserve about his Jewishness has been discussed in several studies, including Alan Wald, *The New York Intellectuals* (Durham: University of North Carolina Press, 1987), 33–37; Terry Cooney, *The Rise of the New York Intellectuals: Partisan Review and Its Circle* (Madison: University of Wisconsin Press, 1986), 107–109, 235–

236; and Jonathan Freedman, *The Temple of Culture: Assimilation and Anti-Semitism in Literary Anglo-America* (New York: Oxford University Press, 2000), 192–196. Most recently, see Michael Kimmage, *The Conservative Turn: Lionel Trilling, Whittaker Chambers, and the Lessons of Anti-Communism* (Cambridge, Mass.: Harvard University Press, 2009), 18–20, 31–34, 86–87, 136–137, 150–151. On Trilling's prewar fiction on Jewish identity, including "Impediments" (1925) and "Chapter for a Fashionable Jewish Novel" (1926), each published in the *Menorah Journal*, see especially Wald, *New York Intellectuals,* 35–36.

26. Morris Bober is the honorable, hapless *schlemiel* of Bernard Malamud's *The Assistant* (1957), set in a Brooklyn ghetto amid first- and second-generation Jewish immigrants.

27. Howe, *Margin of Hope,* 258.

28. Podhoretz, *Ex-Friends,* 70–71.

29. Sidney Ahlstrom, *A Religious History of the American People* (New Haven, Conn: Yale University Press, 1972) 599.

30. See Alexander Bloom, *Prodigal Sons: The New York Intellectuals and Their World* (New York: Oxford University Press, 1986), 141–146, 150–157, 166–174; Alan Wald, *New York Intellectuals,* 27–50; Karen Brodkin Sacks, "How did Jews Become White Folks?" in Steven Gregory and Roger Sanjek, eds., *Race* (New Brunswick, N.J.: Rutgers University Press, 1994), 78–102; Michael Rogin, *Blackface, White Noise: Jewish Immigrants in the Hollywood Melting Pot* (Berkeley: University of California Press, 1996), 251–268; Eric Sundquist, *Strangers in the Land: Blacks, Jews, Post-Holocaust America* (Cambridge, Mass.: Harvard University Press, 2005); Joshua M. Zeitz, *White Ethnic New York: Jews, Catholics, and the Shaping of Postwar Politics* (Chapel Hill: University of North Carolina Press, 2007).

31. Will Herberg cites a poll number showing that Jews constitute only 4 percent of the population—1 percent *less* than the category of no religious "preference" that he discounts as negligible. *Protestant-Catholic-Jew* (Garden City, N.Y.: Doubleday, 1955). See also Herberg, "Religion in a Secularized Society: Some Aspect of America's Three-Faith Religious Pluralism," in *The Sociology of Religion* ed. Richard Knudten (New York: Appleton-Century-Crofts, 1967).

32. For Jewish interpretations of Christianity post-Holocaust, including criticism of Reformed teachings, which had bridged to liberal Christianity before World War II, see Prothero, *American Jesus,* 258–265. Rabbi Richard Rubenstein surveys the European response to the Holocaust and develops his own interpretation, in which Jews are the scapegoat of Christianity's sacrificial violence, in *After Auschwitz: History, Theology, and Contemporary Judaism* (Baltimore: Johns Hopkins University Press, 1966). An excellent historical source for tracking theological debates in the period is *Judaism: A Quarterly Journal on Jewish Life and Thought,* which began publication in 1952.

33. In *Spiritual Politics,* Mark Silk shows that the term "Judeo-Christianity," coined in 1899 to designate a "continuity theory" postulating that the Christian Church grew out of the practices of the Second Temple, entered into regular usage in the thirties to denote Christian opposition to fascism; after the

war, it would be used to distinguish the West from Communism (40–53). On the Judeo-Christian tradition as advanced by Jewish scholars, see Prothero, *American Jesus*, 229–266. A major point of difference between Jewish and Christian defenses of Judeo-Christianity concerned the role of Christ. The idea that Jesus was the bridge between the two faiths became harder for Jewish thinkers to defend after the Holocaust. Writers like Herberg chose instead to emphasize the common belief in God the Father, which was consistent with Reinhold Niebuhr's Calvinistic demotion of Christ. See Herberg's remarks on monotheism and law in "From Marxism to Judaism: Jewish Belief as a Dynamic of Social Action" (1947), in *From Marxism to Judaism: Collected Essays of Will Herberg*, ed. David Dalin (New York: Markus Wiener, 1989), 22–37.

34. Peter Duncan, *Russian Messianism: Third Rome, Holy Revolution, Communism and After* (New York: Routledge, 2000), 54–55, 95–100. Herberg describes what happens to "the messianic impulse when it is robbed of its transcendence and diverted to secular goals," in "Socialism, Zionism, and the Messianic Passion" (1956), in *From Marxism to Judaism*, 110–128.

35. J. Edgar Hoover, *The Masters of Deceit: What the Communist Bosses Are Doing Now to Bring America to Its Knees* (Pensacola, Fla.: Beka Book, 1958). See also J. Edgar Hoover, "The Challenge of the Future," *Christianity Today*, May 26, 1958, 3–4.

36. Wyler's film is deliberately unclear whether Ben-hur himself (Charlton Heston) ever actually converts. What Ben-hur clearly has in common with the early Christians and his Jewish kin is a belief in one God and an antipathy for Roman power. In contrast to *Ben-hur*, other biblical epics, such as *The Ten Commandments*, imagine a Christ-centered "pluralism" by portraying ancient Hebrews as proto-Christians united against tyrants of the East; see Alan Nadel, "God's Law and the Widescreen," in *Containment Culture: American Narratives, Postmodernism, and the Atomic Age* (Durham, N.C.: Duke University Press, 1995).

37. Herberg, *Protestant-Catholic-Jew*, 264; Warshow, *Immediate Experience*, 269. Lionel Trilling, suggests that mystical Judaism, as taught by the Pharisaic rabbis of the *Pirke Aboth*, has "Christian qualities and virtues" that "a strong Christianity must take account of, and be easy with, and make use of"; "Wordsworth and the Rabbis," in *The Opposing Self* (New York: Viking, 1955), 106, 108. Trilling argues that the rabbinical sages, with the same perceptiveness as Wordsworth's "strong Christianity," almost seem to retreat from some radical spirit of subversion in their culture, as Wordsworth drew back from the Revolution in France and as Trilling's generation had withdrawn from communism in the thirties. Harvard historian Daniel Boorstin hinted that Judaic iconoclasm easily correlates to America's pragmatism, what he called its respect for the "given" in experience rather than any "ideological idols"; *The Genius of American Politics* (Chicago: University of Chicago Press, 1953), 170. Boorstin starkly distinguishes "our" informal, civil faith—quietly infused with Jewish tradition—from the utopian party religion of the Left and fascistic tribal religions based on blood, race, or the dead. Boorstin's rhetoric glosses over the

problem he gingerly raises (only to drop) earlier in the text: that Jews, like Catholics, have not yet been assimilated into the Protestant establishment despite their patriotic support for the country (136, 141, 147).

38. Herberg, *Protestant-Catholic-Jew*, 254–281. On Niebuhr and Herberg, see Silk, *Spiritual Politics*, 45–50. In the concluding chapter of *Protestant-Catholic-Jew*, titled "Religion in America from the Perspective of Faith," Herberg deplores how nationalism has all but killed the concept of the God of Judgment, a concept, he believes, that Christianity and Judaism once shared (270–280). On Herberg's intellectual debt to Niebuhr, see "Reinhold Niebuhr: Christian Apologist to the Secular World" (1956), in Herberg, *From Marxism to Judaism*, 38–45. See also Abraham Heschel, "A Hebrew Evaluation of Reinhold Niebuhr," in Charles Kegley and Robert Bretall, eds., *Reinhold Niebuhr: His Religious, Social, and Political Thought* (New York: Macmillan, 1956), 391–410. For studies of Jewish theology and Old Testament prophecy after World War II and the Holocaust, see Abraham J. Heschel, *The Prophets* (New York: Harper and Row, 1962); Rubenstein, *After Auschwitz*, 140–159; Bruce Vawter, *The Conscience of Israel: Pre-Exilic Prophets and Prophecy* (New York: Sheed and Ward, 1961); and Prothero, *American Jesus*, 261–265.

39. Reinhold Niebuhr, "Jewish and Christian Relations at Mid-Century," in *Pious and Secular America* (New York: Charles Scribner's Sons, 1958). See also Niebuhr's introduction to Waldo Frank, *The Jew in Our Day* (New York: Duell, Sloan and Pearce, 1944).

40. Reinhold Niebuhr, *The Nature and Destiny of Man*, vol. 2, *Human Destiny* (New York: Charles Scribner's Sons, 1941), 25.

41. Jacob Heilbrun, *They Knew They Were Right: The Rise of the Neocons* (New York: Basic Books, 2008), 7–8, 228–280.

42. Kristol has said: "The notion that a purely secular society can cope with all of the terrible pathologies that now affect our society is unrealistic—and that has made me culturally conservative. . . . I really think that religion has a role now to play in redeeming the country. And liberalism is not prepared to give religion a role. . . . The liberals have had their reforms, and they've led to consequences that they don't know what to do about"; *Arguing the World*, DVD Chapter 23 "Final Arguments" directed by Joseph Dorman (1987; New York: First Run Features, 2005). Norman Podhoretz decries the "new paganism," which he regards as entailing deconstruction, multicultural, situational ethics, all the anomic forces of relativism unhatched by man's prideful, "narcissistic" decision to set up himself as an "idol," to make of himself the center of meaning and value; Podhoretz, *The Prophets: Who They Were, What They Are* (New York: Free Press, 2002), 313–359. On the movement, see "Neoconservativism: A Eulogy," in *Norman Podhoretz Reader*, 269–284; Podhoretz, *Ex-Friends*, 221–233; Irving Kristol, "Human Nature and Social Reform," in *The Essential Neoconservative Reader*. ed. Mark Gerson (Reading, Mass.: Addison Wesley, 1996).

43. Michael Novak, a Catholic and a member of the American Enterprise Institute, claims Niebuhr as philosophical support for neoconservativism, in "Reinhold Niebuhr: Model for Neo-Conservatives," *Christian Century*, Janu-

ary 22, 1986, 69–71; and "Reinhold Niebuhr: Father of Neoconservatives," in Novak, *On Cultivating Liberty: Reflections on Moral Ecology,* ed. Brian C. Anderson (Lanham, Md.: Rowman and Littlefield, 1999), 200–213. In the latter essay, portions of which were originally published in the *National Review,* May 11, 1992, Novak admits to his reader the joy he finds in appalling Left Niebuhrians with what seems to them a monstrous union. In the latter essay, he also cites Will Herberg as a part of neoconservativism's intellectual genealogy. Kristol calls Reinhold Nieuhr and Lionel Trilling "the intellectual godfathers" who pointed him "beyond liberalism," in "My Cold War," *National Interest* 31 (April 1, 1993): 141–144. Podhoretz has often claimed Trilling as an embryotic neoconservative; see, for example, Podhoretz's reflections on Trilling and, in particular, his recoil from "the adversary culture" (a formulation from Trilling's *Beyond Culture* [1965]), in *Ex-Friends,* 57–103; Podhoretz also invokes Trilling's phrase, "moral realism," in *Prophets,* 323–324. See also Gertrude Himmelfarb, "The Trilling Imagination," in "On the centenary of Lionel Trilling," special issue, *Weekly Standard,* February 14, 2005. Himmelfarb, a distinguished historian and emeritus professor at the City University of New York, is Irving Kristol's wife and, like him, an ex-radical who went through phases of disenchantment first with Marxism and then liberalism. The *Weekly Standard,* founded by Himmelfarb and Irving Kristol's son William, has become the premier forum for neoconservative thought.

44. Arendt was herself a student of Christian theology who had studied with Rudolf Bultmann. Her Ph.D. dissertation, *Der Liebesbegriffe bei Augustin* (revised for publication in German, 1929), has recently become available in English translation as *Love and Saint Augustine,* ed. Joanna Vecchiarelli Scott and Judith Chelius Stark (Chicago: University of Chicago Press, 1996). In her biography of Arendt, Elizabeth Young-Bruehl provides a detailed summary of the dissertation's contents; "Arendt's Doctoral Dissertation: A Synopsis," *Hannah Arendt: For Love of the World* (New Haven: Yale University Press, 1982) 490–500; on Arendt's study of Augustine and her interactions with Bultmann and also Paul Tillich, see 48, 61–62, 74–75, 164, 240–242, 251, 284.

45. On secularization theory, see especially Peter Berger, *The Sacred Canopy: Elements of a Sociological Theory of Religion* (Garden City, N.Y.: Doubleday, 1968), 105–174; Hans Blumenberg," The Secularization Thesis as an Anachronism in the Modern Age," in his *The Legitimacy of the Modern Age* (Cambridge, Mass.: MIT Press, 1983); and Charles Taylor, *A Secular Age* (Cambridge, Mass.: Harvard University Press, 2007), 423–538.

46. Hannah Arendt, *The Origins of Totalitarianism,* 417, 465; from the essay "Ideology and Terror," added to the 1958 edition. All quotations in my text are from *The Origins of Totalitarianism* (N.Y.: Harcourt, Inc., 1968). Young-Bruehl, *Hannah Arendt,* 81. For further analyses of ideology as a style of thought or mystique, see Carl J. Friedrich and Zbigniew Brzezinski, *Totalitarian Dictatorship and Autocracy* (New York: Praeger, 1956); lightly revised as *Totalitarian Dictatorship and Autocracy,* 2nd ed. (Cambridge, MA: Harvard University Press, 1965). Citations hereafter from the 1965 edition 85–128;

Carl J. Friedrich, ed., *Totalitarianism* (Cambridge, MA: Harvard University Press, 1954), 88–140.

47. Roger Griffin, "God's Counterfeiters?" in *Fascism, Totalitarianism, and Political Religion,* ed. Roger Griffin (New York: Routledge, 2005), 2.

48. Arendt's remarks on the absence of God from "A Rejoinder to Eric Voegelin," *Review of Politics* 15 (January 1953), 76–84, in response to Voegelin's review of *The Origins of Totalitarianism* in the same issue, 68–76. The phrase, "climax of a secular revolution," from Voegelin's review, 69. On political religion and the history of the concept, see [Burleigh and Burrin as corrected by copy-editor on page 58], Gentile, "The Sacralisation of Politics: Definitions, Interpretations and Reflections on the Question of Secular Religion and Totalitarianism," in *Totalitarian Movements and Political Religions* 1:1 (June 1, 2000), 18–15. Gentile, Chapter 4, "The Invasion of the Idols: Christians Against Totalitarian Religions" in *Politics as Religion* (Princeton: Princeton University Press, 2006), 69–109. In his essay, "The Totalitarian State and the Claims of the Church," *Social Research* (November 1934), 405–32, Tillich describes how National Socialism and German Christianity have hijacked the radical ethos of religious socialism, as theorized by Protestant clergy in the Berlin-based "Kairos" group to which Tillich belonged in the thirties. According to Gentile, who cites this essay in "The Sacralisation of Politics" (44), Tillich took a functionalist view of political religion; totalitarian appeals to myth and symbol are capitalist chicanery to legitimize greater concentration of power. The essay, however, also stresses that totalitarianism provides the masses with a sense of spiritual security, re-integration, and wholeness, and in his Cold War era writings, Tillich depicted Communism, similarly, as a faith helping discombobulated subjects to overcome their spiritual anxieties over fate, death, and non-being; meaninglessness and doubt; guilt and condemnation. The ability of Communism, like National Socialism, to provide religious succor makes it more mystically enthralling than bourgeois liberalism. See Tillich, "Neo-Collectivist Manifestations of the Courage to Be as a Part" in *The Courage to Be* (New Haven: Yale University Press, 1951), 96–103; "Religion in Two Societies: America and Russia" in *Theology of Culture* (New York: Oxford University Press, 1959), 177–187; "Religious Socialism" in *Perspectives on Nineteenth and Twentieth Century Protestant Theology* (Boston: Houghton Mifflin Co., 1967), 234–239. On the Kairos group, see Pauck 70–75.

49. Denis de Rougement, *The Devil's Share,* trans. Haakon Chevalier (New York: Pantheon Books, 1944), 66. Reissued in 1952 by Meridian Books, hardcover; in 1956 by Pantheon, paperback. The text was inspired by conversations with Reinhold Niebuhr and Paul Tillich; see Michael Kimmage, *The Conservative Turn: Lionel Trilling, Whittaker Chambers, and the Lessons of Anti-Communism* (Cambridge, Mass.: Harvard University Press, 2009) 363n76.

50. Michael Burleigh, "Political Religion and Social Evil," *Totalitarian Movements and Political Religions,* 3, no. 2 (Autumn 2002): 1–61, esp. 1–17; see also Philippe Burrin, "Political Religion: the Relevance of a Concept," *History*

and Memory 9 (1997): 321–349. Voegelin's thesis, *Political Religion,* was published in Vienna in 1938, and Voegelin subsequently expanded its ideas in such books as *The New Science of Politics* (1952) and *Science, Politics, and Gnosticism* (1968), which contained essays from 1959 and 1960. Arendt objected to Voegelin's reduction of liberalism, positivism, pragmatism, Marxism, and fascism to common gnostic heresies. She would maintain that the emergence of totalitarianism did not warrant a wholesale indictment of secular rationality or a resort to religion as antigen; see "Religion and the Intellectuals," *Partisan Review* 17:1 (February 1950): 113–116, and "Religion and Politics," *Confidence* 2:3 (1953), 105–112. The second essay was originally written for the conference, "Is the Struggle between the Free World and Communism Essentially Religious?" (Harvard University 1953). For discussion of "Religion and Politics," see *Three Women in Dark Times: Edith Stein, Hannah Arendt, Simone Weil,* ed. Sylvie Courtine-Denamy (Ithaca, NY: Cornell University Press, 2000), 125–126. Arendt did, however, positively review de Rougement's *The Devil's Share* because the book emphasized that evil would be the dominant intellectual problem of her generation; see Arendt, "Nightmare and Flight," *Partisan Review* 12, no. 2 (Spring 1945): 259.

51. Augustine, *Confessions* (New York: Classic Books America, 2009), 2.
52. Richard Steigmann-Gall, Voegelin, reivew of *The Origins of Totalitarianism,* 74. Richard Steigmann-Gall, "Nazism and the Revival of Political Religion" in Griffin, *Totalitarianism and Political Religion,* 85. On the rise of German Christianity, see Frank H. Little, "The Protestant Churches and Totalitarianism, 1935–1945" in Friedrich, *Totalitarianism,* 108–119; Robert P. Ericksen, *Theologians Under Hitler* (New Haven: Yale University Press, 1985).
53. Robert Service, *Stalin: A Biography* (Cambridge, Mass.: Harvard University Press, 2004), 242, 256, 268, 370, 442–444, 447, 496.
54. On the myths of the Holy Rus and Third Rome, see Peter Duncan, *Russian Messianism.* In his conclusion, Duncan argues that there is insufficient evidence to prove that either of these concepts had a formative impact on Bolshevik or Soviet policy.
55. Edward Roslof, *Red Priests: Renovationism, Russian Orthodoxy, and Revolution, 1905–1946* (Bloomington: Indiana University Press, 2002), 169–200. In 1922, the renovationists (who said that they formed "the Living Church") led a revolution in the Orthodox Church and supported Bolshevism even though it was atheistic. From 1922–1928, the Bolsheviks tolerated renovationism for the purpose of fracturing the R.O.C. During the Stalinist Revolution and through 1943 the state had the renovationist movement liquidated, and many of the movement's priests during the Great Terror were eliminated for allegedly subversive activity.
56. Service, *Stalin,* 443; Roslof, *Red Priests,* 192–194. See Service, *Stalin,* 443.
57. *Ivan the Terrible,* Part I (1944; U.S. release 1947), commissioned by Stalin, was very well liked at the Kremlin. Throughout, it tracks the power struggle between the Church and the Tsar, with Ivan cagily manipulating the clergy for Russia's advancement. The film sometimes figures Ivan III as parodically

Christ-like, but it does not cloak him heroically in the religious messianism that attended his historical counterpart Peter's assumption to Tsar. His epic stature derives from his skills as a master tactician and charismatic leader, whose wiles exceed his enemies, including the disloyal archbishop. *Ivan the Terrible,* Part II (1946; released U.S.S.R. 1958), the second part of a planned trilogy, is a much darker film and strikes subversive parallels between its historical subject and the Soviet regime's Great Terror. Stalin caught his reflection unfavorably in this film and prevented Eisenstein from making another sequel. On the film's suppression by Stalin, see Sergei Eisenstein, *Ivan the Terrible* (London: Faber & Faber, 1989), 16–21.

58. Roslof, *Red Priests,* 171, 178; Service, *Stalin,* 442–443.
59. Niebuhr defined Soviet communism as a "demonic" "politically oriented religion" in John Lewis, Karl Polanyi, and Donald K. Kitchin, eds. *Christianity and the Social Revolution* (London: Gollancz, 1935), 460–469, though, like Tillich in Germany and Christian socialists in England, such as John Lewis, he attributed the success of Marxism to the failure of the liberal churches to provide a coherent social ethic and not only to metaphysical attacks on religion by Western enlightenment. Niebuhr cited in Gentile with discussion, *Politics as Religion,* 82–83. See also references to totalitarian "secular religions" and "political religions" in "God's Design and the Present Disorder of Civilization" in *The Church and the Disorder of Society,* Vol. III, American Assembly Series (New York: Harper and Brothers, 1949), 18–21; *Faith and History: A Comparison of Christian and Modern Views of History* (New York: Charles Scribner's Sons, 1949), 162; and *The Irony of American History* (New York: Charles Scribner's Sons, 1952), 141; and *The Self and the Dramas of History* (New York: Charles Scribner's Sons, 1955), 207–208. Like his colleagues Paul Tillich and John Bennett, Niebuhr thought of Communism as distinct from Nazism insofar as it was a religious heresy rather than a cynical creed that denied human equality; Communism regurgitated the Gospel's "final realm of perfect love in which life is related to life without the coercion" as material paradise realized on earth. It crucially erred because it lacked a corresponding symbol of original sin or the Last Judgment, and so immanentized the Kingdom of God (an eschatological symbol emphasizing the transcendence of perfect good and true peace) as a worldly possibility; see Reinhold Niebuhr, *The Irony of American History* (New York: Scribner's, 1952), 12–13. By John Bennett, see *Christianity and Communism* (New York: Association Press, 1948), 33–35, 46–53. For comparison, see ex-Marxist Russian exile Nicholas Berdyaev's *The Russian Idea* (1946), the principal interpretation of Soviet Communism as deriving from Russian messianism; trans. R. M. French (London: G. Bles, 1947).
60. Friedrich and Brzezinski define totalitarian movements as "secular religions," *Totalitarian Dictatorship and Autocracy* 106, 301, 314; versus Christianity, 93, 105–106, 115, 299–315. For another influential interpretation, see Waldemar Gurian, "Totalitarianism as Political Religion" (1953) in Carl J. Friedrich, ed., *Totalitarianism* (Cambridge, MA: Harvard University Press, 1954), 119–

129. Gurian, a refugee intellectual, born to a Russian-Jewish family in St. Petersburg, was the founder of *The Review of Politics* (1939) and professor of political science at the University of Notre Dame. Gurian's 1953 essay condenses claims from his book, *Bolshevism: An Introduction to Soviet Communism* (Notre Dame, IN: University of Notre Dame, 1952). The concept of "totalitarianism," and especially the equation of Nazism and Stalinism it assumed, came under serious attack by revisionists in the sixties. Elizabeth Young-Bruehl surveys the revisionists in *Hannah Arendt: For Love of the World* (New Haven: Yale University Press, 1982), 406–412. See also Friedrich's *Totalitarianism in Perspective: Three Views* (New York: Praeger Publishers, 1969); Young-Bruehl also comments on these essays, 409. The terms "totalitarianism" and "political religion" have since been revived in the new theorization of fascism by such sociologists as Emilio Gentile and such historians as Roger Griffin. Emilio Gentile, "Fascism, Totalitarianism, and Political Religion: Definitions and Critical Reflections on Criticism of an Interpretation," *Fascism, Totalitarianism, and Political Religion,* ed. Roger Griffin (New York: Routledge, 2005) and Roger Griffin, *The Nature of Fascism* (London: Routledge, 1993); "God's Counterfeiters?" *Fascism, Totalitarianism, and Political Religion,* Ibid. Carl J. Friedrich and Zbigniew Brzezinski, *Totalitarian Dictatorship and Autocracy* (New York: Praeger, 1956).

61. Griffin, "God's Counterfeiters" 6.

62. Raymond Aron, *The Opium of the Intellectuals,* trans. Terence Kilmartin (Garden City, N.Y.: Doubleday, 1957), 105–134, 265–294; Aron had conceptualized Nazism as a "political religion" and a "secular religion" before applying these definitions to Communism, making part of a common totalitarian mentality; see Gentile, *Politics as Religion,* 57–62, 113. Czeslaw Milosz, *The Captive Mind,* trans. Jane Zielonko (1953; repr, New York: Vintage, 1990), 3–24, 75–81, 205–222. Aron had no religious affiliation or stated beliefs, and Milosz came from a Catholic school education. A former member of the Red Army who had been sent to Siberia, Solzhenitsyn renounced his Marxism and became a repentant Christian during his imprisonment. Solzhenitsyn's account of his conversion is "The Soul and Barbed Wire," which is the fourth part of his magnum opus, *The Gulag Archipelago, 1918–1956* (published 1973–1978). Solzhenitsyn made his religious beliefs clear in two famous speeches delivered in the United States during his Soviet-imposed exile: "A World Split Apart" (Commencement address, Harvard University, Cambridge, Mass., June 8, 1978) and "Godlessness, the First Step to the Gulag" (Templeton Prize address, London, May 10, 1983). His traditional Christianity, favoring the Russian Orthodox Church, was discernible in his first published work, *Ivan Denisovich.*

63. Milosz, *Captive Mind,* 206.

64. Daniel Bell has also credited Aron with shaping his own work, *The End of Ideology: On the Exhaustion of Political Ideas in the Fifties* (Glencoe, Ill.: Free Press, 1960). See his new introduction, "The Resumption of History in the New Century," to the 2000 edition (Cambridge, Mass.: Harvard University Press, 2000), xi. Subsequent quotations are from the 1960 edition.

65. Aron, *Opium of the Intellectuals*, 284.

66. Milosz, *Captive Mind*, 40.

67. T. S. Eliot, *Christianity and Culture* (New York: Harcourt, 1948), 10–32; by C. S. Lewis, see his Cold War–era sequel to *The Screwtape Letters* (1942), *Screwtape Proposes a Toast* (1959), in which the Devil, aligned with Communism, is busy at work corroding Western thought from within.

68. Eliot, *Christianity and Culture*, 17.

69. Paul Carter describes the "distrust of reason," "despair in reason," and "death of reason" in the "murky, world-weary Weltanschuanng" of Toynbee and other intellectuals in "History, Mystery, and the Modern World," *Another Part of the Fifties*, 150–154, 163–167. The "intellectual defeatism" of the "many diagnosticians of our age" compelled Sidney Hook, in his article "Intelligence and Evil in Human History," *Commentary* v.3 (March 1947), 210–221, to argue that the re-discovery of evil did not render liberalism, progressivism, and the scientific mind "bankrupt."

70. Howe, *A Margin of Hope*, 203.

71. Daniel Bell, "The End of Ideology in the West," *The End of Ideology*, 370–371.

72. Hoover, *Masters of Deceit*, 98–99, 106. Hoover's reputation as an earnest Judeo-Christian was such that in 1949, the book jacket of first edition of *The Greatest Story Ever Told*, a popular retelling of Christ's life (later made into a soporific film by George Stevens), included the FBI director's endorsement: the book was "not only a design for living, but for eternity."

73. See Michael Rogin, "Kiss Me Deadly: Communism, Motherhood, and Cold War Movies," *Representations* 6 (Spring 1984): 1–5.

74. Alan Nadel, *Containment Culture: American Narratives, Postmodernism, and the Atomic Age* (Durham, N.C.: Duke University Press, 1995); Ann Douglas, "Periodizing the American Century," *Modernism/Modernity* 5, no. 3 (September 1998):71–98.

1. Christianity, Reason, and the National Character

1. Kennan quoted from *Foreign Affairs*, 25 (1947): 582. Anders Stephanson describes the Cold War conception of totalitarianism as the Other of the Free World, *George F. Kennan and the Art of Foreign Policy* (Cambridge, Mass.: Harvard University Press, 1980), 57. Reinhold Niebuhr, *The Irony of American History* (New York: Scribner's, 1952), 4.

2. William Appleman Williams, *The Tragedy of American Diplomacy* (New York: W. W. Norton, 1959), 108–161, 229–243.

3. The classic account of the Open Door is William Appleman Williams, *The Tragedy of American Diplomacy*, which defined the policy as "imperial anti-colonialism" 18–47. Williams's book was a pathbreaking work for revisionist historians of the Cold War because it made two major claims: (1) it argued that the United States had consciously sought international power and that the Cold War extended this will; (2) it challenged the thesis that postwar Russia imagined no possibility of coexistence with capitalist countries and was poised

to wage war with the United States (202–276). I am markedly influenced by the revisionist school. The most prodigious critic of the revisionist narratives is Yale historian John Lewis Gaddis, whose first work, *The United States and the Origins of the Cold War* (1972) is a postrevisionist touchstone. Among the substantive criticisms of Gaddis's work is that he refuses to consider economic factors and focuses instead on the constraints of public opinion, security concerns, and, increasingly in his subsequent books, on the personality of Stalin. Whereas Gaddis dismissed the revisionists, calling them economic determinists, his own work from the seventies onward has consistently excluded economic interests, and therefore the hypothesis of anticolonial imperialism, from consideration.

4. Marty Jezer, *The Dark Ages: Life in the United States, 1945–1960* (Boston: South End Press, 1982), 21–23.

5. Williams, *Tragedy of American Diplomacy*, 61–62.

6. George Kennan describes the Spanish-American War and the subsequent annexation of the Philippines as ill-advised and misfired imperial experiments that demonstrate the irresponsibility of American moralism and idealism in the nation's past; *American Diplomacy* (Chicago: University of Chicago, 1984 [1951]), 3–21. By Robert Osgood, see *Ideals and Self-interest in America's Foreign Relations, the great transformation of the twentieth century* (Chicago: University of Chicago Press, 1953). By Hans Morgenthau, see *Politics Among Nations: the Struggle for Power and Peace* (New York: Knopf, 1948) and *In Defense of the National Self-interest: a critical examination of American Foreign Policy* (New York: Knopf, 1951); Kenneth W. Thompson, *Christian Ethics and the Dilemmas of Foreign Policy* (Durham: Duke University Press, 1959); *Political Realism and the Crisis of World Politics: An American Approach to Foreign Policy* (Princeton, NJ: Princeton University Press, 1960). For points of agreement, regarding U.S. interests, between the realists and "idealists," see Robert Tucker & David Hendrickson, *The Imperial Temptation: The New World Order and America's Purpose* (New York: The Council on Foreign Relations Press, 1992), 183–188.

7. George Orwell, "The Managerial Revolution" (1946) and "Burnham's View of the Contemporary World Struggle" (1947), in *The Collected Essays, Journalism and Letters of George Orwell*, ed. Sonia Orwell and Ian Angus (Boston: Nonpareil Books, 2000), 4:160–181, 4:313–325.

8. For an often-quoted statement of Niebuhr's Cold War realism, see "For Peace, We Must Risk War," *Life* 25, September 20, 1948, 38–39. According to Daniel Bell, moralism culminated the process of the dilution of New England theology in America: "Moralism and moral indignation are characteristic of religions that have abandoned other-worldly preoccupations and have concentrated on this-worldly concerns." In "The Dispossessed" (1955), *The Radical Right*, ed. Daniel Bell, 3rd edition (New York: Transaction, 2002), 62. On the Cold War realists at *Christianity and Crisis*, see Hultheser, *Building a Protestant Left* 24–48, 67–92, 114–134. Having strong memories of the Social Gospel, Bennett was more circumspect about the post-war liberal anti-Communist consensus at *Christianity and Crisis* than Ramsey, Lefever, Thompson,

and Niebuhr. When Bennett became Niebuhr's co-chair at *Christianity and Crisis* in 1954, he began moving it toward a center-left position, turning the magazine's realist philosophy against Cold War truisms. He showed leadership on issues—coexistence, arms control, criticism of nuclear deterrence, the anti-revolutionary application of the Truman Doctrine in Asia—to which Niebuhr came round belatedly. When *Christianity and Crisis* turned anti-war in the mid-sixties, again under Bennett's helmsmanship, Lefever and Ramsey left the magazine to become neo-conservatives, and Lefever went on to shepherd the Ethics in Public Policy Center in 1976. By Kenneth W. Thompson, the magazine's foremost hawk, see *Christian Ethics and the Dilemmas of Foreign Policy* (1959) and *Political Realism and the Crisis of World Politics: An American Approach to Foreign Policy* (1960). Though not formally religious, Morgenthau was a member, along with Bennett and Thompson, of the Council on Religion and International Affairs (CRIA) and credited Christian thinkers, including Niebuhr, for their profound insights into man's tragic condition; see Christoph Frei's discussion of *Scientific Man versus Power Politics* (Chicago, 1946) in *Hans J. Morgenthau: An Intellectual Biography* (Baton Rouge: Louisiana State University Press, 2001), 188–189; also Hans J. Morgenthau, "Niebuhr's Political Thought," in Harold R. Langdon, ed., *Reinhold Niebuhr: A Prophetic Voice in Our Time* (Greenwich, CT: Seabury, 1962), 99–109.

9. In Augustine's *City of God*, real peace—"a tranquil order of rest" ruled by Love—belongs to Eternity. "Actually existing peace on Earth, meanwhile, [is] . . . a sort of simulacrum of the real thing," because "life on Earth after the Fall [is] inherently tainted by sin, by definition merely temporal"; qtd. in Anders Stephanson, "Fourteen Notes on the Very Concept of the Cold War," in *Rethinking Geo-Politics*, ed. Simon Dalby and Gearoid O. Tuathail (London: Routledge, 1998), 69.

10. James Burnham, *The Struggle for the World* (New York: John Day, 1947); and *The Coming Defeat of Communism* (New York: John Day, 1950). Burnham became a contributor to the *National Review* after William F. Buckley founded it in 1956. On Burnham's pre–Cold War career, see Alan Wald, *The New York Intellectuals* (Chapel Hill: University of North Carolina, 1987), 175–192.

11. Ronald Pruessen, *John Foster Dulles: The Road to Power* (New York: Free Press, 1982), 214.

12. Stephanson, *George F. Kennan*, 249.

13. Pruessen has discovered Dulles's Christianity in *John Foster Dulles*, 124–125, 178–217, 444–448; see also Townsend Hoopes, "Death and Assessment," in *The Devil and John Foster Dulles* (Boston: Little, Brown, 1973), 480–491; William Lee Miller, *Piety along the Potomac: Notes on Politics and Morals in the Fifties* (Boston: Houghton Mifflin, 1964), 161–174.

14. The phrase comes from a speech, "The Soviet Way of Thought and Its Effect on Foreign Policy," which was so successful that *Foreign Affairs* invited Kennan to submit it for publication; we know it now as the "X" article, or "The Sources of Soviet Conduct"; cited in Stephanson, *George F. Kennan*, 68.

15. The "profoundly Calvinist" attributes in Kennan's personality have been traced by Stephanson, *George F. Kennan*, 249–250.

16. Kennan opposed NATO because he was afraid a Western military alliance would feed Russian fears that the USSR was being encircled by enemies.

17. Pruessen, *John Foster Dulles,* 278. Dulles and Luce, who was the son of missionaries to China, wanted to free the Eastern bloc from Soviet control and eventually wanted to liberate Russia from international Communism; see Hoopes, "Death and Assessment," 170–173. Dulles had been one of Truman's foreign policy planners before becoming Eisenhower's secretary of state.

18. Walter LaFeber compares Niebuhr's and Kennan's analyses of Communism, in *America, Russia, and the Cold War, 1945–1966* (New York: Wiley, 1967), 54.

19. George F. Kennan, *Memoirs, 1925–1950* (New York: Pantheon, 1967), 358.

20. Kennan, "Russia—Seven Years Later," in *Memoirs,* 530.

21. Kennan, *Memoirs,* 70. Burnham makes a similar diagnosis, that Communism fundamentally distorts reality, in *Struggle for the World:* "the words used publicly by communists about themselves and what they do are particularly misleading, because deliberate deception of others, as well as the normal unconscious self-deception, are an integral part of communism" (56).

22. Walter Lippmann, *Essays in Public Philosophy* (Boston: Little Brown, 1955), 142, 154. Lippmann's series of twelve articles on the containment strategy and the Truman Doctrine were published together as *The Cold War: A Study in U.S. Foreign Policy* (New York: Harper, 1947). The term "Cold War" was not coined by Lippmann. According to some accounts, it was first used by Truman adviser Bernard Baruch before Congress in April 1947. Lippmann was, like Kennan, an antiglobalist and a conservative believer in the balance of power. However, he thought that Kennan was greatly overplaying the role of Communist ideology in determining the Red Army's actions or Stalin's goals. According to Lippmann, Russia's ambition in postwar Europe, the desire for a pan-Slav empire, was one it had historically held, and this could be satisfied through a settlement that would be feasible (and less costly, militarily and economically) to both sides and that would also protect America's Atlantic allies. On the disputed origin of the term, "Cold War," see Stephanson, "Fourteen Notes on the Very Concept of the Cold War," 65. Lippmann was a humanist who called fundamentalism theocratic and liberal Christianity faithless in *A Preface to Morals* (New York: Macmillan, 1929). He admired Niebuhr as an ethicist, and he too perceived totalitarianism as a secular religion, but he sharply disagreed with the bipolar view of the world that the theologian shared with Kennan. For Lippmann's views on religion, see D. Steven Blum, *Walter Lippmann: Cosmopolitanism in the Century of Total War* (Ithaca: Cornell University Press, 1984), 85–90, 91–93; on the "totalitarian church," see *Essays,* 154.

23. Stephanson, *George F. Kennan,* 67–79.

24. Walter Lafeber, *America, Russia, and the Cold War, 1945–1966* (New York: John Wiley & Sons, 1967).

25. Lippmann, *Cold War.* Orwell, an anti-Communist socialist, traced a continuity from Burnham's *The Managerial Revolution* (1941), written in his immediate ex-Trotskyite phase, to his postwar call for Western rearmament under American leadership, in *Struggle for the World* (1947). Burnham's volte-face,

his turn from the apocalyptic, disenchanted, and isolationist vision of "managerialism" to the equally apocalyptic, but Machiavellian, vision of a world struggle for survival between American empire and Communist empire, rested upon the assumption that man is "an animal that can act morally when he acts as an individual, but becomes unmoral when he acts collectively" (Orwell, "Managerial Revolution," 170).

26. In fact, Burnham was dissatisfied with containment because he considered it a purely defensive strategy. He also believed it was spiritually deliquescent, since it summoned no one to high, heroic, sacrificial purposes. See George Nash's discussion of Burnham's *Containment or Liberation? An Inquiry into the Aims of United States Foreign Policy* (1953), in George Nash, *The Conservative Intellectual Movement in America Since 1945*, 35th anniv. ed. (Wilmington, Del.: ISI, 2008), 144–145.

27. Stephanson, "Fourteen Notes," 69.

28. Niebuhr, *Irony*, 173.

29. John Bennett, *Christianity and Communism* (New York: Haddam House, 1948), 41.

30. John Bennett, *Christians and the State* (New York: Charles Scribner's Sons, 1958), 131. See also Dwight MacDonald, "The Unconscious War," in *Memoirs of a Revolutionist*, qtd. in Lasch, *The New Radicalism in America, 1889–1963* (New York: Alfred Knopf, 1965), 329; Pruessen, *John Foster Dulles*, 216; Jacques Maritain, *Man and the State* (Chicago: University of Chicago Press, 1953).

31. Bennett, *Christians and State*, 99.

32. Hannah Arendt, *The Origins of Totalitarianism* (1951; repr., New York: Harcourt, 1966), 464. In 1958, Arendt expanded her analysis of the ideological character of mass movements in an addendum to *The Origins of Totalitarianism*, "Ideology and Terror"; the quotations on ideology are drawn from this addendum.

33. Dulles, one of the advocates for creating the United Nations, was also a representative at the convocation of the World Council of Churches; see Paul Carter, *Another Part of the Fifties* (New York: Columbia University Press, 1983), 137.

34. In 1948, President Truman requested his secretary of state and his secretary of defense to carry out a complete review of America's postwar options for dealing with Russia. The resulting report, NSC-68, issued a number of recommendations (military, economic, and political) that were all based on the erroneous conclusion that Russia was not only capable of launching an assault on the United States and fomenting worldwide revolution but also desirous of waging this conflict in the imminent future. Because Europe was in the process of recovering from massive destruction, only the United States, NSC-68 asserted, had the resources to contain the threat and, if necessary, engage in a full-scale confrontation. Whether the United States would strike offensively to protect its interests was an option the document left open. NSC-68 was revised in 1950, after Russia exploded a nuclear bomb, depriving America of its nuclear supremacy. The document was not declassified until 1975. The documents are

reprinted in Nelson Drew, ed., *NSC-68: Forging the Strategy of Containment* (Washington, D.C.: National Defense University Press, 1996), 22–130. The Committee for the Present Danger, first convened in 1950 to implement the recommendations of NSC-68, was reassembled in 1976 with many of its original members; these anti-Communist hawks would form the core of Ronald Reagan's administration. See Martin Walker, *The Cold War: A History* (New York: Holt, 1995), 248.

It should be noted that while the "X" article" was an evident influence on NSC-68, the concept of totalitarianism was never central to Kennan's foreign policy, as it was (explicitly) to the writers of the secret document; see Stephanson, *George F. Kennan*, 63; Drew, *NCS-68*, 25, 45–47, 50, 57, 66. Kennan did accept the concept, however, and he gave the opening address conference held at the American Academy of Arts & Sciences, Boston on March 1953, entitled "Totalitarianism and Freedom," which was attended by Hannah Arendt; see Elizabeth Young-Bruehl, *Hannah Arendt: For Love of the World* (New Haven: Yale University Press, 1982), 289.

35. John Foster Dulles, "Dynamic Peace" (address before the Associated Press of New York, April 22, 1957).

36. Ronald Pruessen, *John Foster Dulles: The Road to Power* (New York: Free Press, 1982), 204, 270, 290; Niebuhr, *Irony*, 136–137. See also Niebuhr, "The Myth of World Government," *Nation* 162 (March 16, 1946): 312–311; "The Illusion of World Government," *Foreign Affairs* 27 (April 1949): 379–388; and his pamphlet, "The Moral Implications of Loyalty to the United Nations," Hazen Pamphlet 29 (New Haven: Edward Hazen Foundation, 1952). On Kennan's opinion of the vagaries of international law, see *American Diplomacy*, 91–103. Morgenthau sounded a dissonant note among this chorus. Though he agreed that a functioning supra-national government could not be created by legal fiat or under existing post-war conditions, the idea of a democratic, peace-making world state remained for him a long-term aspiration. Where Kennan and Niebuhr held fast to rejecting moralistic rhetoric and underscoring the agonism of international life, Morgenthau strove to theorize how a "functioning supranational society" and "cosmopolitan political identity" could be forged from common interests. He foresaw this would involve supplanting the sovereignty of the nation-state, a political unit which Kennan accepted as axiomatic. In *The Irony of American History* (1952), Niebuhr, in the midst of complimenting Kennan's *American Diplomacy*, added the qualification that concern exclusively for self-interest would lead only to egotism. His own position, that America must develop a concern for the opinions of other nations, essentially restates Kennan's recommendation that his country should not behave unilaterally in a spirit of moral arrogance. Niebuhr's 1952 text assumes a position stated in the final chapter of *The Children of Light and the Children of Darkness* (1944), and not significantly modified in the years intervening; for the imminent future, the forces most likely to unite nations would be the sense of a common foe. Aside from ad hoc defensive arrangements, Niebuhr speculated, UNESCO's projects to raise literacy and education levels

in smaller nations might go some way to laying the basis for a world community in "the very long range." See Hans J. Morgenthau, *Politics among Nations: The Struggle for Power and Peace,* Fifth Edition, Revised (New York: Alfred A. Knopf, 1978), Part 8, 448–488, and Part 9, 489–525. For discussion of *Politics Among Nations,* see William E. Scheuerman, *Morgenthau* (Cambridge, UK: Polity Press, 2009), 118–130. Quotations from Scheuerman, p. 126, 127. By Niebuhr, see *The Irony of American History* (1952), 148–149; Niebuhr, *The Children of Light and the Children of Darkness* (New York: Charles Scribner's Sons, 1944), 153–190; Niebuhr, "The Theory and Practice of UNESCO," in *International Organization,* vol. 4 (February 1950), 6, 8–10.

37. Niebuhr, *Irony,* 137; Bennett, *Christians and the State,* 190.

38. H. P. Lippincott, "World Government and Christianity," *Christianity Today,* February 3, 1958, 5.

39. Stephanson, *George F. Kennan,* 186.

40. Thompson quoted in *Christian Ethics,* 75, and in Hultheser, *Building a Protestant Left,* 84. To cite an example of what Thompson considered a "moralistic" response to the problem of imperialism, he fiercely objected to America's siding with the U.N.'s withdrawal order to Israel during the Suez Crisis. Given the strategic significance of its alliances with Israel, Britain, and France, Thompson argued, America should have taken a stronger hand with Egypt's President Gamal Nasser, instead of standing on anti-colonial principle (*Political Realism* 230; *Christian Ethics* 63–64). Niebuhr agreed, calling America's reasoning idealistic (Hultheser 84). Both Niebuhr and Thompson thought that Nasser's policies were giving the Soviet bloc a geopolitical advantage in the Middle East, even though Nasser had attended, and supported, the 1955 Bandung Conference of non-aligned Third World nations: Asian and African countries that did not want to be spheres of influence for either side in the Cold War. For an incisive report on the Bandung Conference, see Richard Wright, *The Color Curtain* (Cleveland: World Publishing, 1956).

41. Stephanson, *Kennan* 202; George F. Kennan, "Is War with Russia Inevitable?" in Kenneth W. Thompson and Hans J. Morgenthau, eds. *Principles and Problems of International Politics* (New York: Alfred Knopf, 1950), 379. On the weak judgment and importunate influence of democratic public opinion, see Kennan, *American Diplomacy,* 20, 37, 62, 66, 93; Kenneth Thompson, *Political Realism,* 212–214; Hans Morgenthau, "Conduct of American Foreign Policy," *Principles and Problems of International Politics,* 171–172. On the association of the prophetic symbols of Eden and New Israel (Zion) in American thought and how this close association developed, see Ernest Lee Tuveson's study, *Redeemer Nation: the Idea of America's Millennial Role* (Chicago: University of Chicago, 1968).

42. "The Challenge of the Future," *Christianity Today,* May 26, 1958, 3–4; "Communism: The Bitter Enemy of Religion," *Christianity Today,* June 22, 1959, 3–5.

43. Bennett, *Christians and the State,* 146.

44. For another exposition of these ideas by a distinguished theologian, see H. Richard Niebuhr, "The Idea of Covenant and American Democracy," *Church History* 23 (1954): 126–35; see also "The Idea of Original Sin in American Culture" (1949), delivered for the Program of Studies in American Civilization at Princeton, and "The Relation of Christianity and Democracy" (1940), given at Berkeley Divinity School; reprinted in *Theology, History, and Culture,* ed. William Stacy Johnson (New Haven: Yale University Press, 2007). See also his brother Reinhold's essay, "Democracy, Secularism, and Christianity" in *Christian Realism and Political Problems* (New York: Charles Scribner's Sons, 1953), 95–104.

45. Cornel West called Reinhold Niebuhr "the most influential cultural critic in mid-century America," in *The American Evasion of Philosophy* (Madison: University of Wisconsin Press, 1989), 150; in *Billy Graham: Revivalist in a Secular Age* (Ronald Press, 1959); William McLoughlin reports that by 1958, Gallup Poll's annual survey of "the most admired man in the world" placed Graham behind only three other persons: Dwight Eisenhower, Winston Churchill, and Albert Schweitzer (5).

46. See Niebuhr's essay, "The Assurance of Grace" (1934), reprinted in *The Essential Reinhold Niebuhr* (New Haven: Yale University Press, 1986); on Lutheran dualism, see *Moral Man and Immoral Society* (New York: Charles Scribner's Sons, 1932), 77; and *The Nature and Destiny of Man,* vol. 2 *Human Destiny* [hereafter, *Human Destiny*] (New York: Charles Scribner's Sons, 1941), 185–198, 277–278.

47. Portions of this section have been published as Jason Stevens, "Should We Forget Reinhold Niebuhr?" *boundary 2,* 34, no. 2 (Summer 2007): 135–148.

48. See Richard Fox, *Reinhold Niebuhr: A Biography* (San Francisco: Harper, 1985); George Stephanopoulos, *All Too Human: A Political Education* (Boston: Little, Brown, 1999) 69; and Arthur Schlesinger, Jr., "Forgetting Reinhold Niebuhr," *New York Times,* September 18, 2005. For an earlier attempt to refute the New Right with Niebuhr during the Reagan era, see Robert Preston's "Reinhold Niebuhr and the New Right," in *Reinhold Niebuhr and the Issues of Our Time,* ed. Richard Harries (Grand Rapids, Mich.: Eerdmans, 1986), 88–104.

49. David Brooks, "Obama, Gospel and Verse," *New York Times,* April 26, 2007, select.nytimes.com/2007/04/26/opinion/26brooks.html

50. Full reference for Forum: "Public Theology in Contemporary America" featured in *Religion and American Culture* 10:1 (Winter 2000) 1–27.

51. David Brooks, "Man on a Gray Horse," *Atlantic Monthly,* September 2002, www.theatlantic.com/past/issues/2002/09/brooks.htm. One such hawk is Democrat Peter Beinhart, former editor of the *New Republic,* a onetime supporter of the American-Iraqi war, and now member of the Council on Foreign Relations, whose endorsement graces the cover of the reissue of *The Essential Reinhold Niebuhr.* Reinhold Niebuhr, alongside Harry Truman, emerges as the hero of Peter Beinhart's *The Good Fight: Why Liberals and Only Liberals Can Win the War on Terror and Make America Great Again* (New York: Harper Collins, 2006). Beinhardt's account of the Cold War, which provides a tem-

plate in his text for winning "the war on terror," conforms to the triumphalist view of the American-Russian conflict that John Lewis Gaddis, another self-proclaimed Niebuhrian, had taken since the nineties. Leo Ribuffo thoughtfully compares Niebuhr with Gaddis, and each of these thinkers with William Appleman Williams, in "Moral Judgements and the Cold War," *Cold War Triumphalism*, ed. Ellen Schrecker (New York: New Press, 2004).

52. Sidney Hook said that Niebuhr's view of man "has been won by reflection on social and political experience" and hence, that it is coherent apart from any belief in any "dogmatic revelation of the nature of Deity. . . . Here is a prophet who does not want to save souls or preach supernatural truths." See "The Moral Vision of Reinhold Niebuhr" and "Pragmatism and the Tragic Sense of Life," in Hook, *Pragmatism and the Tragic Sense of Life* (New York: Basic Books, 1974), 185, 188. From the lecture series, "Know Your Roots: American Evangelicalism Yesterday, Today, and Tomorrow" (Trinity Evangelical Divinity School 1991, n.d.); *The Christian Catalyst Collection: Carl F. H. Henry and Kenneth S. Kantzer* (Vision Video, 2006). Henry's speech is in Part I of the recording.

53. "Evangelicals and Fundamentals," *Christianity Today*, September 16, 1957, 20–21; Geoffrey Bromiley, "Fundamentalism-Modernism: A First Step in the Controversy," *Christianity Today*, November 11, 1957, 3–5. See also Carl F. H. Henry, "Dare We Revive the Modernist-Fundamentalist Conflict?" *Christianity Today*, June 10, 1957, 3–6; June 24, 1957, 23–26; July 8, 1957, 15–18.

54. Carl F. H. Henry, (speech, part 2 of "Evangelicalism: Yesterday, Today, and Tomorrow," Trinity Evangelical Divinity School, Ellendale, N.D., 1991).

55. Billy Graham, qtd. in McLoughlin, *Billy Graham: Revivalist*, 482.

56. Billy Graham, qtd. in William Martin, *A Prophet with Honor: The Billy Graham Story* (New York: William Morrow, 1991), 146.

57. Moyers, qtd. in Martin, *Prophet with Honor*, 303. William Lee Miller, writer and editor for *The Reporter* magazine, contrasts Niebuhr's sobriety to the "popular," "salable," and "moralizing" national religious revival, embodied for him by Billy Graham and Norman Vincent Peal, in "The 'Religious Revival' and American Politics" (1954) and "The Irony of Reinhold Niebuhr" (1955) reprinted in *Piety along the Potomac*, 125–131, 146–160. Thompson laments Billy Graham's "perfectionism" and praises Christian Realism for being "free of all the illusions and confusion of the presently fashionable revival trend" in *Christian Ethics*, 113–114.

58. Edward Carnell, "Can Billy Graham Slay the Giant?" *Christianity Today*, May 13, 1957, 4.

59. Carnell addressed Niebuhr's work at length in *The Theology of Reinhold Niebuhr* (Grand Rapids, Mich.: Eerdmans, 1950), one of the earliest books on the topic.

60. See Reinhold Niebuhr, *The Irony of American History*; see also *Faith and History: A Comparison of Christian and Modern Views of History* (New York: Scribner's Sons, 1949), especially Chapters 7–10. On the meaning of the Cross, see *Human Destiny*, 47–92; and "The Power and Weakness of God," in *Discerning the Signs of the Times* (New York: Charles Scribner's Sons, 1946; repr. Niebuhr Press, 2007), 132–151. Niebuhr begins to limn the distinction he

would make between tragic and comic modes of conceiving irony in history, in the sermonic essay "Humor and Faith," in *Discerning the Signs of the Times,* III–I3I.

61. Hayden White, *Metahistory: the Historical Imagination in Nineteenth-Century Europe* (Baltimore: Johns Hopkins University Press, 1975), I–44; see also White's essay, "The Value of Narrativity in the Representation of Reality," in *The Content of the Form: Narrative Discourse and Historical Representation* (Baltimore: Johns Hopkins University Press, 1987).

62. Niebuhr, *Irony,* 169.

63. See Ernest May, "The Structure of Public Opinion" and introduction to *American Imperialism: A Speculative Essay* (1967; repr. Chicago: Imprint 1991), 17–43, ix–xi, xviii–xix.

64. During the late thirties, Reinhold Niebuhr published prointervention articles in such journals as the *Christian Century,* the *Nation,* the *New Statesmen,* and *Scribner's.* These writings were quickly collected as *Christianity and Power Politics* (New York: Charles Scribner's Sons, 1940). The main task of these essays was to rebuke the plurality of liberal clergy who were arguing that pacificism was the only morally pure position for Christians to take, especially after the disillusion over World War I.

65. NSC-68 followed a parallel logic, suggesting that the American public would not be easily persuaded to support wars, or even preparation for wars, to prevent the spread of Communism and eventually defeat it. The expansion of presidential power under Roosevelt and Truman, along with the postwar creation of policy-shaping agencies above public review (the CIA, the NSC, and the NSA), also reflected convictions that discussion in the public sphere could not dependably reach the correct conclusions for national self-interest. In the (hyped) state of crisis—when the "post" in " postwar" seemed practically a misnomer—necessity dictated that decision-making be concentrated in highly undemocratic fashion.

66. Mark Silk discusses Reinhold Niebuhr's printed remarks about Graham, and Graham's mild-mannered response, in *Spiritual Politics: Religion and America since World War II* (New York: Simon and Schuster, 1988), 101–107.

67. Reinhold Niebuhr, "Literalism, Individualism, and Billy Graham," *The Christian Century,* May 23, 1956, 641. "Frustration in Mid-Century," in *Pious and Secular America* (New York: Scribner's, 1958), 22. Ten years later, in the Nixon era, Niebuhr would accuse Graham of being an establishment figure unworthy of the prophet Amos's example; see "The King's Chapel and the King's Court," *Christianity and Crisis,* August 4, 1969, 211–212.

68. Niebuhr specified that perfectionism had been a feature, in the eschatological sense, of revolutionary Protestantism (the Diggers, the Anabaptists, Cromwell's Puritans), and in the pietistic sense, of evangelicalism and Roman Catholicism; see *Human Destiny,* 135–178.

69. Niebuhr, "Frustration in Mid-Century," 22.

70. Graham's fullest discussion of sanctification can be found in a later work, *The Holy Spirit: Activating God's Power in Your Life* (Nashville, Tenn.: Thomas Nelson, 1978), especially Chapters 6–8.

71. Niebuhr: "The idea of grace can be stated adequately only in mythical terms"; "The Assurance of Grace," in *The Essential Reinhold Niebuhr* 67–68.

72. Augustine, *The City of God* (London: Penguin, 1984), 593–597. See Reinhold Niebuhr, "Augustine's Political Realism," in *The Essential Reinhold Niebuhr;* reprinted from Niebuhr's *Christian Realism and Political Problems* (1953). See also Reinhold Niebuhr, *The Nature and Destiny of Man,* vol. 1, *Human Nature* [hereafter, *Human Nature*] (Upper Saddle River, NJ: Prentice Hall, 1964), 16–17, 57–61, 178–219, 241–264.

73. Niebuhr, *Human Nature,* 260.

74. Benedict Anderson, *Imagined Communities: Reflections on the Origin and Spread of Nationalism* (New York: Verso, 1983), 141, 143.

75. Niebuhr, *Moral Man,* 154–168. *Human Nature,* 208–219.

76. Czeslaw Milosz, *The Captive Mind,* trans. Jane Zielonko (New York: Vintage, 1990), 3–24. Milosz is careful to state that "Diamat" is not Marxism (52, 74). In his socialist phase, Niebuhr had also differentiated Marxism from Communist Party orthodoxy: "Marxism, in its pure form, has been the most potent critic of liberal illusions" (*Christianity and Power Politics,* 91). After he co-founded the American Committee for Democratic Action (ADA) in 1947 Niebuhr made no such careful distinction between the ideology of the Communist Party and Marxist theory.

77. Langdon Gilkey, *On Niebuhr* (Chicago: University of Chicago Press, 2001), 216. In support of his thesis that a diverse laity deeply read Niebuhr, Andrew Finstuen produces letters from Niebuhr's admirers, who represent a cross-section of American society in the fifties and sixties, but the contents of the letters, as Finstuen describes them, do not demonstrate that the writers, apart from the seminary students and the clergymen perhaps, understood that Niebuhr was demythologizing the Bible; see Finstuen, *Original Sin and Everyday Protestants* (Chapel Hill: University of North Carolina Press, 2009), 96, 99, 101, 106–107, 108, 117–118, 121.

78. Reinhold Niebhur, "Humor and Faith," in *Discerning the Signs of Times,* 114.

79. Arthur Koestler, *The Yogi and the Commissar and Other Essays* (London: Jonathan Cape, 1945). Koestler, Hungarian-born, was a correspondent in the Soviet Union during the 1930s. He was for some years a member of the Communist Party, but broke with it at the time of the Moscow trials. He still counted himself a socialist after the war and enjoyed extended correspondence with George Orwell. As a novelist and co-author of *The God That Failed,* he became a member of the CIA-subsidized American Committee for Cultural Freedom. For insight into Koestler's postwar career, see George Orwell's essay, "Catastrophic Gradualism" (1946) and his correspondence with Koestler in *The Collected Essays, Journalism and Letters of George Orwell,* 4:15–19.

80. Niebuhr, "Humor and Faith," 123.

81. Quotations from *Moral Man and Immoral Society,* respectively 42, 44, 32. For contemporary criticisms of Reinhold Niebuhr's concept of grace and its relation to sin and human freedom, see H. D. Lewis, *Morals and the New Theology* (New York: Harper, 1949); Daniel Day Williams, *God's Grace and Man's*

Hope (New York: Harper, 1949); A. J. Muste, "Theology of Despair" originally published in *Fellowship,* April 21, 1948, 4–8, and reprinted in *The Essays of A. J. Muste,* ed. Nat Hentoff (New York: Bobbs-Merrill, 1967), 305–306; H. Richard Niebuhr, "Reinhold Niebuhr's Interpretation of History" (1949), in *Theology, History, and Culture.* See also the essays on Reinhold Niebuhr's Christology by Paul Lehman, Daniel Williams, Paul Fitch, and Henry Nelson Weiman in *Reinhold Niebuhr: His Religious, Social, and Political Thought,* ed. Charles Kegley (New York: Macmillan, 1956).

82. Billy Graham, *Peace with God* (New York: Doubleday, 1953), 214, 215. Graham became a fast friend and defender of John Foster Dulles and Richard M. Nixon (Republican), both of whom encouraged Graham to use his revival missions abroad to act as an ambassador for American economic and political interests, especially in the Third World. Graham's first official recognition, in fact, had been the State Department's sponsorship of his crusade in Korea (for which sponsorship Harold Ockenga had lobbied), which in turn became the precedent for a spiritual campaign in India that Dulles and Nixon facilitated in 1955. Global Christianity could act as a pathbreaker for global Americanization.

83. Billy Graham, qtd. in McLoughlin, *Modern Revivalism,* 508, 510.

84. Graham, *Peace with God,* 190.

85. Steven Miller's recent monograph, *Billy Graham and the Rise of the Republican South,* gives a balanced account of Graham's cautious relation to the civil rights movement, proposing that Graham paved a route for white Southern moderates to abandon Jim Crow without seeming to be traitors to Southern pride. See Miller, *Billy Graham and the Rise of the Republican South* (Philadelphia: University of Pennsylvania Press, 2009), 64–124.

86. Irving Horowitz, *Ideology and Utopia in the United States, 1956–1976* (New York: Oxford University Press, 1977), 133–161.

87. The clarion call of the new conservative movement was *God and Man at Yale* (Washington, D.C.: Regnery, 1951). William F. Buckley co-founded the *National Review* with Russell Kirk in 1955.

88. A note on terminology: "New Conservative" should not be confused with "Neoconservative." The former designates an intellectual movement, closely associated with Russell Kirk, which was anti-Communist, traditionalist, and politically elitist, but uneasy with industrial capitalism, individualism, and interventionist foreign policy; Nash, *Conservative Intellectual Movement,* 85–126. Kirk was the author of *The Conservative Mind: From Burke to Santayana* (Washington, D.C.: Regnery, 1953), which traces an intellectual genealogy for "New Conservatism." See also Peter Viereck's "The Philosophical 'New Conservatism,'" in Daniel Bell, ed., *The Radical Right,* 3rd ed. (1963; repr., New York: Transaction, 2002), 186–194. Viereck coined the term "New Conservative" in his *Conservativism Revisited: The Revolt Against Revolt* (1949), but later criticized Kirk for failing to see the benefits of limited social welfare spending. A number of traditionalists in the postwar conservative movement were Southern apologists, including Richard Weaver, Allen Tate, and John Crowe Ransom; in addition to Nash, *Conservative Intellectual Movement,* 306–318, see Eugene D. Genovese, *The Southern Tradition: The Achievement*

and Limitations of an American Conservatism (Cambridge, Mass.: Harvard University Press, 1994). Kirk's master's thesis for Duke University, which became his first book, was on John Randolph of Roanoke and developed his interest in Southern history.

89. Nash, *Conservative Intellectual Movement*, 284.
90. Michael Kimmage, *The Conservative Turn: Lionel Trilling, Whittaker Chambers, and the Lessons of Anti-Communism* (Cambridge, Mass.: Harvard University Press, 2009), 144–147, 270–272, 275–276.
91. In his autobiography, *Just As I Am* (San Francisco: HarperCollins, 1997), Graham follows up his narrative of his 1960 trip to Israel with this statement: "I have always believed that the Jews were God's special people, chosen to preserve the Hebrew Scriptures through the centuries and to prepare the way for the coming of Christ" (354). Graham would befriend Golda Meir, Israel's former Prime Minister, and in 1977, he won the first interreligious award from the American Jewish Committee. The autobiography does not acknowledge, much less address, his privately tape-recorded conversations with President Nixon from 1972 in which he voices the opinion that the administration must do something to stop the "satanic Jews" who are dominating the American media. These tapes were made public in 2002. James Warren, "Nixon & Billy Graham Anti-semitism Caught on Tape" in *Chicago Tribune* March 1, 2002 www.rense.com/general20/billy.html. On Graham's improved relations with Roman Catholics, see Martin, *Prophet with Honor*, 309–310, 338–339.
92. Reinhold Neibuhr quotes from *The Structure of Nations and Empires* (New York: Charles Scribner's Sons, 1959), 13, 24, 25, 259; see also 10–17, 21–25.
93. Echoing many "tough-minded" liberals of his age, Niebuhr's criticisms of his government's foreign policy sounded increasingly like the Right's. By 1956, he was calling Eisenhower, the former Supreme Allied Commander, a "new pacifist," "the Chamberlain of our day" (Fox, *Reinhold Niebuhr*, 265). The Eisenhower doctrine of "massive retaliation" sounded like foolish blustering to Niebuhr, who believed it tied the United States to a reactive, purely defensive position, even as Dulles's brinksman-like statements seemed to be daring Russia to strike first. In an editorial for *Christianity and Society* Niebuhr had cautioned that a preventative war would be tantamount to "play[ing] God" (Summer 1948: 7). Niebuhr's demands in the fifties, however, that America "take risks" to cow Russia and prevent it from winning allies in Asia or the Middle East, leave one to wonder whether he would have actually opposed such an action if Eisenhower had been as bold as Dulles's rhetoric or if Niebuhr had estimated that democracies could flourish in countries where "feudal injustices," "low efficiency," "Oriental . . . dishonesty," and "moral resentment" of the West's non-communist "hegemony" had not congealed into a particularly resistant strain of nationalism (Niebuhr, *Irony*, 113–118). Niebuhr did criticize the Eisenhower administration for threatening the USSR and China with massive nuclear retaliation, but he did so on the grounds only that the strategy was politically inefficient. Even hawkish Christian realist Paul Ramsey, whose doctrine of "deferred redemption" allowed Christians ("on occasion") to support their "nation's preparation for unjust warfare," was exasperated with the Eisenhower administration's "more bang for the buck"

approach to the arms race because the indiscriminate destructive capacity of nuclear megaton bombs and I. C. B. M.s rendered moot the principle of non-combatant immunity, which Ramsey derived from Augustine's just war argument. Niebuhr, on the other hand, offered only the admonition that America should never again strike first with a nuclear weapon. Ramsey, who favored limited warfare with tactical nuclear weapons, objected to Niebuhr's failure to morally condemn total war or the threat of massive retaliation, which could push enemies to the brink of a conflict in which civilian casualties would be raised to horrifying totals. Ramsey is responding in particular to Niebuhr's "The Church and the World: Nuclear War and the Christian Dilemma" *Theology Today*, 15:4 (Jan. 1959), 543. Ramsey quotations from *War and the Christian Conscience/How Will Modern War Be Conducted Justly?* (Durham, N.C.: Duke University Press, 1961), 310. Paul Boyer examines Judeo-Christian ethical discourse on the issues of nuclear deterrence and total war in *By Bomb's Early Light: American Thought and Culture at the Dawn of the Atomic Age* (Durham: University of North Carolina Press, 1994), 211–229; see also Margot Henriksen, *Dr. Strangelove's America: Society and Culture in the Atomic Age* (Berkeley: University of California Press, 1997), xv, xvi, 1–11, 61, 183–192, 204–205, 211–213, 225–227; the "more bang for the buck" quotation comes from John Foster Dulles, qtd. in Henriksen, 91. Mark Hultheser covers internal debates in *Christianity and Crisis* over the logic of nuclear deterrence in *Building a Protestant Left*, 89–91.

94. Niebuhr, *Irony*, 162.
95. Niebuhr was also nominated by CIA director (and John Foster Dulles's brother) Allen Dulles for membership in the Council on Foreign Relations (Fox, *Reinhold Niebuhr*, 238).
96. Fox, *Reinhold Niebuhr*, 265; LaFeber, *America, Russia, and the Cold War*, 196. "Mr. Dulles's universe," Niebuhr said, makes "everything clear, too clear" and leads to "simple moral judgments, placed in the service of moral complacency." See "The Moral World of John Foster Dulles" *The New Republic*, Vol. 139 (December 1, 1958), 1.
97. Graham's position did not uniformly define the viewpoints expressed in *Christianity Today*. See the pro and con arguments for the resettlement of Palestine expressed by Oswald T. Allis, "Israel's Transgression in Palestine," and Wilbur Smith, "Israel in Her Promised Land," both in *Christianity Today*, December 24, 1956, 6, 8, 9; 7, 9, 10, 11.
98. Reinhold Niebuhr, "Relations of Christians and Jews in Western Civilization," published for the first time in Niebuhr, *Pious and Secular America* (New York: Charles Scribner's Sons, 1958), 86–112; and "Jews after the War," *Nation* (August 31, 1946): 214–216. On Bennett's differences with Niebuhr over Israel-Palestine, see Hertzel Fishman, *American Protestation and a Jewish State* (Detroit, MI: Wayne State University Press, 1973), 148–149, 171. See also Hultheser, *Building a Protestant Left*, 84–85, 87.
99. Niebuhr, *Irony*, 128. See also John Foster Dulles, who in 1946, before a national convention of Presbyterian ministers said: "Communism, like Islam centuries before, is now challenging the whole Christian world" (Pruessen, *John Foster Dulles*, 287).

100. See Niebuhr's retort to "plutocratic" critics of Truman's legislative expansions of the New Deal and his defense of the political economy of these reforms, in "Halfway to What?" *Nation* 170, January 14, 1950, 26–28. He is careful to specify that a state-administered planned economy, feared by business leaders, is not what either he or Truman envisions.
101. Niebuhr, *Irony,* 108.
102. Reinhold Niebuhr, "The Social Myths in the 'Cold War,'" *Journal of International Affairs* 21 (1967): 46, 47; "Vietnam: Study in Ironies," *New Republic* (June 24, 1967): 11; "Toward New Intra-Christian Endeavors," *Christian Century* 86, 1969, 1662, 1663; *Christianity and Crisis* 30 1970, 70, 71, 72 (cited in *Irony and Consciousness,* 119). Richard Reinitz, *Irony and Consciousness: American Historiography and Reinhold Niebuhr's Vision* (Lewisburg, PA; Bucknell University Press, 1980). Morgenthau and Kennan were more prescient realist critics of American involvement in Vietnam than Niebuhr. For late summations of their cases, see Hans J. Morgenthau, "We Are Deluding Ourselves in Vietnam," *New York Times Magazine,* 18 April 1965; George F. Kennan, "Our Push-Pull Dilemma in Vietnam," *Washington Post* December 12, 1965. Kennan supported the anti-Vietnam platform of Eugene McCarthy in 1968, while Niebuhr reluctantly supported Hubert Humphrey; see Fox, 288. Bennett, in contrast to Ramsey and Thompson at *Christianity and Crisis,* was a more clear-eyed assessor of the situation in South Vietnam who protested what he rightly perceived to be U.S. aggression against popular insurgency. He became a dove, and an anti-war conscience at the magazine, in advance of Niebuhr; see Mark Hultheser, *Building a Protestant Left,* 115, 125–134.
103. Muste, "Theology of Despair," 305–306.

2. Origins of an Ailing Polemic

1. William McLoughlin, *Modern Revivalism: Charles Grandison Finney to Billy Graham* (New York: Ronald Press, 1959); *Billy Graham: Revivalist in a Secular Age* (Ronald Press, 1959). Twenty years later, McLoughlin revisited Billy Graham, in *Revivals, Awakenings, and Reform: An Essay on Religion and Social Change in America, 1607–1977* (Chicago: University of Chicago Press, 1977); his estimate of the revivalist had not changed (186–193).
2. McLoughlin, *Billy Graham: Revivalist,* 120.
3. McLoughlin, *Modern Revivalism,* 511.
4. McLoughlin, *Billy Graham: Revivalist,* 214, 88.
5. The National Council of Churches included four Eastern Orthodox denominations, but no participating Catholics, and even ecumenists Reinhold Niebuhr and John Bennett had reservations about Catholicism because its "perfectionist" doctrine of grace served to legitimate a much too powerful papal authority; see Niebuhr, *The Nature and Destiny of Man,* vol. 2, *Human Destiny* (New York: Charles Scribner's Sons, 1941), 122–131, 135–151, 250–256; and Bennett, *Christians and the State* (New York: Charles Scribner's Sons, 1958), 215–216. Much of the Protestant reservation about Catholicism, and whether it was as compatible with democracy as its counterpart, returned to

an old allegation that the Church, pre–Vatican II, would make the state an arm of Roman authority, a complaint that was given new clothes by Cold War images of totalitarian states and conspiracies; the best-known example is Paul Blanshard's *Communism, Democracy, and Catholic Power* (1951). On Protestant-Catholic tensions in the period, see also Andrew McGreevey, *Catholicism and American Freedom* (New York: WWW Norton, 2003), 166–188. Donald Crosby, *God, Church, and Flag: Senator Joseph R. McCarthy and the Catholic Church* (Chapel Hill: University of North Carolina Press, 1987), 118–146; and Paul Carter, *Another Part of the Fifties,* (New York: Columbia University Press, 1983), 126–134. These clashes, recorded in such publications as the *Nation, Commonweal, Christian Century,* the *Sunday Visitor,* and *Catholic World,* distracted from common themes of Catholic and Protestant leaders, who mutually laid claim to being more anti-Communist than the other. See, for example, Fulton J. Sheen, *Life is Worth Living* (New York: Popular Library, 1953), 54, 155, 95–96, 174, 181–182, 190. The book is a collection of sermons delivered on the bishop's popular "Catholic Hour" radio-television show.

6. Leon Ribuffo, *The Old Christian Right: The Protestant Far Right from the Great Depression to the Cold War* (Philadelphia: Temple University Press, 1983).

7. George Marsden, *Fundamentalism in American Culture,* 2nd ed. (New York: Oxford University Press, 2006), 41–183.

8. Randall Balmer, *Blessed Assurance: A History of Evangelicalism in America* (Boston: Beacon Press, 2000) 54, 94–111. Liberal triumphalism in the aftermath of the trial belied how much of a cultural force fundamentalism remained, especially in the South; see Edward J. Larson, *Summer for the Gods: The Scopes Trial and America's Continuing Debate Over Science and Religion* (New York: Basic Books, 2006), 225–238.

9. Consciously raising the profile of their theology, New Evangelicals numbered in their ranks such scholars as Edward Carnell, Arnold Hearn, and Carl F. H. Henry. Carnell, a Harvard-educated theologian and president of Fuller Theological Seminary, proposed modifications to the doctrine of biblical inerrancy, clarifying that verbal inspiration did not mean every word of Scripture could be taken literally, which helped to dissociate evangelical biblical exegesis from the easily mocked "dictation theory," as if, Harry Emerson Fosdick said, "the original documents of the scripture, which of course we no longer possess, were inerrantly dictated to men a good deal as a man might dictate to a stenographer." Harry Emerson Fosdick, "Shall the Fundamentalists Win?" *Christian Work* 102 (June 10, 1922): 716–722. Reprinted in *The Riverside Preachers,* ed. Paul H. Sherry (New York: Pilgrim Press, 1978), 27–38. This sermon was preached in First Presbyterian Church, New York City, May 21, 1922. Carnell proceeded to criticize fundamentalist literalism for sundering reason from revelation; see *The Case for Orthodox Theology* (Philadelphia: Westminster, 1959) and his article "Post-Fundamentalist Faith," *Christian Century,* August 26, 1959, 171. Billy Graham actually endorsed the New Revised Standard Bible; see William Martin *A Prophet with Honor: The Billy Graham Story* (New York: William Morrow, 1991), 219–220. For a statement of the New Evan-

gelicals' modified theory of inerrancy, as well as a summary statement of New Evangelicalism's differences from Scopes-era fundamentalism, see Harold J. Ockenga's foreword to Harold Lindsell's *The Battle for The Bible* (Grand Rapids, Mich.: Zondervan, 1976). See also John R. W. Stott *Understanding the Bible* (Minneapolis: World Wide Publications, 1972), 181–242.

10. On the Brown Scare, see Ribuffo, *Old Christian Right,* 180–225.

11. Richard Hoftstadter, "Pseudo-Conservatism Revisited," *The Radical Right* 3rd ed. (Doubleday, 1962 repro. New York: Transaction, 2002), 80. In "The Dispossessed" (1962), Daniel Bell says that the present-day upsurge of the right is most directly paralleled to that of twenties, as in the Scopes trial. *The Radical Right,* 24. See also David Riesman and Nathan Glazer, "The Intellectuals and the Discontented Classes" (1955); intellectuals, Riesman and Glazer say, have become too timid to be so bold as Mencken and the American press were when they greeted Bryan in Tennessee with derision. Daniel Bell ed., *The New American Right* (New York: Doubleday, 1955) 131, n 15. Riesman and Glazer's 1955 essay is also included in *The Radical Right,* 105–136.

12. Chris Hedges, *American Fascists: The Christian Right and the War on America* (New York: Free Press, 2006).

13. The film's peculiar mix of supernaturalism and liberal social message designed to offer a panacea attracted the attention of sociologist Frederick Elkin, whose essay-length treatment of it, "God, Radio, and the Movies," was later featured in Bernard Rosenberg and David Manning White, eds. *Mass Culture: The Popular Arts in America* (New York: Free Press, 1957) 308–314.

14. Sidney Hook, "Religion and the Intellectuals" *Partisan Review* 17, no. 3 (March 1950): 230.

15. Sidney Hook, "Rejoinder to Ernst van den Haag" *Partisan Review,* 17:5 (Spring 1950) 615. Hook expands his case for "secularism" in *Religion and Secular Society* (Lincoln: University of Nebraska Press, 1967), especially 27–58. In these lectures, given at the University of Nebraska, March 23 and 25, 1964, he defines the term to designate a position that not only supports the democratic state's religious neutrality and deduces that morality is autonomous from religion, but also makes a necessary distinction between the rightful exercise of one's religion and the unallowable use of political processes to further one's religion.

16. Herberg observes, for instance, that Graham is an "immense" man, but his preaching, emphasizing individualistic piety, is a relic of bygone frontier revivalism unsuitable for modern industrial life; Will Herberg, *Protestant-Catholic-Jew* (Garden City, N.Y.: Doubleday, 1955), 120.

17. Billy Graham, *The Jesus Generation* (Minneapolis: World Wide Publications, 1971), 147–160.

18. Lawrence Levine points out that the Imperial Wizard and Emperor of the Klan, Hiram Wesley Evans, was a fundamentalist; see *Defender of the Faith: William Jennings Bryan: The Last Decade, 1915–1925* (Cambridge, Mass.: Harvard University Press, 1987), 256.

19. In *The Uneasy Conscience of Modern Fundamentalism* (Grand Rapids, MI: William B. Eerdmans, 1947; repro. 2003), Carl Henry actually highlights the

immorality of racism as an issue that New Evangelicals should address "with a Gospel emphasis . . . condemning racial hatred and intolerance, while at the same time protesting the superficial view of man which overlooks the need of individual regeneration" (88).

20. Martin, *Prophet with Honor*, 294–295; McLoughlin, *Billy Graham*, 257n27.

21. Martin, *Prophet with Honor*, 148.

22. Ribuffo, *Old Christian Right*, 83–87.

23. Mark Noll, *America's God* (New York: Oxford University Press, 2003). On millennialism as a dominant Protestant logic, see Ernest Lee Tuveson, *Redeemer Nation: the Idea of America's Millennial Role* (Chicago: University of Chicago Press, 1968), 26–91; Marsden, in *Fundamentalism in American Culture*, explains the distinction between pre-millennialism and post-millennialism, 227–252.

24. Rev. John Kater, *Christians on the Right: The Moral Majority in Perspective* (New York: Seabury, 1982), 9–10.

25. See Paul Carter, *Another Part of the Fifties*, 120–131. The infamous "Reds in Our Churches" flap passed over McCarthy and fell on his subcommittee staff director, Joseph Matthews, an ex-Methodist evangelist to Malay who incurred the displeasure of Eisenhower when he stated that the Protestant clergy was full of Communists. See Murray Kempton's reflection, "J. B. Matthews and the Multiple Revelation," in *Part of Our Time: Some Monuments to the Ruins of the Thirties* (New York: Dell, 1955), 151–180; and Jon Lance Bacon, "Jesus Fanatics and Communist Foreigners," in *Flannery O'Connor and Cold War Culture* (New York: University of Cambridge Press, 1993), 61–86; Crosby, *God, Church, and Flag*, 126–132.

26. New Evangelicals deepened the impression of being America's spiritual compass by engineering numerous Washington-centered activities between 1950 and 1954, the more significant including (1) the Washington Revival Crusade and (2) the first ever sermon for the nation conducted on the steps of the Capitol building, an event that required a special act of Congress (Martin, *Prophet with Honor*, 143, 145).

27. In addition to the Birch Society, other far-right Christian voices of the period included Carl McIntire (of the Bible Presbyterian Church and the *Christian Beacon*), Billy James Hargis (of the Christian Crusade), and Fred Schwartz (of the Christian Anti-Communism Crusade). McIntire, a longtime foe of modernism who had been formally deposed from the Presbyterian Church after protesting its liberalization movement, frequently assailed Graham in the fifties for being a "liberal" on doctrine and for being ecumenical (Martin, *Prophet with Honor*, 218, 220, 222, 334–335). On the careers of McIntire, Schwartz, Hargis, and Robert Welch (founder of the Birch Society), see Brooks R.Walker, *The Christian Fright Peddlers* (Garden City, N.Y.: Doubleday, 1964); in the chapter "Sources of the Radical Right," (233–253) Walker cites *The New American Right* and *The Radical Right*, though he is also influenced by David Danzig, who published articles on fundamentalism in *Commentary*, including "The Radical Right and the Rise of the Fundamentalist Minority," vol. 33, April 1962, 291–298 and by Ralph Lord Roy, author of *Apostles of Discord:*

A Study of Organized Bigotry and Disruption on the Fringes of Protestantism (Boston: Beacon Press, 1953). Covering such "Protestant underworld" figures as Winrod, Smith, and McIntire, whom he distinguishes from "the legitimate fundamentalist movement," including Charles E. Fuller, NAE President Paul Rees, and Billy Graham, Roy heavily documents anti-semitism, anti-"Popery," and hatred of the National Council of Churches and modernists (x, 35, 51, 183, 226, 349). Danzig links the appeal of Hargis-McIntire-Schwartz to "nativist nationalism" (Walker, *Christian Fright Peddlers*, 244–246).

28. See Melanie McAlister, "Prophecy, Politics, and the Popular: The *Left Behind* Series and Christian Fundamentalism's New World Order," *South Atlantic Quarterly*, 102, no. 4 (Fall 2003): 773–798; Paul Boyer, *When Time Shall Be No More: Prophecy Belief in American Culture* (Cambridge, Mass.: Harvard University Press, 1992), 152–292.

29. For a statement of this view on the extreme Right, militantly advocating for an American theocracy created by new laws, see the discussion of the school of Christian Reconstructionism, based on Dominion Theology, as outlined by R. J. (Rousas John) Rushdoony (1916–2001), in *Roots of Reconstruction* (Vallecito, Calif.: Ross House Books, 1991) and *The Institutes of Biblical Law* (Nutley, N.J.: Craig Press, 1973). In its stress on co-opting elite political and business power to achieve religious goals, the New Right is preceded by the International Christian Leadership (ICL) group (known, since 1972, as the Fellowship Foundation and informally as "the Family"). This fundamentalist organization, founded by Abram Vereide, was originally formed in 1935 to oppose the New Deal and subsequently influenced Cold War policy by bringing together right-wing evangelicals with high-placed officials through forums including the presidential prayer breakfasts begun in 1953. Among the ICL's controversial elements are Vereide's successor Doug Coe's fascination with right-wing European dictators and the organization's inception with anti-Rooseveltian businessmen sympathetic to fascist ideologies. The ICL, however, disliked publicity and, consistent with its elitist ideology of great men, preferred to operate quietly behind the doors of power. It was not concerned with altering public opinion, reaching the American masses, or changing the terms of religious discussion in America. I am concerned here with the cultural and political influence of neofundamentalists who broadly endeavored to transform the image of what an evangelical was and what it meant to be a Christian American. Those interested in the clandestine strategies of the ICL and its influence on Cold War politics should consult journalist Jeff Sharlet's powerful exposé, *The Family: The Secret Fundamentalism at the Heart of American Power* (New York: HarperCollins, 2008), especially 120–143, 152–180, 187–195.

30. James Davison Hunter, *Culture Wars: The Struggle to Define America* (New York: Basic Books, 1991). Hunter is disputing not only Herberg, but also sociologist Robert Bellah. See especially Bellah's famous article, "Civil Religion in America," *Daedalus* 96 (Winter 1967): 1–21; see also Bellah's *Habits of the Heart: Individualism and Commitment in American Life* (Berkeley: University of California Press, 1985).

31. Harold Ockenga, NAE press release, December 8, 1957.
32. See Charles Marsh, *Wayward Christian Soldiers* (New York: Oxford University Press, 2007), 22. Since opponents of secular humanism believe that public schools as well as most private universities purvey ideas inimical to their values, many homeschool their children or send them to Christian academies or enroll them in summer youth recruitment programs, as depicted in Heidi Ewing and Rachel Grady's 2006 documentary, *Jesus Camp* (Magnolia Home Entertainment).
33. A term of Pierre Krebs, guru of the European New Right; see "The Metapolitical Rebirth of Europe," in *Fascism,* ed. Roger Griffin (New York: Oxford University Press, 1995), 348–349.
34. Marsh, *Wayward Christian Soldiers,* 24–25.
35. Jim Wallis's account of contemporary fundamentalism and the Religious Right makes no mention of Billy Graham's legacy to either; see *God's Politics* (San Francisco: Harper, 2005), xv–xxvi, 3–20, 56–71, 137–158; Marsh, 24–25; Hedges, *American Fascists,* 20, 140, 141.
36. Nancy Gibbs, "Interviewing the preacher to the Presidents," *Today's Pentecostal Evangel,* December 30, 2007, 12–13. Steven Miller also addresses Graham's often overlooked legacy to the contemporary Christian Right in *Billy Graham and the Rise of the Republican South* (Philadelphia: University of Pennsylvania Press, 2009), 202–203, 207, 217.
37. Ribuffo, *Old Christian Right,* 181.
38. Richard Hofstadter, "The Pseudo-Conservative Revolt," in *New American Right,* ed. Daniel Bell, 44.
39. The methods and findings of *The Authoritarian Personality* have been greatly criticized by social psychologists. See Roger Brown, "The Authoritarian Personality and the Organization of Attitudes," in *Social Psychology,* 1st ed. (New York: Free Press, 1965), 477–548; "Farther Out: Extremists and Activists," Alan C. Elms, in *Personality in Politics* (New York: Harcourt Brace Jovanovich, 1976), 26–57; William P. Kreml, "The Authoritarian Model," *The Anti-Authoritarian Personality* (Oxford, N.Y.: Pergamon Press, 1977), 14–35.
40. Leo Lowanthal and Norbert Gutterman, introduction to *Prophets of Deceit: A Study of the Techniques of the American Agitator,* Studies in Prejudice 5 (New York: Harper, 1949), xii; see also 1–4, 18, 24–27, 65–89, 107–108, 123–129.
41. Leo Lowenthal, qtd. in Paul Apostolidis, *Stations of the Cross: Adorno and Christian Right Radio* (Durham N.C.: Duke University Press, 2000), 62–64; see also Paul Apostolidis' discussion of *Prophets of Deceit,* 62–64.
42. Lowenthal and Guterman, *Prophets of Deceit,* qtd. in Hofstadter, "The Pseudo-Conservative Revolt," 85n7.
43. Richard Hofstadter, *Anti-Intellectualism in American Life* (New York: Vintage Books, 1962), 118. Hofstadter actually cites McLoughlin's *Billy Graham: Revivalist in a Secular Age* in his introduction to *Anti-Intellectualism,* and Billy Graham himself is Exhibit 1 of fundamentalist extremism (15).
44. Seymour Lipset, "Three Decades of the Radical Right: Coughlinites, McCarthyites, and Birchers" in *The Radical Right,* ed. Daniel Bell, 405.

45. The studies do allow for the possibility that Catholics might begin to imitate extreme anti-Communist Protestants to achieve national status and counteract fundamentalist bigotry. This could lead to an alliance within the Republican party between Protestant and Catholic fundamentalism; see Riesman and Glazer, "The Intellectuals and the Discontented Classes," 138–139, 148; Westin, "The John Birch Society," in *Radical Right,* 260; Lipset, "The Sources of the 'Radical Right,'" in *New American Right,* 353.

46. Lipset, "The Sources of the 'Radical Right,'" 351–354; Riesman and Glazer, "Intellectuals and Discontented Classes," 142–147.

47. Daniel Bell, "Interpretations of American Politics," in *New American Right,* 18.

48. Richard Hofstadter, *The Age of Reform: From Bryan to FDR* (New York: Vintage Books, 1995), 22.

49. Richard Hofstadter, "The Democrat as Revivalist," in *The American Political Tradition* (New York: Knopf, 1948); and *Age of Reform,* 94–95, 132–133, 362; see also Bell, "Interpretations of American Politics," 19.

50. Hofstadter, *American Political Tradition,* 288. Hofstadter also strongly implies that Bryan was a bigot. Although he was neither a Klansman nor a Klan sympathizer, Bryan did not repudiate the KKK in public, and this left him open to charges that he had lost his moral nerve. Hofstadter makes a special point of noting Bryan's failed speech before the Klansmen at the Democratic Convention in New York in "The Democrat as Revivalist" (199–200). In *The Age of Reform,* Hofstadter seems to hold Bryan partly responsible for the fact that some Klansmen and nativists were attracted to him because he defended fundamentalism (288–289). On Bryan's differences with the Klan, see Levine, *Defender of the Faith,* 257–258. For Bryan's friendly relations with Jews and Catholics as well as his service with the Committee on the Rights of Religious Minorities, see Levine, *Defender of the Faith,* 258–259. On Bryan's differences with other fundamentalist leaders, see Levine, 251–254, 273–276. Quotations from 275, 276.

51. *The Radical Right* several times cites sociologist (and cowriter, with Talcott Parsons, of *A Theory of Social Action* [1937]) Edward Shils's *The Torment of Secrecy: The Background and Consequences of American Security Policies* (1956), itself a key Cold War analysis of the causes of McCarthyism. As in *The Radical Right,* William Jennings Bryan is a prominent target, and McCarthyism shares with the populist and fundamentalist traditions that merge in Bryan's career an inclination toward dualism, tribalism, "intense emotion," and "hostility" to the political order. Apocalyptic prophecy and conspiracy theory interpenetrate to explain any resistance to their values and goals as devilish: "They regard the world around them as evil and as capable of cure only by violent purgation and conversion"; Shils, *The Torment of Secrecy* (Chicago: Elephant Paperbacks, 1996), 232.

52. Richard Hofstadter, "The Paranoid Style in American Politics," *Paranoid Style in American Politics and Other Essays* (Cambridge, MA: Harvard University Press, 1996), 30. Pursuing a similar tack as Hofstadter in *The Age of Reform,* Schlesinger, interestingly, discredits critics of the Kennedy administration by

calling them millennialists whose intellectual forefathers were Jonathan Edwards and George Fox; see "The Administration and the Left," *New Statesman* 65, February 8, 1961, 185.

53. David Plotke, "Introduction to the Transaction Edition" of *The Radical Right*, iv.

54. Ribuffo extends Rogin's argument that the mirroring strategy had a Cold War advantage for liberals; *Old Christian Right*, 241–242.

55. See, for example, David Riesman's remarks characterizing the politics of the thirties as religious demagoguery, powered by the "fanatical search for scapegoats" and preparation for "election Armageddons"; "Our Country and Our Culture" in *A Partisan Century: Political Writings from "Partisan Review,"* ed. Edith Kurzweil (New York: Columbia University Press), 121. Shils, in *Torment of Secrecy*, bluntly states that Communism in America was the rediscovery of populism. Both drive to achieve "equality of status" at the cost of "equality of opportunity" (230), which is another way of saying that inequality is a functional lesser evil in a "free and open society."

56. Michael Rogin, *The Radical Specter: McCarthy and the Intellectuals* (Cambridge Mass.: MIT Press, 1967), 16–20, 26–31, 173, 183–184. Hofstadter's seriously flawed analysis also results from a fundamental misunderstanding of McCarthy's base of support. As Michael Rogin has definitively shown in *The Radical Specter*, McCarthyism was not a mass movement. In 1962, Lipset reviewed the findings in *The New American Right* and concluded that, contrary to the earlier study, McCarthy never achieved any widespread support. Lipset, "The Decades of the Radical Right: Coughlinites, McCarthyites, & Birchers" (1962) in *The Radical Right*, 420. In this regard, his critical review of The *New American Right* concurs with Rogin's findings later in *The Radical Specter*. See also C. Vann Woodward's critical review, "The Populist Heritage and the Intellectual" in *The Burden of Southern History*, 3rd ed. (Baton Rouge: Louisiana State University Press, 1993), 141–163.

57. Hofstadter, *The New American Right*, 120; Riesman, *The Radical Right*, 121, 131, 142.

58. On the function of populism in the Popular Front, see Michael Denning, *The Cultural Front* (New York: verso, 1998), 123–136.

59. Even on the Far Christian Right today, most exponents describe a conservative authoritarian movement rather than a fascist one: a "strong, but limited state"; "traditional, intermediary bodies" (families, churches, associations); "traditional pillars for social control"; "enhanced roles" for the military and the Church. See Robert O. Paxton, *The Anatomy of Fascism* (New York: Vintage, 2004), 120, 217, 253n34). Even Christian Reconstructionism does not express a totalitarian will to create a new state identified, as in European-style fascism(s), as the direct emanation of the New Man. The state would remain a disciplinary instrument, a scourge for order.

60. In distinction to the current theorization of "political religion," Chip Berlet proposes the term "politi*cized* religion." It is a clerical faith, with an already existing institutional presence, that sacralizes a political ideology as an extension of its theology. Provisionally, as Berlet suggests, we might apply this definition to most of the contemporary Christian Right without entailing the term

"fascism"; Chip Berlet, "Christian Identity: The Apocalyptic Style, Political Religion, Palingenesis, and Neo-Fascism," in *Fascism, Totalitarianism, and Political Religion* Roger Griffin, ed. (New York: Routledge, 2005).

3. Guilt of the Thirties, Penitence of the Fifties

1. Daniel Bell, *The End of Ideology: On the the Exhaustion of Political Ideas in the Fifties* (1959; repr., Cambridge, Mass.: Harvard University Press, 1960), 300; Whittaker Chambers, "The Devil," *Life,* February 2, 1948, reprinted in *Ghosts on the Roof: Selected Journalism from Whittaker Chambers, 1931–1959,* ed. Terry Teachout (Washington, D.C.: Regnery Gateway, 1989), 166–174.
2. Cornell West, *The American Evasion of Philosophy: A Genealogy of Pragmatism* (Madison: University of Wisconsin Press, 1989), 112–124, 151–181.
3. Bell, *End of Ideology,* 302.
4. Hook highlights Niebuhr for giving pragmatism its newfound tragic sense. See "The Moral Vision of Reinhold Niebuhr" and "Pragmatism and the Tragic Sense of Life," in Sidney Hook, *Pragmatism and the Tragic Sense of Life* (New York: Basic Books, 1974), 184–189, 3–25.
5. From the first World Congress of the Third Communist International, March 1919.
6. Hook helped to launch the American Worker's Party after calling, in 1933, for a new revolutionary Marxist party; Alan Wald, *The New York Intellectuals* (Chapel Hill: University of North Carolina Press, 1987), 3.
7. Irving Howe, *A Margin of Hope* (San Diego: Harcourt Brace Jovanovich, 1982), 205. Alan Wald discusses Howe's quarrel with Bell, who believed a merger between labor and the Democratic Party's left wing was necessary to achieve reforms, in *New York Intellectuals,* 311–321. Sidney Hook, having already broken with anti-Stalinist Communism by 1943, took the postwar position that the New Deal's mixed economy was a transitional phase to social democracy. He therefore saw pragmatic reasons to support the Democratic Party. See Wald, *New York Intellectuals,* 3–16; and Bloom, *Prodigal Sons* (New York: Oxford University Press, 1986), 129–131, 182–184.
8. George Lukács, *Theory of the Novel* (Berlin: P. Cassirer 1920). Trans. Anna Bostock (Cambridge, Mass.: MIT Press, 1971). Quotation from 41, 61.
9. See Christopher Lasch, *The New Radicalism in America* (New York: Alfred Knopf, 1965), 292.
10. Czeslaw Milosz, *The Captive Mind,* trans. Jane Zielonko (New York: Vintage, 1990), 205–206; Raymond Aron, *The Opium of the Intellectuals,* trans. Terence Kilmartin (Garden City, N.Y.: Doubleday, 1957), 66–93, 294, 310–314. Edmund Wilson, *To the Finland Station* (1940, repro. New York: New York Review Books, 2003), 192, 194, also 186–188, 192–194. Malcom Cowley says the Left traded the religion of art for the religion of politics in *Exile's Return* (London: Penguin, 1969), 293. Originally published New York: Viking Press, 1934. For further discussion of revolutionary writers and debates on the question of whether Communism was a "church" or a "proletarian religion," see Daniel Aaron, *Writers on the Left* (New York: Columbia University Press,

1992), 188–189, 241, 252–253, 256, 258–261, 268. Michael Denning discusses rebuttals to Eastman by Sidney Hook and other American Marxists in *The Cultural Front* (New York: Verso, 1998), 425–431. He also describes Eastman's subsequent influence on Wilson, 433. Reinhold Niebuhr agreed with Eastman, but, at the time, believed the "religious determinism" Eastman found in revolutionary Russian Marxism was necessary to generate "moral energy"; *Reflections on the End of an Era* (New York: Charles Scribner's Sons, 1934), 131–132.

11. Milosz, *Captive Mind*, 205–206; Aron, *Opium of the Intellectuals*, 264–294.

12. The most well-known exception is Lillian Hellman; see Podhoretz, *Ex-Friends: Fallling Out With Allen Ginsberg, Lionel and Diana Trilling, Lillian Hellman, Hannah Arendt, and Norman Mailer* (San Francisco: Encounter Books, 2000), 103–138; Thom Andersen, "Red Hollywood" (1985), in *'Un-American' Hollywood: Politics and Film in the Blacklist Era*, ed. Frank Krutnick (New Brunswick, N.J.: Rutgers University Press, 2007), 232–235, 240–241. Others include Paul Robeson, who believed any public condemnation of the USSR would be construed as support for the racist and imperialist policies of the United States and European colonial powers, as well as certain unfriendly witnesses before HUAC when it convened in Hollywood; see Martin Duberman, *Paul Robeson: A Biography* (New York: New Press, 1995), 415–419; and Andersen, "Red Hollywood," 240–241.

13. Murray Kempton, *Part of Our Time: Some Monuments and Ruins of the Thirties* (New York: Modern Library, 1998), 190–227; Wald, *New York Intellectuals*, 176–177; Martin Marty, *Modern American Religion, v. 11, The Noise of Conflict, 1919–1941* (Chicago: University of Chicago Press, 1991), 321. On Matthiessen's Leftism, see William E. Cain, *F. O. Matthiessen and the Politics of Criticism* (Madison: University of Wisconsin Press, 1988), 117; Frederick C. Stern, *F. O. Matthiessen: Christian Socialist as Critic* (Chapel Hill: University of North Carolina Press, 1981), 78, 84, 89, 155, 231–232. On Niebuhr and Matthiessen, see F. O. Matthiessen, *From the Heart of Europe* (New York: Oxford University Press, 1948), 82. See Matthiessen's references to Niebuhr ("the strongest renewal in our theology today") in his review of *The Yogi and the Commissar* by Arthur Koestler, *New York Times*, May 27, 1945.

14. See Bloom, *Prodigal Sons*, 50.

15. See Bell's application of *Moral Man and Immoral Society*, along with Niebuhr's discussions of Lutheran dualism, in "The Failure of American Socialism: The Tension of Ethics and Politics," in *The End of Ideology*, 275–298. (For further references to Niebuhr in the text, see 300, 302, 311.)

16. On the transatlantic trend of intellectuals converting to religion, mysticism, or spiritual philosophies, see Columbia University philosophy teacher Irwin Edman's "Religion Without Tears," *Commentary*, vol. 1, April 1946, 1–6.

17. After the Puritans had been misrepresented in nineteenth-century nationalist historiography and then lampooned in the twenties, Harvard literary historian Perry Miller, a proud atheist who admired the Protestant dissenting tradition, rescued the Puritans' reputation for the generation that knew totalitarian dictatorship. The first volume of Miller's magnum opus, *The New England Mind,*

was published in 1939, preceded by *Orthodoxy in Massachusetts* in 1936. Miller's iconoclastic scholarship helped to elevate Calvinism in the academy, but it was Matthiessen's *American Renaissance: Art and Expression in the Age of Emerson and Whitman* (New York: Oxford University Press, 1941), in which the Puritan-scarred tragedians must remind optimists of democracy's precarious fate, that set out the master narrative for subsequent, postwar accounts of the American literary canon: Richard Chase's *Herman Melville: A Critical Study* (1949), R. W. B. Lewis's *The American Adam: Innocence, Tragedy, and Tradition in American Literature* (1955), Harry Levin's *The Power of Blackness: Poe, Hawthorne, Melville* (1958), and Leslie Fiedler's *Love and Death in the American Novel* (1960). In his study *Visionary Compacts*, Donald Pease notes that the flurry of canon-building scholarship after World War II was effectively a meditation on F. O. Matthiessen's classic; see "Visionary Compacts and the Cold War Consensus," 3–48 and "Melville and Cultural Persuasion," 235–267 in *Visionary Compacts: American Renaissance Writings in Context* (Madison: University of Wisconsin, 1987).

18. Kempton, *Part of Our Time*, 41.

19. Bell, *End of Ideology*, 303.

20. Schlesinger was never a socialist or a member of the Communist Party. His defense of the New Deal and his membership in Americans for Democratic Action did not represent a move to the Right.

21. Arthur Schlesinger, Jr., *The Vital Center* (New York: De Capo, 1949), 181–183, 243–257.

22. On Wallace and the ADA, see Marty Jezer, *The Dark Ages: Life in the United States, 1945–1960* (Boston: South End Press, 1982), 24–32. See also Reinhold Niebuhr, "Mr. Wallace's Errors," *Christianity and Crisis*, October 28, 1946, 6, 1–2.

23. Alger Hiss was accused of spying for the Communist Party while he was a federal employee; though not tried for treason, he was indicted for perjury. In 1950, after a previous mistrial, he was found guilty and his appeal was denied. On the Hiss trial, see, in addition to Chambers's *Witness*, Sam Tanenhaus's review of the evidence in his appendix to *Whittaker Chambers: A Biography* (New York: Random House, 1997), 515–520. The Rosenbergs were found guilty of leaking atomic secrets to the USSR; they were executed in 1953. On the case and its impact on American culture, see Marjorie Garber and Rebecca Walkowitz, eds. *Secret Agents: The Rosenbergs, McCarthyism, and Fifties America* (New York: Routledge, 1995). For a biographical account sympathetic to the Rosenbergs, see Ilene Philipson, *Ethel Rosenberg: Beyond the Myths* (New Brunswick, N.J.: Rutgers University Press, 1992).

24. Murray Kempton, "A Sheltered Life," in *Part of Our Time: Some Monuments to the Ruins of the Thirties*. Edition *being cited* is (New York: Modern Library, 1998), 17–45. Original was published (New York: Simon and Schuster, 1955). Leslie Fiedler, "Afterthoughts on the Rosenbergs" (*Encounter*, October 1953) and "Hiss, Chambers and the Age of Innocence" (*Commentary*, December 1950) in *An End to Innocence: Essays on Culture and Politics* (Boston: Beacon Press, 1955), 3–24, 25–45.

25. Leslie Fiedler, "A Prophet Out of Israel" and "Living with Simone Weil," in *The Collected Essays of Leslie Fiedler* (New York: Stein and Day, 1971), 2:5–30, 2:31–35. "A Prophet Out of Israel" was the introduction to the first American edition of Fiedler's *Waiting for God* (New York: G. P. Putnam's Sons, 1951), vii–xxxiv, 5, 26.

26. An earlier exposition of this point of view is William Barrett's editorial, "The Liberal Fifth Column," *Partisan Review* 13, no. 3 (Summer 1946): 279–293, which, like Diana Trilling's "Memorandum on the Hiss Case," *Partisan Review* 17, no. 5 (May–June 1950): 484–500, accuses the misguided "liberals" (the word is placed in quotations throughout the editorial) of drawing suspicion upon the true liberals and giving a political opening to the Right.

27. Fiedler, "Hiss, Chambers," 23.

28. Norman Mailer, *Barbary Shore* (Vintage: New York, 1951), 151, 310.

29. Peter Viereck argued that Hiss was a symbol of the intellectual guilt of the 1930s precisely because he, and his defenders, denied he had done wrong in supporting Stalinism; see Viereck, *Shame and Glory of the Intellectuals: Babbitt Jr. vs. the Rediscovery of Values* (Boston: Beacon Press, 1953). Nash places Viereck's book in the context of Cold War anti-Communism(s), in *The Conservative Intellectual Movement in America since 1945,* 35th anniv. ed. (Wilmington, Del.: ISI, 2008), 160–161. Cold War liberal Robert Warshow, in "The Liberal Conscience in *The Crucible,*" disputes the implied historical analogy—McCarthyism/Calvinist witch hunt—of Arthur Miller's play because it suggests that the accused are guilty of no wrongdoing and heroically resist trumped-up charges when, in fact, Hiss and many of his fellow-traveling liberal brethren were guilty, at the very least, of egregious moral judgments. Though McCarthy uses a blunderbuss, his scattershot methods do not discredit anti-Communism as a position. The liberal desire to equate anti-Communism with extreme, paranoid, sin-obsessed "Calvinism" bespeaks the desire of the intellectuals to see themselves as morally innocent, falsely accused about the nature of the Left in the 1930s; see Warshow, *The Immediate Experience,* enl. ed. (Cambridge, Mass.: Harvard University Press, 2001), 159–176. Warshow's piece was written for *Commentary* (March 1953), a magazine that took a hard-line anti-Communist position until young Norman Podhoretz took the editorial helm in 1960. Warshow became an editor for *Commentary* beginning in 1946.

30. Richard Fox, *Reinhold Niebuhr: A Biography,* (San Francisco: Harper and Row), 201. The review was titled "Sin Re-Discovered," *Time,* March 24, 1941, 38.

31. Whittaker Chambers, *Witness* (Chicago: Regnery, 1952), 507.

32. Harold Rosenberg, "Couch Liberalism and the Guilty Past," in *The Tradition of the New* (Chicago: University of Chicago Press, 1960) 221–240.

33. Chambers, *Witness,* 21.

34. Kempton, *Part of Our Time,* 35. Sidney Hook, "The Faiths of Whittaker Chambers," *New York Times Book Review,* May 25, 1952, 6. "The New Failure of Nerve" was a wartime symposium in *Partisan Review* published in 1943; Hook's was the lead-off essay, 10, no. 1 (January–February 1943): 2–23;

see also "In Defense of Enlightenment," in Hook, *Pragmatism and the Tragic Sense of Life* (New York: Basic Books, 1974) 195–207. On Hook's career after his defection from the revolutionary Left, see Richard Pell, *The Liberal Mind in a Conservative Age: American Intellectuals in the 1940s and 1950s* (New York: Harper and Row, 1985), 285–300; and Bloom, *Prodigal Sons*, 239–242.

35. Philip Rahv, "The Sense and Nonsense of Whittaker Chambers," *Partisan Review* 19, no. 4 (1952): 472–482; republished in *A Partisan Century: Political Writings from the Partisan Review,* ed. Edith Kurzweil (New York: Columbia University Press 1996), 137–145. It was one of Rahv's missions to rescue T. S. Eliot's art, as well as the works of other authors (Hawthorne, Kafka, Dostoevsky, Tolstoy), from "critics of the school of 'original sin,'"; *Partisan Review* 17, no. 2 (March 1950): 237. Defending individual authors, see Rahv's *Image and Idea* (1949; repr., New York: New Directions, 1957), 49–50, 103–104, 105–119, 141, 196–202. For additional discussions of Chambers's literary tastes, particularly his love for Dostoevsky, see Tanenhaus, *Whittaker Chambers,* 333, 452–453, 454, 466, and Michael Kimmage *The Conservative Turn: Lionel Trilling, Whittaker Chambers, and the Lessons of Anti-Communism* (Cambridge, Mass.: Harvard University Press, 2009), 205, 241.

36. Arthur Schlesinger, Jr., "Whittaker Chambers and His *Witness*" (1952), in his *The Politics of Hope* (Boston: Houghton Mifflin, 1963), 193. Schlesinger refers to a passage in Chapter 1 of *Witness,* in which Chambers says that a voice from Heaven urged him to testify against Alger Hiss (see Chambers, *Witness,* 84–85). Irving Howe commented: "From *Witness* an unsympathetic reader might, in fact, conclude that God spent several years as a special aide to the House Un-American Activities Committee"; Howe, "God, Man, and Stalin," *Nation* 174, no. 21 (May 24, 1952): 20.

37. Daniel Bell states in Chapter 13 of *The End of Ideology:* "the generation of the thirties, whose representative men are Lionel Trilling and Reinhold Niebuhr, were prodigal sons who, in terms of American culture, had turned home" (302). Bell alludes to the Gospel parable of the prodigal son in Luke 15:11–32.

38. Michael Kimmage details Trilling's acquaintance with Chambers in *Conservative Turn,* 15–16, 173–202, 301–302.

39. Lionel Trilling, *The Middle of the Journey* (1947; repr., New York: Scribner, 1976); see Trilling's introduction, xv–xxxiv.

40. Tanenhaus, *Whittaker Chambers: A Biography,* 171.

41. Trilling, *Middle of the Journey,* 300.

42. On Trilling's Marxist period, see Bloom, *Prodigal Sons,* 46–48, 108; Wald, *New York Intellectuals,* 61–65, 72, 102, 112; Kimmage, *Conservative Turn,* 55–65; Podhoretz, *Ex-Friends,* 57–102. It was Alfred Kazin in *New York Jew* (1978) who called Trilling "the most successful leader of deradicalization" (qtd. in Wald, *New York Intellectuals,* 231). Trilling became a member of the anti-Communist American Committee for Cultural Freedom; see Frances Stonor Saunders, *The Cultural Cold War: The CIA and The World of Arts and Letters* (New York: New Press, 1999), 157–158. See also Trilling's attack on F. O. Matthiessen for being a fellow traveler in Bloom, *Prodigal Sons,* 233.

43. "Lionel Trilling's Anxious Humanism: The Search for Authenticity," in Nathan Scott, Jr., *Three American Moralists: Mailer, Trilling, Bellow* (Notre Dame, Ind.: University of Notre Dame Press, 1973), 168.

44. See Lionel Trilling, *Matthew Arnold* (1939; repr., New York: Columbia University Press, 1965); "Reality in America," in *The Liberal Imagination* (1950; repr., New York: Charles Scribner's Sons, 1976), 3–22; "Little Dorrit," in *The Opposing Self* (New York: Viking, 1955), 50–65. "The Fate of Pleasure," in *Beyond Culture* (New York: Viking, 1965), 57–87. On Trilling's attitudes toward Christianity, see Kimmage, *The Conservative Turn,* 149–150, 249–250, 259–260.

45. Matthew Arnold, "Dover Beach," *New Poems* (1867).

46. Writing an open letter to Sidney Hook in the "Religion and the Intellectuals" symposium, Ernst van den Haag endorsed the Catholic Church as a rampart of the democratic state against such seditious "secular religions" as Communism; *Partisan Review* 17, no. 5 (Spring 1950): 607–612. See Hook's "Rejoinder to Mr. van den Haag" in the same issue (612–618). Contrary to some widely cited critics, such as Shadia Drury, Strauss did not treat religion as merely a pious fraud or a tool of the state. He maintained that religion and philosophy, or revelation and reason, made fundamentally different claims and that the claims of each challenged the other's. As even a very sympathetic interpreter, Peter Minowitz, has admitted, however, Strauss did "tend to highlight religion's role as a prop to social order" in a weak democracy. For Strauss's views on religion, see "Reason and Revelation" (1948) in Heinrich Meier, *Leo Strauss and the Theologico-Political Problem* (New York: Cambridge University Press, 2006), 141–180; *Spinoza's Critique of Religion* (New York: Schocken, 1965), particularly "The State and the Social Function," 224–250; and, with Eric Voegelin, *Faith and Political Philosophy: The Correspondence between Leo Strauss and Eric Voegelin, 1934–1964* (Columbia: University of Missouri, 2004), 109–138, 217–234. See Shadia Drury, *Leo Strauss and the American Right* (New York: St. Martin's Press, 1999). For responses to Strauss's critics, especially regarding his statements on religion, see Peter Minowitz, *Straussophobia* (Lanham, Maryland: Lexington Books, 2009), 103–107. Minowitz quoted in Scott Horton, "Straussophobia—Six Questions for Peter Minowitz," *Harper's* (September 29, 2009) http://harpers.org/archive/2009/09/hbc-90005789.

47. Meyer Schapiro, "Religions and the Intellectuals," *Partisan Review* (May/June 1950): 335.

48. Trilling, *Opposing Self,* 49.

49. Trilling, *Matthew Arnold,* 342–346. Puritanism was a hyperthyroidic outgrowth of the "Hebraic" contribution to human development and a crosscurrent to the dominant "Hellenic" tide of progress since the Renaissance. See Matthew Arnold, "Hebraism and Hellenism," Chapter 6 of *Culture and Anarchy* (1869).

50. Trilling, *Middle of the Journey,* 355.

51. Mr. Gurney's characterization may refer to the liberal Protestant ministers who advocated socialism during the thirties, though Gurney's perception of the Christlikeness of the Communist Party was unusual. See the examples of Harry Ward, the young Joseph Matthews, and the members of the United

Front in Martin Marty, *Modern American Religion*, vol. 2, *The Noise of Conflict, 1919–1941* (Chicago: University of Chicago Press, 1991), 288–302; see also Lord Roy's chapter, "The Hammer and Sickle Behind the Cross," in *Apostles of Discord: A Study of Organized Bigotry and Disruption on the Fringes of Protestantism* (Boston: Beacon Press, 1953) 251–284; Roy discusses the post-war afterlife of Christian Communism in America.

52. Trilling, *Middle of the Journey*, 288.

53. West, *American Evasion of Philosophy*, 175, 178. For further discussion of Trilling's theory of modern man, see Scott, *Three American Moralists*, 185–189, 203–209.

54. Trilling, *Middle of the Journey*, 25.

55. *The Middle of the Journey* possibly alludes to Hook's essay "The New Failure of Nerve" in an exchange between Maxim and Kermit Simpson. After Simpson witnesses Maxim kneeling and loudly saying the Lord's Prayer, he asks him, "Have you lost your nerve to that extent?" (339).

56. Philip Rahv's essay, "Dostoevsky in 'The Possessed,'" originally titled "Dostoevski and Politics" in *Partisan Review* 5, no. 2 (July 1938): 25–36, was published in the original 1949 edition of *Image and Idea*, a collection of Rahv's writings from the thirties and forties. See also Rahv's reference to *The Possessed* and the zeal of anti-Stalinism, in "American Intellectuals in the Postwar Situation" (1952), reprinted in *Image and Idea* (1957 edition), 228.

57. Trilling, *Middle of the Journey*, xx.

58. Reinhold Niebuhr, *The Children of Light and the Children of Darkness: A Vindication of Democracy and a Critique of its Traditional Defense* (New York: Scribner, 1945).

59. Trilling, *Middle of the Journey*, 354.

60. At Purdue University in 1971 Trilling acknowledged Erskine as the source of this quotation.; see *The Moral Obligation to be Intelligent*, ed. Leon Wieseltier (Chicago: Northwestern University Press, 2008), ix.

61. For a comparison of Trilling's pragmatism and Rorty's, see James Seaton, "Liberalism and Literature: Richard Rorty and Lionel Trilling," in *Cultural Conservatism, Political Liberalism* (Ann Arbor: University of Michigan Press, 1996) 29–35.

62. Trilling, *Middle of the Journey*, 355.

63. Lionel Trilling, "The Poet as Hero: Keats in His Letters," in *Opposing Self*, 33. See also the preface to *Liberal Imagination*, xiii–xv.

64. Cornel West, in *American Evasion of Philosophy*, argues that "The Poet as Hero" rejects the tragic vision because it is not acceptable to Trilling's kind of liberalism (175, 178). On the contrary, Trilling relies on Keats to present a version of tragedy that excises tragic hubris: "For all his partisanship with social amelioration he had no hope whatever that life could be ordered in such a way that its condition might be anything but tragic" ("Poet as Hero," 35).

65. Trilling, "Poet as Hero," 43.

66. Trilling cites Reinhold Niebuhr (on Kant in *The Nature and Destiny of Man*, vol. 1, *Human Nature* (Upper Saddle River, NJ: Prentice Hall, 1964), 120n12,

in "Art and Fortune," in *Liberal Imagination,* 276; Michael Kimmage details their relationship in *Conservative Turn,* 142, as does Richard Fox in *Reinhold Niebuhr,* 234, 247, 259, 273.

67. Chambers, *Witness,* 16.

68. Trilling, *Middle of the Journey,* 305.

69. See Lionel Trilling, "Our Country and Our Culture: Lionel Trilling Comment," *Partisan Review* 19:3 (May 1952), 318–326; reprinted in *Partisan Century,* 131.

70. Richard Pells, *The Liberal Mind in a Conservative Age* (New York: Harper and Row, 1985), 183–261.

71. Diana Trilling, "The Radical Moralism of Norman Mailer," in *Norman Mailer: A Collection of Critical Essays,* ed. Leo Braudy (Englewood Cliffs, N.J.: Prentice Hall, 1972), 53, 57.

72. Robert J. Begiebing, *Acts of Regeneration: Allegory and Archetype* (Columbia: University of Missouri Press, 1980), 13–32.

73. Lionel Trilling, "Greatness with One Fault In It," *Kenyon Review* 4, no. 1 (1942): 99–102.

74. Trilling, *Matthew Arnold,* 226–227.

4. McCarthyism through Sentimental Melodrama and Film Noir

1. Richard Rovere, *Senator Joseph McCarthy* (New York: Harcourt Brace, 1959), 66, 72; *The Night of the Hunter,* DVD, directed by Charles Laughton (1955; Santa Monica, MGM, 01/25/00).

2. See the following essays: Leo Braudy, *The World in a Frame: What We See in Films* (New York: Doubleday, 1976); Michael Brunas, "The Night of the Hunter," *Scarlet Street,* 1, no. 3 (Summer 1991): 33–38, 64; Paul Hammond, "Melmoth in Norman Rockwell Land . . . on *The Night of the Hunter,*" *Sight and Sound* 48 no. 2 (Spring 1979): 105–109; Robin Wood, "Charles Laughton on Grubb Street," in *The Modern American Novel and the Movies,* ed. Gerald Peary and Roger Shatzkin (New York: Frederick Ungar, 1978), 204–215; Simon Callow, *The Night of the Hunter* (London: BFI Film Classics, 2000). Once United Artists agreed to finance *Night of the Hunter,* director Charles Laughton traveled to New York with the express purpose of screening all of D. W. Griffith's films at MOMA. Also fans of Griffith, his cinematographer, Stanley Cortez *(The Black Cat, Secret Beyond the Door),* and his screenwriter, James Agee, became students of the director along with Laughton, as the three of them together reviewed the whole oeuvre. Agee refers to these sessions in a letter to Paul Gregory, January 14, 1955, *The Night of the Hunter* Archive, National Library of Congress, Washington, D.C. Elsa Lanchester, Laughton's widow, donated his papers.

3. See Arthur Schlesinger, Jr., *The Vital Center* (New York: De Capo, 1949), 161–163.

4. Reinhold Niebuhr, *The Nature and Destiny of Man,* vol. 1, *Human Nature* [hereafter, *Human Nature*] (1964, repr. New York: Charles Scribner's Sons, 1941), 266, 268. For scriptural references associating children with corruptibility, see Matthew 19:4, Mark 10:14, and Luke 18:6.

5. Reinhold Niebuhr, "America's Precarious Eminence," in *American Defense Policy,* 8th ed., ed. Paul J. Bolt (Baltimore: Johns Hopkins University Press, 1965), 16–23. Reprinted from *Reinhold Niebuhr on Politics,* ed. Harry Davis and Robert C. Good (New York: Charles Scribner's Sons, 1960), 269–283.

6. Leslie Fiedler, "Afterthoughts on the Rosenbergs," in *A Fiedler Reader* (Amherst, N.Y.: Prometheus Books, 1999), 62.

7. See Richard Hofstadter, *The Age of Reform* (New York: Vintage, 1955), 60–81; *The Paranoid Style in American Politics* (Cambridge, Mass.: Harvard University Press, 1996), 29–36; and *Anti-Intellectualism in American Life* (New York: Vintage Books, 1962), 134–136.

8. Lionel Trilling, *The Middle of the Journey* (1947; repr., New York: Scribner, 1976), 139–141.

9. Trilling's introduction, "Huckleberry Finn: 1948," is reprinted in *The Moral Obligation to Be Intelligent: Selected Essays* (New York: Farrar, Straus and Giroux, 2000).

10. Whittaker Chambers, *Witness* (Chicago: Regnery, 1952), 3.

11. Hiss's attorneys recruited Dr. Carl Binger and a Harvard psychiatrist, Dr. Henry A. Murray, who had psychoanalyzed Hitler (in absentia!), to testify that Chambers was a psychopath who, by his mental condition, could not help but tell lies. In *Witness,* Chambers reverses the charges of the defense team, accusing Hiss and his liberal supporters of suffering from psychosis (790, 793). On the psychiatrists' testimonies, see Alan Nadel, *Containment Culture: American Narratives, Postmodernism, and the Atomic Age* (Durham, N.C.: Duke University Press, 1995), 82; Sam Tanenhaus, *Whittaker Chambers: A Biography* (New York: Random House, 1997), 425.

12. Despite his support for investigations into the backgrounds of all suspected Communists, ex-Communists, and fellow-travelers, Chambers regarded McCarthy as a "raven of disaster," because the senator's bludgeoning, reckless approach risked trivializing an issue of national—and world—security; see Derek Leebaert, *The Fifty-Year Wound: The True Price of America's Cold War Victory* (New York: Little, Brown, 2002), 113. Chambers's attitude toward McCarthy is congruous with Niebuhr's and the American Committee for Democratic Action's; see Richard Fox, *Reinhold Niebuhr: A Biography* (San Francisco: Harper and Row, 1985), 252–255.

13. According to Ralph de Toledano (an anti-Communist and a *Newsweek* journalist), liberals dishonestly identified with the criminal Hiss yet protested he was innocent; "The Liberal Disintegration—A Conservative View," *Freeman* 1 (November 13, 1950): 109, 110. De Toledano followed up with a book-length best seller, co-written with Victor Lasky, *Seeds of Treason: The True Story of the Hiss-Chambers Tragedy* (New York: Funk and Wagnalls, 1950). Irving Kristol, though no defender of McCarthy, augmented the perception, already set by Chambers and de Toledano, that liberals bore a good deal of responsibility for McCarthy's successful raids on their reputations since they had not sufficiently distanced themselves from Communists; "'Civil Liberties' 1952—A Study in Confusion," *Commentary,* March 1952, at www.commentarymagazine .com/viewarticle.cfm/-civil-liberties-1952-a-study-in-confusion-br-em-do-we-

defend-our-rights-by-protecting-communists-em-1445 (accessed December 8, 2009). Norman Podhoretz defends Kristol's controversial essay in Podhoretz, *Ex-Friends: Falling out with Allen Ginsberg, Lionel and Diana Trilling, Lillian Hellman, Hannah Arendt, and Norman Mailer* (San Francisco, Encounter Books, 2000), 10–11.

14. Joseph McCarthy, Lincoln Day radio address (Republican Women's Club, Wheeling, W.Va., February 9, 1950). The term "McCarthyism" was probably coined by political cartoonist Herbert Block (Herblock), but it was subsequently taken up by McCarthy himself, who in 1952, published *McCarthyism: The Fight for America* (New York: Devin-Adair, 1952). For commentary, see J. Ronald Oakley, *God's Country: America in the Fifties* (New York: Dember Books, 1986), 59–69.

15. See the rhetoric throughout *McCarthyism: The Fight for America*.

16. Qtd. in David Halberstam, *The Fifties* (New York: Fawcett Columbine, 1994), 234.

17. Nadel, *Containment Culture*, 77.

18. Michael Rogin, "Kiss Me Deadly: Communism, Motherhood, and Cold War Movies," *Representations* 6 (Spring 1984): 1–36.

19. See J. Edgar Hoover, *Masters of Deceit* (Pensacola, Fla.: Beka Book, 1958), 87, 185–196. See also James Burnham, *The Web of Subversion: Underground Networks in the U.S. Government* (New York: J. Day, 1954).

20. Harry Truman publicly referred to McCarthy as a liar, and Washington columnists wrote that "'McCarthy is the only major politician in the country who can be labeled 'liar' without fear of libel'"; Oakley, *God's Country,* 61–62; and Ellen Schrecker, *Many Are the Crimes: McCarthyism in America* (New York: Little, Brown, 1998), 242. For one of the key liberal attacks on McCarthy's Washington influence, see "Cultivation of Fear," *Christian Century,* April 5, 1950, 423–424. For a survey of the rumors imagining McCarthy's operatives and backstage counselors, see Robert Ellwood, *The Fifties Spiritual Marketplace* (New Brunswick, N.J.: Rutgers University Press, 1997), 27–30. See also the VHS *Point of Order!* directed by Emile de Antonio (1964; New Yorker Video, 1998), a documentary compilation of clips from the Army-McCarthy Hearings, wherein the Wisconsin Senator consistently refuses to reveal his sources. The most amusing of all the paranoid theories about McCarthy is, of course, director John Frankenheimer's *The Manchurian Candidate* (MGM/UA, 1962), which looks back on the Korean War period from the vantage of the Kennedy years.

21. Edward Shils, *The Torment of Secrecy: The Background and Consequences of American Security Policies* (1996, repr. Chicago: Elephant Paperbacks, 1956), 197.

22. Fiedler, "Afterthoughts on the Rosenbergs," 55–56.

23. Leslie Fiedler, "Hiss, Chambers, and the Age of Innocence," in *An End to Innocence* (Boston: Beacon Press, 1995), 24. "McCarthyism and the Intellectuals," in *An End to Innocence,* 46–87. The characterization of McCarthy's "melodrama" and Fiedler's allusion to Dostoevsky's "the Grand Inquisitor," 54, 67. Other quotes, 71, 72.

24. Morris Dickstein, *The Gates of Eden* (New York: Basic Books, 1977), 42–43.
25. Fiedler, "Hiss, Chambers," 23.
26. Dickstein, *Gates of Eden,* 42.
27. In "McCarthyism and the Intellectuals," Fiedler warns that the liberal must not adopt the "self-righteousness" of the ex-Communist James Wechsler who still holds to the "legendary melodrama he had believed in as a youth"; *An End to Innocence,* 74, 84.
28. Williams, "Melodrama Revisited," *Refiguring American Film Genres,* ed. Nick Browne (Berkeley: University of California Press, 1998), 50–51; and Peter Brooks, *The Melodramatic Imagination* (New Haven: Yale University Press, 1976), 11–23, 32.
29. See Leslie Fiedler's *Love and Death in the American Novel* (New York: Delta Books, 1966); and Ann Douglas's *The Feminization of American Culture* (New York: Anchor Books, 1977).
30. Sergei Eisenstein, "Dickens, Griffith, and the Film Today," in *Film Form,* ed. and trans. Jay Leyda (New York: Harcourt, Brace, 1949), 229.
31. D. W. Griffith, qtd. in Robert Lang, *American Film Melodrama* (Princeton, N.J.: Princeton University Press, 1980), 58.
32. Thomas Elsaesser, "Tales of Sound and Fury," *Monogram* 4 (1972); reprinted in Bill Nichols, ed. *Movies and Methods* (Berkeley: University of California Press, 1985) 2:165–194.
33. Jonathan Munby, *Public Enemies, Public Heroes: Screening the Gangster from "Little Caesar" to "Touch of Evil"* (Chicago: University of Chicago Press, 1998), 215. See also J. P. Telotte, *Voices in the Dark: The Narrative Patterns of Film Noir* (Urbana: University of Illinois Press, 1989) 1–41; and Dana Polan, *Power and Paranoia: American Narrative and Film, 1940–1950* (New York: Columbia University Press, 1986), 193–249.
34. For discussion of noir as "a sensibility or a worldview that results from the death of God," see the essays in Mark Conrad, ed., *The Philosophy of Film Noir* (Lexington: The University Press of Kentucky, 2006), 7–22, 41–48, 91–106, 107–124, 187–206, 232–238. Most of these essays take as their point of departure Robert Porfirio's classic essay on the anti-Enlightenment, yet secular, mood of noir, "'No Way Out': Existential Motifs in the *Film Noir*" (1976), collected in Alain Silver and James Ursini, eds., *Film Noir Reader* (New York: Limelight Editions, 1996), 77–93. James Naremore discusses the influence of T. S. Eliot and Graham Greene's views of the faux Christian West in the chapter "Modernism and Blood Melodrama," in his *More Than Night: Film Noir in its Contexts* (Berkeley: University of California Press, 1998), 40–81.
35. Noir's critics argue that it rejects classical Hollywood conventions and, more arguably, that it presents a full-fledged oppositional view of the country. Since "film noir" entered critical vocabulary, it has been associated with subversive politics, more than any other Hollywood form except, perhaps, the pre-Code gangster films. See James Naremore, "From Dark Films to Black Lists," in *More Than Night,* 96–135; Jonathan Munby, "*Noir:* the Un-American Film Art," in *Public Enemies, Public Heroes,* 186–220; and Paule Buhle and Dave Wagner, "Politics and Mythology of Film Art—The *Noir* Era," in *Radical Hol-*

lywood: The Untold Story Behind America's Favorite Movies (New York: New Press, 2002), 321–368. For incisive criticism of Buhle and Wagner's work, see Thom Andersen's afterword to Frank Krutnik, ed., *'Un-American' Hollywood: Politics and Film in the Blacklist Era* (New Brunswick, N.J.: Rutgers University Press, 2007), 264–275. Andersen's important essay, "Red Hollywood" (1985), reprinted in the same volume, defines a much shorter list of movies from the noir canon, works he categorizes as *film gris,* that show a manifest Marxist impact on their style, content, and sensibility: "noir films in which a social critique carries more weight than a psychological diagnosis" (267).

36. Robert Lindner, *Must You Conform?* (New York: Rinehart, 1956), 161. Richard Rovere cites several psychological studies of McCarthy and also compares the senator to Lindner's profile of the psychopathic personality in *Rebel Without a Cause* (1944). See Rovere, *Senator Joseph McCarthy,* 66–70. Having first emerged in nineteenth century European psychology, the psychopath type, which became ubiquitous in American culture and social discourse throughout the forties and fifties, delineated a deviant extrovert whose seemingly dysfunctional conscience challenged the assumptions of both rational ethics and Christian morality; see Hervey M. Cleckley, "Psychopathic States," *American Handbook of Psychiatry,* ed. Silvero Arieti, v. 1, Chapter 28 (New York: Basic Books, 1959), 567–588.

37. Callow, *Night of the Hunter,* 32. The term "two-fisted tough guy" is from Mort Nathanson, "The Night of the Hunter," a fifty-nine-page feature story manual commissioned by Paul Gregory and United Artists; in Lanchester's *The Night of the Hunter* Archive. On Mitchum's career, see Lee Server, *Robert Mitchum: "Baby, I don't care."* (New York: St. Martin's Press, 2001).

38. Wood, "Charles Laughton on Grubb Street," 213–214; and Braudy, *The World in a Frame,* 234.

39. In Gerd Oswald's 1956 adaptation of Ira Levin's novel, *A Kiss Before Dying* (1953), the college psychopath (Robert Wagner) plots the murder of his pregnant fiancée while a humanities professor lectures sonorously on Jonathan Edwards and the problem of free will.

40. Nadel, *Containment Culture,* 34.

41. Shils, *Torment of Secrecy,* 197.

42. James Agee, *Agee on Film: Five Film Scripts* (Boston: Beacon Press, 1960), 292–293.

43. Brooks, *Melodramatic Imagination,* 47.

44. Roberta Pearson, *The Modesty of Nature: Performance Style in the Griffith Biographs* (Ph.D. dissertation, New York University, 1987); Brooks, "The Text of Muteness," in *Melodramatic Imagination,* 56–80; Lang, *American Film Melodrama,* 58–59, 72–73; Tom Gunning, *D. W. Griffith and the Origins of Film Narrative: The Early Years at Biograph* (Urbana: University of Illinois Press, 1991), 106–107.

45. The phrase "a sentimental picture" comes from *The Night of the Hunter* screenplay, which Laughton revised; see James Agee, *Agee on Film,* vol. 2, *Screenplays* (New York: Grosset and Dunlap, 1958), 266.

46. Brooks, *Melodramatic Imagination,* 29. See, for comparison, the opening scenes of *Orphans of the Storm* (1921), which show the two sisters, soon to be caught up in the French Revolution, peacefully at play.

47. Richard Rubenstein, *After Auschwitz* (Baltimore: Johns Hopkins University Press, 1966), 141.

48. The phrase comes from Charles Laughton's 1955 recording for RCA Victor, *"The Night of the Hunter":* Narrated by Charles Laughton, CD Bear Family Records, 1998.

49. On the iconography of Depression-era Left populism, especially the common man turned reluctant criminal, see Richard Slotkin's *Gunfighter Nation* (Norman: University of Oklahoma Press, 1998), 293–303. See also Michael Denning, *The Cultural Front* (New York: Verso, 1997), 123–129, 151–159, 222–229; Richard Pells, *Radical Visions and American Dreams* (Chicago: University of Chicago Press, 1998), 202–219, 246–252, 310–319.

50. On the identification of thirties' Left liberal and radical intellectuals with male laborers, see Pells, *Radical Visions and American Dreams,* 151–193, 202–218, 246–262.

51. The scene showing Ben's sentencing has no correlate in Grubb's novel, and it may echo a moment from "The Mother and the Law," one of the four parallel stories in Griffith's *Intolerance* (1916). A young married man (the Boy) loses his job, amidst mounting labor struggles with factory owners, and ends up becoming involved in crime and tried for murder. When the judge hands down the sentence, he denies pleas for mercy and tells the Boy, "You will be hanged by the neck until you are dead, dead, dead."

52. Producer Paul Gregory's publicity team included a 1920 photograph of Gish and the cast from *Way Down East* in *Hunter*'s press package, and the press release for Lilian Gish highlights *Way Down East* among her "classic films"; both are available in Elsa Lanchester's *Night of the Hunter* Archive.

53. Griffith's first film, *The Adventures of Dollie* (in the MOMA Collection), has as its central action a child's river journey. The playful little girl, stolen from her family garden by a gypsy, floats downriver in a basket, as the currents fortuitously carry her back to her loving home.

54. The river sequence contains some of *Hunter*'s most extraordinary imagery. See George Turner, "Creating 'Night of the Hunter,'" *American Cinematographer* v. 62 (December 1982): 1271–1276, 1335–1342.

55. The phrase comes from Charles Laughton's 1955 recording for RCA Victor, *"The Night of the Hunter."*

56. Callow, *Night of the Hunter,* 74.

57. Qtd. in Laughton's revised screenplay for *Night of the Hunter;* see Agee, *Agee on Film,* vol. 2, *Screenplays,* 327.

58. Wood, "Charles Laughton on Grubb Street," 211–213.

59. Lionel Trilling, *Sincerity and Authenticity* (New York: Harcourt Brace, 1974), 14, 16.

60. Rovere, *Senator Joseph McCarthy,* 71–73.

61. Fiedler, "Hiss, Chambers, and the Age of Innocence," 23. David Riesman, who had never been a fellow traveler, deemed the rhetoric of confession pes-

simistic and misleading, but his own model of communication in the Cold War climate just as firmly rejects the "contemporary cult of sincerity," which he finds pronounced among youth; see Riesman, *Individualism Reconsidered* (New York: Free Press, 1954), 12, 19–21, 47–54. Anticipating the liberal critique of the New Left in the sixties, Riesman expresses apprehension over these benighted Holden Caulfields. Their ideology of transparency is not a mode of self-disclosure alternative to coerced confession, but a habituated middle-class style of overweening frankness, subjectively affirming perhaps, but ultimately inauthentic and guilt-motivated (12, 19, 22, 47–50, 52–54). Riesman, as in so many other cases, does little to change the confessional discourse that he examines, as if he is an optimistic outsider; the utopian insight he affords is that even sincerity is a form of inauthenticity.

62. Shils, *Torment of Secrecy*, 197.
63. Reinhold Niebuhr, *The Irony of American History* (New York: Scribner's, 1952), 146, 170.
64. Qtd. in Laughton's revised screenplay for *Night of the Hunter;* see *Agee on Film*, vol. 2, *Screenplays*.
65. The phrase "senses in a flash" comes from Charles Laughton's 1955 recording for RCA Victor, *"The Night of the Hunter."*
66. Braudy, *World in a Frame*, 95, 234–245.
67. Simon Callow, *Charles Laughton: A Difficult Actor* (London: Methuen, 1987), 229, 233–234.
68. Callow, *Night of the Hunter*, 75–76.
69. Larry Ceplair and Steven Englund, *The Inquisition in Hollywood: Politics in the Film Community, 1930–1960* (New York: Doubleday, 1980), 328–331, 336–339.

5. The Mass Culture Critique's Implications for American Religion

1. Thomas Merton, *The Seven Storey Mountain* (San Diego: Harcourt Brace and Jovanovich, 1948).
2. I am using phraseology from Merton's gloss to his 1948 essay, "Poetry and Contemplation," in *The Literary Essays of Thomas Merton* (New York: New Directions, 1981), 339.
3. For some classic formulations on mass culture and the mass society, see Bernard Rosenberg and David White's anthology, *Mass Culture: The Popular Arts in America* (New York: Free Press, 1957), especially the essays by Clement Greenberg, Leo Lowenthal, Dwight MacDonald, and Irving Howe (whose response typifies the line taken by *Dissent*). See also Alfred Kazin, "Religion and the Intellectuals," *Partisan Review* 17, no. 4 (April 1950): 234 and the statements in the 1952 *Partisan Review* symposium, "Our Country and Our Culture," especially those by Lionel Trilling, Philip Rahv, Norman Mailer, and C. Wright Mills; in *A Partisan Century*, ed. Edith Kurzweil (New York: Columbia University Press 1996), 115–136. By Mills, see also *White Collar: The American Middle Classes* (New York: Oxford University Press, 1951), 332–340; and *The Power Elite* (New York: Oxford University Press, 1956), 311–

320. Mailer's key statements on mass culture, aside from his contribution to the *Partisan Review*'s 1952 symposium, are "From Surplus Value to the Mass Media" and "A Riddle in Psychic Economy," in *Advertisements for Myself* (1959; repr., Cambridge, Mass.: Harvard University Press, 1992), 434–438.

4. T. S. Eliot, *Christianity and Culture* (New York: Harcourt, 1948). See also Eliot's remarks on "the insidious influence" of "popular novelists," "popular plays," "amusement," and "the cheap and rapid–breeding cinema," in "Religion and Literature" (1935) and "Marie Lloyd" (1922), in *Selected Prose of T. S. Eliot*, ed., Frank Kermode (New York: Farrar, Straus and Giroux, 1975), 103, 172–174. Dwight MacDonald coined the term "mass culture" in his essay "A Theory of 'Popular' Culture'" (1944) and expanded the idea in "A Theory of Mass Culture" (1953). Eliot cites MacDonald's 1944 essay in his *Notes towards the Definition of Culture*, which is the second part of *Christianity and Culture*.

5. Editorial preface, "Our Country and Our Culture," *Partisan Review* 19 no. 3 (May–June 1952): 282–287. After his disenchanting experience with the factionalized Council for a Democratic Germany and his blacklisting by the U.S. Army for his affiliation with the mistakenly identified "pro-Communist" Council, Tillich withdrew from active interest in politics, and his religious socialism became basically a spiritual orientation lamenting what he took to be an aimless American emphasis on technological mastery and productivity for the sake, merely, of producing ever more things without regards to ultimate ends (love, justice). Over the course of the fifties, in such books as his best–selling *The Courage to Be* (1952), Tillich's ideas—deftly mixing Christian theology, existentialism, depth psychology, and high modernism—made him a favorite figure of universities, the mass media (especially *Newsweek* and *Time*), and the college–educated middle class. On Tillich's career in America after World War II, see Wilhelm and Marion Pauck, *Paul Tillich: His Life and Thought* (New York: Harper and Row, 1989), 218–285. British humanist William Empson dubbed American academics Hugh Kenner (Catholic) and New Critic Cleanth Brooks (Anglican) "neo-Christians," a term he coined in reference to the revival of orthodoxy among literary critics after World War II; see John Haffenden, *William Empson*, vol. 2, *Against the Christians* (London: Oxford University Press, 2006), 432–453, 560–605; for Empson's disputes with Hugh Kenner, see 432, 545. Niebuhr, "Our Country and Our Culture," *Partisan Review* 19:3 (1952), 303. Though its focus was politics and theology, *Christianity and Crisis* did review arts and entertainment in the 1950s and 1960s. The magazine's writers, who included Nathan A. Scott, Jr. and Robert McAfee Brown, preferred highbrow culture (Shakespeare, Camus, Faulkner, Kafka, Fellini, Pasolini) and gave scant attention to popular music, TV, or films. See Mark Hultheser, *Building a Protestant Left: Christianity and Crisis Magazine, 1941–1993* (Knoxville: University of Tennessee Press, 1999), 94–100. *The Christian Century* carried capsule reviews of movies and occasional articles on the churches' competition with, and regrettable secularization by, mass media and entertainment. See the editorial, "Cur Vadis?" 69 no. 13, March 26, 1952, 359–361; also Charles Eliot Morrison, "Protestantism and Commercialized Entertainment," 63 no. 18, May 1, 1946, 553–556.

6. T. S. Driver, Melanie J. Wright, *Religion and Film* (London: I. B. Tauris, 2008), 73. Several ministers wrote letters to *Christian Century* taking exception to Driver's "'neo-orthodox'" comments (74–75); William Whyte, *The Organization Man* (New York: Simon and Schuster, 1956), 254, 255, 256; Elkin, "God, Radio, and the Movies," in Rosenberg, *Mass Culture*, 314; William Phillips, "The Success of Faith—Or Is It the Faith of Success?" in *Commentary* (March 1954), 272–275.

7. R. Laurence Moore, *Selling God: American Religion in the Marketplace of Culture* (New York: Oxford University Press, 1994), 147.

8. Paul Gorman, *Left Intellectuals and Popular Culture* (Chapel Hill: University of North Carolina Press, 1996), 20–33.

9. Frances Stonor Saunders, *The Cultural Cold War: The CIA and The World of Arts and Letters* (New York: New Press, 1999); and Frank Ninkovich, *The Diplomacy of Ideas: U.S. Policy and Cultural Relations, 1938–1950* (Cambridge: Cambridge University Press, 1981), 176.

10. Moore, *Selling God*, 239; and Stephen Prothero, *American Jesus: How the Son of God Became a National Icon* (New York: Farrar, Straus and Giroux, 2003), 117–118.

11. Ninkovich, *Diplomacy of Ideas*, 119–120. See Jackson Lears, "A Matter of Taste: Corporate Cultural Hegemony in a Mass-Consumption Society," in *Recasting America: Culture and Politics in the Age of Cold War*, ed. Lary May (Chicago: University of Chicago Press, 1989), 41–42.

12. Eliot's Anglo-Catholicism and his joint concern with the living organ of tradition have roots in scholasticism and in the Oxford movement of the Church of England (especially as refracted in Henry Newman and Matthew Arnold). He also had strong affinities with the agrarian movement of the American South, as Eliot acknowledged in the opening of the first of his three Page-Barbour lectures given at the University of Virginia in 1933, collected by Faber and Faber as *After Strange Gods: A Primer of Modern Heresy* (1934). Russell Kirk's *The Conservative Mind from Burke to Eliot* (Washington, D.C.: Regnery, 1953) stated: "His books *The Idea of a Christian Society* (1939) and *Notes towards the Definition of Culture* (1948) are among the most significant conservative writings of recent years" (411). The two texts by Eliot were also published together as *Christianity and Culture* (see note 4).

Cleanth Brooks, John Ransom, and Allen Tate, like Kirk and Eliot, shared grave reservations about the tendency of industrial society to uproot accumulated customs and an associated sense of ultimate ends, enabling them to be replaced with abstract identities and disciplines of efficiency that "collectivized" men by reducing them to means or consigning to them the functions of things. See Ransom's *God Without Thunder: An Unorthodox Defense of Orthodoxy* (New York: Harcourt Brace and Co. 1930); Tate's essays "Religion and the Old South," in *On the Limits of Poetry, Selected Essays, 1928–1948* (Athens, Ohio: Swallow Press, 1948), and "What Is a Traditional Society?" in *Reason and Madness* (New York: G. P. Putnam, 1941); and Cleanth Brooks's "The Enduring Faith," in *Why the South Will Survive, By Fifteen Southerners* (Athens: University of Georgia Press, 1981) and "A Plea to the Protestant

Churches," in *Who Owns America? A New Declaration of Independence,* ed. Herbert Agar and Allen Tate (Boston: Houghton Mifflin, 1936), 323–333 ("A Plea" originally published as "The Christianity of Modernism," *American Review* 6 [November 1935–March 1936]: 435–436.) Brooks embraces Tillich's and Eliot's analyses of industrial mass culture in *The Hidden God* (New Haven: Yale University Press, 1963), originally five lectures Brooks delivered for the 1955 Faculty Conference on Theology at Trinity College, Connecticut; the preface and conclusion were added in 1963.

A native Canadian and professor of English at Santa Barbara (and subsequently at Johns Hopkins and the University of Georgia), Hugh Kenner, a Catholic convert, was chapleted as a don of English modernism with the publication of *Dublin's Joyce* (1956). A central feature of this study is Kenner's predilection for, and knightly defense of, scholasticism, which can be credited with beginning the "Catholic recuperation of Joyce" from apostasy, signaled by the publication, two years later, of Jesuit priest William Noon's *Joyce and Aquinas* (1958).

13. Gabriel Vahanian, *The Death of God: The Culture of Our Post-Christian Era* (New York: George Braziller, 1961) 73; Martin Marty, *The New Shape of American Religion* (New York: Harper, 1959), 73 no. 28, 32, 88.

14. Paul Tillich, "Communicating the Christian Message: A Question to Christian Ministers and Teachers," first published in *Union Seminary Quarterly Review* 7, no. 4 (June 1952): 3–11; reprinted as the conclusion to Tillich's *Theology of Culture* [collected essays from 1946 TO 1957], ed. Robert C. Kimball (New York: Oxford University Press, 1959), 201–213. On "the Protestant principle," see "The Protestant Principle and the Proletarian Situation" (1931), in *The Protestant Era* (Chicago: University of Chicago Press, 1948) 161–181; "Protestantism and Artistic Style"(1955), in *On Art and Architecture,* ed. John and Jane Dillenberger (New York: Crossroad, 1987) 119–125; and "Protestantism" (1957), in *The Essential Tillich,* ed. C. Forrester Church (Chicago: University of Chicago Press, 1987), 69–86.

15. Tillich, *Theology of Culture,* 40–51, 68–75; "Art and Ultimate Reality" (1951) 139–157 and "Existentialist Aspects of Modern Art" (1955) 89–101, in *On Art and Architecture.* See also Tillich's "The Courage of Despair in Contemporary Art and Literature," part of the fifth chapter of his popular *The Courage to Be* (1952). As a measure of Tillich's notoriety as a philosopher of art, MOMA asked him in 1959 to write a preface for an exhibition catalogue, *New Images of Man,* on the human figure in the "revolutionary styles in the visual arts," by curator Peter Selz and published New York: MOMA, 1959. Quotation is from Tillich's preface in the catalog, 9.

16. The author of *The Age of Anxiety* (1947, started in 1944), the long poem whose title came to stamp the Cold War era, Auden converted, or returned, to Christianity in 1940. Though Barth, Reinhold Niebuhr, and Tillich were, and remained, significant tutors to his faith, Auden had mellowed on Protestant neoorthodoxy and the Kierkegaard revival that had transfixed him around the period of his conversion. On Auden's Anglo-Catholicism, see Edward Mendelson. *Late Auden* (New York: Farrar, Strauss and Giroux, 1999), 129–163; and

the most complete treatment, Arthur Kirsch's *Auden and Christianity* (New Haven: Yale University Press, 2005).

17. Cleanth Brooks, "Discourse to the Gentiles" (on T. S. Eliot), in *Hidden God,* 72.

18. There have been several recent monographs on popular culture and religious subculture, specifically conservative evangelicalism. The following studies focus on entertainment produced by conservative evangelicals intended not only for insiders to the subculture but also encouraging (and eliciting) cross-over audiences: Heather Hendershot, *Shaking the World for Jesus: Media and Conservative Evangelical Culture* (Chicago: University of Chicago Press, 2004); and Hillary Warren, *There's Never Been a Show Like Veggie Tales: Sacred Messages in a Secular Market* (Walnut Creek, Calif.: Altamira Press, 2005).

19. The actual Scopes trial happened in Dayton, Tennessee, where Kramer filmed *Inherit the Wind*'s exterior scenes. The name change to *Hills*boro evokes the rural hick.

20. Frank Capra's pre-Code *The Miracle Woman* (Columbia, 1931) is inspired by the career of faith-healing revivalist Aimee Simple MacPherson.

21. For treatments of the liberal conscience films, see Peter Biskind, *Seeing is Believing* (New York: Henry Holt, 1983), 9–33; Richard Maltby, *Hollywood and the Ideology of Consensus* (Metchuen, N.J.: Scarecrow Press, 1983), 240–290; Michael P. Rogin, *Blackface, White Noise* (Berkeley: University of California Press, 1996), 209–250; and Larry Ceplair and Steven Englund, *The Inquisition in Hollywood: Politics in the Film Community, 1930–1960* (New York: Doubleday, 1980), 73–74, 245, 317–318, 441–444.

22. Stanley Kramer with Thomas Coffey, *A Mad, Mad, Mad, Mad World: Kramer on Kramer* (New York: Harcourt, Brace, 1997), 174.

23. Reflecting on the Scopes trial some thirty years after he covered it as a correspondent for the *Nation,* Joseph Wood Krutch expressed disappointment with Lawrence and Lee's play *Inherit the Wind* because it saw the event as "a witch trial" "in terms of the grim ideological conflicts of our own day"—mistaking "Bryanism" for "McCarthyism." Krutch's remarks apply equally well to Kramer's adaptation of the play; see Krutch's autobiography, *More Lives Than One* (New York: William Sloane, 1962), 145–146, 159–160. On the play's and the film's connection to the cultural legacy of the Scopes Trial, especially those aspects of the legacy effecting the image of fundamentalism, see Edward J. Larson, *Summer for the Gods: The Scopes Trial and America's Continuing Debate Over Science and Religion* (New York: Basic Books, 2006) 234–246.

24. The pogrom was added by screenwriters Nathan Smith and Harold Douglas, who had worked with Kramer on *The Defiant Ones.* There is no comparable scene in Lawrence and Lee's play.

25. Adorno's "Culture Industry: Enlightenment as Mass Deception" essay was not available in English until the early seventies, when *The Dialectic of Enlightenment* was finally translated.

26. Theodor Adorno, *The Psychological Technique of Martin Luther Thomas' Radio Addresses* (Stanford, Calif.: Stanford University Press, 2000). The text,

originally written in English, was first published by a German house, Suhrkamp Verlag, in 1975. According to the text's internal dates (Adorno refers to the present time as 1943 on p. 122), it was written during World War II, prior to the completion of Adorno and Horkheimer's long essay on "Elements of Anti-Semitism," which became the last chapter of *The Dialectic of Enlightenment.* The text, as Adorno indicates, offers many previews of the more famous essay, notably the theory that the fascist imitates what he wants to destroy. For a close discussion of Adorno's study of Thomas, in light of Adorno's subsequent writings on fascism and the culture industry, see Paul Apostolidis, *Stations of the Cross: Adorno and Christian Right Radio* (Durham, N.C.: Duke University Press, 2000), 57–89.

27. Adorno, *Psychological Technique,* 81, 83, 84, 75–76.
28. See Leo Lowenthal, *Prophets of Deceit: A Study of the Techniques of the American Agitator* (New York: Harper, 1949), xi, 1–19, 137. Apostolidis discusses subtle, but telling, differences in the methods of the two studies, in *Stations of the Cross,* 71–75.
29. The Institute, established in Frankfurt, Germany, was temporarily relocated to New York City from 1933 to 1950.
30. Martin Jay, *The Dialectical Imagination: A History of the Frankfurt School and the Institute of Social Research, 1923–1950* (Berkeley: University of California Press, 1973), 217. The most incisive critique of Adorno's theses on the culture industry is Andreas Huyssen's essay, "Adorno in Reverse: From Hollywood to Richard Wagner," in *After the Great Divide: Modernism, Mass Culture, Postmodernism* (Bloomington: Indiana University Press, 1986), 16–43.
31. Lawrence Levine, *Highbrow and Lowbrow: The Emergence of Cultural Hierarchy in America* (Cambridge, Mass.: Harvard University Press, 1990), 171–242, quotations 149. Dwight MacDonald coined the term "mass culture" in "A Theory of 'Popular' Culture," published in his magazine, *Politics* vol. 1, no. 1 (February 1944), 20–23. On the development of cultural hierarchy, see also Susan Hegeman, *Patterns for America: Modernism and the Concept of Culture* (Princeton: Princeton University Press, 1999), 129ff; Gorman, *Left Intellectuals and Popular Culture,* 20–54, 54–81; Alan Trachtenberg. *The Incorporation of America: Culture and Society in the Gilded Age* (1982; repr., New York: Farrar, Straus and Giroux, 2007), 158–161. On the celebration of movie culture, see Robert Sklar, *Movie-Made America* (New York: Vintage, 1975).
32. John Dewey, *Art as Experience* (New York: Penguin, 1934), 4–10, 21–27, 84, 258, 298, 356–358.
33. After the war's end, Adorno expressed diminishing hope that the collective agent of Marxism could be the negating agent that its historical dialectic required; Eugene Lunn, *Marxism and Modernism; An historical study of Lucács, Brecht, Benjamin, and Adorno* (Berkeley: University of California Press, 1982), 199, 207, 209. The resistance of individual subjectivity thus took primacy over political praxis in Adorno's cultural theory, though he never sacrificed Marxist analytical categories.

34. Raymond Williams persuasively classes Eliot as a critic (in the line of Burke, Coleridge, Arnold, and Ruskin) who sees culture as "a whole way of life" that radically protests the conditions of liberal society, with its haphazard merging of democracy and industrialism; *Culture and Society, 1780–1950* (New York: Columbia University Press, 1983), esp. 232–243.

35. T. S. Eliot, "Religion and Literature," in *Selected Prose*, 104.

36. As Peter Bürger argues, autonomous art came to act as a "profane salvation"; see the essay "Literary Institution and Modernization," in his *The Decline of Modernism* (University Park: Pennsylvania State University Press, 1992), 1–18, which, while it makes many good historical points, overstates the thesis that during the Enlightenment art became the functional equivalent of religion (17–18). See also Herbert Marcuse's classic essay, "The Affirmative Character of Culture" (1937) in his *Negations* (Boston: Beacon Press, 1968), 88–133, which takes Marx's ideological critique of religion as a model for his own critique of bourgeois culture's treatment of art as a separate value sphere. See also Raymond Williams's account of the nineteenth–century invention of "culture" as a domain transcending society; *Culture and Society*, 34–47. Lawrence Levine and T. Jackson Lears each describe the emerging belief in the nineteenth century that art/religion had same sources and that both were in decline; see "The Sacralization of Culture" in *Highbrow/Lowbrow*, 83–168; T. Jackson Lears, *No Place of Grace: Anti-Modernism and the Transformation of American Culture, 1880–1920* (Chicago: University of Chicago Press, 1994), 183–216, 251–260.

37. Lionel Trilling, "Art and Fortune," in *The Liberal Imagination* (New York: Viking Press, 1950), 255–281.

38. See Daniel Bell, "America as a Mass Society: A Critique," in *The End of Ideology* (1959; repr., Cambridge, Mass.: Harvard University Press, 2000) esp. 32–38.

39. Lionel Trilling, "Elements That Are Wanted," *Partisan Review* 5 (September–October 1940): 367–378. This essay reviews Eliot's "Idea of a Christian Society."

40. See David Riesman, "Our Country and Our Culture," in *Partisan Century*, 121–122; "The Saving Remnant," "Movies and Audiences" (with Evelyn Riesman), "Some Observations on Changes in Leisure Attitudes," "New Standards for Old: From Conspicuous Consumption to Conspicuous Production," in *Individualism Reconsidered* (New York: Free Press, 1954), 99–120, 194–231; Robert Warshow, *The Immediate Experience* (New York: Doubleday, 1962); and Leslie Fiedler, "The Middle Against Both Ends" (1955), in *Mass Culture: The Popular Arts in America*, ed., Bernard Rosenberg and David Manning White (New York: Free Press, 1957). The phrase "taste market" is from Fiedler, 537–547. On Marxist diagnoses of mass culture in the thirties, see Hegeman, *Patterns for America* (131–137, 146, 171–173) and Gorman, *Left Intellectuals and Popular Culture* (112–154). The Left in the thirties was not uniformly arrayed against mass culture. Michael Denning discusses a few intellectuals (Elizabeth Hawes, Sidney Finkelstein, C. L. R. James) of the Popular Front who imagined a democratization of mass culture that would con-

nect it aesthetically to the labor movement. He contrasts the optimism of these intellectuals to the hostility to mass culture found in the Communist magazines, such as *The Daily Worker* and *The New Masses; The Cultural Front* (New York: Verso, 1998), 454–462.

41. Andrew Ross, "Containing Culture in the Cold War," in *No Respect: Intellectuals and Popular Culture* (New York: Routledge, 1989), 53–59; and Gorman, *Left Intellectuals and Popular Culture*, 149–155.

42. Robert Warshow, "The Legacy of the 30s" (*Commentary*, v. 4 December 1947, 538–545), in *Immediate Experience*, 39.

43. Reisman, *Individualism Reconsidered*, 99–120, 194–231. In addition to Fiedler's "The Middle Against Both Ends," see his *Love and Death in the American Novel*, (Cleveland, Ohio: World Publishing Co., 1962), 248–253, 315–320, 342–343, 350, 449–452, 472–482. Of the Cold War critics who wrote somewhat sympathetically about mass culture, Robert Warshow showed the least condescension and most deftness in handling the content of specific texts. Warshow's essays on "The Western" and "The Gangster as Tragic Hero," in *The Immediate Experience*, remain classics of genre study and rank, along with James Agee's reviews for *Time* and the *Nation* and Manny Farber's for the *New Republic* and the *Nation*, as the period's best film criticism in what was then a nonprofessionalized field.

44. Philip Rahv, "Our Country and Our Culture," in *Image and Idea*, rev. ed. (New York: New Directions, 1957), 230.

45. Richard Hofstadter, *Anti-Intellectualism in American Life* (New York: Vintage Books, 1962), 86.

46. In America, Protestant churches struggled to hold on to their cultural authority as arbiters of morality and centers of community life during the same period that mass culture enjoyed its first major expansion as the industrializing country began shifting to a consumer economy. The popular press provided the first major encounter between mass culture and organized faith, but in the twentieth century, the clergy would face still more distractions from urban mass entertainments, such as the movies, vaudeville, and amusement parks.

    On the popularity of sentimental Christian fiction and Jesus novels, see, in addition to Ann Douglas's *The Feminization of American Culture;* Stephen Prothero, *American Jesus: How the Son of God Became a National Icon* (New York: Farrar, Strauss and Giroux, 2003), 64–74; Allene Stuart Phy, "Retelling the Greatest Story Ever Told: Jesus in Popular Fiction," in *The Bible and Popular Culture in America* (Philadelphia: Fortress Press, 1985), 41–83. In the silent era, churches, Catholic and Protestant, Reformed and evangelical, liberal and (even) fundamentalist, had begun producing their own "sanctuary cinema," successful at attracting parishioners, though having limited distribution outside of congregations; see Terry Lindvall, *Sanctuary Cinema: Origins of the Christian Film Industry* (New York: New York University Press, 2007). By the mid-thirties, the Catholic Legion of Decency—under the aegis of the Breen Office—managed to get considerable leverage over mainstream film content; see Gregory Black, *Hollywood Censored: Morality Codes, Catholics, and the Movies* (Cambridge: Cambridge University Press, 1994); and Frank Walsh, *Sin and Censorship* (New Haven: Yale University Press, 1996). Seminaries and Christian quarterlies as well as the secular media charged revivalists with commercialism; William McLoughlin, *Modern Revivalism: Charles Grandison Finney to Billy Graham* (New York: Ronald Press, 1959), 216–281, esp. 219–221.

47. Sinclair Lewis, *Elmer Gantry* (New York: Signet, 1967), 416. William Thomas Ellis's Depression-era biography of Billy Sunday, published the same year as *It Can't Happen Here,* inspired Adorno to remark that "detailed study of the literature on revivalism . . . would yield a great many of the psychological devices of modern fascist propaganda"; see Ellis, *Billy Sunday: The Man and His Message* (Philadelphia: John C. Winston, 1936); cited in Adorno, *Psychological Techniques,* 80.

48. Dwight MacDonald, "A Theory of Mass Culture" in *Mass Culture,* 58.

49. W. E. Sangster, "The Christian Use of Leisure," *Christianity Today,* June 10, 1957, 11–13; S. Richey Kamm, "Is America Losing Her Cultural Distinctives?" *Christianity Today,* July 8, 1957, 3–5; Richard C. Halverson, "Any Good—From Hollywood?" *Christianity Today,* December 23, 1957, 8–10; Editorial, "The Ten Commandments as a Religious Epic," *Christianity Today,* May 27, 1957, 25; Editorial, "Churches and Hidden Persuaders," *Christianity Today,* May 25, 1959, 20–22.

50. Andrew Ross discusses the shift from a class society model to a mass society model of politics in his essay, "Containing Culture in the Cold War," 47–55.

6. Jeremiads on the American Arcade and its Consumption Ethic

1. Kate Buford, *Burt Lancaster: An American Life* (New York: Knopf, 2000), 200; and Robyn Karney, *Burt Lancaster: A Singular Man* (London: Bloomsbury, 1996), 119–120.

2. Richard Brooks's credits include the antifascist prison noir *Brute Force* (1947) (writer only), *Storm Warning* (1951) (writer only) about the Klu Klux Klan; *The Blackboard Jungle* (1955), about juvenile delinquency in inner-city high schools; *Something of Value* (1957), concerning British colonialism in Kenya; and his 1967 adaptation of *In Cold Blood,* stressing Capote's indictment of capital punishment.

3. Karney, *Burt Lancaster,* 120.

4. In addition to *The Lonely Crowd,* see Riesman's *Individualism Reconsidered* (New York: Free Press, 1954), especially its essays "Some Observations on Changes in Leisure Attitudes," 202–218, and "The Social and Psychological Setting of Veblen's Economic Theory," 273–285.

5. See Riesman, "The Saving Remnant," in *Individualism Reconsidered,* 99–120.

6. Riesman, *Individualism Reconsidered,* 221.

7. Fredric Jameson, *Postmodernism or, The Cultural Logic of Late Capitalism* (Durham, N.C.: Duke University Press, 1991), 271.

8. Since the Progressive era, conservative evangelicals have been cautiously pro-capitalist, but antimonopoly and suspicious of usury (the sin to which Calvin

reluctantly consented, and one that populism has historically despised); see Willard Cantelon, *New Money or None?* (Plainfield, N.J.: Logos International, 1979). Conspiracy theories of the New World Order have not exposed free-market ideology to criticism. Instead, evangelicals like Pat Robertson imagine using the market to protect America's national sovereignty and to promote the churches' principles of stewardship and evangelism. The evangelical antidote to the concentration of economic power has been to reduce foreign debt, thus restoring a "strong dollar" and giving the market the Providential role Smith envisioned in *The Wealth of Nations.*

9. Marxists have classically comprehended this blockage, or disconnect, in social consciousness by the concept of the commodity fetish and the associated notion, developed by George Lucács, of "reification": the rationalistic process of effacing the traces of production, and alienated labor, from the commodity; see *History and Class Consciousness* (Cambridge, Mass.: MIT Press, 1971), 83–222. Liberals like Riesman, by explaining conformity as arising from the social and economic *gains* of the middle class since the thirties, contributed to the impression that the nation as a whole had enjoyed the trickle-down benefits of that economic sector, a misdiagnosis perceptively challenged by other, more perspicuous, non-Marxist critics. In his classic of advocacy journalism, *The Other America* (1962), Michael Harrington, former associate editor of the *Catholic Worker* (1951–1953) and contributing editor to *Dissent,* eloquently witnessed to "the new segregation of poverty," the creation of "the first minority poor in history," victims of the greater productivity who were removed from "the living, emotional experience of millions upon millions of middle-class Americans"; *The Other America: Poverty in the United States* (Baltimore: Penguin, 1962), 12, 14, 19. Harvard economist John Kenneth Galbraith, in *The Affluent Society* (1958), objurgated the Cold War economy for its dependence on the creation of artificial needs and ambrosial goods, to maximize profit, and its consequent neglect of poverty and sacrifice of public interest; see *The Affluent Society* (Cambridge, Mass.: The Riverside Press, 1958), 308–348. For the adverse effects of the corporate economy on American labor, in both its workplace and its leisure time, see George Lipsitz, *Rainbow at Midnight: Labor and Culture in the Forties* (Champaign: University of Illinois Press, 1994), 182–203, 253–279, 335–349; and Stanley Aronowitz, *False Promises* (Durham, N.C.: Duke University Press, 1992), 323–394.

10. The hard-boiled, whisky-drinking, bare-knuckled news-reporter "Jim Lefferts" is actually an amalgam of two characters, Elmer's skeptical college roommate from Chapters 1–3 and Bill Kingdom, the reporter for the Zenith *Advocate-Times.*

11. Burt Lancaster, qtd. in Karney, *Burt Lancaster,* 123.

12. Sinclair Lewis, *Elmer Gantry* (New York: Signet, 1967).

13. Buford, *Burt Lancaster,* 201.

14. William Martin, *A Prophet with Honor: The Billy Graham Story* (New York: William Morrow, 1991), 120.

15. Peter Berger, *The Sacred Canopy: Elements of a Sociological Theory of Religion* (Garden City, N.Y.: Doubleday, 1968), 127–150.

16. Walter Benjamin, "The Work of Art in the Age of Mechanical Reproduction," in *Illuminations,* trans. Harry Zohn (New York: Schocken Books, 1968), 217–252.

17. Billy Graham, *Just as I Am* (San Francisco: Harper Collins, 1997), 187. Graham devotes a chapter of *Just As I Am,* his autobiography, to his film and radio ministry; see "Building for the Future," 172–187.

18. William McLoughlin, *Modern Revivalism: Charles Grandison Finney to Billy Graham* (New York: Ronald Press, 1959), 362; *Billy Graham: Revivalist in a Secular Age* (Ronald Press, 1959), 131. Mass manipulation is not unique to Graham's style of revivalism, McLoughlin argues, though Graham may be the most adept at exploiting it, as he pits "the individual against the crowd."

19. Notable boardroom dramas (which originated in the fifties) include *Patterns,* directed by Fielder Cook (United Artists, 1956), from Rod Serling's teleplay; *Executive Suite* directed by Robert Wise (MGM, 1954); *Man in the Grey Flannel Suit* directed by Nunnally Johnson (Twentieth Century Fox, 1956); and *Madison Avenue,* directed by Bruce Humberstone (Twentieth Century Fox, 1961).

20. Billy Graham, *Peace with God* (New York: Doubleday, 1953), 15.

21. Billy Graham, *World Aflame* (New York: Pocket Books, 1965), 33.

22. Paul Tillich, "The Divine Name" (1963), in *The Essential Paul Tillich,* ed. F. Forrester Church (Chicago: University of Chicago Press, 1987), 58, 60.

23. Graham, *World Aflame,* 185.

24. The view of culture in *Christianity and Today* is largely that culture is good if it produces good persons, though the fine arts, including irreligious modernists such as Beckett and Faulkner, offer more effective means than entertainment of persuading people to the meaning or necessity of Christian faith, even when artists purvey a view inconsistent with the kerygma. See, for example, "Dali's Place in Religious Art," *Christianity Today,* December 10, 1956, 26–27, 34; Calvin D. Linton, "The Nativity Theme in English Poetry" [covering Jonson, Crashaw, Milton, Auden, and Eliot], *Christianity Today,* December 10, 1956, 6–8; Virginia Ramey Mollenkott, "The Church and Modern Literature," *Christianity Today* (Feb. 16, 1959), 16–17; Robert D. Knudsen, "Milton's 'Paradise Lost'," *Christianity Today,* February 16, 1959, 14–16; Harry Jaeger, "The Clergy in Modern Fiction" [canvassing Hardy, Samuel Butler, Harold Frederic, H. G. Wells, Dreiser, and Steinbeck], *Christianity Today,* February 15, 1960, 14–18; Fred E. Luchs, review of *Waiting for Godot, Christianity Today,* June 6, 1960, 6–8; Cynthia Pearl Maus, "The Fine Arts and Christian Education," *Christianity Today,* August 29, 1960, 9–10. In these articles, the writers' academic accreditations and institutions are nearly always specified to demonstrate intellectual authority. Mollenkott enlists T. S. Eliot's *Religion and Literature* to defend modern literature; Maus offers a scholastic definition of beauty; and Linton and Knudsen show an awareness of literary genre and poetic lineage. They cover many of the same cultural texts that *Christianity and Crisis* approved for their "modern scripture" and their nearness to modern man's "dread, despondency, anguish, and alienation." *Christianity Today* was also willing, as was *Christianity and Crisis,* to criticize high culture on

theological grounds. Compare Mellenkott, in *Christianity Today,* and Nathan Scott, in *Christianity and Crisis,* on Faulkner's image of man; both applaud his profound sense of sin but find him lacking a positive doctrine of grace; Scott's remarks in Mark Hultheser, *Building a Protestant Left: Christianity and Crisis Magazine, 1941–1993* (Knoxville: University of Tennessee Press, 1999), 97. Other quotatons, also by Scott, cited in Hulsether, 96.

25. In *World Aflame,* Graham actually expresses disdain for theologians such as Tillich, who call God "the ground of being"; they are part of "a strong movement, especially in Protestantism, to recast the Christian message in order to make it acceptable to modern man" (71–72). Such men are "false prophets" and "false teachers" (72).

26. Bell quoted in Leon Ribuffo, *The Old Christian Right: The Protestant Far Right from the Great Depression to the Cold War* (Philadelphia: Temple University Press, 1983), 241. See also Daniel Bell, "Is There a Ruling Class in America? *The Power Elite* Reconsidered," *The End of Ideology* (Cambridge, Mass.: Harvard University Press, 2001), 47–74, and David Reisman, "Culture: Popular and Unpopular," in *Individualism Reconsidered,* 180.

27. Compare McLoughlin's description of the thoughtless audiences at Graham's rapid fire, jolting revivals, experiencing immediate relays to their viscera (*Modern Revivalism,* 513; *Billy Graham: Revivalist,* 131). In effect, he is saying that they are experiencing "enthusiasms," the Puritans' name for false conversions affected by the imagination and nervous excitement.

28. On the definition and sources of cultural capital, see Pierre Bourdieu, *Distinction: A Social Critique of the Judgment of Taste* (Cambridge, Mass.: Harvard University Press, 1984).

7. Controversies over Therapeutic Religion

1. William March, *The Bad Seed* (New Jersey: Ecco Press, 1997), 5. The epigraph is from William McLoughlin, *Billy Graham: Revivalist in a Secular Age* (New York: Ronald Press, 1959), 85, 87.

2. Dr. Fredric Wertham was the psychiatric nemesis of the horror comics (the E. C. titles, such as *Tales from the Crypt* and *The Haunt of Fear,* were the most accomplished) that found huge circulation after the war. See David Skal, *The Monster Show: A Cultural History of Horror* (New York: Faber and Faber, 2001), 233.

3. Elaine Tyler May, *Homeward Bound: American Families in the Cold War Era* (New York: Basic Books, 1998), 26.

4. March, *Bad Seed,* 6.

5. Charles J. Rolo derisively uses the phrase "secular religion" in "The Freudian Revolution" the preface to "Psychology in American Life," special supplement, *Atlantic Monthly,* July 1961, 61–111. See also O. Hobart Mowrer, "Psychiatry and Religion," 88–91, in the same issue.

6. The phrase "Baby Gorgon" is from a review of *The Bad Seed* in "Books— Mystery and Crime," *New Yorker,* April 10, 1954, 151; cited in William Paul, *Laughing Screaming* (New York: Columbia University Press, 1994), 475n24.

For the novel's critical reception, see Roy S. Simmonds's biography, *The Two Worlds of William March* (Tuscaloosa: University of Alabama Press, 1984), 302. *The Bad Seed* was William March's only experiment with fantastic horror fiction in a thirty-year writing career. March did not long savor his success. He died in 1955 before seeing either the movie or play versions of *The Bad Seed*, and he never learned that the National Institute of Arts and Letters had approved him for a writer's grant. On the film, see William Paul's chapter, "Postwar Malaise and the Ontogeny of Evil Children: *The Bad Seed* and *Village of the Damned*," in *Laughing Screaming*, 267–286.

7. Philip Rieff, a sociologist and a Catholic, wrote *Triumph of the Therapeutic: Uses of Faith After Freud* (New York: Harper and Row, 1966); Karl Menninger, a psychoanalyst of Protestant background, asked *Whatever Became of Sin?* (New York: Hawthorne Books, 1973); Paul Vitz, a psychologist and conservative Catholic, followed with *Psychology as Religion: The Cult of Self-Worship* (Grand Rapids, Mich.: William B. Eerdmans, 1977); and Christopher Lasch, a Leftist sociologist, criticized the mental health movement as the cornerstone of social liberalism's secular faith, in *The Culture of Narcissism: American Life in an Age of Diminishing Expectations* (New York: Norton, 1978).

8. For an enormously influential general theory of the middle-class interest in psychology, particularly the Freudian talking cure, see Michel Foucault's *The History of Sexuality*, vol. 1 (first American edition, New York: Pantheon Books, 1978) and *Mental Illness and Psychology* (1976). On the specific wartime and Cold War applications of psychology, see Ellen Herman, *The Romance of American Psychology: Political Culture in the Age of Experts* (Berkeley: University of California Press, 1995), 238–241, 257–265.

9. Herman, *Romance of American Psychology*, 119–120, 124–136, 245–249.

10. On the growth of the mental health industry and its prehistory in World War II, see Catherine Lutz, "Epistemology of the Bunker: The Brainwashed and Other New Subjects of the Permanent War," in *Inventing the Psychological*, ed. Joel Pfister and Nancy Schnog (New Haven: Yale University Press, 1997).

11. C. Kevin Gillespie, S. J., *Psychology and American Catholicism, From Confession to Therapy?* (New York: Crossroad Publishing, 2001), 15.

12. Lionel Trilling, *Freud and the Crisis of Our Culture* (Boston: Beacon Press, 1955), 41–42.

13. Psychoanalysis had enjoyed vogues among the Northern middle class, bohemia, and the elite southwest during the twenties and early thirties, but its wobbly status as science, hermeneutic, or social fad had prevented it from receiving accreditation by the American Psychological Association until 1947, "when it made clinical training a mandatory element of graduate education in psychology;" see Herman, *Romance of American Psychology*, 259. On the reception of psychoanalysis in the United States, see Joel Pfister, "Glamorizing the Psychological: The Politics of the Performances of Modern Psychological Identities," in *Inventing the Psychological*, 167–213; Frederick Hoffman, *Freudianism and the Literary Mind* (1945; repr., New York: Grove Press, 1959), 44–86; Nathan Hale, Jr., *The Rise and Crisis of Psychoanalysis in the*

United States: Freud and the Americans, 1917–1985 (New York: Oxford University Press, 1995); John Seeley, *The Americanization of the Unconscious* (New York: International Science Press, 1967).

14. See Sigmund Freud, "Obsessive Actions and Religious Practices," vol. 9 (1907); *Totem and Taboo*, vol. 13 (1913); *The Future of an Illusion*, vol. 21 (1927); and *Moses and Monotheism*, vol. 23 (1938), in *The Standard Edition of the Complete Psychological Works of Sigmund Freud*, ed. and trans. by James Strachey (London: Hogarth Press, 1957–1974). Freud saw all religions as illusions (wish-fulfilling ideas), but he had particular distaste for Christianity. Judaism proudly bore the guilt of having murdered its "father" Moses, but Christianity, being an adaptation for weaker souls, had provided a guilt-remitting mechanism in the substitutionary sacrifice of the Father's Son. In *Civilization and Its Discontents,* Freud singles out liberal theology for contempt because it attempts to accommodate science (a far superior cultural accomplishment) and thus surrendered any of the psychic benefits of hard religion's irrational myths and disciplines; see David Riesman, *Individualism Reconsidered* (New York: Free Press, 1954), 393.

15. Allison Stokes, *Ministry After Freud* (New York: Pilgrim Press, 1985), 109–143. The New York Psychology Group was a seminar that met monthly from 1942 to 1945 at Union Theological Seminary. Many members were academics from Union Theological Seminary or Columbia University, and the two dozen core members included Erich Fromm, Seward Hiltner, Rollo May, David Roberts, Carl Rogers, and Paul Tillich. The expressed purpose of the seminars was to exchange ideas about the relation of Christian theology to Freudian ideas being brought to the public by the secular liberal intelligentsia (139). Topics they discussed included "The Psychology of Conscience" (1943–1944 session).

16. Robert Lindner, "Come Over, Red Rover," in *The Fifty-Minute Hour: A Collection of True Psychoanalytic Tales* (New York: Bantam, 1982), 67–113. Lindner died at age 56; the essays were collected posthumously and first published in 1956. In his preface to his third book, *Must You Conform?* (New York: Rinehart, 1956), Lindner—an orthodox Freudian—pommels St. Paul and Augustine, and, in two psychopathic case studies of *The Fifty-Minute Hour* ("Songs My Mother Taught Me," 1–66, and "Destiny's Tot," 169–220), he underscores that each patient is made unhealthy by a strict religious background, particularly a fundamentalist one. Lindner sees religion as on the model of *Totem and Taboo*, where psyche and culture both obey "the law of the talion"; someone must always pay the sacrifice for one's suffering.

17. The key American revisionists in the field of psychotherapy were Harry Stack Sullivan, Franz Alexander, Karen Horney, Erik Erikson, Carl Rogers, Abraham Maslow, Erich Fromm, and Rollo May. The term "ego-psychology" was often used in this period as a close associate, if not a synonym, of neo-Freudianism, as in the *Atlantic Monthly* issue discussed later in this chapter. In this context, we will allow the association. "Ego-psychology" precisely refers to the school of thought developed by Heinz Hartman and David Rapaport (stressing the autonomy of ego functions from unconscious conflict) rather than

neo-Freudianism, though it shares antecedents, particularly Alfred Adler and Anna Freud, with the latter. The sociology of Talcott Parsons helped to shape Hartman's conception of the ego's adaptational role to its environment, whereas neo-Freudians tended to emphasize self-realization rather than adaptation. Erik Erikson is a neo-Freudian who is also frequently cited as an ego-psychologist because of his "psycho-social" stage theory. Carl Rogers—though often discussed in the same breath as Horney, Sullivan, et al.—did not practice the clinical method of psychoanalysis (premised on transference), nor did he believe in dynamic repression (in which memories and fantasies, and the psychic energies attached to them, are forced into the unconscious where they cannot be retrieved through primary thinking processes). Of these theorists, Rollo May placed the least emphasis on early family life. His "existential psychoanalysis" treats images and memories of the past only so far as they reveal something about the patient's anxieties over his future; see Rollo May, "The Origins and Significance of the Existential Movement in Psychology," 3–36 and "Contributions of Existential Psychotherapy," 37–91 in his *Existence: A New Dimension in Psychiatry and Psychology* (New York: Basic Books, 1958).

18. Prior to the fifties, Niebuhr's most extensive disquisition on Freud appeared in *Human Nature* (New York: Scribner's, 1941), where he treats his subject as a philosopher, rather than a clinician, and states that Freud's critique of bourgeois morality is not at all radical, for it simply nurtures middle-class decadence (53). Niebuhr's own psychoanalysis with Erik Erikson and Dr. Edgerton Howard, which occurred in the summer of 1955, somewhat improved his view of psychotherapy, though reservations about its underlying theory of man remained, as his preface to the Scribner Library edition of *The Nature and Destiny of Man* (New York: Charles Scribner's Sons, 1964) attests. Niebuhr's most involved statement on Freud's link to the contemporary therapeutic movement appears in *The Self and the Dramas of History* (1955), written before he undertook his analysis with Erikson and one year before his home base, Union Theological Seminary, decided to hire a full-time chair to manage its roster of psychology classes. See the book's chapters on neurosis, "The Internal Dialogue of the Self" and "The Climax of an Empirical Culture."

19. On the efforts of Protestants to adapt psychotherapy (including especially psychoanalysis), see these pioneering works: O. Hobart Mowrer, *The Crisis in Psychiatry and Religion* (New York: Van Rostrand Reinhold, 1961); and Samuel K. Klausner, *Psychiatry and Religion, A Sociological Study of the New Alliance of Ministers and Psychiatrists* (Glencoe, Ill.: Free Press of Glencoe, 1964). Two books have addressed the topic at length since Mowrer and Klausner published their studies in the sixties. These are Allison Stokes's *Ministry After Freud* and Donald Meyer's, *The Positive Thinkers, Religion as Pop Psychology from Mary Baker Eddy to Norman Vincent Peale and Ronald Reagan* (New York: Harper and Row, 1988), originally published as *The Positive Thinkers, A Study of the American Quest for Health, Wealth, and Personal Power from Mary Baker Eddy to Norman Vincent Peale* (New York: Doubleday, 1965).

20. Stokes, *Ministry after Freud,* 61–63, 77, 130, 144–146, 158. Stokes takes the phrase "the modernist impulse" from William Hutchison, *The Modernist Impulse in American Protestantism* (New York: Oxford University Press, 1976).

21. Philip Rieff, *Freud: The Mind of the Moralist* (New York: Viking Press, 1959), 194.

22. See Freud, *Group Psychology and the Ego,* trans. James Strachey, in *Standard Edition.*

23. Trilling's source is "Considerations Regarding the Loyalty Oath as a Manifestation of Current Social Tension and Anxiety: A Statement Formulated by the Committee on Social Issues of the Group for the Advancement of Psychiatry and a Panel Discussion," G.A.P. Symposium, Topeka, Kans., October 1954. His comments were published in Lionel Trilling, *Freud and the Crisis of Our Culture* (Boston: Beacon Press, 1955), 43.

24. Riesman identified himself as a neo-Freudian and had received training from Erich Fromm, though he deradicalized his mentor's Marxist humanism. In *Individualism Reconsidered,* he published four essays on Freud from 1946 and 1947, written while he was lecturing on social sciences at the University of Chicago: "Themes of Work and Play in the Structure of Freud's Thought," 310–333, "Authority and Liberty in the Structure of Freud's Thought," 334–364; "Themes of Heroism and Weakness in the Structure of Freud's Thought," 365–387; "Freud, Religion, and Science," 388–408. Riesman found Freud wanting where his theory resists adaptation to "creative consumption." His imagination still lodged in the nineteenth-century gentleman's work ethic, Freud is too ascetic. His reality principle administers "scarcity economics," and his theory of the ego is outmoded, for it does not admit for the new psychic formations possible in the "society of abundance" (339, 344–346, 404).

25. Karen Horney, *Neurosis and Human Growth: The Struggle toward Self-Realization* (New York: W.W. Norton, 1950), 373.

26. Riesman, *Individualism Reconsidered,* 351–354.

27. D. E. Roberts, *Psychotherapy and a Christian View of Mind* (New York: Charles Scribner's Sons, 1950), 9–10.

28. Erik Erikson, *Childhood and Society* (New York: WW Norton, 1950), 257.

29. Roger Johnson, "Psychohistory as Religious Narrative: The Demonic Role of Hans Luther in Erikson's Saga of Human Evolution," in *Psychohistory and Religion: The Case of Young Man Luther,* ed. Roger Johnson (Philadelphia: Fortress Press, 1977), 127–161. Hans Luther's resemblance to the Nazi fathers in Erikson's "The Legend of Hitler's Childhood" has also been remarked by Johnson. See also Erikson, *Young Man Luther* (New York: Norton, 1958), 103–110.

30. Erikson, *Childhood and Society,* 258.

31. See Doctor Spock's *Baby and Child Care* (1945; repr., New York: Hawthorn and Dutton, 1976), 374; see also 364–368. For an overview of the psychoanalytic impact on parental awareness that "emotional health and pathology are determined in early childhood," see Peter B. Neubauer's "The Century of the Child," *Atlantic Monthly* (July 1961), 84–87. Neubauer was director of New York's Child Development Center.

32. See Karen Horney, "The Concept of the Super-Ego," 207–231; and "Neurotic Guilt Feelings," 232–245; in *New Ways in Psychoanalysis* (New York: W.W. Norton, 1939); and "Neurotic Guilt Feelings," 230–258, in Horney, *The Neurotic Personality of Our Time* (New York: W.W. Norton, 1937).

33. Horney, *Neurosis*, 376.

34. Erich Fromm, *Man for Himself* (New York: Rinehart, 1947), 159.

35. Fromm's colleague Herbert Marcuse also concludes that Luther and Calvin support the legitimacy of any authority that maintains order, even if the order be unjust, and restrict dissent to private conscience; see his section on the Reformation from "A Study on Authority," in *Studies in Critical Philosophy*, trans. Joris De Bres (Boston: Beacon Press, 1973), 49–156.

36. Erikson was influenced by Fromm's "The Protestant Era," in *Escape From Freedom* (New York: Henry Holt, 1941), which he cites in *Young Man Luther*, 239; he differs from Fromm in assigning the authoritarian mentality to excesses within the Reformation rather than the movement's essential character. See also Erikson's discussion of the history of religion in "Wholeness and Totality: A Psychiatric Contribution" in Carl J. Friedrich, ed., *Totalitarianism* (Cambridge, MA: Harvard University Press, 1954), 156–171.

37. Erikson, *Young Man Luther*, 108–109.

38. Fromm, *Man for Himself*, 149.

39. Horney, *Neurosis*, 375.

40. "Psychology in American Life," ed. Charles Rolo, special supplement, *Atlantic Monthly*, July 1961, 61–111. Contributors include Rolo, "The Freudian Revolution," 61–68; John R. Seeley, "The Americanization of the Unconscious," 68–72; Alfred Kazin, "The Language of Pundits," 73–78; Peter B. Neubauer, "The Century of the Child," 84–87; O. Hobart Mowrer, "Psychiatry and Religion," 88–91; Ira Progoff, "The Psychology of Personal Growth," 102–104; and Philip Rieff, "The American Transference: From Calvin to Freud," 105–107.

41. Charles Rolo, "The Freudian Revolution," *Atlantic Monthly* (July 1961), 69.

42. Mowrer, "Psychiatry and Religion," 89. Mowrer makes this argument at full length in his book, *The Crisis in Religion and Psychology* (New York: Van Nostrand, 1961).

43. Rieff, "The American Transference," 107, 106. Compare Rieff, *Freud: The Mind of the Moralist*, 77.

44. Rieff's Catholicism is exposed, though never explicitly pronounced, in his characterization of the "therapeutic" as a direct outgrowth of the Reformation's "failure" to create a unified community. He finds a modernist impulse at the heart of Protestantism, which was always, in his estimate, a cultural religion. "The new psychology is simply old heresy"—antinomianism, in fact; see *Triumph of the Therapeutic*, 128. "The rise of psychological man" in America would stimulate some well-known conservative Christian critiques of psychoanalysis in the seventies, beginning with Paul Vitz's *Psychology as Religion: The Cult of Self-Worship* (1977); for like titles, see Vitz's copious bibliographic references. According to Vitz, the pathbreaker for all of these volumes was *Triumph of the Therapeutic*. Vitz's discussion of original sin has been suggestive for my remarks here on Freud and Calvinism; in addition to *Psychology as Religion*, see Vitz's "Christian Theory of Personality," in *Mind and Man*, ed.

T. Burke (Hillsdale, Mich.: Hillsdale College Press, 1987), 199–122. Also very suggestive for the Freud/Calvin parallel has been Ann Douglas's discussion of Freud and the Puritan Legacy in 1920s New York, *Terrible Honesty* (New York: Farrar, Straus and Giroux, 1996), 94–95, 149–155; John Demos, "Historical Perspectives on the Reception of Oedipus in the United States," (1978) and "History and the Psychosocial: Reflections on 'Oedipus and America,'" (1997) in *Inventing the Psychological*, 63–78, 79–83; and Riesman's comments in "Authority and Liberty in the Structure of Freud's Thought," *Individualism Reconsidered*, 340–341. Riesman had carried on discussions with Rieff while at the University of Chicago; see *Individualism Reconsidered*, 305.

45. Vitz, *Psychology as Religion*, 7, 11.
46. For biographical details on May and Rogers, see Vitz, *Psychology as Religion*, 7, 11; and Stokes, *Ministry after Freud*, 124–128, 132–133. For Rogers's essays, see *The Carl Rogers Reader*, ed. Kirschenbaum and Henderson (Boston: Houghton Mifflin, 1989).
47. Alongside these examples, it is worth noting that one of Freud's first sponsors in America, G. Stanley Hall, had been a theologian; see Rieff, *Freud: The Mind of the Moralist*, 191. In a footnote, Rieff adds that Hall "was president of Clark University when Freud delivered his lectures there in 1909" (377n11).
48. Horney, *Neurosis*, 377–378.
49. For discussions of the European psychoanalysts who broke with Freud because they insisted on the psychological utility of faith (Adler, Rank, Jung, Reich), see Hans Küng, *Freud and the Problem of God* (New Haven: Yale University Press, 1979), 63–66; and Ernest Becker, *The Denial of Death* (New York: Free Press, 1973), 175–206.
50. Fromm, *Man for Himself*, 44. Fromm interpreted the myth of the Fall in *Genesis* as a symbolization of the "awareness of human separation, without reunion by love"—the source of "shame," "guilt and anxiety"—but added that this separateness could be healed by human love, while original sin, in Christian doctrine, can be overcome only by divine love and grace. Freud did not endow human love with the same healing and integrative powers as Fromm did. Quotations on love and interpretation of *Genesis* in Fromm, *The Art of Loving* (1956; repr. New York: Harper Perennial, 2006), 9. David Riesman, who had been mentored by Fromm, also acknowledges a "metaphorical" resemblance between the doctrine of original sin and Freud's "primal crime of Oedipus" (*Individualism Reconsidered*, 334–335, 396–397), though he works hard to rescue Freud from the "neo-orthodox" implications of the comparison (395, 396).
51. Rogers, *The Carl Rogers Reader*, 402.
52. Joshua Loth Liebman, *Peace of Mind* (New York: Simon and Schuster, 1946), 15. *Peace of Mind* was "the most successful American inspirational book of the twentieth century" before it was supplanted by Peale's *The Power of Positive Thinking* (1952); see Jonathan Sarna, *American Judaism* (New Haven: Yale University Press, 2005), 281. David Reynolds discusses additional rabbis, Louis Binstock and Israel Chados, who contributed to the inspirational genre in the fifties; see *The Positive Thinkers*, 327–330.
53. Gregory Zilboorg, *Freud and Religion* (Westminster, MD: Newman Press, 1958), 90–91; Fromm, *Man for Himself*, 18, 107, 152–153, 206. Among other

sources, Fromm cites Nahum Glatzner's *In Time and Eternity: A Jewish Reader* (New York: Schocken Books, 1946). For attempts to connect psychoanalysis to antecedents in Jewish teaching, see the following articles, also cited in Robert Ellwood's *The Fifties Spiritual Awakening* (New Brunswick, N.J.: Rutgers University Press, 1997): Lillian Blumberg McCall, "The Hidden Springs of Sigmund Freud," *Commentary,* August 1954, 102–110; and David Bakan, "Freud's Jewishness and His Psychoanalysis," *Judaism* 3, no. 1 (Winter 1954), 20–26. Bakan subsequently published *Freud and the Jewish Mystical Tradition* (1958). Stanley Edgar Hyman, an atheist, calls Freud a "secular rabbi" in his review of Volume 1 of Ernest Jones's biography, 264–267; "Freud and Boas: Secular Rabbis?" review of *The Life and Work of Sigmund Freud, Commentary,* March 1954; Robert Lindner, one of the decade's best-selling psychoanalytic authors, also remained militantly secular. In a hectoring piece written for *Commentary,* Irving Kristol casts Jews as eager suitors in "the current love affair between psychoanalysis and religion": "the Catholic Church has shown itself to be a rather frigid partner. But, all in all, things have gone well, and the occasional Catholic reserve has been more than made up for by Protestant acquiescence and Jewish ardor." Kristol's impatience with secular reductions of faith (he asks his reader to ponder whether truth is with God rather than faith and reason) is already evident, but, withal, psychoanalysis did not play the central apologetic role for Judaism that it did for liberal Protestantism; Kristol, "God and the Psychoanalysts: *Can Freud and Religion Be Reconciled?*" *Commentary,* November 1949, 434–443. See also the reader letters by rabbis Abraham Cronbach and Roland Gittelsohn, January 1950, 87–89. Will Herberg does not drive a wedge between psychoanalysis and Judeo-Christianity, as Kristol does, but he also favors Freud to the more "conciliatory" "post-Freudians," in "Freud, Religion, and Social Reality," *Commentary,* March 1957, 277–284.

54. Gillespie, *Psychology and American Catholicism,* 90–93, 168–169.

55. Louis Gross, *God and Freud* (New York: David McKay, 1959), 21.

56. Gillespie, *Psychology and American Catholicism,* 84–86. In 1943, Twentieth Century Fox released *The Song of Bernadette,* a lavishly produced religious biopic adapted from Franz Werfel's best seller about the miracle of Lourdes. The production was closely monitored by the Catholic Breen Office, and the film treats psychoanalysis contemptuously, though it is an anachronism in the nineteenth-century setting. The hamlet's committed atheist (who else but Vincent Price?) hires an odious psychologist (Alan Napier) to persecute the pious peasant child Bernadette and convince her that the vision of the Holy Mother is no miracle, only a neurotic delusion. The Church ejects the quack doctor, and God punishes the loquacious atheist by plucking his vocal cords.

57. Pius XII, "The Moral Limits of Medical Research and Treatment" (address, First International Congress on the Histopathology of the Nervous System, September 14, 1952).

58. Benjamin Wolman, ed., *Psychoanalysis and Catholicism* (Northvale, N.J.: Jason Aronson, 1995), viii.

59. Gillespie, *Psychology and American Catholicism,* 54–68, 90–92; Ellwood, *Fifties Spiritual Awakening,* 61.

60. Fulton Sheen, *Life Is Worth Living* (New York: McGraw-Hill, 1953), 226, 93, 89, 234, 71, 121. This is a selection of transcripts from Sheen's eponymous TV show; see esp. 2, 71, 86, 89, 93, 119, 121, 141, 172–173, 226, 234. Sheen also attacks Freud at length in *Peace of Soul,* one of his fifty-odd books.

61. Gillespie, *Psychology and American Catholicism,* 16–18.

62. Pius XII, "On Psychotherapy and Religion" (address, Fifth International Congress on Psychotherapy and Clinical Psychology, April 13, 1953); see also Pius XII, "Applied Psychology" (address, Rome Congress of the International Association of Applied Psychology, April 10, 1958).

63. Unknown author, "Freud and the Catholic Church," *Time,* August 4, 1947.

64. Gillespie, *Psychology and American Catholicism,* 106–113.

65. Foucault, *History of Sexuality,* 1:57–73.

66. In addition to Gillespie, see Liebman, "Psychoanalysis and Confessional" from the chapter, "Conscience Doth Make Cowards," in his *Peace of Mind;* Karl Menninger, *Whatever Became of Sin?* (New York: Hawthorn Books, 1973), 218; John McNeill, "A Short History of the Cure of Souls," in *The Church and Mental Health,* ed. Paul Maves (New York: Charles Scribner's Sons, 1953) 43–60; and William H. Whyte, *The Organization Man* (New York: Simon and Schuster, 1956), 374.

67. Positive thinking religious books were among the best sellers of the fifties and reached interdenominational and interfaith audiences. Some well-known titles include Norman Vincent Peale's *The Power of Positive Thinking* (1952), Sheen's *Peace of Soul* (1949), Graham's *Peace with God* (1953), Rabbi Joshua Loth Liebman's *Peace of Mind* (1946), and Ira Progoff's *The Death and Rebirth of Psychology* (1956). While Liebman's and Progoff's books are heavily influenced by psychoanalysis, the others are not; Peale's book owes much to the tradition of Mary Baker Eddy's Christian Science. On Peale and mind cure, see Reynolds, *Positive Thinkers,* 259–289.

68. David Roberts, *Psychotherapy and the Christian View of Man,* 93.

69. Gross, *God and Freud,* 18–19.

70. Menninger, *Whatever Became of Sin?* 226.

71. My source for these facts is Louis Gross's *God and Freud,* 17–19.

72. For information on evangelical responses to the therapeutic movement, in magazines, novels, advice literature, and seminary courses, I am grateful to Eliza Barstow for sharing Chapter 3 of "Godly Adults: The Rhetoric of Maturity for Evangelical Young Adults, 1945–1965" (Ph.D. diss. Harvard University, 2010). Evangelicals gingerly advised Christians that it was permissible to seek advice from secular psychology so long as their problems remained in the medical domain and not the spiritual. This would cordon off many of the areas where liberal Protestants sought to apply the insights of therapy. Evangelicals never regarded psychology, least of all psychoanalysis, as apologetic evidence for their faith. Articles in *Christianity Today* are generally receptive to psychologists' criticisms of the church and, like Tillich and Roberts, the magazine's writers reject perfectionism; however, in arguing for a realistic view of man, the writers are sensitive to the perception that evangelicals, like unreconstructed fundamentalists, make a point of pillorying people for their sins. For example, Clyde

Narramore, Ph. D. Columbia University and author of *Psychology of Counseling* (1960), caricatures a liberal who misunderstands evangelical theology: "Do you think it's harmful to frighten boys and girls with those Bible stories about hell? Won't teaching young people that they're sinners give them a guilt complex?" According to Narramore, this voice represents a parent who thinks guilt *per se* is bad and therefore discredits the necessity of regenerative grace. See Narramore, "What a Psychologist Thinks about Sunday School," *Christianity Today* (February 29, 1960), 28. From the first five years of *Christianity Today's* publication, see also Bernard Ramm, "Christian Experience and Psychology" (May 26, 1958), 13–14, 22; Johannes D. Plekker, "Psychology and Pastoral Care" (November 9, 1959), 7–9; Norvell L. Peterson, "Christianity and Psychiatry" (November 9, 1959), 9–12; Theodore J. Jansma, "Christian Psychotherapy" (June 20, 1960), 9–10; Theodore J. Jansma, "Pastoral Counseling" (July 6, 1959), 16–18, 23. Gross's *God and Freud* was reviewed by Lars Granberg in *Christianity Today;* "Religion and Psychiatry" (May 25, 1959), 36–37.

73. Pratt, "The Parish Minister and the Psychiatrist," 215.

74. The distinction is from William James, Lecture 4, "The Religion of Healthy-Mindedness," in *The Varieties of Religious Experience;* cited by Roberts, *Psychotherapy,* 66.

75. Paul Tillich, *The Courage to Be* (New Haven: Yale University Press, 1951); and "The Theological Significance of Existentialism and Psychoanalysis," *Faith and Freedom,* 9, no. 25 (Autumn 1955); reprinted in Tillich, *Theology of Culture* (New York: Oxford University Press, 1959), 112–126.

76. Tillich, *Courage,* 77–78. For other attempts to define the joint role of the clergy and the psychotherapist, see from *The Church and Mental Health* the following articles: Seward Hiltner, "The New Concern of Recent Years," 61–74 [an abbreviated version of his thesis in *Pastoral Counseling* (1949)]; Gene Bartlett, "Preaching and Pastoral Rules," 109–128; and Dallas Pratt, "The Parish Minister and the Psychiatrist," 193–218. Hiltner was the executive secretary of the Department of Pastoral Services of the Federal Council of Churches (FCC) (1938–1950) and then Associate Professor of Pastoral Theology on the faculty of the University of Chicago; Bartlett was the pastor of the First Baptist Church in Los Angeles; and Pratt was a New York psychiatrist.

77. An idea central to Tillich's good friend D. E. Roberts's theology as well. See D. E. Roberts, "Paul Tillich's Doctrine of Man," in *The Theology of Paul Tillich,* ed. Charles Ogley (New York: Macmillan, 1952), 125–129.

78. On dreaming innocence, see Paul Tillich, "The Political Meaning of Utopia" (1951), in *The Political Expectation,* ed. James Luther Adams (New York: Harper, 1971), 131–132, 156, 171–173; and "The Unity of Love, Power, and Justice" in *The Essential Tillich,* ed. F. Forrester Church (Chicago: University of Chicago Press, 1987), 149; excerpted from *Love, Power, and Justice* (London: Oxford University Press 1954), 108–125. On man's reunion with his essence through the power of Christ (that which reconciles what has been estranged from itself and from its depth), see the title sermon and "Our Ultimate Concern," in Tillich, *The New Being* (Lincoln: University of Nebraska Press, 1955), 15–24, 152–160.

79. Tillich's "complete self-acceptance" provided a refrain for Carl Rogers's work; see especially Rogers, *On Becoming a Person* (New York: Houghton Mifflin, 1961), 87–90, 207.

80. Tillich, *Essential Tillich*, 77.

81. Roberts, "Tillich's Doctrine of Man," 120, 128–129.

82. See David Roberts's discussion of demythologization in *Psychotherapy and the Christian View of Man*, 86–88, 115.

83. Director Ida Lupino's little-known film for RKO, "Outrage" (1950), nods to the revival of the priestly concept of the ministry, as *cura animarum*, by having characters refer to the young Protestant minister as "Doc" rather than "reverend." Jacques Tourneur's beautifully detailed *Stars in My Crown* (1950), adapted from Joe Don Baker's popular religious novel, continuously parallels the soul healing of the Presbyterian pastor, Josiah Grey (Joel McCrea), with the medicine of the town's skeptical physician, Daniel Harris; each professional makes house calls, to the same patients/parishioners, and often minister from alternate sides of the same needy person's bed. Says the parson to Dr. Harris: "souls don't always enjoy perfect health, any more than bodies do."

84. Ministers, for instance, experimented with asking family members to set aside "rule-based" moral judgments about each other and to look at their relationships from a "depth psychology approach" emphasizing free association. Some churches made extensive use of mental hygiene. See the liberal organ, "Great Churches of America: First Community Church, Columbus, Ohio," *Christian Century*, December 20, 1950, 1515–1516. For Seward Hiltner's description of the separation of functions, see, in addition to *Pastoral Counseling*, Dallas Pratt's article, "The Parish Minister and the Psychiatrist," which gives a concise summation of Hiltner's book.

85. Ellwood, *Fifties Spiritual Awakening*, 222; Gross, *God and Freud*, 15.

86. Hiltner, "New Concern," 70–71; Howe, "A More Adequate Training for Ministers," 240–243, 249–251; Pratt, "Parish Minister," 193–218.

87. Gross, *God and Freud*, 66–67.

88. Roberts, *Psychotherapy*, 96, 100.

89. C. S. Lewis, hardly a liberal, came to a similar conclusion in *Mere Christianity*, arguing that there is no necessary antagonism between psychotherapy and orthodoxy: "Now what psychoanalysis undertakes to do is to remove the abnormal feelings, that is, to give the man the better raw material for his acts of choice: morality is concerned with the acts of choice themselves"; Chapter 4, "Morality and Psychoanalysis," in *Mere Christianity* (New York: Macmillan, 1952), 84.

90. Gross, *God and Freud*, 73.

91. See Kant, "The Failure of All Philosophical Theodicies" (1791).

92. Gross, *God and Freud*, 144–149.

93. The *Church and Mental Health* features essays by Gene Bartlett, pastor of Los Angeles's First Baptist Church, and Daniel Blain, medical director of the APA. In light of new insights into the enslaving power of neurotic guilt, they recommend psychotherapy for ministers and new preaching rules for pastors; see Bartlett, "Preaching and Pastoral Rules," 109–128; and Blain, "Fostering the Mental Health of Ministers," 253–268.

94. Herman, *Romance of American Psychology,* 20–30.

95. Other Left Freudians include Herbert Marcuse and Erich Fromm, whose *Eros and Civilization* and *Escape from Freedom,* respectively, Norman O. Brown addresses as if they were heretics in *Life Against Death* (Middletown, Conn.: Wesleyan University Press, 1959). Subsequent citations will refer to the Second Edition, 1985.

96. Theodore Roszak, *The Making of a Counter Culture* (New York: Doubleday, 1969), 115.

97. Brown connects Luther's image of man as Faust to Tillich's concept of the demonic (*Life Against Death,* 210, 224), though the source he cites is not *The Courage to Be* or *Systematic Theology,* but the much earlier work from Tillich's socialist phase, *The Protestant Era.* Nowhere in *Life Against Death* does Brown acknowledge Tillich's writings on theology and psychology, which clearly show the influence of Freud's revisionists, and he does not seem to be cognizant of Tillich's relationship to figures like Erich Fromm.

98. Brown, *Life Against Death,* 233.

99. Roszak, *Making of a Counter Culture,* 107.

100. Herbert Marcuse' *Reason and Revolution* (1941), cited in Roszak, *Making of a Counter Culture,* 118. In his review of Norman O. Brown's *Love's Body* (1966), Marcuse accuses Brown of "mystification," since his "metaphysical utopia" never translates into a "historical utopia." Calling for the abolition of "the reality principle," Brown succeeds only in renouncing the historical universe: "the only one that, in any meaningful sense, can ever be the universe of freedom and fulfillment." In *Negations: Essays in Critical Theory* (Boston: Beacon Press, 1968), 227–243. Quotations from 236, 239.

101. Roberts, *Psychotherapy,* 101.

102. On the "*kairos* circle," see Wilhelm and Marion Pauck, *Paul Tillich: His Life and Thought* (Harper and Row, 1989), 70–75. Ruth Levitas discusses how Tillich's conception of utopia was shaped by Marxist philosopher Ernst Bloch, particularly his *The Principle of Hope* (1937–1947), but she is also careful to note how Tillich's contrasting belief in man's radical estrangement leads him to different conclusions about the potential power of utopian aspiration. See Levitas, *The Concept of Utopia* (Hertfordshire, U.K.: Philip Allan, 1990), 103–104.

103. Mailer's valorization of psychopathic states follows the progress of his friend Robert Lindner's work, recorded in best-selling works inspired by his clinical case studies, beginning with *Rebel Without a Cause: The Hypnoanalysis of a Criminal Psychopath* (1944) [inspiration for the 1954 James Dean film]; *Prescription for Rebellion* (New York: Rinehart, 1952); and *Must You Conform?* (New York: Rinehart, 1956). In *Prescription,* The psychopath mutinies against an insane society that makes adjustment its "Eleventh Commandment": "such, indeed, has become the injunction: You Must Adjust!" (167). On the relationship between Norman Mailer and Robert Lindner, see Mary Dearborn, *Mailer: A Biography* (New York: Houghton Mifflin, 1999), 92, 112–113, 128. Mailer pays tribute to Lindner, with excerpts from his work, in *Advertisements for Myself* (Cambridge, Mass.: Harvard University Press, 1992), 303–305.

104. Seeley, *Americanization of the Unconscious*, 16, 421, 422. Seeley imagines a marriage of psychology and sociology that would lead to the removal of utopian thinking. The shaping of human nature and social reconstruction would proceed hand in hand. For his vision, and specific reform proposals, see further in *The Americanization of the Unconscious*, 18–35, 48–63, 239–266, 280–295, 418–435.

105. Reinhold Niebuhr, in *Human Nature*, praises Horney for calling Freud's theory of anxiety too narrowly biological, but then chides her for replacing Freud's explanation with a too narrowly socioeconomic one. He directs her instead to Kierkegaard for a proper education in the meaning of *angst* (43–44, 44n4).

106. The terms "surplus repression" and "repressive desublimation" are Marcuse's, from *Eros and Civilization* (1955), revisited in *One-Dimensional Man* (1964).

107. Roberts, *Psychotherapy*, 113–114.

108. Throughout *The Mind of the Moralist*, Rieff uses Freud to tame liberalism and the ideology of progress, much as Niebuhr uses Augustine; see "Politics and the Individual," 220–256.

109. Pratt, "The Parish Minister" 202; David E. Roberts, "Concluding Remarks" 278–279.

110. Roberts, *Psychotherapy*, 133, 134, 135.

111. Caption for *Time*, March 8, 1948, which featured Reinhold Niebuhr's photograph on the cover and Chambers's story "Faith for a Lenten Age" inside.

112. In "A Note on 'The Nature of Man,'" (1957), Carl Rogers addresses an essay by fellow psychologist D. E. Walker, proposing that Rogers is as much a modern-day Rousseau as Freud was a modern-day Augustine. Rogers says that his own experiences in client therapy do not justify early Freudianism, and he speculates that most modern psychologists would agree with him. See "A Note on 'The Nature of Man'" (1957), in *Carl Rogers Reader*, 401–409. D. E. Walker's essay, "Carl Rogers and the Nature of Man," appeared in *The Journal of Counseling and Psychology* 3 (1956): 89–92.

113. Lasch, *The Culture of Narcissism*, 166.

114. Article cited in Menninger, *Whatever Became of Sin?* 44. By the mid-fifties, the APA was concerned over the number of pastors without medical accreditation who were offering amateur consultations.

8. Locating the Enigma of Shirley Jackson

1. Judy Oppenheimer, *Private Demons: The Life of Shirley Jackson* (New York: Fawcett Columbine, 1988), 125; on Jackson's upbringing, see 11–20. Jackson's career was cut short by her heart failure in 1965. Oppenheimer cites Jackson's unsent letter, quoted in the epigraph (233).

2. S. T. Joshi, "Domestic Horror," *The Modern Weird Tale* (Jefferson, NC: McFarland, 2001), 42–46.

3. Harvey Breit, "Talk with Miss Jackson," *New York Times Book Review*, June 26, 1949, 15.

4. Jackson was an avid reader on the subject of witchcraft, and she had a private library on the subject amounting to some five hundred volumes. Oppenheimer

also reports that when Jackson was a college student, she once attempted to conjure the Devil with magic; see Oppenheimer, *Private Demons*, 36–37, 49, 188–190.

5. There is no date available for "The Smoking Room," which was previously unpublished. Jackson's children, Laurence Jackson Hyman and Sarah Hyman Stewart, collected the story in an anthology they edited, *Just An Ordinary Day* (New York: Bantam, 1996), 3–8.

6. It is a mark of her novelty, and of her provocation, that Jackson's contemporaries responded to her with a mixture of admiration, bewilderment, and condescension. See Lenemaja Friedman, annotated bibliography to *Shirley Jackson* (Boston: Twayne Publishers, 1975), 167–177.

7. Leslie Fiedler, *Love and Death in the American Novel* (1960; repr., New York: Delta Books, 1966); and Harry Levin, *The Power of Blackness* (New York: Vintage Books, 1958).

8. Fiedler, *Love and Death*, xxii; and Levin, *Power of Blackness*, 236.

9. Levin, *Power of Blackness*, xii, 236. Mr. Smooth-It-Away is a character in Hawthorne's homage to Bunyan, "The Celestial Railroad" (1843), and the statement, "No, in Thunder!" is from Melville's letter to Hawthorne, April 16, 1851, upon reading *The House of Seven Gables*. These are Levin's allusions.

10. In the first book-length treatment of Jackson's work since Joan Wylie Hall's *Shirley Jackson: A Study of the Short Fiction* (New York: Twayne Publishers, 1993), Darryl Hattenhauer argues, on scant evidence, that Jackson was a Marxist whose fiction interrogates her ideology, "reveal[ing] the cracks" in its "foundation"; *Shirley Jackson's American Gothic* (Albany, N.Y.: State University of New York Press, 2003), 173. It is true that Stanley Hyman (then her boyfriend) introduced her to Marxism while she was a student at Syracuse University (1937–1940), that she briefly joined the Young Communist League, and that she and Stanley named the campus magazine the *Spectre* after Marx's famous metaphor in *The Communist Manifesto*. However, her involvement with radical politics (which, according to Jackson's biographer, Judy Oppenheimer, never reflected a deep commitment) coincided with her years at Syracuse in the late thirties. There is no biographical evidence supporting Hattenhauer's assumption that Jackson continued to be preoccupied with Marxism in her postwar career. If her fiction is sensitive to class divisions (as in *The Road Through the Wall* or the story "IOU"), this is insufficient evidence to support the inference that Jackson "holds to the Marxist notion of a largely determinate base underlying an apparently disordered surface" (6). I follow Oppenheimer's well-researched biography in portraying the postwar Jackson as a left-of-center liberal whose Marxist politics belonged to her college years. On Jackson's campus radicalism, see Oppenheimer, *Private Demons*, 60, 61, 64, 66–68, 73, 76–79, 83, 106.

11. The phrase "domestic containment," referring to the antifeminist rollback following World War II, is Elaine Tyler May's from her study *Homeward Bound: American Families in the Cold War Era* (New York: Basic Books, 1998). Psychology played a large role in normalizing a new cult of domesticity on the model of the nuclear, suburban family. This normalization was accomplished

in part by pathologizing deviance from traditional gender roles. According to Ellen Herman, "wartime preoccupations with 'normal neurosis' in ordinary male soldiers faded after 1945 and expert attention shifted decisively toward the female gender. The new focus on women revealed a plethora of gender disorders eating away at the domestic tranquility and national security of the country"; *The Romance of American Psychology* (Berkeley: University of California Press, 1995), 277–278.

12. See Jackson's stories "A Fine Old Firm" (1944), disclosing anti-Semitism, and "After You, My Dear Alphonse" (1943), showing up white stereotypes of blacks, and "The Flower Garden" (1948), concerning white prejudice in a Vermont country town.

13. Carol A. Warren, *Madwives: Schizophrenic Women in the Fifties* (New Brunswick, N.J.: Rutgers University Press, 1997), 8.

14. Richard Pascal adapts the Freudian term "reality principle," to contrast the customary ways people see the world to the "fantastic inversions" Jackson and her heroines perform on conventional perceptions; Richard Pascal, "'Farther than Samarkand': The Escape Theme in Shirley Jackson's 'The Tooth,'" *Studies in Short Fiction* 19 (1982): 133–39. See also James Egan, "Sanctuary: Shirley Jackson's Domestic and Fantastic Parables," *Studies in Weird Fiction* 6 (1989), 15–24.

15. The best feminist interpretations of "The Lottery" are Fritz Oelschlaeger, "The Stoning of Miss Hutchinson: Meaning and Context in 'The Lottery,'" *Essays in Literature* 15 (1988): 259–65; and Peter Kosenko, "A Marxist/Feminist Reading of Shirley Jackson's 'The Lottery,'" *New Orleans Review* 12 (Spring 1985): 27–32.

16. See Seymour Lainoff, "Jackson's 'The Lottery,'" *Explicator* 12 (March 1954): 34; Helen Nebeker, "'The Lottery': Symbolic Tour de Force," *American Literature* 46 (1974): 100–7; and James M. Gibson, "An Old Testament Analogue for 'The Lottery,'" *Journal of Modern Literature* 11 (March 1984): 193–195. Gibson identifies a comparable lottery from Joshua 7.

17. The Christian allusions in "The Lottery" have been highlighted by Helen Nebeker, "'The Lottery.'" These include the name of one of the village clans, "Delacroix" ("of the Cross") and the three-legged stool (the trinity) on which the box of lots rests.

18. Oppenheimer, *Private Demons*, 125.

19. On the social and religious functions of the sacrificial victim, see René Girard's classic *Violence and the Sacred*, trans. Patrick Gregory (Baltimore: Johns Hopkins University Press, 1972) and his follow-up study, *Things Hidden Since the Foundation of the World*, trans. Stephen Bann and Michael Metteer (Stanford, Calif.: Stanford University Press, 1987).

20. Jackson's unsent letter to Nemerov, *Private Demons*, 233.

21. Jackson seemed to respond well to the treatment—though no such positive relationship exists between a therapist and a patient in her fiction. See Oppenheimer, *Private Demons*, 237, 240–242, 245–262.

22. The term "momism," was coined by Philip Wylie in *Generation of Vipers* (1942; reissued 1955; repr., Normal, Ill.: Dalkey Archive, 1996). Certain clin-

ical psychologists adopted the term as a diagnostic category for gender disorder; see Herman, *Romance of American Psychology,* 276–284. On cultural
momism, see Michael Rogin, "Kiss Me Deadly: Communism and Cold War
Movies," *Representations* 6 (Spring 1984): 1–36.

23. Mary Ann Doane has noted that the woman's imagination seems to be disease-
producing, her daydreaming the instigator of turmoil; "Clinical Eyes: The
Medical Discourse," in *The Desire to Desire: The Woman's Film of the 1940s*
(Bloomington: Indiana University Press, 1987), 53. With few exceptions, such
as Hitchcock's *Spellbound*, the mental patients of case-study films were usually
female; see Krin Gabbard and Glen Gabbard, *Psychiatry and the Cinema* (Chicago: University of Chicago Press, 1987), 60–114. Several of these films had
literary sources; these include the MGM production *Lizzie* (1957), adapted
from Jackson's *The Bird's Nest*.

24. Oppenheimer, *Private Demons,* 162.

25. Warren, *Madwives,* 58, 73, 79, 81.

26. Shirley Jackson, *Hangsaman* (New York: Farrar, Straus, and Giroux, 1975),
425.

27. See Paul Ricoeur, "Defilement," *The Symbolism of Evil,* trans. Emerson Bu-
chanan (New York: Harper and Row, 1967), 25–46.

28. Wyatt Bonikowski, "'Only One Antagonist . . . Only One Enemy': The Feminine Experience in the Work of Shirley Jackson," Cornell University (paper
presented at the panel, "Shirley Jackson: Beyond *The Lottery,*" thirty-fourth annual convention of the Northeast Modern Language Association, Boston, Mass.,
March 7, 2003; panel chaired by Lynn Parker, Framingham State College).

29. Jackson, *Hangsaman,* 288.

30. In the tarot deck, the Hanging Man is pictured as a body inverted on "a tree
of sacrifice" (Jackson, *Hangsaman,* 522). If the card is upright, the allegory
reads, "life in death. Joy of constructive death" (522). If reversed, it means
one's own death rather than regeneration. In Natalie's life at least, its meaning
is reversed.

31. Joan Wylie Hall has argued persuasively that the character's name alludes to
Elizabeth Style, a witch whose partnership with the Devil is a showpiece of
Glanville's *Saducismus Triumphatus;* see Hall, *Shirley Jackson,* 7–8.

32. Shirley Jackson, *The Bird's Nest* in *The Magic of Shirley Jackson,* Stanley Edgar Hyman, ed. (New York: Farrar, Strauss, & Giroux, 1975), 189. (Further
references will be cited as Jackson, *The Bird's Nest*.

33. Freud, *The Standard Edition of the Complete Psychological Works,* vol. 7,
1901–1905: A Case of Hysteria, ed. and trans. James Strachey (London: Hogarth Press, 1953), 109. Jackson may have also been aware that Freud compared
medieval demonology and the psychoanalytic theory of hysteria, saying that
modern science had merely discovered the truth behind the older metaphors.
This was a claim that psychological medicine had been making about the myth
of demon possession since the late nineteenth century; see Thomas Szasz, *The
Manufacture of Madness* (New York: Harper and Row, 1970), 73–75.

34. Shirley Jackson, *The Bird's Nest,* 364.

35. Girard, *Violence and the Sacred,* 165.

36. Jackson, *Bird's Nest*, 378.
37. Thomas Szasz, "Theology, Witchcraft, and Hysteria," in *The Myth of Mental Illness*, rev. ed. (1960; repr., New York: Harper and Row, 1974); and "The Inquisition and Institutional Psychiatry" 3–134 and "The Expulsion of Evil," 260–275 in *Manufacture of Madness*. For background on Szasz and Chesler, see Herman. "Psychiatry Constructs the Female," in *Romance of American Psychology*, 280–290.
38. Szasz, *Myth of Mental Illness*, 186.
39. See Phyllis Chesler, *Women and Madness* (Garden City, N.Y.: Doubleday, 1972), esp. 9–10n, 27n, 101–106. Chesler also draws on Michel Foucault's *Madness and Civilization* (1961), as does Szasz in *The Manufacture of Madness*.
40. On the theory of witchcraft power, see Walter Stephens, *Demon Lovers: Witchcraft, Sex, and the Crisis of Belief* (Chicago: University of Chicago Press, 2002), 180–207.
41. Shirley Jackson, "The Tooth," *The Lottery and Other Stories* (New York: Farrar, Straus, & Giroux, 1949), 265–286.
42. Jackson alludes to the belief that blood-drinking is damnable in *The Witchcraft of Salem Village* (New York: Landmark Books, 1956), when she recounts the last words of Sarah Goode, who warned her confessors that if she were hung, then they, not she, would be cursed: "I am no more a witch than you are a wizard, and if you take away my life, God will give you blood to drink!" (129). Blood-drinking is also a blasphemous witches' rite in Hawthorne's *The House of Seven Gables* (1851). For an alternative interpretation of this passage, which erroneously reads the blood-drinking as an expiation, see Richard Pascal, "Farther than Samarkand," 133–139.
43. Francis Child's ballad no. 243, "James Harris, the Daemon Lover," provides the epilogue to *The Lottery; or the Adventures of James Harris* (1949), subsequently reprinted, against Jackson's intentions, as simply *The Lottery and Other Stories*. Joan Wylie Hall shows how the ballad, in which a mysterious stranger, James Harris (an alias for the devil), seduces a young woman and swirls her down to hell, provides a connective device between the tales, several of which feature or allude to the Harris figure (Hall, *Shirley Jackson*, 11–16, 17–18).
44. Many readers of *The Haunting of Hill House* have read the novel as if it were an account of a neurotic's breakdown. In fact, Nelson Gidding, screenwriter of Robert Wise's acclaimed 1963 film adaptation, *The Haunting*, actually mistook the novel for a Caligari-like Chinese box, in which all the events turned out to be a female mental patient's colored perceptions of a hospital; see Nelson Gidding, foreword to *Robert Wise on His Films*, ed. Sergio Leemann (Los Angeles: Silman-James Press, 1995).
45. Shirley Jackson, *The Haunting of Hill House* (New York: Penguin Books, 1959), 3, 246.
46. See Leviticus 14:47, 49–53. In *Powers of Horror*, Julia Kristeva discusses Leviticus at length, arguing that the taboos against unclean flesh ultimately repudiate the maternal body; see "Semiotics of Biblical Abomination," in *Powers of Horror* (New York: Columbia University Press, 1982). Tricia Lootens as-

sociates Nell's mother with defilement and asserts that the disgusting plasma in Theo's room is "clearly menstrual imagery," in "'Whose Hand Was I Holding?': Familial and Sexual Politics in Shirley Jackson's *The Haunting of Hill House*," in *Haunting the House of Fiction: Feminist Perspectives on Ghost Stories by American Women*, ed. Lynette Carpenter and Wendy Kolmar (Knoxville: University of Tennessee Press, 1991), 183. On the old house as a theological metaphor of the profane body, see Victor Sage's chapter, "Dark House: Theology and the Picturesque," in his *Horror Fiction in the Protestant Tradition* (New York: St. Martin's Press, 1988) 1–25.

47. Jackson, *Haunting of Hill House*, 75.

48. Lootens, "'Whose Hand Was I Holding?'" 183.

49. Jackson, *Haunting of Hill House*, 123, 213.

50. Judie Newman, *"On The Haunting of Hill House," Gothic Horror: A Reader's Guide from Poe to King and Beyond* ed. Clive Bloom (New York: St. Martin's Press, 1998), 159.

51. Jackson, *Haunting of Hill House*, 137, 166–167, 180.

52. Like Sandra Gilbert and Susan Gubar in *The Madwoman in the Attic* (1979), Oppenheimer dubiously turns insanity and self-annihilation into signs of feminine assertiveness (*Private Demons*, 164).

53. See R. D. Laing, *The Politics of Experience* (New York: Pantheon Books, 1967).

54. See George Steiner, foreword to *The Death of Tragedy* (New Haven: Yale University Press, 1996), v. See also Paul Ricoeur's discussion of the wicked God, *The Symbolism of Evil* (New Yorker: Harper and Row, 1967), 89.

55. "O-gape," a pun on "agape" connoting void and narcissistic orality, appears in Plath's "The Moon in the Yew Tree." See "Piranha Religion: Plath's Theology," in Tim Kendall, *Sylvia Plath: A Critical Study* (London: Faber and Faber, 2001), 117, 118, 122.

56. Jackson, *Haunting of Hill House*, 3.

57. Jackson once explained that she was writing about the possibilities of "order" and "adjustment" in "an inhuman world" (Oppenheimer, *Private Demons*, 125).

9. Voices of Reform, Radicalism, and Conservative Dissent

1. Epigraph from Jacques Maritain, *Man and the State* (Chicago: University of Chicago Press, 1953), 143. Maritain has actually traced the notion of natural law in Christian theology to St. Paul's statement from Romans 2:14, "When the Gentiles who have not the Law, do by nature the things contained in the Law, these, having not the Law, are a law unto themselves"; see Maritain, *Man and the State*, 84–85.

2. James Darsey's intelligent study, *The Prophetic Tradition and Radical Rhetoric in America* (New York: New York University Press, 1997), falters when it attempts to identify natural law with prophetic ethos. On higher law, see Greg Crane, "Human Law and Higher Law" in Maurice Lee, ed. *The Cambridge Companion to Frederick Douglass* (Cambridge, UK: Cambridge University Press, 2009), 89–102

3. Bertrand Russell, *Authority and the Individual* (1949; repr., New York: AMS Press, 1968), 69.

4. See Reinhold Niebuhr's famous critique of natural law theory in *Human Destiny* (New York: Scribner's Sons, 1964), 278–298. In addition to *The Genius of American Politics* (Chicago: University of Chicago Press, 1953), 73, see Niebuhr's editorial, "We Need an Edmund Burke," *Christianity and Society* 16 (Summer 1951), and his tribute to Burke in *Christian Realism and Social Problems* (New York: Scribner, 1953), 72. Niebuhr shows a Burkean aversion to the abstractness of laws creating new rights in his reflections on *Brown vs. Board of Education*, stating that the law, in most instances, cannot communicate new moral claims, but only catch up to the "mores of the community": "The law sometimes plays a creative role, as it has in this instance [*Brown vs. Board*]. But usually the law merely regularizes and symbolizes realities and power relations that have been achieved by gradual accommodation"; Niebuhr, "Justice to the American Negro from State, Community, and Church," in *Pious and Secular America* (New York: Scribner's, 1958), 79–82. See Cornel West's gloss on Niebuhr's essays regarding desegregation, in *The American Evasion of Philosophy* (Madison: University of Wisconsin Press, 1989), 163.

   John Bennett denies that Niebuhr has become one of the many so-called "New Conservatives" who also quote Burke, such as Russell Kirk; "Reinhold Neibuhr's Social Ethics," in *Reinhold Niebuhr: His Religious, Social, and Political Thought*, ed. Charles Kegley (New York: MacMillan, 1956), 75–77. Peter Viereck seconds Bennett; as distinct from the Southern Agrarians, who are merely nostalgic for roots, the authentic "Burkean new conservative" is Reinhold Niebuhr for "his view of history" and "anti-modernist, anti-liberal" theology; see Viereck, "The Philosophical 'New Conservativism'" (1962), in *The Radical Right*, 3rd ed., ed. Daniel Bell (New York: Transaction, 2002), 199–200.

5. See David Riesman's fulsome appeal for a reconstructed "utopianism" befitting the values of the rising middle class, in "A Philosophy for Minority Living," in *Individualism Reconsidered* (New York: Free Press, 1954), 99–120; see also "Some Observations Concerning Marginality," 153–165; and "Marginality, Conformity, and Insight," 166–178. The Old Testament prophets teach upwardly mobile minorities, including Jews and blacks, to resist the pressures of conformity (Reisman, *Individualism Reconsidered*, 67–68). The ethic of resistance that Riesman learns from the Old Testament has less to do with *The Book of Amos* and more with *Guess Who's Coming to Dinner?*

6. In the early twentieth century, Reformed Judaism's social justice advocacy and involvement in union labor struggles derived from "the words of the prophets" and "contemporary American liberalism"; Lloyd P. Gartner, "American Judaism, 1880–1945," in *The Cambridge Companion to American Judaism*, ed. Dana Evan Kaplan (Cambridge, UK: Cambridge University Press, 2005), 53. See also Michael Meyer, *Response to Modernity: A History of the Reformed Movement in Judaism* (New York: Oxford University Press, 1988), 286–289. Meyer argues that the Social Gospel's influence on the American rabbinate effected a transformation from "prophetic idealism" to "applied social justice." Scholar and rabbi Abraham Heschel, of German Hasidic background, was a

theological critic of Reform Judaism, but he nonetheless identified himself very visibly as a prophet for whom the theological and the political were intertwined. In the civil rights era, he befriended Martin Luther King, Jr., and linked "the black struggle to the biblical Exodus," much as King himself; qtd. in Jonathan Sarna, *American Judaism* (New Haven: Yale University Press, 2005), 311.

7. The New Right's Jewish allies in the neoconservative movement stress duality of the teleological-utopian and eschatological-apocalyptic interpretations of the prophets, and find the former irreconcilable with the content of the Hebrew books and with rabbinical tradition. At book length, in *The Prophets* (2002), Podhoretz has attacked "liberological" misreadings of the Old Testament, and Kristol has said that Jewish liberals and socialists alike have secularized Hebrew prophecy, "paving the way for the extinction of Judaism in America itself"; Kristol, qtd. in Jacob Heilbrun, *They Knew They Were Right: The Rise of the Neocons* (New York: Anchor Books, 2009), 12. In the fifties, Nathan Glazer, later associated with the neoconservative movement, made the case that within Judaism there had been no version of the Christian Social Gospel. Jewish concerns for social justice were not drawn from, at the most only mildly influenced by, ancestral religion: "I believe that Jewish social attitudes derive more from nineteenth century liberalism and socialism than from the Hebrew prophets" (Glazer quoted in Sarna, *American Judaism*, 141). Judaism, Glazer says, had been a religion of laws and observances, a way of being Jewish in the world, not an inspiration for reforming the world, much less radically changing it, as in some Christian sects.

8. Timothy Smith, *Revivalism and Social Reform: American Protestantism on the Eve of the Civil War* (Gloucester, Mass.: Peter Smith, 1976), 188–223.

9. Walter Rauschenbusch, *A Theology of the Social Gospel* (New York: Mac-Millan, 1917), 21.

10. Walter Rauschenbusch, *The Righteousness of the Kingdom* (New York: Abingdon, 1968), 230.

11. Rauschenbusch, *Theology*, 147, 149.

12. Rauschenbusch, *Theology*, 195. See also Rauschenbusch, *Righteousness*, 118–132; "The Holy Spirit, Revelation, Inspiration, Prophecy," in *Theology*, 188–196; and "The Historical Roots of Christianity: The Hebrew Prophets," in *Christianity and the Social Crisis* [1907] *in the 21st Century,* ed. Paul Rauschenbusch (New York: HarperCollins, 2007), 1–31. Rauschenbusch's images of Jesus and the Old Testament prophets as social revolutionaries bears close comparison to the tradition of nineteenth-century religious socialism in Europe and in antebellum America; for types of the revolutionary Christ, see Theodore Ziolkowski, "The Christian Socialist Jesus," in *Fictional Transfigurations of Jesus* (Princeton, N.J.: Princeton University Press, 1972), 55–97.

13. On the Protestant theory that the prophets were filled with the Holy Ghost, see Abraham Heschel, *The Prophets* (New York: Harper and Row, 1962), 343–344. The theory is likely derived from 1 John 4, where the apostle separates true from false prophets based on whether they are filled with the Holy Ghost. For a contemporary example, see John Rea, Th. D., *Charisma's Bible Handbook on the Holy Spirit* (Lake Mary, Fla.: Creation House, 1998). The handbook is endorsed by the renowned, conservative Fuller Theological Seminary.

14. Rauschenbusch, *Theology,* 148, 150, 146–166; see also 158, 192, 250–252, 274–275.

15. Rauschenbusch, *Righteousness,* 178.

16. Rauschenbusch, *Theology,* 40. See Romans 5 and 1 Corinthians 15.

17. Rauschenbusch, *Righteousness,* 191.

18. Rauschenbusch, *Theology,* 229.

19. The Social Gospel movement was basically progressivist in its orientation, and Rauschenbusch's "Communism" and "socialistic political economy" is to the left of Teddy Roosevelt's Bull Moose Party mainly in its calls for some public ownership (versus Teddy Roosevelt's trust-busting in the name of private competition) and for the organization of working-class protest groups to compel some divestment of private wealth (versus elite regulatory management of big business). His most radical proposal is for labor's collective ownership of production and its yield, though he asks that the transfer of economic power happen by gradualistic rather than revolutionary means; see Rauschenbusch, *Christianity and the Social Crisis,* 301, 312, 314, 322–330.

20. Reinhold Niebuhr, *Human Nature* (Upper Saddle River, NJ: Prentice Hall, 1964), 246, 246n3.

21. In *Reflections on the End of an Era* (1934), for example, Reinhold Niebuhr had joined the legacy of the Old Testament prophets with the Reformation and the Marxist theory of historical crisis. See also "Christian Radicalism," *Radical Religion* (Winter 1936): 8–9; "Marx, Barth, and Israel's Prophets," *Christian Century,* LII, no. 5 January 30, 1935, 138–140; and *Christianity and Power Politics* (New York: Charles Scribner's Sons, 1940), 181–182, 222. See also Arthur Schlesinger, Jr., "Reinhold Niebuhr's Role in American Political Thought and Life" (1956), in *The Politics of Hope* (Boston: Houghton Mifflin, 1963), 111.

22. Niebuhr, *Christianity and Power Politics,* 163–165, 167–175.

23. Reinhold Niebuhr, *Moral Man and Immoral Society* (New York: Charles Scribner's Sons, 1932), 152, 154–168, 220–223.

24. Niebuhr, *Human Nature,* 224–226.

25. For earlier instances of this opinion, see Niebuhr, *Christianity and Power Politics,* 25, 36, 163–165, 167–175.

26. *Reader in Public Opinion and Communication,* ed. Bernard Berelson and Morris Janowitz (Glencoe, Ill.: The Free Press, 1953), 278–288, 407–422, 465–468; Howard Lasswell, *The Analysis of Political Behavior* (Hamden, Conn.: Archon, 1947); Leon Festinger, Henry W. Reicken, and Stanley Schachter, *When Prophecy Fails* (Minneapolis: University of Minnesota Press, 1956); Norman Cohn, *Pursuit of the Millenium,* rev. ed. (1957; repr., New York: Oxford University Press, 1970), 285–286; Arthur Schlesinger, Jr., *The Politics of Upheaval* (Boston: Houghton Mifflin, 1960), 42–68. For a description of the impact Weber's theories had on political philosophy and history in American academies, see Arthur Schlesinger, Jr.'s "On Heroic Leadership," in *The Politics of Hope* (Boston: Houghton Mifflin, 1963). See also Schlesinger's "Messiah of the Rednecks" (1960), on Huey Long, and Robert Penn Warren's Pulitzer prize–winning novel, *All the King's Men* (New York: Harcourt, Brace, 1946), in which Willie Stark is the prophet demoagogue who tragically defies

the irony of history; "Messiah of the Rednecks," in *Huey Long,* ed. Hugh
Davis Graham (Englewood Cliffs, N.J.: Prentice-Hall, 1970), 145–161.

27. For a discussion of these sociologists' work on Weber, see S. N. Eisenstadt's
introduction to Max Weber, *On Charisma and Institution Building,* ed. S. N.
Eisenstadt (Chicago: University of Chicago Press, 1968), x–xi. On the context
of Weber's reception in the age of fascism, see "Max Weber and the Contemporary Political Crisis" (1942) in Talcott Parsons, *Talcott Parsons on National
Socialism,* ed. Uta Gerhardt (New York: Walter de Gruyter, 1993), 159–187.
A pioneering study quickly issued, as Columbia University sociologist Theodore Abel used Weberian categories to describe Hitler's leadership in the Na-
tional Socialist movement; Abel, *Why Hitler Came Into Power* (New York:
Prentice-Hall, 1938). For further discussion of charisma in totaliatarian sys-
tems, see Alex Inkeles, "The Totalitarian Mystique," in Carl J. Friedrich, ed.,
Totalitarianism (Cambridge, MA: Harvard University Press, 1954), 47–60.
Friedrich and Brzezinski call Hitler and Stalin "pseudo-charismatic" because
their religions lack "genuine religious context" and "transcendent faith in
God" in *Totalitarian Dictatorship and Autocracy,* 2nd ed. (Cambridge, MA:
Harvard University Press, 1965), 41, 44.

28. The English word "charisma" derives from the Church Latin, which in turn
derives from the Greek *kharisma,* translated "divine gift." In the Greek texts,
the word occurs several times in the epistles to the churches in Corinth (the
first letter), Rome, and Ephesus. For exact references and interpretation, see
Robert Banks, *Paul's Idea of Community,* 2nd ed. (Peabody, Mass.: Hendrickson, 1994), 88–109. In Weber, "charisma," always stated in the singular, accomplishes the inverse of Pauline fellowship, for, by its nature, it is accessible
only to a chosen avatar. Compare Rauschenbusch's own Pauline conception of
the primitive church's "charismatic life": "The new thing in the history of
Pentecost is not only the number of those who received the tongue of fire but
the fact that the Holy Spirit had become the common property of a group.
What had seemed to some extent the privilege of aristocratic souls was now
democraticized" (*Theology,* 189).

29. Weber, *On Charisma,* 20, 24, 40, 51.

30. Maritain, *Man and the State,* 140, 139.

31. C. Vann Woodward, *The Burden of Southern History* (Baton Rouge: Louisiana State University Press, 1993), 1–25, 41–68, 187–211. Robert Penn Warren, *The Legacy of the Civil War* (Lincoln: University of Nebraska Press,
1961), 71–76; *Democracy and Poetry* (Cambridge, Mass.: Harvard University
Press, 1975), 15–22, 54–55; and "The Use of the Past" (1978), in *New and
Selected Essays* (New York: Random House, 1989), 32–34. Richard Reinitz
discusses Niebuhr's impact on C. Van Woodward in his *Irony and Consciousness: American Historiography and Reinhold Niebuhr's Vision* (Lewisburg,
PA: Bucknell University Press, 1980).

32. For examples of Warren's demagogic prophets, see, in addition to *All The
King's Men,* his history, *John Brown: The Making of a Martyr* (New York:
Payson and Clark, 1929); his novel *Night Rider* (Boston: Houghton Mifflin,
1939); his discussion of abolitionism in his extended essay, *Legacy of the*

Civil War, 20–33; and his portrait of Malcom X in his journalistic *Who Speaks for the Negro?* (New York: Random House, 1965). Warren tended to treat biblical prophets as themselves bloodthirsty; see his portrayal of Elijah in "Saul at Bilboa," Part 1 of a pair of poems, "Holy Writ," from *Tale of Time: Poems 1960–1966,* included in *The Collected Poems of Robert Penn Warren,* ed. John Burt (Baton Rouge: Louisiana State University Press, 1998), 207–214.

33. On Southern conservatism's and traditionalist Catholicism's common criticism of impersonal market relations, bourgeois individualism, and liberal theology, see Eugene D. Genovese, *The Southern Tradition: The Achievement and Limits of an American Conservatism* (Cambridge, Mass.: Harvard University Press, 1994), 14–15, 22–23.

34. Ralph C. Wood, "Flannery O'Connor's Strange Alliance with Southern Fundamentalists," *Literature and Belief* 17 nos. 1–2 (1997), 75–98.

35. Section epigraph from Flannery O'Connor, *Mystery and Manners* (New York: Farrar, Straus and Giroux, 1961).

36. The best overall discussion of Southern fundamentalism in O'Connor's writing is Robert Coles's "Hard, Hard Religion," in his *Flannery O'Connor's South* (Athens: University of Georgia Press, 1980), 57–108. See also Brad Gooch, *Flannery: A Life of Flannery O'Connor* (New York: Little, Brown, 2009), 222–223, 269–270, 279–307, 323–325.

37. O'Connor, *Mystery and Manners,* 131.

38. Coles, *Flannery O'Connor's South,* 5.

39. "Revelation" in *The Complete Stories* (New York: Farrar, Straus and Giroux, 1992), 488–509. At the close of "Revelation," Mrs. Turpin has a vision that causes her to transcend her usual vanity about having been born white and landowning rather than "white-trash," "common," or "nigger" (491). In the vision, people of all classes tumble towards heaven, reminding Mrs. Turpin that the grace through Christ can raise anyone regardless of their earthly station.

40. O'Connor, *Mystery and Manners,* 203.

41. Much of O'Connor criticism devotes some space to the prophecy theme in her fiction and essays. The most helpful of these works is Sister Kathleen Feeley's "The Tatooed Christ: The Prophet's View of Reality," in *Voice of the Peacock* (New York: Fordham University Press, 1982), 140–178, which documents some of O'Connor's scholarly and theological sources on the biblical prophets: Bruce Vawter's *The Conscience of Israel* (1961), Eric Voeglin's *Order and History,* vol. 1, *Israel and Revelation* (1956), and Thomas Aquinas's *Der Veritate.*

42. Thomas Hill Schaub, *American Fiction in the Cold War* (Madison: University of Wisconsin Press, 1991); and Jon Lance Bacon, *Flannery O'Connor and Cold War Culture* (New York: University of Cambridge Press, 1993).

43. Bacon, *Flannery O'Connor,* 115–116, 137–138.

44. Henry Luce, "Wanted: An American Novel" *Life,* September 12, 1955, 48.

45. On O'Connor's attitude towards "interleckchuls," see Robert Coles's essay, "A Southern Intellectual," in *Flannery O'Connor's South,* 112–161. Coles does an excellent job of balancing O'Connor's extraordinary erudition and curiosity against her wariness of the Northern intellectuals who helped to

build her reputation. She was, of course, also promoted by the Southern New Critical school in such premiere literary journals as *Sewanee Review* and *Kenyon Review;* see Sarah Fodor, "Marketing Flannery O'Connor: Institutional Politics and Literary Evaluation," in *Flannery O'Connor: New Perspectives,* ed. Sura P. Rath and Mary Neff Shaw (Athens: University of Georgia Press, 1996), 12–37.

46. O'Connor, *Mystery and Manners,* 26, 30, 33.

47. O'Connor declined even calls from the Catholic press for "'positive novel[s] based on the Church's fight for social justice'"; see *Mystery and Manners,* 195.

48. On the sentimentalization of ethical judgment, see O'Connor, *Mystery and Manners* (43, 49, 146–149, 192, 227). See also for instance, O'Connor's strong exception to Steinbeck's statement: "In the end was the word and the word was with men" (159).

49. On O'Connor's association of sentimentality with "bourgeois" values, see *Mystery and Manners,* 41.

50. According to Graham, Sheen introduced himself on a train from Washington, D.C. to New York: "We talked about our ministries and our common commitment to evangelism, and I told him how grateful I was for his ministry and his focus on Christ"; see Billy Graham, *Just As I Am* (San Francisco: HarperCollins, 1997), 692–694. The meeting was the beginning of a friendship that lasted until Sheen's death in 1979. Graham recalls that the meeting occurred in "the early years of his ministry" and while Sheen's prime-time television series, *Life Is Worth Living,* was still on air (692).

51. Flannery O'Connor to "A" (addressee not otherwise identified), July 25, 1959, in *Habit of Being,* ed. Sally Fitzgerald (New York: Farrar, Straus and Giroux, 1979), 342.

52. Flannery O'Connor, *The Violent Bear It Away* (New York: Noonday Press, 1988), 21, 39; and *Mystery and Manners,* 227.

53. O'Connor, *Mystery and Manners,* 39. O'Connor is obviously inspired by the vivid anagogical imagery in the Old Testament prophecies as well as their many references to special vision (Ezekiel's "opened heavens," Daniel's dreams, the preambles to Isaiah, Obadiah, or Nahum), but she describes the gift of prophetic sight in nonbiblical categories borrowed from the modernist and New Critical theories of the symbol she had imbibed at the Writer's Workshop, University of Iowa, as when she describes "the Hebrew genius for making the absolute concrete" (202). For a discussion of O'Connor's New Critical aesthetics, see P. Albert Duhamel, "The Novelist as Prophet," in *The Added Dimension: The Art and Mind of Flannery O'Connor,* ed. Melvin Friedman and Lewis Lawson (New York: Fordham University, 1977), 88–93. On the New Critical reception of O'Connor's work, see Fodor, "Marketing Flannery O'Connor," 26–32.

54. Flannery O'Connor, review of *The Conscience of Israel,* by Bruce Vawter, in the Georgia diocesan *Bulletin,* March 1962; cited in Feeley, "The Tatooed Christ," 141–142. Even though she subscribed to the Church's exegesis of the Old Testament, O'Connor was well aware that the Old Testament prophets were addressing the tribulations of Israel's history in periods of imperial conquest. The first half of O'Connor's short story "The Displaced Person" actu-

ally builds its central irony around a false prophet's ignorance that biblical books like Ezekiel were written for a displaced people. The Guizacs, Polish refugees who have been exiled by Nazi invaders, are in an analogous position to the Israelites in the time of Assyria's and Babylon's expansion.

55. O'Connor, *Mystery and Manners*, 47.

56. O'Connor, *Habit of Being*, 350.

57. Frederick Crews, "The Power of Flannery O'Connor," *New York Review of Books* (April 26, 1990): 49–55. Sarah Fodor answers Crews in her essay, "Marketing Flannery O'Connor" 12–14, 29–32.

58. O'Connor, *Habit of Being*, 42, 404, 412, 499, 549–551, 580.

59. Janet Egleson Dunleavy points out the many details in the story that betray Rayber's insincerity toward blacks; "A Particular History: Black and White in Flannery O'Connor's Short Fiction," in *Critical Essays on Flannery O' Connor*, ed. Melvin Friedman and Beverly Clark (Boston: G. K. Hall, 1985), 186–201.

60. O'Connor, *Mystery and Manners*, 132.

61. Ezekiel ingests the book, and Jeremiah eats God's words (Ezekiel 3:1–3; Jeremiah 15:16). In Revelation, John of Patmos is commanded to eat his message in the form of a book (10:9).

62. On O'Connor and civil rights, see Gooch, *Flannery*, 331–334. On O'Connor's representation of race relations, see Alice Walker, "Beyond the Peacock: The Reconstruction of Flannery O'Connor," in *Critical Essays on Flannery O'Connor*, 71–84; Jon Lance Bacon, "The Segregated Pastoral," *Flannery O'Connor and Cold War Culture*, 87–114; and Robert Coles, *Flannery O'Connor's South*, 6–13, 32–44, 149.

63. "About the Negroes, the kind I don't like is the philosophizing prophesying pontificating kind, the James Baldwin kind"; Flannery O'Connor to Maryat Lee, May 21, 1961, in *Habit of Being*, 580.

64. Flannery O'Connor, "Judgement Day," in *Stories*, 545.

65. The French Catholic novelist George Bernanos, whom O'Connor admired, also viewed poverty as a perennial reminder of human sin and as an occasion for the servant of God to administer to the weak, thus disciplining him in both charity and humility. See, for example, *The Diary of a Country Priest* (1936).

66. O'Connor wrote the introduction to *A Memoir for Mary Ann* (New York: Farrar, Straus and Cudahy, 1961), at the request of Sister Evangelist, the Sister Superior of Our Lady of Perpetual Help Free Cancer Home in Atlanta. The Cancer Home had for nine years sheltered a terribly deformed child. The introduction to the memoir is reprinted in *Mystery and Manners*, 213–228. For more background on O'Connor's introduction to the memoir, which was written by the attendant nuns, see Harold C. Gardiner, S. J., "Flannery O'Connor's Clarity of Vision," in *The Added Dimension*, esp. 184–189.

67. O'Connor, *Mystery and Manners*, 218–219.

10. James Baldwin and the Wages of Innocence

1. Epigraph and quotations from James Baldwin, "In Search of a Majority," in *James Baldwin: Collected Essays* (New York: Library of America, 1998), 215–

216. On the prophetic meanings of black preaching, see James Cone, *God of the Oppressed* (New York: Seabury Press, 1975), 17–24, 51–61, 183–194; W. E. B. Du Bois, "Of the Faith of the Fathers," in *The Souls of Black Folk* (New York: Penguin, 1996), 154–168; Henry Mitchell, *Black Preaching* (New York: J. B. Lippincott, 1970); and Albert J. Raboteau, *Slave Religion: The "Invisible Institution" in the Antebellum South* (New York: Oxford University Press, 1978), 290–318. In an interview with Budd Schulberg, Baldwin mentioned the Old Testament heritage of his youth in a black Pentecostal church. He says that he "really *did* grow up in the Old Testament" and had been taught by his father, the minister, to regard "himself as a Jew in terms of the children of Israel coming out of Egypt," as in the black spiritual "I Wish I Had Died in Egypt Land."; see James Baldwin and Budd Schulberg, "Dialogue in Black and White," (1964–1965) in *James Baldwin: The Legacy,* ed. Quincy Troupe (New York: Simon and Schuster, 1989), 143.

2. Critics who accuse Baldwin of preaching reverse racism do not appreciate that he believes "whiteness" is fundamentally a choice of identity; see Jonathan Yardley, "The Writer and the Preacher," 240–243 and Julius Lester, "Some Tickets Are Better: The Mixed Achievement of James Baldwin," 244–249, in *Critical Essays on James Baldwin,* ed. Fred L. Stanley and Nancy V. Burt (Boston: G. K. Hall, 1988).

3. Taylor Branch, *Parting the Waters: America in the King Years, 1954–63* (New York: Simon and Schuster, 1988), 69–104.

4. *The Irony of American History* mentions slavery only glancingly and makes no note of the Hays-Tilden Compromise of 1876, the Supreme Court victories for "Jim Crow" legislation, or the tokenism of social democracy from the Progressive era through the New Deal. Niebuhr had been the chairman (1926–1927) of the Interracial Committee initiated by Detroit mayor (and Catholic) John W. Smith. See Richard Fox, *Reinhold Niebuhr: A Biography* (San Francisco: Harper and Row, 1985), 90–94. For selections from Niebuhr's several articles on civil rights, from 1942 to 1958, see *Reinhold Niebuhr on Politics,* ed. Harry R. Davis and Robert C. Good (New York: Charles Scribner's Sons, 1960), 228–238, 354–355. His magazine *Christianity and Crisis* generally maintained a prudently gradualist stance until its radicalization in the late sixties; see Mark Hulsether, *Building a Protestant Left: Christianity and Crisis Magazine* (Knoxville: University of Tennessee Press, 1999), 49–55, 69–74, 117–125. Hearing echoes of his earlier work in King's teachings, Niebuhr said that King was the best Protestant alternative to Black Power leaders; see Fox, *Reinhold Niebuhr,* 281–283. During a 1963 televised meeting, titled the "Missing Face of God," Baldwin and Niebuhr debated the ethics, and the effectiveness, of nonviolence in the current struggle; see Branch, *Parting the Waters,* 896. In his conclusions, Niebuhr showed far more sympathy to the movement than Will Herberg, who condemned King for violating custom and the rule of law, in "'Civil Rights' and Violence: Who Are the Guilty Ones?" *National Review,* September 7, 1965, 769–770.

5. Harold Cruse, *The Crisis of the Negro Intellectual* (New York: William Morrow, 1967), 195.

6. In *The Evidence of Things Not Said: James Baldwin and the Promise of American Democracy* (Ithaca, N.Y.: Cornell University Press, 2001), Lawrie Balfour makes a formidable case against white innocence (see Chapter 4, "Presumptions of Innocence," 87–112), but neglects Baldwin's Christian sources, as does Louis Pratt, who contends that the prophet persona is a mode of address that Baldwin assumes only in order to assail his audience about social issues; see Pratt, *James Baldwin* (Boston: G. K. Hall, 1978), 53. The most comprehensive discussions of Baldwin's theology are Clarence E. Hardy's *James Baldwin's God: Sex, Hope, and Crisis in Black Holiness Culture* (Knoxville: University of Tennessee Press, 2003), and a trio of essays by Michael Lynch: "Just Above My Head: James Baldwin's Quest for Belief," *Literature and Theology*, 11, no. 3 (September 1997): 284–298, is a revised and expanded version of Lynch's earlier piece, "A Glimpse of the Hidden God: Dialectical Visions in Baldwin's *Go Tell It on the Mountain*," 29–58, in *New Essays on Go Tell It on the Mountain*, ed. Trudier Harris (Cambridge: Cambridge University Press, 1996). Lynch has written a sequel to the piece, focusing on one of Baldwin's plays: "Staying Out of Temple: Baldwin, the African American Church, and *The Amen Corner*," in *Re-Viewing James Baldwin: Things Not Seen*, ed. D. Quentin Miller (Philadelphia: Temple University Press, 2000). Prior to Lynch's trio of essays, the most ambitious reading of Baldwin's theology was James Macebuh's chapter, "Baldwin's Quarrel with God," in *James Baldwin: A Critical Study* (New York: Third Press, 1973). See also Patricia Lorine Schnapp, *The Liberation Theology of James Baldwin* (Ph.D. diss., Bowling Green State University, December 1987). David Hempton summarizes these studies in "James Baldwin: Preacher and Prophet," in *Evangelical Disenchantment* (New Haven: Yale University Press, 2008), 163–186.

7. George Shulman, *American Prophecy: Race and Redemption in American Political Culture* (Minneapolis: University of Minnesota Press, 2008), 132.

8. Baldwin, who left the Pentecostal church as a youth, became a member of Washington, D.C.'s largest Baptist church near the end of his life.

9. The phrase "theology of terror" is from Baldwin's essay "Everybody's Protest Novel," which equally indicts *Uncle Tom's Cabin* and *Native Son* for being possessed of a "theological terror, a terror of damnation." Baldwin argues that Stowe's "good Negro" Uncle Tom and Wright's "bad Negro" Bigger Thomas are two inverse stereotypes that whites require together in order to preserve the image of their innocence. Together, these complementary types assure whites of their "salvation," for Uncle Tom shows how much good America intends as surely as Bigger displays why those good intentions founder; *James Baldwin: Collected Essays*, 15.

10. Shailer Matthews saw the Bible merely as "the germplasm" of Christianity and an expression of a stage in its changing consciousness; Matthews, *The Faith of Modernism* (New York: Macmillan, 1924), 53.

11. James Baldwin, *The Fire Next Time* (1963; repr., New York: Vintage, 1993), 47.

12. The modernists were proponents of "Anglo-Saxon civilization," though some, including Walter Rauschenbusch, expressed concern that racial hatred at home

would undercut evangelistic missions abroad. For an informed account of the churches' internal disputes over Jim Crow and antilynching laws as well as some rudimentary bridge building between black and white clergy (especially in the Federal Council of Churches), see Martin Marty, *Modern American Religion*, vol. 1, *The Irony of It All* (Chicago: University of Chicago Press, 1986), 98–105; and vol. 2, *The Noise of Conflict* (Chicago: University of Chicago Press, 1991), 110–122.

13. The later King disagreed with younger black militants chiefly on political methods; he continued to assert that nonviolence was the only morally defensible means to revolution; see James Cone, *Martin and Malcom: A Dream or a Nightmare* (Maryknoll, N.Y.: Orbis Books, 1991), 266–271.

14. Baldwin said in 1961 that King "was playing the role" that the black church "had always played in Negro life," but he had given it "a new power," answering its "prayers" for a leader who would not stay in the sanctuary; see Baldwin, "The Dangerous Road Before Martin Luther King," in *James Baldwin: Collected Essays*, 643.

15. On Pentecostalism, see Randall Balmer, *Blessed Assurance: A History of Evangelicalism in America* (Boston: Beacon Press, 1999); and Harvey Cox, *Fire from Heaven: The Rise of Pentecostal Spirituality and the Reshaping of Religion in the Twenty-First Century* (New York: Addison-Wesley, 1995).

16. Cox, *Fire from Heaven*, 45–81, 306–331.

17. On the impact of black preaching on African American literature, including Baldwin, see Bernard Bell, *The Afro-American Novel and Its Tradition* (Amherst: University of Massachusetts Press, 1987), 29–32, 215–235.

18. James Baldwin, *Go Tell It on the Mountain* (New York: Delta, 1953), 12.

19. For Baldwin's retrospective on the liberal conscience films, see Chapter 2 of *The Devil Finds Work* (New York: Dial, 1976), 50–76. Black soldiers did not receive full benefits under the G.I. Bill; they were not eligible for the college educations or low-interest loans that helped many working-class whites move up in income and out to the suburbs. The Federal Housing Authority (FHA) redlined black neighborhoods and supported racial segregation as policy. The FHA's discrimination, when combined with urban renewal and suburbanization, actually encouraged ghettoes of the kind that Baldwin describes in "Fifth Avenue Uptown"; see George Lipsitz, "The Possessive Investment in Whiteness: Racialized Social Democracy and the 'White' Problem in American Studies," *American Quarterly* 47, no. 3 (September 1995): 369–387; the essay forms the first chapter of Lipsitz, *The Possessive Investment in Whiteness: How White People Profit from Identity Politics* (Philadelphia: Temple University Press, 2006), 1–23.

20. Baldwin, *Go Tell It on the Mountain*, 15.

21. Gabriel cites the same passage, Revelation 22:11, when he prophesies that blacks are a lost, bastard people (136).

22. Barbara Olson, "'Come-to-Jesus-stuff' in James Baldwin's *Go Tell It on the Mountain* and *The Amen Corner*," *African American Review* 31, no. 2 (Summer 1997): 295–301. The affirmative camp accepts the subjective experience of characters as truth, without regard to the narrator's oscillation between

empathy and distance; the narration is never first person, but indirect, which allows Baldwin to share consciousness at the same time that he contrasts characters' perceptions with the brutal realities of the South and the Northern ghetto.

23. The Gospel of John also relates that John was the one of the original five disciples and the follower whom Christ loved most; 13:23, 19:26, 20:2, 21:7, 21:20.

24. The story of the angel rescuing the Apostles from the Roman dungeon may itself allude to passages in Isaiah 40, 45 and Jeremiah 38, 40, in which the prophets are placed in shackles for telling truth.

25. Although *The Fire Next Time* was first published by Dial Press in 1963, its two parts—"My Dungeon Shook" and "Down at the Cross"—were originally printed separately in the winter of 1962. "My Dungeon Shook" (first titled "Letter to My Nephew") appeared in *The Progressive*, and "Down at the Cross" (first titled "Letter from a Region in My Mind") in *The New Yorker*. (My citations are taken from the Vintage International reprint of the Dial Press edition; see note 11.)

26. Shulman, *American Prophecy*, 154–159.

27. Baldwin, *Fire Next Time*, 6.

28. Harold Bloom, introduction to *James Baldwin, Modern Critical Views* (New York: Chelsea House, 1986), 6.

29. On the theology of God's pathos in the prophetic books, see Abraham Heschel, *The Prophets* (New York: Harper and Row, 1962), 221–268.

30. See Lamentations 1:11–12; 5:1, 2, 21; see also Claus Westermann, "The Lament," in *Basic Forms of Prophetic Speech*, trans. Hugh Clayton White (Cambridge, UK: Westminster, 1991), 202–203. For another example of the long prayer form in the prophetic books, compare Habbakuk 3. On the interplay between first-person singular and second-person plural pronouns in the prophetic books, see James Darsey, *The Prophetic Tradition and Radical Rhetoric in America* (New York: New York University Press, 1997), 22–24.

31. See Ezekiel 3:26, 24:27, 33:22; 4:5–6, 15, 24:16–18; Hosea 1, 2.

32. John F. Kennedy, qtd. in Branch, *Parting the Waters*, 823–824.

33. Baldwin, *Fire Next Time*, 93–94, 89–90.

34. Robert Penn Warren, *Who Speaks for the Negro?* (New York: Random House, 1965), 254, 255, 257. The book, a work of advocacy journalism, is a sequel, of sorts, to his earlier work, *Segregation: The Inner Conflict in the South* (1956). Warren alludes to a passage from *The Fire Next Time* in which Baldwin, echoing playwright Lorraine Hansberry, asks why blacks should join American society when it is a "burning house." Warren likens this statement to a "Black Muslim prophecy of destruction" and later describes such thinking as "black Armageddon" and "history conceived as doom." (254)

35. Balfour, *Evidence of Things Not Said*, 107.

36. Baldwin, *Fire Next Time*, 97.

37. Balfour analyzes the ways Baldwin's representations of suffering make black disenfranchisement visible to whites; see *Evidence of Things Not Said*, 60–86.

38. Baldwin, *Fire Next Time,* 88.
39. Baldwin, "Everybody's Protest Novel" and "Many Thousands Gone," in *James Baldwin: Collected Essays,* 13–18, See also *The Fire Next Time,* 91–92.
40. Baldwin, "Many Thousands Gone," in *James Baldwin: Collected Essays,* 33. See also, in *Collected Essays,* "A Stranger in the Village," 120–123, 128–129.
41. Baldwin, "Everybody's Protest Novel," 15.
42. James Baldwin, "Alas, Poor Richard," in *Nobody Knows My Name,* in *James Baldwin: Collected Essays,* 267.
43. In "Everybody's Protest Novel," Baldwin says that "the fear of the evil so often symbolized racially by blackness, or the terror of the theological damnation signified by darkness of complexion," is a "warfare waged daily in the heart"; and "Alas, Poor Richard" refers to "the powers of darkness" that "the illusion of safety" demands we forget (266–267). In "Many Thousands Gone," American liberals are extravagantly optimistic about the future of race relations because they will not see the human fact that in the valley of life, of pain and blood-lust and guilt, "no one has clean hands" (CE, 34).
44. James Baldwin, "Notes of a Native Son," in *James Baldwin: Collected Essays,* 72; Baldwin's italics.
45. Baldwin, *Fire Next Time,* 87.
46. Warren, who was always deeply suspicious of the prophetic, meditates on charismatic leadership and the uses of inspired rhetoric in *Who Speaks for the Negro?* (1965). In the section "Leadership from the Periphery," Warren describes Baldwin, in terms that echo the egoistic, all-seeing stare of Willie Stark, as having a voice filled with apocalyptic frisson and theological absolutism. While Baldwin does not preach violence, his collective condemnation of white society may be used, Warren fears, to rationalize revolutionary hatred of the kind Warren associates with Malcom X (the book's least sympathetic portrait); see *Who Speaks for the Negro?* 254, 255, 257, 281–282, 291, 295, 442.
47. Schnapp, *Liberation Theology,* 96.
48. Baldwin, *Fire Next Time,* 67–68.
49. Hannah Arendt, *Eichmann in Jerusalem: A Report on the Banality of Evil* (London: Penguin, 1962), 296–97.
50. Baldwin, *Fire Next Time,* 104.
51. Bloom, introduction to *James Baldwin,* 6; Warren, *Who Speaks,* 281–282, 291.
52. Baldwin, *Fire Next Time,* 105–106. According to editor Toni Morrison, the lines come from a spiritual called "Got a Home in That Rock"; "Notes on the Texts," in *James Baldwin: Collected Essays,* 864.
53. Bloom, introduction to *James Baldwin,* 6.
54. On Ham, see Stephen R. Haynes, *Noah's Curse: The Biblical Justification of American Slavery* (New York: Oxford University Press, 2002).
55. By "nemesis" I refer to "the tendency in nature to recover its balance" after "human aggression" has disturbed its proportions; from Northrop Frye, *The Great Code* (San Diego: Harcourt Brace and Jovanovich, 1983), 120.
56. See Bloom, introduction to *James Baldwin,* 6. Here Baldwin seems to show some debt to King; on the centrality of black suffering to King's theology, see

Cornel West, *Prophesy Deliverance*, (Westminster: John Knox Press, 1982), 74–75.

57. James Baldwin, "Princes and Powers," in *James Baldwin: Collected Essays*, 147–148, 154, 157. Kevin Birmingham, "Letters in 'History's Ass Pocket': James Baldwin and Cultural Privacy of the South" (paper presented at the James Baldwin Conference, Queen Mary, University of London, June 2007). On the perspective on American identity and race relations Baldwin gained during his years in western Europe, see also Bryon R. Washington, *The Politics of Exile: Ideology in Henry James, F. Scott Fitzgerald, James Baldwin* (Boston: Northeastern University Press, 1995), 95–108. After 1961, Baldwin spent much of the next decade living in Turkey; see Magdalena Zaborowska, *James Baldwin's Turkish Decade: Erotics of Exile* (Durham, N.C.: Duke University Press, 2008).

58. Baldwin, *Fire Next Time*, 83.

59. In 1964, there were over one hundred race riots nationwide; statistic cited in Robert Ellwood, *The Sixties Spiritual Awakening* (New Brunswick, N.J.: Rutgers University Press, 1994), 119.

60. James Baldwin, "The Crusade of Indignation," *James Baldwin: Collected Essays*, 609

61. Baldwin, *Fire Next Time*, 67–68.

62. Russell Banks, "John Brown's Body: James Baldwin and Frank Shatz in Conversation," *Transition*, 81/82, (2000) 250–266; cited in Shulman, *American Prophecy*, 269n49.

63. The source for this account of Baldwin's meeting with the Black Panthers is *No Name in Street* in *Collected Essays*, 450–464. Although *No Name* was published in 1972, Baldwin began drafting it in 1969, after King's assassination, and it covers the years from 1963 to the end of the decade.

64. In the winter of 1965–1966, Carmichael, a Howard University student who had joined the Freedom Riders project in 1961, helped to author a position paper, "SNCC Speaks for Itself," which announced the organization's break with King's nonviolence philosophy and its turn toward what Carmichael would shortly call "Black Power" (BP). Although Carmichael and the BP leaders were, after Malcom X's assassination, America's most audible voices of black anticolonialism, such theorists as *Freedomways'* Jack H. Dell and Britain's C. L. R. James provided historical models also supporting the case that the condition of American blacks was economically analogous to the colonized in nations dominated by Western empire. See Malcom X, "The Ballot or the Bullet" (1964), Stokely Carmichael's "What We Want"(1966), and The Black Panthers' "Party and Platform" in *The Sixties Papers*. See also J. H. Dell, "Colonialism and the Negro American Experience," *Freedomways* 6, no. 4 (Fall 1966): 296–308; J. H. Dell, "Foundations of Racism in American Life," *Freedomways* 4, no. 4 (Fall 1964): 513–535; C. L. R. James, "Black Power," in *The C. L. R. James Reader*, ed. Anna Grimshaw (Oxford: Blackwell, 1992), 362–374.

In this same period, Martin Luther King himself became increasingly attracted to socialism and speculated that the economic conversion of black communities might require a temporary, nationalistic separation from the white-run business structure and perhaps the creation of an independent third party; see Cone, *Martin and Malcom*, 245–271; and Branch, *Parting the Waters*, 215–216. As he came out against the U.S. involvement in Vietnam, King, much as Stokely Carmichael, linked his protest of the war to a worldwide campaign against the economic and racial oppression of the poor.

65. Baldwin, *Fire Next Time*, 47.

66. Baldwin, *Go Tell It on the Mountain*, 173.

67. Shulman, *American Prophecy*, 139.

68. See H. Richard Niebuhr, *Theology, History, and Culture*, ed. William Stacy Johnson (New Haven: Yale University Press, 2007), 10. Bryan R. Washington and Michael Lynch have argued that in *Go Tell It on the Mountain* Elisha represents a potential beloved for John. See Washington, "Wrestling with the 'Love that Dare Not Speak its Name': John, Elisha, and the 'Master'" 77–95; and Lynch, "A Glimpse of the Hidden God: Dialectical Visions in Baldwin's *Go Tell It on the Mountain*," *New Essays on Go Tell It on the Mountain*. The same-sex love theme is more pronounced in Baldwin's short story, "The Outing" (1951), which also features John Grimes. In his next two novels, *Giovanni's Room* and *Another Country*, Baldwin uses the queer or bisexual lover/artist to symbolize the potential for human salvation, through freely accepting the freedom of another; on *Another Country*, see Lynch, "Beyond Guilt and Innocence: Redemptive Suffering and Love in Baldwin's Another Country," *Obsidian II: Black Literature in Review*, 7, nos. 1–2 (1992): 1–18. Clarence E. Hardy describes how Baldwin uses sexual imagery to explore religious practices and the language of religion to explore sex, in *James Baldwin's God*, 59–76. See also Shulman's "Queering Prophecy and Dishonoring Prophets," which responds to Eldridge Cleaver's attack on Baldwin's homosexuality in *Soul on Ice* (1970), in *American Prophecy*, 159–163. Bryan Washington takes a much a much less favorable view than I do of Eric, and the sexual politics of *Another Country*, in his *The Politics of Exile*, 17–34, 70–94, 127–142.

69. James Cone, *God of the Oppressed* (New York: Seabury, 1975), 49–50, 107.

70. Baldwin, *Fire Next Time*, 44.

71. James Baldwin, "White Racism or World Community," in *James Baldwin: Collected Essays,* 755–756. The NCC leadership nominated Albert Cleague for president of the organization in 1969. Baldwin was speaking to an audience receptive to his message, though he still wrathfully intones it. On the NCC's cooperation with sixties radicalism, see Ellwood, *Sixties Spiritual Awakening*, 111–112, 222, 274–278.

72. Carmichael was a Christian when he joined King's Southern Christian Leadership Conference (SCLC), prior to his involvement in SNCC. Baldwin does not intend to impugn the SCLC (which Carmichael had since rejected for "Uncle Tomism"), but he does wish to underline how the resistance of a so-called Christian culture outside the SCLC compelled Carmichael to make a conscientious decision to abandon the religion. According to Baldwin, Carmichael abandoned the formal and ideological aspects of the religion rather than its spiritual substance ("White Racism," 752–753).

73. J. Edgar Hoover was obsessed with Baldwin, and he monitored the author for his homosexuality as well as for Communist ties the Bureau erroneously at-

tributed to his past; see James Campbell *Talking at the Gates: A Life of James Baldwin* (Berkeley, Calif.: University of California Press, 2002), 157–158, 167–169, 172.

74. James Baldwin, *No Name in the Street,* in *James Baldwin: Collected Essays,* 462.

75. Malcom X had stated that Jesus was a black man and a revolutionary. See Cone, *Martin and Malcom* 231.

76. Baldwin, *No Name,* 474.

77. Niebuhr differentiated perfect, or "unprudential" love from what he termed, "mutual love." The latter refers to the reciprocity of mutual interests as these are continually replenished by grace. Perfect love is the final norm of all human life, but mutual love is the highest possibility of the social life. Since it involves self-love and some calculation of advantage, mutual love falls short of perfect love, which is heedless, self-sacrificial, and exemplified by the crucified Christ. On the definition of mutual love and its difference from perfect love, see *Faith and History* (New York: Charles Scribner's Sons, 1949), 185; "Love and Law in Protestantism and Catholicism" in *Christian Realism and Political Problems* (New York: Charles Scribner's Sons, 1953), 159–164; *The Nature and Destiny of Man,* vol. 11, *Human Destiny* (1943 repro. New York: Charles Scribner's Sons, 1964), 81–87.

Epilogue

1. Norman Mailer, *The Presidential Papers* (New York: Bantam, 1964), 189.

2. William Hamilton's essay, "Mailer," in *On Taking God Out of the Dictionary* (New York: McCraw-Hill, 1974), is, next to Chapter 3 of Robert Solarotoff's *Down Mailer's Way* (Chicago: University of Illinois Press, 1974), the best overall discussion of Mailer's self-styled Theology of Dread up to the point it had developed by the seventies. For its subsequent expansion, see Mailer's last completed novels, *The Gospel According to the Son* (1997) and *The Castle in the Forest* (2008), and his interview book with Michael Lennon, *On God: An Uncommon Conversation* (New York: Random House, 2007).

3. Stephen Prothero, "Superstar," in *American Jesus* (New York: Farrar, Straus and Giroux, 2003), 124–157.

4. Thomas Altizer and William Hamilton, *Radical Theology and the Death of God* (Indianapolis, Ind.: Bobbs-Merrill, 1966), 5, 9, 48, 164–165.

5. Theodor Roszak, *The Making of a Counter Culture* (Garden City, N.Y.: Anchor Books, 1969), 192–193.

6. Robert Ellwood, *The Sixties Spiritual Awakening* (New Brunswick, N.J.: Rutgers University Press, 1994), 28.

7. Norman Podhoretz, *Making It* (New York: Random House, 1967), 281.

8. See especially Paul Goodman, *Growing Up Absurd: Problems of Youth in the Organized Society* (New York: Random House, 1960).

9. Leslie Fiedler, "The New Mutants," *Partisan Review* 32, no. 6 (Nov. 26, 1965): 505–525; and *The Return of the Vanishing American* (New York: Stein and Day, 1968).

10. On the cultural programs of the Popular Front, especially its positive valuation of local, indigenous popular culture, see Richard Pells, *Radical Visions and American Dreams* (New York: Harper and Row, 1973), 195–219, 246–251, 310–319.

11. Norman Mailer, *Armies of the Night* (New York: Plume, 1994 originally New York: New American Library, 1968), 121.

12. "The Port Huron Statement," in *The Sixties Papers: Documents of a Rebellious Decade*, ed. Judith Clavir Albert and Stewart Edward Albert (Westport, Conn.: Praeger, 1984), 121.

13. For an account of the ways the New Left drew inspiration from the counterculture, see Todd Gitlin, *The Sixties: Years of Hope, Days of Rage* (New York: Bantam, 1993), 195–245; and Morris Dickstein, *Gates of Eden* (New York: Basic Books, 1977), 3–24. See also C. Wright Mills, "Letter to the New Left," in *The Sixties Papers,* and *The Power Elite* (New York: Oxford University Press, 1956); and Herbert Marcuse, *One Dimensional Man* (Boston: Beacon Press, 1964).

14. Douglas Rossinow, *The Politics of Authenticity: Liberalism, Christianity, and the New Left in America* (New York: Columbia University Press, 1998).

15. I am suggesting a parallel to Baldwin, but the intellectual source for the CFLC's idea of community was the Lutheran pastor, theologian, and—for his stance against National Socialism in Germany—martyr Dietrich Bonhoeffer's *Life Together* (1954), especially, it seems, Chapter 5, "Confession and Communion." The book was published posthumously. Bonhoeffer was executed by the Nazis in 1945 for his involvement in a conspiracy to assassinate Hitler.

16. The CFLC was not compelled by Tillich's theology where it overlapped with neoorthodoxy and realism; in his redefinition of original sin, man's freedom still estranges him from God, giving him angst. The CFLC preferred Tillich's call to "the New Being" in Christ. See the title sermon in *The New Being* (Lincoln: University of Nebraska, 2005), 15–24.

17. "Reinhold Niebuhr's Theology of History" (1949), in H. Richard Niebuhr, *Theology, History, and Culture,* ed. William Stacy Johnson (New Haven: Yale University Press, 1996), esp. 95–96, 100.

18. A. J. Muste, "Pacificism and Perfectionism" (1948), 308–321. Muste alludes to 1 John: 3. After keeping alive the peace movement post–World War II as the executive secretary of the Fellowship for Reconciliation, Muste became the country's leading religious critic of nuclear deterrence as the head of the Committee for Non-Violent Action (1958). He was also an important activist in the civil rights movement whose ministry extended back to the pre–World War II era. Bayard Rustin, James Lawson, Robert Moses, and James Farmer were each at one time a member of Muste's Fellowship of Reconciliation, which combined the philosophies of Gandhi and Quaker pacifism. See Taylor Branch, *Parting the Waters: America in the King Years, 1954–63* (New York: Simon and Schuster, 1988), 171–173, 179, 298–99, 330, 389–90. For some of Muste's key writings on nonviolent resistance, see Muste, "Pacifism and Class War" (1928), 179–184; "Sit-downs and Lie-downs" (1937), 203–206; "The World Task of Pacifism" (1941), 215–233; and "Of Holy Disobedience"

(1952), 355–377, in *The Essays of A. J. Muste,* ed. Nat Hentoff (New York: Bobbs-Merrill, 1967).

19. Gitlin, *Sixties,* 22–24, 92–101.

20. Todd Gitlin, "Enclaves of the Elders," in *Sixties,* 45–80; see also Gitlin's account of the ill-fated 1963 meeting between Irving Howe and Tom Hayden, 171–177.

21. Irving Howe, *A Margin of Hope* (San Diego: Harcourt Brace Javonovich, 1982), 292–298; and Irving Howe, ed. *Beyond the New Left* (New York: McCall, 1970), 19–32.

22. Lionel Trilling introduces the phrase "adversary culture" (referring to the avant-garde) in the preface of *Beyond Culture* (New York: Harcourt Brace Jovanovich, [1978] ca. 1965), ix–xviii, to rue how academics have legitimized the "subversive." Sixties radicals were doing "modernism in the streets"; quoted in Marshall Berman, "Modernism in the Streets," *Dissent* (Fall 2008). www.dissentmagazine.org/article/?article-1310.

23. Paul Goodman, "The New Reformation," in *Beyond the New Left,* 320–321. Compare also, in the same volume, Michael Harrington's essay, "The Mystical Militants," esp. 33–39. For Goodman's earlier reflection on the religious core of youthful alienation, see the chapter, "Faith," in *Growing Up Absurd* (New York: Random House, 1960), 133–158.

24. Paul Goodman, *Adam and His Works: Collected Stories* (New York: Vintage, 1963), 424, 430, 432. Taylor Stoehr places this story in the development of Goodman's career in his introduction to *The Galley to Mytilene: Stories, 1949–1960,* ed. Taylor Stoehr (Santa Barbara: Black Sparrow Press, 1980), 13–15. In the story, the speaker says, "I do not like it when people speak of Adam's fall; there is no such language in the Bible. How did he fall? from what dignity? how humiliated before whom? . . . It is possible to construe the Biblical sentences about nakedness and knowing to mean that Adam has lost his innocence; but to me at least, this does not seem to be our universal fact" (429).

25. Goodman, *Beyond the New Left,* 89.

26. Howe, *Margin of Hope,* 321.

27. He was also rebuking his younger self. "Howe's articles in Labor Action . . . were marked by stridency and an occasional utopianism with religious overtones"; see Alan Wald, *The New York Intellectuals* (Chapel Hill: University of North Carolina, 1987), 314.

28. Billy Graham, *The Jesus Generation,* special crusade ed. (Zondervan: Grand Rapids, Mich. 1971), 16. "The Jesus Revolution" received its name from *Time* magazine in its June 21, 1971 cover story.

Two years later, a prominent liberal Protestant, Martin Marty, would argue that the Christian Left had committed the "errors" of abandoning the Church's historic purpose of providing people with identity, community, and a sense of ultimate purpose. In exchanging the sacred symbols and spiritual capital of Christianity for social relevance, the Christian Left had followed secular messianists in projecting religious meanings onto political causes, Marty argued. In the process, he added, it had rendered the mainline liberal churches obsolete and ceded the field to the likes of Billy Graham and the Right. Marty's case was overstated. Evangelical churches did experience high growth rates in the 1950s and 1960s, but this was attributable to their greater success retaining youth. During the same period, the majority of those who switched denominations moved from the right to left theologically. There was no mass defection from the mainline, which was already a numerical minority of parishioners at the outset of the Cold War. These facts cited in Hulsether, *Building a Protestant Left,* 145. See Martin Marty, *The Fire We Can Light* (Garden City, NY: Doubleday, 1973), 113–116, 165–177.

29. For a recent, and eloquent, defense of utopian thought in ethics, politics, and American culture after the Clinton and Bush, Jr., administrations, see Rabbi Michael Lerner, *The Left Hand of God* 3rd ed. (New York: Harper One, 2006).

30. Gitlin, *Sixties,* 195–245.

31. Robert Fogel, qtd. in Nicholas Kristof, "God, Satan, and the Media," *New York Times,* east coast edition, March 4, 2003.

32. Hans Küng, "Why We Need a Global Ethic," in *The Postmodern Reader,* ed. Charles Jencks (New York: St. Martin's Press, 1995), 409–414.

Acknowledgments

M ANY FRIENDS and colleagues have contributed their thoughts to
this book over the course of its development beginning eight years
ago. Maura Spiegel, from my graduate days, took an early interest in my
work and encouraged me to pursue my long-standing love of film and
cultural history. Ann Douglas's "Cold War American Culture" seminar at
Columbia University changed the direction of my career. Ann, Jonathan
Arac, and the late Karl Kroeber were dedicated, empathetic, and inspiring
advisers. I never expected to have an adviser whose interests and passions
aligned so closely with mine, but with Ann, I was blessed. Jonathan commented meticulously on every draft of the manuscript, which seemed, at
times, to be endlessly expanding; I keep his example before me as a model
of collegial generosity. Karl was a wise raconteur, a hilarious storyteller,
and an irreplaceable friend. I do not think I would have made it through
Columbia without him.

Wayne Proudfoot and James Livingston offered brilliant criticism, and
Paul Bové, by email and in person, carried on scholarly conversations with
me regarding Niebuhr, secularism, and the academic Left. At Harvard, I
found many readers who helped me to reshape and substantially revise the
manuscript in its multiple versions. For their support of young scholars
and my career in particular, I am indebted to John Stauffer, James Engell,
and Luke Menand. James Simpson conversed with me about the Reformation, America's Calvinist legacy, Protestant iconoclasm, and the CIA.

Lawrence Buell, Philip Fisher, and Lisa New also deserve thanks. I had the pleasure of meeting Michael Kimmage when he visited Harvard to discuss his own work on Lionel Trilling, Whittaker Chambers, and Cold War liberalism, and I have since benefited indispensably from his learning.

I cannot neglect to mention the many students whose papers, classroom comments, and conversations outside of class have stimulated me over the past five years. The undergraduates in my classes "Religion in American Film" and "Protestantism in American Literature" have been an intellectual boon to me. They have reminded me how much matters of faith continue to touch this generation's lives. In the 2008 version of "Religion in American Film," Mark Scott was not a teaching assistant so much as he was a co-instructor, and our work together deepened my appreciation for theological studies. Harvard's graduate students have also inspired me through their work and their professional examples. George Blaustein knows all the back-stories of the Cold War liberals who were involved in the making of American Studies, and Kevin Birmingham is one of James Baldwin's sharpest readers. Eliza Barstow approaches evangelicalism with a combination of sympathy and deep understanding that is rare.

Lindsay Waters, my editor at Harvard University Press, first read a draft of this manuscript five years ago. It has been a long journey, and I'm thankful to him for championing the book through to the finish.

Lastly, there are those who have encouraged me with their love. My old friend Jefferson Gatrall read the germ of the book when it was only a proposal; he has heard more iterations of this project than anyone else and he has always listened with patience and discernment. His expertise on Russian history and literature supplemented gaps in my knowledge, and his scholarship on liberal Christianity and the arts spurred me to look at sources that I might have otherwise overlooked. His spouse, and my good friend, Rupa Bhattacharya, was a source of tolerant levity during long hours when she was subjected to our musings on Jesus, figuration, and Bible adaptations. My dear parents, Wayne and Rebecca Stevens, and my wonderful grandparents, Rayetta Brown and Roy C. and Gladys M. Stevens, have instilled in me a lasting respect for religious and spiritual questions. I could not have traveled this far in my vocation without their love, their sacrifice, their encouragement, and the example of their own convictions. My brother, Justin, remains my favorite conversationalist on all things cinematic, and his sense of humor has buoyed me when I have been in low spirits. My fiancé, Rita, has been understanding at every step of this past year, during which I spent more evenings than most poring over revisions. When my words seemed to be failing me on the page, her caring and her laughter kept me grounded and happy.

Index